LOCAL CONTENT AND SUSTAINABLE DEVELOPMENT IN GLOBAL ENERGY MARKETS

Local Content and Sustainable Development in Global Energy Markets analyses the topical and contentious issue of the critical intersections between local content requirements (LCRs) and the implementation of sustainable development treaties in global energy markets including Africa, Asia, Europe, North America, Latin America, South America, Australasia and the Middle East.

While LCRs generally aim to boost domestic value creation and economic growth, inappropriately designed LCRs could produce negative social, human rights and environmental outcomes, and a misalignment of a country's fiscal policies and global sustainable development goals. These unintended outcomes may ultimately serve as disincentive to foreign participation in a country's energy market. This book outlines the guiding principles of a sustainable and rights-based approach – focusing on transparency, accountability, gender justice and other human rights issues – to the design, application and implementation of LCRs in global energy markets to avoid misalignments.

Damilola S. Olawuyi is an associate professor of petroleum, energy and environmental law at Hamad Bin Khalifa University (HBKU) College of Law, Doha, Qatar. He is also Chancellor's Fellow and Director of the Institute for Oil, Gas, Energy, Environment and Sustainable Development (OGEES Institute), Afe Babalola University, Ado Ekiti, Nigeria. He is an Independent Expert of the Working Group on Extractive Industries, Environment, and Human Rights Violations in Africa formed by the African Commission on Human and Peoples' Rights.

"A thorough analysis of local content. A go-to reference book. Having a robust local content policy is one tool to avoid the resource curse. But to succeed it must be carefully tailored to the circumstances of the country and must gradually evolve as local vendors, services, and employee capabilities are enhanced. "Local" content is necessarily just that—local, not truly national and certainly not global, but this book, while covering the globe, recognizes the need to tailor local content to local circumstances. Every host government and investor can benefit from the many wisdoms imparted in this book and from about the local-content experiences of various countries. The story of local content is a cautionary tale. Because the petroleum industry is capital, not labor, intensive, a local-content policy, no matter how robust, cannot provide full employment—especially in a country with a large population. Thus, every petroleum-producing country must avoid the resource curse, especially Dutch disease, which can lead to more unemployment than the petroleum industry can make up—no matter how robust the local-content program may be. Thus, a host government must pay equal attention to sustainability, which necessarily includes keeping an eye on competitiveness, as the title of this important book emphasizes."

Professor Owen L. Anderson, Distinguished Oil & Gas Scholar and Co-Academic Director, KBH Center for Energy Law & Business, the University of Texas at Austin, and Eugene Kuntz Chair in Oil, Gas & Natural Resources, Emeritus and George Lynn Cross Research Professor Emeritus, The University of Oklahoma, United States of America

"Damilola Olawuyi has brought together a group of leading energy and natural resources law scholars to address the important subject of local content requirements. These requirements are often contentious, and the contributions in this book unravel the many legal challenges that attend them. The contributors identify the value of measures that increase the benefits that flow to a host country or community from oil and gas operations, and, to a lesser extent, renewable electricity. At the same time the contributors explore the many difficulties. Local content requirements may be economically inefficient and inequitable in gender and wealth terms or as between regions; they may be hard to reconcile with environmental aspirations in sustainable development, and they may contravene international trade rules. In the course of 21 chapters, the contributing authors have analyzed the experience of a number of countries, and have identified a number of ways that careful legislative design can address the challenges, minimize misalignments and maximize the potential to reap local benefits and grow industries and employment opportunities. The book is a valuable contribution to the scholarship of energy and natural resources law, and it will be a key point of reference globally for researchers and policy makers interested in the characteristics high-quality local content requirements."

Professor Barry Barton: Professor of Law and Director of the Centre for Environmental, Resources and Energy Law at the University of Waikato, Hamilton, New Zealand.

"There is a growing body of literature on local content requirements. No doubt because of the speed and importance of various developments in this area. This book provides a detailed and comprehensive account of local content policies and their interaction with sustainable development trends in energy markets. It provides an overview of the current state of play around the world and discusses future developments in great detail. The book is clearly essential reading for students in energy law, policy makers and international energy law practitioners. More generally, it should be read by those interested in direction of global energy markets."

Professor Kim Talus, McCulloch Chair in Energy Law and Director of Tulane Center for Energy Law (Tulane University, United States); Professor of European Economic and Energy Law, UEF Law School; Professor of Energy Law, University of Helsinki, Finland

"The importance of local content enterprises to national or regional economies cannot be overstated. In their best forms, local content programmes enable countries or regions to capitalise on their comparative advantage to transform primary industries into competitive industries that are a valuable part of global supply chains and a catalyst for sustainable development. Resource-rich countries therefore rightfully rely on local content programmes to transform or enhance their economies. However, resource-rich countries tend to focus on the fiscal or economic benefits derived from local content policies, without paying commensurate attention to the externalities of such policies.

This book offers an excellent exposition and comparative analysis of local content requirements in the energy sector, as well as highlights the often-neglected issues for sustainable development, such as gender injustice, social exclusion, transparency, corruption, accountability, corporate social responsibility, environmental justice, climate change, human rights, and participatory development. It also appropriately considers the impact of current geopolitics and international treaty obligations and offers constructive recommendations for designing, applying and implementing local content requirements. For the African Legal Support Facility, whose mandate includes ensuring balanced negotiations and contracts between its regional member countries and investors in the energy, extractives and infrastructure sectors, the issues and recommendations discussed in this volume are relevant for advising on appropriate legal and regulatory frameworks, building capacity, and negotiating contracts that will ensure sustainable development. The initiative by Dr. Damilola Olawuyi and his esteemed colleagues to publish this insightful volume is not only commendable, but also timely as our countries strive to achieve the UN Sustainable Development Goals (SDGs) by 2030.'

Stephen Karangizi, Director & Chief Executive Officer, African Legal Support Facility, African Development Bank

"Olawuyi has brought together an impressive number of renowned specialists to discuss local content experiences in light of international treaty obligations on trade, investment, business and human rights. This much needed innovative approach provides solid understanding of several legal and fiscal regimes as well as valuable insights on how to design sustainable, transparent and effective local content requirements in global energy markets. This is an important book for policymakers, scholars, stakeholders, lawyers and any interested observer."

André Giserman, Deputy Superintendent of Local Content, Brazilian National Agency of Petroleum, Natural Gas and Biofuels

"Professor Olawuyi's germinal scholarly work in creating the conceptual apparatus for, editing, and integrating the various chapters of this book, more or less closes a yawning gap in the literature by tackling an extremely important topic that lies close to the heart of the longstanding effort of resource-rich countries (mostly in the Global South) to benefit much more than has generally been the case from their natural resource endowments. The book sparkles with disciplinary cross-fertilization, creativity and insight in putting into a highly productive conversation, several bodies of knowledge and policymaking that are all-too-often incorrectly viewed and treated as isolated and disparate. In the result, he has produced a work of scholarship that will be just as useful to human rights, environmental, indigenous rights, and sustainable development scholars and practitioners as it will be to their counterparts who focus more closely on fields such as energy, trade, investment, or corporate law and policy."

Professor Obiora Chinedu Okafor, United Nations Independent Expert on Human Rights and International Solidarity and York Research Chair in International and Transnational Legal Studies, Osgoode Hall Law School, Canada

TREATY IMPLEMENTATION FOR SUSTAINABLE DEVELOPMENT

Over the past three decades, a series of international treaties have entered into force to address pressing global concerns of social and economic development and environmental protection. On climate change, biodiversity and biosafety, desertification, agriculture and seeds, and trade and investment liberalisation, new regimes have been established to implement global commitments related to sustainable development, many with nearly universal membership. Successful domestic implementation of these international treaty regimes is one of the most significant challenges facing international law today. Although much has been written on the content and form of treaty law, there is relatively little that examines the transition from international legal theory and treaty texts to domestic regulation and practice.

This series of books addresses this need and provides a serious contribution to ongoing global debates by conducting a detailed analysis of how myriad new treaty regimes that cover the future's most pressing concerns can be made to work in practice.

Series Editors:

Marie-Claire Cordonier Segger
Markus Wilheim Gehring

Volumes in the Series:

Sustainable Development, International Aviation, and Treaty Implementation edited by Armand de Mestral, Paul Fitzgerald, Tanveer Ahmad (2018)
NAFTA and Sustainable Development edited by Hoi L. Kong and L. Kinvin Wroth (2015)
Legal Aspects of Implementing the Cartagena Protocol on Biosafety edited by Marie-Claire Cordonier Segger, Frederic Perron-Welch, and Christine Frison (2013)
Sustainable Development, International Criminal Justice, and Treaty Implementation edited by Sébastien Jodoin and Marie-Claire Cordonier Segger (2013)

Local Content and Sustainable Development in Global Energy Markets

Edited by

DAMILOLA S. OLAWUYI

Hamad Bin Khalifa University

CAMBRIDGE
UNIVERSITY PRESS

University Printing House, Cambridge CB2 8BS, United Kingdom

One Liberty Plaza, 20th Floor, New York, NY 10006, USA

477 Williamstown Road, Port Melbourne, VIC 3207, Australia

314–321, 3rd Floor, Plot 3, Splendor Forum, Jasola District Centre, New Delhi – 110025, India

79 Anson Road, #06–04/06, Singapore 079906

Cambridge University Press is part of the University of Cambridge.

It furthers the University's mission by disseminating knowledge in the pursuit of education, learning, and research at the highest international levels of excellence.

www.cambridge.org
Information on this title: www.cambridge.org/9781108495370
DOI: 10.1017/9781108862110

© Cambridge University Press 2021

This publication is in copyright. Subject to statutory exception and to the provisions of relevant collective licensing agreements, no reproduction of any part may take place without the written permission of Cambridge University Press.

First published 2021

A catalogue record for this publication is available from the British Library.

Library of Congress Cataloging-in-Publication Data
NAMES: Olawuyi, Damilola S. (Damilola Sunday), 1983– author.
TITLE: Local content and sustainable development in global energy markets / edited by Damilola S. Olawuyi, Hamad Bin Khalifa University, Doha.
DESCRIPTION: Cambridge, United Kingdom ; New York, NY : Cambridge University Press, 2021. | Series: Treaty implementation for sustainable development | Includes index.
IDENTIFIERS: LCCN 2020028442 (print) | LCCN 2020028443 (ebook) | ISBN 9781108495370 (hardback) | ISBN 9781108862110 (ebook)
SUBJECTS: LCSH: Energy consumption – Law and legislation. | Energy conservation – Law and legislation. | Sustainable development – Law and legislation. | Power resources – Law and legislation. | Renewable energy sources – Law and legislation. | Energy policy.
CLASSIFICATION: LCC K3981 .O43 2021 (print) | LCC K3981 (ebook) | DDC 343.08/4228–dc23
LC record available at https://lccn.loc.gov/2020028442
LC ebook record available at https://lccn.loc.gov/2020028443

ISBN 978-1-108-49537-0 Hardback

Cambridge University Press has no responsibility for the persistence or accuracy of URLs for external or third-party internet websites referred to in this publication and does not guarantee that any content on such websites is, or will remain, accurate or appropriate.

Contents

Preface and Acknowledgements	*page* xiii
List of Abbreviations	xvi
Editor	xx
List of Contributors	xxi

PART I   INTRODUCTORY CONTEXT AND PRINCIPLES

1   Local Content and the Sustainable Development Nexus   3
Damilola S. Olawuyi

2   Defining the 'Local' in Local Content Requirements
in the Oil and Gas Sector   16
Chilenye Nwapi

3   Local Content Measures and the WTO Regime:
Addressing Contentions and Trade-offs   41
Mandy Meng Fang

4   Local Content Requirements in Extractive Industries:
A Human Rights Analysis   63
Susan L. Karamanian

5   Upgrade of Local Suppliers in the Global Production
Network: The Success or Otherwise of Local Content
Regimes   83
Alexander Ezenagu and Chidiebere Eze-Ajoku

x   *Contents*

PART II   CASE STUDIES

AFRICA

6   Expressing Local Content through Black Economic
     Empowerment in the South African Petroleum Industry   107
     Hanri Mostert and Meyer van den Berg

7   Local Content Frameworks for Petroleum Industry Operations
     in the CEMAC Region: An Evaluation of Their Functionality,
     Sustainability and Normative Underpinnings   130
     George K. Ndi

8   Local Content, *Angolanização*, and Sustainable Development
     in Angola   156
     Jesse Salah Ovadia

9   Local Content and the Sustainable Development of Oil
     and Gas Resources in Nigeria   167
     Damilola S. Olawuyi and Ayobami J. Olaniyan

10   Local Content Requirements and Treaty Implementation
     in Kenya's Petroleum Sector   188
     James O. Kirwa and Melba K. Wasunna

AUSTRALIA AND ASIA

11   Sustainability and Local Content Requirements in Australian Oil
     and Gas Development: Has the Ship of Opportunity Sailed?   206
     Tina Soliman Hunter

12   Local Content for Sustainable Development in Middle East
     and North Africa: Current Legal Approaches and Future Directions   228
     Damilola S. Olawuyi

EUROPE

13   Local Content and Sustainable Development in Norway   245
     Catherine Banet

SOUTH AMERICA

14   Local Content and Sustainable Development in Argentina   264
     Marcelo Neuman

Contents

15   The Latin American Experience in Designing Local Content
Policies in the Oil and Gas Sectors: Strengths, Limitations,
and Future Perspectives   280
Amir Lebdioui and Marcela Morales

16   Local Content and Sustainable Development in Brazil
Eduardo G. Pereira, Rafael Baptista Baleroni, Fernanda Delgado,
Jose Vicente Duncan de Miranda, Aaron Koenck, and Pedro   300
Henrique Neves

NORTH AMERICA

17   Industrial Policy and Local Content Rules in US Energy Policy   320
Zachary Sturman and Timothy Meyer

18   Oil and Gas Sector Local Content Decision Processes: Canadian
Indigenous Participation   343
Alastair R. Lucas and David K. Laidlaw

PART III   LESSONS LEARNED AND FUTURE DIRECTIONS

19   Local Content, Community Content, and Sustainable Development
in the Oil and Gas Industry: Perspectives from Legislation, Policy,
and Community Development Agreements   369
Ibironke T. Odumosu-Ayanu

20   Local Content Requirements and Social Inclusion in Global Energy
Markets: Towards Business and Human Rights Content   392
Oyeniyi Abe and Ada Ordor

21   Advancing Sustainable Development in Local Content Initiatives:
Summary for Policy Makers   413
Damilola S. Olawuyi

Index   424

Preface and Acknowledgements

Determined to incentivise and maximise the use of local goods and services in their energy industries, resource-rich countries across the world are increasingly introducing local content requirements (LCRs) into their regulatory framework, legislation, guidelines, industry contracts and bidding practices. A number of studies have compiled the importance of LCRs as revolutionary and innovative regulatory measures that can unlock the competitiveness of the local economy, while allowing a country to strengthen its national industry and achieve other social benefits. However, notwithstanding the importance and prevalence of LCRs in global energy markets, LCRs have also been linked in a number of countries with producing conflict and misalignments with extant national obligations under core international treaty provisions on trade, investment, gender, environment, human rights and sustainable development.

Despite the tensions and trade-offs between LCRs and sustainable development–related treaties, a comparative analysis and evaluation of the normative underpinnings, functionality and sustainability of legal and fiscal regimes on LCRs, in the light of international treaty obligations on environment, trade, investment, business and human rights, has yet to receive a book-length, exhaustive and rigorous exposition and analysis. This book fills that gap. It provides an authoritative exposition of legal, fiscal and institutional frameworks on LCRs in global energy markets. It explores the values, assumptions and guiding principles that underpin LCRs and explores how questions of social exclusion, transparency, gender injustice, corruption, accountability, corporate social responsibility, environmental justice and participatory development in LCR formulation and implementation have been, and could be better, addressed.

Overall, the book aims to: enhance an understanding of the intersectional nature of, and the relationship among, LCRs, sustainable development, distributive justice, gender justice, social licence to operate and corporate social responsibility in the energy sector, especially the question of whether LCRs aid or hinder the domestic implementation of sustainable development treaties and norms in energy markets;

xiii

analyse how LCRs may result in misalignment with World Trade Organization agreements and other international trade and investment treaties; analyse the general legal, fiscal and contractual framework governing LCRs, highlighting examples of contractual provisions and clauses such as employment of nationals, training, procurement, technology transfer and project participation requirements; explore how LCRs may result in negative social, human rights and environmental outcomes if not backed by robust legal and governance safeguards; and highlight how lessons learned from surveyed jurisdictions can influence the design of sustainable, transparent and effective LCRs in global energy markets.

The book is prepared in a user-friendly style to enhance its utility among its primary audience, namely students, corporations, energy departments and ministries, law firms, courts and arbitrators, notably international and regional committees and tribunals before whom arguments over local content clauses and policies often come for resolution. The book analyses the key roles that international institutions such as the Organization for Petroleum Exporting Countries, Gas Exporting Countries Forum, Organization for the Harmonization of Business law in Africa (OHADA), International Energy Agency, International Maritime Organization, World Trade Organization, and national institutions such as national oil companies, the Ministry of Petroleum Resources, Department of Petroleum Resources, Local Content Development and Monitoring Boards, and National Extractive Industry Transparency Initiatives, play in developing and implementing high-leverage LCRs. This book provides a worldwide audience of business leaders, policy makers and administrators an authoritative and invaluable guidebook and toolkit to access, understand and appreciate theoretical, legal, fiscal and institutional frameworks applicable to the effective design, application and implementation of LCRs.

Any writing process requires significant planning and organisation. In this regard, I must register my profound gratitude to many helping hands, without whom the publication of this book would not have been possible. First and foremost, my thanks and appreciation go to God the Almighty for the successful publication of this book. Secondly, I appreciate the kind motivation and support of the President and Founder of Afe Babalola University – Aare Afe Babalola, OFR, CON, SAN, FNIALS, FCIArb., LL.D – for his unflinching support of me and my family. Aare Afe Babalola's journey and global achievements provide reinforcing pillars and instructive pathways that one could only aspire to follow.

Furthermore, I am especially indebted to everyone at Qatar Foundation and Hamad Bin Khalifa University (HBKU), Doha, Qatar, for their exceptional love and support over the years. Special thanks to Dean Susan L. Karamanian for being ever so kind and supportive, and to Professor Clinton W. Francis, the founding Dean of the HBKU College of Law, for providing remarkable opportunities and support to organise the 2018 Doha Energy Experts' Workshop that greatly furthered my interest in this area.

Preface and Acknowledgements xv

This book was conceived during my time as Herbert Smith Freehills Visitor at the University of Cambridge Law Faculty. I am therefore deeply grateful for research funding and support from Herbert Smith Freehills LLP, Cambridge Law Faculty, the Lauterpacht Centre for International Law and, most importantly, my host faculty, Dr. Markus Gehring and his wonderful family, for the warm hospitality, insights and support that facilitated the initial framing of this book. Special thanks are also due to the editors of this series, as well as editorial staff of Cambridge University Press for the smooth and professional review process which guided this book through to its timely completion. A thank you also goes to Sarah L. Macleod (Schulich School of Law, Dalhousie University, Canada) as well as Umair Dogar (Qatar Foundation) for providing remarkable and thoughtful research assistance. They assisted greatly in collating chapters at the submission, review and editing stages. I also acknowledge the dedication and collegiality of all the contributing authors, whose substantial research and commitment to leading-edge scholarship in this field has been pivotal to the production of this book.

Finally, I would like to thank my dear wife Oluwabunmi and our amazing twin girls, Titilayo and Oluwatoni, for their love, support and inspiration. Thanks are also due to my exceptional students whose class contributions and ideas served as timely seeds that blossomed into this book. I thank you all for your support and kindness, and I commit this book to your scholastic minds.

This book has endeavoured to state the position of the law as of 30 June 2020, although authors have been able to take into account subsequent developments in one or two instances.

Damilola S. Olawuyi
Doha, Qatar
30 June 2020

Abbreviations

AECID	Spanish Agency for International Development Cooperation
AEP	Angola Enterprise Program
AMC	Australian Marine Complex
ANC	African National Congress
ANP	National Petroleum Agency
ANPG	Angola's National Oil, Natural Gas and Biofuels Agency
APPEA	Australian Petroleum Production & Exploration Association
ASCM	Agreement on Subsidies and Countervailing Measures
BBBEE	Broad-Based Black Economic Empowerment
BEE	Black Economic Empowerment
BHRU	Business and Human Rights Unit
BITs	Bilateral Investment Treaties
BNDES	National Bank for Economic and Social Development
BREXIT	British Exit from the European Union
CAMA	The Companies and Allied Matters Act 1990 of Nigeria
CBD	Citizens and Business Department
CCIA	Angolan Chamber of Commerce and Industry
CDAs	Community Development Agreements
CDBs	Community Development Boards
CEDAW	Convention on the Elimination of All forms of Discrimination against Women
CEMAC	Central African Economic and Monetary Community
CEPA	Comprehensive Economic Partnership Agreement
CER	Canadian Energy Regulator
CFRN	Constitution of the Federal Republic of Nigeria
CNL	Chevron Nigeria Limited
CNPE	National Council for Energy Policies
CRES	Centre de Recherches Enterprises et Societies
CSB	Ceduna Sub-Basin

List of Abbreviations

CSG	Commercial-Scale Coal Seam Gas
DEC	Directorate of Economy and Concessions
D.PRO	Directorate of Production
DSB	Dispute Settlement Body
ECCAS	Communauté Économique des États de l'Afrique Centrale
EEA	Employment Equity Act
EEA	European Economic Area
EGA	Environmental Goods Agreement
EGASPIN	Environmental Guidelines and Standards for the Petroleum Industry in Nigeria
EIA	Environmental Impact Assessment
EOPS	Early Oil Pilot Scheme
EPRA	Energy and Petroleum Regulatory Authority
EU	European Union
FISO	Fideicomiso Público para Promover el Desarrollo de Proveedores y Contratistas Nacionales para la Industria Energética
FPIC	Free, Prior, Informed Consent
GAB	Great Australian Bight
GATS	General Agreement on Trade in Services
GATT	General Agreement on Tariff and Trade
GMOU	Global Memorandum of Understanding
GPs	United Nations Guiding Principles on Business and Human Rights
HRBA	Human Rights Based Approach
HDSA	Historically Disadvantaged South Africans
HIPC	Heavily Indebted Poor Country
HLCS	Housing and Living Conditions Standard
IAAC	Impact Assessment Agency of Canada
IBA	Impact and Benefit Agreement
ICCPR	International Covenant on Civil and Political Rights
ICESCR	International Covenant on Economic, Social and Cultural Rights
IFC	International Finance Corporation
IGFMMMSD	Intergovernmental Forum on Mining, Minerals Metals and Sustainable Development
IKTVA	In Kingdom Total Value Add
ILUAs	Indigenous Land Use Agreements
ILO	International Labour Organization
IMF	International Monetary Fund
IOCs	International Oil Companies
IPIECA	International Petroleum Industry Environmental Conservation Association

ICTSD	International Centre for Trade and Sustainable Development
JOA	Joint Operating Agreement
JVs	Joint Ventures
LNG	Liquefied Natural Gas
LCRs	Local Content Requirements
NAFTA	North American Free Trade Agreement
NCDMB	Nigerian Content Development and Monitoring Board
NDDC	Niger Delta Development Commission
NDP	National Development Plan
NEITI	Nigerian Extractive Industries Transparency Initiative
NERSA	National Energy Regulator of South Africa
NLNG	Nigerian Liquefied Natural Gas Company
NOSDRA	National Oil Spill Detection and Response Agency Act
OECD	Organisation for Economic Co-operation and Development
OFEPHI	Organización Federal de Estados Productores de Hidrocarburos
OHADA	Organization for the Harmonization of Business law in Africa
OIC	Organization of Islamic Cooperation
OLADE	Latin-American Energy Organization
OPA	Ontario Power Authority
OPAGGSA	Offshore Petroleum and Greenhouse Gas Storage Act
OPEC	Organization of Petroleum Exporting Countries
PAL	Petroleum Activities Law
PDO	Plan for Development and Operation
PDVSA	Petróleos de Venezuela, S.A.
PEDEFOR	Program for Stimulus to Competitiveness in the Supply Chain, Development and Enhancement of Suppliers in the Oil and Natural Gas Sector in Brazil
PIGB	Petroleum Industry Governance Bill
PPAs	Power Purchase Agreements
PPAD	Public Procurement and Asset Disposal
PRODEPRO	Programa de Desarrollo de Proveedores
PROMINP	Program for the Mobilization of the Oil and Gas Industry
PSA	Production Sharing Agreement
PSC	Production Sharing Contract
SDA	Skills Development Act
SNH	Société Nationale des Hydrocarbures
SNPC	Société Nationale des Hydrocarbures du Gabon
SOI	Report Sea of Indifference: Australian Industry Participation in the North West Shelf Project
SPDC	Shell Petroleum Development Company
SRP	Supplier Relationship Programme

TIVET	Technical, Industrial, Vocational, and Entrepreneurship Training
TVET	Technical and Vocational Education and Training
TRIMs	Trade-Related Investment Measures
UDEAC	Uniòn Douanière et Éconmique de l'Afrique Centrale
UDHR	Universal Declaration of Human Rights
UNCTAD	United Nations Conference on Trade and Development
UNDP	United Nations Development Programme
UNFCCC	United Nations Framework Convention on Climate Change
USAID	US Agency for International Development
WTO	World Trade Organization

Editor

Damilola S. Olawuyi is an associate professor of petroleum, energy and environmental law at Hamad Bin Khalifa University (HBKU) College of Law, Doha, Qatar. He is also Chancellor's Fellow and Director of the Institute for Oil, Gas, Energy, Environment and Sustainable Development (OGEES Institute), Afe Babalola University, Nigeria. A prolific and highly regarded scholar, Professor Olawuyi has practised and taught energy law in Europe, North America, Asia, Africa and the Middle East. He has served as a visiting professor at Columbia Law School, New York, and the China University of Political Science and Law, and as senior visiting research fellow at the Oxford Institute for Energy Studies. In 2019, he was a Herbert Smith Freehills visiting professor at Cambridge University. He was formerly an international energy lawyer at Norton Rose Fulbright Canada LLP where he served on the firm's global committee on energy investments in Africa. He has delivered lectures on energy law in over forty countries. Professor Olawuyi has published close to a hundred articles, book chapters and books on petroleum law, energy and international environmental law. His most recent book publications include *The Human Rights-Based Approach to Carbon Finance* (Cambridge University Press, 2016) and *Extractives Industry Law in Africa* (Springer, 2018). Professor Olawuyi serves on the executive committees and boards of several organisations. He is Vice Chair of the International Law Association; co-chair of the Africa Interest Group of the American Society of International Law (2016–2019); and member of the Academic Advisory Group of the International Bar Association's Section on Energy, Environment, Natural Resources and Infrastructure Law (SEERIL). He is the Editor-in-Chief of the *Journal of Sustainable Development Law and Policy*. Professor Olawuyi holds a doctorate (DPhil) in energy and environmental law from the University of Oxford; a master of laws (LLM) from Harvard University; and another LLM from the University of Calgary. He has been admitted as Barrister and Solicitor in Alberta, Canada; Ontario, Canada; and Nigeria. Professor Olawuyi is a regular media commentator on all aspects of natural resources, energy and environmental law. Further information about his profile and publications can be found at www.damilolaolawuyi.com.

Contributors

Oyeniyi Abe: Research Associate, Centre for Comparative Law in Africa, Faculty of Law, University of Cape Town, South Africa, and Research Fellow (Business and Human Rights), Institute for Oil, Gas, Energy, Environment and Sustainable Development (OGEES), Afe Babalola University, Ado Ekiti, Nigeria.

Rafael Baptista Baleroni: lawyer in Brazil; Bachelor of Law (Juris Doctorate Equivalent) at the Rio de Janeiro State University (UERJ), where he held a scholarship from the Brazilian oil agency, as well as a Master of Laws (LL.M.), University of Chicago, and a Master of International Law (UERJ).

Catherine Banet: Associate Professor, Scandinavian Institute for Maritime Law, Energy and Resources Law Department at the University of Oslo, Norway; affiliated to the Oslo Centre for Research on Environmentally friendly Energy (CREE).

Meyer van den Berg: Attorney of the High Court of Namibia; Consultant, Koep & Partners, Windhoek, Namibia; Lecturer, Faculty of Law, University of Namibia and Adjunct Associate Professor at the SARChI Chair: Mineral Law in Africa, University of Cape Town, South Africa.

Fernanda Delgado: Full-time professor and research coordinator at FGV Energia, one of Brazil's main think tanks; and an affiliated professor of Oil Geopolitics in the Brazilian Navy Officers University, Brazil.

Jose Vicente Duncan de Miranda: Bachelor of Law (Juris Doctorate Equivalent) at the Federal University of Rio de Janeiro (UFRJ). Specialisation in Civil-Constitutional Law (UERJ) and Upstream Management Projects (IBP). Currently a lawyer in Brazil, and has held senior positions in the legal departments of Chevron Brazil, Angola LNG Ltd., and as former chairman of IBP (Brazilian Petroleum and Natural Gas Institute)'s legal committee.

Alexander Ezenagu: Assistant Professor of Taxation and Commercial Law, College of Law, Hamad Bin Khalifa University, Qatar.

xxii *List of Contributors*

Chidiebere Eze-Ajoku: Barrister and Solicitor of the Supreme Court of Nigeria; Bachelor of Law at Igbinedion University, Okada, Nigeria, as well as a Master of Tax Law (LL.M), Queen Mary, University of London.

Tina Soliman Hunter: Professor of Petroleum and Resources Law, University of Aberdeen, and Director of Centre for Energy Law, University of Aberdeen, Scotland.

Susan L. Karamanian: Dean, College of Law, Hamad Bin Khalifa University, Qatar.

Amir Lebdioui: Fellow, Department of International Development and in the Latin American and Carribean Centre, London School of Economics, United Kingdom.

James Ombaki Kirwa: Program Officer, Research and Publication, Strathmore Extractives Industry Centre, Strathmore Law School, Kenya.

Alastair R. Lucas QC: Professor Emeritus and Senior Research Fellow, Canadian Institute of Resources Law (CIRL), Faculty of Law, University of Calgary, Canada.

David K. Laidlaw: Research Fellow, CIRL, University of Calgary, Canada.

Mandy Meng Fang: Assistant Professor, School of Law, City University of Hong Kong, Hong Kong.

Timothy Meyer: Professor of Law, Vanderbilt University Law School, United States.

Marcela Morales: Research Associate at On Think Tanks; Independent consultant working on natural resource management, gender and education.

Hanri Mostert: DST/NRF SARChI Research Chair: Mineral Law in Africa and Professor of Law, University of Cape Town, South Africa.

Marcelo Neuman: Associate Professor and Research Coordinator of the Energy for Sustainable Development Area, Institute of Industry, National University of General Sarmiento, Buenos Aires, Argentina.

Chilenye Nwapi: Research Fellow, Canadian Institute of Resources Law, University of Calgary, Canada.

George Ndi: Senior Lecturer in Law, University of Huddersfield, United Kingdom.

Ada Ordor: Associate Professor and Director, Centre for Comparative Law in Africa, Faculty of Law, University of Cape Town, South Africa.

Jesse Salah Ovadia: Associate Professor, Department of Political Science, University of Windsor, Canada.

Damilola S. Olawuyi: Associate Professor of Law, Hamad Bin Khalifa University, Qatar, and Director, Institute for Oil, Gas, Energy, Environment and Sustainable Development (OGEES Institute), Afe Babalola University, Ado Ekiti, Nigeria.

List of Contributors

Ayobami J. Olaniyan: Senior Lecturer, College of Law and Research Fellow (Oil and Gas Law & Policy), Institute for Oil, Gas, Energy, Environment and Sustainable Development (OGEES), Afe Babalola University, Ado Ekiti, Nigeria.

Ibironke Odumosu-Ayanu: Associate Professor of Law, College of Law, University of Saskatchewan, Canada.

Eduardo G Pereira: is a Professor of Natural Resources and Energy Law as a full-time scholar at the Siberian Federal University, Russia and part-time, adjunct and/or visiting scholar in a number of leading academic institutions around the world (including the University of West Indies, University of São Paulo, Strathmore University, Agostinho Neto University, University of Aberdeen and among others).

Aaron Koenck: attorney in the United States; Juris Doctorate, Diploma in Comparative Law and LL.M. in Energy, Environment, and Natural Resources.

Pedro Henrique Neves: Master of Chemical Engineering candidate at Fluminense Federal University, Brazil, and a researcher at FGV Energia, focused on oil & gas market intelligence.

Zachary Sturman: PhD Candidate in Law and Economics, Vanderbilt University Law School, United States.

Melba K. Wasunna: External Affairs Manager, Base Titanium Ltd, Kenya, and Sessional Lecturer, LL.M. Program in Oil and Gas Law, Strathmore Law School, Kenya.

PART I

Introductory Context and Principles

1

Local Content and the Sustainable Development Nexus

Damilola S. Olawuyi

1 INTRODUCTION

Energy is inextricably linked to all aspects of human life: the ability to work, live, survive and execute tasks. Given the significance of energy to human life and the global economy, global energy markets are rapidly growing and have witnessed significant transformations over the last few decades.[1] Technological innovation; the diversification of the main primary energy sources (conventional and unconventional oil and gas, coal, renewables, nuclear and solid minerals); rise in global primary energy demand; changes to established means of energy supply and distribution; geopolitical uncertainties; environmental pollution; climate change; sharp drop in the price of oil since 2014; outbreak of the novel Coronavirus Disease of 2019 (COVID-19) pandemic; and the increasing demand for the equitable distribution of the benefits and risks of energy production amongst other things are rapidly transforming the field of energy law.[2] Furthermore, important political changes such as United Kingdom's exit from the European Union (Brexit); the rise of America-first policies in the United States under President Donald Trump; the abrupt diplomatic isolation and blockade of Qatar by several Gulf countries; as well as the global quest for low-carbon energy transition in alignment with the United Nations Sustainable Development Goals (SDGs) have all resulted in

---

[1] The global energy market consists of people, companies, financial institutions, trade organisations and national authorities involved in the production, distribution and sale of energy. The energy market consists of three key sectors: production (upstream), networks (midstream) and retail (downstream). There are various sub-industries encompassed in each key sector, including the petroleum industry, gas industry; mining industry, electrical power industry; coal industry; renewable energy industry; drilling, equipment/service industry; refining/marketing industry amongst others. See R. Heffron, *Energy Law: An Introduction* (Springer, 2015) 1–3; see also D. Olawuyi, *Extractives Industry Law in Africa* (Cham, Switzerland: Springer, 2018) 1–5.

[2] See D. Zillman, M. Roggenkamp, L. Paddock and L. Godden, 'Introduction: How Technological and Legal Innovation Are Transforming Energy Law' in D. Zillman, M. Roggenkamp, L. Paddock and L Godden (eds.) *Innovation in Energy Law and Technology: Dynamic Solutions for Energy Transitions* (Oxford University Press, 2018) 1–16.

4   *Damilola S. Olawuyi*

fundamental shifts in domestic national energy policies.[3] In response, countries have evolved legal innovations, policies and measures aimed at maximising the gains of resource production in the energy sector, while lowering the negative social, economic, environment and geopolitical impacts. One key revolution in energy law and policy over the last decade is the rise in the adoption of local content requirements and policies (LCRs) – regulatory measures, contractual provisions and policies that require energy market participants and operators to give priority to nationals, domestic companies and locally produced materials, in the procurement of goods and services used for energy operations.

Given the international nature of the global energy industry, design and application of LCRs have taken diverse forms and standards in different jurisdictions. One consistent aim of LCRs in global energy markets is the desire to incentivise and maximise the use of local and in-country goods and services in energy operations. Despite this clear and uniform overall policy driver of LCRs in global energy markets, the practical outcomes of LCRs in terms of boosting productivity, developing value chains and advancing sustainable development have yielded mixed results to date. LCRs have been linked in a number of countries with producing conflict and misalignments with extant national obligations under core international treaty provisions on trade, investment, gender, environment, human rights and sustainable development.[4] Similarly, the application of LCRs in the renewable energy sector has provided mixed results, with studies showing that protectionist and trade-restrictive LCRs may slow down the development of the renewable energy sector thereby stifling progress in environmental and sustainable development objectives.[5] Furthermore, despite the rise in LCRs in terms of providing employment and participation opportunities for nationals, there remains a considerable gender gap in the distribution of benefits and risks, as well as access to socio-economic opportunities, for women in key sectors of the energy industry.[6] Similarly, on-the-ground problems relating to the implementation of LCRs, such as lack of available technology, capacity and material at the local level, may delay projects and may ultimately result in loss of foreign direct

---

[3] See D. Olawuyi, 'International Energy Law and the Gulf Crisis' in Rory Miller (ed.), *The Gulf Crisis: The View from Qatar* (Doha: HBKU Press, 2018) 127–35.

[4] See B. Asiago and M. Wasunna, 'Are Local Content Requirements in Developing Petroleum Sectors Sustainable? Managing Expectations while Aligning Sustainable Principles with Regulatory Policy' (2018) OGEL, www.ogel.org/journal-advance-publication-article.asp?key=572.

[5] Ibid. See also J.-C. Kuntze and T. Moerenhout, 'Local Content requirements and the Renewable Energy Industry: A Good Match?' International Centre for Trade and Sustainable Development (2013) 6–11.

[6] African Development Bank, *Women's Economic Empowerment in Oil and Gas Industries in Africa*, www.afdb.org/fileadmin/uploads/afdb/Documents/Publications/anrc/AfDB_WomenEconomics Empowerment_V15.pdf, noting the need to address the considerable gender bias in the distribution of the risks, costs and benefits in extractive industries in Africa.

investment (FDIs) to less restrictive jurisdictions.[7] Such an outcome may delay a country's path to wealth creation and sustainable development.

The undertone of conflict between domestic-level LCRs and the coherent implementation of sustainable development law and treaty provisions raise fundamental questions of policy and practice. This book provides a multijurisdictional and systematic exposition of how LCRs have evolved in energy markets across the world, with case studies from Africa, Asia, Europe, North America, Latin America, South America and Australasia. It then provides comparative analysis of the key implementation challenges that arise, and legal and negotiation techniques for managing those challenges.

This chapter provides foundational information, which would help readers to firmly grasp the underpinning concepts and terminologies relating to the sustainable development questions in the design and implementation of LCRs. After this general introduction, Section 2 provides an overview of the essential features of LCRs in global energy markets. Section 3 outlines the overall aim and structure of the book, providing information on the work that our thirty-two authors have done to examine the core intersections between LCRs, treaty implementation and sustainable development in global energy markets.

2 LCRS IN GLOBAL ENERGY MARKETS: LEGAL CONTEXT AND OVERVIEW

There is no uniform definition of LCRs. In this book, our working definition of LCR is regulatory measures, contractual provisions and policies that require energy market participants and operators to give priority to nationals, domestic companies and locally produced materials, in the procurement of goods and services used for energy operations. Although LCRs have been extensively discussed with respect to the oil and gas sector, LCRs have been widely applied in mining, renewable energy and other energy subsectors.[8] Irrespective of the subsector, LCRs are generally utilised by governments to generate broader economic benefits for the local economy, beyond fiscal benefits.[9]

LCRs can be in form of preferential rates for local industries; mandatory procurement requirements to source goods from local industries; preferential tax and tariff

---

[7] See D. Olawuyi, 'Local Content Policies and Their Implications for International Investment Law' in J. Chaisse et al. (eds.), *Handbook of International Investment Law* (Springer, 2019) 1–21.

[8] See Organisation for Economic Co-operation and Development (OECD), Working Party of the Trade Committee, 'Local Content Policies in Minerals-Exporting Countries' (OECD 2017); also C. Banet, 'Techno-nationalism in the Context of Energy Transition: Regulating Technology Innovation Transfer in Offshore Wind Technologies' in D. Zillman, M. Roggenkamp, L. Paddock and L Godden (eds.), *Innovation in Energy Law and Technology: Dynamic Solutions for Energy Transitions* (Oxford University Press, 2018) 74–98.

[9] D. Olawuyi, 'Local Content and Procurement Requirements in Oil and Gas Contracts: Regional Trends in the Middle East and North Africa' (2019) 37(1) *Journal of Energy and Natural Resources Law* 93–117.

6   *Damilola S. Olawuyi*

schemes that confer financial benefits on goods or energy produced with local equipment; preference for local goods and services as part of the conditions for approving contracts, permits or licenses; or performance requirements and targets designed to confer benefits on nationals and local industries.[10] Slightly over 90 per cent of resource-rich countries have at least one form of LCR as regards their energy industries, 50 per cent of which impose quantitative performance targets to achieve certain threshold of local participation and utilisation of human and material resources indigenous to that economy.[11] Famous examples include 'Buy American' provisions in the United States, which typically require government contractors to purchase their supplies from American companies even if those supplies are more expensive than the same products purchased from non-American companies.[12] Also, the Feed-in-Tariffs Scheme (FIT Programme) in Ontario, Canada, which mandated project operators to procure 'minimum amount of goods and services that come from Ontario' in order to be able to participate in the price guarantees and grid access granted by the FIT.[13] In Australia, Indigenous Land Use Agreements (ILUAs) in the mining sector have stipulated that at least 40 per cent of the workforce at the mine will at all times be comprised of local Aboriginal people.[14] Similarly, as far back as 1959, the Government of Nigeria established indigenisation policies which gave priority to Nigerians, Nigerian companies and locally produced material in critical sectors of the Nigerian economy, including the oil and gas sector.[15] Likewise, in the early 1990s, Spain developed a renewable energy legislation that encouraged regions in the country to apply LCRs as a condition for awarding concessions.[16] A number of other prominent energy markets, such as Brazil, the United Kingdom, Norway, Qatar and several other

[10] See United Nations Conference on Trade and Development (UNCTAD), 'Foreign Direct Investment and Performance Requirements: New Evidence from Selected Countries', 2003, p. 2, which defines performance requirements as 'stipulations, imposed on investors, requiring them to meet certain specified goals with respect to their operations in the host country'. In other words, they are measures requiring investors to behave in a particular way or to achieve certain outcomes in the host country. Agreement on Trade-Related Investment Measures, April 15, 1994, Marrakesh Agreement Establishing the World Trade Organization, Annex 1A, 1868 UNTS 186 [TRIMs], Preamble.

[11] Olawuyi, note 7.

[12] T. Meyer, 'How Local Discrimination Can Promote Global Public Goods' 95 *Boston University Law Review* 1937–2001.

[13] See, Ontario Ministry of Energy, 'Feed-in Tariff Program Two-Year Review', www.energy.gov.on.ca /en/fit-and-microfit-program/2-year-fit-review/.

[14] See the Australian Native Title Act 1993 (Cth) see Division 3, Subdivisions B-E. See T. Hunter, *Legal Regulatory Frameworks for the sustainable Extraction of Australian Offshore Petroleum Resources: A Critical Functional Analysis* (University of Bergen, 2010), ch. 4.

[15] For a discussion on the history of the development of legal and policy regimes to promote local content in the Nigerian oil and gas industry, see U. J. Orji, 'Towards Sustainable Local Content Development in the Nigerian Oil and Gas Industry: An Appraisal of the Legal Framework and Challenges-Pt I' (2014) *International Energy Law Review* 30–5.

[16] International Renewable Energy Agency (IRENA) and Global Wind Energy Council (GWEC), '30 Years of Policies for Wind Energy: Lessons from 12 Wind Energy Markets', Spain 2013.

Local Content and Sustainable Development Nexus

countries in Africa and the Middle East, have implemented various forms of LCRs in oil, gas, mining, power and/or renewable energy sectors.[17] LCRs are generally designed to unlock the competitiveness of the local economy and workforce, while allowing a country to diversify and strengthen its national industry. Such LCRs can also promote other social benefits such as job creation, development of endogenous technology and infrastructure and the redistribution of wealth and authority to address concerns of particular minority, indigenous or disadvantaged communities.[18]

LCRs have been increasingly framed as a revolutionary strategy and framework through which resource-rich countries can utilise resource exploitation to increase public welfare, advance sustainable development and diversify growth in other important sectors of their domestic economies, especially by creating local employment, skills development and the participation of local communities in the energy industry.[19] As Ezenagu and Eze-Ajoku argue in this book, 'if developing countries are to develop, upgrade their products, and compete favourably in today's globalized economy, protectionist policies, in the form of LCRs, are inevitable'.[20] Furthermore, if carefully designed and implemented, LCRs can provide a basis for energy companies and indigenous communities to negotiate mutually beneficial terms that could address social, economic and environmental concerns of production operations in indigenous communities.[21]

However, despite the clear drivers, scope and policy objectives of LCRs in global energy markets, approaches taken to enforce and implement LCRs may conflict with core international treaty provisions on sustainable development, especially in countries with unclear and unspecific legal frameworks on LCRs. Here we define sustainable development, specifically sustainable resource management (SRM), as development that balances social and economic development and environmental protection in the management and use of petroleum, solid minerals and other natural resources.[22] Sustainable development law therefore encompasses treaties, regulatory instruments and frameworks that aim to advance economic, social and environmental

---

[17] Ibid. See also, T. Acheampong, M. Ashong and V. C. Svanikier, 'An Assessment of Local Content Policies in Oil and Gas Producing Countries' (2016) 9 *Journal of World Energy Law & Business* 282; S. Tordo et al., Local Content Policies in the Oil and Gas Sector (World Bank 2013); also P. Heum, 'Local Content Development – Experiences from Oil and Gas Activities in Norway' (2008) SNF Working Paper No 02/08, Institute for Research in Economics and Business Administration, Bergen.

[18] See Intergovernmental Forum on Mining, Minerals Metals and Sustainable Development, *Designing Local Content Policies in Mineral Rich Countries* (2018), www.iisd.org/sites/default/files/publications/local-content-policies-mineral-rich-countries.pdf, p. 2–3.

[19] See Meyer, note 12, arguing that 'the use of these discriminatory subsidies at the subnational level can sometimes increase global welfare'.

[20] See Chapter 5 of this book.

[21] See Odumosu-Ayanu in Chapter 19 of this book.

[22] See the Brundtland Report, which defines sustainable development as 'development which meets the needs of the present without compromising the ability of future generations to meet their own needs'. G. Brundtland, Report of the World Commission on Environment and Development: Our Common Future (United Nations General Assembly document A/42/427, 1987) para 27. Also, Para. 1.2 of the ILA

8   Damilola S. Olawuyi

development for current and future generations. The principle of SRM, which seeks to address inconsistencies and overlap between economic instruments and their overall social and environmental development outcomes, especially in the energy sector, has become one of the most-recognised and important principles of international law, and has found its way into several international declarations, treaties and domestic law.[23] In its simplest practical application, SRM requires a coherent and systemic integration of core instruments and treaties on energy, environment, trade, investment, economic growth, human rights and development to encourage mutual supportiveness and avoid overlap.[24] This includes promoting (1) participation and inclusion, (2) access to information, (3) non-discrimination and equality, (4) empowerment and accountability and (5) legality and access to justice (the 'PANEL Principles') in the design and implementation of energy policies and programs to prevent social and human rights trade-offs.[25]

New Delhi Declaration on Sustainable Development stating that 'states are under a duty to manage natural resources, including natural resources within their own territory or jurisdiction, in a rational, sustainable and safe way so as to contribute to the development of their peoples, with particular regard for the rights of indigenous peoples, and to the conservation and sustainable use of natural resources and the protection of the environment, including ecosystems. States must take into account the needs of future generations in determining the rate of use of natural resources. All relevant actors (including States, industrial concerns and other components of civil society) are under a duty to avoid wasteful use of natural resources and promote waste minimization policies.' See also the 2012 Sofia Guiding Statements on the Judicial Elaboration of the 2002 New Delhi Declaration of Principles of International Law Relating to Sustainable Development, RESOLUTION No. 7/2012 noting in para. 3 that 'the sustainable use of all natural resources represents an emerging rule of general customary international law, with particular normative precision identifiable with respect to shared and common natural resources'.

[23] For a comprehensive list of these instruments, see the United Nations Sustainable Development Knowledge Platform. See also N. Schrijver, 'Advancements in the Principles of International Law on Sustainable Development', in M. C. Cordonier Segger and C. G. Weeramantry (eds.), *Sustainable Development Principles in the Decisions of International Courts and Tribunals, 1992–2012* (Routledge, 2017) 99–102 (providing an overview of the ways that sustainable development principles have been incorporated into and operationalised by international treaty regimes and tribunals); D. French, 'The Sofia Guiding Statements on sustainable development principles in the decisions of international tribunals', in Cordonier Segger and Weeramantry, *infra*, 177–84 (highlighting how sustainable development has been incorporated into the juridical activities of international bodies convened under the auspices of UN associated and influenced treaty regimes).

[24] See D. Olawuyi, *The Human Rights Based Approach to Carbon Finance* (Paperback Edition, Cambridge University Press, 2018) 1–25, discussing the need for systemic integration and harmonisation of core trade, environment, climate change, energy and human rights treaties to achieve broader goals of sustainable development.

[25] See D. Olawuyi, 'Energy (and Human Rights) for All: Addressing Human Rights Risks in Energy Access Projects', in R. Salter, C. G. Gonzalez and E. K. Warner, *Energy Justice: US and International Perspectives* (Edward Elgar, 2018) 73–104. See also the preamble to chapter 23 of Agenda 21, approved by the UN Conference on Environment and Development on 13 June 1992: UN doc A/CONF.151/26 (vols. I–III) (1992), stating that fundamental prerequisites for the achievement of sustainable development is broad public participation in decision-making. 'This includes the need of individuals, groups, and organizations to participate in environmental impact assessment procedures and to know about and participate in decisions, particularly those that potentially affect the communities in which they live and work.'

SRM and the need for policy coherence have assumed greater significance and urgency as the United Nations' 2030 Agenda for Sustainable Development places great emphasis on the need for enhanced partnership – globally, regionally and nationally – to support the ambitious targets of the 2030 Agenda.[26] SDG 17.14 specifically encourages all stakeholders to enhance policy coherence for sustainable development. For example, in recognising the importance of trade to the attainment of the SDGs, SDG 17.10 encourages countries to promote a 'universal, rules-based, open, non-discriminatory and equitable multilateral trading system under the World Trade Organization, including through the conclusion of negotiations under its Doha Development Agenda'.[27] Similarly, SDG 2.B calls on countries to correct and prevent trade restrictions and distortions in world agricultural markets, through – amongst other measures – the elimination of export subsidies.[28] These and other SDGs recognise the need to strengthen and advance ongoing efforts to promote partnerships and mutual supportiveness between trade, energy, human rights and environment regimes as a prerequisite for achieving the 2030 Agenda.[29]

However, as shown in chapters of this book, LCRs, if not properly designed and implemented, can result in significant overlap and misalignment in the domestic implementation of a number of international treaties relating to trade, investment, energy, human rights, the environment and sustainable development. For example, domestic level LCRs can present major inconsistencies and risks to the application of international trade and investment law. Forests of literatures have analysed the conflicts between LCRs and the provisions of the General Agreement on Tariffs and Trade (GATT, 1994, 1947); the Agreement on Trade-Related Investment Measures (TRIMS); the Agreement on Government Procurement (GPA); and the General Agreement on Trade in Services (GATS).[30] Many of these instruments expressly prohibit the use of certain performance requirements – especially those related to local content, export controls, foreign exchange restrictions, purchase of raw materials, domestic equity/ownership, technology transfer, research and development (R&D), employment and domestic equity/ownership – that can cause trade restriction or price-distorting effects.[31] For example, in 2013, the WTO Appellate Body

---

[26] Ibid.; see also D. Olawuyi, 'Sustainable Development and the Water-Energy-Food Nexus: Legal Challenges and Emerging Solutions' (2020) 103 *Environmental Science and Policy* 1–9.

[27] United Nations, 'Transforming Our World: The 2030 Agenda for Sustainable Development', GA Res. 70/1, 25 September 2015 (2030 Sustainable Development Agenda).

[28] Ibid.

[29] Olawuyi, note 25.

[30] Olawuyi, note 7; also L. Nielsen, 'The Legality of Local Content Measures under WTO Law' (2014) 48 *Journal of World Trade Law* 3, 553–91, 557–65.

[31] Article 2.1 of the TRIMs Agreement requires WTO members to refrain from applying any TRIMs (Trade-Related Investment Measures) that are inconsistent with the national treatment obligation under Article III or XI of the GATT Treaty (1994). See Trade-Related Investment Measures (TRIMs) Agreement. Agreement on Trade-Related Investment Measures, Apr. 15, 1994, Marrakesh Agreement Establishing the World Trade Organization, Annex 1A, 1868 U.N.T.S. 186; also General Agreement on Tariffs and Trade (GATT) (1994) TS 56 (1996) Cm 3282; 33 ILM 28.

10 *Damilola S. Olawuyi*

ruled that Canada's LCRs violate the obligation not to discriminate against foreign products contained in the GATT.[32] A number of other decisions have highlighted the deep tensions and trade-offs between domestic LCRs and the implementation of trade, investment and environment treaties.[33] In addition to creating misalignment with trade and investment treaty obligations, discriminatory and protectionist LCRs in the energy sector can stifle progress in the transfer of environmentally preferable technologies and products needed to advance environmental protection, energy security and sustainable development.

Similarly, restrictive LCRs can be detrimental to the flow of foreign direct investment (FDIs) to energy-producing countries.[34] Several energy-producing countries have intensified efforts to attract FDIs in all sectors of national economies, as key ways to improve economic diversification, create jobs and eliminate poverty in line with SDG 8 on decent work and economic growth, and SDG 1 on poverty eradication.[35] However, while LCRs may specify the portion of total expenditures that must be comprised of locally sourced goods and services, lack of available capacity and material at the local level may delay projects and may ultimately result in loss of FDIs to less restrictive jurisdictions.[36] Such an outcome may ultimately stifle a country's path to sustainable development. For example, complying with product mandating requirements could mean project delays or higher costs on the part of the operator, especially when suitable and reasonably priced alternatives are not immediately available locally.[37] This can have a distorting effect on the profitability and viability of a project from the investor's standpoint or affect the timeline for investment activities. The imposition of domestic-level LCRs in the absence of required supporting capacity, institutional resources or adequate technological capabilities could ultimately reduce the attractiveness of a country as a desirable location for FDIs.[38] According to a study by the Organisation for Economic Co-operation and Development (OECD), total imports and total exports have declined in every region of the world as

---

[32] Appellate Body Reports, Canada: Certain Measures Affecting the Renewable Energy Generation Section, Canada: Measures Relating to the Feed-in Tariff Program, 5.85, WTO Doc. WT/DS412/AB/R, WT/DS426/AB/R (adopted May 24, 2013) [hereinafter Canada: Renewable Energy] (finding that Canada's LCR programs – 'Minimum Required Domestic Content Levels' – violate Article III:4 of the GATT 1994 standards).

[33] See a full discussion in Chapter 3.

[34] J. Jensen and D. Tarr, 'Impact of Local Content Restrictions and Barriers against Foreign Direct Investment in Services: The Case of Kazakhstan's Accession to the World Trade Organization' (2008) 46 *Eastern European Economics* 5–26.

[35] UN General Assembly, Transforming Our World: The 2030 Agenda for Sustainable Development, 21 October 2015, UN Doc. A/RES/70/1.

[36] See Chapters 9 and 12 of this book for detailed discussion.

[37] P. Peek and P. Gantès, 'Skills Shortages and Local Content in the Sub-Saharan African Oil and Gas Industry: How to Close the Gap', Centre de recherches enterprises et societies (CRES), 2008.

[38] See United Nations Conference on Trade and Development (UNCTAD), 'Elimination of TRIMS: The Experience of Selected Developing Countries', 2007, pp. 9–10.

Local Content and Sustainable Development Nexus

a result of LCRs and have shrunk world imports and exports by USD 12 billion and USD 11 billion, respectively.[39] Furthermore, according to the study, almost all cases where LCRs are introduced, final goods exports have been reduced from 0.05 per cent to as much as 5.0 per cent.[40] Investors that are unable to meet a country's LCRs may seek alternate and less restrictive markets for their investments. Such an outcome could impact the ability of energy-rich countries to meet their sustainable development aims.

Furthermore, LCR implementation, especially obligations relating to state involvement in procurement processes, compliance reporting and data localisation requirements, as seen in some LCRs in Africa and the Middle East, could raise the legal risks, cost and feasibility of investing in energy sectors in those regions.[41] For example, recent studies show that LCR compliance costs can increase an investor's information technology expenditure by as much as 40 per cent.[42] Likewise, the cost of training local employees and meeting mandatory corporate social responsibility (CSR) obligations of local communities, especially in indigenous communities, can be very significant and must therefore be carefully considered by energy operators at contract negotiation stages in order to avoid fines, protracted litigation and community protests. Analysing the general legal, fiscal and contractual framework governing LCRs, especially understanding contractual provisions and clauses such as employment of nationals, training, procurement, technology transfer and project participation requirements, is now very important to effective risk management and due diligence in the design and implementation of energy projects.

Additionally, despite the rise in LCRs in terms of providing employment and participation opportunities for nationals, there remains a considerable gender gap in the distribution of benefits and risks associated with the sector, as well as access to socio-economic opportunities for women across the energy industry value chain, especially in developing countries where the energy industry remains overwhelming male dominated.[43] LCR implementation in a number of countries has yet to pay sufficient attention to studying, analysing and unpacking patterns of opportunity

---

[39] S. Stone, J. Messent and D. Flaig, 'Emerging Policy Issues: Localisation Barriers to Trade', OECD Trade Policy Papers, No. 180, 2015, pp. 10–11.

[40] Ibid.

[41] See National Board of Trade (NBT), 'No Transfer, No Trade: The Importance of Cross-Border Data Transfers for Companies Based in Sweden', 2014.

[42] Ibid.; Ponemon Institute, 'The True Cost of Compliance' January 2011.

[43] For example, according to a report, the Nigerian 'oil and gas industry is still overwhelmingly male, with surveys showing that the executive boardrooms of petroleum companies are mostly a boys' club'. See BBC News, 'Nigeria's Growing Number of Female Oil Bosses', September 11, 2014, www .bbc.com/news/business–29127436. See also African Development Bank, Women's Economic Empowerment in Oil and Gas Industries in Africa, www.afdb.org/fileadmin/uploads/afdb/docu ments/publications/anrc/afdb_womeneconomicsempowerment_v15.pdf, stating that in African extractive industries, 'while benefits accrue mostly to men in the form of employment and compensation, the costs (e.g. family or social disruption, environmental degradation) fall most heavily on women'.

and wealth (non)creation for women in key sectors of the energy industry. The number of local content opportunities and outcomes, such as jobs, financing, procurement contracts and training, provided for women in the energy industry is hardly measured, assessed or documented against LCRs objectives and legislative provisions in a clear and transparent manner.[44] Furthermore, the critical linkages between gender justice and overall sustainable development are yet to be given serious consideration in decision-making, program planning, public procurement practices, financing, training, capacity development and program implementation in several global energy markets and industries, cutting across government, industry and non-governmental agencies. Lack of reliable information gathering and assessment makes it difficult, if not impossible for countries to develop tailored programs, projects and opportunities for girls and women, even though they are some of the most affected by industry-related pollution, displacements and conflicts. As demonstrated in this book, well-intended LCRs may result in negative social, human rights and environmental outcomes if not backed by robust legal and governance safeguards, especially the PANEL Principles.[45]

The undertone of conflict between domestic-level LCRs and the coherent implementation of sustainable development law and treaty provisions raise fundamental questions of policy and practice that require dynamic legal solutions. Are the two mutually supportive or in tension with one another? To the extent that conflicts arise, how should they be addressed? Can the objectives of LCRs and sustainable development law be reconciled, or are conflicts inevitable? And if the latter, what is the appropriate balance between the two? These questions, tensions and trade-offs highlight, on the broader level, the need to continually measure and balance the policy aims of LCRs with practical outcomes in terms of contributions to economic, social and environmental development outcomes.

Despite the importance and prevalence of LCRs in global energy markets, a comparative analysis and evaluation of the normative underpinnings, functionality and sustainability of LCRs and regimes, in the light of emerging international law norms on trade, investment, business and human rights, has yet to receive a book-length, exhaustive and rigorous exposition and analysis. While earlier scholarship has focused on surveying existing laws and policies on LCRs in select countries, the multi-dimensional, intersectional nature of LCRs and sustainable development, especially in the Global South, has yet to receive detailed, book-length exposition. This book fills this gap. It unpacks the legal interactions and fundamental tension points between international sustainable development law and domestic-level LCRs. In so doing, the book will shed new light on the oft-neglected social dimension of the design, application and implementation of LCRs, especially the question

---

[44] See Chapter 9 of this book for a detailed discussion.
[45] Olawuyi, note 25.

Local Content and Sustainable Development Nexus   13

whether LCRs aid or hinder the implementation of sustainable development treaties and norms in energy markets.

3 AIM, SCOPE AND STRUCTURE OF THE BOOK

As noted earlier, while most of the earlier legal scholarship on LCRs has focused on surveying existing laws and policies on LCRs in select countries, the multi-dimensional, intersectional nature of LCRs and sustainable development, especially in the Global South has yet to receive detailed, book-length exposition. This analytical gap and the ensuing regulatory disconnect have not allowed for systemic and comparative evaluation of the normative underpinnings, functionality and sustainability of LCRs, in the light of emerging international law norms and treaties on trade, investment, business and human rights. With case studies from Africa, Asia, Europe, North America, Latin America, South America and Australasia, this book provides a far more complete theoretical analysis and exposition of how LCRs have evolved in key global energy markets. It will then provide comparative analysis of LCRs in these countries, in order to determine optimal and sustainable local content policies, the context of their implementation and barriers to their application. It will also include recommendations on the guiding principles of a sustainable and rights-based approach to the design, application and implementation of LCRs.

While this book offers a scan of the sources and underpinning principles of LCRs in key energy jurisdictions, it is clearly acknowledged that the substantive chapters cannot unpack and analyse every applicable legislation and instrument in all energy-producing countries. Given the range of intersecting issues involved and the sheer number of local content legislation, regulations, policies and contracts around the world, this book focuses on select case studies in key energy markets with publicly accessible legal instruments and information to illustrate the legal and policy aspects of designing and implementing LCRs. The twenty-one chapters of this book provide multijurisdictional and systematic exposition of how LCRs have evolved in energy jurisdictions across the world, as well as a comparative analysis of the key implementation challenges that arise, and legal and negotiation techniques for managing those challenges. The central organising principle and aim of this book therefore is to: enhance an understanding of the guiding principles of laws, applicable instruments, regulatory framework and institutions on LCRs in the surveyed jurisdictions; explore common legal and sustainable development challenges and risks that apply with respect to LCRs in key global energy markets; and provide practical viewpoints on how governments, corporations and their lawyers alike, can identify, mitigate and prevent legal challenges and risks when negotiating contractual provisions relating to LCRs.

4 STRUCTURE

Each of the chapters of the book provides a detailed and rigorous background of the regulatory context of LCRs in the surveyed region or country, especially how LCRs have contributed to sustainable development, the barriers that remain and approaches for integrating sustainable development, gender justice, transparency and accountability amongst others into the design and implementation of LCRs.

This book is organised into three parts to reflect a transition from theoretical concepts to key practical discussions. Part I of the book, comprising five chapters, introduces the evolution and conceptualisation of LCRs in global energy markets. It explains the relationship amongst LCRs, sustainable development, participatory development, distributive justice, social licence to operate and corporate social responsibility, and introduces some of the normative frameworks that have been utilised to analyse the conceptualisation, design and implementation of LCRs.

The thirteen chapters in Part II of the book consist of a series of geographical case studies that apply these frameworks to selected energy markets in the Global North and the Global South. The case studies identify concerns of social exclusion, environmental trade-offs, corruption, lack of transparency and use of performance requirements – incoherent application of LCRs that have been raised in different energy markets. This part also identifies compatible and high-leverage local content strategies, the contexts in which they are being implemented, barriers to their effective implementation and innovative legal approaches to promote such strategies. The chapters demonstrate how inappropriately designed and implemented LCRs can produce distributive injustice, local resistance, misalignment of a country's fiscal policies and sustainable development goals, and may ultimately serve as disincentive to foreign participation in a country's extractive market. The case studies then discuss innovative legal strategies to address these misalignments and inequities.

Part III of the book, comprising three chapters, offers reflections on the case studies and addresses how lessons from the diverse jurisdictions may inform thoughts on how to effectively design, apply and implement sustainable and rights-based LCRs. By evaluating gaps in extant instruments, Part III provides a consolidation of the findings reached by the thirty-two authors and analyses practical ideas that could influence and guide emerging efforts by national authorities and international organisations, such as the OECD, the Extractive Industries Transparency Initiative (EITI) and the African Development Bank aimed at adopting transparent, consistent and regional best practices on local content in extractive industries.

5 CONCLUSION

Without adequate sustainable development safeguards, LCRs designed to expand economic benefits from energy operations and projects, risk exacerbating treaty violations, social exclusion, corruption, lack of transparency, human rights violations, delayed progress on climate and environmental action and loss of FDIs in many countries. A comprehensive analysis and study of key sustainable development trade-offs and tensions that arise in the design, application and implementation of LCRs in global energy markets can help us plot a comprehensive path for achieving policy coherence and reform.

The systemic and multijurisdictional survey of the unique and underlying features of LCRs in diverse jurisdictions offered by this book can simplify the task of negotiating measurable, collaborative and sustainable LCRs in global energy markets.

2

Defining the 'Local' in Local Content Requirements in the Oil and Gas Sector

Chilenye Nwapi[*]

1 INTRODUCTION

Local content is broadly understood as the overall value added to, or created in, a given economy by firms operating in that economy, through the conscious utilisation of human and material resources indigenous to that economy, as distinct from resources imported from foreign lands. As defined by the International Petroleum Industry Environmental Conservation Association (IPIECA), it is:

> the local resources a project or business utilizes or develops along its value chain while investing in a host country. This may include employment of nationals, goods and services procured from companies resident in the host country, partnerships with local entities, development of enabling infrastructure, the improvement of local skills and capacity of local businesses, or the improvement of local techno-logical capabilities.[1]

Despite this seemingly clear definition, the conceptual question of what constitutes 'local' is not without ambiguity. For instance, what is meant by 'local resources', 'local goods and services', 'local entities', 'local skills', 'local businesses' (local companies or firms) or 'local technological capabilities'? Is 'local' synonymous with 'national'? Or does 'local' refer to the subnational locality (the community or broader local area, such as the municipality) where the oil and gas resources are extracted or produced, or to the subnational 'region' (the state or province, or group of them within a subnational geopolitical zone) where the resources are located? These questions are important from a policy perspective because how local is conceptualised has a significant role to play in determining the type and scope of persons who would directly benefit from the imposition of local content

---

[*] This chapter is an expanded version of the author's original article: C. Nwapi, 'Defining the "Local" in Local Content Requirements in the Oil and Gas Industry in Developing Countries' (2015) 8 *Law and Development Review* 187–216. The author has the permission of the journal to publish this revised version in this edited book.

[1] IPIECA, 'Local Content: A Guidance Document for the Oil and Gas Industry', Second Edition, April 2016.

requirements (LCRs) on companies. In addition, while there are no hard and fast rules about how 'local' is to be defined, it is important for LCRs to be guided by a clear understanding of 'local', as such clarity enhances the ability of the government not only to design LCRs in a strategic way but also to formulate other socio-economic policies in the country in a more focused or targeted manner. The conceptualisation of 'local' is especially relevant for developing countries where the benefits of oil and gas development have concentrated historically in the hands of a few at the centre, while the communities and regions where the resources are located, and which suffer most severely the negative externalities of resource extraction, are excluded or marginalised from those benefits.[2] Such a developing country that is desirous of addressing such historical marginalisations may have to take seriously how 'local' is defined.

This chapter does two principal things. First, it reviews local content legislation from select jurisdictions with oil and gas resources to ascertain how 'local' *is* defined and/or understood. Second, it engages with the policy question of how 'local' *should be* defined to enable those jurisdictions to maximise the sustainable development potential of LCRs, especially broad-based economic and social development. Its central argument is that an affirmative policy perspective that embeds community content and national content into LCRs has a uniquely viable path to inclusive, broad-based development, especially in developing countries where oil-bearing communities have seen only marginal benefits from the development of the resources.

A key finding of this chapter is that while LCRs are proliferating, particularly in the oil and gas sector, there is little critical analysis of the meaning of 'local' in LCRs. A review of the laws of most jurisdictions adopting LCRs shows that very little thought has been given to the term 'local'. Most jurisdictions have adopted a centralist or national approach that defines local content in terms of first consideration being given to their 'nationals'. There is scarcely any reference to the local populations around the location of the resource extraction. This approach impedes the potential of LCRs to engender broad-based economic development. Given that revenues from oil and gas resources are managed by national governments (in most jurisdictions), a nuanced approach to LCRs that recognises the historical grievances of local resource communities can provide a mechanism for meeting the demands of those communities and other subnational stakeholders, such as states/provinces and local governments. This will in turn foster the ability of companies to obtain the social license to operate from their host communities. Community dissatisfaction resulting from watching lucrative jobs going to 'outsiders' can stir up conflicts. A localist approach to LCRs can serve as a mechanism for reducing conflict over control of natural resources, ensuring simultaneously that the subnational constituent

---

[2] See F. Okpanachi and N. Andrews, 'Preventing the Oil Resource Curse in Ghana: Lessons from Nigeria' (2012) 68 *World Futures* 430–50.

18   *Chilenye Nwapi*

where the resource extraction takes place does not depend for its development solely on revenues from the resources that flow back to it from the national government. To ground these claims, this chapter will utilise four interconnected theoretical frameworks: localism, the 'shared value' principle, subnational economic development theory and subnational competitiveness theory.

Apart from localist and national perspectives to the understanding of local, another relatively recent proposal calls for the adoption of a regional integration strategy to boost regional, rather than merely (subnational or) national, growth and competitiveness. The argument is that given the complex structure of the international trading system, acting alone, individual countries (in the global south) may not achieve much with LCRs. Rather, a regional content policy would enable a region to share expertise and boost intraregional trade.[3] The regional integration approach has received only scant scholarly attention but this chapter is not the proper forum to deal with it: the shape it should take, its guiding principles and its implementation structures.[4] The focus of this chapter is on how 'local' is defined in various national laws and regulations, whereas an examination of the regional integration approach will have to deal with the strategies of supranational institutions.

The policy context, as well as the arguments for and against the adoption of LCRs, has been well discussed by Olawuyi in Chapter 1 of this book and need not be repeated here. Following this introduction, then, the balance of this chapter is divided as follows: Section 2 considers local content provisions in the national laws and policies of a number of jurisdictions to ascertain the manner in which 'local' is understood in various jurisdictions. The jurisdictions considered are primarily African. This is mainly because most of the local content laws enacted within the past decade in the oil and gas sector were enacted by African countries. Section 3 makes a case for the adoption of a localist perspective to the definition of 'local' in LCRs, drawing on the four theoretical frameworks mentioned earlier (i.e., localism, the 'shared value' principle, subnational development theory and subnational competitiveness theory). Section 4 discusses the likely problems associated with a localist approach to LCRs and provides potential responses to those problems. Section 5 is the conclusion.

2 THE 'LOCAL' IN LOCAL CONTENT: A REVIEW OF LEGAL PROVISIONS ACROSS JURISDICTIONS

The question of what constitutes local content is subject to different interpretations across jurisdictions and varies with the context, although a common thread running through all the legal definitions is 'value-addition' in the country. For example,

---

[3] See C. Nwapi, 'A Survey of the Literature on Local Content Policies in the Oil and Gas Sector in East Africa' (2016) 9 *University of Calgary, School of Public Policy Technical Paper* 18–20.
[4] Preliminary thoughts on this have been provided by Nwapi, ibid.

Defining 'Local' in Local Content Requirements

under the Nigerian Oil and Gas Industry Content Development Act, 2010, Nigerian content is defined as 'the quantum of composite value added to or created in the Nigerian economy by a systematic development of capacity and capabilities through the deliberate utilization of Nigerian human, material resources and services in the Nigerian oil and gas industry'.[5] The Act requires that 'first consideration shall be given to services provided from within Nigeria, to goods manufactured in Nigeria', and in matters of 'training and employment'.[6] To meet the Nigerian LCR, therefore, it is essential that the indigenous company utilised, or the individual employed, is *a Nigerian* or that the raw materials used in the production of goods and services are sourced within Nigeria, regardless of which part of Nigeria they come from. There is no requirement that any proportion of the content must be sourced from within the locality where the company operates. However, Section 27 of the Act gives the content Board power to require a company to maintain an office in a community where it has significant operations. Yet, there is no requirement that in matters of employment in that office, first consideration must be given to members of that community.

Ghana's Petroleum (Local Content and Local Participation) Regulations, 2013 defines local content as 'the quantum or percentage of locally produced materials, personnel, financing, goods and services rendered in the petroleum industry value chain and which can be measured in monetary terms'.[7] The regulation speaks about granting 'first consideration' to services provided within Ghana, goods manufactured in Ghana (where they meet established specifications), and to qualified Ghanaians in employment matters.[8] There is no requirement in the Regulation for any consideration to be given to communities located in the proximity of the resources.

Tanzania's Petroleum Act, 2015 defines local content as:

> the quantum of composite value added to, or created in, the economy of Tanzania through deliberate utilization of Tanzanian human and material resources and services in the petroleum operations in order to stimulate the development of capabilities indigenous of Tanzania and to encourage local investment and participation.[9]

The Act stipulates that preference shall be given to goods 'produced or available in Tanzania' as well as to services provided by Tanzanians or Tanzanian local companies. Where required goods and services are unavailable in Tanzania, they are to be provided by a foreign company which has entered into a joint venture with a local company that has no less than a 25 per cent participating share in the venture.[10] The

---

[5] Nigerian Oil and Gas Industry Content Development Act, 2010, s. 106 [NOGICD Act].
[6] Ibid., s. 10(1).
[7] Petroleum (Local Content and Local Participation) Regulations, 2013, LI 2204, Reg. 49 [Ghana Local Content Regulation].
[8] Ibid., Reg. 9(1).
[9] The Petroleum Act, 2015 (Tanzania), No. 8 of 2015, s. 3. See, also, the Petroleum (Local Content) Regulations 2017, regulation 3.
[10] Ibid., s. 220(1)–(3).

Act defines 'local company' by reference mainly to local registration and ownership, namely, a company incorporated in Tanzania and that is 100 per cent owned by Tanzanians, or a company that has 'a joint venture partnership with a Tanzanian citizen or citizens whose participating share is not less than 15 per cent'.[11] There are also provisions mandating the employment and training of Tanzanians.[12] Companies are required to submit employment and training programmes that take into account gender equity, the condition of persons with disabilities and the needs of host communities.[13] The Act defines 'Host communities' as the 'inhabitants of the local area in which petroleum operations or gas activities take place'.[14]

The above provisions of the Tanzanian Petroleum Act may be contrasted with the provisions of an April 2014 published draft of the Tanzanian Local Content Policy for the Oil and Gas Industry. The draft policy defines local content as:

> [t]he added value brought to the country in the activities of the oil and gas industry in the United Republic of Tanzania through the participation and development of local Tanzanians and local businesses through national labour, technology, goods, services, capital and research capability.[15]

Elsewhere, the draft policy defines local content as 'the added value brought to a host nation (and regional and local areas in that country) through the activities of the oil and gas industry'.[16] The reference to 'regional and local areas' suggests that there is specific recognition of the need to consider to the localities or regions where the resources are extracted in the implementation of LCRs. However, 'local' is defined under the policy as '[t]he Tanzania Mainland and its people', indicating that as long as the person employed or engaged to provide services is a Tanzanian national, the requirement of local content will have been met.[17] The policy also requires that 'deliberate preference' be made in favour of Tanzanians in matters of employment and supply of goods and services.[18] Remarkably, the policy recognises the need to develop 'local local content'.[19] This will give corporations the 'social licence to operate' and contribute to the growth of local communities to achieve a 'mutually beneficial and sustainable' business environment.[20] Despite these expressly recognised advantages, however, the idea of 'local local content' was abandoned in the Petroleum Act. Thus, neither the policy nor the Petroleum Act

---

[11] Ibid., s. 220(9).
[12] Ibid., s. 221.
[13] Ibid., s. 221(2)–(3), (5).
[14] Ibid., s. 221(5).
[15] Ministry of Energy and Minerals (United Republic of Tanzania), *Local Content Policy of Tanzania for the Oil and Gas Industry*, Draft One, Dar es Salaam, April 2014, p. iii [Tanzania Draft Local Content Policy].
[16] Ibid., p. 7.
[17] Ibid., p. iii.
[18] Ibid., p. 21–2.
[19] Ibid., p. 25.
[20] Ibid.

Defining 'Local' in Local Content Requirements 21

requires that any preference be given to local communities or regions over other Tanzanians. The draft policy, however, encourages companies to, 'as far as possible', procure their workforce, materials and services from the communities in which they operate.[21] This provision is partially reflected in the Petroleum Act's provision that requires oil and gas licence holders and contractors to take into account host community needs in their employment and training programs.[22]

In Mozambique, local content in the oil and gas industry is governed by the Petroleum Law No 21/2014 of 8 August 2014 and the Petroleum Operations Regulations (Decree No 33/ 2015). 'Local content' is not defined in either of these two instruments. However, Article 26(4) of the Petroleum Law stipulates that Mozambican legal entities and 'foreign legal entities that associate with Mozambican legal entities' shall be given first consideration in the granting of petroleum concession contracts. The foreign entities, however, must be registered in Mozambique and in the Mozambique Stock Exchange.[23] Mozambican goods and services are also to receive first consideration by petroleum rights holders provided the quality of those goods and services are comparable to the quality of goods and services available abroad and their costs are not more than those of the foreign goods and services by more than 10 per cent.[24] In matters of employment, however, while petroleum rights holders are required to provide employment and training to Mozambican nationals, there is no requirement for this to be provided preferentially to Mozambican nationals.[25] The only stipulated preference relates to residents of the concession area.[26] Under the Petroleum Operations Regulations, however, the use and domestic consumption of natural gas shall be based on the principle that local resources, such as raw materials and services shall be used and that Mozambican manpower shall be given priority.[27] As Andrews and Nwapi have argued, the statutory language employed in the Regulations implies that preference for local employees is applicable only to natural gas and not to all aspects of petroleum operations.[28] Thus, in Mozambique, 'local' is sometimes, for preferential purposes, viewed as national and other times viewed as residents of the petroleum concession area.

There are local content provisions in Uganda's major oil and gas statutes: the Upstream Act[29] and the Midstream Act,[30] the details of which are fleshed out in

[21] Ibid., p. 25–6.
[22] See The Petroleum Act, note 9, s. 221(2)–(3), (5).
[23] Mozambique Petroleum Law No. 21/2014 of 8 August 2014, Article 13(1).
[24] Ibid., Article 41(4); Mozambique Petroleum Operations Regulations (Decree No. 33/ 2015), Article 54(3)).
[25] Mozambique Petroleum Law, Article 12(2).
[26] Ibid., Article 15(b).
[27] Mozambique Petroleum Operations Regulations, note 24, Article 108(3)(h)).
[28] N. Andrews and C. Nwapi, 'Bringing the State Back in Again? The Emerging Developmental State in Africa's Energy Sector' (2018) 41 Energy Research and Social Science 51.
[29] Petroleum (Exploration, Development and Production) Act, 2013 [Uganda Upstream Act].
[30] Petroleum (Refining, Conversion, Transmission and Midstream Storage) Act, 2013.

Regulations passed in 2016.[31] Under the Regulations, local content is viewed nationalistically rather than localistically. In fact, the Regulations adopt the term 'national content' rather than 'local content', and define national content as

> (a) the level of use of Ugandan expertise, goods and services, Ugandan citizens, business and financing in midstream operations; and (b) the substantial combined value added or created in the Ugandan economy through the utilisation of Ugandan human and material resources for the provisions of goods and services to the petroleum industry in Uganda.[32]

Under the Upstream Act, operators shall give first consideration to 'goods produced or available in Uganda' and to services provided by 'Ugandan citizens and companies'.[33] Where goods and/or services are not available in Uganda, the operator shall acquire them from a company which has a joint venture with a Ugandan company, provided the Ugandan company owns not less than 48 per cent of the joint venture.[34] This requirement for priority consideration for Ugandan goods and services contrasts with provisions requiring employment and training of Ugandans in that the latter is not mandated to be provided to Ugandans on a preferential basis.[35] However, the employment and training provisions require that account shall be taken of 'gender, equity, persons with disabilities and host communities', host communities being defined as 'the inhabitants of the district in which petroleum activities take place'.[36] This provision is similar to the 'as far as possible' provision of the Tanzanian draft local content policy. However, the 2016 Regulations, enacted pursuant to the Midstream Act, and applicable only to midstream operations, require midstream licence holders to ensure that Ugandans are given priority in employment matters.[37] Furthermore, midstream licence holders shall take into account the importance of promoting the participation of specific groups, such as women, persons with disabilities and persons from diverse geographical and ethnic origins. Thus, while for upstream operations, there is an emphasis on the need to promote the participation of the localities where the operations take place, for midstream operations the emphasis is instead on the need to carry the entire country along by promoting the participation of persons from different geographical and ethnic areas of the country. Uganda thus does not have uniform LCRs for upstream and midstream operations. LCRs for midstream operations are more nationalistic than LCRs for upstream operations (which are slightly more localistic).

---

[31] Petroleum (Refining, Conversion, Transmission and Midstream Storage) Regulations, 2016 [Uganda Petroleum Regulations].
[32] Ibid., Reg. 4.
[33] Uganda Upstream Act, note 29, s. 125(1).
[34] Ibid., s. 125(2). The Upstream Act does not, however, define a 'Ugandan company'.
[35] Ibid., s. 126.
[36] Ibid., s. 126(2) and (3).
[37] Uganda Petroleum Regulations, note 31, Reg. 17.

Defining 'Local' in Local Content Requirements   23

In Norway, believed to be about the most successful LCR jurisdiction,[38] there is no definition of local content; however, its local content practice suggests that it prefers the national understanding of 'local'.[39] In Trinidad and Tobago, local content is defined in terms of 'maximizing the level of usage of local goods and services, people, businesses and financing'.[40] The emphasis is on 'local value-added', which is viewed in terms of 'ownership, control and financing by the citizens of Trinidad and Tobago'.[41] There is no reference to the local areas where the oil and gas resources are located, meaning that Trinidad's approach is nationalistic rather than localist. This also represents the position in most other jurisdictions, including Mexico,[42] Angola,[43] Equatorial Guinea,[44] and the Middle Eastern countries Qatar, UAE, Oman, Saudi Arabia and Jordan.[45] It has been pointed out that in other Middle Eastern countries Yemen, Iran, Lebanon and Iraq, as well as in Algeria, 'a more expansive' understanding of 'local' prevails that includes 'services by locally registered firms and entities and the employment of local manpower' and that this allows for consideration not only for nationals of the countries but also for residents of the oil-bearing regions in those countries.[46] It must be noted, however, that this understanding of 'local' is not incorporated in legislation in any of these countries. In fact, LCRs lack explicit statutory rendition in some of these countries but are established in oil and gas contracts concluded between the governments and companies. Moreover, a look at some of those contracts, such as Iraq's Technical Service Contract for the Rumaila Oil Field, concluded in 2009, shows a wholly national perspective to the understanding of local.[47] Thus, at least in principle, the

---

[38]   See B.C. Asiago, 'Norwegian Local Content Model a Viable Solution?' (2017) 14 *US-China Law Review* 471–497; I. Olegovna Semykina, 'Managing Regional Economic Development through Local Content Requirements in the Oil and Gas Industry' (2017) 13 *Ekonomika regiona [Economy of Region]* 457 at 460; T. Acheampong, M. Ashong and V. C. Svanikier, 'An Assessment of Local-Content Policies in Oil and Gas Producing Countries' (2016) 9 *The Journal of World Energy Law and Business* 282–302.

[39]   See, generally, Asiago, ibid.

[40]   Republic of Trinidad and Tobago, 'Local Content and Local Participation Policy and Framework for the Republic of Trinidad and Tobago Energy Sector', 7 October 2004, p. 6.

[41]   Ibid.

[42]   Methodology for measuring national content in Allocations and Contracts for Exploration and Extraction of Hydrocarbons, as well as for the Permits in the Hydrocarbons Industry, 13 November 2014.

[43]   Republic of Angola, Decree-Law No. 17/09 of July 26: Rules and Procedures to Observe in Recruitment, Integration, Training and Development of Workers from the Oil Sector.

[44]   Hydrocarbons Law of the Republic of Equatorial Guinea, Hydrocarbons Law No. 8/2006, of 3 November 2006, ss. 80–93.

[45]   See D. Olawuyi, 'Local Content Requirements in Oil and Gas Contracts: Regional Trends in the Middle East and North Africa' (2019) 37 *Journal of Energy and Natural Resources Law* 93–117. See also D. Olawuyi, *Extractives Industry Law in Africa* (New York: Springer Publishing, 2018), pp. 233–64.

[46]   Ibid.

[47]   'Technical Service Contract for the Rumaila Oil Field between South Oil Company of the Republic of Iraq and BP Iraq Limited and CNPC International (Iraq) Limited and Somo', 27 July 2009. Article 30 of the contract, for example, provides: 30.1: Works and services performed in the Republic of Iraq

Chilenye Nwapi

national, rather than the subnational locality where the oil and gas activities take place, is the legal focus of LCRs in Iraq.

Also, in Iran, local content is governed by the Law on Maximum Use of the Productive and Service Capacity of the Country and Protection of Iranian Products, a law adopted by the Iranian Parliament in May 2019. The law applies to all public and government-affiliated entities, as well as all private entities and cooperatives that execute projects using funds provided or guaranteed by the government of Iran. It prohibits all entities from purchasing foreign goods and services which are found in Iraq, unless approved by the Ministry of Industry, Mines and Commerce or, in some cases, by the Ministry of Agriculture. Where it is necessary to procure the services of a non-Iranian firm, it must be from a company in which Iranians own at least 51 per cent of the shares. Even then, the approval of the Supervisory Board established under the law must first be obtained. But the law also recognises that it may be necessary to procure the services of a company where Iranians hold less than 51 per cent of the shares, or even from a wholly foreign company. In such a case, the approval of the Iranian Economic Council must first be obtained.[48] There is, however, no indication in the law that the subnational locality where the (oil and gas) activities are carried out shall be given any special recognition in the procurement of goods and services. In the absence of any such indication, and going by the overall tenor of the legislation, it can be assumed that a wholly national perspective is meant by the term.

TABLE 2.1 *Survey of the definition of local in frontier oil and gas jurisdictions*

Country	Definition of Local	Comment
Nigeria	No definition of 'local'	Local content is defined in terms of in-country value. No reference to the localities where the resources are produced.
Ghana	No definition of 'local'	Local content is defined in terms of in-country value. No reference to the localities where the resources are produced.

through sub-contracts shall be carried out on a competitive basis. Preference shall be given to Iraqi entities and firms, or foreign firms in association therewith, provided that their relevant capabilities and prices are competitive with those available in the international market. 30.2: Preference shall be given to locally manufactured and/or available goods, materials, equipment, consumables and the like provided that their technical specifications, availability, prices and time of delivery are comparable to those available in the international market.

[48] This law repeals the Maximum Utilization of Production and Services Potency in Providing Country's Needs and Promotion of Exports, a law passed by the Iranian Parliament in 2012, Article 4 of which states that 'Companies and organizations mentioned in this Act must ensure that a minimum of 51 percent of the cost of every project is executed through domestic labour (local content) in all construction, installation, supply and service projects'.

Defining 'Local' in Local Content Requirements   25

TABLE 2.1 *(continued)*

Country	Definition of Local	Comment
Tanzania	No definition of 'local'	Local content is defined in terms of in-country value. 'Host communities' are to be taken into account in matters of employment.
Mozambique	No definition of 'local'	Local content is defined in terms of in-country value. Employment and training are to be provided preferentially to residents of the concession area.
Uganda	No definition of 'local'	Local content is defined in terms of in-country value. In fact, the Regulation employs the term 'national content' rather than 'local content'. Upstream Act requires that 'host communities' be taken into account in matters of employment. Midstream Act requires that people in diverse geopolitical areas be taken into account in matters of employment. Therefore, local content is more nationalistic in midstream petroleum than in upstream.
Other countries: Angola, Algeria, Equatorial Guinea, Jordan, Mexico, Norway, Oman, Iraq, Iran, Saudi Arabia, Trinidad and Tobago, UAE	No definition of 'local'	Local content is either not defined or defined in terms of in-country value.

SOURCE: Author

One aspect of the definition of 'local' needing further examination is the meaning of 'local company'. The literature has identified the following characteristics of a local company: (1) local registration (company is registered under local law); (2) local ownership (a certain percentage of the shares of the company is owned by citizens [include corporate citizens] of the country); (3) local labour force (majority of the company's labour force, both regular and contract, are citizens of the country); and (4) local value added (a certain percentage of the goods and services of the company is produced within the country).[49] These characteristics are not all to be found in any single definition of local company by any country or institution. For instance, the Nigerian local content law defines a Nigerian company for the purposes of local content as a company registered in Nigeria and in which Nigerians hold 'not less than 51% equity shares'.[50] Tanzania's Local Content Regulations defines a local company as 'a company or subsidiary company incorporated under the Companies Act, which is one hundred percent owned by a Tanzanian citizen or a company that is in a joint venture partnership with a Tanzanian citizen or citizens whose participating share is not less than fifteen percent'.[51] In Ghana, an 'indigenous Ghanaian company' is a company incorporated under the [Ghanaian] Companies Act 1963', has at least 51 per cent Ghanaian equity shareholding, 'and that has Ghanaian citizens holding at least eighty percent of executive and senior management positions and one hundred percent of non-managerial and other positions'.[52] In Uganda, a Ugandan company is 'a company incorporated under the Companies Act, 2012 and which (a) provides value addition to Uganda; (b) uses available local raw materials; (c) employs at least 70 percent of Ugandans; and (d) is approved by the [Ugandan Petroleum] Authority under regulation 10(3)'.[53] World Bank's definition for 'domestic preference qualification' is based on the percentage of the shares of the firm that is locally owned.[54] The African Development Bank's definition of 'local firms' is based on place of registration, the nationality of a majority of board members of the firm and the percentage of shares held by nationals of the country.[55]

Esteves, Coyne and Moreno argue that ownership of a company or the country of its registration should not play any critical role in the formulation of local content policies. What matters, according to them, is the contribution a company makes to building the domestic economy in which it operates (at both national and subnational levels) and whether those contributions meet the public policy objectives of that country.[56] This view derives credibility from the experiences of Norway and Malaysia where local content has been viewed mainly in terms of value addition, without emphasis on the nationality of the company adding the value. It is however attractive in appearance but fails in principle. It has the potential to preserve global

[49] A. M. Esteves, B. Coyne and A. Moreno, 'Local Content Initiatives: Enhancing the Subnational Benefits of the Oil, Gas and Mining Sectors' Natural Resource Governance Institute Briefing', Natural Resource Governance Institute, 2–3 July 2013.

[50] NOGICD Act, note 5, s. 106.

[51] Tanzania Petroleum (Local Content) Regulations, 2017, reg. 3.

[52] Ghana Local Content Regulation, note 7, Reg. 49.

[53] Petroleum (Refining, Conversion, Transmission and Midstream Storage) (National Content) Regulations, 2016, Regulation 4 (Uganda).

[54] World Bank, 'Increasing Local Procurement by the Mining Industry in West Africa', Report No. 66585-AFR, January 2012, p. 29.

[55] Ibid.

[56] Esteves et al., note 49, p. 3.

economic inequality in an era of neoliberal capitalism. Especially in the extractive sector in developing countries where the key players are foreign multinationals more economically powerful than their host governments, it is imperative for host developing countries to chart a path for taking ownership of the development of their resources. Ownership and registration requirements provide a potent avenue for them to regain control over their resources. This regaining of control, however, cannot occur in the short term, but will follow a gradual process that will materialise in the long term. Nevertheless, it is hard to conceive a better way in which foreign companies can contribute to building the domestic economy of their host countries than by empowering locally owned and registered businesses to thrive and blossom side by side with them. Locally owned and registered businesses are more likely to hire local people than foreign-owned companies would hire and thereby would, potentially, more effectively fight unemployment and poverty than foreign-owned companies. Fighting poverty and unemployment is an important public policy objective of developing countries.

3 A CASE FOR A LOCALIST PERSPECTIVE TO LCRS IN THE OIL AND GAS INDUSTRY

A localist perspective to LCRs aligns with what Warner has termed 'community content': 'the strategic deployment of local participation and local capability development opportunities arising from an oil or gas project, specifically directed to strengthen the sustainability, relevance and political visibility of community investment programmes'.[57] Warner writes that '[u]ltimately, community content is about realising a competitive advantage for the oil company in the eyes of both the local population and the country's guardians of economic policy'.[58] He regards community content programs as a 'merit good' targeted at those negatively impacted by extractive resource development whereas local content programs are regarded as a 'public good'. Both programs are 'exclusionary' although local content programs are less so because they exclude only foreigners whereas community content excludes both foreigners and non-community members.[59] Warner seems to suggest that community content should be pursued as a policy distinct from local content. However, it may still be possible to pursue community content as an aspect or subset of local content. This may require giving special consideration to local labour force, local contractors and local service providers *vis-à-vis* other nationals. To achieve this successfully would require consciously building the capability of local skills at the

---

[57] M. Warner, 'Community Content: The Interface of Community Investment Programmes with Local Content Practices in the Oil and Gas Development Sector' *Overseas Development Institute (ODI)* Briefing note 9 (2007), p. 5.
[58] Ibid.
[59] Ibid.

28 *Chilenye Nwapi*

community level to enable the communities to access the procurement and employ-ment opportunities brought by resource development.

Discussed in the following sections are four theoretical frameworks (namely, localism, the 'shared value' principle, subnational economic development theory and subnational competitiveness theory) which might be used to explain the import-ance of a localist approach to LCRs.

3.1 *Localism*

Localism is about the empowerment of local areas. It is rooted in a set of arguments about the role of local governments in promoting efficiency in the provision of public goods and services as well as in promoting democracy and community.[60] The efficiency argument posits that local autonomy permits public policy decisions to be tailored to the distinctive circumstances, needs and preferences of local areas.[61] This promotes efficiency because it reduces the cost of governance and promotes 'inter-local competition'.[62] When decisions are made by the very people who are to be directly affected by them, the decisions have the potential to reflect the yearnings and aspirations of the people more fully. The democracy argument posits that true democracy offers people an opportunity to participate in the decisions and political processes that affect them. Lastly, the community argument takes the view that 'localities are not simply arbitrary collections of small groups of people', but instead 'communities' with shared and distinct values and identities and bound by common historical experiences.[63] A country that values its diversity must therefore promote local autonomy because it allows localities to preserve their distinct identities. Decentralisation guarantees that local policies are adapted to the circumstances of heterogeneous populations.[64] The focus is therefore on 'governance relations', particularly on 'subsidiarity, devolution and decentralisation of the state's powers and responsibilities'.[65] It is regulation from below upward. Especially since the Brexit vote in the United Kingdom, localism has risen to the forefront of debates in many countries.[66]

---

[60] R. Briffault, 'Localism and Regionalism' (1999) *Columbia Law School Public Law and Legal Theory* Working Paper No. 1 at 18.

[61] A. Anas, 'The Costs and Benefits of Fragmented Governance and the New Regionalist Policies', Paper prepared for presentation at 'Regionalism: Promise and Problems', a symposium held at the State University of New York at Buffalo School of Law, 6 March 1999.

[62] Briffault, note 60, p. 20.

[63] Ibid.

[64] A. S. Kessler, N. A. Hansen and C. Lessmann, 'Interregional Redistribution and Mobility in Federations: A Positive Approach' (2011) 78 *Review of Economic Studies* 1345.

[65] S. Davoudi and A. Madanipour, 'Localism and Neo-liberal Governmentality' (2013) 84 *Town Planning Review* 551.

[66] See, for example, Independent Commission on the Future of Localism, *People Power: Findings from the Commission on the Future of Localism*, 23 January 2018, www.powertochange.org.uk/wp-content /uploads/2018/01/LOCALITY-LOCALISM-FULL-ONLINE-REPORT.pdf.

Defining 'Local' in Local Content Requirements 29

But localism is more than local autonomy. It is a theory 'which reverses the trend of globalisation by discriminating in favour of the local'.[67] It favours support for local businesses, use of local resources, employment of locals and services for local consumers.[68] LCRs designed to give first consideration to local populations in the proximity of the resources, who are most directly affected by the resource development externalities, are consistent with these demands of localism. Since these demands cannot be described as illegitimate or unconscionable, a local community-oriented local-content policy can serve as a vehicle to build the capability of local skills to access the opportunities brought by extractive resource development as well as mitigate its negative impacts. It has in fact been pointed out that 'a society of many small [local] businesses is more resilient, more empowering and more in keeping with the spirit of capitalism and of the market' than a society of big businesses and that government policy should turn to localism rather than nationalism.[69]

There are further advantages. A localist approach to LCRs would reduce the exodus of local people to overcrowded urban centres in search of greener pastures that, more recently, are increasingly in very short supply. It has the potential to improve company–community relations, enabling companies to obtain the social license to operate,[70] thereby contributing positively to the public perception of extractive companies.[71] Given the socioecological impacts of oil and gas resource development, a localist approach to LCRs has the potential to compensate local communities afflicted by resource externalities by promoting job creation and value addition for the communities.[72] During a social impact assessment of oil, gas and mining projects, Esteves, Coyne and Moreno found that community discontent arising from seeing only basic jobs being offered to local communities poses a significant challenge to the success of the projects.[73] This is arguably because such discontents quite often lead to violent conflicts that disrupt extractive operations. A localist approach can also help conflict-ridden developing countries' governments to achieve political

---

[67] C. Hines, *Localisation: A Global Manifesto* (London: Earthscan, 2000), p. 27.
[68] E. Frankova and N. Johanisova, 'Economic Localization Revisited' (2012) 22 *Environmental Policy and Governance* 309.
[69] K. Albertson, 'Hate Globalisation? Try Localism, Not Nationalism', 9 November 2017, http://theconversation.com/hate-globalisation-try-oi-not-nationalism-86870.
[70] A. M. Esteves and M. Barclay, 'Enhancing the Benefits of Local Content: Integrating Social and Economic Impact Assessment into Procurement Strategies' (2011) 29 *Impact Assessment and Project Appraisal* 205.
[71] For a discussion of social licence to operate, see C. Nwapi, 'Can the Concept of Social Licence to Operate Find Its Way into the Formal Legal System' (2016) 18 *Flinders Law Journal* 349–75.
[72] R. Ado, 'Local Content Policy and the WTO Rules on Trade-Related Investment Measures (TRIMS): The Pros and Cons' (2013) 2 *International Journal of Business and Management Studies* 142. See, generally, J. Pegram, G. Falcone and A. Kolios, 'A Review of Job Role Localization in the Oil and Gas Industry' (2018) 11 *Energies* 2779.
[73] Esteves et al., note 49, p. 6.

30 *Chilenye Nwapi*

harmony by promoting peaceful coexistence among communities and preventing or reducing resource conflicts.[74] It can be used to promote inclusiveness with regard to the resource-rich communities that often feel excluded from the benefits of the resources located within their territory and as a mechanism to reallocate resource wealth within the country.[75] The United Nations Conference on Trade and Development has found that 'community relations issues are a significant obstacle to the implementation of a speedy, strife-free local content development in the oil and gas industry in Nigeria'.[76] Oguine (former General Counsel of Chevron Nigeria) has described the absence of a local community content requirement in Nigeria's local content law as 'a serious shortcoming'.[77] This supposedly stems from his experience of the agitations of local communities in Nigeria's oil-bearing region.

3.2 The 'Shared Value' Principle

'Shared value' focuses on the link between societal progress and business success. It is the principle that business success is inextricably bound up with the prosperity of host nations and the communities in which the businesses are located.[78] Accordingly, it proclaims that businesses should carry out their activities in a manner that creates value for the society in which they operate by recognising, and contributing to providing, the needs of that society and addressing its challenges. The principle was developed in response to the situation whereby businesses are seen to be prospering at the expense of the society in which they operate despite huge investments in corporate social responsibility.[79] The principle allows us to redefine 'profit' and 'business success' generally in a manner that recognises that it is societal needs, rather than traditional economic needs (such as corporate profits), that define

---

[74] Ado, note 72, p. 142; M. Warner, *Local Content in Procurement: Creating Local Jobs and Competitive Domestic Industries in Supply Chains* (Sheffield, UK: Greenleaf Publishing, 2011).

[75] See World Trade Institute (WTI) Advisors, 'Local Content Requirements and the Green Economy', Paper presented at the Ad Hoc Expert Group Meeting on Domestic Requirements and Support Measures in Green Sectors: Economic and Environmental Effectiveness and Implications for Trade, 13–14 June 2013, p. 10 (positing that LCRs can be used to 'redistribute rents arising from economic activities', such as 'to ensure that the profits and employment from natural resource extraction are felt directly in the communities where the extraction is done'). See, also, A. Wennmann, 'Sharing Natural Resource Wealth during War-to-Peace Transitions' in P. Lujala and S. A. Rustad (eds.), *High Value Natural Resources and Peace Building* (London: Earthscan, 2012), pp. 225–50.

[76] United Nations Conference on Trade and Development (UNCTAD), 'UNCTAD/CALAG African Oil and Gas Services Sector Survey, Volume 1–Nigeria: Creating Local Linkages By Empowering Indigenous Entrepreneurs' (UNCTAD, 2006), p. 79.

[77] I. Oguine, 'Nigerian Content in the Nigerian Petroleum Industry: Legal and Policy Issues' (2011) 29 *Journal of Energy and Natural Resources Law* 428.

[78] M. E. Porter and M. R. Kramer, 'The Big Idea: Creating Shared Value How to Reinvent Capitalism – and Unleash a Wave of Innovation and Growth' (2011) *Harvard Business Review* 1 at 4.

[79] See P. Wójcik, 'How Creating Shared Value Differs from Corporate Social Responsibility' (2016) 24 *Journal of Management and Business Administration. Central Europe* 32 at 33.

markets.[80] What is to be shared, however, is not corporate profits. Nor is it revenues derived by the government from economic activity. These are both already-created values, which can only be redistributed. Rather, the concept of shared value has to do with expanding the range of values to be created out of an economic activity so that more people – the broader society – can share in them.[81] As Porter and Kramer explain it:

> [t]he concept of shared value can be defined as policies and operating practices that enhance the competitiveness of a company while simultaneously advancing the economic and social conditions in the communities in which it operates. Shared value creation focuses on identifying and expanding the connections between societal and economic progress.[82]

The shared value principle supports the deliberate consideration of local community perspectives in the formulation and implementation of LCRs. In fact, LCRs provide an opportunity for the implementation of the principle – a principle that has been criticised for providing no clear implementation criteria for businesses.[83] According to IPIECA, shared value is 'a business strategy designed to achieve both project competitiveness, and stability and economic development in the local community and host country'.[84] IPIECA recognises the importance of integrating community content into local content strategies and supports a shared vision of local content that takes into consideration 'the costs and benefits' to stakeholders at all levels: at the national, regional, host community and marginalised/targeted group levels.[85] Similarly, the Organisation for Economic Co-operation and Development's operational guidance for shared value creation emphasises the need for host governments to 'develop plans for an inclusive local workforce and supplier participation, focusing on increasing the participation of vulnerable groups, such as women and indigenous peoples'.[86] The shared value principle thus allows for the values (viewed in terms of opportunities, such as job creation) created though LCRs in the oil and gas industry to be shared among all stakeholders, including the local communities where oil and gas operations take place. A strictly nationalistic approach to LCRs would unfairly limit value sharing, whereas recognition of community content would ensure that the needs of the local communities are addressed by the very businesses that contributed to the creation of those needs.

---

[80] Porter et al., note 78, p. 5.
[81] Ibid.
[82] Ibid., p. 6.
[83] See K. Dembek, P. Singh and V. Bhakoo, 'Literature Review of Shared Value: A Theoretical Concept or a Management Buzzword?' (2015) 137 *Journal of Business Ethics* 231–7.
[84] IPIECA, note 1, p. 5.
[85] Ibid., p. 25.
[86] Organisation for Economic Co-operation and Development, 'Collaborative Strategies for In-Country Shared Value Creation: Framework for Extractive Projects', OECD *Development Policy Tools* (OECD Publishing, 2016), p. 12.

3.3 Subnational Economic Development Theory

Subnational economic development theory calls for a regional or local approach to development. This involves decentralisation of power and resources from central governments to subnational governments. In an increasingly globalising world economy, this call seems counterintuitive. However, it has been necessitated by the transformations brought by globalisation upon the economic landscape of many (particularly developing) countries.[87] Those transformations include, perhaps most remarkably, economic disparities among the various regions of many countries. As Libman has noted, economic development theory shows that intracountry differences in political and economic institutions among the constituent units of a country can be almost as varied as intercountry differences.[88] It follows that assessing a country's economic development based solely on national economic statistics may be misleading. It also suggests that 'distance and geography' matter for economic development in a globalised world and that 'national economic growth tends to be driven by the performance of a limited number of local economies within nation-states'.[89] The increasing demand for regionalisation and localisation is therefore an 'acknowledgement that regional forces and characteristics are strongly relevant in shaping local development trajectories in a context of increasing globalisation'.[90]

Studies have demonstrated that national institutions do have an impact on subnational development, but that this occurs only when the subnational constituent is close to the national capital.[91] According to one study, this is partly because law enforcement is stronger in areas closer to the national capital and weaker in more remote areas.[92] The distance problem has also been associated with infrastructure issues, such as transportation.[93] Thus, for an oil and gas deposit in a remote region to be developed rather than deposits in less remote alternative regions, the geological features of the more remote region must produce 'sufficiently low unit costs of production' to compensate for the higher costs to be paid to transport the products from the region to the market.[94] Other studies have shown that the interplay of

---

[87] A. Ascani, R. Crescenzi and S. Iammarino, 'Regional Economic Development: A Review', WPI/03 Search Working Paper, European Community's Seventh Framework Programme, January 2012, p. 3.

[88] A. Libman, 'Natural Resources and Sub-National Economic Performance: Does Sub-national Democracy Matter?' (2013) 37 *Energy Economics* 82. See, also, A. Libman and V. Kozlov, 'Sub-National Variation of Corruption in Russia: What Do We Know About It?' (2013) 2 *Region* 153–80.

[89] Ascani et al., note 87, p. 5.

[90] Ibid., p. 3.

[91] S. Michalopoulos and E. Papaioannou, 'National Institutions and Subnational Development in Africa' (2014) 129 *Quarterly Journal of Economics* 157.

[92] Ibid.

[93] R. G. Eggert, 'Mining and Economic Sustainability: National Economies and Local Communities', Mining, Minerals and Sustainable Development, International Institute for Environment and Development, World Business Council for Sustainable Development, October 2001, v19.

[94] Ibid.

Defining 'Local' in Local Content Requirements

subnational institutions and resources is a determinant of economic growth at the subnational level.[95] These studies speak to the need to ensure that national policies are tailored to the needs of the constituent units of a country.

In addition, the history of economic development shows that oil and gas development has made significant contributions to the development of local communities and regions in many countries but has also contributed significantly to the underdevelopment of many other communities.[96] The Niger Delta region of Nigeria is one of the most notorious examples of socioeconomic and environmental degradation occasioned by oil and gas development, despite the huge revenues the Nigerian government has gained from the resources over several decades. There has been continuing conflict in Nigeria over the negative socioenvironmental impacts of oil extraction and the distribution of the resource wealth between the resource-bearing region and the federal government.[97] Among the factors identified as responsible for this is 'the historical failure of governance at all levels'.[98]

The extent to which a region would benefit from oil and gas development is therefore a function of the balance between the benefits of the resources and their costs. This can be achieved through strengthening the capacity of oil and gas resources to contribute positively to economic development while at the same time reducing their capacity to produce negative externalities. The impact of oil and gas operations on the local economy will be limited when goods and services supplied to the operators are imported when they could have been sourced locally. Local economies will develop more speedily if the non-extractive sectors are encouraged to grow and the extractive companies are encouraged to focus their local content energies on strengthening local businesses.[99] Being close to the site of oil and gas operations thus becomes a legitimate advantage for a local firm.

Oil and gas development can contribute to local economic development both directly, through the employment of local workforce, and indirectly, through its links to other economic activities within the locality (linkages). These linkages arise, for instance, from oil and gas companies' continuing need to purchase equipment to build or repair their facilities, the need by local firms to acquire equipment from the foreign firms operating within their locality to upgrade their facilities and the need of their workers to purchase personal goods and services for their upkeep while living in the extractive region. LCRs that give special consideration to local suppliers within

---

[95] Libman, note 88, pp. 8 and 45.

[96] See J. G. Frynas, 'The False Developmental Promise of Corporate Social Responsibility: Evidence from Multinational Oil Companies' (2005) 81 *International Affairs* 581–98; K. Omeje (ed.), *Extractive Economies and Conflicts in the Global South: Multi-regional Perspectives on Rentier Politics* (UK: Routledge, 2017).

[97] C. Nwapi, 'A Legislative Proposal for Public Participation in Oil and Gas Decision-Making in Nigeria' (2010) 54 *Journal of African Law* 184.

[98] United Nations Development Programme, 'Niger Delta Human Development Report' (2006), p. 17.

[99] A. M. Esteves and G. Ivanova, 'Using Social and Economic Impact Assessment to Guide Local Supplier Development Initiatives' in C. Karlsson and M. Andersson (eds.), *Handbook of Research Methods and Applications in Economic Geography* (Cheltenham: Edward Elgar, 2013), pp. 571–96.

34   *Chilenye Nwapi*

the subnational region where the resources are exploited can help to strengthen the contributions of oil and gas resource development to subnational economic development. Given the serious negative impact of resource development on the subnational region where the resources are located, a subnational approach to LCR could help to compensate the affected subnational region for the damage to its development. On the other hand, a strictly nationalistic or centralist approach could marginalise the affected subnational region.

3.4 *Subnational Competitiveness Theory*

Economic geographers have considered the impact of foreign direct investment (FDI) on interregional inequality. Lessmann argues that FDI might increase regional inequality since FDI is not equally distributed among the many different regions of a country.[100] He scrutinises cross-country time-series data on FDI and regional inequalities. Based on data collected on regional inequalities covering fifty-five countries that were at different stages of development between 1980 and 2009, he finds that FDI increases regional inequality more strongly in low- and middle-income countries than in high-income countries; in fact, that FDI has 'almost no significant effect on regional inequality in high-income countries'.[101] The underlying reason, according to Lessmann, is the degree of 'redistribution' of FDI across the country. Countries with high redistribution rates will experience lower regional inequality than countries with low redistribution rates. Two factors decisive for the degree of FDI redistribution are factor mobility and government policies (e.g., subsidies and tax policies). Lessmann finds that the higher factor mobility of developed countries and their government policies are the factors bridging interregional gap within those countries.[102]

Following the influential writings of Michael Porter on the competitive advantage of nations, which theorise that '[a] nation's competitiveness depends on the capacity of its industry to innovate and upgrade',[103] scholars have turned to consider competitiveness at the subnational level and to theorise and measure its impact on national economic development. Ascani, Crescenzi and Iammarino have argued that 'territorial competition represents an opportunity for poorer regions to manage local economic development since devolution allows them to play an active role in designing their own strategies'.[104] A study by the Asia Competitiveness Institute on

---

[100] C. Lessmann, 'Foreign Direct Investment and Regional Inequality: A Panel Data Analysis' (2013) 24 *China Economic Review* 130. Earlier studies on regional inequality in China came to the same conclusion. See, for example, B. Fleisher, H. Li and M. Q. Zhao, 'Human Capital, Economic Growth, and Regional Inequality in China' (2010) 92 *Journal of Development Economics* 215–31; R. Kanbur and X. Zhang, 'Fifty Years of Regional Inequality in China: A Journey through Central Planning, Reform, and Openness' (2005) 9 *Review of Development Economics* 87–106.

[101] Lessmann, note 100, p. 100.

[102] Ibid.

[103] M. E. Porter, 'The Competitive Advantage of Nations' (1990) 68 *Harvard Business Review* 73.

[104] Ascani et al., note 87, p. 13.

subnational competitiveness in Indonesia's thirty-three provinces shows that subnational competitiveness has helped to boost Indonesia's economic performance.[105] Subnational growth is viewed as 'a generative process' and national growth as 'an aggregate' of subnational growth.[106] National policies should therefore focus on optimising growth at the subnational level, as this would generate national growth eventually. Subnational economic growth is seen as contributing favourably to Indonesia's national economic growth.[107] The study takes a panoramic view of subnational competiveness, dividing it into four major environments: macroeconomic, microeconomic, governance and quality of life.[108]

In their study of the role of subnational competitiveness in Indonesia's national performance, Tan and Amri divide subnational competitiveness into four major quadrants: macroeconomic stability, microeconomic environment (finance, business and manpower conditions), government and institutional setting, and quality of life and infrastructure development.[109] The macroeconomic environment speaks to the economic viability of the region, the region's openness to trade and services and its attractiveness to foreign investors. The microeconomic environment relates to the performance of firms and the challenges they face in their operations.[110] Government and institutional setting encompasses the 'efficacy of government institutions' and addresses such issues as government policies and fiscal sustainability, governance, leadership, competition, regulatory standards and rule of law. Quality of life and infrastructure development cover both physical and technological infrastructure and general 'standard of living,' education and social stability'.[111] A region's competitiveness is therefore to be looked for not only in the competitiveness of the firms operating within the region, but also in the broader assets and socioeconomic and institutional characteristics of the particular region. In another, related, study, it is found that provinces rich in natural resources have the potential to be more competitive than others, but not in the absence of good governance.[112] The study finds that while the top competitive provinces in Indonesia did not get to the top relying on one competitiveness characteristic, governance was a critical factor for all the

---

[105] See, for example, K. G. Tan and M. Amri, 'Overview' in K.G. Tan, M. Amri, L. Low and T. K. Yam (eds.), *Competitiveness Analysis and Development Strategies for 33 Indonesian Provinces* (Singapore: World Scientific Publishing Company, 2013), p. 35

[106] S. Nazara, M. Sonis and G.J.D. Hewings, 'Interregional Competition and Complementarity in Indonesia', Discussion Paper 01-T-02, The Regional Economic Applications Laboratory (2000), p. 3.

[107] Ibid.

[108] Ibid., p. 1.

[109] Tan et al., note 105, p. 1.

[110] Ibid., p. 2.

[111] Ibid.

[112] K. G. Tan and M. Amri, 'Subnational Competitiveness and National Performance: Analysis and Simulation for Indonesia' (2013) 6 *JCC: The Business and Economics Research Journal* 188.

36   Chilenye Nwapi

provinces, for lack of good governance was a major factor that barred some of the rich provinces from getting to the top.[113] Subnational competition does not mean regions competing with one another in the ordinary sense. Rather it is 'the promotion of local economic development in competition with other territories'.[114] It is the actions that economic agents within a territory take to enhance the standard of living of their territory. It is thus the economic agents that actually carry out the competition.[115] The territories as such are not in competition with one another, for the growth of one does not come at any cost to another.[116] The role of the government in the competition is to create a playing field for the agents within each territory that would enable them to compete favourably with agents in other territories.[117] This entails 'promoting the territory as a competitive place to do business and [this] may be more directed at improving the environment for existing local businesses and fostering new firm formation, than in trying to attract inward investment'.[118] No doubt, of course, attraction of inward investment will be the natural consequence of improving the business environment of a territory.

LCRs can be used to promote subnational competitiveness. A localist perspective carries the potential to even do so more effectively. This can be explained by the efficiency arguments (discussed earlier) supporting localism. As noted, one of the arguments is that localism promotes interlocal competition. It does this by fostering interlocal mobility. Because each locality adopts a governance model that matches its characteristics, needs and preferences, individuals will be able to choose among different localities to live, based on the assortment of benefits, such as taxes and services, each locality offers and the corresponding obligations each locality imposes on its residents.[119] If local decisions do not match an individual's preferences, the individual can move to another locality. The possibility that people can move acts as a check on government policies. Local governments would therefore have to vie for taxpayers, much as producers vie for consumers. As Briffault puts it, '[i]t is interlocal mobility that enables people to select the community that best matches their needs, and it is the possibility of mobility that gives rise to the interlocal competition that promotes efficiency'.[120]

---

[113] Ibid. These studies may be used to explain the key to Indonesia's transformation from a low-income economy to a middle-income economy. Upon the turn of the twenty-first century, Indonesia underwent democratic and political restructuring whereby it adopted an approach to boost its economic performance by allowing healthy competition among its provinces.

[114] P. C. Cheshire and I. R. Gordon, 'Territorial Competition: Some Lessons for Policy' (1998) 32 *Annals of Regional Science* 321.

[115] J. Poot, 'Reflections on Local and Economy-Wide Effects of Territorial Competition' in P.W.J. Batey and P. Friedrich (eds.), *Regional Competition* (Berlin: Springer Verlag, 2000), p. 205.

[116] Nazara et al., note 106, p. 14.

[117] Ibid.

[118] Cheshire et al., note 114, p. 322.

[119] Briffault, note 60, p. 18.

[120] Ibid., p. 22.

Defining 'Local' in Local Content Requirements

LCRs can promote competition and facilitate local economic development because they provide an incentive to local governments as well as local residents to protect the industries operating on their territory and to help to guard company facilities. A local community-oriented LCR gives local governments and residents a greater incentive to do so because they stand to benefit most from the growth of the companies operating on their territory. The death of the companies would have detrimental consequences on the local people's socioeconomic well-being. Every local government, every state/province and every region of a country would therefore be compelled to create a favourable operational environment for the companies operating in its area so as to ensure their sustenance. This is not to say, however, that subnational governments will have to create their own LCRs. This might lead to a race to the bottom. Rather, the LCR is to be designed and managed from the national level while the subnational units would be competing to ensure that firms operating within their respective territories are retained. Actions of subnational governments in this regard would include strengthening subnational institutions for the promotion of rule of law, protection of property rights, law enforcement and provision of security to ensure the protection of companies' properties located within their territories. These actions align with Tan and Amri's finding that good governance is a critical factor in the competitiveness of Indonesia's provinces.[121]

4 THE PROBLEMS WITH A LOCALIST APPROACH TO LCRS

Since oil and gas resources are not located evenly within a country, and since regions with more deposits of extractive resources are likely to attract more FDI than those with fewer deposits, giving first consideration to workers and suppliers within the subnational region where the resources are located might produce interregional inequality within a country. This must be disconcerting because interregional inequality affects interpersonal income inequality.[122] Moreover, conflict studies suggest that interregional inequalities contribute to the causes of conflicts.[123] But interregional inequality may also be the result of factors unrelated to FDI inflow, such as national marginalisation or ethnic discrimination. A state-centric local content policy may also promote interregional inequality because, by not requiring companies to give first consideration to the localities where they operate, companies

---

[121] Tan et al., note 105.

[122] Kessler et al., note 64, p. 1347; R. Yemtsov, 'Quo vadis? Inequality and Poverty Dynamics across Russian Regions' in R. Kanbur and A. Venables (eds.), *Spatial Inequality and Development* (Oxford University Press, 2005), pp. 348–408; C. Elbers, P. Lanjouw, J. Mistiaen, B. Ozler and K. Simler, 'Are Neighbours Equal? Estimating Local Inequality in Three Developing Countries' in R. Kanbur and A. Venables (eds.), *Spatial Inequality and Development* (Oxford University Press, 2005), pp. 37–76.

[123] See, for instance, H. Buhaug, K. Skrede Gleditsch, H. Holtermann, G. Ostby and A. Foro Tollefsen, 'It's the Local Economy, Stupid! Geographic Wealth Dispersion and Conflict Outbreak Location' (2012) 55 *Journal of Conflict Resolution* 814–40; C. Deiwiks, L. Cederman and K. Gleditsch, 'Inequality and Conflict in Federations' (2012) 49 *Journal of Peace Research* 289–304.

38   Chilenye Nwapi

may decide to utilise indigenous firms in other parts of the country in the provision of goods and services and employ other nationals of the country, leaving local populations around the resources unemployed. Given the deleterious socioenvironmental effects of extractive development on local populations, this would have a negative developmental effect on the locality or region where the companies operate and would affect their ability to compete with other regions.[124]

There are several ways in which the risk of interregional inequality arising from a local community-oriented LCR can be reduced. These are encapsulated in the two factors identified by Lessmann: factor mobility and government policy.[125] The higher the mobility of factors and the more effective government policies geared toward reallocating FDI inflows among regions, the less interregional inequality a country would have. Factors that can facilitate factor mobility include better infrastructure, better transport facilities and a more highly skilled workforce. Other measures include tax holidays in favor of disadvantaged regions, subsidies for specific industries and public investments in public goods.[126] In a number of countries, such as Canada and Germany, redistribution measures specifically designed to bridge regional inequality have taken the form of interregional 'equalisation grants'.[127] In the United States, redistribution has been carried out in a more indirect and less explicit manner through the use of federal grants.[128] In Canada, the equalisation mechanism is anchored in Section 36(2) of the Constitution Act, 1982[129] and is aimed at addressing fiscal inequalities among Canadian provinces by 'enabl-[ing] less prosperous provincial governments to provide their residents with public services that are reasonably comparable to those in other provinces, at reasonably comparable levels of taxation'.[130] The Canadian government has transferred billions of dollars to less prosperous provinces under the program.[131] In Germany, it is traceable to Articles 72, 106 and 107 of the German constitution and takes the

---

[124]   This is the case with many communities in Nigeria's Niger Delta region where Nigeria's oil is explored.

[125]   Lessman, note 100, does not say which (if any) of the two factors is more decisive. But even factor mobility can be addressed through government policies at both the national and the subnational levels. He also does not indicate whether by government policies, he refers to policies of national governments or those of subnational (or regional) governments. Given the context of his study, however, one can assume that it is to the policies of national governments that he refers.

[126]   Lessmann, note 100, p. 139.

[127]   Kessler et al., note 64, p. 1346; R. Hepp and J. von Hagen, 'Fiscal Federalism in Germany: Stabilization and Redistribution before and after Unification', ZEI Working Paper No B 02–2010, Center for European Integration Studies, University of Bonn (2010).

[128]   Ibid.

[129]   The section provides that 'Parliament and the government of Canada are committed to the principle of making equalization payments to ensure that provincial governments have sufficient revenues to provide reasonably comparable levels of public services at reasonably comparable levels of taxation'.

[130]   Department of Finance (Canada), 'Equalization Program', 19 December 2011, www.fin.gc.ca/fed prov/eqp-eng.asp.

[131]   See Department of Finance (Canada), 'Federal Support to Provinces and Territories', December 2013, www.fin.gc.ca/fedprov/mtp-eng.asp.

Defining 'Local' in Local Content Requirements 39

form of interstate transfers under the program known as Länderfinanzausgleich whose constitutional goal is to 'equalize living standards' across the nation.[132]

But there can never be perfect equality across geographical boundaries. There will always be some degree of inequality, not caused by human action per se, but by what Soja calls '[t]he friction of distance and related physical properties' of the earth.[133] Location always comes with relative advantages or disadvantages, some significant, others of little or no importance.[134] The uneven location of natural resources (or particular natural resources) across geographies is thus a natural foundation for inequality that would be difficult for redistributive efforts to white-wash. The goal of redistribution therefore is to reduce inequality, not necessarily to eradicate it.

Promoting subnational competitiveness through a bottom-up approach to LCRs will not necessarily increase the burden of redistribution. Since it has the potential to facilitate economic development in every region of a country, it will most likely reduce the burden of redistribution because it will make redistribution more effect-ive by compelling receiving regions to make effective use of the resources redistrib-uted to them. Since subnational competitiveness can enhance both national and subnational economic development, it may be optimal to promote it through LCRs and accompany it with a scheme of interregional redistribution, preferably at the constitutional level where all the regions would vote over its governance.[135]

Besides, regional inequality is not inherently evil. If it is the result of healthy competition among the various regions of a country, there is nothing to be said against it provided there is a level playing field for all regions. A level-playing field should not be seen in terms of equal interregional endowment with natural resources since natural resources are gifts of nature and are not created by the State. But a level playing field can be seen in terms of government policies to encourage regional economic development without discrimination. The remaining inequality can be addressed, as far as possible, through redistribution programs, the impact of which take time to materialise discernibly.

In addition to these, a localist approach comes with certain trade-offs. One trade-off is that local community content may not promote supplier diversification; however, its benefits outweigh the value of supplier diversification. Another, related, trade-off is that it may not offer adequate opportunity to the country's best, in terms of technical, entrepreneurial and managerial know-how, to participate in the devel-opment of the extractive sector in the country.[136] However, the benefits of maintain-ing social stability in the extractive region may be more important for national

---

[132] Kessler et al. note 64, p. 1346; Hepp, note 127, p. 7.
[133] E. W. Soja, *Seeking Spatial Justice* (University of Minnesota Press, 2010), p. 72.
[134] Ibid., p. 73.
[135] This idea is adapted from Kessler, Hansen and Lessmann's suggestion that 'decentralization accom-panied by a scheme of interregional financial aid at a constitutional stage where the entire population votes over its governance structure' may produce an optimal result. Kessler et al., note 64, p. 1347.
[136] UNCTAD, note 76, p. 79.

economic development than the benefits of providing an equal playing field for all nationals. Moreover, a localist approach to LCRs does not mean excluding other nationals from consideration. Rather, it may be implemented through the creation of a quota system that allocates a certain percentage of local procurement or employment to the local populations while other nationals compete for the rest.

To be mentioned also is the possibility that a local community-oriented LCR may be subject to capture by local elites. But so can a central-oriented LCR be subject to capture by national elites. The capture problem may be more easily addressed at the local level than at the national level. This is because many local communities (particularly in Africa) have already-existing systems and institutions for equitable allocation of resources and distribution of burdens and benefits, based mostly under native law and custom. Giving such local institutions legal recognition as well as financial, managerial and institutional support can help to strengthen them to more effectively address the problem of capture. At the national level, such institutional arrangements are seldom to be found, and where a semblance of them is found, such as in the federal character principle under the Nigerian constitution, they apply in limited circumstances (mostly in the appointment of public office holders) and private actors are not bound by them.

5 CONCLUSION

The question of what constitutes 'local' in LCRs in the oil and gas industry around the world has not received precise legislative consideration and very little policy attention. The prevailing view, based on the general tenor of the respective laws and policies considered, is that 'local' is understood as synonymous with 'national' rather than the subnational locality where the oil and gas resources are located. In fact, in the few instances where the subnational is alluded to (such as in Tanzania and Uganda), companies are merely encouraged, rather than mandated, to give consideration to those subnational localities. This chapter highlights the importance of considering subnational localities in the design and implementation of LCRs. Since they are the primary bearers of the negative impacts of oil and gas development, considering subnational localities carries several advantages, including reducing local community discontent over the negative impacts of extractive resource development, reducing resource conflicts, making subnational regions less dependent on revenues from the central government for their survival, enabling companies to obtain the social license to operate and promoting interregional competition. All of these have the effect of fast-tracking national and subnational economic development in the manner demon-strated in this Chapter. Such an approach, though, comes with its trade-offs, such as efficiency and market distortion; however, its potential gains outweigh these trade-offs, particularly for developing countries where community dissatisfaction with the impact of extractive resource development and the inequitable allocation by the State of the benefits from the resources have been a major trigger of resource conflicts.

3

Local Content Measures and the WTO Regime: Addressing Contentions and Trade-offs

Mandy Meng Fang

1 INTRODUCTION

This chapter analyses how local content requirements (LCRs) may result in misalignment with World Trade Organization (WTO) agreements. Drawing examples from the application of LCRs in the renewable energy sector, it argues that LCRs not only violate the principle of non-discrimination enshrined in the WTO regime, but may also slow down the diffusion of renewable energy technologies in global energy markets by erecting trade barriers and driving up the cost. It also examines prevailing rationales, such as political and economic ones, that still exist for the use of renewable energy LCRs, particularly in emerging and developing economies.

LCRs have been introduced widely by both developed and developing countries in a variety of sectors including automotive, oil and gas and renewable energy, especially after the 2008 financial crisis.[1] As trade-related measures that require the investor to purchase a certain amount of local materials for incorporation in the investor's product, LCRs are designed and implemented to benefit domestic firms at the expense of foreign competitors.[2] In this vein, the compatibility of using LCRs with obligations as set by the WTO regime has been highly controversial due to the discriminatory implications the measures can have on international trade.[3]

Enhancement of manufacturing competitiveness in the renewable energy industry is widely perceived to bring substantial benefits from economic, social and environmental perspectives, such as export growth, tax revenue, employment opportunities and emissions reduction. Along with the intensification of global

---

[1] See G. C. Hufbauer, J. J. Schott and C. Cimino, *Local Content Requirements: A Global Problem* (Washington, DC: Peterson Institute for International Economics, 2013), p. 3.

[2] See D. Olawuyi, 'Local Content and Procurement Requirements in Oil and Gas Contracts: Regional Trends in the Middle East and North Africa' (2019) 37 *Journal of Energy and Natural Resources Law* 93–117.

[3] See H. Hestermeyer and L. Nielson, 'The Legality of Local Content Measures under WTO Law' (2014) 48 *Journal of World Investment and Trade* 553–91. See also, D. Olawuyi, 'Local Content Policies and Their Implications for International Investment Law' in J. Chaisse, et al. (eds.), *Handbook of International Investment Law* (Springer, 2019) 1–21.

competition in renewable energy industry, LCRs adopted in renewable energy policies have proliferated worldwide, notably in the wind and solar manufacturing sectors.

The forms of LCRs used to boost renewable energy manufacturing tend to vary between different countries. They can be imposed as a precondition for access to financial support schemes provided to renewable energy generators, such as feed-in tariffs (FITs) or direct financial transfers, or public tenders. In many scenarios, LCRs are not standalone policies but adopted to complement other renewable energy incentive measures. Therefore, a case-by-case analysis to examine the specific design and implementation of LCRs is much needed.

Since the imposition of LCRs has the immediate effect of making foreign renewable energy manufacturers less competitive, escalating trade frictions seem to be inevitable when the use of LCRs shows no sign of diminishing. This is particularly so among major renewable energy producer countries that happen to be big trading nations, such as the United States, China, the European Union, Japan, Canada and India. Ever since Japan and the EU began the first-ever WTO dispute against Canada for its renewable energy supportive measures that included LCRs, the litigiousness in this area has been mounting rapidly. Six WTO disputes have been filed so far concerning the legality of LCRs adopted in renewable energy policies, of which three have been adjudicated by the WTO Panel or/and the Appellate Body. The WTO rulings can shed important light on the scope of policy space that the Members have in making use of LCRs to boost their domestic manufacturing industry without running afoul of the WTO law.

As a new facet of a long-running debate on the interaction between trade-related values and environment-related ones, the use of trade-related renewable energy measures with restrictive implications on international trade becomes a testing ground of the compatibility of trade regime and climate regime. In light of the extreme difficulty, if not entire impossibility, of justifying the use of LCRs as WTO-consistent, the case law that has been established sends a clear message that blatantly discriminatory renewable energy measures cannot survive the scrutiny of the WTO law. A following question to ask is how to assess the stringent rules being imposed by the WTO on the use of LCRs. Put differently, whether the overall benefits that could be generated through the use of LCRs in the renewable energy sector would outweigh the costs incurred is important to explore before analysing whether the policy space under the WTO regime for LCRs is too narrow or not.

If left unchecked, the use of LCRs can lead to worldwide proliferation of trade protectionism in the renewable energy sector and cast negative impacts on climate change mitigation. Therefore, the rather narrowed policy space that the WTO regime has for blatantly discriminatory LCRs would be conducive in shaping a level playing field for renewable energy manufacturers and can create an enabling environment for the expansion of renewable energy. This is much needed in reducing carbon emissions and achieving the goal of sustainable development.

Local Content Measures and the WTO Regime 43

This chapter consists of four sections. Section Two discusses LCRs in the renewable energy sector, including the arguments for and against renewable energy LCRs. It also discusses criteria for LCRs in renewable energy production to be effective and efficient in achieving objectives, such as jobs creation, economic growth and innovation. Section Three analyses the interaction between renewable energy LCRs and the WTO regime by examining the jurisprudence established in three disputes that addressed the legality of renewable energy LCRs. This Section also explores the possible policy space under the WTO regime that Members can have in making use of renewable energy LCRs. Section Four concludes.

2 LCRS AND THE RENEWABLE ENERGY SECTOR

This section examines key debates surrounding the use of LCRs in the renewable energy sector. Assessing the full costs and benefits of LCRs is an essential step in helping policymakers to apprehend policy trade-offs, which is also an important factor to be considered when analysing the reaction of the WTO to such measures. In other words, whether the WTO regime should provide sufficient policy scope for renewable energy measures that can contribute to climate change mitigation even when trade restrictions exist requires a holistic assessment of the measure's implications.

LCRs have increasingly been used by developed countries and emerging economies to favour domestic renewable energy manufacturers, especially since 2008.[4] Governments, at both national and local levels have designed and implemented LCRs as a component of green industrial policies to nurture and promote the development of domestic manufacturing capacity in renewable energy sector, notably the solar photovoltaic and wind turbines.[5] LCRs can take different forms that vary among countries. They can be imposed as a precondition for access to financial support schemes provided to renewable energy generators, such as FITs or direct financial transfers, or public tenders.[6] The ratio of LCRs can be set at different levels as well, which calls for case-by-case analysis. It is estimated that LCRs implemented in the renewable energy sector probably impact over USD 100 billion of trade annually.[7]

In light of the popularity of LCRs in the renewable energy sector and the implications on international trade, a few questions can be asked. What is the rationale of using LCRs in the eyes of renewable energy policymakers? What are

---

[4]   OECD, 'Green Finance and Investment: Overcoming Barriers to International Investment in Clean Energy', OECD Report to G20 Finance Ministers and Central Bank Governors, September 2015, p. 50.
[5]   Ibid., p. 64.
[6]   Ibid., p. 50.
[7]   S. Stephenson, 'Addressing Local Content Requirements: Current Challenges and Future Opportunities' (2013) 7 *Biores.*

the arguments against LCRs? Are LCRs effective in achieving the underlying objectives? What are the implications that LCRs generate on international trade?

Moerenhout and Kuntze list four primary reasons that can justify the imposition of LCRs by policymakers in renewable energy policies.[8] First, LCRs augment public support for renewable energy projects because of the alleged capacity to create jobs and value added locally in manufacturing sector. Particularly at subnational level, the use of LCRs seems to be even more appealing. Second, there is a need to protect infant industries, especially in developing countries, until they can compete on the international market. Third, LCRs will lead to an increased tax base for governments because of a larger local manufacturing industry, which allows countries to have more income in a time of financial need. Fourth, LCRs can generate positive environmental impacts in the medium term because they can eventually bring more, new mature players to the global market and benefit a certain transfer of technology and knowledge. Besides these justifications, Shadikhodjaev raises another point – the use of LCRs imposes insignificant cost to the government budget, which makes it politically appealing.[9] In Meyer's paper, how the use of LCRs can promote global public goods and increase welfare is analysed by examining renewable energy LCRs being adopted in a number of states in the United States.[10] It is argued that local governments should be provided with policy space under international trade law to implement discriminatory measures that can contribute to global public goods, such as climate change mitigation.[11] Otherwise, the potential to substantially curtail the large number of renewable energy supportive programs at local level exists.[12]

Opponents of LCRs in renewable energy policies cast doubts on the measures mainly from economic, trade and environmental perspectives.[13] To start, a measure without a trade-distorting discriminatory provision is always preferable in an economic sense to the same measure with the discriminatory provision. LCRs can lead to inefficient allocation of resources because they distort the level playing field between domestic products and foreign ones by making the latter less attractive.[14] As a direct consequence, renewable energy power prices will be inflated at least in the short term due to the increased price of renewable energy generation equipment, the burden of which will be passed partially or fully to the domestic consumer. Concerns about overall job increases exist because higher price of power generation

---

[8] J.-C. Kuntze and T. Moerenhout, 'Local Content Requirements and the Renewable Energy Industry – A Good Match?' ICTSD, Global Green Growth Institute, May 2013.

[9] S. Shadikhodjaev, *Industrial Policy and the World Trade Organization between Legal Constraints and Flexibilities* (Cambridge University Press, 2018), p. 147.

[10] See, T. Meyer, 'How Local Discrimination Can Promote Global Public Goods' (2015) 95 *Boston University Law Review* 1937.

[11] Ibid., p. 2012.

[12] Ibid.

[13] Kuntze et al., note 8.

[14] Olawuyi, note 3.

Local Content Measures and the WTO Regime 45

can lead to less production and less employment. Although employment can be boosted in renewable energy equipment manufacturing, the size of job losses in the downstream sectors, such as maintenance, service and installation, is very likely to be larger. In addition, LCRs act as trade barriers with the effect of reducing competition between domestic manufacturers and their foreign competitors to the detriment of the latter, which impedes trade liberalisation. The higher the level of LCRs, the more trade restrictive the measures are. From an environmental perspective, particularly a climate-related one, LCRs could increase the cost of renewable energy production and slow down the diffusion of renewable energy technologies, which contradicts the goal of climate change mitigation.[15] To meaningfully contribute to emissions reduction, renewable energy technologies need to be made more competitive than fossil fuels so as to increase the share of renewable energy.

Some researchers have laid out criteria for LCRs in renewable energy production to be effective in achieving objectives, such as enhancing innovation and capacity in the renewable energy industry, and promoting job opportunities and economic growth.[16] These include: stability and size of market;[17] restrictiveness of LCRs;[18] cooperation between government and firms;[19] and technology and knowledge transfers.[20] It is essential for policy makers to identify practical challenges that might negatively impact the efficiency and effectiveness of LCRs adopted in the renewable energy sector.

3 THE INTERACTIONS BETWEEN THE USE OF LCRS IN RENEWABLE ENERGY POLICIES AND THE WTO REGIME

The use of LCRs in renewable energy policies has not gone unnoticed by affected trading partners, and in recent years the number of WTO disputes filed concerning this matter has been rapidly growing.[21] Not only developed countries, but also developing ones, have increasingly resorted to the WTO dispute-settlement system

---

[15] Hestermeyer et al., note 3.

[16] Kuntze et al., note 8, pp. 11–12.

[17] Ibid. LCRs need a stable market with sufficient size and potential, without which there will be little incentive to invest in building up the necessary manufacturing capacity.

[18] Ibid. LCRs should not be set too high or too quickly.

[19] Ibid. Dialogue and information sharing can help governments set targets based on realistic assessments of supply and demand; financial assistance from governments to help firms meet targets can also help improve positive outcomes, though care needs to be taken to ensure costs of any subsidies are tailored to (and do not outweigh) their benefits, and that subsidies are appropriately limited in duration.

[20] Ibid. LCRs can produce benefits when technologies from or needed by the project spill over into the domestic economy and increase competitiveness of domestic suppliers. For technology and knowledge transfers to occur, there must be adequate absorptive capacity in the host country, and a bridgeable gap between foreign and domestic technologies

[21] In chronological order, WTO Request for Consultations by India, United States – Certain Measures Relating to the Renewable Energy Sector, WT/DS510/1, submitted on 9 September 2016; WTO Request for Consultations by the United States, India – Certain Measures Relating to Solar Cells

46   Mandy Meng Fang

to challenge trading partners' use of LCRs. The rising litigiousness in the renewable energy sector has been remarkable. In Asmelash's paper, he laid out two possible reasons that can explain this phenomenon.[22] The first is the likelihood of success in winning a dispute concerning the use of discriminatory renewable energy measures against trading partners. Some renewable energy measures, such as LCRs, are blatantly trade-restrictive and amount to a breach of the WTO obligation. The second is the pressure from domestic interest groups, such as politically influential renewable energy equipment manufacturing industries. These groups are inclined to petition their governments to initiate an investigation or file a formal WTO dispute against other Members. Perhaps the era when the Members were restrained from filing disputes against others' renewable energy measures out of the fear that resulting jurisprudence is likely to come back as precedent against their own policies in the same area had ended.

The expanding jurisprudence on the use of trade-related renewable energy policies can shed important light on the scope of policy space under the WTO regime for measures designed to support industrial development in this area. From a broader perspective, this relates to the debate around trade and climate change, with possible indications of how to ensure the compatibility of the WTO law with the objective of sustainable development. The following sections provide a critical review of three WTO disputes that have been addressed by the WTO adjudicators so far.

3.1 Canada – Renewable Energy *(DS412 and DS426)*

As the first case that has ever been filed with the WTO Dispute Settlement Body concerning the use of LCRs in renewable energy policies, *Canada – Certain Measures Affecting the Renewable Energy Generation Sector* and *Canada – Measures Relating to the Feed-in Tariff Program (Canada – Renewable Energy)* can advance the WTO case law in this regard.[23]

---

and Solar Modules, WT/DS456/1, submitted on 6 February 2013; WTO Request for Consultations by China, European Union and Certain Member State – Certain Measures Affecting the Renewable Energy Generation Sector, WT/DS452/1, submitted on 5 November 2012; WTO Request for Consultations by the European Union, Canada – Measures Relating to the Feed-in Tariff Program, WT/DS426/1, submitted on 11 August 2011; WTO Request for Consultations by United States, China – Measures Concerning Wind Power Equipment, WT/DS419/1, submitted on 22 December 2010; WTO Request for Consultations By Japan, Canada – Certain Measures Affecting the Renewable Energy Generation Sector, WT/DS412/1, submitted on 13 September 2010.

[22] H. B. Asmelash, 'Energy Subsidies and WTO Dispute Settlement: Why Only Renewable Energy Subsidies Are Challenged?' (2015) 18 *Journal of International Economic Law* 261 at 267.

[23] WTO Request for Consultations by Japan, *Canada – Certain Measures Affecting the Renewable Energy Generation Sector*, WT/DS512/1, submitted on 13 September 2010; WTO Request for Consultations by the European Union, *Canada – Certain Measures Affecting the Renewable Energy Generation Sector*, WT/DS512/1, submitted on 11 August 2011.

3.1.1 Dispute Facts and the Legal Complaints

In *Canada – Renewable Energy*, the challenged measure consisted of LCRs, which were adopted by the Canadian Province of Ontario and attached in the FIT Program applicable to solar and wind power generation facilities.[24] Established by the Ontario Power Authority (OPA),[25] the FIT Program provided generators of renewable energy electricity a guaranteed price for twenty to forty years. The Province of Ontario would enter into contractual arrangements with producers of solar and wind energy via FIT, and micro-FIT contracts. Access to FIT contracts was predicated on meeting the minimum LCRs for power generation equipment.[26] The underlying policy objectives were threefold:[27] First was to support climate change initiatives in North America by phasing out coal-fired electricity generation by 2014 and improve air quality. Second was to create renewable energy industries and employment opportunities. Third was to boost Ontario's economic activity and the development of renewable energy technology.

Japan and the European Union filed the litigation regarding Canada's measures relating to LCRs in the FIT Program under the WTO's Dispute Settlement System in September 2010 and August 2011, respectively. Japan and the EU challenged the consistency of the FIT Program with LCRs attached under the GATT,[28] the TRIMs[29] and the SCM Agreement,[30] of the WTO.[31] To be specific, the complaining parties claimed that the measure constituted a violation of the national treatment principle, as set out in Article III:4 of the GATT[32] and Article 2.1 of the TRIMs.[33] Another claim of violation of SCM Articles 3.1(b) and 3.2,[34] which forbid subsidies contingent on the use of domestic over imported goods, was premised on being able

[24] Panel Reports, *Canada – Certain Measures Affecting the Renewable Energy Generation Sector / Canada – Measures Relating to the Feed-in Tariff Program*, WT/DS412/R / WT/DS426/R, adopted 19 December 2012, para 2.1.
[25] The OPA was established under Ontario's Electricity Restructuring Act of 2004 as a government agency responsible for managing Ontario's electricity supply.
[26] The LCRs mandated the use of a minimum of domestic content ranging from 25 per cent to 60 per cent in large installations. Those levels range from 25 per cent for wind projects over 10 kilowatts in 2009 to 2011 to 60 per cent for solar projects over 10 kilowatts starting in 2011. For instance, if a company producing wind power wants to receive the price guarantees and grid access granted by the FIT, it needs to ensure that at least 25 per cent of the equipment used to produce that energy, including wind turbine and other equipment, and respective services comes from Ontario.
[27] See, Ontario Ministry of Energy, 'Feed-in Tariff Program Two-Year Review', www.energy.gov.on.ca /en/fit-and-microfit-program/2-year-fit-review/.
[28] General Agreement on Tariffs and Trade 1994, 15 April 1994, Marrakesh Agreement Establishing the World Trade Organization, Annex 1A, 1867 UNTS 187, 33 ILM 1153 (1994) [GATT].
[29] Agreement on Trade-Related Investment Measures, 15 April 1994, Marrakesh Agreement Establishing the World Trade Organization, Annex 1A, 1868 UNTS 186 [TRIMS].
[30] Agreement on Subsidies and Countervailing Measures, 15 April 1994, Marrakesh Agreement Establishing the World Trade Organization, Annex 1A, 1869 UNTS 14 [SCM].
[31] Panel Reports, *Canada – Renewable Energy*, paras. 3.1–3.6.
[32] GATT, note 28, Article III:4.
[33] TRIMS, note 29, Article 2.1.
[34] SCM, note 30, Articles, 3.1(b) and 3.2.

48   *Mandy Meng Fang*

to prove that the FIT incentives were subsidies under the SCM Agreement. Since the focus of this Chapter is the use of LCRs in renewable energy policies, the subsidy claim concerning the measure of FITs raised in the dispute is not relevant and not addressed.

3.1.2 Legal Decisions

The WTO Panel began its evaluation under the TRIMS Agreement by considering whether the FIT Program was in fact an investment program and, if so, whether it was trade related. It is noted that the TRIMS Agreement lacks any substantive disciplines independent of the GATT; therefore, evidencing a violation of GATT Article III or XI[35] is necessary to show a violation of TRIMS Article 2.[36] On the basis of the legislative record and the evidence that Ontario's scheme had in fact attracted investment in equipment manufacturing, the Panel decided that the FIT was an investment measure.[37]

Canada made its counterargument by invoking the GATT Article III:8(a)[38] and contending that the FIT Program amounted to 'laws and requirements that govern the procurement of renewable energy electricity for governmental purpose of securing an electricity supply for Ontario from clean sources ... [and] not with a view to commercial resale or with a view to use in the production of goods for commercial sale'.[39] As noted, Article III:8(a),[40] which is a provision of government procurement derogation, became the only defence Canada made in this dispute. If Canada could successfully avail itself of Article III:8(a),[41] even the discriminatory LCRs would have been exonerated.[42] Therefore, the key question before the Panel and the Appellate Body was how to apply the language in Article III:8(a),[43] which became the central feature of the TRIMS and GATT analysis in this dispute.

Whether Article III:8(a)[44] was available or not was nearly a *tabula rasa* for the WTO dispute system, as *Canada – Renewable Energy* was the first dispute in which this provision was brought up.[45] Dormant for more than six decades, the GATT Article III:8(a)[46] became a focal point of *Canada – Renewable Energy*. Both the

---

[35]   GATT, note 28, Articles III and XI.
[36]   TRIMS, note 29, Article 2; S. Charnovitz and C. Fischer, 'Canada–Renewable Energy: Implications for WTO Law on Green and Not-So-Green Subsidie' (2015) 14 *World Trade Review* 177 at 184.
[37]   Panel Reports, *Canada – Renewable Energy*, para 7.112.
[38]   GATT, note 28, Article III:8(a).
[39]   Appellate Body Report, *Canada – Renewable Energy*, para. 1.10.
[40]   GATT, note 28, Article III:8(a).
[41]   Ibid.
[42]   A. Cosbey and P. C. Mavroidis, 'A Turquoise Mess: Green Subsidies, Blue Industrial Policy and Renewable Energy: The Case for Redrafting the Subsidies Agreement of the WTO' (2014) 17 *Journal of International Economic Law* 11 at 15.
[43]   GATT, note 28, Article III:8(a).
[44]   Ibid.
[45]   Charnovitz et al., note 36, p. 190.
[46]   GATT, note 28, Article III:8(a).

Panel and the Appellate Body invested considerably in applying the specific case facts to the understanding of Article III:8(a),[47] after which they rejected Canada's defence on the basis of different reasoning.[48] The Panel found that the Government of Ontario and the municipal governments did 'profit from the resale of electricity that is purchased under the FIT Program' and that the resale of electricity was made 'in competition with the licensed electricity retailers, which amounted to "commercial resale" and failed to satisfy the last requirement'.[49] In disagreement with the Panel, the Appellate Body decided that the reading of Article III:8(a)[50] must be understood in relation to the obligations stipulated in GATT Article III[51] as a whole.[52] This means the product of foreign origin that is allegedly discriminated against must be in 'a competitive relationship' with the product purchased by governmental agencies.[53] Therefore, whether the LCRs could be regarded as a legal requirement 'governing' the procurement of electricity within the meaning of Article III:8(a)[54] depends on the existence of a competitive relationship between the two products. According to the Appellate Body, it was renewable energy generation equipment that was subject to discrimination and electricity that was purchased under the FIT Program, which were not in a competitive relationship. The mere existence of 'a close relationship', as contended by the Panel between products cannot replace the requirement of 'a competitive relationship' in order to successfully invoke Article III:8(a). Thus, the challenged measures did not qualify as 'laws, regulations or requirements governing the procurement by government agencies' of electricity under Article III:8(a).[55] Canada's attempt to exonerate the deviation from the national treatment obligation via GATT Article III:8(a)[56] failed and the use of LCRs breached the WTO rules.

---

[47] Ibid.

[48] Literature on the WTO jurisprudence of Article III:8(a) includes K. Dawar, 'Government Procurement in the WTO: A Case for Greater Integration' (2016) 15 *World Trade Review* 645–70; A. Davies, 'The Article III:8(a) Procurement Derogation and *Canada – Renewable Energy*' (2015) 18 *Journal of International Economic Law* 543–54; A. Yanovich, 'Canada – Renewable Energy and Canada – FIT Program – Debunking the Myth that the GATT 1994 Provides Carte Blanche to Discriminate in Government Procurement' (2013) 8 *Global Trade and Customs Journal* 430–4; M. Meng Fang, 'Shades of Green: Mapping the Parameters of the Article III:8(a) Government Procurement Derogation in the Renewable Energy Transition' (2019) 20 *Journal of World Investment and Trade* 553–77.

[49] Panel Report, *Canada – Renewable Energy*, para. 7.151. The Panel found out that Hydro One, a provincial government entity, and municipal public utilities resold the renewable electricity procured by the OPA.

[50] GATT, note 28, Article III:8(a).

[51] Ibid., Article III.

[52] Appellate Body Report, *Canada – Renewable Energy*, para. 5.58. To be in a competitive relationship, the two products should be identical or 'like', or directly competitive to or substitutable.

[53] Appellate Body Report, *Canada – Renewable Energy*, para. 5.74.

[54] GATT, note 28, Article III:8(a).

[55] Ibid; Appellate Body Report, *Canada – Renewable Energy*, para. 5.79

[56] GATT, note 28, Article III:8(a).

50   *Mandy Meng Fang*

The key divergence between the Panel and the Appellate Body in interpreting Article III:8(a)[57] lies in how to understand the relationship between products being discriminated against and products being purchased. The Appellate Body's reversal of the Panel's findings, which were more lenient towards the availability of derogation, would reduce the scope of Article III:8(a)[58] and, thus, the likelihood that WTO Members can rely on this provision to justify the use of LCRs.[59] From a broader perspective, this decision has put 'an important gloss' on how to understand government procurement derogation in specific WTO disputes.[60] The rather restrictive interpretative approach adopted by the Appellate Body in this dispute has largely widened the scope of Article III[61] obligation beyond what some commentators had believed.[62] To what extent the jurisprudence established by the adjudicators in *Canada – Renewable Energy* would be followed is an open question, while it is widely acknowledged that the Appellate Body's decisions could create security and predictability among Members and carry weight when relevant disputes occur in future.[63] To sum up, *Canada – Renewable Energy* created a WTO precedent ruling that the use of LCRs in renewable energy sector amounts to a blatant violation of national treatment obligation.

3.2 *India – Solar Cells and Modules (DS456)*

Not too long after the initiation of *Canada – Renewable Energy*, the United States filed a case against India concerning certain measures relating to domestic content requirements[64] under the Jawaharlal Nehru National Solar Mission (JNNSM) for solar cells and solar modules.[65] Rulings issued in *India – Certain Measures Relating to Solar Cells and Solar Modules*

---

[57] Ibid.
[58] Ibid.
[59] Hestermeyer et al., note 3, p. 577.
[60] Charnovitz et al., note 36, p. 178.
[61] GATT, note 28, Article III.
[62] Cosbey et al., note 42.
[63] This reflects that the Appellate Body has succeeded in producing a consistent body of interpretation of WTO rules, despite the absence of a strict notion of *stare decisis*. See, I. Van Damme, 'Treaty Interpretation by the WTO Appellate Body' (2010) 21 *European Journal of International Law* 605 at 614.
[64] Domestic content requirements are used interchangeably with local content requirements. For the sake of clarity and consistency, this article adopts the phrase 'local content requirements' (LCRs).
[65] The JNNSM adopted three successive Phases (Phase I, Phase II and Phase III), with each phase being further divided into Batches. The 11th Plan and first year of the 12th Plan (up to 2012–13) has been considered as Phase I, the remaining 4 years of the 12th Plan (2013–17) are included as Phase II and the 13th Plan period (2017–22) is envisaged as Phase III. A mandatory LCR was imposed on solar power developers participating in both Phase I and Phase II of the NSM. However, the scope and coverage of the LCR measures in Phase I and Phase II differed. Under Phase I (Batch 1), it was mandatory for all projects based on crystalline silicon (c-Si) technology to use c-Si modules manufactured in India, while the use of foreign c-Si cells and foreign thin-film modules or concentrator photovoltaic (PV) cells was permitted. Under Phase I (Batch 2), it was mandatory for all projects based on c-Si

Local Content Measures and the WTO Regime

(*India – Solar Cells*)[66] would further expand the WTO jurisprudence on the interaction between the use of LCRs and the multilateral trading regime. A critical analysis of the Panel and the Appellate Body decisions in *India – Solar Cells* is essential in understanding how the use of LCRs in renewable energy policies would be defined by the WTO regime.

3.2.1 Dispute Facts and Legal Complaints

This dispute concerned LCRs stemming from India's JNNSM, a programme launched in 2010 with the goal of deploying 20,000 MW (later revised upwards to 100,000 MW) of solar panels through an interconnected grid by 2022.[67] Under the scheme, the government of India would enter into twenty-five-year power purchase agreements (PPAs) with solar power developers, which guaranteed that electricity generated by the domestic solar power developers would be purchased at a preferential rate.[68] Access to the preferential rate of tariff for electricity and other forms of supportive schemes under the JNNSM was conditioned on the use of solar components manufactured only in India. The stated objective of the JNNSM is 'to establish India as a global leader in solar energy, by creating the policy conditions for its diffusion across the country as quickly as possible'.[69] In the eyes of Indian policy makers, the growth of a domestic solar manufacturing industry is strategically important.[70] As a consequence, solar products imported from foreign countries would be disfavoured. The US Trade Representative complained that solar exports from the USA to India had fallen by more than 90 per cent due to the LCR measures as mandated by the JNNSM.[71] With no

---

technology to use c-Si cells and modules manufactured in India, while the use of domestic or foreign modules made from thin-film technologies or concentrator PV cells was permitted. Under Phase II (Batch 1-A), any solar cells and modules used by the solar power developers had to be made in India, irrespective of the type of technology used.

[66] See, WTO Request for Consultations by United States, India – Certain Measures Relating to Solar Cells and Solar and Solar Modules, WT/DS456/20, submitted on 6 February 2013.

[67] Government of India Ministry of New and Renewable Energy, 'Ministry of New and Renewable Energy – Scheme / Documents', February 2012, www.mnre.gov.in/solar-mission/jnnsm/introduction-2. This objective later was revised upward to 100,000 MW. According to India's Ministry of New and Renewable Energy, the scheme aims to reduce the cost of solar power generation in India, specifically via long-term policy, large-scale deployment targets, intensive research and development and domestic production of the necessary raw materials and components.

[68] Panel Report, India – Solar Cells, para. 7.2. Two Indian electricity regulatory commissions, the Central Electricity Regulatory Commission at the national level and the State Electricity Regulatory Commission at each state level, determine the guaranteed rate of electricity produced under the PPAs.

[69] See Government of India, Ministry of New and Renewable Energy, 'Resolution No. 5/14/2008, Jawaharlal Nehru National Solar Mission', www.mnre.gov.in/solar-mission/jnnsm/resolution-2/.

[70] Energética India, 'Solar Manufacturing in India', January/February 2015, p. 4.

[71] 'US Emerges Victorious Over India in WTO Solar Panel Dispute', September 17, 2016, www .dnaindia.com/money/report-us-emerges-victorious-over-india-in-wto-solar-panel-dispute-2255915.

52 Mandy Meng Fang

surprise, it was the LCRs contained in the schemes that led the USA to litigate against India at the WTO.[72]

On 6 February 2013, the USA requested consultations with India concerning certain measures of India relating to LCRs under the JNNSM for solar cells and solar modules. Later, in 2014, the USA requested supplementary consultations concerning certain measures of India relating to LCRs under 'Phase II' of the JNNSM for solar cells and solar modules. The USA claimed that the LCR measures for solar cells and solar modules under the JNNSM constituted violations of the GATT Article III:4[73] and Article 2.1 of the TRIMs[74] since these measures accorded less-favourable treatment to foreign solar cells and modules than that accorded to like domestic products.[75] The conditions of competition would be modified in favour of solar cells and modules manufactured in India to the detriment of imported ones. Although the USA made claims pursuant to Articles 3.1 (b), 3.2, 5(c), 6.3(a), 6.3(c) and 25 of the SCM Agreement[76] in its first consultation request, these claims were withdrawn later in the second consultation request, which seems to be 'a strange absence'.[77] Nevertheless, the underlying cause of the change of allegations made by the USA is beyond the scope of this research.

3.2.2 Legal Decisions

In its defence, India submitted that the challenged measures should be exonerated by the means of the GATT Article III:8(a),[78] which was the second time that government procurement derogation was invoked in the WTO dispute settlement. In addition, India also sought justification by arguing for the applicability of the GATT Article XX(d) and (j).[79] Therefore, *India – Solar Cells* represents a first-time litmus test of the applicability of Article XX[80] for LCRs. In resemblance to the jurisprudence established in *Canada – Renewable Energy*, the adjudicators in the present case deemed the use of LCRs as a breach of national treatment obligations within the meaning of the GATT and TRIMs Agreement. Therefore, the focal point of the WTO decisions becomes whether India's defences made under GATT Article III:8(a), the GATT Article XX(d) and (j) would be valid.[81]

---

[72] Ibid.
[73] GATT, note 28, Article III:4.
[74] TRIMS, note 29, Article 2.1.
[75] Panel Report, *India – Solar Cells*, para. 7.39.
[76] SCM, note 30, Articles 3.1 (b), 3.2, 5(c), 6.3(a), 6.3(c) and 25.
[77] M. Benitah, 'India – Solar Cells, the Strange Absence of the SCM in the US Claim', 29 February 2016, https://ielp.worldtradelaw.net/2016/02/india-solar-cells.html.
[78] GATT, note 28, Article III:8(a); See, India's first written submission, paras. 101–164.
[79] GATT, note 28, Article XX(d) and (j).
[80] Ibid., Article XX.
[81] Ibid., Article III:8(a), XX(d) and (j).

Local Content Measures and the WTO Regime 53

3.2.2.1 THE DECISIONS ON THE GATT ARTICLE III:8(A). In applying Article III:8 (a)[82] to the case facts of *India – Solar Cells*, the Panel followed the jurisprudence established by the Appellate Body in *Canada – Renewable Energy*, despite that India argued for a different interpretation of Article III:8(a)[83] on the basis that the challenged measure in the present dispute and the one in *Canada – Renewable Energy* were distinguishable from each other.[84] The Panel also dismissed India's assertion that that as 'integral inputs' to the generation of electricity, solar cells and modules were relevant to the analysis under Article III:8(a)[85] since these were issues that the Appellate Body left undecided in *Canada – Renewable Energy*.[86] The Appellate Body upheld the Panel's decisions and rejected India's proposition. In doing so, the Appellate Body reiterated that products purchased under Article III:8(a)[87] by way of procurement must be 'like', or 'directly competitive' with, or 'substitutable' for the foreign products being discriminated against.[88] The reliance on a competitive relationship test in determining the applicability of Article III:8 (a)[89] has been even reinforced by the Appellate Body in the dispute. India's attempt to exempt the use of LCRs in its renewable energy sector from the WTO obligation could not be accepted because the discrimination did not directly refer to what India was purchasing, which was electricity. The Appellate Body in *India – Solar Cells* squeezed the availability of Article III:8(a)[90] by refusing to consider 'inputs and processes of production' used to produce the product as a parallel to the competitive relationship test, although the Appellate Body in *Canada – Renewable Energy* did not explicitly rule out this possibility. The established jurisprudence in relation to understanding Article III:8(a)[91] seems to indicate that it is extremely difficult, if not entirely impossible, that LCRs adopted to promote renewable energy industry can be justified under this provision.

3.2.2.2 THE DECISIONS ON THE GATT ARTICLE XX(D)[92]. India also defended the challenged measure by referring to the GATT Article XX(d),[93] which requires measures to be 'necessary to secure compliance with laws or regulations which are not inconsistent with the provisions of this Agreement, including those

[82] Ibid., Article III:8(a).
[83] Ibid.
[84] Appellate Body Report, *India – Solar Cells*, para. 5.19.
[85] GATT, note 28, Article III:8(a).
[86] Panel Report, *India – Solar Cells*, paras. 7.118–7.120.
[87] GATT, note 28, Article III:8(a).
[88] Appellate Body Report, *India – Solar Cells*, para. 5.40.
[89] GATT, note 28, Article III:8(a).
[90] Ibid.
[91] Ibid.
[92] Ibid., Article XX(d).
[93] Ibid.

54   *Mandy Meng Fang*

relating to customs enforcement, the enforcement of monopolies operated under paragraph 4 of Article II and Article XVII, the protection of patents, trademarks, and copyrights, and the prevention of deceptive practices'.[94] This exceptional clause has been invoked by the Members and addressed by the adjudication bodies many times in the past.[95] Therefore, a large body of jurisprudence concerning the application of Article XX(d)[96] exists, on the basis of which the Panel and the Appellate Body in *India – Solar Cells* could rely.[97]

India referred to a wide range of certain international and domestic instruments[98] as the laws and regulations with which the LCR measures were to secure compliance, as well as its obligations to address climate change and ensure ecologically sustainable growth.[99] However, the Panel decided that the executive branch implementing action without express legislative sanction did not speak to the question of whether international obligations, as assumed by India, would automatically be incorporated into domestic law and have a 'direct effect' in India.[100] Therefore, India failed to meet its burden of demonstrating that any of the international instruments at issue had 'direct effect' in India and thus, they cannot be characterised as 'laws or regulations' within the meaning of Article XX(d).[101]

---

[94]   Ibid., Articles II and XVII.
[95]   See GATT Panel Reports, *US – Spring Assemblies*, 1982; *Canada – FIRA*, 1983; *Japan – Agricultural Products I*, 1987; *US – Section 337 Tariff Act*, 1998; *EEC – Parts and Components*, 1990; *US – Tuna (Mexico)*, 1991; *US – Malt Beverages*, 1992; *US – Taxes on Automobiles*, 1994; *US – Tuna (EEC)*, 1994; WTO Panel Reports, *US – Gasoline*; *Canada – Periodicals*; *Korea – Various Measures on Beef*; *Argentina – Hides and Leather*; *Canada – Wheat Exports and Grain Imports*; *EC – Trademarks and Geographical Indications* (Australia); *Dominican Republic – Import and Sale of Cigarette*; *Mexico – Taxes on Soft Drink*; *Brazil – Retreaded Tyres*; *US – Customs Bond Directive*; *US – Shrimp (Thailand)*; *China – Autos Parts*; *Colombia – Ports of Entry*; *Thailand – Cigarettes (Philippines)*; Appellate Body Reports, *Korea –Various Measures on Beef*; *Dominican Republic – Import and Sale of Cigarettes*; *Mexico – Taxes on Soft Drinks*; *US – Shrimp (Thailand)* / *US – Customs Bond Directive*; *Thailand – Cigarettes (Philippines)*.
[96]   GATT, note 28, Article XX(d).
[97]   Following the two-tier test as established in previous case law, the defending party needs to show that the challenged measure is designed to secure compliance with laws or regulations that are not themselves inconsistent with some provision of the GATT 1994. Second, it must be shown that the measure is necessary to secure such compliance.
[98]   The international instruments identified by India were as follows: the preamble of the WTO Agreement; UN General Assembly, *United Nations Framework Convention on Climate Change*, 20 January 1994, UN Doc. A/RES/48/189; UN, *1992 Rio Declaration on Environment and Development*, 14 June 1992, UN Doc. A/CONF.151/26; UN General Assembly, *The Future We Want*, 11 September 2012, UN Doc. A/RES/66/288. The domestic instruments identified by India were as follows: Electricity Act, Act No. 36 of 2003, 26 May 2003, s 3; National Electricity Policy, 12 February 2005, No. 23/40/2004-R&R (Vol. II), para. 5.12.1; Government of India, Ministry of Power, Central Electricity Authority, 'National Electricity Plan', January 2018, S 5.2.1; and Government of India, 'National Action Plan on Climate Change', 2008.
[99]   India's first written submission to the Panel, para. 240.
[100] Panel Report, *India – Solar Cells*, paras. 7.298.
[101] GATT, 28, Article XX(d); Appellate Body Report, *India – Solar Cells*, para. 5.98.

Local Content Measures and the WTO Regime   55

The Appellate Body pointed to a few indicators that should be taken into consideration when assessing what constitute eligible 'laws and regulations' within the meaning of Article XX(d).[102] Among domestic instruments identified by India, only Section 3 of the Electricity Act, 2003 qualified as a 'law' within the meaning of Article XX(d).[103] However, the Appellate Body found that India failed to establish a 'link or nexus' between the LCR measures and Section 3 of the Electricity Act, 2003.[104] This means that India cannot prove that LCR measures were employed to 'secure compliance' with the legal obligations in Section 3 of the Electricity Act.[105] With respect to international instruments, the Appellate Body recognised that international instruments could be valid 'laws or regulations' within the meaning of Article XX(d) in two circumstances.[106] The Appellate Body agreed with the Panel that there was no evidence showing that the international instruments had direct effect in India.[107] Therefore, India failed to satisfy the requirement of Article XX(j).[108]

3.2.2.3 THE DECISIONS ON THE GATT ARTICLE XX(J).[109] *India – Solar Cells* represents the first time that Article XX(j)[110] had been invoked by a WTO Member before the Dispute Settlement Body, therefore, the decisions made by the adjudicators could have far-reaching implications on future jurisprudence. Article XX(j) requires measures to be 'essential to the acquisition or distribution of products in general or local short supply, provided that any such measures shall be consistent with the principle that all contracting parties are entitled to an equitable share of the international supply of such products, and that any such measures, which are inconsistent with the other provisions of the Agreement shall be discontinued as soon as the conditions giving rise to them have ceased to exist'.[111]

---

[102] Ibid., para. 5.113. These indicators include: (i) the degree of normativity of the instrument and the extent to which the instrument operates to set out a rule of conduct or course of action that is to be observed within the domestic legal system of a Member; (ii) the degree of specificity of the relevant rule; (iii) whether the rule is legally enforceable, including, e.g. before a court of law; (iv) whether the rule has been adopted or recognised by a competent authority possessing the necessary powers under the domestic legal system of a Member; (v) the form and title given to any instrument or instruments containing the rule under the domestic legal system of a Member; and (vi) the penalties or sanctions that may accompany the relevant rule.

[103] Electricity Act, note 98; GATT, note 28, Article XX(d); Panel Report, *India – Solar Cells*, para. 7.318.

[104] Panel Report, *India – Solar Cells*, para. 7.329; Electricity Act, note 98.

[105] Ibid.

[106] Appellate Body Report, *India – Solar Cells*, paras. 5.140 and 5.141. The first circumstance is when these international instruments become part of the Members' domestic legal system by means of incorporation or having direct effect within the domestic system without such implementation, or in other ways available under that system. The other circumstance is when the international instruments operate with 'a sufficient degree of normativity and specificity under the domestic legal system ... so as to set out a rule of conduct or course of action'.

[107] Appellate Body Report, *India – Solar Cells*, para. 5.145.

[108] GATT, note 28, Article XX(j).

[109] Ibid.

[110] Ibid.

[111] Ibid.

India asserted that 'lack of domestic manufacturing capacity of solar cells and modules amounts to a situation of local and general short supply of solar cells and modules in India'.[112] In addition, India also pointed out the 'risk of a shortage' would cause solar cells and modules 'being products in general or local short supply'.[113] The contentious point became whether the lack of domestic manufacturing capacity and the risk of a shortage would meet the definition of 'general or local short supply' within the meaning of Article XX(j).[114] The Panel ruled that the terms 'products in general or short supply' referred to 'a situation in which the quantity of available supply of a product does not meet demand in the relevant geographical area or market'.[115] In addition, the Panel held that 'products in general or local short supply' did not mean 'products at risk of becoming in short supply' and 'only imminent risks of such shortage' would fall under the ambit.[116] Therefore, the Panel found the products subject to the challenged LCR measures were not 'products in general or local short supply' within the meaning of Article XX(j) of the GATT 1994.[117]

The Appellate Body mandated an assessment of the relationship between the challenged measure and 'the acquisition or distribution' of products on the basis of the measure's design and its essentiality to such acquisition or distribution was required.[118] The term 'essential' was understood to be similar to the word 'necessary' in Article XX(d),[119] which means that the process of 'weighing and balancing' of relevant factors in a necessity test would also be pertinent under Article XX(j).[120] Therefore, it is important to assess the challenged measure's contribution to addressing 'the acquisition or distribution' of the products in short supply and its trade restrictiveness in comparison to reasonably available alternatives.[121] In conceptualising the terms 'general or local short supply', the Appellate Body held that insufficient supply from all sources, whether domestic or foreign to meet demand in the relevant market would satisfy.[122] There are a number of factors in assessing the issue of short supply: the level of domestic production of a particular product, the relevant product and geographical market, potential price fluctuation, accessibility of international supplies and other factors demonstrating the availability and sufficiency of a given product.[123] The Appellate Body also acknowledged that a Member's development status as indicative of production capacity and exposure to supply disruptions – stressing that the measure's policy rationales, for instance, energy security and

---

[112] See, India's first written submission, para. 213.
[113] Ibid., para. 236.
[114] GATT, note 28, Article XX(j).
[115] See, Panel Report, *India – Solar Cells*, para. 7.218.
[116] Ibid.
[117] GATT, note 28, Article XX(j); Panel Report, *India – Solar Cells*, para. 7.265.
[118] Appellate Body Report, *India – Solar Cells*, para. 5.58 and 5.60.
[119] GATT, note 28, Article XX(d).
[120] Ibid., Article XX(j); Appellate Body Report, *India – Solar Cells*, paras. 5.62 and 5.63.
[121] Appellate Body Report, *India – Solar Cells*, paras. 5.62 and 5.63.
[122] Ibid., para. 5.83.
[123] Appellate Body Report, *India – Solar Cells*, para. 5.71.

Local Content Measures and the WTO Regime

sustainable development – could be given certain consideration in the analysis of short supply.[124]

India's argument that a lack of 'sufficient' domestic manufacturing of a given product could be taken as evidence of 'short supply' of that product was not endorsed by the Appellate Body ruling.[125] India failed to justify the challenged measures by relying on Article XX(j), which does not distinguish between imported and domestic product.[126] Therefore, the status of LCRs was ruled again as unacceptable under the WTO regime.

3.3 *US – Renewable Energy (DS 510)*

It seems that tit-for-tat trade disputes are at the heart of mercantile trading regimes.[127] Soon after India lost a case brought by the USA concerning the LCR measures in India's JNNSM, India brought the USA to the WTO dispute settlement system regarding its government programmes that protected domestic renewable energy manufacturers.[128] This dispute also marks the latest development in a long-running debate over how to design and enact supportive policy measures for the development of renewable energy without running afoul of the WTO rules.[129] As of writing, the Panel report has been issued and it is highly uncertain whether and when the Appellate Body Report could be circulated since both parties have made the appeal to the Appellate Body.[130] This section develops analytical analysis on the basis of the rulings made by the Panel in this dispute.

3.3.1 Dispute Facts and Legal Complaints

Perhaps as a retaliation to a similar move made by the USA against India's plan to deploy solar power generation projects with mandatory LCRs,[131] India challenged eleven renewable energy measures adopted by eight US States (Washington, California, Montana, Connecticut, Michigan, Delaware, Minnesota and Massachusetts) to have discriminatory treatment on imported

---

[124] Ibid., paras. 5.72, 5.78 and 5.79.
[125] Ibid., para. 5.88.
[126] GATT, note 28, Article XX(j).
[127] R. K. Devarakonda, 'India Challenges WTO Ruling against Solar Technology Development', 28 May 2016, https://thewire.in/39217/india-challenges-wto-ruling-against-solar-technology-development.
[128] WTO Request for Consultations by India, the *United States – Certain Measures Relating to the Renewable Energy Sector*, WT/DS510/1, submitted on 19 September 2016.
[129] ICTSD, 'India Files WTO Challenge against US State Programmes for Renewable Energy', September 15, 2016, www.ictsd.org/bridges-news/bridges/news/india-files-wto-challenge-against-us-state-programmes-for-renewable-energy.
[130] The Panel Report was circulated on 27 June 2019. The US submitted the notification of an appeal on 15 August 2019.
[131] See previous Section's discussion of *India – Solar Cells*.

58   *Mandy Meng Fang*

goods.[132] In India's arguments, the US measures adopted at the subnational level violated the GATT Articles III:4 and Article XVI:1,[133] Article 2.1 of the TRIMs Agreement,[134] Articles 3.1(b), 3.2, 5(a), 5(c), 6.3(a), 6.3(c) and 25 of the SCM Agreement.[135]

3.3.2 Legal Decisions

Unlike the defendants in *Canada – Renewable Energy* and *India – Solar Cells*, the USA in this dispute did not refer to any WTO derogation/exceptions as justification for the challenged measures at issue. Instead, the USA, in its submissions, argued that India failed to meet the legal burden necessary to establish each and every element of Article III:4 of the GATT,[136] Article 2.1 of the TRIMs Agreement[137] and Articles 3.1(b) of the SCM Agreement[138] with respect to each measure at issue.[139] Simply put, the adjudicators are left to assess whether the challenged measures constitute breach of the obligations that the USA has to assume under the three WTO agreements. Why the USA did not make any defence by referring to possible justifications provided by the WTO regime appears to be quite bizarrely intriguing, which unfortunately is beyond the scope of this Chapter and merits further analysis in future.

The Panel decided that India has successfully established that the challenged measures fulfil all three elements of the legal test under the GATT Article III:4.[140] First, the Panel found that the relevant domestic and imported products under each measure at issue are like products within the meaning of Article III:4.[141] Second, each measure at issue is a law, regulation or requirement affecting the internal sale, offering for sale, purchase, transportation, distribution or use of the relevant products. Third, each measure at issue accords to relevant imported products treatment less favourable than that accorded to like domestic products within the meaning of the GATT Article III:4.[142]

Having found that the measures at issue constitute violation of Article III:4,[143] the panel decided to exercise judicial economy[144] on India's claims under Articles 2.1

---

[132]   Panel Report, *United States – Certain Measures Relating to the Renewable Energy Sector*, WT/DS510/1, para 2.2.
[133]   GATT, note 28, Article III:4 and Article XVI:1.
[134]   TRIMS, note 29, Article 2.1.
[135]   SCM, note 30, Articles 3.1(b), 3.2, 5(a), 5(c), 6.3(a), 6.3(c) and 25.
[136]   GATT, note 28, Article III:4.
[137]   TRIMS, note 29, Article 2.1
[138]   SCM, note 30, Article 3.1(b).
[139]   United States Trade Representative, 'U.S. Second Integrated Executive Summary', 3 May 2019.
[140]   GATT, note 28, Article III:4; Panel Report, *United States – Renewable energy*, paras 7.331.
[141]   GATT, note 28, Article III:4.
[142]   Ibid.
[143]   Ibid.
[144]   Judicial economy refers to the discretion of a Panel to address only those claims that must be addressed in order to resolve the matter in issue in dispute.

and 2.2 of the TRIMS Agreement[145] and Articles 3.1(b) and 3.2 of the SCM Agreement.[146] As mentioned in the beginning of this section, the USA did not invoke any WTO exceptions to justify the challenged measures once they were found to be WTO-inconsistent. The renewable energy measures challenged by India in the present dispute are ruled as breach of national treatment under the WTO. The USA is recommended to bring the measures into conformity with its obligations under the GATT Article III:4.[147]

Although both parties have submitted an appeal to the Appellate Body, it is highly uncertain when or even whether the dispute would be addressed by the Appellate Body in light of the current crisis. Put differently, the USA has successfully blocked the reappointment of new panel members, and so by the end of 2019, the panel's membership fell below the threshold necessary to render decisions.[148] Consequently, any losing party can prevent the adoption of a WTO Report simply by making an appeal to the Appellate Body.[149]

3.4 Reflections

The ever-expanding WTO jurisprudence concerning the legality of the use of LCRs in renewable energy policies sends a clear signal that it is extremely hard, if not entirely impossible, for such measures to survive the scrutiny of the WTO law. LCRs represent the textbook example of blatantly discriminatory measures that amount to breach of national treatment obligation, which is one of the cornerstones of the WTO law. The chance for LCRs to be void of WTO disciplines is to prove the applicability of carve-outs that can justify the use of LCRs when they violate WTO principle. However, the case law established so far suggests the chance is rather limited.

Firstly, the government procurement derogation has been narrowly interpreted by the Appellate Body in *Canada – Renewable Energy* and *India – Solar Cells*, which will carry weight when relevant disputes occur in future. The myth that governments had carte blanche to favour domestic producers over foreign ones in government procurement was debunked.[150] As a result, the scope of national treatment obligation has been largely widened. Secondly, the GATT Articles XX(d) and (j)[151] cannot be applied in justifying the use of LCRs, although Article XX[152] is widely perceived to

---

[145]   TRIMS, note 29, Articles 2.1 and 2.2
[146]   SCM, note 30, Articles 3.1(b) and 3.2; Panel Report, *United States – Renewable energy*, paras. 7.347–7.354 and 7.356–7.372.
[147]   GATT, note 28, Article III:4; Panel Report, *United States – Renewable energy*, para. 8.7.
[148]   R. Steinberg, 'The Impending Dejudicialization of the WTO Dispute Settlement System?' (2018) 112*American Society of International Law Proceedings* 316.
[149]   J. Pauwelyn and R. J. Hamilton, 'Exit from International Tribunals' (2018) 9 *Journal of International Economic Law* 679 at 683.
[150]   Yanovich, note 48, p. 434.
[151]   GATT, note 28, Article XX(d) and (j).
[152]   Ibid., Article XX.

60   *Mandy Meng Fang*

provide wide scope of policy space for Members to protect non-trade values. It is hard to prove LCRs are 'necessary to secure compliance with laws or regulations which are not inconsistent with the provisions of this Agreement' within the meaning of Article XX(d)[153] or 'essential to the acquisition or distribution of products in general or local short supply' within the meaning of Article XX(j).[154]

However, the use of LCRs in the renewable energy sector does not come without any merits, as discussed in Section 2. The scenarios are: when the imposition of LCRs is viewed as necessary for the passing of certain renewable energy supportive policies, or when the use of LCRs has the potential to nurture local renewable energy industries to become competitive players in global market. Particularly for developing and emerging economies that also face urgent need to take action on climate change and energy issues, the use of LCRs can turn out to be politically necessary in fostering investment in this sector.

In light of the ongoing stalemate in the Doha round negotiation and the difficulty to strike any new agreement concerning renewable energy, it is critically important to identify possibly available policy space that WTO Members can have in using LCRs to develop renewable energy and mitigate climate change. This Chapter recommends one option that policymakers can take into consideration when designing and implementing renewable energy LCRs.

The option is to incorporate renewable energy LCRs in government procurement schemes in line with the requirements as set in the GATT Article III:8(a).[155] It is noted that countries that are parties to the Government Procurement Agreement (GPA),[156] which is a plurilateral agreement within the framework of the WTO, need to ensure procurements are conducted in a competitive, non-discriminatory and transparent manner. The scope and coverage of the GPA is not unrestricted because the number of 'government entities' in acceded Members covered by the agreement is limited as well as the product and service.[157] Nevertheless, a large number of the WTO Members still have the discretion to discriminate in their government procurement activities. For instance, it is WTO-consistent for governments to procure wind farms for governmental purposes and not with a view to commercial resale and require the farm to be domestically made. In this case, domestic wind turbine

---

[153]   Ibid., Article XX(d).
[154]   Ibid., Article XX(j).
[155]   Ibid., Article III:8(a).
[156]   See, Agreement on Government Procurement Annex 4(b) of the WTO Agreement, reprinted in Uruguay Round of Multilateral Trade Negotiations: Legal Instruments Embodying the Results of the Uruguay Round, Vol. 31, GATT Secretariat, Geneva, 1994. The first agreement on government procurement (the so-called 'Tokyo Round Code on Government Procurement') was signed in 1979 and entered into force in 1981. After three rounds of amendments, the Agreement has nineteen parties comprising forty-seven WTO Members as of 2019.
[157]   The principles and procedural requirements set out by the text of the GPA do not automatically apply to all the procurement activities of each party but those that specified in the parties' coverage schedules have to comply with the rules of the GPA. See, the WTO GPA coverage schedules, www .wto.org/english/tratop_e/gproc_e/gp_app_agree_e.htm#revised.

Local Content Measures and the WTO Regime 61

manufacturers could be provided with more competitive advantages and thus, opportunities to grow and compete with foreign counterparts.

4 CONCLUSIONS

An examination of the WTO case law developed so far concerning the use of LCRs in renewable energy policies suggests the difficulty that LCRs face in passing muster in WTO disciplines. The high chance for complaining parties to win a WTO dispute concerning the use of LCRs in renewable energy policies also explains the rising litigiousness in this area. However, not providing breathing room for LCRs does not mean that the WTO regime is hostile towards non-trade values, namely climate change mitigation. Quite the contrary. Striking down blatantly discriminatory measures, such as LCRs, can be conducive from the perspective of climate change mitigation. Furthering trade liberalisation in the renewable energy sector can meaningfully contribute to the reduction of renewable energy price and diffusion of renewable energy technologies, which is much needed to combat climate change.

In addition, when an increasing number of Members turn to trade-discriminatory measures, such as LCRs, to boost their own renewable energy industry, a 'beggar-thy-neighbour' scenario featuring trade-inhibiting consequences would emerge. In other words, if left unchecked, the rampant use of LCRs can open the floodgate to rising protectionism in the renewable energy sector that can encourage the adoption of various forms of trade-restrictive measures. The trade disputes between WTO Members with respect to how to develop renewable energy with trade-related measures would always take years to simmer down, which can cast chilling effects on trade and investment in renewable energy.

However, the usefulness and effectiveness of LCRs in fostering infant industries, including the renewable energy industry, should not be entirely dismissed. In the presence of the urgent need to take action on climate change and energy issues, the use of LCRs can be politically salient, particularly in emerging and developing economies. This is not to argue that the WTO regime should give a pass to LCRs as long as they are adopted in renewable energy production. Instead, this Chapter points out that there is still policy space for the WTO Members to make use of LCRs without running afoul of the trade law. The rather limited scope of policy space under the GATT Article III:8(a)[158] can effectively reduce the abusive use of government procurement to serve protectionist objectives, while still allowing the Members to nurture domestic renewable energy industries. If properly designed and implemented, renewable energy LCRs can not only survive the scrutiny of the WTO law, but also contribute to goals such as promoting industrial growth and creating green jobs.

[158] GATT, note 28, Article III:8(a).

To sum up, renewable energy LCRs entail discriminatory effects in favour of local manufacturers to the detriment of foreign competitors, which can easily contravene a number of WTO disciplines. As established in the WTO jurisprudence, the policy space that Members have in making use of renewable energy LCRs is very limited, though not entirely absent. Therefore, it is crucial for policymakers to bear in mind the limits to policy space so as to design and implement LCRs in a way that is in conformity with the WTO rulebook. By restricting Members' attempts to discriminate in renewable energy measures while still providing breathing space for those with a need to enhance renewable energy industrial competitiveness and tackle climate change, the WTO regime plays a positive role in enhancing the synergy between trade values and climate-related ones.

4

Local Content Requirements in Extractive Industries: A Human Rights Analysis

Susan L. Karamanian[*]

1 INTRODUCTION

As a condition to accessing its oil, gas, and mineral resources, a State may require a foreign investor to purchase or procure local goods or services in the extraction or production process.[1] Known as local content requirements (LCRs), these State laws and regulations are non-tariff barriers to trade.[2] They may specify targets, such as percentages, of local resources used in the process, or they may take a broader approach and generally mandate use of locally sourced goods and services.[3]

LCRs seek to ensure that the benefits of a State's natural resources flow to its citizens and inhabitants. The traditional view is that, although counter to trade liberalization, LCRs promote the local community through job creation and enhancement of domestic entities, including infrastructure development.[4] They also prevent reallocation of rents attributed to the State's assets from that State to foreigners with the expectation that the assets will stay under the control of the host State.[5]

---

[*] I thank my colleague Dr. Damilola Olawuyi for his feedback on earlier drafts of this chapter as well as for encouraging me to write on this subject. I also thank Ms Sarah L. MacLeod, J.D. candidate, Schulich School of Law, Dalhousie University, Canada, for her careful review and suggested edits.

[1] See D. S. Olawuyi, *Extractives Industry Law in Africa* (Switzerland: Springer Nature Switzerland, 2018), pp. 233–260 (identifying and analysing LCRs in the energy sectors of various States in Africa and States outside of Africa, such as Canada, Saudi Arabia, and the United Kingdom).

[2] See C. Cimino, G. C. Hufbauer, and J. J. Schott, "A Proposed Code to Discipline Local Content Requirements," Peterson Institute for International Economics Policy Brief No. PB14-6, February 2014, p 1.

[3] See H. P. Hestermeyer and L. Nielsen, "The Legality of Local Content Measures under WTO Law" (2014) 48 *Journal of World Trade Law* 553; I. Ramdoo, "Unpacking Local Content Requirements in the Extractive Sector: What Implications for the Global Trade and Investment Frameworks?" International Centre for Trade and Sustainable Development, September 2015, pp. 2–4.

[4] See C. G. Ackah and A. S. Mohammed, "Local Content and Practice: The Case of the Oil and Gas Industry in Ghana," WIDER Working Paper 2018/152, p. 2 (recognizing that liberal economists have assumed that "growth in the extractive sector will induce economic growth through increased government revenues, used to finance poverty alleviation programmes and facilitate the improvement of infrastructure").

[5] G. C. Hufbauer, J. J. Schott, C. Cimino-Isaacs, M. Vieiro, and E. Wada, *Local Content Requirements: A Global Problem* (Washington, DC: Peterson Institute Press, 2013).

63

The implications of LCRs, however, are unsettled. What is their effect on the dynamic and wide-reaching area of human rights? Since World War II, States have joined a network of treaties, establishing duties to individuals based on their status as human beings.[6] The treaties recognize civil and political rights, such as the right to equality, the right to life, the right to liberty, and the right to freedom of expression.[7] They also include economic, social, and cultural rights, such as the right to work, the right to equal pay, and the right to an adequate standard of living.[8] State Constitutions and national laws may also acknowledge these rights.[9] The enjoyment of human rights, such as the right to life, assumes a sustainable environment.[10] It also means elimination of corruption, as its role in the allocation of natural resources could mean that members of a society are without food, water, or electricity: "[t]he right of peoples to dispose freely of their national wealth and natural resources" is "among the inalienable rights."[11] Hence, removing impediments to the realization of human rights is essential.

Because LCRs protect local resources and reallocate the benefits of production to a State's citizens, presumably they promote the indigenous community's economic and social rights.[12] Further, LCRs could benefit the political and civic realm as stability enables the broader development of the individual within the State.[13] The more resources that stay in the home State, the greater the opportunity for their allocation to fund schools and hospitals. In addition, LCRs targeted to specific industries, such as solar energy, could lead to affordable and sustainable sources of energy.[14]

By definition, however, LCRs discriminate based on national origin, so they defy the principle of equality. Second, in their implementation, LCRs have spawned new

---

[6] R. Higgins, *Problems and Process: International Law and How We Use It* (Oxford University Press, 1994), p. 96 (noting that "[h]uman rights are rights held simply by virtue of being a human person").

[7] UN General Assembly, *International Covenant on Civil and Political Rights*, 16 December 1966, 999 UNTS 171, arts. 3, 6, 9 and 19(2) [ICCPR]. See also Council of Europe, *European Convention for the Protection of Human Rights and Fundamental Freedoms*, 4 November 1950, 87 UNTS 103, arts. 2, 5, 10(1) and 14 [ECHR].

[8] UN General Assembly, *International Covenant on Economic, Social and Cultural Rights*, 16 December 1966, 993 UNTS 3 [ICESCR].

[9] See, for example, notes 79 and 81 (discussing Constitution of the Federal Republic of Nigeria 1999 and Constitution of the Republic of Ghana, respectively).

[10] United Nations Human Rights Office of the High Commissioner, "Special Rapporteur on Human Rights and the Environment: Introduction," www.ohchr.org/en/Issues/environment/SRenvironment/Pages/SRenvironmentIndex.aspx (observing that "[a] safe, clean, healthy and sustainable environment is integral to the full enjoyment of a wide range of human rights").

[11] N. Kofele-Kale, "Patrimonicide: The International Economic Crime of Indigenous Spoliation" (1995) 28 *Vanderbilt Journal of Transnational Law* 45 at 75. (emphasis in original).

[12] G. F. Moon, "Capturing the Benefits of Trade? Local Content Requirements in WTO Law and the Human Rights-Based Approach to Development" (April 2009) *SSRN Electronic Journal*.

[13] See Ackah et al., note 4.

[14] T. Meyer, "How Local Discrimination can Promote Global Public Goods" (2015) 95 *Boston University Law Review* 1937 at 1940 (noting that laws of various US states protect renewable energy, and arguing that they "sometimes increase global welfare").

Local Content Requirements in Extractive Industries 65

circumstances, particularly as to the relationship between indigenous companies, which may build their existence and relationship based upon LCRs, and foreign investors. These relationships could implicate basic human rights principles, such as the right to work and payment for work.

This chapter argues that States should embed human rights principles in LCRs to enable the State to achieve its developmental objectives, broadly defined. This action is essential given States' obligations to promote, protect, and fulfill human rights. The chapter sets forth how to accomplish this goal. After first analyzing LCRs under the recent experience of two States, Nigeria and Ghana, the chapter establishes the human rights framework and considers LCRs in its light. Building principally on the UN Guiding Principles on Business and Human Rights, the chapter recognizes that business enterprises and others in the extractive process, such as the government that awards bids and entities in supply chains, have specific human rights obligations. It establishes these obligations and demonstrates how LCRs can help satisfy them.

2 UNDERSTANDING LOCAL CONTENT REQUIREMENTS

2.1 *Overview*

The story of how States, or groups within them, have implemented measures to ensure that local communities benefit from the natural resources of the respective States is not a new one. In fact, it has existed as long as explorers have traveled the world in search of resources or cheaper ways of gaining access to them.

For example, in the 1600s, the East India Company from England arrived in India in search of spices. The Company developed a vibrant trade in Indian cotton for importation into England.[15] Indian cotton, however, threatened local English textile production.[16] Under the Calico Acts of 1701 and 1721, England prohibited the import of Indian and certain other foreign cotton.[17] The English trade restriction was a non-tariff barrier to trade in the form of an embargo. Years later, within India, as the British partitioned Bengal, India initiated a movement to encourage the purchase of locally produced goods. Known as the Swadeshi Movement, it spread beyond Bengal. In 1915, Mahatma Gandhi led the effort to encourage Indians to purchase local cotton only woven by local weavers. As he wrote:

> If we follow the Swadeshi doctrine, it would be your duty and mine to find out neighbours who can supply our wants and to teach them to supply them where they do not know how to proceed, assuming that there are neighbours who are in want of healthy occupation. Then every village of India will almost be a self-supporting and

---

[15] A. W. Douglas, "Cotton Textiles in England: The East India Company's Attempt to Exploit Developments in Fashion 1660–1721" (May 1969) 8 *Journal of British Studies* 28 at 28–29.
[16] J. E. Orchard, "Oriental Competition in World Trade" (1936–1937) *Foreign Affairs* 707 at 708.
[17] Douglas, note 15, at 35–36.

66 Susan L. Karamanian

self-contained unit, exchanging only such necessary commodities with other villages where they are not locally producible.[18]

Another example involves sugar. In 1811, Napoleon jump-started the French sugar industry by issuing a decree dedicating 79,000 acres of French land to beet production.[19] His action responded to British blockade of European ports, which prevented the importation of cane sugar from the West Indies. It would lead to the development of the European beet industry, which "was fed on bounties."[20]

How do LCRs fit into this picture? First, unlike the Swadeshi Movement, which encouraged Indians to buy from local suppliers, LCRs are typically mandatory. Second, unlike the Calico Acts, LCRs do not wholesale ban entry of foreign products in the State market. Under LCRs, entry of foreign investors into certain sectors is conditional; the investors must engage certain local resources. Third, in contrast to Napoleon's land decree, LCRs do not mandate State seizure of local resources to help build a local market. Instead, they steer the purchasing power of foreign investors to local workers, suppliers, and manufacturers.

LCRs are not solely creatures of developing countries that seek to build or strengthen a locale around their oil, gas, and mineral resources. Developed countries with mineral resources have enacted LCRs.[21] In recent years, a number of countries, such as Argentina, China, France, India, Russia, and the United States (at the State level), have used LCRs as a way to build their wind and solar energy industries.[22] Various countries have long attempted to use laws and regulations in the procurement process, such as the Buy American Act in the United States, which dates back to 1933.[23] Under the Buy American Act, the federal government gives "a price preference for domestic end products and construction materials" in the procurement process.[24]

In short, LCRs take various forms. Their use is prevalent and independent of the economic status of the enacting State. They target a wide range of business activity. Their effect, depending upon the targeted sector and its significance in any given State, could be substantial.

---

[18] M. K. Gandhi, *India of My Dreams* (Delhi, India: Rajpal and Sons, 2009), p. 120.

[19] F. Schneider, Jr., "Sugar" (1925–1926) 4 *Foreign Affairs* 311 at 313.

[20] Ibid., p. 314.

[21] Organisation for Economic Co-operation and Development (OECD), Trade and Agriculture Directorate Trade Committee, Working Party of the Trade Committee, "Local Content Policies in Minerals-Exporting Countries," June 2, 2017, TAD/TC/WP(2016)3/PART1/FINAL, p. 10 (observing that "[m]easures that aim to increase local content and procurement in the extractive industries are pervasive, including in OECD countries").

[22] OECD, "Green Finance and Investment: Overcoming Barriers to International Investment in Clean Energy," OECD Report to G20 Finance Ministers and Central Bank Governors, September 2015, pp. 53–54.

[23] Buy American Act, 41 U.S.C. ss. 8301–8305.

[24] K. M. Manuel, "The Buy American Act Preferences for 'Domestic' Supplies: In Brief," Congressional Research Service Report, April 26, 2016, p. 2.

Local Content Requirements in Extractive Industries 67

2.2 *LCRs in the Extractives Industry: The Experience of Nigeria and Ghana*

Two resource-rich countries in Africa, Nigeria and Ghana, have broad-sweeping LCRs applicable to foreign investors in extractive industries. Their respective LCRs are the Nigerian Oil and Gas Industry Content Development Act, 2010 (NOGICD Act)[25] and Ghana's Petroleum (Local Content and Local Participation) Regulations, 2013 (LI 2204).[26] Both laws have received considerable attention.[27] Further, these LCRs apply in the context of transition economies, which enables a better understanding of their application to differing constituencies, including local workers, one of the intended beneficiaries of LCRs.

2.2.1 Nigeria: The NOGICD Act

Nigeria's commitment to an aggressive local content policy began in earnest in the early part of the twenty-first century.[28] The NOGICD Act reflects the culmination of extensive efforts over at least a decade to enact an LCR in Nigeria's booming oil and gas business.[29]

Under the NOGICD Act, any entity or person involved in any aspect of the Nigerian oil and gas industry "shall consider Nigerian content as an important element of their overall project development and management philosophy for project execution."[30] The Act defines "Nigerian content" as "the quantum of composite value added to or created in the Nigerian economy by a systematic development of capacity and capabilities through the deliberate utilization of Nigerian human, material resources and services in the Nigerian oil and gas industry."[31]

The definition is opaque. For example, it measures Nigerian content of any activity based on a macroeconomic effect, namely, the benefit to the Nigerian economy. Second, it requires a "systematic" and "deliberate" approach to promote Nigerian resources. Activity in the oil and gas industry, which is not pursuant to a plan yet has the desired effect of promoting use of indigenous capacity, simply does not fit within the definition.

Attached to the NOGICD Act is a Schedule, which establishes the minimum Nigerian content to be included in any such project.[32]

---

[25] Government of Nigeria, Nigerian Oil and Gas Industry Content Development Act, 2010 Act No. 2 [NOGICD Act].

[26] Government of Ghana, Petroleum (Local Content and Local Participation) Regulations, 2013, LI 2204 [LI 2204].

[27] See, for example, Olawuyi, note 1.

[28] J. N. E. Nwaokoro, "Nigeria's National Content Bill: The Hype, the Hope and the Reality" (2011) 55 *Journal of African Law* 128 at 131–37 (discussing history of local content legislation and activity in Nigeria).

[29] Ibid.

[30] NOGICD Act, note 25, s. 2.

[31] Ibid., s. 106.

[32] Ibid., s. 11 (specifying that "the minimum Nigerian content in any project to be executed in the Nigerian oil and gas industry shall be consistent with the level set in Schedule to this Act").

Nigerian independent operators have first consideration in the award of access to oil resources.[33] Further, "Nigerian indigenous service companies which demonstrate ownership of equipment, Nigerian personnel and capacity" are given "exclusive consideration" to "bid on land and swamp operating areas of the Nigerian oil and gas industry for contracts and services" in a referenced schedule attached to the Act.[34]

Compliance with the Act and "promotion of Nigerian content development" is a "major criterion" to access the oil and gas sector, such as awarding of licenses and bids.[35] Any bidder must submit a Nigerian Content Plan, and can only operate after the Plan has been approved as evidenced by the issuance of a Certificate of Authorization. Under the Plan, "first consideration shall be given to services provided from within Nigeria and to goods manufactured in Nigeria" and "Nigerians shall be given first consideration for training and employment in the work programme for which the plan was submitted."[36] The lowest bidder is not entitled to the award of a contract; instead, preference is to a "Nigerian indigenous company" so long as its bid is no greater than 10 percent of the lowest bid.[37]

A key aspect of the NOGICD Act is the establishment of the Nigerian Content Development and Monitoring Board, which is responsible for implementing the Act, including reviewing Nigerian Content Plans and issuing Certificates of Authorization when appropriate.[38] The Act does not specify a detailed standard for the awarding of a contract; instead, the Board need only be "satisfied" that the Nigerian Content Plan complies with the Act.[39]

Further, the Board is responsible for implementing regulations of the Minister of Petroleum Resources,[40] who can also issue directives relating to the work of the Board.[41] The Board's Governing Council includes a number of government officials, including from the Ministry of Petroleum Resources. The Board is expressly authorized to "accept gifts of money, land or other property on such terms and conditions, if any, as may be specified by the person or organization making the gift" so long as the conditions are not "inconsistent with the functions of the Board."[42] These governance provisions have raised concerns about the potential for bias and corruption within the Board.[43] As Nwapi has observed:

---

[33] Ibid., s. 3. First consideration is given "in the award of oil blocks, oil field licenses, oil lifting licences and in all projects for which contract is to be awarded in the Nigerian oil and gas industry." Ibid.

[34] Ibid., s. 3(2).

[35] Ibid., s. 3(3).

[36] Ibid., s. 10(a), (b).

[37] Ibid., s. 16.

[38] Ibid., s. 8.

[39] Ibid. For a critique of this aspect of the NOGICD Act, see Nwaokoro, note 28, pp. 140–142.

[40] NOGICD Act, note 25, s. 70(b).

[41] Ibid., s. 100.

[42] Ibid., s. 92(1), (2).

[43] Nwaokoro, note 28, pp. 141–43. See also C. Nwapi, "Corruption Vulnerabilities in Local Content Policies in the Extractive Sector: An Examination of the Nigerian Oil and Gas Industry Content Development Act, 2010" (2015) 46 *Resources Policy* 92.

Local Content Requirements in Extractive Industries 69

Allowing the Nigerian Content Board charged with overseeing the implementation of the local content policy and supervising companies' compliance with the requirements of the policy to accept gifts from the very companies it is charged to supervise creates a potential conflict of interest within the Board.[44]

Another critical aspect of the NOGICD Act concerns technology transfer. Under the Act, operators are to "give full and effective support to technology transfer" to the Board's satisfaction.[45] Each operator is required to submit an annual report to the Board "describing its technology transfer initiatives and their results," which will enable the Minister to "make regulations setting targets on the number and type of such joint venture or alliances to be achieved for each project."[46] It is far from clear what effect the technology transfer requirement has on the intellectual property of the foreign investor in oil and gas. For example, could Nigeria require the complete transfer of intellectual property without royalties or other forms of compensation to the investor? Such action could have severe consequences for a foreign operator, particularly as to its right to property, including intellectual property.

2.2.2 Ghana: LI 2204

A second example of an LCR is Ghana's Petroleum (Local Content and Local Participation in Petroleum Activities) Regulations of 2013, known as LI 2204.[47] Designed to maximize "value-addition and job creation" as well as "develop local capacities" in the petroleum industry, LI 2204 gives first preference to an "indigenous Ghanaian company" in the awarding of contracts and licenses in the petroleum business.[48] Any entity "carrying out a petroleum activity" is required to "ensure that local content is a component of the petroleum activities" in which it is engaged.[49] An indigenous Ghanaian company is to have at least a 5 percent equity in a petroleum agreement or license.[50] Yet, the Minister Responsible for Energy is free to adjust the 5 percent threshold "where an indigenous Ghanaian company" cannot meet it.[51] The determination of the 5 percent equity also rests with the Minister.[52] Further, a non-Ghanaian entity that provides goods and services to another entity is required to do so by way of a joint venture with an indigenous Ghanaian company and provide the latter with an equity interest of at least 10 percent.[53]

---

[44] Nwapi, note 43, p. 93.
[45] NOGICD Act, note 25, s. 45.
[46] Ibid., s. 46.
[47] LI 2204, note 26.
[48] Ibid., ss. 1, 4(1).
[49] Ibid., s. 3.
[50] Ibid., s. 4(2).
[51] Ibid., s. 4(3).
[52] Ibid., s. 4(4).
[53] Ibid., s. 4(6).

70 *Susan L. Karamanian*

Like the Nigerian law, Ghana requires submission of a local content plan to the appropriate authority, in this case the Petroleum Commission.[54] The Local Content Committee, which the Commission establishes, reviews the plan to determine compliance with LI 2204, and, if it is compatible, the Committee sends it to the Commission with a recommendation for approval.[55] LI 2204 has a schedule of the required level of local content.[56] The awarding of a bid does not go to the lowest bidder; instead, like the NOGICD Act, a Ghanaian bidder within 10 percent of the lowest bid will be awarded the contract.[57]

Further, as in the NOGICD Act, the foreign entity awarded a contract is required to support training for Ghanaian employees.[58] It is also required to submit a Technology Transfer Sub-Plan to promote "the effective transfer of technology" from the contractor or a related entity "to a Ghanaian entity or citizen."[59]

3 HUMAN RIGHTS QUESTIONS IN IMPLEMENTING LCRS IN NIGERIA AND GHANA

Whether Nigeria's NOGICD Act or Ghana's LI 2204 has resulted in the use of indigenous resources as contemplated in each law, with the anticipated changes in each economy, is beyond the scope of this Chapter. What is relevant for the analysis is the extent to which new problems, mainly those affecting human rights, have surfaced due to the mere fact of the LCRs.

Both legal regimes protect and empower certain local entities, namely those with the statutory minimum level of indigenous resources. These local entities are positioned to capture substantial business from the foreign investor as they are essential to the latter's ability to enter the Nigerian or Ghanaian oil and gas markets. As a result, LCRs have arguably emboldened these entities merely due to their status, effectively making them immune from normal economic forces.

For example, in Nigeria, small and medium enterprises (SMEs) provide products and services to larger Nigerian companies, which, in turn, have substantial contracts with foreign investors. The contracts have arisen largely due to the NOGICD Act. In recent years, SMEs have reported that the Nigerian companies are months behind in payments to them, resulting in the demise of many Nigerian SMEs.[60] Hence, the very system that was designed to protect and promote Nigerian resources is undermining less powerful and smaller Nigerian enterprises. As many of the latter are self-owned,

---

[54] Ibid., s. 7(1).
[55] Ibid., s. 8(2).
[56] Ibid., First Schedule.
[57] Ibid., s. 12(3).
[58] Ibid., s. 17.
[59] Ibid., s. 24.
[60] M. Eboh, "Local Content, Local Troubles: How Big Firms Kill Small Businesses," December 24, 2018, https://oglinks.news/nigeria/news/local-content-local-troubles-how-big-firms-kill-small-businesses.

Local Content Requirements in Extractive Industries 71

individual livelihoods in Nigeria are insecure.[61] The significance of the damage to SMEs must not be understated. A recent study shows that corruption in Nigeria has a substantial effect on SMEs.[62]

A second development is the emergence of indigenous shell entities, designed solely to secure contracts with foreign investors without providing substantial benefits to the indigenous community. This phenomenon, known as "fronting," has surfaced in Ghana in the aftermath of LI 2204. As Ghana's Minister of Energy remarked, due to the common practice of fronting, Ghanaians are not engaging in the oil and gas industry.[63] In Nigeria, LCRs have been "misused" with supply contracts "awarded to shell companies, inflating costs and increasing the project cycle."[64] In short, LCRs are fueling the masking of identity in an effort to obtain wealth. They are defying the fundamental human rights principle of equality, rewarding corruption, and reallocating valuable resources based on fraud.

A third aspect affecting the human dimension of LCRs concerns labor and education. A study regarding LI 2204 has shown that indigenous Ghanaians are simply unaware of local content requirements in Ghana's upstream oil and gas industry.[65] This situation is not attributable to the mere fact of the LCR, yet it reflects LI 2204's largely economic, as opposed to human, focus.

The fourth aspect concerns corruption. As noted, the NOGICD Act expressly authorizes payments to the very entity that approves the Nigerian Content Plan.[66] A regulation that ties ownership of the supplier to nationality, subject to the approval of a State body that can accept gifts, is ripe for abuse.

4 HUMAN RIGHTS: LEGAL FRAMEWORK

When a State opens access of its natural resources to non-State entities, it engages in more than an economic or political exercise. The State's decision could affect each individual or entity in and outside the State. For example, if the State does not consider the environmental consequences of its decision, lives may be lost or impaired. As

---

[61] Ibid. (describing the financial destitution because local Nigerian companies are protected under LCRs).

[62] M. Page and C. Okeke, "Stolen Dreams: How Corruption Negates Government Assistance to Nigeria's Small Businesses," Carnegie Endowment for International Peace, Working Paper, March 2019.

[63] "Stop Fronting for Foreign Companies-Amewu Tells Local Firms," September 10, 2018, www .ghanaweb.com/GhanaHomePage/NewsArchive/Stop-fronting-for-foreign-companies-Amewu-tells-local-firms-683602#.

[64] M. Martini, "Local content policies and corruption in the oil and industry," Transparency International, September 12, 2014, p. 6.

[65] Global Energy Insight, "Ghana's Human Resource Prevailing Local Content in the Upstream Petroleum Sector: Meeting the Requirements of the Petroleum (Local Content & Local Participatory) Regulation, L.I. 2204," http://geinsight.com/en/categories/the-industry/452-ghana-s-human-resource-prevailing-local-content-in-the-upstream-petroleum-sector-meeting-the-require ments-of-the-petroleum-local-content-local-participatory-regulation-l-i-2204.

[66] Nwapi, note 43.

Susan L. Karamanian

another example, if the State's framework for access to natural resources deprives individuals of their jobs, it could be depriving citizens of their right to work.

Most States seek to control access to natural resources on their own terms, consistent with their exercise of sovereign power. Yet, these very States likely have obligations under a series of treaties, namely in the human rights field, that cannot, or at least, should not, be ignored. They may also have these rights reflected in their respective Constitutions.

For example, Nigeria and Ghana are parties to core United Nations human rights treaties, including the International Covenant on Civil and Political Rights (ICCPR)[67] and the International Covenant on Economic, Social and Cultural Rights (ICESCR).[68] Furthermore, Nigeria and Ghana are parties to the African Charter on Human and Peoples' Rights.[69]

Equality is a foundational principle of these treaties. The rights under the ICCPR are to be respected and ensured as to "all individuals within" and subject to the jurisdiction of the territory of the States, "without distinction of any kind," including as to "national or social origin."[70] State parties to the ICCPR are obligated "to ensure the equal right of men and women to the enjoyment of all civil and political rights" in the treaty.[71] One of those rights is equality itself: "All persons are equal before the law and are entitled without any discrimination to the equal protection of the law."[72] The ICCPR prohibits discrimination based on national origin.[73]

The ICESCR has a similar equality provision, requiring that State Parties provide equal treatment in ensuring treaty rights.[74] It does recognize, however that developing countries "may determine to what extent they would guarantee the economic rights" in the Covenant to non-nationals.[75]

Equality is also a bedrock of the African Charter, with every individual being "equal before the law" and being "entitled to equal protection of the law."[76] Further,

---

[67] ICCPR, note 7. Nigeria acceded to the ICCPR in 1993 and Ghana acceded to it in 2000. See UN Human Rights, Office of the High Commissioner, "Status of Ratification Interactive Dashboard," http://indicators.ohchr.org/</u> [UN Dashboard].

[68] ICESCR, note 8. Nigeria acceded to the ICESCR in 1993 and Ghana acceded to it in 2000. UN Dashboard, note 67.

[69] African Charter on Human and Peoples' Rights (Banjul Charter), 27 June 1981, OAU Doc. CAB/LEG 6713/Rev.5, 21 ILM 58 (1982) [African Charter]. Nigeria ratified the African Charter on June 22, 1983. See F. Viljoen, "Application of the African Charter on Human and Peoples' Rights by Domestic Courts in Africa" (1999) 43 *Journal of African Law* 1 at 8. In 1990, Nigeria enacted the African Charter on Human and Peoples' Rights (Ratification and Enforcement) Act. Ibid. Ghana ratified the African Charter in 1989. Ratification Table: African Charter on Human and Peoples' Rights, www.achpr.org /ratificationtable?id=49.

[70] ICCPR, note 7, art. 2(1).

[71] Ibid., art 3.

[72] Ibid., art 26.

[73] Ibid.

[74] ICESCR, note 8, art. 3.

[75] Ibid., art. 2(3).

[76] African Charter, note 69, art. 3.

Local Content Requirements in Extractive Industries 73

the African Charter expressly guarantees "the right to property" and does not limit such right to citizens of Africa States.[77] It recognizes, however, limits to the right: "[i]t may only be encroached upon in the interest of public need or in the general interest of the community and in accordance with the provisions of appropriate laws."[78]

Both Nigeria and Ghana have sophisticated legal systems that work within a constitutional framework, which rely on the principle of equality. The Constitution of Nigeria prohibits discrimination in many forms, including as to place of origin.[79] Equality of rights, however, applies only to citizens.[80]

Chapter Five of the Constitution of Ghana, titled "Fundamental Human Rights and Freedoms," applies to [e]very person in Ghana."[81] It recognizes that "[a]ll persons shall be equal before the law"[82] and prohibits discrimination based on a variety of factors, including ethnic origin.[83] The Constitution expressly recognizes that "'discriminate' means to give different treatment to different persons attributable only or mainly to their respective descriptions by race, place of origin."[84]

Further, the Constitution of Ghana imposes affirmative obligations on the State to "take all necessary action" to maximize economic development "and to secure the maximum welfare, freedom and happiness of every person in Ghana."[85] The State is obligated to guarantee "a fair and realistic remuneration for production and productivity" so to encourage continued and higher growth.[86]

As to Nigeria, the significance of human rights within the context of foreign investment has a novel twist. In 2016, Nigeria entered into a bilateral investment treaty (BIT) with Morocco.[87] Although the BIT applies to an investor from Morocco that invests in Nigeria, its legal standards shed important insights into Nigeria's understanding of the significance of international human rights as to foreign investors and their investments.

The BIT focuses on ensuring that foreign investment conforms to human rights. The BIT's Preamble recognizes investment's role in promoting sustainable development, including "furtherance of human rights and human development" and the importance of a State's ability to regulate investments so as to maintain the appropriate balance of "rights and obligations among the State Parties, the investors, and

---

[77] Ibid., art. 14.
[78] Ibid.
[79] Constitution of the Federal Republic of Nigeria 1999, Act No. 24, 5 May 1999, art. 15(2).
[80] Ibid., art. 17(2).
[81] Constitution of the Republic of Ghana, 7 January 1993, art. 12(2).
[82] Ibid., art. 17(1).
[83] Ibid., art. 17(2).
[84] Ibid., art. 17(3).
[85] Ibid., art. 36(1).
[86] Ibid., art. 36(2)(a).
[87] Reciprocal Investment Promotion and Protection Agreement between the Government of the Kingdom of Morocco and the Government of the Federal Republic of Nigeria, 3 December 2016 [Morocco-Nigeria BIT].

74   *Susan L. Karamanian*

the investments."[88] Given these objectives, is the NOGICD Act such an exercise of Nigeria's regulatory authority?

The BIT obligates Nigeria to "high levels of labour and human rights protection appropriate to its economic and social situation" while striving to improve.[89] Nigeria's "laws, policies and actions" are to conform to international human rights treaties to which it is a party.[90] Surely, in light of this provision, every law of Nigeria, including the NOGICD Act, should conform to Nigeria's international human rights obligations.

A unique feature of the Morocco-Nigeria BIT is the imposition of duties on investors, both pre- and post-establishment.[91] Pre-establishment they are to "comply with [applicable] environmental assessment screening and assessment processes," whether as per the host State or the home State, whichever is "more rigorous."[92] This provision does more than impose a duty; it ensures that the law of the investor's home State follows the investor abroad.[93] Also, pre-establishment, investors and investments that engage in corruption are to have violated the domestic law of the host State.[94] Post-establishment, investors are to "maintain an environmental management system."[95] Further, "[i]nvestors and investments shall uphold human rights in the host state" and adhere to ILO labour standards. In their operations, investors and investments "shall not ... circumvent[] international environmental, labour and human rights obligations" to which Nigeria is a party.[96]

Finally, under Article 24 of the Morocco-Nigeria BIT, titled Corporate Social Responsibility, investors and their investments "should strive to make the maximum feasible contributions to the sustainable development of the Host State and local community through high levels of socially responsible practices."[97] Shaping the CSR concepts are the priorities of the host State and the UN Sustainable Development Goals.[98] Further, investors "should apply" the ILO Tripartite Declaration on Multinational Investments and Social Policy and other appropriate standards for responsible conduct.[99]

---

[88]   Ibid., Preamble.

[89]   Ibid., art. 15(5).

[90]   Ibid., art. 15(6).

[91]   This approach is also reflected in Supplementary Act A/SA.3/12/08 Adopting Community Rules on Investment and the Modalities for their Implementation with Economic Community of West African States (ECOWAS), December 19, 2008.

[92]   Morocco-Nigeria BIT, note 87, art. 14(1). The environmental impact assessment is to apply the precautionary principle, art. 14(3).

[93]   See R. McCorquodale and P. Simons, "Responsibility beyond Borders: State Responsibility for Extraterritorial Violations by Corporations of International Human Rights Law" (2007) 70 *Modern Law Review* 598.

[94]   Morocco-Nigeria BIT, note 87, art. 17(2),(4).

[95]   Ibid., art. 18(1).

[96]   Ibid., art. 18(2)–(4).

[97]   Ibid., art. 24(1).

[98]   Ibid.

[99]   Ibid., art. 24(2).

Local Content Requirements in Extractive Industries 75

Notably, none of the obligations in the Morocco-Nigeria BIT refers to the NOGICD Act, nor does the NOGICD Act refer to Nigeria's obligations under investment treaties. Yet, with the Morocco-Nigeria BIT, Nigeria has embraced the concept that foreign investors have human rights duties. Why are those duties not acknowledged in the NOGICD Act or applied to any business enterprise, whether foreign or indigenous, that operates in the oil and gas industry?

5 LCRS AND HUMAN RIGHTS: MINDING THE GAPS

The phrase "human rights" does not appear in the NOGICD Act or Ghana's LI 2204. The human rights implications of these LCRs, however, are multifold. The most relevant perspective is their effect on the rights of individuals within the State that enacted the LCR. LI 2204 has a lengthy Section 1, which sets out its purpose and signals some of the human rights implications of the act. The closest reference to human rights is indirect, as the LCR seeks to promote maximum job creation, develop local capacity through education, achieve a minimum level of employment, and enable Ghanaians to "achieve and maintain a degree of control ... over development initiatives for local stakeholders."[100] In addition, Section 1 addresses the need for transparency in the LCR process.[101]

An LCR scheme enables foreign investors' access to a State's resources and thus affords the State the opportunity to impose obligations on investors. Accordingly, like the Morocco-Nigeria BIT, a State could identify specific human rights and related laws with which it would expect foreign investors to comply. Second, the LCR could build into it the obligation of the State to protect, promote, and fulfill human rights.

Further, LCRs also affect the rights of those outside of this State, principally foreign investors. The latter statement may appear odd as foreign investors are typically international oil companies and thus far removed from the "human." Yet certain human rights treaties recognize the right to property; also, the right to be free from non-discriminatory treatment based on national origin is recognized under international human rights law.

In particular, LCRs could implicate the foreign investors' right to property, particularly when imposed after an investor has entered the local market. Does this fact give rise to a human rights violation? Of note, the Universal Declaration of Human Rights recognizes the right of everyone "to own property alone as well as in association with others" and prohibits arbitrary deprivation of property.[102] The ICCPR and the ICESCR, however, do not recognize the right to property. As

---

[100] LI 2204, note 26, s. 1 (b), (c), and (f).
[101] Ibid., s. 1(g) (recognizing the need "for a robust and transparent monitoring and reporting system to ensure delivery of local content policy objectives").
[102] UN General Assembly, *Universal Declaration of Human Rights*, 10 December 1948, UN Doc. GA/RES/217A(iii), art. 17 [UDHR].

76 Susan L. Karamanian

noted, the African Charter, however, expressly recognizes the right to property and does not limit that right to the individual.[103] Further, Article 1 of Protocol 1 to the European Convention on Human Rights recognizes that "[e]very natural or legal person is entitled to the peaceful enjoyment of his possession."[104] Accordingly, in the European human rights systems, corporations have asserted claims against European States based on deprivation of the right to property.[105]

6 INTEGRATING HUMAN RIGHTS INTO LCRS

6.1 Rationale

Given the human rights implications, it is only appropriate that States revise their LCRs to give effect to their obligations under international human rights law. In particular, States have a duty to respect, protect, and fulfill human rights.[106] At a minimum, the State should examine every law based on its impact on human rights, and this is particularly true as to a law that governs foreign investment.[107]

An approach that recognizes the human rights dimensions of State restrictions on access to markets is essential for three reasons. First, embedding human rights into LCRs would better enable States to fulfill the LCRs' overall objective of improving the condition of the local population. The assumption that mere reallocation of economic resources leads to the betterment of humankind is incorrect. The additional assumption that such reallocation could not harm humankind is also in error.

Second, a focus on human rights, along with local content, would minimize the possibility that the LCR itself and its implementation would violate fundamental human rights. The LCR is an opportunity to harmonize foreign investment and human rights, or at least to minimize the apparent conflict between them. In so doing, a State would enable the integration of human development with economic growth.

Third, such an approach would be in line with the human rights obligations of States, whether reflected in treaties or national laws, including Constitutions. In short, human rights are legal constraints against the State to which exceptions are limited.

---

[103] African Charter, note 69, art. 14.

[104] UN, *Protocol [No 1] to the European Convention for the Protection of Human Rights and Fundamental Freedoms*, 20 March 1952, 213 UNTS 262, art 10. As in African Charter, note 69, art. 14, the right to property is not absolute.

[105] M. Emberland, *The Human Rights of Companies: Exploring the Structure of ECHR Protection* (Oxford University Press, 2006).

[106] F. Mégret, "Nature of Obligations" in D. Moeckli, S. Shah, and S. Sivakumaran (eds.), *International Human Rights Law* (Oxford University Press, 2018), pp. 86, 97–99.

[107] See note 90 (in the Morocco-Nigeria BIT, Nigeria is obligated to take such an undertaking to respect, protect, and fulfill human rights).

Local Content Requirements in Extractive Industries   77

6.2 Guiding Principles of a Human Rights–Based Approach to LCRs

In tackling LCRs from a human rights angle, the State must first adhere to its fundamental obligation to respect human rights. Accordingly, any LCR should state that one of its purposes is to enable development of local content, described using a human rights angle, consistently with the State's obligations to respect human rights. The LCR should also acknowledge at the outset the relevant human rights norms implicated in the overall regulatory scheme. The challenge in identifying the human rights norms is that LCRs are inherently discriminatory and they discriminate based on national origin. Yet the LCR could acknowledge the State's purpose in engaging in such discrimination and mention that it is being done to minimize any harmful effects with appropriate safeguards to protect human rights. Other human rights norms, or related ones that the LCR should identify, include applicable labor rights, right to remuneration for work, and right to education. The LCR should also emphasize the goals of promoting transparency and sustainability.

Under the United Nations Guiding Principles on Business and Human Rights,[108] the State is required to take measures to "protect against human rights abuse" by business enterprises.[109] This statement is a recognition that "under the international human rights regime" States are obligated "to protect against human rights abuses by third parties within their jurisdiction."[110] Accordingly, the LCR should also acknowledge that its purpose is to ensure that business enterprises operating in the oil and gas industry, whether foreign or indigenous, respect human rights. If the State does not do this, and enables third parties, such as business enterprises, to engage in human rights abuses, such a State could be in violation of Principle 1 of the Guiding Principles. Actually, it could be worse than a mere violation of Principle 1, to the extent that the LCR is the root cause of human rights violations.

Further, under the Guiding Principles, business enterprises "should respect human rights."[111] According to this additional foundational principle of the Guiding Principles, business enterprises "should avoid infringing on the human rights of others and should address adverse human rights impacts with which they are involved."[112] The obligation to respect means that business enterprises are to have "policies and processes" that reflect a "commitment to meet their responsibility to

---

[108] UNOHCHR, *Report of the Special Representative of the Secretary General on the issue of human rights and transnational corporations and other business enterprises, John Ruggie: Guiding Principles on Business and Human Rights: Implementing the United Nations 'Protect, Respect and Remedy' Framework*, 21 March 2011, UN Doc. A/HRC/17/31 [Guiding Principles]. See also UN News, "UN Human Rights Council endorses principles to ensure businesses respect human rights," June 19, 2011, https://news.un.org/en/story/2011/06/378662.

[109] Ibid., Principle 1.

[110] J. G. Ruggie, "The Social Construction of the UN Guiding Principles on Business and Human Rights Corporate Responsibility Initiative," Working Paper No. 67, p. 12.

[111] Guiding Principles, note 108, Principle 11.

[112] Ibid.

respect human rights" and a "human rights due diligence process to identify, prevent, mitigate and account for how they address their impacts on human rights."[113] Senior management must approve a statement of policy reflecting the commitment to human rights, which must be based on appropriate expertise, be applicable to a wide constituency that is affiliated with the business entity, be publicly available, and be fully operational.[114] In addition, business enterprises are to conduct "human rights due diligence," which should entail "assessing actual and potential human rights impacts, integrating and acting upon the findings, tracking responses, and communicating how impacts are addressed."[115]

6.3 A Proposed Model

The LCR must do more than simply express the goal of having human rights protected by the State or respected by enterprises when the State promotes local content in oil and gas sectors. It should specify ways to achieve the goal. Four core elements should be included:

(1) recognition of the State's duty to protect human rights and its obligation to protect against human rights abuses by third parties, namely, business entities;
(2) establishment of an LCR-Human Rights Compliance Body;
(3) enactment of measures to ensure that business enterprises and other third parties fulfill their obligation to respect human rights; and
(4) commitment to transparency and anti-corruption throughout the entirety of the process.

6.3.1 Human Rights Recognition

The LCR should state that its purpose is to promote the LCR objectives while fulfilling the State's well-established human rights obligations.[116] As to the substantive obligations of the LCR, the State should recognize that it has a duty to protect human rights. These rights include, but are not limited to, those in the Universal Declaration on Human Rights,[117] the International Covenant on Civil and Political Rights,[118] the International Covenant Economic and Social Rights,[119] and the other

[113] Ibid., Principle 15.
[114] Ibid., Principle 16.
[115] Ibid., Principle 17.
[116] A purpose clause could elucidate the human rights aspects of the LCR. See C. Llewellyn, "Remarks on the Theory of Appellate Decision and the Rules or Canons about How Statutes are to be Construed" (1950) 3 *Vanderbilt Law Review* 395 at 400 (stating that "[i]f a statute is to make sense, it must be read in the light of some assumed purpose. A statute merely declaring a rule, with no purpose or objective, is nonsense").
[117] UDHR, note 102.
[118] ICCPR, note 7.
[119] ICESCR, note 8.

Local Content Requirements in Extractive Industries   79

treaties to which the State is a party. The State should set out the specific treaties and other governing law establishing its human rights obligations.[120] The State should also expressly acknowledge that, in implementing its LCR, it will ensure that business enterprises do not engage in human rights abuses. In short, the State recognizes that it is obliged to protect against human rights abuses by business enterprises, whether foreign or indigenous. Such recognition is consistent with Principle 1 of the UN Guiding Principles.[121]

6.3.2 LCR-Human Rights Compliance Body

The State should establish an LCR-Human Rights Compliance Body to determine the laws and other actions needed to ensure that business enterprises respect human rights; examine on an annual basis the human rights implications of the LCR; and propose steps to cure any shortcomings. The Body should consist of experts in the area of business and human rights and report to the law-making authority of the State. It should have two public meetings on an annual basis to gather information from all affected persons or entities. It should issue an annual report, designed for submission to the law-making authority as well as the public. Further, the Body should make a human rights assessment of a proposed license to an investor and provide the assessment to the designated local content committee or other license-issuing body. Finally, it should have the authority to refer matters to the appropriate human rights bodies, and, when appropriate, criminal authorities.

The establishment of the Body with the referenced authority is consistent with multiple aspects of the Guiding Principles. First, it fulfills Principle 1's mandate that the State take "appropriate steps to prevent [and] investigate" human rights abuse.[122] The Body would play a major role in deterring human rights abuses in the first instance, and promoting public awareness about human rights, in general. Second, the Guiding Principles require States to enable those affected by human rights abuses to have access to an effective remedy.[123] Principle 27 acknowledges that "non-judicial grievance mechanisms," such as national human rights institutions, complement judicial mechanisms.[124]

6.3.3 Human Rights Duties of Business Enterprises

All business enterprises, whether foreign or indigenous, are to respect human rights while conducting their business in the territory or jurisdiction of the State. Under

---

[120] See, for example, Republic of France, "National Action Plan for the Implementation of the United Nations Guiding Principles on Business and Human Rights," pp. 12–14 (identifying the UN website that lists human rights treaties to which France is a party; also identifying other relevant treaties).
[121] Guiding Principles, note 108.
[122] Ibid., Principle 1.
[123] Ibid., Principle 25.
[124] Ibid., Principle 27.

80 — Susan L. Karamanian

the UN Guiding Principles, they are to respect "the International Bill of Human Rights, and the principles concerning fundamental rights set out in the International Labour Organization's Declaration on Fundamental Principles and Rights at Work."[125] Specifically, they are to avoid "causing or contributing to adverse human rights impacts" and are to "prevent or mitigate adverse human rights impacts that are directly linked to their operations, products or services."[126]

This innovative aspect of the Guiding Principles requires the engagement of the State and business enterprises. As for the State, in addition to acknowledging the obligations of business enterprises, it must enact laws to enable the full investigation, punishment, and redress of human rights violations.[127] The laws should apply to any business enterprise, whether foreign or indigenous. This approach is consistent with Guiding Principle 26, under which States "should take appropriate steps to ensure the effectiveness of domestic judicial mechanisms."[128]

Second, any business enterprise, whether foreign or indigenous, should have in place a human rights policy and process, indicating its commitment to respect human rights, a due diligence process, and a remediation process.[129] The policy should be approved by senior management, reflect relevant expertise, confirm its application throughout the business enterprise, be publicly available, and be reflected in operations.[130] Submission of the policy, and a record of compliance with it, should be a condition to any entity benefiting from an LCR, whether a foreign licensee or a local vendor.

Any business enterprise, whether foreign or indigenous, should annually conduct a human rights due diligence exercise and issue a report covering the items in Principle 17 of the UN Guiding Principles.[131] It should also integrate findings into its practices consistently with Principles 18-21 of the UN Guiding Principles.[132] In this regard, focus should be on human rights risks and adverse human rights impacts, including tracking effectiveness of responses to them.

6.3.4 Transparency and Anti-corruption

Public awareness of government activity is critical to the realization of human rights. As the Constitutional Court of South Africa has noted, "[a]ccess to information is fundamental to the realization of the rights guaranteed in the Bill of Rights" such as

---

[125] Ibid., Principle 12. The International Bill of Human Rights consists of the UDHR (note 102), the ICCPR (note 7), and the ICESCR (note 8).

[126] Ibid., Principle 13.

[127] Ibid., Principle 1 Commentary (States are to have "effective policies, legislation, regulations and adjudication" to address human rights abuses).

[128] Ibid., Principle 26.

[129] Ibid., Principle 15.

[130] Ibid., Principle 16.

[131] Ibid., Principle 17 (detailing items to be covered in the assessment).

[132] Ibid., Principles 18–21.

Local Content Requirements in Extractive Industries 81

freedom of expression.[133] Accordingly, any records of any meeting of a public entity charged with activity under the LCR, whether the body granting a license to develop oil, gas, and minerals resources or the proposed LCR-Human Rights Compliance Body, shall be public and all records of such meeting made available to the public. As noted, all business enterprises are to have a human rights policy, and make that policy and compliance reports available to the public.

In activity related to the extractive industries, in particular, corruption is rampant, leading to mismanagement of natural resources and resultant destabilization of development.[134] The NOGICD Act's tolerance of gifts to members of the Nigerian Content Development and Monitoring Board should be eliminated. Instead, an LCR should expressly prohibit any government official from accepting anything of value from someone involved in the extractive industries.

These proposed measures would establish the LCR as a means for the State to fulfill its entrenched human rights obligations. Second, they would signal to any business enterprise that foreign investment and business activity, particularly in the oil and gas sectors, should go hand-in-hand with human rights. Third, the specific proposals should not be so overwhelming as to stymie the otherwise legitimate business objectives of the LCR.

The proposal is not without downsides. For example, it adds more complexity to already long and detailed laws. Second, it opens the door to possibly more ambiguity as the human rights norms are evolving and, in many instances, subject to a wide range of interpretations. Third, it would require those working largely in the business realm to have expertise in the human rights field and vice versa. The last impediment could also be a benefit, however, as experts from the two fields would at least be engaged in a dialogue.

7 CONCLUSION

Any major economic activity of a State will necessarily lead to the engagement of the State in human rights. Why? Too much is a stake when a State decides who gets access to resources and on what terms, and the situation is magnified when the allocation is of the State's valuable natural resources. Salaries, jobs, and access to essential resources for survival could come into play. The regulatory conduct itself likely serves to restrict essential freedoms, as well. Ultimately, for those affected, human dignity could be on the line.

Further, a State's attempt to restrict markets, in particular, is likely to have a range of human rights consequences. The regulations or conduct could affect the citizens

---

[133] *Brümmer v. Minister of Social Development and Others*, Judgment of 13 August 2009, Case CCT 25/09, para. 63.

[134] A. M. Truelove, "Oil, Diamonds, and Sunlight: Fostering Human Rights through Transparency in Revenues from Natural Resources" (2003–2004) 35 *Georgetown Journal of International Law* 207 at 222.

of the State, such as impairing their access to meaningful work or an income, or those outside the State, such as foreign investors. A State that ignores human rights in their entirety, as in certain LCRs, could face a legitimacy crisis. The same holds true if LCRs, while acknowledging human rights, do not address them to enable the State to help meet its obligation to respect, protect, and fulfill human rights as per international standards.

This Chapter is the first step in what will likely be a long, contentious conversation about mainstreaming human rights norms into LCRs.[135] The issue is one that has implications beyond LCRs, as well, particularly in an era in which States are becoming even more protectionist. Thus, the lessons learned today about LCRs and human rights will have growing relevance into the future.

---

[135] See also Chapter 20 of this book, on the need for business and human rights content in LCRs.

5

Upgrade of Local Suppliers in the Global Production Network: The Success or Otherwise of Local Content Regimes

Alexander Ezenagu and Chidiebere Eze-Ajoku

1 INTRODUCTION

The aim of this chapter is to examine how the defensive use of local content requirements (LCRs) and policies in the construction of national development may lead to the upgrade of local products and services, competitiveness, and stronger relevance of local suppliers in the global production network. Drawing examples from LCRs in the USA and Nigeria, the Chapter demonstrates how LCRs must be supported by additional considerations in order to minimize the potential negative externalities of protectionism.

The increase in a nation's per capita GDP has been shown to decrease the country's poverty level over time.[1] Most government policies are directly or indirectly focused on the nation's development. However, a more direct approach than others would be the use of LCRs, which are primarily targeted at promoting the domestic economy and creating competitive value.[2] It is therefore not a new strategy for governments to strategically place local policies in a defensive position towards the protection of local businesses and skills against international competition within the nation's borders. Indeed, the need to promote and protect domestic skills and industries cannot be overstated. However, in light of free trade, which provides the option to procure resources from outside the country, how does a nation promote and protect its resources from capital flight?

---

[1] Speech by Justine Greening, UK Development Secretary (2013), "Investing in Growth: How DFID Works in New and Emerging Markets," Delivered at the London Stock Exchange on economic growth and the role of business in international development, www.gov.uk/government/speeches/investing-in-growth-how-dfid-works-in-new-and-emerging-markets. "The facts are compelling – wherever long-term per capita growth has been higher than 3 per cent, we have also seen significant falls in poverty. Look at China – in 1981, 84 per cent of China's population lived under $1.25 per day. By 2008, this proportion had fallen dramatically to 13 per cent. This was principally driven by the tenfold increase in per capita GDP over the period. Look at Vietnam – a three-fold increase in per capita GDP resulted in poverty levels falling from 64 per cent in 1993 to 17 per cent in 2008."

[2] J. Geipel and D. Hetherington, "Local Content Policy: What Works, What Doesn't Work," DFID Business Environment Reform Facility, October 2018.

84 Alexander Ezenagu and Chidiebere Eze-Ajoku

This Chapter is divided into four sections. After this introduction, Section 2 discusses the ways in which various countries have historically attempted to balance the protection of local skills and services through LCRs and free trade across national borders. Drawing examples from Nigeria, this section also examines how the implementation of LCRs can result in the upgrade of local suppliers. Section 3 provides recommendations on handling the negative externalities of LCRs. Section 4 sets out the conclusion.

2 FREE TRADE, PROTECTIONISM, AND LCRS

Free trade represents elimination of barriers to trade and investments among countries.[3] Fouda defines free trade as "a system in which the trade of goods and services between or within countries flows unhindered by government-imposed restrictions and interventions."[4] The debate on the ideal economic model – capitalism vs. socialism; free trade vs. quasi-regulation/regulated market, etc. – is as important today as it was in the Adam Smith era.[5] With examples of successful protectionist regimes in today's global economy, proponents of free trade have seen the veracity of their claims questioned.[6]

As the UK Development Secretary once remarked, "So, international trade works in creating prosperity, but what about individual countries?"[7] This statement continued the debate on how much developing countries truly benefit from international trade. It was an equidistant point between an argument for continued foreign investment in developing nations and the need for countries to encourage domestic productivity. It was her belief that a more balanced and resilient economy will not only come from trading between nations, but also from developing and unlocking potentials at home.[8]

On the other hand, protectionism, as an economic policy, restricts trade between nations through tariffs on imported or exported goods, quotas, government regulations, and anti-dumping laws. Protectionism is defined as "the practice of nations to protect domestic industries and their workers by providing subsidies for their production and imposing tariffs on competing foreign

---

[3] R. Fouda, "Protectionism and Free Trade: A Country's Glory or Doom?" (2012) 3 *International Journal of Trade, Economics and Finance*.

[4] Ibid.

[5] "Since the nineteenth century, economic liberalism has been the dominant theoretical perspective on international trade. Liberal economic theorists maintain that free markets establish prices that result in the most efficient allocation of factors of production, such as land, labour, and capital. Thus, from the time of Adam Smith (1723–1790), they have concluded that free trade is the surest path to economic prosperity and growth." B. Moon, "Dilemmas of International Trade" in G. Lopez (ed.), *Dilemmas in World Politics* (2nd ed., University of Notre Dame, 2018).

[6] F. Block and P. Evans, "The State and the Economy" in N. Smeiser and R. Swedberg (eds.), *The Handbook of Economic Sociology* (2nd ed., Princeton University Press, 2005).

[7] Greening, note 1.

[8] Ibid.

Upgrade of Local Suppliers in Production Network 85

products."[9] Protectionism is deployed to protect infant industries from adverse competition from well-established and better-suited foreign companies.[10] The "infant industry agreement" claim has been debunked by Milton Friedman as a "smoke screen," who argued that the "so-called infants never grow up."[11] Yet countries around the world use one form of protectionist regime or another to protect infant industries or start-ups.[12] Amsden claims "China, India, South Korea, and Taiwan began to invest heavily in their own proprietary national skills, which helped them sustain national ownership of business enterprises in mid-technology industries and invade high-technology sectors based on national leaders."[13] In the next section, we discuss two forms of protectionist policies: protection of local goods and protection of local skills and services.

2.1 *Protection of Local Goods*

In 2009, there was much ado about the US government's introduction of the protectionist policy commonly called "Buy America" into the American Recovery and Reinvestment Act.[14] The clause was introduced with the aim of stimulating the economy and creating more jobs for Americans by ensuring that "not one dollar" of federal funds should be spent on foreign steel.[15] The US Senate and House of Representatives recognized that the steel industry was important for the development of any economy.[16] In particular, the steel industry was more capital than labor intensive. Without a protectionist policy in place, the USA would miss out on not just job creation opportunities, but also on capital.

Protectionism was not a new concept for the Americans, as the principles of the Buy America provisions were already introduced to the legal landscape by President Hoover in 1933 through the Buy American Act.[17] However, popular arguments around this domestic preference policy were two-fold: (1) whether the provision

[9] L. Teeboom, "Free Trade vs. Protectionism," February 12, 2019, https://smallbusiness.chron.com /trade-vs-protectionism-3830.html.
[10] C. Nwapi, "A Survey of the Literature on Local Content Policies in the Oil and Gas Industry in East Africa," SPP Research Paper No. 9/16, 2016.
[11] M. Friedman and R. Friedman, "The Case for Free Trade," October 30, 2007, www.hoover.org /research/case-free-trade.
[12] Protectionist regimes increased globally after the financial crisis of 2008–2009. S. Evenett, "Africa Resists the Protectionist Temptation: The Fifth Global Trade Alert Report," May 28, 2010, http://voxeu .org/article/africa-resists-protectionist-temptation-fifth-global-trade-alert-report.
[13] A. Amsden, "Industrializing Late" in *"The Rise of 'The Rest': Challenges to the West from Late-Industrializing Economies"* (Oxford University Press, 2001).
[14] American Recovery And Reinvestment Act of 2009: Law, Explanation and Analysis: P.L. 111–5, as Signed by the President on February 17, 2009. Chicago, Ill.: CCH, 2009.
[15] G. C. Hufbauer and J. J. Schott, "Buy America: Bad for Jobs, Worse for Reputation," Peterson Institute for International Economics, Policy Brief 09–2, February 2009.
[16] Ibid.
[17] P. B. Dixon, M. T. Rimmer, and R. G. Waschik, "Evaluating the Effects of Local Content Measures in a CGE Model: Eliminating the U.S. Buy America(n) Programs" 68 *Economic Modelling*, 156–166.

86 *Alexander Ezenagu and Chidiebere Eze-Ajoku*

would really be beneficial for the US economy bearing in mind international trade agreements already in place, as well as retributive actions likely to be meted out against the USA by its international trade partners; and (2) if retributive actions are meted out, whether the negative impact of job losses and loss of business to the export-focused manufacturers in the USA was significantly commensurate to the proposed job and market creation to be introduced by this provision.[18] To avoid claims of violation of international trade agreements, which allow for participation of other signatory countries in government procurement, the federal government funds these transportation projects by way of grants or loans to the state and local governments.[19]

The US Congressional Research Service, in July 2019, released its report for members of the US Congress on the effects of the Buy America provisions on the US economy so far and it was recorded that the effects on steel manufacturing were small compared to the rise in the demand for steel and global economic growth.[20] On the basis of this, the proposed positive impact of the Buy America protectionist policy on the US economy remains debatable.[21] Notwithstanding, Buy America provisions are still in use in 2019 in laws regulating various public transportation projects like aviation, intercity passenger rail, and Amtrak. Proposals for the expansion of its applicability is also being explored by the Trump administration.[22]

Another perspective can be seen with the Nigerian Oil and Gas Industry Content Development Act of 2010 (NOGICDA).[23] This law requires that, from the commencement of the Act, "all operators, project promoters, contractors and any other entity engaged in the Nigerian oil and gas industry shall carry out all fabrication and welding activities in the country."[24]

However, unlike the US's Buy America legislation, it has been reported that six years into the inception of the Nigerian Content Act, local capacity utilization in the oil and gas sector grew by about 400 percent and was reportedly responsible for attracting about $5 billion into the economy while creating over 38,000 local jobs.[25] One can argue that this is attributable to two major factors: the policy and the implementation. The NOGICDA does not stop at limiting the use of foreign skills and infrastructure, but also provides for the training and development of local skills

---

[18] Ibid.

[19] The USA is a signatory to the World Trade Organization Agreement on Government Procurement, but individual states are excluded.

[20] Data obtained from Congressional Research Service, "Effects of Buy America on Transportation Infrastructure and US Manufacturing," July 2, 2019. "Buy America Fact Sheet," www.transit.dot.gov /buyamerica.

[21] Ibid., note 15.

[22] Ibid., note 20.

[23] Government of Nigeria (2010), Nigerian Oil and Gas Industry Content Development Act, 2010 Act No. 2 [NOGICDA].

[24] Ibid., s. 53.

[25] N. McCulloch, N. Balchin, M. Mendez-Parra, and K. Onyeka "Local Content Policies and Backward Integration in Nigeria," The Nigerian Economic Summit Group, October 2017.

in order to cater to the skills requirements of the industry. In practice also, the implementation body set up by the NOGICDA is hands-on to the best of its abilities in ensuring compliance with local content requirements and regular reporting. It also does not hold back in penalizing non-compliant companies.

2.2 Protection of Local Skills and Services

With talks of BREXIT in the United Kingdom, renewed vigor in clamping down on illegal migrants in the United States,[26] and increased agitation and violence against foreign workers in South Africa,[27] the beats seem like they come from the same drum. Countries are increasingly trying to protect local jobs and have started to point fingers at non-indigenous workers as the reason for lack of sufficient jobs in the society.

Expatriate quotas are not new in Africa and are commonly used to limit the number of jobs that foreigners can take up in a company. The inclusion of transfer of skills and technology to local companies and citizens as a condition for granting expatriate quotas and work visas to companies is one of the most popular methods of protecting the domestic work force, especially within developing countries.[28] In the Democratic Republic of Congo (DRC), for example, the number of expatriate employees working in any organization must never exceed 15 percent of the total workforce and certain positions are reserved exclusively for Congolese nationals.[29] Also, Article 31 of the Investment Code goes further to provide an obligation on investors to not only give priority to the employment of nationals over expatriates, but also to train and upgrade the skills of nationals up to managerial competences.[30]

Likewise, Nigeria also has a requirement for all companies that desire expatriates to obtain an expatriate quota from the Nigerian Immigrations Service. The Citizens and Business Department (CBD) of the Nigerian Immigration Service was set up with responsibility to review each company's application for an expatriate quota on a case-by-case basis. The CBD will also designate specific positions that can be occupied by an expatriate on certain conditions, including the condition that Nigerians be employed to understudy the foreign experts for the purpose of training,

---

[26] K. Clausing, "The Progressive Case against Protectionism: How Trade and Immigration Help American Workers," November/December 2019, www.foreignaffairs.com/articles/united-states/2019–10-15/progressive-case-against-protectionism.

[27] N. Ncana and M. Cohen, "Xenophobic Attacks in South Africa Leave Migrants Living in Fear," September 4, 2019, www.bloomberg.com/news/articles/2019–09-04/xenophobic-attacks-in-south-africa-leave-migrants-living-in-fear.

[28] F. Katende-Magezi, "The Legal Regime Governing Presence of Natural Persons (Mode 4) In SADC Member States", for GFA Consulting Group GmbH in the GIZ/GFA project "*Strengthening of economic and trade policy capacities and competences in SADC Phase II – Trade in Services*" (Final Report, 2013).

[29] Similar restrictions apply in Mozambique and Botswana.

[30] Investment Code, Law no. 004/2002, 21 February 2002 (Democratic Republic of Congo).

88 *Alexander Ezenagu and Chidiebere Eze-Ajoku*

to enable the understudies to acquire relevant skills for the eventual take-over of the expatriate quota positions.[31]

Although these measures are geared towards strategically preserving local jobs and creating opportunities for citizens to develop and utilize their skills, introducing protectionist policies, like expatriate quotas, without first addressing the issue of skills and capability may be likened to placing the cart before the horse. There is no guarantee that if a nation's borders are closed to work migration or if expatriate quotas are implemented to limit this migration there will be sufficient local skilled manpower to immediately fill the need in the skills market. This is more so especially when the role requires advanced technical or specialized skills.

2.3 *The Upgrade of Local Suppliers Using Protectionist Policies*

The integration and multiplicity of effective economic models is fast becoming the norm, thereby leading to the rise of mixed-economy theory, globally.[32] The shift to "national capitalism" from the ideal "capitalism" represents the harsh reality that the influence and popularity of free-rein capitalism may be waning with the geometric rise of the mixed economy model. China presents a perfect example of the rise of a mixed economy.[33] Zhang Weiwei[34] describes China's model key features as: down-to-earth pragmatic concern with serving the people; constant trial and error experimentation; gradual reform rather than neoliberal economic shock therapy; a strong and pro-development state; and a pattern of implementing easy reforms first, difficult ones later. Core to the Chinese model is the protection of the nation state and the economy of China. It is in light of this shift in economic policies that we argue protectionist regimes are important to the upgrade of products and services of developing countries and their competitiveness in the global economy.[35]

The NOGICDA provides another illustration of how, through its protectionist regime, local suppliers are able to upgrade their products and services and compete in the global economy.[36] We will use data obtained from the Nigerian Content Development and Monitoring Board (NCDMB)[37] in line with the focus of this discourse.

---

[31]   The Nigeria Immigration Service, "Visa Types," https://portal.immigration.gov.ng/?p=about.
[32]   R. Nelson, "Capitalism as a Mixed Economic System" in D. C. Mueller (ed.), *The Oxford Handbook of Capitalism* (Oxford University Press, 2012), 277–298.
[33]   R. Nelson, "Roles of Government in a Mixed Economy" (1987) 6 *Journal of Policy Analysis and Management* 540–557.
[34]   W. Zhang, "The Allure of the Chinese Model," November 1, 2006, www.nytimes.com/2006/11/01/opinion/o1iht-edafrica.3357752.html.
[35]   A. Esteves, B. Coyne, and A. Moreno, "Local Content Initiatives: Enhancing the Subnational Benefits of the Oil, Gas and Mining Sectors," Natural Resource Governance Institute, Briefing, July 2013.
[36]   J. S. Ovadia, "The Role of Local Content Policies in Natural Resource-Based Development," Österreichische Entwicklungspolitik. Rohstoffe und Entwicklung, 2015, p. 37.
[37]   Nigerian Content Development and Monitoring Board, https://ncdmb.gov.ng/. The data is from June 2015 and includes random NCDMB progress reports.

2.4 Industrialization Boom and the Statutory Inclusion of Indigenous Companies

In the past, all manufacturing jobs in the Nigerian oil and gas sectors were carried out abroad. However, as a result of the NOGICDA, there is a visible increase in manufacturing activities taking place in the oil and gas sector within the borders of Nigeria. For instance, Total Exploration and Production Nigeria Limited, between December 2018 and January 2019, started its Egina Ultra-Deep Offshore Project using the biggest floating, production, storage, and offloading (FPSO) Total has ever built.[38] More than half of the workforce used in building the Egina FPSO were Nigerian, with manufacturing, assembling, and production of the FPSO taking place mainly in the cities of Lagos and Port-Harcourt. This project utilized a record level of local contractors in Nigeria, with over 77 percent of project hours spent within the country.[39] Likewise, in April 2016, the Nigerian Liquefied Natural Gas Company (NLNG) celebrated the arrival of a new vessel named *Abuja II*, which recorded appreciable Nigerian Content achievements in the course of its construction.[40] Also, there is an ongoing construction of an integration yard for FPSO in Nigeria, valued at $300 million, being built by Lagos Deep Water and Logistics Base (LADOL), a Nigerian company.[41] This comes fifty years after oil discovery in Nigeria and over fourteen FPSOs have been built for the Nigerian oil and gas industry in foreign yards. Upon completion of the yard, it is expected that over 100,000 Nigerians will be employed directly and indirectly.

In addition, Total Exploration and Production Nigeria Limited reported in August 2015, to have exceeded Nigerian content targets in the execution of Oil Mining Lease 58 upgrade projects, located onshore in Rivers State, Nigeria.[42] The upgrade projects were designed to improve oil recovery, boost gas supply for industrial and domestic use, and increase deliveries to the NLNG. Some of the projects carried out include the upgrade of the Ogbogu Flow Station, erection of a new field Logistics Base, construction of a new Obite Gas Treatment Centre, construction of the 42-kilometer O.U.R Pipeline from Obite to Rumuji, and the construction of the 50-kilometer, 24-inch Northern Option Pipeline (NOPL).[43] These projects witnessed Nigerian Content of over 70 percent.[44] Finally, it was reported in

---

[38] "Nigeria: Total Starts Up Production of the Giant Egina Field," January 2, 2019, www.total.com/en/media/news/press-releases/nigeria-total-starts-production-giant-egina-field.

[39] Ibid.

[40] O. Ajayi, "Nigerian Content: NLNG Celebrates Arrival of New Vessel," April 24, 2016, https://ncdmb.gov.ng/2016/04/nigerian-content-nlng-celebrates-arrival-of-new-vessel/.

[41] O. Ajayi, "Oil Industry No Longer Exporting Jobs, Spend-Kentebe," July 22, 2015, https://ncdmb.gov.ng/2015/07/oil-industry-no-longer-exporting-jobs-spend-kentebe/.

[42] O. Ajayi, "Total Completes OML 58 Projects, Records High Nigerian Content Achievements," July 22, 2015, https://ncdmb.gov.ng/2015/07/total-completes-oml-58-projects-records-high-nigerian-content-achievements/.

[43] Ibid.

[44] Ibid.

November 2016, by the Executive Secretary of the Board Mr. Simbi Wabote, that the implementation of the NOGICDA had attracted investment commitments worth $2 billion in 2016,[45] while a previous statement, credited to the former Executive Secretary of the Board Ernest Nwapa, put the sum at $5 billion from 2009 to 2015.[46] These investments have gone towards localizing fabrication and construction, manufacturing of component parts, equipment, spare parts, accessories, drilling fluid, Sub-sea production systems, line pipes, design engineering, project management, shipping and logistics, etc.; activities that, prior to the enactment of the NOGICDA, were carried out abroad.[47]

Under the NOGICDA, all operators and project promoters are required to consider Nigerian content when evaluating any bid; where bids are within 1 percent of each other at the commercial stage, the bid containing the highest level of Nigerian content shall be selected provided the Nigerian content in the selected bid is at least 5 percent higher than its closest competitor.[48] By section 16 of the NOGICDA, the award of contract shall not be solely based on the principle of the lowest bidder where an indigenous Nigerian company has capacity to execute such a job and the company shall not be disqualified exclusively on the basis that it is not the lowest financial bidder, provided the value does not exceed the lowest bid price by 10 percent.[49] In compliance with this legislation, the NLNG, in its contract bidding guidelines, included a criteria for companies to:

> give first consideration to materials, manufactured as well as assembled goods of Nigerian origin which shall include a breakdown of all materials to be utilized and identifying those that are found locally, finished products and materials that will be procured from Nigerian manufacturing and assembly plants, finished goods that order can be placed from outside Nigeria through Nigerian authorized vendors and accredited agents and those that would be directly imported.[50]

Furthermore, the NOGICDA requires all operators, contractors, and other entities in the Nigerian oil and gas industry to carry out fabrication and welding activities in-country.[51] In practice, this bidding process is closely monitored by the NCDMB which carefully scrutinizes each contract bidding process to ensure compliance.

The NOGICDA promotes indigenous asset ownership, infrastructure development, research and development, manufacturing, development of local suppliers,

---

[45] O. Ajayi, "Nigerian Content Attracts $2bn Investment in Oil and Gas Sector," September 27, 2016, https://ncdmb.gov.ng/2016/09/nigerian-content-attracts-2bn-investment-in-oil-and-gas-sector/.

[46] O. Ajayi, "Nwapa: Nigerian Content Attracted $5bn Investment in 4 years," July 18, 2015, https://ncdmb.gov.ng/2015/07/nwapa-nigerian-content-attracted-5bn-investment-in-4-years/.

[47] I. Ramdoo, "Unpacking Local Content Requirements in the Extractive Sector: What Implications for the Global Trade and Investment Frameworks?" E15Initiative, International Centre for Trade and Sustainable Development (ICTSD), World Economic Forum, September 2015.

[48] NOGICDA, note 23, s. 14.

[49] Ibid., s. 16.

[50] Nigeria NLG Limited, "General Nigerian Content Requirements," para. 5.

[51] NOGICDA, note 23, s. 53.

and training of Nigerians in the oil and gas sector. One of the ways it achieves this is by prescribing minimum Nigerian content levels with respect to various goods and services utilized by the oil and gas industry.[52] Upon commencement of the NOGICDA, all subsequent oil and gas agreements, contracts, or memoranda of understanding relating to any operation or transaction in the Nigerian oil and gas industry had to conform with the NOGICDA,[53] as set out in Schedule A.[54] The NOGICDA further requires a "Nigerian Content Plan" (the Plan) prior to the execution of any project in the Nigerian oil and gas industry.[55] The Plan is to contain information intended to ensure first consideration will be given to services provided from within Nigeria and goods manufactured in Nigeria; and Nigerians, with regard to training and employment in the work program for which the plan is submitted.[56] Operators[57] are equally required to submit to the Board,[58] annual Nigerian Content Performance Reports covering all their projects and activities for the year under review.[59] The report is to specify by category of expenditure, Nigerian content on both a current and cumulative cost basis; as well as set out employment achievements in terms of hours or days worked by Nigerian and foreign workers and their status.[60] The Report is also required to set out procurement achievements in terms of quantity, tonnage of locally manufactured materials, and foreign origin.[61] From practice, these reports require stakeholders to frequently provide comprehensive information on their local content plans. For example, some reports require information on all subcontractors and vendors supporting each project under that reporting year. This information would typically also include information on the amount of local manpower to be utilized, as well as the percentage of project funds that would be expended on local content.[62] The NCDMB also regularly invites project personnel and company executives from joint-venture partner companies (IOCs) for project clarification meetings and can go as far as halting the execution of a project where its reports show that the project falls short of local content requirements.

---

[52] Oil and gas industry means all activities connected with the exploration, development, exploitation, transportation, and sale of Nigerian oil and gas resources including upstream and downstream oil and gas operations (NOGICDA, note 23, s. 109).

[53] Ibid., s. 6.

[54] Ibid., Schedule A.

[55] Ibid., s. 7.

[56] Ibid., s. 10.

[57] The term *operator* means the Nigerian National Petroleum Corporation ("NNPC"), NNPC subsidiaries and joint venture partners, and any Nigerian and foreign international oil and gas company operating in the Nigerian oil and gas industry (Ibid., s. 109).

[58] Nigerian Content Development Monitoring Board (NCDMB) is the government body established to administer the Act and monitor its application.

[59] NOGICDA, note 23, s. 60.

[60] Ibid., s. 61.

[61] Ibid.

[62] Ibid., note 59

2.5 Capacity Building, Training, and Research and Development

The NOGICDA has copious provisions for the training of Nigerians, technology transfer, investment in research and development, and an open innovation policy.[63] Six years after the enactment of the law, some progress has been recorded in this aspect. In June 2016, Nigerian Agip Energy Limited (NAE) concluded the training of fifteen youths on manifold construction and design.[64] The training, which lasted for six months, saw ten Nigerians trained on engineering design and fabrication engineering while five trainees were trained on welding and fabrication.[65] The NCDMB is also collaborating with the Imperial College London and four leading Nigerian universities on research for the oil and gas industry.[66]

In May 2016, Esso Exploration and Production Nigeria Limited (ExxonMobil) and OneSubsea Offshore Systems Nigerian Limited marked the graduation of sixty trainees from its skill acquisition program and commissioned solar-powered boreholes, virtual laboratories and science library projects.[67] In February 2016, Chevron Nigeria Limited (CNL) celebrated the graduation of 169 Nigerians trained in process engineering and document control, among other things.[68] Oilserv Limited, in January 2016, completed the training of twenty-eight Nigerian youths in auto-welding, manual welding and fitting, and rigging activities as part of its technical training scheme,[69] thus further domiciling these activities in-country.[70]

In the open innovation drive, in August 2015, the Board sent twenty-two Nigerians to the Peoples Republic of China to acquire critical skills needed to operate and maintain machines that will be used at the pipe mill being set up at Polaku, Bayelsa State, by Mainland Pipe Mill Nigeria.[71] This training, which took place at the facilities of Baoji Petroleum Steel Pipe Company Limited in Shaanxi Province, provided opportunities for exchange of innovation ideas. Corredoira and McDermott posit that, "in these contexts of scarce resources and inferior

---

[63] For example: S. 10(b), S. 28(1), S. 29(c) and S. 30

[64] O. Ajayi, "Nigerian Agip Concludes Training for 15 Youths," June 26, 2016, https://ncdmb.gov.ng /2016/06/nigerian-agip-concludes-training-for-15-youths/.

[65] Ibid.

[66] O. Ajayi, "NCDMB, Imperial College Collaborate on Research for Oil and Gas Industry," May 24, 2016, https://ncdmb.gov.ng/2016/05/ncdmb-imperial-college-collaborate-on-research-for-oil-and-gas-industry/.

[67] O. Ajayi, "OneSubsea, Esso Train 60 Youths, Commission Projects in Anambra," May 25, 2016, https://ncdmb.gov.ng/2016/05/onesubsea-esso-train-60-youths-commission-projects-in-anambra/.

[68] O. Ajayi, "169 Youths Complete Capacity Development Programmes," February 24, 2016, https:// ncdmb.gov.ng/2016/02/169-youths-complete-capacity-development-programmes/.

[69] O. Alayi, "Oilserv Graduates 28 Technical Trainees," January 24, 2016, https://ncdmb.gov.ng/2016/01/ oilserv-graduates-28-technical-trainees/.

[70] C. Ayonmike and B. Okeke, "The Nigerian Local Content Act and Its Implication on Technical and Vocational Education and Training (TVET) and the Nation's Economy" (2015) 3 *International Journal of Education Learning and Development* 26–35.

[71] O. Ajayi, "NCDMB Begins Training of Nigerians for Steel Pipe Manufacturing Technology in China," July 22, 2015, https://ncdmb.gov.ng/2015/07/ncdmb-begins-training-of-nigerians-for-steel-pipe-manufacturing-technology-in-china/.'

technologies, upgrading depends on the ways in which organizational and institutional networks enable firms to integrate imported advanced knowledge with local applied knowledge."[72] Open innovation drive remains a core element of the local content policy of the Nigerian government.

Furthermore, in the area of research and development, in June of 2015, General Electric signed a memorandum of understanding (MoU) with the government of Cross River State to upgrade and equip the mechanic/electrical workshops of the Government Technical College, Calabar, Cross River State, Nigeria.[73] The project, estimated at $2 million, is aimed at developing a pipeline of talents that could take up employment in the oil and gas industry and offer innovative solutions to the problems plaguing the sector.

In addition, the NOGICDA requires operators to have an Employment and Training Plan (E&T Plan) which shall outline the hiring and training needs of the operator/project promoter and major contractors, with a breakdown of skills required and anticipated shortage in the Nigerian labor force; and a time frame for employment opportunities for each phase of project development and operations to enable members of the Nigerian workforce prepare themselves for such opportunities.[74] The NOGICDA further requires that where Nigerians are not employed because of their lack of training, the operators shall ensure, to the satisfaction of the NCDMB that every reasonable effort is made within a reasonable time to supply such training locally or elsewhere and such effort and the procedure for its execution shall be contained in the operator's E&T Plan.[75] Section 31 requires operators to submit a succession plan for any position not held by Nigerians and the plan shall provide for Nigerians to understudy each incumbent expatriate for a maximum period of four years and at the end of the four-year period the position shall become "Nigerianised."[76] Section 32 provides that for each of its operations, an operator or project promoter may retain a maximum of 5 percent of management positions as may be approved by the Board as expatriate positions to take care of investor interests.[77]

Section 34 requires that all projects or contracts whose total budget exceeds $100 million shall contain a "Labour Clause" mandating the use of a minimum percentage of Nigerian labor in specific cadres as may be stipulated by the Board.[78] Section 35 of the NOGICDA requires all operators and companies operating in the

---

[72] R. Corredoira and G. McDermott, "Adaptation, Bridging and Firm Upgrading: How Non-Market Institutions and MNCs Facilitate Knowledge Recombination in Emerging Markets" (2014) 45 *Journal of International Business Studies* 699–722.

[73] O. Ajayi, "GE Boosts Craftsmanship with $2m Investment in Technical School," July 18, 2015, https://ncdmb.gov.ng/2015/07/ge-boosts-craftsmanship-with-2m-investment-in-technical-school/.

[74] NOGICDA, note 23, s. 29.

[75] Ibid., s. 30.

[76] Ibid., s. 31.

[77] Ibid., s. 32.

[78] Ibid., s. 34.

Nigerian oil and gas industry to employ only Nigerians in their junior and intermediate cadre or any other corresponding grades designated by the operator or company.[79]

In the area of research and development, section 37 of the NOGICDA requires an operator to carry out a program and make expenditure to the satisfaction of the NCDMB, for the promotion of education, attachments, training, and research and development in Nigeria in relation to its work program and activities.[80] An operator is to submit to the operator's Research and Development Plan (R&D Plan) to the NCDMB and update it every six months.[81] The R&D Plan is required to outline a revolving three- to five-year plan for oil and gas related research and development initiatives to be undertaken in Nigeria, together with a breakdown of expected expenditures that will be made in implementing the R&D Plan.[82] Also, the R&D Plan is to provide for public calls for proposals for research and development initiatives associated with the operator's activities.[83] Section 39 mandates the operator to report to the NCDMB, on a quarterly basis, with respect to its R&D activities and the NCDMB shall compare these activities to the operator's R&D Plan.[84] Furthermore, each operator is required to carry out a program in accordance with the country's own plans and priorities, to the satisfaction of the NCDMB, for the promotion of technology transfer to Nigeria in relation to its oil and gas activities.[85] The operator shall annually submit to the NCDMB a plan, satisfactory to the NCDMB, setting out a program of planned initiatives aimed at promoting the effective transfer of technologies from the operator and alliance partners to Nigerian individuals and companies.[86]

In relation to the services industry, the NOGICDA requires that all operators, project promoters, alliance partners, and indigenous Nigerian companies engaged in any form of business, operations, or contracts in the Nigerian oil and gas industry are to insure all insurable risks related to their oil and gas business, operations, and contracts, with an insurance company, through an insurance broker, registered in Nigeria under the provisions of the Insurance Act, as amended.[87] Also, all operators, contractors, and other entities engaged in any operation, business, or transaction in the Nigerian oil and gas industry requiring legal services shall retain only the services of a Nigerian legal practitioner or a firm of Nigerian legal practitioners whose office is located in any part of Nigeria.[88] In the same vein, section 52 of the Act mandates all

---

[79] Ibid., s. 35.
[80] Ibid., s. 37.
[81] Ibid., s. 38.
[82] Ibid.
[83] Ibid.
[84] Ibid., s. 39.
[85] Ibid., s. 43.
[86] Ibid., s. 44.
[87] Ibid., s. 49.
[88] Ibid., s. 51.

Upgrade of Local Suppliers in Production Network   95

operators, contractors, and any other entity engaged in any operation, business, or transaction in the Nigerian oil and gas industry requiring financial services to retain only the services of Nigerian financial institutions or organizations, except where, to the satisfaction of the Board, this is impracticable.[89] The NOGICDA equally mandates operators to submit Legal Services Plans (LSP) and Financial Services Plans (FSP).[90]

2.6 Employment Opportunities, Localization of Services, and Improved Life

The Niger-Delta region, home to Nigeria's oil and gas resources, remains a volatile region. The agitations of the people range from exploitation of their resources without commensurate returns to the region, environmental pollution, and the unemployment of their people. They blamed the IOCs for not employing indigenes of the regions and ignoring local service providers for foreign service providers.[91] The consequences of these agitations have been destruction of oil and gas assets, kidnap of foreigners, occasional murder of oil and gas workers, and general unrest in the region. With the introduction of the NOGICDA, some of these issues have been and are still being addressed. In June 2015, the Board claimed to have created over 30,862 jobs since 2012.[92] These jobs were in the areas of manning rigs, fabrication yards servicing, design engineering firms, and oil and gas equipment manufacturing. As is the practice in recruitment in the oil and gas sector in Nigeria, indigenes of the oil-producing communities were favored in the recruitment process. General Electric, in June 2015, pledged to create 2,300 jobs for Nigerians through its operations in the next five years.[93] This significantly increases the number of Nigerians in the economy and leads to domiciliation of knowledge, earnings, and growth potentials of the company.

The participation of Nigerian firms in the oil and gas industry has increased, resulting in indigenous in-country capacity development, credited to the enactment of the NOGICDA.[94] The result of this is that Nigerian firms are now engaged in the exploration, production, and service segment of the oil and gas industry, thereby localizing services and increasing the standard of living of Nigerians. This equally addresses capital flight, which the NCDMB put at $380 billion between 1956, when oil was discovered, and 2006.[95] The NCDMB further claimed, in June 2015, that

[89] Ibid., s. 52.
[90] Ibid., ss. 51 and 52.
[91] U. Ihua, O. Olabowale, K. Eloji, and C. Ajayi, "Entrepreneurial Implications of Nigeria's Oil Industry Local Content Policy: Perceptions from the Niger Delta Region" (2011) 5 Journal of Enterprising Communities: People and Places in the Global Economy 223–241.
[92] O. Ajayi, "Local Content, Best Option for Job Creation – Experts," July 18, 2015, https://ncdmb.gov.ng/2015/07/local-content-best-option-for-job-creation-experts/.
[93] O. Ajayi, "Nigerian Content: GE to Create 2300 Jobs in Five Years," July 22, 2015, https://ncdmb.gov.ng/2015/07/nigerian-content-ge-to-create-2300-jobs-in-five-years/.
[94] O. Ajayi, "Local Content Gives Succour to Indigenous Players," July 18, 2015, https://ncdmb.gov.ng/2015/07/local-content-gives-succour-to-indigenous-players/.
[95] Ibid.

96 Alexander Ezenagu and Chidiebere Eze-Ajoku

with the coming into place of the NOGICDA, $107 billion procurement, $20 billion fabrication, $20 billion engineering, $14 billion technical services, and $7 billion research and development are domiciled in Nigeria.[96]

As a result of the localization of services and increased employment of Nigerians, especially indigenes of the Niger-Delta region, the Movement for the Survival of the Ijaw Ethnic Nationality in the Niger Delta (MOSIEND) pledged to continue supporting the Board in its implementation of the Nigerian Content Act.[97] Such support from indigenous organizations like MOSIEND implies peaceful coexistence between the oil companies and the host communities, guaranteeing smooth and continuous operations in the oil and gas sector, a critical factor in the country's development.

Concluding, protectionism has become important in the economic development of Nigeria, faced with the pressures of liberalization and free-market rhetoric from supranational bodies like the World Bank, IMF, and neoliberalists.[98] While not adopting fully the neo-statist view, we strongly believe in "tempered capitalism" – where government or the state acts as umpire or co-captain of the ship.[99] Sadly, African governments are too quick to cede all economic rights and gains to gifts-bearing foreigners and doom-mongering supranational bodies.[100] In an era where international trade, investment, and finance govern foreign policies, Nigeria, and indeed most African countries, still remain mere resource countries, with little or no value added to the global pool.[101]

2.7 Handling the Negative Externalities of Protectionism: Recommendations

The negative effects of LCRs are being discussed at length in one way or another on various platforms, especially given current world events, such as BREXIT and the building of walls along State borders.[102] These potential negative effects include unemployment, increase in the cost of goods and services, loss of competitiveness of protected firms, and inefficient local firms.[103] Notwithstanding, protectionism is not

---

[96] Ibid.

[97] O. Ajayi, "Ijaw Group, Journalists Pledge Support for Nigerian Content Implementation," July 22, 2015, https://ncdmb.gov.ng/2015/07/ijaw-group-journalists-pledge-support-for-nigerian-content-implementation/.

[98] R. Lawrence and P. Draper, "Trade Policy, Protectionism and the Global Economic Crisis," CDE Conversations, No. 3, 2009, p. 1.

[99] D. Stark and L. Bruszt, "Markets, States and Deliberative Actions: East Meets West" in *Post Socialist Pathways: Transforming Politics and Property in East Central Europe* (Cambridge University Press, 1998). J. Braithwaite, "Tempered Power, Variegated Capitalism, Law and Society" (2019) 67 *Buffalo Law Review* 527.

[100] F. Edoho, "Globalization and Marginalization of Africa: Contextualization of China-Africa Relations" (2011) 58 *Africa Today* 103–124.

[101] G. Gereffi, "The Global Economy: Organization, Governance, and Development" in N. J. Smelser and R. Swedberg (eds.), *The Handbook of Economic Sociology* (2nd ed., Princeton University Press, 2005), 160–182.

[102] Clausing, note 26.

[103] F. Ng and A. Yeats, "Open Economies Work Better! Did Africa's Protectionist Policies Cause Its Marginalization in World Trade?" Policy Research Working Paper 1636, The World Bank, 1996.

Upgrade of Local Suppliers in Production Network   97

always the bringer of doom as the literature suggests. In this Chapter, various examples have been given that show some of the negative impacts of the enforcement of LCRs, as well as some LCRs that are working to boost the economy. It has become even more evident that LCRs in themselves are not the enemy. Strategic planning and timely response to the negative effects of LCRs can go a long way to further ensure growth of the economy.

For example, when the Chinese government noticed a rise in imports in the beginning of the twenty-first century, they introduced stricter import license constraints as a protectionist measure in support of local producers.[104] However, a recent study reveals that "relaxing policies that prioritize domestic production in 2016, when the average price of Chinese oil imports was US$42 per barrel, could have increased China's import demand by 0.29 million barrels per day" but reduced the cost of supply by US$2.8 billion because "imported oil has more direct access to the country's pipeline network."[105] In light of the need to balance encouraging international trade with protecting local production, protectionist policies should be closely monitored to ensure that the administration and enforcement of the LCRs are not burdensome and that there is measurable impact of the policy on the local economy.

For example, the US's Buy America Act encouraged the use of local steel, but this did not guarantee the rise in demand for local steel or the creation of more jobs in the steel industry. In reality, the July 2019 report by the US Congressional Research Service revealed that "eliminating Buy America requirements would result in 57,000 fewer U.S. manufacturing jobs, including about 1,600 fewer jobs in the United States in iron and steel production" and it was estimated that "the U.S. economy overall would gain more than 300,000 jobs if Buy America were terminated."[106] One key reason for the misalignment between the policy and the end result is the insufficient availability of locally made resources to support the demand for steel within America. More time was being spent applying for waivers than actual compliance with Buy America. The delay caused by local supply inefficiencies, as well as the time spent in administering and enforcing its requirements, made Buy America very expensive to implement.[107] At this point, the government ought to have reassessed the viability of the legislature towards either halting the enforcement of the legislation or making certain changes to the administrative process to ensure ease of compliance with the legislature.

One of the flexible measures applied by states and local governments to avoid the federal requirements that were attached to federal funding under Buy America was

---

[104] B. Rioux, P. Galkin, and K. Wu, "An Economic Analysis of China's Domestic Crude Oil Supply Policies" (2019) 17 *Chinese Journal of Population Resources and Environment* 217–228.

[105] Ibid.

[106] Ibid; Congressional Research Service, note 22, p. 10.

[107] Obtaining waivers where necessary, and documenting steel origins can extend the life span of a project, thereby increasing project costs.

98   *Alexander Ezenagu and Chidiebere Eze-Ajoku*

to enact legislations that reduced the number of projects that rely on federal funds, thereby reducing the amount of transactions that would suffer the negative impacts of the Buy America legislation.[108]

3 BALANCING LCRS TO ACHIEVE SUSTAINABLE DEVELOPMENT: RECOMMENDATIONS

As discussed in Section 2 of this chapter, protectionism may lead to unintended consequences, such as jeopardizing growth prospects, industrial development, and discouraging new innovations. Piore and Sabel argue "political intervention in the economy – ranging from the formation of a cartel of oil exporters to the operation of the welfare state – has at worst, aggravated a crisis, that has other, deeper issues."[109] They conclude that while there are instances of unsuccessful state intervention, not all state intervention leads to disaster.[110] We concur that there are other factors at play in the success or otherwise of state intervention in the economy. However, in this section, we explore ways to minimize the potential negative externalities of protectionism.[111]

3.1 *Cluster Formation and Networks*

To guard against negative externalities, cluster formation and network among firms must be promoted.[112] Paolo Perez-Aleman elaborates on "how public and private actors create institutions through an interactive process that transforms their products, organizations, relationships, and connections to global markets."[113] She argues that institutions are key to knowledge creation and knowledge building, and the facilitation of same. Citing Chile's tomato-processing and farmed-salmon clusters, she reveals the state's role in providing a space for exploration of new business ideas and production and setting new expectations. She concludes by stating that, "growth and development associated with clusters will depend on building institutions that foster collective learning and firm capabilities. These institutions emerge from the interactions between private and public actors as they collectively explore

---

[108]   For example, Nebraska's Federal Funds Purchase Program, https://dot.nebraska.gov/business-center /lpa/projects/programs/ffpp/.

[109]   M. Piore and C. Sabel, *The Second Industrial Drive: Possibilities for Prosperity* (New York: Basic Books, 1984).

[110]   Ibid.

[111]   Ovadia, note 36.

[112]   A. Saxenian, "IT Enclaves in India" in *The new Argonauts: Regional Advantage in a Global Economy* (Harvard University Press, 2006); A. Saxenian "Taiwan as Silicon Sibling" in *The New Argonauts: Regional Advantage in a Global Economy* (Harvard University Press, 2006).

[113]   P. Perez-Aleman, "Cluster Formation, Institutions and Learning: The Emergence of Clusters and Development in Chile" (2005) 14 *Industrial and Corporate Change* 651–677. See also, P. Perez-Aleman, "Collective Learning in Global Diffusion: Spreading Quality Standards in a Developing Country Cluster" (2011) 22 *Organization Science* 173–189.

Upgrade of Local Suppliers in Production Network 99

possibilities, identify and strategize to solve them."[114] We agree, and argue further that the need for public–private partnership in building institutions that foster collective learning and firm capabilities cannot be overemphasized; cluster formation offers economies of scale, avenues for collective bargaining, and stronger influence on policy formation. It is our advice that local firms in the oil and gas sector form clusters and engage in the exchange of information, promoting cooperation while being competitive.

Baldwin, Scott, and Hood divide regulation into three concepts: (1) regulation as authoritative rules; (2) regulation as efforts of state agencies to steer the economy; and (3) regulation as mechanisms of social control.[115] The NOGICDA addresses the efforts of state agencies to steer the economy and as a mechanism of social control.[116] Prior to the NOGICDA, as in most African countries, the Nigerian economy was susceptible to extreme foreign domination, represented by multinational corporations.[117] Thus, it was important to wean the country's economy off the hold of foreign actors and create an economy that provided greater opportunities for Nigerian people.[118] Achieving this is no easy task. How do firms upgrade products? How can firms maximize exploitation for all in a society seemingly trapped in a history of dysfunctional institutions and social capital? Peter Evans argues, "without an organized business community, even an organized state cannot promote structural change."[119] Achieving structural change in the implementation of LCRs in Nigeria calls for a healthy relationship between state actors and investors, both local and foreign. This, the NCDMB also tried to achieve by introducing the research and development council who will be in charge of establishing "research clusters covering engineering studies, geological and physical studies, local material substitution and technology."[120] However, to date, clusters are yet to be declared or formed.

Integral to guarding against negative externalities from protectionist regimes is the centrality of networks to the discourse. Networks provide three broad categories of benefits: access, timeliness, and referrals.[121] Cooperation among indigenous firms

[114] Ibid.
[115] R. Baldwin, C. Scott, and C. Hood, "Introduction" in R. Bardwin, C. Scott, and C. Hood (eds.), *A Reader on Regulation* (Oxford University Press, 1998), 1–55.
[116] B. Schneider and S. Maxfield, "Business, the State, and Economic Performance in Developing Countries" in S. Maxfield and B. R. Schneider (eds.), *Business and the State in Developing Countries* (Cornell University Press, 1997).
[117] G. Helleiner, "Marginalization and/or Participation: Africa in Today's Global Economy" (2002) 36 *Canadian Journal of African Studies/Revue Canadienne Des Etudes Africaines* 531–550.
[118] A. Subramanian and N. Tamirisa, "Is Africa Integrated in the Global Economy" (2003) 50 *IMF Staff Papers.*
[119] P. Evans, "State Structures, Government-Business Relations, and Economic Transformation" in S. Maxfield and B. R. Schneider (eds.), *Business and the State in Developing Countries* (Cornell University Press, 1997).
[120] O. Ajayi, "Oil Industry to Get Research & Development Council-NCDMB," September 27, 2017, https://ncdmb.gov.ng/2017/09/oil-industry-to-get-research-development-council-ncdmb/.
[121] R. Burt, *Structural Holes* (Harvard University Press, 1992).

100   *Alexander Ezenagu and Chidiebere Eze-Ajoku*

promotes healthy competition; promotes innovations and development, especially in open societies; and guarantees public information flows.[122] Indigenous firms can jointly set up research and development consortia, which will drive growth for all.[123] However, these networks must not be closed to new membership to prevent static innovation but must allow for dynamism. More training centers should be built in-country to develop more indigenous skills and increase local capacity.

3.2 Promotion of Learning and Monitoring among Firms

A major argument against protectionism is that the infant industries, being protected, never grow up. This may be attributed to the use of blanket policies and the absence of capacity, knowledge, investment in research and development, and closed innovation policies. The development of sectors of the economy and empowering local production through protectionist methods, such as local content regulations, cannot work without an enabling environment to upgrade the local goods and services being supplied as well. Without an upgrade in the local commodity and skill set, local business owners and service providers would be responding to demand with substandard and inferior goods and services, thereby discouraging long-term foreign investments.

For example, although the NCDMB may be vigilant in ensuring that local content plans are submitted and regularly reported by the IOCs,[124] there are no substantial reports of their enforcement actions with respect to ensuring compliance from smaller indigenous contractors, especially with regard to the transfer of skill and technology.

It has therefore become industry practice for local contractors to submit comprehensive local content plans for upstream projects without actually hiring the local resources to carry out the work. The ripple effect of the lack of enforcement is that local contractors have to partner with foreign subcontractors to provide the skills to the IOCs, rather than building the skills in-house, thereby jeopardizing their growth prospects. This means that although an employee has worked for a local contractor for 10 years, that employee may have gained skills in subcontractor management more than in any specialized skills. For the contractor company, it is more frequently a boost of the quantity and quality of partnerships rather than technical capabilities and experience. In addition, local contractors continue to suffer reduction in their negotiating strength with regard to profit sharing on the project when negotiating with the foreign subcontractor. At the end of the day, a great chunk of the

---

[122]   R. Nelson, *National Innovation System* (Oxford University Press, 1993); N. Sharif, "Emergence and Development of the National Innovation Systems Concept" (2006) 35 *Research Policy* 745–766.

[123]   G. McDermott, R. Corredoira, and G. Kruse, "Public-Private Institutions as Catalysts of Upgrading in Emerging Market Societies" (2009) 52 *The Academy of Management Journal* 1270–1296.

[124]   NCDMB, "Guidelines on Application for Expatriate Quota, Succession Plan and Deployment of Expatriates in the Nigerian Oil and Gas Industry," Public Notice NC-LEG-01EQ/17.

Upgrade of Local Suppliers in Production Network 101

funds to be paid to the local contractor is often taken out of the country by the foreign subcontractor.

Tied to the establishment of clusters and networks is the importance of promoting continuous learning and monitoring in the formed clusters. Paola Perez-Aleman defines learning as "the process of firms catching up to the international standards of quality and productivity."[125] She further defines monitoring as "actors continually assessing each other's performance according to the agreed standards."[126] The international standard for the procurement of goods and services is constantly changing and more driving factors are being recognized in the selection process than value-for-money, economy, integrity, and fit-for-purpose.[127] In 2016, the World Bank revised its Procurement Rules, recognizing other "non-commercial" factors in a procurement process.[128] This reform saw the introduction of more "sustainable procurement" guidelines that encourage the procurers to look out for compliance with "international sustainability standards."[129] To keep up with local regulations and remain internationally competitive, firms in clusters can regulate one another by ensuring that established standards are frequently updated and adhered to by members of the cluster.[130] This firm-based regulation addresses free riding and rent seeking by exploitative firms.[131] Constant monitoring of activities and operations of the sectors guarantees economic development. Also, where a government board exists, such as Nigeria's NCDMB, the board would be well positioned to be a knowledge bridge between "previously isolated producer communities"[132] and must provide necessary guidance to the sector.[133]

3.3 Collaborative Governance

Another safeguard against negative externalities of protectionism is the use of collaborative governance in the formulation of policies and laws. Collaborative governance provides a shift in traditional planning of top-down management to a more effective bottom-up approach by giving local producers a voice in policy

[125] Perez-Aleman, note 113.
[126] Ibid.
[127] The World Bank, "Procurement Regulations for IPF Borrowers: Procurement in Investment Project Financing: Goods, Works, Non-consulting and Consulting Services," July 2016, Points 1.3 and 2.4, Annex VII, 3.5, Directive 2014/24, Annex X, Directive 2014/25, and Annex XIV.
[128] Ibid.
[129] Ibid.; J. Górski, "The Reform of World Bank's Procurement Rules," Chinese University of Hong Kong, Centre for Financial Regulation and Economic Development, Working Paper No. 20, November 7, 2016.
[130] Tim Bartley, "Institutional Emergence in an Era of Globalization: The Rise of Transnational Private Regulation of Labor and Environmental Conditions" (2007) 113 *American Journal of Sociology* 297–351.
[131] Schneider et al., note 116.
[132] McDermott et al., note 123.
[133] F. Fuchs, "Rethinking the Role of the State in Technology Development: DARPA and the Case for Embedded Network Governance" (2010) 39 *Research Policy* 1133–1147.

development.[134] This will assist governments with addressing sector-specific challenges, while setting up local standards that are internationally competitive and more easily implementable. It empowers the beneficiaries of policies, regulation, planning, and public management to be involved in the conception, design, execution, and maintenance of government actions.

Ansell and Gash define collaborative governance as, "a governing arrangement where one or more public agencies, directly engage non-state stakeholders in a collective decision-making process that is formal, consensus-oriented, and deliberative and that aims to make or implement public policy or manage public programs or assets."[135] From their definition, a few important elements stand out:

(a) *Collaborative governance must be formal*: The formalization of collaborative governance breeds accountability and removes deniability. This is important in African countries, plagued by cronyism and what we call "undue-influence-wielding-bigmanism." By formalizing the process, interested parties are given the opportunity to air their views in an open, not bullish, environment; interests are aligned; and differences decentralized.[136]

(b) *The opportunity to arrive at a consensus-oriented policy or plan*: This grants the affected communities a sense of ownership; and common to every property owner, is the commitment to protect his property. In communities where people are allowed to "own" government plans, policies, and infrastructure, there is a concerted effort to guard the assets and protect decisions arrived at, exuding pride and belonging. This is the case in oil communities of the Niger-Delta region of Nigeria.

(c) *The opportunity to "deliberate"*: In most developing countries, which have experienced military rule or a form of dictatorship, one major opposition to such governments has been the top-down approach of management, with no room for discussion or people participation. A deliberative structure of governance results in efficient resilience for the communities and the policies and plans. Quick and Feldman argue, "resilience involves the ability to reassemble resources and activities in ways that enable systems to continue to work despite disruption and adversity."[137] Beyond this, deliberative governance structure enhances insulation of plans/policies from individuals, thereby converting possible boundaries to junctures for competing interests.[138]

---

[134] D. Olawuyi, "Local Content and Procurement Requirements in Oil and Gas Contracts: Regional Trends in the Middle East and North Africa" (2019) 37 *Journal of Energy and Natural Resources Law* 93–117.

[135] C. Ansell and A. Gash, "Collaborative Governance in Theory and Practice" (2008) 18 *Journal of Public Administration Theory and Practice* 543–571. See also D. Olawuyi, *Extractives Industry Law in Africa* (Springer Nature Switzerland, 2018) pp. 118–121, 260–264, and 303–308.

[136] K. Quick and M. Feldman, "Boundaries as Junctures: Collaborative Boundary Work for Building Efficient Resilience" 24 *Journal of Public Admin Research and Theory* 673–695.

[137] Ibid.

[138] Ibid.

4 CONCLUSION

The primordial politico-economic territorial structure and division of the world is changing. The advancement of technology, expansion of e-commerce, and birth of the internet economy necessitate that resource-based economies set out to maximize in-country returns from the exploitation and exploration of their resources, while they still can. As the world further globalizes and countries rely further on international trade, investment, and finance, it becomes more important to safeguard against economic vultures and renegotiate the terms of international coexistence.

Regular interactions between the state and the economy are inevitable. Protectionist regimes present a viable tool for maximizing in-country returns. Protectionist regimes have the potentials to upgrade products and services and promote relevance and competitiveness of local suppliers. However, protectionist policies, such as LCRs, may suffer negative externalities, and to effectively address these, some elements must be present prior to the enforcement of protectionist policies namely: clusters, networks, learning and monitoring, and collaborative governance.

PART II

Case Studies

6

Expressing Local Content through Black Economic Empowerment in the South African Petroleum Industry

Hanri Mostert and Meyer van den Berg[*]

1 INTRODUCTION

The main aim of this chapter is to examine the measures imposed in South Africa, under a constitutional reform mandate, to achieve Black Economic Empowerment (empowerment or BEE). We argue that, as a policy, BEE has held sway over South African understandings of what it means to promote local content.[1] Our focus here is only on the relationship between BEE and local content requirements in South Africa's petroleum industry. More specifically, because of scope limitations, we home in on only one requirement: that of black ownership or holding.

The link between empowerment and local content policy is expounded in Section 2, followed by an overview of the law and policy supporting upstream and downstream transformation in Section 3. Section 4 then scrutinises the success of such endeavours by considering current challenges, before some insights and recommendations are shared in Section 5, the concluding section.

2 THE LINK BETWEEN EMPOWERMENT AND LOCAL CONTENT

A main motivation for including provisions on local content in, for instance, South Africa's procurement policy framework, is to strengthen the country's industrial base and promote the development of new industries.[2] A further motivation is to stimulate growth of expertise to eradicate skills shortages or misappropriations.[3] While local

---

[*] The authors wish to acknowledge the research assistance of Kennedy Chege and Analisa Ndebele with gratitude. The financial support of the National Research Foundation and the University of Cape Town is gratefully acknowledged. Opinions expressed here, and errors made, should not be attributed to either of these institutions.

[1] Compare, for example, the OECD's understanding of local content with the requirements of the code and scorecard approach discussed below. See J. Korinek and I. Ramdoo, 'Local content policies in mineral-exporting countries' (2017) OECD Trade Policy Papers, No. 209, OECD Publishing, Paris.

[2] W. Nyakabawo, 'South Africa's Local Content Policies: Challenges and Lessons to Consider', Trade and Industrial Policy Strategies (TIPS), Policy Brief: 7/2017, July 31, 2017, p. 2.

[3] See I. Ramdoo, 'Local Content Policies in Mineral-Rich Countries' (2016) European Centre for Development Policy Management, Discussion Paper No 196 2; Nyakabawo, note 2, p. 2; also D. Olawuyi,

content policy thus usually embodies an effort to redirect economic rents away from foreign entities and towards specific interest groups within a country hosting natural resource extraction, such policy may also be harnessed to achieve sociopolitical objectives.[4]

In South Africa, socio-economic transformation and redress of past injustice and discrimination has been high on the agenda for over two decades. This objective is the very fabric of the society emerging from its broken past. Political and economic events unfolding in the wake of discoveries of vast deposits of hard mineral resources in the late 1800s, left South Africa with a complicated and inherently skewed social structure.[5] Competition for scarce resources was driven and managed by race and class categorisations; racial discrimination in the distribution of such resources was characteristic.[6] The effect of those political choices is palpable even today, more than a century later. The bottom line is that in South Africa, one cannot deal with local content policies outside the context of socio-economic transformation.

Empowerment is the vehicle through which socio-economic transformation must be achieved in South Africa. The negotiated Constitution from 1996[7] mandates the state to respond to the systematic discrimination of the past by enabling redress and social and economic transformation.[8] The Constitution's reliance on 'legislative and other measures' to achieve its ideal of an equal society[9] is the mainstay of its transformative intent.[10] Legislatively driven reform is how the Constitution envisions that those who were previously disadvantaged by unfair discrimination can be protected and/or advanced.[11] This lies at the heart of the Constitution's desired socio-economic transformation to a society built on dignity, equality and freedom.[12]

'Local Content and Procurement Requirements in Oil and Gas Contracts: Regional Trends in the Middle East and North Africa' (2019) 37 *Journal of Energy and Natural Resources Law* 93–117.

[4] S. Silva, 'Local content requirements and the green economy', United Nations Conference on Trade and Development (UNCTAD), UNCTAD/DITC/TED/2013/7, pp. 11–14; Nyakabawo, note 2, p. 2. See also, D. Olawuyi, 'Local Content Policies and Their Implications for International Investment Law' in J. Chaisse, et al. (eds.), *Handbook of International Investment Law* (Springer, 2019) pp. 1–21.

[5] See C. H. Feinstein, *An Economic History of South Africa: Conquest, Discrimination and Development* (Cambridge University Press, 2005), pp. 99–100; H. Giliomee and B. Mbenga, *New History of South Africa* (Tafelberg: NB Publishers, 2007), p. 199.

[6] H. Mostert and C. L. Young, 'Between Custom and Colony: Social-Norm Based Property Law in South Africa's Post-Constitutional "No-Man's Land" in P. Babie and J. Viven-Wilksch (eds.), *Léon Duguit and the Social Norm of Property* (New York: Springer 2019) 371–402; P. S. Benjamin, M. Taylor, and T. N. Raditapole, *Black Economic Empowerment: Commentary, Legislation & Charters* (Cape Town: Juta Legal and Academic Publishers, 2014), pp. 1–3.

[7] Constitution of the Republic of South Africa 1996 (hereafter 'Constitution'). See the Preamble, sections 25 (6–8), 29(2)(c), and 195(1)(i).

[8] Mostert et al., note 6; Benjamin et al., note 6, pp.1–4.

[9] Constitution, note 7, section 9(1). Remedial measures must be used as a means to achieve equality, not as an exception to the principle of equality. See Benjamin et al., note 6, pp. 1–4.

[10] Constitution, note 7, section 9(2); T. Balshaw and J. Goldberg, *Broad-Based Black Economic Empowerment: Amended Codes and Scorecard* (Tafelberg: NB Publishers, 2014), p. 69.

[11] Constitution, note 7, section 9(2).

[12] Constitution, note 7, section 7(1).

Expressing Local Content through Black Empowerment

For the petroleum industry, as for many other industries,[13] legislative measures have been implemented systematically over the past twenty years in an attempt to give expression to the Constitution's transformative mandate to achieve a society based on dignity, equality and freedom. As we will show, these attempts included provisions for enabling local content initiatives through the empowerment policies of the Government. The policy and legislative frameworks to achieve the interrelated goals of transformation, empowerment, and local benefit in the extractive sector are interwoven in a complex and layered way, as will be further discussed. Several of the tenets of those frameworks overlap with the purposes for which a local content policy is established. In both the mineral and petroleum industries, for instance, there is a strong focus on local procurement policies, a typical pillar of local content provisions.[14] However, the focus is meant to ensure meaningful economic participation by historically disadvantaged South Africans (HDSAs) in these industries,[15] thus targeting a specific part of the population,[16] and making the link between black economic empowerment and local content provisions inalienable. These provisions are prevalent in many policy documents,[17] some of which[18] will be considered. There are

---

[13] For example, land reform has been top of the agenda for policy makers since 1991 and is mandated by section 25, Constitution of the Republic of South Africa, note 7. See , for example, D. James, *Gaining Ground?: 'Rights' and 'Property' in South African Land Reform* (Abingdon: Routledge-Cavendish, 2007), pp. 3–4; Institute for Poverty, Land and Agrarian Studies, University of the Western Cape, 'Diagnostic Report on Land Reform in South Africa', Commissioned Report for High Level Panel on the Assessment of Key Legislation and the Acceleration of Fundamental Change, An Initiative of the Parliament of South Africa, September 2016, pp. 3–6.

[14] The other pillars of local content include: rights application, training and employment, implementation, and monitoring and enforcement. The 2018 Mining Charter aligns with each of these pillars in certain respects. For example, in terms of the Mining Charter, it is required that HDSAs must own 15 per cent of mining companies with mineral rights that have been converted from old-order rights, and 26 per cent of companies under the current regime. In respect of training and development, mining companies are legally required to achieve a minimum percentage of HDSA representation at senior management level. The enactment of the Mining Charter is a manifestation of the implementation pillar of local content, as it contains provisions requiring the implementation of local content principles. The Charter also incorporates a scorecard to assess, monitor and evaluate compliance by companies. In spite of regulating each of these pillars, it is evident that the Charter places more emphasis on local procurement. See Minister of Mineral Resources, 'Broad-Based Socio-Economic Empowerment Charter for the Mining and Minerals Industry, 2018', Government Gazette, September 27, 2018, paras. 2.2 and 4.5 ['Mining Charter 2018'].

[15] Mineral and Petroleum Development Act 28 2002, section 2 (d) ['MPRDA'].

[16] See, for example, Minister, Department of Natural Resources, 'Implementation Guidelines for the Broad-Based Socio-Economic Empowerment Charter for the Mining and Minerals Industry 2018', Government Gazette, 19 December 2018, paras. 5.1.1 and 5.13.2 ['Implementation Guidelines for the Mining Charter 2018]. In the mining sector, companies are required to ensure that 21 per cent of their total mining goods procurement and 50 per cent of procurement spent on services, are sourced from companies that are owned and controlled by HDSAs, including women. Mining Charter 2018, note 14, paras. 5.13.1 and 5.6.2.

[17] For example, Department of Minerals and Energy, 'Publication of the Codes of Good Practice for the Minerals Industry', Government Gazette, April 29, 2009.

[18] Sasol, 'Charter for the South African Petroleum and Liquid Fuels Industry: Empowering Historically Disadvantaged South Africans', June 2018 ['Liquid Fuels Charter' or 'Petroleum Charter'].

requirements localizing a component of the rights that can be awarded and held; further requirements pertaining to training and employment, as well as the procurement of goods and services. In this Chapter, the focus is largely on the localizing of resource holding patterns (i.e. title/ownership and licencing).

Access to resources is an important empowering factor in any sector of the economy, including the minerals and petroleum industries. In South Africa, historically, access was controlled through discriminatory laws that reserved ownership of land to a racially determined minority. Without access to the land whence resources could be extracted, the black majority of the population had limited opportunities to develop and diversify economically useful skills and to engage in wealth-creating activity. The effects are visible in both the upstream and downstream petroleum sectors.

Opportunities for transformation in the upstream petroleum industry have been limited, due to the historical composition of this sector of the industry: the upstream industry was dominated by the then national oil company, the Southern Oil Exploration Corporation (Pty) Ltd ('Soekor'), until 2002,[19] which placed control of the sector firmly within the hands of the State. In view of recent discoveries and the new technical ability to extract hitherto inaccessible reserves of petroleum, however, South Africa stands a chance to improve its position as a player in the global petroleum industry.[20] It will have to consider its choices around partnerships with local and foreign investors in shaping the upstream petroleum industry into one that supports inclusive and sustainable growth.

In the downstream sector, two business models prevailed during Apartheid.[21] The distinction between these models lay in who owned the land on which petrol service stations were situated: the distribution companies or the operating dealers.[22] Either way, the strict race limitations on landownership under Apartheid meant that the industry could only be accessed by those who were eligible to own land: predominantly white persons.[23] This Chapter relies on findings in existing scholarship,[24] which scrutinized progress made on socio-economic transformation in the

[19] See PetroSA, 'Historic Milestones', www.petrosa.co.za/discover_petroSA/Pages/Historic-Milestones-PetroSA.aspx.

[20] Total's recent discovery of approximately 1 billion barrels of off-shore gas in the Brulpadda basin off the Southern coast has aroused optimism, particularly as regards energy security and development potential. See, for example, South African Government, 'President Cyril Ramaphosa: 2019 State of the Nation Address', 7 February 2019, www.gov.za/speeches/president-cyril-ramaphosa-2019-state-nation-address-7-feb-2019-0000.

[21] The two retail models were the Dealer Owned-Dealer Operated (DODO) and Company Owned-Dealer Operated (CODO) models. See M. Makiva, I. Ile and O. M. Fagbadebo, 'Evaluating Transformation Progress of Historically Disadvantaged South Africans: Programme Perspective on the Downstream Petroleum Industry' (2019) 7 African Evaluation Journal 2.

[22] Ibid., p. 2.

[23] James, note 13.

[24] [24] See D. Olawuyi, Extractives Industry Law in Africa (Switzerland: Springer Nature Switzerland, 2018) 233–260 (identifying and analyzing LCRs in the energy sectors of various States in Africa and States outside Africa, such as Canada, Saudi Arabia and the United Kingdom).

Expressing Local Content through Black Empowerment 111

downstream petroleum sector by focusing on the extent to which these holding patterns have shifted under new licencing and operating requirements. These findings allow us to evaluate the legal framework that should enable the socio-economic transformation embodied by provisions dealing with empowerment and local content requirements.

3 LEGISLATIVE MEASURES FOR LOCAL CONTENT AND EMPOWERMENT IN SOUTH AFRICA

Under constitutional mandate,[25] various legislative measures have been initiated to promote equality and redress past discrimination.[26] In the petroleum industry, both industry-specific laws and generic laws contribute to creating a framework for empowerment through affirmative action, employment equity and skills development. These provisions activate the local content requirements in the industry. Primary legislation is accompanied by a code-and-scorecard approach and supplemented by the partnership between Government and the petroleum industry, embodied in the sectoral Charter.

To understand the local content requirements in the petroleum industry, it is necessary to acknowledge, briefly, the broader framework within which they are positioned. Accordingly, the following paragraphs deal cursorily with South Africa's law and policy for black economic empowerment (Section 3.1) and employment equity, competition and skills development (Section 3.2) before undertaking a more detailed analysis of the provisions applicable to the petroleum industry (Section 3.3).

3.1 *Broad-Based Black Economic Empowerment*

An initial strategy document, *South Africa's Economic Transformation: A Strategy for Broad-Based Black Economic Empowerment* (Empowerment Strategy,[27] laid the groundwork for transformation initiatives.[28] In its wake followed legislation[29] to

---

[25] Constitution, note 7, section 9.

[26] Several provisions in the Constitution expressly mandate the legislature to take legislative and other measures to redress past discrimination. One of the most significant legislative measures taken under this mandate is the Promotion of Equality and Prevention of Unfair Discrimination Act 4 of 2000 (PEPUDA or the Equality Act). See further *Minister of Finance v Van Heerden* [2004] (6) SA 121 (CC), para. 36.

[27] Department of Trade and Industry, 'South Africa's Economic Transformation: A Strategy for Broad-Based Black Economic Empowerment', ['Empowerment Strategy'].

[28] The purpose of this initiative is 'to facilitate growth, development and stability in the South African economy'. Ibid., para. 3.1.1.

[29] Broad-Based Black Economic Empowerment Act 53 2003 ('BEE Act'), section 1, sv 'broad-based black economic empowerment'. The rationale for referring to 'broad-based black economic empowerment' rather than to 'black economic empowerment' is to emphasise that empowerment is not only for an elite few, but for all black persons. See Benjamin et al., note 6, pp. 1–6.

achieve broad-based BEE.[30] The aim of the BEE initiative is to enable meaningful economic participation by black people[31] by significantly increasing the number of 'black people that manage, own and control the country's economy', and to combat income inequality.[32]

'Black persons' is a generic term in the Strategy, describing African, coloured, and Indian South Africans.[33] In subsequently enacted laws, as we shall discuss, different terms are used to refer to these or similar groupings of people benefitting from empowerment initiatives.

The BEE process comprises several modalities that largely mirror typical local content requirements: human resource development, employment equity, enterprise development, preferential procurement, investment, ownership and control of enterprises, and economic assets.[34] The BEE framework goes beyond conventional local content requirements, though, in that it obliges the involvement not only of locals, but of *marginalized* locals,[35] in the economic opportunities created, among others, by resource extraction.

The main law, applicable to all industries, is the Broad-Based Black Economic Empowerment Act (BBBEE Act),[36] supplemented by a code and a scorecard.[37] These instruments must facilitate the economic empowerment of all black people,[38] women, people with disabilities, workers, youth and people living in rural areas.[39] The BEE Act's accompanying Code of Good Practice (Code), most recently republished in 2013,[40] applies to 'all organs of state and public entities',[41] also to the Minister(s) of Mineral Resources and Energy. The Code contains a broad-based BEE generic scorecard.[42] Businesses that do not comply with the basic thresholds set out in the scorecard can effectively not pursue business opportunities, with

---

[30]   R. Southall, 'The ANC and Black Capitalism in South Africa' (2004) 31 *Review of African Political Economy* 315; P. J. Badenhorst and H. Mostert, *Mineral and Petroleum Law of South Africa* (Cape Town: Juta Law, 2004), pp. 23–4.

[31]   Balshaw, note 10, pp. 13.

[32]   Empowerment Strategy, note 27, para. 3.2.2.

[33]   Ibid., para. 3.1.1.

[34]   As envisaged by ibid., para. 3.2.3. See also para 3.3, which outlines a number of policy objectives for BEE.

[35]   Compare R. Matey, 'A Comparison of Public-Private Partnerships in Nigeria & South Africa' (2019) 18 *Washington University Global Studies Law Review* 691 at 715.

[36]   See BEE Act, note 29, section 11. The Act empowers the Minister to issue a strategy aimed at realising black economic empowerment in South Africa, and it sets the guidelines for the content of such a strategy; Benjamin et al., note 6, pp. 1–3.

[37]   See, in general, Balshaw, note 10, p. 70.

[38]   For envisaged actions, BEE Act, note 29, section 2.

[39]   The new Codes of Good Practice of the Broad-Based Black Economic Empowerment were gazetted in 2007, along with several sector scorecards, general guidelines and definitions. The definition of BEE remained as it was under the BEE Act, note 29.

[40]   Department of Trade and Industry, 'Codes of Good Practice on Broad Based Black Economic Empowerment', Government Gazette, 24 February 2016 ['Code'].

[41]   Ibid., Statement 000, para. 3.1.1.

[42]   Ibid., Statement 000, para. 8.

Expressing Local Content through Black Empowerment

concomitant detrimental effects. BEE compliance is benchmarked on the basis of the scorecard, as against the shape and size of a particular business entity (Measured Entity).[43] The Code promotes a substance-over-form approach in measuring BEE compliance.[44] The Code applies to Measured Entities engaging in economic activity with state organs and public entities and also with other Measured Entities subject to the Code.[45]

The five pillars of empowerment in the generic scorecard each carry a specific weighting. Ownership:[46] 25 points; management control:[47] 15 points; skills development:[48] 20 points; enterprise and supplier development:[49] 40 points; socio-economic development:[50] 5 points. To be fully compliant, the Measured Entity requires 100 scorecard points made up of these modalities. The different pillars add up, however, to 105 points. It is therefore possible for an entity to be fully compliant without meeting all the criteria.[51] The degree of compliance with the BEE scorecards is measured in 'Levels', with 'level-1 status' representing a 135 per cent BEE recognition.[52] Start-up enterprises are generally treated preferentially, but not those applying for rights to petroleum.[53] In the petroleum industry, start-up enterprises are subject to the same provisions that apply to tendering for contracts, where the Minister of Mineral Resources determines qualification criteria for the issuing of rights to petroleum.[54]

Legislatively mandated sectoral codes[55] require all government departments, state-owned enterprises, and public agencies to determine and implement their preferential procurement policy.[56] Sector-specific scorecards can measure progress in achieving BEE.[57] These scorecards use defined elements

---

[43]   Ibid. Defined in Schedule 1 to the Code and in Code, Statement 000, para. 3.2.3.

[44]   Ibid., Statement 000, para. 2.1.

[45]   Ibid., Statement 000, paras. 3.1.2. and par 3.1.3.

[46]   Points for direct/indirect participation by black people in the Measured Entity's rights of ownership. Ibid., Statement 100, para. 3.1.1.

[47]   Measuring participation on board level, other executive management, senior management, middle management, junior management and employees with disabilities. Ibid., Statement 200, para. 2.

[48]   Measured through various categories of compliance targets on the scorecard. Demographic representation of Black people forms the basis of these targets. Ibid., Statement 300, paras. 2.1, 2.2 and 2.3.

[49]   Precipitating the vision in the Empowerment Strategy, note 27, para. 3.5.5., preferential procurement is regarded as the policy instrument that may effectively promote BEE in the South African economy. Ibid., Statement 400, paras. 3.1.1 and 3.1.2.

[50]   Ibid., Statement 500, para. 2.3.

[51]   Measured Entities also get scored on any socio-economic development contributions that are quantifiable in monetary terms. Ibid., Statement 500, para. 3.1.1.

[52]   Ibid., Statement 000, para. 8.2.1; W. Scholtz and C. Van Wyk, *BEE Service Empowermentor* (Durban, SA: LexisNexus South Africa, 2013), pp. 1–3. See special dispensation for 'Exempt Micro-Enterprises'.

[53]   Code, note 40, Statement 000, para. 6.3.

[54]   Ibid., Statement 000, para. 6.4 read with the BEE Act, note 29, section 10(a).

[55]   BEE Act, note 29, sections 9 and 10(a) to (c). The codes weigh the BEE indicators and provide guidelines for sectoral or industry charters. See Scholtz et al., note 52, 1–1.

[56]   Empowerment Strategy, note 27, para. 3.5.5.

[57]   Ibid., para. 3.5.3.1.

and sector-specific contributions from which to construct such measurement.[58] All organs of state and public entities are bound to consider such code where applicable.[59] The Minister must also publish and promote separate transformation charters for particular sectors of the economy,[60] each of which must be developed by major stakeholders in a specific sector. These charters therefore arise from the collaborative efforts of stakeholders within a given industry, rather than being instruments imposed by the state.[61] Such charters must advance the objectives of the BEE Act.[62] An example of such sector-based consensus is the *Charter for the South African Petroleum and Liquid Fuels Industry on Empowering Historically Disadvantaged South Africans in the Petroleum and Liquid Fuels Industry* (Petroleum Charter), which will be discussed further in Section 3.2. For the petroleum industry, the BBBEE Act effectively obliges the Minister of Mineral Resources to consider the codes of good practice when granting and issuing rights in respect of petroleum.[63]

3.2 *Employment Equity, Competition and Skills Development*

Further-supplementing legislation and policy instruments support the operation of the BBBEE Act.[64] The Employment Equity Act 55 of 1998, Competition Act 89 of 1998 and Skills Development Act 97 of 1998 deserve mention.

The Competition Act regulates the anti-competitive conduct of companies,[65] among others.[66] It aims specifically to increase the participation and the ownership stakes of black people – referred to in the Competition Act as 'historically disadvantaged South Africans' in the economy.[67] Pursuant to section 10(2)(a) of this Act, the Competition Commission exempted the petroleum and refinery industry between January 2016 and June 2016, and subsequently extended the exemption until

---

[58] Scholtz et al., note 52.

[59] BEE Act, note 29, section 10.

[60] Ibid., section 12.

[61] Benjamin et al., note 6, pp. 1–12.

[62] BEE Act, note 29, section 12.

[63] The BEE Act requires every organ of state and public entity, including the Department of Mineral Resources and Energy, to take into account and apply the codes of good practice, where applicable to *inter alia*, the issuing of licences, concessions or other authorisations in terms of any law. See BEE Act, note 29, section 10(1).

[64] Empowerment Strategy, note 27, paras. 3.5.1 – 3.5.3

[65] See Competition Act 89 of 1998, sections 4–9 ['Competition Act'].

[66] The objectives of the Competition Act are set out in section 2.

[67] Competition Act, note 65, Preamble note 79. Under this Act, the Competition Commission granted an exemption to the petroleum and refinery industry, which covered several agreements and practices that would otherwise be perceived as 'cartel conduct' in the petroleum and refinery industry dealing with logistics and bulk supply. Until December 2016, participants in the liquid fuels supply chain were thus permitted a collaborative exchange of information needed for stability of supply and efficient use of supply chain facilities. This form of coordination would also ensure security of supply.

Expressing Local Content through Black Empowerment 115

December 2016.[68] The effect of this exemption was that participants in the liquid fuels supply chain could have a collaborative exchange of information needed for stability of supply and efficient use of supply chain facilities.[69]

The Employment Equity Act (EEA)[70] covers all employees,[71] including those employed by petroleum companies. It prohibits direct and indirect unfair discrimination,[72] on a broad range of listed grounds, including 'race, ... ethnic or social origin, colour, ... culture, language and birth'.[73] It further, more controversially,[74] introduces a new system of social engineering,[75] compelling certain classes of employers[76] to implement affirmative action measures[77] and to have a plan in place that articulates their intended progress towards employment equity.[78] Rather than requiring quotas, this Act mandates preferential treatment, specifically to promote South Africans who are black and/or female and/or have disabilities.[79] These individuals are from 'designated groups',[80] which is a variation on the description of 'historically disadvantaged South Africans' used in other empowerment legislation.

The Skills Development Act (SDA)[81] facilitates the creation of an institutional and financial framework[82] to redress and overcome past injustices by concentrating on education and skills development.[83] Public–private partnerships are encouraged

---

[68] Economic Development Department, 'Competition Commission: Notice in terms of Section 10(7) of the Competition Act 89 of 1998 (as amended): South African Petroleum Industry Association granted conditional exemption', Government Gazette, 12 October 2018.

[69] Ibid.

[70] Employment Equity Act 55 1998 ['EEA'], which gives effect to right to equality guaranteed by section 9 of the South African Constitution.

[71] The EEA does not cover independent contractors. See ibid., section 1, sv 'employee'.

[72] See J. Grogan, *Dismissal, Discrimination, and Unfair Labour Practices* (2nd ed., Cape Town: Juta and Co., 2007), p. 163.

[73] EEA, note 70, section 6 (1).

[74] Grogan, note 72, p. 163. The Constitutional Court has provided clarity on the application of affirmative action in *South African Police Service v Solidarity obo Barnard* CCT 01/14 [2014] (6) SA 123 (CC).

[75] Ibid.

[76] The classes of employees referred to in this provision are those with annual turnovers above a certain prescribed threshold, and more than 50 employees. EEA, note 70, section 12.

[77] Ibid., ch. III; Grogan, note 72, p. 163.

[78] EEA, note 70, sections 5, 13, and 20, read with Schedule 4.

[79] Ibid., section 15(3).

[80] The EEA uses the term 'designated groups' to refer to Black people, women and people with disabilities. See ibid., section 1, sv 'designated groups'.

[81] Skills Development Act 97 1998 ['SDA'].

[82] Ibid., section 2(2)(a). The institutional and financial framework comprises: (a) the National Skills Authority; (b) the National Skills Fund; (c) a skills development levy-financing scheme as contemplated in the Skills Development Levies Act; (d) sector education and training authorities; provincial offices of the Department of Labour; (e) labour centres of the Department of Labour; (f) accredited trade test centres; (g) skills development institutes; (h) the Quality Council for Trades and Occupations; (i) a skills development forum for each province; (j) a national artisan moderation body; and (k) Productivity South Africa.

[83] See ibid., Preamble.

to provide learning in and for the workplace[84] in co-operation with the South African Qualifications Authority.[85] Skills development under the Act is linked to enhancing workers' quality of life,[86] improving employers' productivity and competitiveness[87] and promoting self-employment.[88] The Act encourages transformation of workplaces into active learning environments,[89] among others, to improve employability of those who were unfairly discriminated against in the past.[90] Employers – also petroleum companies – are obliged, under the Skills Development Levies Act,[91] to pay levies towards skills development,[92] thus contributing to socio-economic development and bringing benefit from the industry's operations to the people of South Africa.

3.3 Specific Framework for Empowerment and Local Content in the Petroleum Industry

These Sections described the broader context within which BEE – and through it, local content requirements – must find implementation in South Africa. A series of specific legal and policy instruments were established to give effect to the same objectives in the petroleum industry. They are discussed in the following.

3.3.1 Policy Context

The Energy White Paper of 1998[93] (White Paper) sets out the Government's policy position. It deals with the upstream and the downstream petroleum sectors but does not outline specific transformation objectives for the upstream sector, because the State-owned entity, Soekor, was the only significant upstream player when the White Paper was released.[94] The downstream sector was different. Substantial earlier investment, supported by investor-friendly policies[95] and significant government support,[96] resulted in a downstream sector with a vertically integrated value chain

---

[84] Ibid., section 2(2)(b).
[85] Ibid., section 2(2)(c).
[86] Ibid., section 2(2)(a)(i).
[87] Ibid., section 2(2)(a)(ii).
[88] Ibid., section 2(2)(a)(iii).
[89] Ibid., section 2(2)(b) and 2(c).
[90] Ibid., section 2(2)(e).
[91] Skills Development Levies Act 9 of 1999.
[92] At a rate of 1% of the leviable amount. Ibid., section 3(1)(b).
[93] White Paper on the Energy Policy of the Republic of South Africa 1998 ['White Paper'].
[94] Ibid., para. 3.4.3.
[95] A. Paelo, G. Robb and T. Vilakazi, 'Competition and Incumbency in South Africa's Liquid Fuel Value Chain' in J. Klaaren, S. Roberts and I. Valodia (eds.), *Competition Law and Economic Regulation in Southern Africa: Addressing Market Power in Southern Africa* (Wits University Press, 2017), pp. 172–173.
[96] Ibid.

Expressing Local Content through Black Empowerment 117

of activities[97] and a few big, key players: large multinational oil companies with refining capacity in strategic port locations, alongside Sasol, the government's own internal fuel producer.[98] For downstream, the White Paper committed, among others, to meaningful inclusion of the interests of those who have been HDSAs.[99] The key milestone for deregulating the petroleum industry would be enduring or sustainable HDSA ownership or control of about roughly a quarter of all facets of the liquid fuels industry.[100]

In the wake of the White Paper, the *Charter for the South African Petroleum and Liquid Fuels Industry on Empowering Historically Disadvantaged South Africans in the Petroleum and Liquid Fuels Industry*[101] (generally known as either the Petroleum Charter or the Liquid Fuels Charter in upstream and downstream parlance, respectively)[102] was finalised and signed in 2000. Some subsequent alignment became necessary after the release of the BEE Codes of Practice, and the amendments to these in 2013.[103]

The Charter's purpose is summarized in its title: to drive the empowerment of HDSAs[104] in the industry.[105] Signatories committed to targets facilitating empowerment in the petroleum industry, which align largely with the generic targets, but have been tailored to include commitments not only to ownership,[106] management and control, employment equity,[107] procurement[108] and capacity

[97] Ibid.
[98] Ibid.
[99] White Paper, note 93, para. 7.4.2.
[100] Or plans towards this target. Ibid., para. 7.4.16.
[101] Sasol, note 18.
[102] Henceforth, in service of brevity, the reference is to the 'Petroleum Charter', regardless of whether the discussion is focused on upstream or downstream.
[103] BEE Act, note 29, section 9(1). The Petroleum Charter also had to be aligned with several other pieces of empowerment legislation. See the Public Proclamation No. 31 2017, 'Codes of Good Practice on Broad-Based Black Economic Empowerment', Government Gazette, 13 September 2017.
[104] HDSA is defined in the Petroleum Charter as 'all persons and groups who have been discriminated against on the basis of race, gender and/or disability'. See the Petroleum Charter under the heading *Interpretation*.
[105] Benjamin et al., note 6, pp. 1–12.
[106] The Petroleum Charter attempts to reform access to and ownership of joint facilities in the petroleum industry. Owners of such facilities must provide third parties with non-discriminatory access to uncommitted capacity. HDSA companies must be given fair opportunity to acquire ownership in such facilities. See Petroleum Charter under the heading *Access and Ownership of Joint Facilities*.
[107] Under the Petroleum Charter, companies publish their employment equity targets and achievements and subscribe to the following: (a) South African subsidiaries of multinational companies and South African companies focus their overseas placement and/or training programmes on HDSAs; (b) identifying a talent pool and fast-tracking it; (c) ensuring inclusiveness of gender; (d) implementing mentorship programmes; and (e) setting and publishing 'stretch' (i.e. demanding) targets and their achievement. Ibid., under the heading *Capacity Building*.
[108] Procurement is promoted in that participants in the petroleum industry subscribe to and adopt supportive procurement policies favouring procurement companies to facilitate and leverage the growth of HDSA companies. The scope of procurement must include supplies, products and all

118   *Hanri Mostert and Meyer van den Berg*

building,[109] and also to sustainability, financing[110] and development of certain sectors such as synfuels, retailing and enterprise, as well as fostering a supportive culture,[111] for HDSA companies.[112] The focus in this Section is on the ownership requirement and its link to the availability of licences.

3.3.2 Legal Context

While the White Paper represents the Government's policy statement, and the Petroleum Charter embodies the agreement between industry and government on how to translate the policy goals into action, legislation provides the framework within which the policy goals are converted into reality. The following Section attends to the main applicable laws in the upstream sector (Section 3.3.2.1) and the downstream sector (Section 3.3.2.2).

3.3.2.1 UPSTREAM: MINERAL AND PETROLEUM RESOURCES DEVELOPMENT ACT 28 OF 2002. The Mineral and Petroleum Resources Development Act 28 of 2002 (MPRDA)[113] has specific socio-economic empowerment objectives for the mineral and petroleum sectors. In force since 2004, and generally acknowledged as a clear legislative commitment to transforming the extractives industry in terms of equity

---

other goods and services. HDSA companies are accorded preferred supplier status as far as possible. Government liaises with State Tender authorities to alert them to the White Paper milestones as regards economic empowerment of HDSAs. The aim is to give effect to supportive procurement policies. Ibid., under the heading *Private Sector Procurement*.

[109] Standing consultative arrangements further enable the industry to dovetail its efforts with the work of statutory bodies (such as sectoral education and training authority) in the development of skills development strategies. Ibid., under the heading *Capacity Building*.

[110] In the Petroleum Charter, note 18 under the heading *Financing*, the South African Government commits to assist industry in explaining the milestones in the White Paper as well as explaining the needs and characteristics of the industry to financing institutions, both private and public. Companies must investigate and implement internal and external financing mechanisms for giving HDSA companies access to equity ownership within the South African context. Companies must also consider engaging HDSA companies in viable strategic partnerships. Industry participants also acknowledge that terms of credit are important to HDSA companies and agree to take this into account in bilateral activities.

[111] Petroleum Charter, note 18, under the heading *Supportive Culture*, acknowledges the need for buy-in from those with the responsibility for managing the transformation process within the industry, to create a supportive and enabling environment for business success. The necessary support is gleaned from various undertakings in the Charter itself: First, member companies and Government undertake to appoint managers with an understanding of the spirit of and historical motivation for the Petroleum Charter. Member companies commit to fostering a supportive culture for HDSAs in the context addressed by the Charter. Companies commit to transformation and a change of culture in their statements of business principles.

[112] Access to refining capacity also represents a key weakness in HDSA companies' supply chain. Ibid., under the heading *Access and Ownership of Joint Facilities*.

[113] With a previous attempt at amending the MPRDA, note 15 (in 2013) abandoned, the State is now once again developing an amendment to the legislative regime that would regulate the upstream petroleum sector and affect State participation in the petroleum industry.

Expressing Local Content through Black Empowerment   119

and representativity,[114] its preamble affirms the State's commitment to reform, to 'bring about equitable access to the country's mineral and petroleum resources'.[115] Section 3(1) provides that 'mineral and petroleum resources are the common heritage of all the people of South Africa' and the State is 'the custodian thereof for the benefit of all South Africans'.[116]

The MPRDA's preamble, like its Section 2, elucidates its objectives of socio-economic empowerment. It seeks to promote equitable access to the nation's mineral and petroleum resources to all the people of South Africa,[117] to make good on past discrimination in the industry.[118] The objects include substantially and meaningfully expanding access to the mineral and petroleum industries for historically disadvantaged persons, including women and communities, and to benefit from extractive activity.[119] The MPRDA also intends to promote employment and advance the social and economic welfare of all South Africans.[120] These objects bear interpretative weight[121] for several other provisions dealing with applications for and granting of rights to petroleum.[122] Finally, the MPRDA holds the holders of mining and production rights responsible to contribute towards the socio-economic development of the areas in which they are operating.[123] This is where the dovetailing of the transformative agenda with local content provisions becomes noticeable.

These objectives trickle into various further empowerment provisions, some of which align with or even go beyond typical local content requirements, hence their description in this chapter as 'transformation requirements'. For one, for applications received on the same day, preference must be given to applications by HDSAs.[124] Further, the grant of exploration and production rights is dependent

[114] H. Mostert, *Mineral Law: Principles and Policies in Perspective* (Cape Town: Juta and Co., 2012), p. 79; M. O. Dale, A.B.W. Cox, M. Ash et al., *South African Mineral and Petroleum Law* (Durban: LexisNexis South Africa, 2015), MPRDA-3; Badenhorst et al., note 30, pp. 1–2; *AgriSA v Minister for Minerals and Energy* [2013] (4) SA 1 (CC).

[115] MPRDA, note 15, Preamble.

[116] Ibid., section 3(1).

[117] Ibid., section 2(c).

[118] Dale et al., note 114, MPRDA-117.

[119] MPRDA, note 15, section 2(d).

[120] Ibid., section 2(f).

[121] Ibid., section 4(1). See also Dale et al., note 114, above) MPRDA-118.

[122] The MPRDA requires applicants for petroleum and other mining rights to submit a Social and Labour plan, among other requirements such as a Mining Work Programme and an Environmental Management Programme. The Social and Labour plan requires applicants to initiate programmes in the mining communities, with the aim of enhancing transformation in the mining industry by promoting social and economic development, including creating employment opportunities. See Department Mineral Resources, Republic of South Africa, 'T Guideline for the Submission of a Social and Labour Plan as required in terms of Regulation 46 of the Mineral and Petroleum Resources Development Act (Act 28 of 2002)', October 2010; The objectives of the Mining Charter, note 14, also apply to the granting of petroleum and mining rights; see Broad-Based Socio-Economic Empowerment Charter for the Mining and Mineral Industry 2018.

[123] MPRDA, note 15, section 2(i).

[124] Ibid., section 69(2) read with section 9(1)(a) and section 9(2). Applications received on different dates must be treated in the order in which they are received. See also Badenhorst, note 30, pp. 23–42;

120   Hanri Mostert and Meyer van den Berg

on, *inter alia* whether it will promote employment and advance the social and economic welfare of all South Africans[125] and will substantially and meaningfully expand access to and benefit from the petroleum resources for HDSAs.[126] Additionally, the granting of the production licence must be in accordance with the Petroleum Charter[127] and the prescribed social and labour plan.[128] As the process of extraction approaches the production phase, therefore, the stringency of the MPRDA's upstream transformation requirements increase.[129] No transformation requirements attach to reconnaissance permits[130] or technical co-operation permits.[131] The contrary is true for exploration rights[132] and production rights.[133] For one, granting of such rights is subject to a requirement of 'substantially and meaningfully' creating access to and enabling benefit from petroleum resources.[134] An award of such rights considers how economic growth is to be promoted. In the petroleum sector, the development of petroleum inputs industries is a particular consideration.[135] The transformation requirements in the petroleum sector hence align well with the typical requirements for local content.

3.3.2.2 DOWNSTREAM: PETROLEUM PRODUCTS ACT 120 OF 1977 AND OTHERS. An array of further laws influence empowerment (and hence also local content) in the downstream sector. Under the Petroleum Products Act[136] (PP Act) as amended, transformation requirements can be grouped into those dealing with vertical integration, licencing, biofuels and tariffs. For present purposes, the licencing requirements are the most interesting. The PP Act prohibits fuel wholesalers of liquefied natural gas from holding commercial retail licenses, other than for training

---

       MPRDA, note 15, section 9(1)(b) read with section 69(2) and section 9(3). As to the meaning of 'receives', see Dale et al., note 114, MPRDA–156. This has given rise to litigation in the minerals context, but not yet in relation to petroleum; *Pan African Mineral Development Company (Pty) Ltd and Others v Aquila Steel (S Africa) (Pty) Ltd* (179/2017) [2017] ZASCA 165; [2018] 1 All SA 414 (SCA); [2018] (5) SA 124 (SCA); *Aquila Steel (South Africa) (Pty) Ltd v Minister of Mineral Resources and Others* [2019] (3) SA 621 (CC).

[125] MPRDA, note 15, section 80(1)(g) and (i) read with section 2(d) and (f).
[126] Ibid., section 80(1)(g) read with section 2(d).
[127] Ibid., section 84(1)(i).
[128] Ibid., section 84(1)(g).
[129] The MPRDA obliges the Minister to grant a production right and exploration right if such granting will 'substantially and meaningfully expand opportunities for historically disadvantaged persons, including women, to enter the mineral and petroleum industries and to benefit from the exploitation of the nation's mineral and petroleum resource'. See ibid., sections 80(1)(g) and 84(1)(i).
[130] Ibid., section 75(1).
[131] Ibid., section 77(1).
[132] Ibid., section 80(1)(g).
[133] Ibid., section 84(1)(i).
[134] In the case of production rights, this requirement is set. In the case of exploration rights, the Minister of Mineral Resources may request that the applicant give effect to this requirement. See ibid., section 80(2).
[135] One of the objectives of the MPRDA is to promote economic growth and mineral and petroleum resources development in South Africa. See ibid., section 2(e).
[136] Petroleum Products Act 120 1977.

Expressing Local Content through Black Empowerment   121

purposes.[137] The effect is that vertical integration in the downstream sector is avoided, which creates more opportunities for new entrants into the industry.

Compliance with the Petroleum Charter is considered in granting manufacturing, wholesale, site or retail licences.[138] Licensed retailers, wholesalers and manufacturers must comply with the Charter and report their compliance progress.[139] Licensed manufacturers, wholesalers and retailers must report annually on, for example: the number of employees distinguished by race, gender and disability; and progress and strategies relating to achieving the objectives of the Petroleum Charter. The inclusion of HDSAs is thus a legal requirement and a prerequisite for the award and retention of petroleum licences.[140]

Entry to the downstream petroleum sector is supported by a dedicated set of regulations[141] for the mandatory blending of bio-ethanol with petrol and biodiesel with petroleum diesel also contain provisions supporting transformation.[142] These regulations effectively prohibit petroleum manufacturers from manufacturing biofuels. This opens the biofuels manufacturing sector to new entrants.[143] Alongside the stringently monitored requirements of BEE, significant opportunities for local content are thereby created.

The Petroleum Pipelines Act[144] (Pipelines Act) was introduced as parties other than the state became owners or operators of petroleum pipelines in South Africa.[145] The Pipelines Act should ensure efficient operation of the pipelines network which was state-managed and state-operated before 2003, but now can be subject to broader ownership and operation. The Pipelines Act should also regulate future development of the network.[146] This aligns the Pipelines Act with the transformation agenda of the White Paper in that it

---

[137]   The Petroleum Products Amendment Act inserted *inter alia* section 2A into the Petroleum Products Act 120 of 1977, which prohibits manufacturers and fuel wholesalers of liquefied natural gas from holding retail licences, except for training purposes. See Petroleum Product Amendment Act 58 2003, section 2A.

[138]   The Petroleum Products Amendment Act inserted section 2C into the Petroleum Products Act 1977, which states that the Commissioner must give effect to the Petroleum Charter when considering licence applications in terms of the Act. See ibid., section 3.

[139]   See Petroleum Products Act Regulations regarding petroleum products site and retail licences No. 286 2006, section 22(3)(c), section 22(3)(g)(iii) and section 26(1)(d).

[140]   See Makiva et al., note 21, p. 2.

[141]   See Regulations regarding the mandatory blending of biofuels with petrol and diesel No. 671 of 2012, section 3.

[142]   The Regulations stipulate that: 'a licensed petroleum manufacturer must only purchase biofuels from a licensed biofuels manufacturer'; and 'a licensed petroleum manufacturer must purchase all bio-ethanol or biodiesel offered for sale by a licensed biofuel manufacturer (provided that the volume of the biofuel can be blended with the volumes of petroleum petrol or petroleum diesel available from the licensed petroleum manufacturer)'. See ibid., section 3(1) and section 3(6).

[143]   Ibid., section 3(1) and section 3(6).

[144]   Petroleum Pipelines Act60 of 2003.

[145]   The Petroleum Pipelines Act permits individuals or private entities to own and operate petroleum pipelines in South Africa. See ibid., section 1, *sv* 'licensee' and section 16(2)(g).

[146]   Ibid., section 2(b).

promotes fair and equitable access to,[147] and competition in, the construction and operation[148] of petroleum pipelines, loading facilities and storage facilities, and by promoting competitiveness of HDSA companies in the petroleum pipeline industry through favourable licencing conditions.[149] Licence conditions and tariffs are the key enablers of transformation in terms of the Pipelines Act.

Compliance is monitored by the National Energy Regulator of South Africa (NERSA).[150] NERSA imposes licence conditions requiring the promotion of HDSAs and provision of information about participation of HDSA in the licence holder's activities. The licence conditions are also geared to provide third parties access to loading facilities, and to sharing capacity proportionate to the needs of all users, and subject to payment. NERSA requires a licence holder to manage vertically integrated companies separately; allows changes in the routing, size and capacity of pipelines to be negotiated; and allows facilities of other licence holders to be interconnected where technically feasible and affordable to the entity requesting the interconnection.

The MPRDA compelled the Minister of Mineral Resources (MMR) to 'develop a code of good practice for the minerals industry', within five years from entering into force. Likewise, after consultation with the Minister for Housing, the MMR had to develop a housing and living conditions standard (HLCS) for the minerals industry.[151] This was duly executed,[152] and these documents play some role in implementing local content and transformation imperatives. The obligation on the Minister to develop a HLCS and Code applies to the petroleum industry too.[153] Nevertheless, no separate standard and code has been developed.[154] The existing HLCS for the minerals industry and mining code of good practice are silent as to whether they apply to the petroleum industry.[155] Commentaries on mineral and petroleum law in South Africa do not provide any further guidance.[156] Since the documents refer only to the minerals industry, it is assumed that they do not apply to the petroleum industry.[157] The introductory section of the Code, however, pays its respects to the petroleum industry.

---

[147] Ibid., section 2(d).
[148] Ibid., section 2(a).
[149] Ibid., section 2(g) and (h).
[150] Transnet, 'Pipelines', 2018.
[151] MPRDA, note 15, section 100(1).
[152] Badenhorst et al., note 30, pp. 23–40.
[153] MPRDA, note 15, section 69(2).
[154] Badenhorst et al., note 30, pp. 23–40.
[155] Ibid.
[156] Ibid.; Dale et al., note 114, MPRDA-590.
[157] This is supported by the fact that these documents themselves only refer to the minerals industry.

4 CURRENT CHALLENGES

This section examines key challenges and struggles experienced in relation to the implementation and enforcement of local empowerment initiatives in the petroleum industry. The main weakness in achieving local benefit in the South African Petroleum context has to do with the disconnect between goals and outcomes in the overarching policy of black economic empowerment. We discuss these in Section 4.1, before looking more closely at the challenges in the upstream and downstream contexts specifically.

4.1 *The Failures of BEE*

The aim of BEE was originally to transform the South African economy by empowering HDSAs. They had to be given a chance – through various pillars of empowerment, including broadening management, control and ownership opportunities – to participate meaningfully in the economy.[158] The initiative has not, however, yielded results that align with that initial goal.[159] In fact, most black South Africans are excluded from BEE ownership; only an elite few are benefitting repeatedly,[160] many of them former ANC activists from before the party came into power.[161] The alleged cronyism and corruption[162] spawned by BEE has lead former Archbishop Desmond Tutu to condemn BEE, claiming it only benefits a small 'recycled elite'.[163] Criticism has led to attempts to promote more 'broad-based' BEE, which is contained in the current framework.[164] Despite this, BEE remains subject to criticism, with some claiming that it is used to enrich already prominent and empowered black people who are politically well connected.[165]

The failure of the BEE initiative is sometimes attributed to its distorted emphasis on the pillars of empowerment, with ownership overshadowing all the other

---

[158] Balshaw et al., note 10, p. 13.

[159] See, for example, R. Tangri and R. Southall, 'The Politics of Black Economic Empowerment in South Africa' (2008) 34 *Journal of Southern African Studies* at 699; L. P. Kruger, 'The Impact of Black Economic Empowerment (BEE) on South African Businesses: Focusing on Ten Dimensions of Business Performance' (2011) 15 *Southern African Business Review* at 212 and 232.

[160] J. Cargill, *Trick or Treat: Rethinking Black Economic Empowerment* (Johannesburg: Jacana Media, 2010) 119.

[161] D. Schneiderman, 'Promoting Equality, Black Economic Empowerment, and the Future of Investment Rules' (2010) 2 *South African Journal on Human Rights* 246 at 252.

[162] S. Newell and O. Okome, *Popular Culture in Africa: The Episteme of the Everyday* (Abingdon: Routledge, 2013), p. 159.

[163] Schneiderman, note 161, p. 253.

[164] Ibid., p. 253.

[165] S. Ndlovu Mpho, 'BEE Cake only for elite few-banker', 21 October 2014, www.pressreader.com /south-africa/sowetan/20141021/281900181467182; M. Collins, 'A New Kind of Apartheid: Analysing South Africa's "Class Struggle"', 19 December 2014, www.rnews.co.za/article/2212/opinion-a-new-kind-of-apartheid-analysing-south-africa-s-class-struggle; B. Sergeant, 'Mines for the Taking', 1 January 2015, www.noseweek.co.za/article/3353/Mines-for-the-taking.

pillars.[166] Indeed, in its early years, BEE's purpose was to deracialise business ownership and to create a black middle class.[167] BEE initiatives of the 1990s certainly focused on transferring the ownership of businesses to black persons.[168] In the mining industry, for instance, shareholding in mining companies was transferred to black persons on a large scale,[169] in the hope that the economic growth of South Africa would be stimulated.[170] Despite adaptations in the current 'broad-based' variation of the BEE framework, criticism persisted.[171] Reforms after the Black Economic Empowerment Commission's[172] Report of 2001 were mindful of the undue reliance on ownership as a means to empowerment. Even so, under current law, businesses have to maintain a certain level of representation of black persons in the equity ownership and management of the business. This requirement is supplemented by others, pertaining to skills development and the development of black enterprises and suppliers by making use of the goods and services of these entities,[173] and also promotion of socio-economic development through financing suitable projects.[174] Even so, there seems to be a continued emphasis on BEE ownership deals, which has led to some discontent.[175]

South Africa's approach to local content and transformation was to opt for an empowerment policy that had to deliver instant gratification, rather than the longer-term empowerment that may arise from typical local content policies. A focus on aspects of local content/empowerment that go beyond the transfer of ownership may have achieved better prospects for long-term prosperity. By comparison, skills development may bring about much more significant changes in wealth-creating patterns, albeit in the long run.[176]

---

[166] H. M. van den Berg, 'Regulation of the Upstream Petroleum Industry: A Comparative analysis and evaluation of the regulatory frameworks of South African and Namibia', PhD thesis, University of Cape Town, 2014, p. 293: R. Horne, 'Patterns of Ownership and Labour Unrest within the South African Mining Sector' (2015) 40 *Journal for Contemporary History* 25 at 32.

[167] BEE Commission, *Black Economic Empowerment Commission Report* (Johannesburg, Skotaville Press 2001) 1; J. Seekings and N. Nattrass, *Class, Race and Inequality in South Africa* (New Haven and London, Yale University Press, 2005) 343–344.

[168] Ibid., pp. 344 and 345.

[169] Tangri et al., note 159, p. 703.

[170] Seekings et al., note 199, p. 343. M. Mbeki, *Architects of Poverty: Why African Capitalism Needs Changing* (Picado Africa, 2011) 74.

[171] Newell et al., note 162, p. 159.

[172] BEE Commission, note 167.

[173] Department of Trade and Industry, 'Amended Code Series 000: Framework for Measuring Broad-Based Black Economic Empowerment, Statement 000: General Principles and the Generic Scorecard, Issued under section 9 of the Broad-Based Black Economic Empowerment Act of 2003', Government Gazette, 11 October 2013 ['Generic scorecard'].

[174] Ibid.

[175] In the mining industry, for instance (in spite of the implementation of BBBEE), the focus on ownership deals is blamed for the labour unrest that took hold of the industry in 2012. See Horne, note 166, p. 32.

[176] S. Tordo, M. Warner, O. E. Manzano and Y. Anouti, *Local Content Policies in the Oil and Gas Sector* (Washington, DC: The World Bank, 2013), p. 2.

From the petroleum perspective, expecting to achieve transformation through an ownership-based empowerment policy is likely to be even less effective, for reasons we will set out. At the outset, though, a significant obstacle is the capital-intensive character of the petroleum industry. Acquiring ownership with debt is not the preferred scenario, although often used.[177] For the petroleum industry, empowerment through the other pillars seem more promising and effective, given the content of the sectoral Charter, the recognition of community interest and the commitment to skills development.

The Department of Energy's last comprehensive audit of BEE compliance in the petroleum industry was in 2011, and resulted in mixed findings:[178] Only 50 per cent of companies to which the Petroleum Charter is applicable had, at that stage, met the 25 per cent ownership obligation. Compliance with management control was good, but companies were not all fully compliant. Average compliance with supportive culture was rated 'medium'. Capacity building scored low in identifying a talent pool and fast tracking, implementing mentoring programs and overseas placement programs. Scores on employment equity were generally low, and only two companies made notable strides in crude procurement. Companies have performed well in terms of providing finance to HDSAs for ownership deals, and the majority of companies are also doing well in terms of offering HDSA customers terms of credit.[179] The results are thus a mixed bag of successes and failures.

4.2 Upstream Pressures

Whereas progress on local empowerment in the downstream sector has been measured and evaluated already, the same cannot be said for the upstream sector. Petroleum upstream being a relatively small sector in comparison with, for example, extraction of hard minerals, and having been dominated by the state and state-owned enterprises thus far, has limited opportunities to create broader entry for new players. However, the petroleum industry is now on the brink of an expected accelerated development. New offshore gas discoveries create new questions about the way in which the upstream sector can align with a transformative agenda. A careful consideration of the role of industry partnerships, and its potential to catalyse reform in favour of local content, will be needed.

Development of the upstream sector is sure to depend on the availability of appropriate capabilities, experience, expertise and especially resources. Government and industry will have to carefully conceptualise their collaboration in shaping a truly transformed petroleum sector. The aim should be for the proceeds and benefits of this industry to serve the South African populace broadly, to contribute to prosperity and

---

[177] Cargill, note 160, p. 120.
[178] Department of Energy, Republic of South Africa 'Petroleum and Liquid Fuels Charter Final Audit Report', 5 August 2011.
[179] Ibid.

equality of opportunities. The private sector must necessarily be a crucial partner in such endeavours, and the legislative regime must be supportive in the way in which it balances national interests with those of investors. The Empowerment Strategy already forecasted that the BEE initiative will fail without support from the private sector.[180] As such, public–private partnerships (PPPs) are key to the formulation and implementation of BEE programmes in different economic sectors.[181]

4.3 Downstream Struggles

The secrecy of operations in the petroleum industry before 1994 made it impossible to establish, at the outset, to what extent the sector lacked transformation, because of how and to whom licenses to operate were issued.[182] This complicates the measuring of transformation progress.

It was envisaged that, by 2010, HDSAs would hold at least 25 per cent ownership and control of all facets of the petroleum industry.[183] The due date has come and gone. Achievement of the objectives has been mixed. The primary objective of 25 per cent ownership and control has not yet been met,[184] although the issuing of retail licences in the downstream industry grew by 44.7 per cent between 2006 and 2013,[185] while the DoE scored a good 67.8 per cent on the licencing aspect of its economic transformation of the HDSA objective. Makiva et al.[186] attribute this failure to the erroneous assumptions in the liquid fuels policy that issuing licences to HDSAs would achieve the required transformation of ownership patterns.[187]

Assuming that changing licence issuance patterns would achieve the required transformation of ownership patterns was not much more than wishful thinking. Makiva et al.[188] point out that 'licences obtained contributed minimally to the desired results, namely meaningful economic ownership by HDSAs'. They are critical of the lack of government support in enabling entry of new players into the petroleum industry. This support must take the shape of 'funding, infrastructure, land availability and vast critical skills'.[189] They further suggest that the government must provide the financial guarantees to overcome the further hurdle of availability of financing for new entrants into the downstream industry, who struggle to access start-up capital due to lacking lending ability.[190] The problem, however, is that the state does not have sufficient funds to channel to its priority areas. The DoE's budget

[180] Empowerment Strategy, note 27, para. 3.5.7.2.
[181] Ibid.
[182] Makiva et al., note 21, p. 10.
[183] Petroleum Charter, note 18, under the heading *Interpretation*.
[184] Dale et al., note 114, RFLS-7.
[185] Makiva et al., note 21, p. 6.
[186] Ibid., p. 7.
[187] Ibid.
[188] Ibid.
[189] Ibid.
[190] Ibid., pp. 7–10.

Expressing *Local Content through Black Empowerment*

allocation had been falling short for several years.[191] Absent an available funding structure to support the policy objective of ensuring transformation, the empowerment of HDSA will keep lagging behind.[192]

Another important (but hitherto largely ignored) component of transformation is education and skills transfer.[193] New recipients of retail licenses were found to lack basic understanding of business principles, as well as negotiating and accounting skills,[194] a shortage foundational to failure.[195]

In view of such findings, Makiva et al.[196] find that although the downstream industry made great strides in changing license-issuing patterns, the impact on the economic ownership of HDSAs as dealers or company owners was comparably minimal. While progress on license-issuing patterns may thus be said to be sustainable, inadequate input from the state has limited its potential to ensure economic transformation of HDSAs.

5 CONCLUDING RECOMMENDATION

Even in jurisdictions with a less traumatic experience of racialising benefit from resource extraction than that of South Africa, addressing local content concerns in the extractive industries requires a careful balancing act between investors' interests and the interests and concerns of local communities and citizens.[197] It relies on careful policy choices about the rate of exploitation and the socio-economic goals and the inherent weaknesses of particular jurisdictions and economic systems.[198] Also, if local content targets are too low, potential opportunities for linkages might be missed. If they are too high, investment may be discouraged, or the system may perversely incentivise evasion of rules and processes.[199]

South Africa must urgently address the material conditions of people living under the triple curse of poverty, inequality and unemployment. These 'evil triplets'[200] are of great concern, in the extractives sector no less than in any other. Ultimately, for

---

[191] Makiva et al., note 21, p. 8; Department of Energy of the Republic of South Africa – Vote 29, 'Annual Report 2013/2014'; Department of Energy of the Republic of South Africa – Vote 29, 'Annual Report 2014/2015';
Report of the Parliamentary Portfolio Committee (PPC) on Energy during the 4th Parliament, May 2009–March 2014.

[192] Makiva et al., note 21, pp. 7–10; Paelo et al., note 95.

[193] Makiva et al., note 21, p. 8.

[194] A. Paelo, G. Robb, and T. Vilakazi, 'Study on Barriers to Entry in Liquid Fuel Distribution in South Africa', Centre for Competition, Regulation and Economic Development, University of Johannesburg, South Africa, 12 November 2014, pp. 18–19.

[195] Makiva et al., note 21, p. 8.

[196] Ibid., p. 9.

[197] Tordo et al., note 176, pp. 159–60.

[198] Ibid.

[199] Ibid., p. 58.

[200] S. Chiwandamira and T. Majoko, 'The Evil Triplets and the Mining Industry' (2011) 11 *Without Prejudice* 53.

128 Hanri Mostert and Meyer van den Berg

South Africa, transformation of the petroleum industry is important, not only as part of the larger attempt to redress historical transgressions, but also because of the imperative of inclusive economic growth and the need to broaden economic participation.[201] Nevertheless, transformation is a difficult concept to measure, even if extrinsic, tangible benchmarks are identified. Economic, social, political and spiritual factors could influence transformation,[202] and the perception of its success.[203]

In the South African context, BEE constitutes a specific form of local content, as it focuses on concentrating benefits on a marginalized section of the population. The objectives of local content policies are implemented mainly through the government's overarching policy of black economic empowerment to redress past injustices and inequality, which are a legacy of apartheid. This is the definition of local content that has been adopted in this Chapter.

Scholarly assessments of some aspects of transformation in the downstream petroleum industry have indicated varied results, some of which are unsatisfactory.[204] What stands out from these assessments is the critique that the empowerment strategy has been based on untenable assumptions about the links between economic ownership and access to the industry. These assumptions have formed the basis for the legislative framework which painstakingly sets out the parameters for transformation. In view of existing findings, a more thorough and detailed scrutiny of the policy and legislative framework needs to be undertaken by the Government, with suitable adjustments in the measurement and monitoring of transformation progress made.

The range of local content interventions include: participation in the sector, ownership and holding, value addition from the development of local industries, and technology transfer from labour market development through knowledge and technical skills transfer.[205] These overlap to a large extent with the broad-based black economic empowerment initiative of the South African government, although the BEE initiative is more limited in some ways and goes much further in others. On the one hand, BEE is limited in its applicability: it targets a specific, historically marginalised section of the population for benefit. Ironically, this section of the population also forms the majority of the South African demographic. What is even more curious is the general perception – as discussed – that BEE has not yet shown results in improving the economic position of the broad base of society it is targeting. On the other hand, BEE is aimed at a more intense, more immediate scheme of benefit,

---

[201] Paelo et al., note 95.
[202] M. Getu, 'Measuring Transformation. Conceptual Framework and Indicators' (2002) 19 *Transformation: An International Journal of Holistic Mission Studies* (SAGE) 92–93.
[203] Makiva et al., note 21, p. 3.
[204] Discussed in Section 4.3.
[205] Nyakabawo, note 2.

compared to typical local content policies. Perhaps this characteristic focus on instantly gratifying outcomes is the Achilles' heel of the BEE initiative. A more diversified local content approach with longer-term targets for enduring and sustainable socio-economic transformation would bring more tangible benefits and meaningful empowerment into the South African society.

7

Local Content Frameworks for Petroleum Industry Operations in the CEMAC Region: An Evaluation of Their Functionality, Sustainability and Normative Underpinnings

George K. Ndi

1 INTRODUCTION

The main objective of this chapter is to appraise the role, functionality and effectiveness of local content requirements (LCRs) in upstream petroleum industry operations in the Central African Economic and Monetary Community (CEMAC) region. It demonstrates how the lack of tailored and context-specific elaboration of LCRs may stifle the sustainable development outcomes of LCRs. Drawing examples from LCRs in the CEMAC region, the chapter discusses the need for greater emphasis on functionality, sustainability and specificity in order to enable effective monitoring and enforcement of LCRs.

The CEMAC region, also known as *Communauté Économique et Monétaire de l'Afrique Centrale*, is a regional economic, customs and monetary union comprising six member states: Cameroon, Central African Republic, Chad, Congo, Gabon and Equatorial Guinea. CEMAC's historical origins date back to the Treaty of Brazzaville of 1964 which established the Union Douanière et Éconmique de l'Afrique Centrale (UDEAC), laying the foundations for a free-trade policy based on customs union and a common tariffs policy.[1] CEMAC itself is currently a subset of the larger Economic Community of Central African States (*Communauté Économique des États de l'Afrique Centrale* or ECCAS). Four more countries (Angola, Burundi, Democratic Republic of Congo and São Tomé and Prìncipe) joined the six member states to form ECCAS.[2] CEMAC's own mission focuses on closer economic integration between member states through the establishment of a common market, a common monetary policy based on the platform of a common currency (the CFA Franc) and the harmonisation of regional commercial and industrial policy.[3] The ultimate goal of

---

[1] N. Jua, 'UDEAC: Dream, Reality or the Making of Subimperial States' (1986) 21 *Africa Spectrum* 211.
[2] D. Avom and M. Njikam, 'Market Integration in the ECCAS Sub-Region' in M. Ncube, I. Faye and A. Verdier-Chouchane (eds.), *Regional Integration and Trade in Africa* (New York: Springer, 2015), pp. 71–90.
[3] M. Bongyu, 'The Economic and Monetary Community of Central Africa (CEMAC) and the Decline of Sovereignty' (2009) 44 *Journal of Asian and African Studies* 389.

CEMAC, ECCAS and the AU is undoubtedly to promote economic integration in the context of the Global South, economic cooperation with the Global North (for example, through the Global South–Global North platform the ACP–EU Cotonou Agreement[4]), thus ultimately facilitating the integration of these regional hubs into the global economy.[5]

With the exception of the Central African Republic which is mainly a mineral producer, the other five members of CEMAC are producers and net exporters of crude oil. With a combined crude oil output amounting to just less than one million bpd, CEMAC's output remains relatively modest by international standards.[6] Apart from landlocked Chad, most of the region's oil production is located offshore in the Gulf of Guinea where oil-producing Cameroon, Congo, Gabon and Equatorial Guinea all share common maritime boundaries. Although there have been significant discoveries of offshore natural gas deposits in the region, these deposits remain largely undeveloped due to the twin constraints of development costs and the adverse logistics of accessing energy markets in developed countries (the 'Global North') – hence the current focus on strategies for developing regional markets for the domestic consumption of natural gas.[7] Notwithstanding the historic success of the landmark Chad–Cameroon pipeline project which has opened access to global markets for Chadian oil production, the CEMAC region as a whole remains a relatively underdeveloped oil province. CEMAC may thus be aptly described in prospecting terms as a 'frontier or emerging region' with still-to-be-explored acreage and a great deal of undeveloped potential. It is in this context that LCRs may be perceived as having a potentially critical role to play in promoting and maximising the value-add chain of upstream petroleum industry operations for local economies, both at the national and regional level.

This chapter embarks on a critical enquiry as to whether LCRs in the CEMAC region can provide an effective tool for enabling local economies to generate value-add economic benefits, beyond direct fiscal and monetary benefits from oil production. The author argues that the promotion of effective LCRs in the CEMAC region's oil industry requires judiciously designed normative frameworks with particular attention paid to their functionality, contribution to sustainable economic development and normative status. LCR frameworks ought to be seen and conceived as critical policy aspects of the petroleum industry in their own right, rather than simply being complementary 'add-ons' to contractual or licensing stipulations

---

[4] See further, the African Caribbean Pacific (ACP)–EU Cotonou Agreement for International Cooperation and Development of 23 June 2000.

[5] A. Ndedi, 'Roadmap for Regional Integration within the Central African Economic and Monetary Community (CEMAC) under the NEPAD Framework' (2015). https://papers.ssrn.com/sol3/papers .cfm?abstract_id=2551739 (accessed on 5 July 2019).

[6] See generally, A. Omolade, 'Crude Oil Price Shocks and Macroeconomic Performance in Africa's Oil-Producing Countries' (2019) 7 *Cogent Economics and Finance* 1.

[7] M. Fulwood, 'Opportunities for Gas in Sub-Saharan Africa', Oxford Institute for Energy Studies, University of Oxford, January 2019, pp. 13–15.

vis-à-vis host state entitlements such as fiscal gains from oil production (acreage fees, royalties, taxation, rentals, etc.), or host state share of oil production. LCR frameworks should, a priori, serve a normative function in facilitating the efficient implementation and enforcement of value chain benefits to the CEMAC region vis-à-vis their contribution to economic and industrial development, while serving as auxiliary platforms for facilitating the attainment of wider policy goals such as distributive justice, social inclusion and gender quality, alongside a wider human rights agenda. They could, and should, also provide an impetus for accelerating the pace of regional economic and social integration.

A perhaps more distant but nonetheless looming challenge, both for the world energy industry and CEMAC, is the task of creating strategic policy linkages between LCR frameworks and environmental sustainability aspirations in light of the increasing currency (and urgency) of the global climate change agenda. Arguably, normative LCR frameworks could be strategically positioned to play an effective contributory role to policies aimed at addressing the problems of environmentally sustainable development and climate change. For example, LCR policies can be used as a platform for the local sourcing of 'green' products for upstream petroleum operations. Normative LCR policies could also serve as platforms for the construction of joint venture projects between Global North and Global South companies for the development of green energy sources in Global South economies such as the CEMAC region. Such innovative uses of LCR frameworks need not be limited to private sector partnerships. It is axiomatically the case that governments which are committed to a 'green' agenda are better placed to promote such an agenda within the framework of equity or non-equity participation in local petroleum industry agreements through partnership agreements with international oil companies in the form of joint ventures, production sharing or service agreement.

Meaningful state participation in oil industry operation can lead to effective monitoring and implementation of LCR policies, which in turn can lead to the prevention of environmental malpractices by private petroleum operators. An example of such malpractices is the growing practice of 'green laundering' or 'green-washing' – that is, the passing-off or misrepresentation of essentially 'brown' or polluting petroleum assets or practices through their deceitful inclusion in an operator's green agenda, in other words, as operations which comply with local environmental protection requirements. The Global South, including countries of the CEMAC region, have a valued role to play in addressing the phenomenon of climate change. It could be further argued that the traditional, but nonetheless emblematic, LCR model of state participation in upstream petroleum operation provides the prospect for Global South economies to develop a strategic vision aimed at proactively exerting a positive regulatory influence through the effective monitoring and implementation of genuinely green policies in their local oil industries.

Local Content Frameworks in the CEMAC Region 133

This chapter is divided into four sections. After this introduction, Section 2 examines the scope and key objectives of local content policies in petroleum industry operations in the CEMAC region, alongside an overview of country specific LCR frameworks. Section 3 discusses the functionality of petroleum industry LCRs in CEMAC countries and assesses their potential to contribute to the economic development of the region. Section 4 identifies some of the key attributes and prerequisites for a new generation of local content frameworks for oil industry operations in the CEMAC region. Section 5 concludes the chapter with final reflections and recommendations.

2 SCOPE AND OBJECTIVES OF LCRS IN THE CEMAC REGION

As earlier discussed in Chapter 1 of this book, petroleum industry LCR frameworks in general tend to exhibit a typical focus on the following policy areas: the employment of nationals; effective sourcing of the domestic market, including the local procurement of goods and services from indigenous companies; infrastructure development; capacity building; skills acquisition; and local business development, as well as expansion of endogenous technological capabilities. This section evaluates how LCRs have been conceptualized in the national petroleum industries of the CEMAC region.

The specific focus of LCR frameworks in CEMAC countries has been on traditional areas such as enhancing capacity building, skills development, local employment and facilitating national participation in upstream exploration and production activities.[8] One of the major flaws in the design of country-specific LCR frameworks in CEMAC resides in the fact that the model retains a predominantly administrative and bureaucratic approach. In practice, the CEMAC models tend to be technically inefficient with very limited normative underpinnings in their practices and enforcement procedures. These regional models rely primarily on administrative sanctions, in the form of financial penalties, for breaches of LCR obligations – an approach susceptible to exploitation through corrupt practices and other rent-seeking behaviours. There is thus a need for a shift away from administrative enforcement towards the adoption of adjudicatory regimes in the enforcement of LCR – this, with a view to promoting greater accountability and transparency. Better still, LCR regimes in the region could focus more on collaborative partnerships with petroleum industry operators in actualising LCR programmes, as opposed to the current emphasis placed by governments in the region on the 'command-and-control' model.

---

[8]   B. Oyewole, 'Overview of Local Content Regulatory Frameworks in Selected ECCAS Countries' in *UNCTAD: Strengthening Development Linkages from the Mineral Resources Sector in Central Africa* (May 2018), pp. 1–2. See also D. Olawuyi, *Extractives Industry Law in Africa* (Switzerland: Springer Nature Switzerland, 2018) pp. 118–21, 260–4 and 303–8.

134 George K. Ndi

2.1 Republic of Cameroon

A comprehensive definition of 'local content' is included in Section 3 of Law No. 2012/006 implementing the Gas Code.[9] This provision defines local content as 'all activities relating to local capacity-building, use of local human and material resources, technology transfer, use of local industrial and service companies, and the creation of measurable value added for the local economy'.[10] Furthermore, Section 2 of the law specifies that one of its purposes is to create an enabling environment for the use of local human, material and industrial resources in every gas resources enhancement project.[11] In addition to the petroleum code and the gas code, the LCR frameworks are also set out in Law No. 99/013 of 22 December 1999, instituting the Petroleum Code (implemented by Decree No. 2000/465/176 of 30 July 2000).[12]

Sections 76 and 77 of the Petroleum Code require operators, contractors and subcontractors to give preference to local enterprises and personnel in petroleum operations, including in construction activities, procurement and other services.[13] On closer examination, however, the language used in these sections appears to be rather generic and vague, with no timelines and benchmarks to facilitate effective monitoring and enforcement. Section 12,[14] on the other hand, sets out in detail the proposed content of any petroleum contract between the State and contractors. Among its requirements is the inclusion in the petroleum contract of 'obligations relating to the training and employment of Cameroonian human resources'.[15] It is also worth noting in this respect that subsection (k) of section 12 makes provision for local participation in petroleum operations via the platform of State participation or through some other entity duly authorised by the State in a joint venture with the contractor.[16]

Comprehensive LCR provisions are included in the Model Petroleum Production-Sharing Contract, section 18[17] of which reinforces the requirement for compliance with the obligation for granting preferences to nationals and local enterprises in the sourcing of staff and services. More intriguing is section 19, which requires contractors to make available to the State party an annual budget for the training of personnel.[18] Notwithstanding the assurances provided in section 19(1) that the State party will furnish the contractor with reasonable accounting evidence in the execution of the training budget,[19] there is still a lingering question

---

[9] The Gas Code (Law no. 2012/006 of April 19, 2012), section 3.
[10] Ibid.
[11] Ibid., section 2.
[12] Petroleum Code (Law no. 99/013 of December 22, 1999).
[13] Ibid., sections 76 and 77.
[14] Ibid., section 12.
[15] Ibid., section 12(l).
[16] Ibid., section 12(k).
[17] Société Nationale des Hydrocarbures (SNH), Cameroon's Model Oil and Gas PSC, section 18.
[18] Ibid., section 19.
[19] Ibid., section 19(1).

Local Content Frameworks in the CEMAC Region 135

as to whether the contractors is not the best placed party to provide such training. The provision[20] also raises ethical questions as to the management of such a training budget, particularly when considered against the background of the endemic corruption for which the country has become notorious internationally.

LCR policies in the Cameroonian context extend to natural gas production and distribution. The Gas Code contains detailed provision on local content, with section 62 providing that the development of natural gas resources must be accompanied by a local content component specifying the benefits of the gas project to national economic, social, industrial, and technological development.[21] Section 63(1) identifies two aspects to local content: a human resources aspect and a local enterprises and industrial development aspect.[22] Section 63(2) builds on this obligation by further identifying illustrative examples such as vocational and technical training for nationals, together with the prioritisation of local enterprises in the sourcing of goods and services.[23]

Viewed as a whole, the LCR frameworks for the petroleum and natural gas industries in Cameroon lack inventiveness in that they retain all the standard features of traditional legal transplants (i.e. wholescale mimicry of provisions from mature legal regimes such as Canada), and hence are ill-adapted to the specific local environment in which they are meant to be implemented. The Cameroonian approach to petroleum industry LCRs is more reminiscent of a rigid and inflexible 'top-down' command-and-control model – as opposed to a flexible and collaborative framework within which the contractor and the State party can work effectively together to ensure clearly defined, measurable and achievable localisation objectives, with a better prospect of ensuring successful outcomes. There is also some degree of misalignment of objectives, with the seeming prioritisation of revenue generation (through training budget contributions from the contractor) over the more substantive policy aspects of the local content agenda. The absence of an institutional framework, in the form of an enforcement agency such as a national local content agency, remains a debilitating handicap for the enforcement process.

2.2 *Chad*

Of all the countries in the CEMAC region, Chad is unique in not having promulgated specific LCR legislation for the petroleum industry. In the absence of sector-specific LCR frameworks, the country relies on its national development plan (NDP)[24] alongside its poverty reduction strategy[25] to promote skills acquisition and

[20] Ibid., section 18.
[21] The Gas Code, note 9, section 62.
[22] Ibid., section 63(1).
[23] Ibid., section 63(2).
[24] National Legislative Bodies / National Authorities, 'Chad: Plan National de Développement (PND) 2017–2021', August 2017.
[25] International Monetary Fund, 'Chad: Poverty Reduction Strategy Paper', IMF Country Report No. 03/209, July 2003.

local employment in its petroleum industry.[26] The country has also relied on petroleum agreements with international oil companies (IOCs) to embed LCR provisions, particularly in contracts for the construction of the Chad–Cameroon pipeline project which generated employment opportunities for over 13,000 Chadian and Cameroonian employees as well as USD680 million in procurement contracts for local enterprises.[27] Chad has fared relatively well in comparison to other countries in the region in terms of progress with its LCR strategy, particularly in the area of skills acquisition and local employment. This is due in part to the significant involvement of the World Bank Group in the financing the development of the Chadian oil industry. A specific example of linkages and value-chain creation promoted by the World Bank's International Finance Corporation is the *Small and Medium Enterprises Initiative* based mainly in the petroleum production area of southern Chad. The initiative, set up as part of the petroleum industry project, has led to the establishment of FINADEV, the first accredited commercial micro-finance institution in Chad.[28] Other technical assistance projects launched as part of the *Small and Medium Enterprises Initiative* include the promotion of agribusiness which has supported the training of over 400 local people and resulted in seven major supply contracts for locally produced food and agricultural products to the petroleum industry, with ExxonMobil as the main buyer.[29]

These gains, however, remain modest by international standards.[30] The NDP, which requires both backward and forward linkages between the petroleum sector and other sectors of the economy, has been a relative success by regional standards with first the national enterprise centre, and now the Chamber of Commerce, assisting and preparing local enterprises in bidding for contracts and participating in petroleum industry operations. One of the remarkable features of the Chadian LCR regime is effective monitoring with up-to-date statistics collated on local enterprises participation in supply contracts for goods and services, as well as in exploration and production licensing through the electronic bidding process. According to the World Bank's International Finance Corporation, the electronic bidding process has greatly improved the participation of local Chadian enterprises in the provision of petroleum industry services.[31] A standard feature of the Chadian regime has been the embedding of local content policies within the strategic framework of corporate social responsibility programmes of IOCs operating in the country. This has enabled the country to attain local content outcomes comparable

---

[26] Oyewole, note 8, p. 6.
[27] See further, International Finance Corporation, 'Chad-Cameroon Pipeline Project: Project Overview' (2012, World Bank Group).
[28] Ibid.
[29] Ibid.
[30] E. Ntsimi, 'The Chad-Cameroon Oil Development and Pipeline Project: A Model for Natural Resource Development in Africa' (2011) 15 *Centre for Energy, Petroleum, and Mineral and Policy Annual Review* 9.
[31] Oyewole, note 8, p. 6.

Local Content Frameworks in the CEMAC Region

to those in Angola and Nigeria, a quite remarkable achievement in view of the fact that Chad has no dedicated local content legislation for the petroleum industry.[32]

The relative success of the Chadian LCR regime is attributable to a number of factors. From a strategy viewpoint, the country had adopted a very focused policy perspective which relies less on multiple legislative sources, but rather draws its main strength from a well-established and relatively robust institutional framework (currently the Chadian Chamber of Commerce). From a geographical perspective, a favourable onshore industry location (which does not require the specific technical skills and demands of an offshore marine environment) provides better avenues and opportunities for broadly based local participation initiatives. Last but not least, when viewed from a process perspective, the implementation of electronic bidding procedures has facilitated effective monitoring of local content, hence the relative success of local enterprise participation in the petroleum industry in Chad.

2.3 Central African Republic (CAR)

Although not an oil producer, CAR nonetheless has significant deposits of minerals such as diamonds, and thus deserves our brief discussion in light of the importance of developing an effective LCR framework for the country's mineral industry. The main legislation regulating mining activity in the country is the Mining Code (Law No.09–005) of 29 April 2009,[33] together with a regulatory instrument in the form of Decree No.09–125 on the application of the Mining Code.[34] The legal framework regulating mining activities in CAR does not contain a specific definition of 'local content' as such, with the focus being on the formation of artisanal cooperatives. Membership of an artisanal cooperative confers on nationals the status of eligibility to apply for an artisanal mining licence. The regulatory entity for the mining sector is the Ministry of Mines, Energy and Water. Various CAR governments have to date failed to capitalise on a readily available pool of semi-skilled artisanal miners whose basic mining skills, if properly harnessed, could provide the springboard for a successful home-grown mining industry.[35] Unlike the petroleum industry in most CEMAC countries with their offshore locations (thus limiting accessibility), the mining industry in CAR has been accessible to indigenes who, over generations, have developed the basic skills required for employment in the industry.[36] The

---

[32] F. Mushemeza and J. Okiira, 'Local Content Frameworks in the African Oil and Gas Sector: Lessons from Angola and Chad' ACODE Policy Research Series No. 72, April 2016.

[33] Mining Code (Law No.09–005) of 29 April 2009.

[34] Decree No.09–125.

[35] A. Richiello, 'Central African Republic: great potential and massive challenges in the heart of the continent', 19 November 2018, https://aspeniaonline.it/central-african-republic-great-potential-and-massive-challenges-in-the-heart-of-the-continent/.

[36] G. Lwanda, 'Central African Republic: Boosting the Potential of Artisanal Diamond Mining', 18 July 2016, www.africa.undp.org/content/rba/en/home/blog/2016/7/Central-African-Republic-Boosting-the-potential-of-artisanal-diamond-mining.html.

138   *George K. Ndi*

mining industry in CAR is, in effect, more readily amenable to the embedding of LCR policies than the petroleum industries in other CEMAC countries, where locals' unfamiliarity with the marine environment can be an obstacle to involvement in the industry. The diamond and gold mining industries in CAR present very good opportunities for the design and implementation of effective LCR frameworks for promoting skills acquisition and the employment of nationals. The various governments have, so far, not been able to make effective use of this potential, partly due to recurrent political instability in the country, caused by resource conflict. However, the prospect for collaborative partnerships between the State and foreign mining operators remains an enduring possibility, which in turn could lead to the development of effective LCR policies for the mining industry in CAR.

2.4 *Republic of Congo*

Compared to other CEMAC countries, there is far less information about the petroleum industry in the Republic of Congo, although its annual crude oil production accounts for 85 per cent of exports and 70 per cent of GDP.[37] This dearth of information is due in part to the lack of transparency in a region where oil industry matters are still considered to be a closely guarded state secret, and in part to corrupt practices which fuel the petroleum industry in the region.[38] Congo has a history of resource conflict centred on the petroleum industry, but it would seem that the lessons of the past have not been learnt as management of the industry remains as opaque as it has ever been.

The country has recently embarked on an economic diversification programme as part of its National Development Plan (NDP) for the period 2017–2021, the aim of which is to reduce Congo's economic overdependence on the oil sector.[39] Its LCR strategy will undoubtedly be expected to play a pivotal role in the plan's actualisation. A new Hydrocarbons Code No. 2016–2 promulgated on 12 October 2016 contains a number of provisions dedicated to the promotion of local content.[40] Noteworthy are Articles 139–147 which require, *inter alia*, the prioritisation of local human and material resources along the hydrocarbons value chain; capacity building through training of nationals, skills acquisition and technology transfer; and promoting the creation of measurable benefits to the wider national economy along the value added chain.

However, it is far from clear how this last aspiration is to be achieved. It is worth noting that the Petroleum Code[41] does not contain any LCR quotas or annual targets.

---

[37] Oyewole, note 8, p. 2.
[38] K. Sharife and P. Engels, 'The Unlikely Partnership that Unlocked Congo's Crude', 7 September 2018, www.occrp.org/en/investigations/8557-the-bribery-network-that-unlocked-congo-s-crude.
[39] Oyewole, note 8, p. 6.
[40] Ibid.
[41] Law n°24–94 (Petroleum Code of Republic of Congo) of 23 August 1994.

Local Content Frameworks in the CEMAC Region   139

Exploration and production permits, on the other hand, tend to focus more on minimum monetary contributions to training budgets (by IOC operators) for skills acquisition with a view to facilitating the employment of nationals. At the same time, IOC operators in the country are required to set up training programmes for nationals, a provision that appears to be at odds with the requirement for contribution to a training budget operated by the government. As is the case with Cameroon, the LCR framework in Congo appears to prioritise revenue generation over authentic local content objectives. In terms of an overall assessment, the success rate of the Congolese LCR policy has been rather modest (even by regional standards), although it is still a developing model. Reforms of the LCR policies in the country's petroleum sector are still ongoing, guided by the aspirations of the National Development Plan.[42]

2.5 *Gabon*

In Gabon, substantive LCR policies are embedded in a mix of petroleum codes (buttressed by a new Hydrocarbons Law promulgated on 15 September 2014[43]), and labour legislation, most notably the Labour Law No. 39/93 of 15 February 1994.[44] The emphasis in legislation has been on local employment as well as the use of local enterprises in subcontracts for downstream petroleum operations. Upstream ventures typically take the form of a *convention d'établissement* (traditional concession agreement) or a production-sharing contract (PSC). Both forms require the contractor to comply with LCR obligations. Under the new Employment and Labour Law of 2019, priority in the sourcing of local goods and services is to be given to subcontractors employing at least 80 per cent Gabonese nationals.[45] This policy places an emphasis on localisation in the narrow sense of national origin (as opposed to a regionalised approach in line with the ethos of an integrated CEMAC common market). The frequency of strikes (led by Gabonese trade unions) protesting the worsening unemployment situation in countries, can correctly be interpreted as evidence of the failure of petroleum industry LCR frameworks to adequately integrate local job seekers into the oil industry. As with all the other CEMAC countries, the local business environment in Gabon remains underdeveloped, and therefore unconducive to the propagation of effective local content policies and strategies.[46] Despite its oil wealth, Gabon's economy remains one of the weakest in sub-Saharan Africa and the country is subject to the International Monetary Fund's Extended Fund Facility.[47]

[42] Oyewole, note 8.
[43] Hydrocarbon Code, Law n°002/2019 dated 16 July 2019; the previous Hydrocarbon Code, Law n°011/2014 dated 28 August 2014.
[44] Labour Law No. 39/93 of 15 February 1994.
[45] Oyewole, note 8, p. 9.
[46] Oyewole, note 8.
[47] International Monetary Fund, Country Report n°19/17 (Gabon), January 2019; see also I. Gill and K. Karakülah, 'Sounding the Alarm on Africa's Debt' *Future Development, Brookings*, 6 April 2018, pp. 1–3.

140 *George K. Ndi*

The country currently ranks at Number 169 in the 'Ease of Doing Business Index'.[48] Industrialisation is weak and the economy is sustained mainly by the export of raw materials, mainly crude oil and timber, with no large-scale industrial projects which could provide linkages to the oil economy and thus ensure a sustainable economic strategy.[49] The institutional framework for LCR remains weak – with LCR monitoring and enforcement placed under the remit of the State oil company and various ministries, including the petroleum ministry and the labour ministry. The ultimate result is poor coordination in the absence of a dedicated LCR national agency.

2.6 *Equatorial Guinea*

Equatorial Guinea is the latest newcomer to the petroleum industry in the CEMAC region with the onset of commercial production in 1995.[50] The country sought from the start to maximise the benefits of oil production beyond traditional revenue generation by adopting policies aimed at promoting the economic development of the country as a whole. Of all the CEMAC countries, it boasts the most extensive LCR frameworks and policies, albeit with limited success on the ground. The earliest legal instrument regulating petroleum operation in the country (Ministerial Order 1/2014) stipulates the inclusion of local content provisions in all petroleum agreements. It aims to promote local employment, skills development and local industry participation in oil activities.[51] Other noteworthy legislation in the context of the case study, includes earlier instruments such as Hydrocarbons Law No. 8/2006, which contains fairly detailed stipulations on local content, including capacity building through the establishment of a national Hydrocarbons Technological Institute.[52] The LCR obligations in this legislation extend to local enterprise participation;[53] activities aimed at promoting the socio-economic development of the country;[54] the sourcing of local goods, services and local employment;[55] contribution towards training and employment of locals;[56] and the funding of projects by the contractor aimed at promoting public welfare.[57] These provisions are further complemented and reinforced by Articles 156 and 157 of the Petroleum Regulations of 20 June 2013.[58]

[48] The World Bank, 'Ease of Doing Business Index', https://data.worldbank.org/indicator/IC.BUS .EASE.XQ. Data cited up-to-date as of 9 November 2019.

[49] L. Söderling, 'After the Oil: Challenges Ahead in Gabon' (2006) 15 *Journal of African Economies* 117.

[50] J.G. Frynas, 'The Oil Boom in Equatorial Guinea' (2004) 103 *African Affairs* 527 at 528.

[51] Oyewole, note 8, p. 7.

[52] Hydrocarbons Law No. 8/2006 of 3 November 2006, Article 88.

[53] Ibid., Article 89.

[54] Ibid., Article 90.

[55] Ibid., Article 91.

[56] Ibid., Article 92.

[57] Ibid., Article 93.

[58] Ministerial Order Number 4/2013, dated, June 20, by which approves and promulgates the Regulations on Petroleum Operations, in application of the Hydrocarbons Law of Equatorial Guinea, Number 8/2006, dated November 3.

Equatorial Guinea has arguably been relatively robust in the CEMAC region in its reaction to perceived breaches of LCR obligations by international operators. International service companies operating in the country's oil and gas industry, such as Schlumberger, Subsea 7 and FMC, have all, in the past, been threatened with outright bans and revocation of their operating licences on account of their perceived non-compliance with local content obligations.[59] Following pressure from the country's authorities, international oil giant Exxon Mobil was also forced to cancel its contracts with CHC Helicopters with the latter accused of breaching local content regulations.[60] In a follow-up measure to this action, in July 2018 the authorities ordered all companies operating in the country's petroleum sector to cancel all contracts with CHC Helicopters due to non-compliance with LCR measures, while giving other companies sixty days to review their subcontracting practices with a view to ensuring full compliance, or face a similar sanction.[61]

This review of country-specific legal frameworks for embedding local content policies in petroleum industry operations reveals an unquestionable potential for such policies to contribute to the economic development of the region. But this potential needs to be fully activated before any meaningful progress can be made. It is noteworthy that, to date, lauded successes in the region on LCRs are still chiefly measured by the yardstick of their potential to achieve stated goals, rather than by their actual achievements; for example, through commonly used pronouncements such as 'these investments are expected to contribute to enhancing domestic backward and forward linkages between the oil and gas sectors and [other] economic sectors, thereby increasing the benefits of the sector to the country'.[62] Highlighted successes also include what are by global industry standards extremely modest indicators, for example, an increase from two to twenty in the number of nationals receiving training annually as part of the skills development project in Equatorial Guinea,[63] or the employment of forty-two graduates by Marathon Oil in the same country over a four-year period from 2010 to 2014.[64] What these modest achievements demonstrate is the absence of effective legal and institutional mechanisms, together with an enabling economic environment, on which to anchor the potential gains of local content policies. Despite the prevalence of LCR frameworks in the CEMAC region, employment opportunities for nationals in the petroleum sector remains limited; local enterprise development

---

[59] See further, 'E. Guinea Minister Orders Operators to Cut Ties with Subsea 7', 22 November 2018, www.offshoreenergytoday.com/e-guinea-minister-orders-operators-to-cut-ties-with-subsea-7/.

[60] See further 'CHC Contracts Cancelled over 'Local Employment' Row', 13 February 2019, www.africanaerospace.aero/chc-contracts-cancelled-over-local-employment-row.html.

[61] Reuters, 'Equatorial Guinea Targets CHC Helicopter in Compliance Crackdown', 18 July 2018, www.reuters.com/article/equatorial-chc-helicopter/equatorial-guinea-targets-chc-helicopter-in-compliance-crackdown-idUSL8N1UF1EC.

[62] Oyewole, note 8, p. 6.

[63] Ibid., p. 8.

[64] Ibid.

142 *George K. Ndi*

remains modest, as evidenced by the exponential growth of the informal economic sector; and the economies of the region remain mired in debt dependency.[65] It is worth noting that of the six member states of CEMAC, Cameroon, Chad, the Central African Republic and Congo all form part of the World Bank's Heavily Indebted Poor Country (HIPC) Initiative.[66]

On reflection, the emphasis placed in LCR frameworks on local employment, local enterprise participation and sustainable development seems unachievable in the long term when viewed against the background of the problem of energy insufficiency and chronic power outages which continue to plague the CEMAC region. And yet this is an often-overlooked aspect when discussing the link between LCRs and sustainable development.[67] Perhaps one way of addressing this problem could be to refocus attention in LCR frameworks on linkages and joint ventures between local enterprises and foreign firms specifically aimed at developing critical infrastructure such as electricity provision, without which the quest for sustainable development will remain illusory. In the section which follows, some of the main institutional and legal obstacles to the achievement of desired local content outcomes in the CEMAC region will be examined.

TABLE 7.1 *Survey of LCR legislation and requirements in the CEMAC region*

Country and Applicable Legislation	Definition of Local	Analysis/Comments
Cameroon Law No. 99/013 of 22 December 1999 instituting the Petroleum Code (sections 76–77). Law No. 2012/006 implementing the Gas Code (Section 3).	All activities relating to local capacity-building, use of local human and material resources, technology transfer, use of local industrial and service companies, and the creation of measurable value added for the local economy.	No dedicated local content regulation. No autonomous local content agency. Regulatory authority is vested in the national oil company (SNH). Definition of 'local' equates to domestic or national, rather than regional (CEMAC). No evidence of progress in achieving LCR outcomes as outcomes are not published.

---

[65] Gill and Karakülah, note 47.

[66] See further, The World Bank, 'Heavily Indebted Poor Country (HIPC) Initiative', 11 January 2018, www.worldbank.org/en/topic/debt/brief/hipc.

[67] See generally, D. Farquharson, P. Jaramillo and C. Samaras, 'Sustainability Implications of Electricity Outages in Sub-Saharan Africa' (2018) 1 *Nature Sustainability* 597.

Local Content Frameworks in the CEMAC Region 143

TABLE 7.1 *(continued)*

Country and Applicable Legislation	Definition of Local	Analysis/Comments
Chad The Oil Revenue Management Law (Law001/PR/99 (as modified by Law002/PR/06); Ordinance No.001/PR/2010 establishing the Model Production Sharing Contract; Decree No.796/PR/PM/ MPE/2010 implementing the Petroleum Law	Local content is broadly defined as comprising of policies promoting local employment, skills development and local enterprise participation.	No dedicated local content regulations. Current LCR obligations are complemented by the National Development Plan, and the Poverty Reduction Strategy. No dedicated local content agency. Regulatory authority vested in the enterprise centre and the Chamber of Commerce. Has made relative progress in the implementation of local content policies, partly due to the part played by the IFC's Small and Medium Enterprise Initiative.
Central African Republic Mining Code (Law No.09–005) of 29 April 2009	No specific definition of local content in legislation. The policy focus has been on the formation of local cooperatives to promote artisanal mining with priority given to the licensing of nationals who are registered members of a cooperative.	No petroleum industry. No autonomous local content agency. Regulatory authority is vested in the Ministry of Mines, Energy and Water Resources Mining sector is dominated by artisanal mining. Resource conflict is rife.
Equatorial Guinea Hydrocarbons Law No. 8/2006 Petroleum Regulations of 20 June 2013 (Articles 156–157) Ministerial Order 1/2014 of 2014.	Capacity building through the establishment of the National Hydrocarbons Technological Institute, local enterprise participation, sourcing of local goods and services, training and employment of nationals, and funding of CSR projects.	The only country in the region to have adopted bespoke local content regulations in the form of ministerial Order 1/2014. No autonomous local content agency. Regulatory authority is vested in the Ministry of Petroleum. Has made the most progress towards institutional development, most notably in the form of the National Hydrocarbons

(continued)

144 George K. Ndi

TABLE 7.1 *(continued)*

Country and Applicable Legislation	Definition of Local	Analysis/Comments
		Technological Institute for the training of nationals. Adopts a fairly robust approach to enforcement of local content obligations, with administrative sanction in tow. Relative progress has been made, with some data published on the employment of nationals, but achievements remain modest.
Republic of Gabon Hydrocarbons Law of 15 September 2014. Employment and Labour Law of 2019	Emphasis is placed on the use of local enterprises in subcontracts for the downstream petroleum subsector. Under the Employment and Labour Law, priority in the sourcing of local goods and services is to be given to subcontractors employing at least 80% Gabonese nationals.	No dedicated LCR framework. No autonomous local content agency, with regulatory authority vested in the national oil company (SNHG). No real evidence of progress made, as measurable data such as progress on employment of nationals is not published.
Republic of Congo Hydrocarbons Code No. 2016–2 of 2016, Articles 139–147.	The prioritisation of local human and material resources along the hydrocarbons value chain; capacity building through training of nationals, skills acquisition and technology transfer; and promoting the creation of measurable benefits to the wider national economy along the entire value chain.	No dedicated local content regulations. No autonomous local content agency, with regulatory author vested in the national oil company (SNPC). Reference is made to measurable benefits in relevant legislation, but there is no evidence or data to support its implementation in practice. There is no transparency in the reporting in local content outcomes. The petroleum industry in Congo is shrouded in secrecy, against a historic background of resource conflict.

3 FUNCTIONALITY, NORMATIVE STATUS AND CONTRIBUTION TO SUSTAINABLE ECONOMIC DEVELOPMENT: AN OVERALL APPRAISAL OF CEMAC'S LCR FRAMEWORKS FOR PETROLEUM INDUSTRY OPERATIONS

The results of LCR policies in the relative short history of petroleum industry operations in the CEMAC have been variable and limited, with some successes registered in Chad and Equatorial Guinea. However, the overall assessment has been largely negative. Undeveloped or underdeveloped value chains, poor market linkages and primitive infrastructure all serve as evidentiary indicators of the failure of LCR policies in the region to make meaningful contributions to the establishment of sustainable development strategies. The petroleum industries in CEMAC serve the traditional function of income generation, with LCR frameworks which exhibit very limited conceptual or normative underpinnings. Rather, they are simply the product of legal plantation, poorly designed and ill adapted to the specific character of the petroleum industry environment of CEMAC with its local conditions and cultural realities. A fundamental misalignment in LCR policies is evidenced by the emphasis placed on administrative enforcement, with financial penalties (as in Cameroon) or cancellation of licence rights followed by the withdrawal of exploration and production rights (as in Equatorial Guinea) serving as ultimate sanctions for breach of LCR obligations by the contractor.[68] The Cameroonian approach, with its bureaucratic approach to enforcement, ultimately reduces the LCR policy to an income-generation model while increasing the opportunity for rent-seeking or corrupt practices.[69] The Equatorial Guinean approach, extreme as it may be, hardly serves as a deterrent against material breaches of LCR obligation – as evidenced by the many recorded instances of non-compliance by operating companies.[70] From a conceptual viewpoint, the question therefore arises as to whether the approach itself is not self-defeating – for it is axiomatically the case that cancellation of a specific petroleum project, in effect, terminates the LCR programme contained therein. Such extreme measures, arguably, amount to a case of throwing out the baby with the bath water.

When measured on the scale of the level of attainability, from the basic to most difficult, local content aspirations in the CEMAC region would range from employment opportunities for locals as the most basic, and then progress on to sourcing of local goods and services; technology transfer; effective participation of local enterprises in exploration and production; environmental protection; and ultimately to effective linkages between the petroleum sector and the wider economy in promoting a sustainable development model for the region as a whole.

---

[68]   Reuters, note 61.

[69]   B. Gauthier and A. Zeufack, 'Governance and Oil Revenues in Cameroon', *Research Paper 38, Oxford Centre for the Analysis of Resource Rich Economies*, 2009, pp. 26–29; see also, *Oil and Gas in Africa: Joint Study by the African Development Bank and the African Union* (2009, Oxford University Press), pp. 105–9.

[70]   Farquharson et al., note 67.

146   *George K. Ndi*

However, a review of available literature would seem to indicate a lack of success even at the most basic level, with widespread dissatisfaction among the populations of the region on account of the lack of jobs and income opportunities in the sector.[71] The increasing involvement of Chinese enterprises in the petroleum and mining sectors of CEMAC countries seems to be exacerbating rather than alleviating the problems of lack of employment opportunities – notwithstanding the much-vaunted contributions of Chinese investment to local economies promoted in official circles. It is evidently the case that the Chinese model of debt-based foreign direct investment (often relying on financing from the China's Exim Bank), sources mainly Chinese personnel and expertise for project implementation. The effect of this debt-based Chinese model of foreign direct investment is arguably to nullify the relevance, application and functionality of LCR obligations within these projects. Chinese funded projects in CEMAC countries are increasingly the subject of conflicts both at the societal level (between the operator and indigenous populations) and at the official level (between the Chinese government or operator and host State governments in the CEMAC region).[72]

The near absence of effective involvement and technical participation by local enterprises in petroleum operations in the CEMAC region remains a pressing concern. In the upstream sector, local involvement has mainly taken the form of non-technical representation by State oil companies.[73] These companies are mainly defined by their bureaucratic structures, with their functions limited to revenue collection and production sharing in joint venture productions with IOC contractors.[74] Participation in petroleum industry operations by private local enterprises remains nominal with very limited participation in bidding rounds for the licensing of exploration or production acreage. The prevailing model of private local enterprise participation is represented by what may be termed the 'oil well ownership' syndrome, with locally acquired exploration or productions rights subsequently assigned to a foreign operation through a joint venture platform.[75] Under this model, exploration or production rights are granted to privileged members of the

---

[71]   L. Miranda, 'Local Content in Cameroon: Myth or Reality?' (2017 November/ December) *Petroleum Africa* pp. 36–9.

[72]   For an example of conflict in the mining sector, see further, www.voanews.com/africa/cameroon-china-look-improve-ties-amid-miners-tensions.

[73]   See further, D. Victor, 'National Oil Companies and the Future of the Oil Industry' (2013) 5 *Annual Review of Resource Economics* 445.

[74]   J.-J. Lecat, 'Conducting Oil and Gas Activities in Cameroon' (2016), www.extractiveshub.org/serve file/getFile/id/5724; see also, M. Hammerson, S. Harwood and J. LaMaster (eds.), *Oil and Gas in Africa: A Legal and Commercial Analysis of the Upstream Industry* (2015); and J. Paterson, 'Production Sharing Agreements in Africa: Sovereignty and Rationality', NUS Working paper 2018/031 (2018, National University of Singapore).

[75]   See generally, A. Fouda, 'Transparency and Value Chain in the Extractive Industries in Central Africa' in J. Runge and J. Shikwati (eds.), *Geological Resources and Good Governance in Sub-Saharan Africa: Holistic Approaches to Transparency and Sustainable Development in the Extractive Sectors* (Taylor & Francis, 2011) 33–6.

Local Content Frameworks in the CEMAC Region   147

political elite in the form of patronage. The rights holders in turn form 'shell' companies which enter into joint venture agreements with IOCs to enable exploitation of rights granted under the licence in return for a share of production and crude oil lifting rights. The performance of local petroleum enterprises therefore remains inadequate in terms of company infrastructure, work force or beneficial linkages (value added) to the local economy.[76] The preferred sector for local enterprises in the CEMAC region remains the downstream petroleum sector. Their ubiquitous presence in retail and distribution of refined petroleum products, when viewed against their near absence of such enterprises in the upstream exploration and production activities, serve as testimony to the failure of LCR policies in promoting the acquisition of the technical knowhow and skills required for effective involvement by local companies in petroleum industry operations.[77]

The World Bank in a key document on local content policies in the oil, gas, and mining industries identified a key aim of LCRs as being to 'leverage the extractive value chain to generate sustained and inclusive growth through economic diversification and employment opportunities'.[78] A second key aim is to generate opportunities for regional integration and international trade, which in turn will reduce countries' dependence on external aid.[79] CEMAC countries' continued reliance on the export of primary raw materials (crude oil, timber and agricultural products) is testimony to the lack of progress on economic diversification.[80] Lack of employment opportunities for nationals both in the petroleum industry and generally (leading to a migration crisis as the region's youth population leave to seek better opportunities abroad[81]), together with dependence on external aid (increasingly from China[82]), provides further evidence of the failure of LCR frameworks to produce the desired results.

The following institutional and legal barriers account for the lack of progress made in the region on capitalising on the utility of petroleum industry LCR frameworks as tools for promoting sustained economic growth.

---

[76] See further, A. Vasquez, 'Four Policy Actions to Improve Local Governance of the Oil and Gas Sector' (2016) 7 *International Development Policy* 1.

[77] See, for example (with reference to Cameroon's national oil company), P. Heller, P. Mahdavi and J. Schreuder, 'Reforming National Oil Companies: Nine Recommendations' *National Resources Governance Institute* (July 2014) p. 3.

[78] The World Bank, 'Local Content in Oil, Gas and Mining', 27 January 2016, www.worldbank.org/en/topic/extractiveindustries/brief/local-content-in-oil-gas-and-mining. See also D. Olawuyi, 'Local Content Policies and Their Implications for International Investment Law' in J. Chaisse et al. (eds.), *Handbook of International Investment Law* (Springer, 2019) 1–21.

[79] Ibid.

[80] Banque de France, '4. Economic Diversification in Central Africa: Overview and Lessons Learnt', 2016.

[81] M-L. Flahaux and H. De Haas, 'African Migration: Trends, Patterns, Drivers' (2016) 4 *Comparative Migration Studies* 1.

[82] See further, A-S. Isaakson and A. Kotsadam, 'Chinese Aid and Local Corruption' (2018) 159 *Journal of Public Economics* 146.

148 *George K. Ndi*

3.1 *Weak Institutional Mechanisms*

The absence of dedicated independent agencies for the monitoring and evaluation of petroleum industry LCR policies in all six CEMAC countries is one of the factors accounting for the slow progress made in the region. Even in Chad, where relative progress has been made, there is no dedicated local content monitoring and evaluation agency and the country has instead had to rely on institutions such as the enterprise centre and the Chamber of Commerce for the monitoring and evaluation of local content policies.[83] In Cameroon, Congo, Equatorial Guinea and Gabon, monitoring and evaluation functions tend to be split between the relevant government ministry and the State oil company, inevitably leading to an overlap or duplication of functions.[84] In the Central African Republic, the regulatory function resides in the Ministry of Mines, Energy and Water.[85] The closeness of these institutions to the governments of the region inevitably translates into a lack of autonomy and authority, with a resulting politicisation of the monitoring and enforcement process as can be seen from the examples in Equatorial Guinea (discussed in Section 2.6). The absence of effective institutional mechanisms in the form of independent regulatory bodies further accounts for the lack of transparency in the monitoring and evaluation of local contents policies. There are no readily published data in the form of annual evaluations of progress made on job creation, local enterprise participation, or on what contribution local content policies have made to economic diversification or to promoting regional integration.

3.2 *Legal Obstacles Arising from the Conception and Design of LCR Frameworks in the Region*

As with the institutional framework, there are no dedicated local content laws and regulations, with relevant local content provisions forming part of the petroleum code (Cameroon, Chad, Equatorial Guinea and Gabon), the mining code (Central African Republic) or a combination of the petroleum code and general labour legislation (Republic of Congo). This inclusion of local content obligations in petroleum legislation can lead to competing objectives, with more pressing objectives such as revenue maximisation ultimately being prioritised over compliance with local content provisions. A more effective approach would have been to have bespoke LCR regulations implemented and monitored by autonomous national agencies, or even a regional agency assigned the task of ensuring a regionalised CEMAC-wide approach to the implementation of local content policies.

[83] Oyewole, note 8, p. 7
[84] Ibid., pp. 17–24.
[85] World Bank, 'Assessment of the Central African Republic Mining Sector' (Washington, DC, 2008), p. 15.

Other design problems arise from the command-and-control approach adopted by governments of the CEMAC region to local content requirements, and to the OIC's role in the petroleum industry in general. In other words, local content obligations are conceived and viewed as part of the OIC's contractual or licensing obligations, rather than as a collaborative framework within which the host state and the contractor can work together to achieve the desired goals. Hence the recourse to administrative penalties for perceived breaches as opposed to corrective measures to remedy to the breach. Ironically, this rather rigid command-and-control model is not often accompanied by clear and transparent criteria for the measurability of outcomes.[86]

3.3 The Absence of a Coordinated and Regionalised Approach

One of the key aims of local content policies in the extractive industries identified by the World Bank is to generate opportunities for regional integration, international trade and reducing dependency on external debt. The absence of a regionalised perspective to the conception and design of petroleum industry LCR frameworks represents one of the main legal obstacles to the effectiveness of local content policies in the region. The national economies of each of the six CEMAC countries are by definition small in size. With the obvious limitations imposed by small market size to the sourcing of labour, goods and services, a regionalised approach to local content whereby 'local' is defined as 'CEMAC' rather than 'national' would have been a more effective conceptual and practical basis for the design of LCR frameworks for the region. However, in matters relating to the petroleum industry, overriding considerations relating to national sovereignty still hold sway over the governments of the region. This continuing focus on domestic or national, as opposed to regional, content, nonetheless represents a missed opportunity for using local content as a platform for promoting regional integration, trade and sustainable growth, while reducing reliance on external debt.

3.4 Lack of Conceptual Underpinning and Guiding Principles

A review of LCR frameworks in CEMAC countries reveals a predominantly contractual character in their design. The focus is on generic outcomes, with no perceptible conceptual or normative underpinnings. Issues such as the promotion of gender equality, distributive justice, social inclusion and inter-generational equity are not often articulated as part of local content provisions. With regard to gender equality in employment, for example, employment figures published by Chad and Equatorial Guinea (the only two countries for which some data is available) are invariably presented in generic form such as 'forty-two graduates employed by

---

[86] Oyewole, note 8, p. 7.

150   *George K. Ndi*

Marathon Oil between 2010 and 2013'[87] without any breakdown of the figures in terms of gender. The guiding principle in the current generation of LCR frameworks in CEMAC countries seem to be centred on ensuring maximum benefits for national economies from petroleum industry operations, to wit: revenue generation.

4 SUGGESTED ATTRIBUTES FOR THE NEXT GENERATION OF LCR FRAMEWORKS FOR PETROLEUM INDUSTRY OPERATIONS IN THE CEMAC REGION

The obvious lack of progress on the actual practice of embedding local content in petroleum operations in the CEMAC region could itself be symptomatic of a misalignment between the viewpoints, understandings, aspirations and expectations of host State governments and IOC operators. To remedy this defect in the design, conception and implementation of LCR frameworks requires a shift away from the command-and-control model currently prevailing in the region to a more collaborative approach aimed at facilitating the involvement of contractors in the conception and design of practical aspects of the LCR regime right from the start of the project. To ensure success in their implementation, LCR frameworks in the region should be designed for the mutual benefit of both the State and IOC operators, as opposed to the current models in the CEMAC region which promote the perception of LCR frameworks as one-sided engagements entailing benefits for the host State and obligations for contractors. OIC contractors need to be made confident of the fact that an appropriately designed and successful LCR framework will open up more commercial opportunities in the local economy for the company, from competitive sourcing of local goods and services (including a well-trained and technically competent labour force) to productive joint ventures with viable local enterprises in the petroleum sector.

As tempting as it may be to try to view LCR frameworks in the CEMAC region in the light of innovative practices and aspiration towards attaining international best practices, it must nonetheless be conceded that current LCR frameworks in the region retain a predominantly basic and elementary character. Given their rudimentary nature, an exercise aimed at appraising LCR frameworks in CEMAC is inevitably limited to a review of their functionality and implementation processes. Innovative features related to substantive policy aspirations are largely absent from CEMAC LCR frameworks, and could therefore guide the conception and design of the next generations of LCR frameworks for the region. Such innovative features include, but are not limited to, the following: promotion of gender equality in petroleum industry operations (improved training and employment prospects for women); policies aimed at promoting distributive justice and social inclusion, thus ensuring access to the benefits of natural resources exploitation for sections of

---

[87]   See Section 2.6.

society; and inter-generational equity with policies aimed at promoting youth employments and building up income reserves for future generations in the form of sovereign wealth funds.

Apart from Chad with its local content agency in the form of the Chamber of Commerce, the institutional frameworks for LCR monitoring and implementation remain weak in the CEMAC region. Regulatory agencies, in the form of State petroleum companies, lack the technical capacity to effectively monitor and implement local content policies. For example, the SNH in Cameroon has, over years, become simply an extension and financier of the ruling party. There is little transparency on the work it is supposed to be doing and it publishes no reports on progress with local content or on the number of nationals employed in the petroleum industry. The same can be said for the State oil companies of Congo (SNPC), Equatorial Guinea (GEPetro) and Gabon (SNPG), all of which, in principle, are tasked with implementing local content policies. However, in practice, the focus of government attention tends to be on acreage promotion and revenue collection. Progress in the region on realising the benefits of LCR will ultimately depend on the introduction of more effective monitoring and enforcement mechanisms, including the establishment of robust institutional frameworks endowed with relevant technical expertise as opposed to the standard bureaucratic constructs.

This case study argues a pressing necessity for a policy shift away from the traditional or standard model in favour of the adoption of more imaginative and innovative approaches in LCR design and formulation. Such a policy shift is undoubtedly a prerequisite for any meaningful progress on embedding local content into petroleum industry operations in CEMAC. The legal framework has a key role in this regard. A first step would be for countries in the region to undertake a comprehensive review of their LCR frameworks. The focus of such a review would be to renovating and streamlining their substantive content and introducing innovative features, such as the promotion of gender equality in oil industry employment, and the promotion of a broader human rights agenda in the context of distributive justice, social inclusion and intergenerational equity. The social dimension of LCR frameworks needs developing beyond the traditional leitmotif of corporate social responsibility, especially in light of growing social unrest and societal strife driven by discontent among the younger generation founded on perceived social injustices and inequities, with an underlying theme of resource conflict. The environmental protection agenda requires concrete actions beyond the standard recitals in model petroleum contracts. From the viewpoint of embedding local content into the environmental protection agenda, local NGOs and environmental activists are well positioned to play a key role in ensuring compliance by oil and gas operators with environmental protection regulations. Local organisations equally have a key role to play in monitoring and reporting corrupt practices in an industry where rent-seeking behaviours on the part of officials could become a tool for leveraging non-compliance by contractors with LCR and environmental protection obligations.

It would certainly be unrealistic of anyone to expect the petroleum industries in CEMAC countries to aspire, at this point in time, to the same high standards as LCR frameworks and strategies of Global North countries. There are, nonetheless, instructive lessons to be learnt in the quest for instilling international best practices into petroleum operations in the region. However, progress can only be possible if local realities are taken into consideration in the design of LCR frameworks in the region – as opposed to wholescale legal transplantation of Global North concepts into the local environment of CEMAC without the necessary adaptation. An illustrative example of this is the traditional coupling of technology transfer with indigenous participation, which in the CEMAC region has turned out to be unlikely bedfellows. This is mainly due to the absence of a local 'technology culture' in the form of a budding technology industry on which to anchor the model. This problem is further exacerbated by the predominantly offshore location of the petroleum industry in CEMAC region with its hostile and uninviting environment. As discussed earlier, the end product of this skewed model has been to reduce the concept of local participation to 'oil well ownership' by a few powerful oligarchs benefitting from political patronage in the allocation of petroleum licences. Other unedifying features of the model include token boardroom membership for political elites and ineffectual State oil companies whose bureaucratic functions are limited to administrative tasks while serving as financial conduits for oil revenues, with little or no technical expertise or involvement in concrete petroleum industry operations. Perhaps a more realistic short-term approach could be to contextualise LCR aspirations by linking petroleum operations with promotion of the financial services sector. This policy would activate participation by oil and gas companies in local banking services via remittances, operating domestic as opposed to foreign accounts and accessing insurance products and capital markets. The question of technology transfer could then become a longer-term objective following the development of a viable and sustainable financial services sector within local CEMAC economies.

From a processes viewpoint, ensuring some measure of success for the next generation of industry LCR frameworks in the CEMAC region would thus require policies imbued with the following key attributes: firstly, there should be clearly stated criteria for measurability in the conception of design of local content polies. Secondly, the adoption of guiding principles aimed at promoting the effective monitoring the attainment of industry milestones on local content should be included in LCR frameworks. Thirdly, CEMAC countries should adopt the practice of conducting effective annual reviews aimed at assessing progress towards the attainment of set targets. Finally, progress towards adopting more effective

LCR regimes that shift away from the traditional emphasis on rigid command-and-control models focusing on administrative sanctions for breach of LCR obligations to a more flexible and inclusive model based on cooperation between the State and the contractors in ensuring the smooth implementation of local content obligations.

On the whole, the conception and design of LCR frameworks in the CEMAC region requires a more innovative, holistic and integrated approach in line with community aspirations towards regional economic and social integration. LCR policies should be guided and informed, both in their form and in substantive content, by the ethos of regional integration founded on common market principles. From a definitional perspective, references in LCR frameworks to local and localisation ought to be construed and interpreted in the light of 'regionalisation'. For example, regionalisation of LCRs would entail the sourcing of regional or CEMAC-wide goods, services and markets (including a regional employment market for the recruitment of CEMAC citizens) rather than the current narrow perspective with its focus on country-specific sourcing. In line with this aspiration towards regionalisation, the use of restrictive terminology such as 'indigenous' ought to be avoided in the text of LCR frameworks. An authentic regionalised approach, coupled with the combined and concerted efforts of CEMAC governments at monitoring, implementation and enforcement, should ultimately produce better results and outcomes than isolated and uncoordinated LCR frameworks specifically designed to serve the petroleum industries of individual countries in the region.

The question of identifying the normative underpinnings for LCR frameworks is an important aspect of the local content regime. A normative status confers on LCR policies legal authority and legitimacy, thus enhancing the prospects for compliance. Normative status also provides a rationale for effective enforcement. For these reasons, it is recommended that the conceptual and normative underpinnings of local content policies be clearly highlighted in LCR frameworks. As an example, obligations relating to local employment in the context of gender equality, distributive justice and social inclusion ought to be anchored in the human rights norm. Equally, participation by local or regional enterprises in petroleum operations could ultimately be grounded on the norm of permanent sovereignty over natural resources, on the basis that it is an aspect of the exercise of such sovereignty. As for the norm relating to environmental protection, this is now deeply rooted in international environmental law – hence providing a ready-made rationale for the involvement of local activists and civil society organisations within the context of LCR frameworks for the monitoring and reporting of breaches relating to environmental protection by oil contractors. The same can be said of anti-corruption strategies which derive their normative status from the various international conventions aimed at combating corrupt practices and money laundering. Local NGOs and activist (including the local chapters of organisations such as Transparency

International), working with the framework of LCR policies and practices, could be a critical component in ensuring the success of anti-corruption practices in the petroleum sector in CEMAC.

As an overall assessment, the future success of petroleum industry LCR policies in the CEMAC region requires a redesign of current frameworks with a view to formulating more effective and resilient local content strategies. This would involve embedding key attributes such as simplicity, clarity, transparency, attainability, measurability and sustainability. With regard to processes and implementation, well-known impediments to their effective actualisation, such as an overwhelming bureaucratic focus, coupled with the nullifying effect of corruption, must be genuinely addressed. An effective LCR strategy would also require explicit linkages to normative underpinnings, with normative international law principles such as human rights, sovereignty over natural resources and sustainable development serving as mainstreams providing a normative link for connecting the various tributaries which consist of LCR policies on gender equality employment, local participation and environmentally sustainable practices in petroleum industry operations.

5 CONCLUSION

The legal and regulatory frameworks for LCRs in the petroleum sector in the CEMAC region as a whole remain relatively underdeveloped. They could even be termed rudimentary in comparison with Global North standards and international best practices. This is due in part to the underdevelopment of local economies and their incapacity to offer opportunities for the local sourcing of goods, manpower and services (a veritable catch-22 scenario). The actualisation of local content opportunities is further hamstrung by poor infrastructure, as well as poor implementation and enforcement in a region where the rule of law itself is underdeveloped.

In principle, petroleum industry LCRs in CEMAC countries undoubtedly have a key role to play beyond promoting sustainable development. They also have the potential to impact positively on much-cherished values such as human rights, gender equality, distributive justice and social inclusion. However, LCR policies need to be carefully designed and properly aligned with national development objectives. Emphasis should be directed towards a well-coordinated sectoral approach founded on efficient monitoring and effective implementation. Certainty and consistency should be at the forefront of the enforcement process as the key attributes informing implementation, as opposed to a piecemeal approach to enforcement founded on administrative discretion.

The success or otherwise of petroleum industry LCR policies in the CEMAC region will ultimately be judged not solely on the basis of their attainment of measurable targets and milestones. Their long-term success will equally be assessed on the basis of evidence on the ground pointing to a meaningful and effective contribution to sustainable economic development, which can only be possible by addressing some of the main symptoms of the resource curse syndrome such as distributive injustice, gender inequality, social exclusion, societal inequities and resource conflicts.

8

Local Content, *Angolanização*, and Sustainable Development in Angola

Jesse Salah Ovadia

1 INTRODUCTION

This chapter evaluates the contributions of Angola's local content requirements and policies (LCRs) to the attainment of sustainable development in the country. It reviews progress made, the barriers that remain, and approaches for better integrating sustainable development into the design and implementation of LCRs in Angola.

Alongside Nigeria, Angola is one of sub-Saharan Africa's two major oil producers. A member of the Organization of Petroleum Exporting Countries (OPEC), Angola has been producing significant oil wealth since the 1970s. However, the country only emerged from thirty long and brutal years of war in 2002. With abundant natural resources and fertile farmland, Angola had been the jewel in the crown of Portugal's colonial empire. No less than three separate movements took up arms in the fight for independence. Aided by Cold War rivals, these groups fought each other after independence was achieved. The war even continued after the fall of the Soviet Union, because by that time, the two major combatants had found new sources of funding to continue their conflict – oil and diamonds.[1]

Angola is one of the key cases for building both academic and popular understandings of the "resource curse" hypothesis.[2] Eventually, the government's oil resources enabled it to gain the upper hand. The state oil company, Sonangol had been the key to victory. Well-run with a reputation as a strong negotiator and stable partner, the company was a black box in which oil revenues disappeared before reaching the treasury, used instead by the president in secret deals for arms and influence.[3]

---

[1] J.S. Ovadia and S. Croese, "Post-War Angola: The Dual Nature of Growth without Development in an Oil-Rich State" in G. Kanyenze, H. Jauch, A.D. Kanengoni, M. Madzwamuse, and D. Muchena (eds.), *Towards Democratic Developmental States in Southern Africa* (Zimbabwe: Weaver Press 2016).

[2] For detailed analysis of the "resource curse" conundrum, see J. S. Ovadia, "Natural Resources and African Economies: Asset or Liability?" in T. Falola and S. Oloruntoba (eds.), *Palgrave Handbook of African Political Economy* (Cham, Switzerland: Palgrave MacMillan, 2020) 667–678. See also D. Olawuyi, *Extractives Industry Law in Africa* (Switzerland: Springer Nature Switzerland, 2018) 1–15.

[3] S. Kibble, "Angola: Can the Politics of Disorder Become the Politics of Democratisation & Development?" (2006) 33 *Review of African Political Economy* 525; R. Soares de Oliveira, "Business

Local Content, Angolanização, and SD in Angola   157

The war destroyed much of the country's infrastructure and farmland.[4] However, Angola was rebuilding at the beginning of a commodity boom that would last over a decade. For a period the world's fastest growing economy, Angola pursued oil-backed development alongside illicit elite accumulation. Sonangol expanded rapidly while actively promoting local content in procurement; the Ministry of Petroleum took primary responsibility for increasing the participation of Angolans in the oil sector with its policies of *Angolanização*.[5]

The Angolan government is elite-driven and dominated by the president and his inner circle. While local content had the potential to foster new industries and diversify an economy heavily dependent on oil, it had a "dual nature" in that it represented a new avenue for elite accumulation.[6] Therefore, as during the war, Sonangol took the lead in an approach that eschewed formal local content legislation and regulations in favour of a more informal approach that better-suited the interests of the Angolan elite. This chapter is divided into five sections. After this introduction, Section 2 discusses the current context for sustainable development in Angola's petroleum industry. Section 3 examines formal local content mechanisms in Angolan legislation and bidding round procedures, while Section 4 examines informal mechanisms such as the Sonangol's internal practices its relationship with international oil companies. Finally, Section 5 summarizes and concludes the analysis.

2 THE CURRENT CONTEXT FOR SUSTAINABLE DEVELOPMENT IN ANGOLA'S PETROLEUM INDUSTRY AND THE PURSUIT OF LOCAL CONTENT

The oil price shock of 2014 brought some reform to the Angolan oil industry, and, within a few years, the country's first new president in thirty-eight years (though the extent to which these events were linked is a matter of debate). The reforms seek to increase Sonangol's efficiency and promote foreign investment in the non-oil economy. Through its decades of increasing oil production, Angola never identified the petroleum reserves of a country like Nigeria. The imperative to prepare for life after oil is therefore much greater.

Success, Angola-Style: Postcolonial Politics and the Rise and Rise of Sonangol" (2007) 45 *Journal of Modern African Studies* 595.

[4] A. de Grassi and J. S. Ovadia, "Trajectories of Large-Scale Land Acquisition Dynamics in Angola: Diversity, Histories, and Implications for the Political Economy of Development in Africa" (2017) 67 *Land Use Policy* 67.

[5] J. S . Ovadia, "The Dual Nature of Local Content in Angola's Oil and Gas Industry: Development vs. Elite Accumulation" (2012) 30 *Journal of Contemporary African Studies* 395.

[6] Ovadia, note 5; J. S. Ovadia, "The Reinvention of Elite Accumulation in the Angolan Oil Sector: Emergent Capitalism in a Rentier Economy" (2013) 25 *Cadernos de Estudos Africanos* 33; Ovadia et al., note 1.

158   Jesse Salah Ovadia

It may seem counterintuitive to discuss sustainable development in the context of the oil and gas industry, however, for Angola, petroleum dominates the economy. While carbon-reliance can never be "sustainable," it may still be possible to think about how the industry can better-serve Angola's economy and its sustainable development targets. Local content policies are undoubtedly central to any such petro-developmental outcomes.[7] The oil price shock was a warning about the dangers of oil dependence. After more than a decade of steadily rising oil output, oil production has begun to fall. In some respects, this creates a "window for real reform,"[8] however it is not clear whether the opportunity is being taken up. While new projects coming online and a stronger oil price mean that the government can rely on oil for a bit longer, the relevance of local content and its central importance in a broader strategy of economic diversification has never been greater.

Local content is difficult in the context of an industry that is largely offshore and in ultra-deep waters where both the technology and skills required by the industry are highly specialized. The bigger challenge, however, is that though local content and *Angolanização* are politically popular and have been priorities for both Sonangol and the Ministry of Petroleum, they can never be as important to the president and his inner circle as the oil revenues upon which their rule is based. Local content continues to be more valuable as a mechanism for elite enrichment. While impressive gains have been made through Angola's largely informal approach to local content, as long as local participation continues to be pursued informally the developmental benefits of local content will fall short of its potential. Furthermore, oil sector reform may paradoxically limit the power of regulators to pursue informal local content gains, thus weakening the developmental outcomes.

3 FORMAL LOCAL CONTENT MECHANISMS

3.1 Legislation, Regulations, and Production-Sharing Agreements

The key legislation governing the oil and gas sector are the Petroleum Activities Law (PAL),[9] Petroleum Customs Law,[10] and the Law on Taxation of Petroleum Activities.[11] These laws contain local content and *Angolanização* provisions, however regulators have a long history of looking the other way when it comes to enforcement. Several other pieces of legislation are related to local content, however they are of secondary importance and adequately discussed in other works. In

---

[7]   J. S. Ovadia, *The Petro-Developmental State in Africa: Making Oil Work in Angola, Nigeria and the Gulf of Guinea* (Hurst 2016) 1-25.

[8]   S. K. Jensen, "Angola Can Mark 40 Years Since Independence with Bold Economic Reforms," November 11, 2015, www.chathamhouse.org/expert/comment/angola-can-mark-40-years-independence-bold-economic-reforms.

[9]   Petroleum Activities Law, Republic of Angola, Law No. 10/2004 of 12 November.

[10]   Petroleum Customs Law, Republic of Angola, Law No. 11/2004 of 12 November.

[11]   Law on Taxation of Petroleum Activities Republic of Angola, Law No. 13/2004 of 24 December.

general, the Ministry of Petroleum, the official regulator, has very little capacity or power. Therefore, in practice, oversight has been carried out by Sonangol, which played a key role in putting in place the legal framework for local content in Angola.[12]

Article 86 of the PAL requires that local and foreign companies employ only Angolan citizens in all categories and functions, except where no Angolan citizens exist in the national market with the required qualifications and experience. It also contains clauses regarding training, local procurement, and social investments. However, these clauses were on the books for several decades in earlier legislation that was never well-enforced and was largely ignored by international oil companies. Training and employment are further governed by Decree-Law 17 of 2009.[13]

Oil operators are also required to procure goods and services from local providers. Article 26.1 of the PAL expressly determines that the Angolan government should adopt measures to "guarantee, promote and encourage investment in the petroleum sector by companies held by Angolan citizens and create the conditions necessary for such purpose." Article 27 of the PAL even requires local procurement when the provider's cost is up to 10 percent higher. However, the Ministry of Petroleum is in no position to monitor such a clause. Instead, it is Sonangol that monitors local procurement through clauses in the Production Sharing Agreements (PSAs) that require its approval of workplans, budgets, and all expenditure beyond a certain amount (between US\$100,000 and US\$250,000 depending on the PSA and when it was signed). Key clauses from the PAL around local employment, training, social investment, and a 10 percent margin of preference for local goods and services, are replicated in the PSAs.[14]

Because the PSAs are contractual agreements with terms that are not necessarily in the public domain, their value in setting local content is in some ways greater – particularly as these contracts set out the terms of oil exploration and production and are considered sacrosanct by both parties. The PSAs are also the only place that policies related to technology transfer can be found. This aspect of local content has not always been emphasised by Sonangol; however, most PSAs do say that contractors need to ensure that Angolans are training on the most appropriate technology, "including proprietary and patented technology, 'know how' and other confidential technology, to the extent permitted by applicable laws and agreements."[15]

There is one final piece of legislation that does play an important role in Angola's local content framework: Decree 127 of 2003,[16] which establishes three regimes for oil industry procurement (see Table 8.1). This system is a stark contrast with the

---

[12] Ovadia, note 7. In 2019 Angola transferred Sonangol's regulatory responsibilities to the newly created National Agency of Petroleum and Gas (ANPG).
[13] Decree-Law No. 17/09 of July 26.
[14] Ovadia, note 5.
[15] Angola Model PSA [2008], Article 36.2.
[16] Order 127/03 of 25 November.

160   *Jesse Salah Ovadia*

TABLE 8.1 *Regimes created by Decree No. 127/03*[18]

Regime	Title	Description
Regime 1	Regime of Exclusion for Angolan Businesses	Activities such as transportation, supply, catering, cleaning, gardening, general maintenance, and so forth are included in this regime. In law (if not in practice), only Angolan companies (51% owned by Angolan citizens and registered with both MINPET and CCIA) can bid on contracts.
Regime 2	Regime of Semi-Compliance	For areas such as the purchasing and processing of data, surveying, drilling, consultancies, operation and maintenance of pipelines, and so forth. In this regime, foreign companies must be in an association with an Angolan company. Although some in the industry argue the law is "confusing" in terms of what this means in practice, Angolan authorities have interpreted this provision to require a formal joint venture (Morgan 2006).
Regime 3	Regime of Competition	For goods or services that involve "a high level of capital in the oil industry and in-depth specialist know-how." Foreign-owned companies are free to participate without entering into a joint venture with an Angolan company. In practice, there are very few activities which fall into this category.

approaches of other African countries, which have focused on specific targets for local participation in various categories of goods and services. As Ovadia explains, the law duplicates provisions around preferential rights in the contracting and sub-contracting of goods and provision of support services provided their proposals are not more than 10 percent higher than other companies. The Ministry of Petroleum and the Angolan Chamber of Commerce and Industry review Angolan capacity annually to determine if activities in the sector can be moved from Regime 3 to 2 or from Regime 2 to 1.[17]

Given that contracting and subcontracting decisions are often not public and tender documents are not reviewed by the Ministry of Petroleum, there is little opportunity for oversight or to monitor the extent to which these provisions are enforced. Anecdotally, Sonangol officials often exercise their discretion – particularly in ways that benefit themselves and their colleagues. They also direct foreign investors to particular local companies and act to exclude others from winning contracts.[19]

In 2012, the government also moved to promote local content in the financial sector, anchoring their reform in the oil sector due to its significance and their

[17] Ovadia, note 5.
[18] Ibid.
[19] Ovadia (2013), note 6; Ovadia (2016), note 7.

influence over petroleum activities. Law 2 of 2012 required taxes as well as payments made to local suppliers to be made through Angolan banks and in the local currency. Generally, payments to foreign suppliers must also be made through Angolan banks. There is little information in the public domain about how successful this policy has been in the wake of the oil price shock and resulting liquidity difficulties in the Angolan economy. In 2019, the government finally followed through with plans to separate regulatory and oversight authority from Sonangol with Decree 48, which created the National Agency of Oil, Gas and Biofuels (ANPG).[20] The impact of the creation of ANPG will have to be explored in future research; however, as will be discussed further, the move may limit the state's ability to pursue local content and sustainable development informally.

What has evaded Angola in its post-war oil-backed development has been a unified approach to local content policy and unified local content legislation. A Ministry of Petroleum official first mentioned the possibility of new local content legislation in 2010. Since then, it has been brought up by government officials, cabinet members, and even Sonangol employees as something that is being studied and is just around the corner.[21] This is also seen in comments made by Mateus Neto in 2014[22] and José Maria Botlho de Vasconcelos in 2017.[23] The lack of movement suggests a strategy that can be considered "piecemeal" with "a lack of coordination between Sonangol, the Ministry of Petroleum and other key stakeholders."[24]

3.2 Local Content in Bidding Rounds

The other formal mechanism for promoting local content is through bidding rounds for new oil blocks. In its terms of reference for bidding rounds, Sonangol has been able to reserve stakes for local companies (though these are often fronts for local elites), reserve a carried stake for Sonangol's Research and Production subsidiary, and evaluate bids according to local content criteria.

The PAL contemplates both bid rounds and open tenders, although typically Sonangol sends a request for proposals to a limited number of (mostly) international oil companies. In recent bid rounds, 20 percent of the bid evaluation was weighted to the proposed social programs. Bid evaluations are done in private and terms of the winning bids are not necessarily made public. This limits the opportunity for local

---

[20] Agencia Angola Press, "Concludio Quadro legal da AMPG," April 19, 2019, www.angop.ao/angola/pt_pt/noticias/economia/2019/3/16/Concluido-quadro-legal-ANPG,6c9a775a-fa91-42a1-9f61-08b18284ifeb.html.

[21] J. S. Ovadia, "Local Content Policies and Petro-Development in Sub-Saharan Africa: A Comparative Analysis" (2016) 49 *Resources Policy* 20.

[22] CAE, "CAE Promotes Petroleum Sector Providers Forum," October 17, 2014, https://caeangola.com/cae-promotes-petroleum-sector-providers-forum/.

[23] "Angola to Set New Local Content Rules," March 23, 2017, www.theoilandgasyear.com/news/angola-to-set-new-local-content-rules/.8.

[24] J. S. Ovadia, "Local Content and Natural Resource Governance: The Cases of Angola and Nigeria" (2014) 1 *The Extractive Industries and Society* 137 at 141.

content, particularly since "Sonangol appears to be one of the lowest performers on the reporting of payments and supplies to governments, procurement services and anti-corruption programmes, but one of the most transparent oil company on the reporting of licensing criteria and licenses."[25]

Evaluation of social investment provision was the main formal local content feature in bid rounds in 2007/08 and 2010/11, other than the fact that PSA templates were provided in the bid documents that contained the standard local content provisions mentioned above. Informally, Sonangol ensured small stakes were given to local companies, whose ownership structures were difficult to ascertain. However, in the 2014/15 bid round, which was for onshore oil blocks in the Kwanza Basin and Lower Congo Basin, steps were taken to ensure even greater participation by local companies. This included reserving 30 percent for Sonangol and 20 percent for local companies. Although road shows were held in Houston, London, and Singapore – and eighty-four companies from twelve countries were pre-qualified and requested to submit their proposals, including ENI, Chevron, and Tullow – 100 percent of the interest in all ten blocks was awarded to indigenous oil companies.[26]

The roadshow presentation specifically mentioned the goal of increasing local content in the petroleum industry. It also noted that under Law 3 of 2012, indigenous oil companies were granted certain tax incentives such as reduced income and petroleum sales tax, as well as exemptions from the payment of signature bonuses, from financing Sonangol's interest in the block, and from contributions to social programs. However, it also noted that companies that benefit from these incentives can not, under penalty of loss of these incentives, assign all or part of their capital to foreign part(s).[27]

Finally, the 2014/15 bid round documents also included an updated model PSA for the onshore blocks. In this PSA, all the same local content provisions are in place around Sonangol approving suppliers for tenders over US$250,000, on annual approvals of work plans and budgets, on social program contributions (for non-Angolan companies), on local procurement, and on recruitment and training. There is one additional clause that is relevant to local content in the model PSA for onshore blocks. The model onshore PSA states, "Except as is appropriate for the economic and efficient processing of data and laboratory studies thereon in specialized centres outside Angola, geological and geophysical studies as well as any other technical studies related to the performance of this Contract, shall be in a percentage not less than 35% (thirty five percent) of their

---

[25] L. C. Mouan, "Governing Angola's Oil Sector: The Illusion of Revenue Transparency?" (PhD Thesis, Coventry University 2015), citing Transparency International, "Promoting Revenue Transparency: 2008 Report on Revenue Transparency of Oil and Gas Companies," 2008.

[26] "Chevron, ENI, Tullow Lose Out in Angolan Bid Round," December 7, 2015, http://africaoilgasreport .com/2015/12/farm-in-farm-out/chevron-eni-tullow-lose-out-in-angolan-bid-round/.

[27] "Roadshow Presentation," February 21, 2014, www.sonangol.co.ao/English/AreasOfActivity/ Concessionary/Pages/Licensing-Rounds.aspx.

Local Content, Angolanização, and SD in Angola   163

value executed in Angola."[28] This provision is noteworthy as it may be the first time in Angola that a hard target has been set for local participation in a specific good or service and it is not found in the 2008 model PSA.

4 INFORMAL LOCAL CONTENT MECHANISMS

If local content (both in terms of personnel and procurement) has been increased in Angola, it is because the government, and Sonangol in particular, have made it clear to international oil companies that local content is important and progress will have to be made if they want to continue to operate in the country without problems. This message has largely been communicated to the oil companies informally and without specific guidance on what local content objectives are most important. Where specific objectives have been communicated to the companies, it is largely to promote a particular local company for personal gain rather than developmental benefit.

Yet local content has risen through these largely informal arrangements. This has happened, firstly, because each international oil company has designed its own local content strategy and sought approval from Sonangol for their efforts; and secondly, because Sonangol staff have made some key interventions on major projects to reject arrangements without what they deemed to be sufficient local content. This intervention has raised local content on those projects and also reinforced the overall message that each international oil company must continue to display progress on local content to avoid running afoul of Sonangol.

In the mid-2000s, Sonangol began to work with each international oil company to identify and undertake a major new local content initiative. The seriousness with which Sonangol pursued local content gains is underlined by Patrick Heller in his summary of the national oil company's activities. Heller writes, "Local content and local staffing are important goals of most NOCs that work with international partners, but most international officials who work in Angola indicate that Sonangol is tougher about local content and places more emphasis on it than counterpart companies in other countries."[29]

Sonangol's pressure led to Chevron Angola launching its Angola Enterprise Program (AEP) in 2004 to develop the local capacity of SMEs, Total Angola launching the Zimbo Fund (a microfinance initiative to help SMEs access to capital) in 2005, BP Angola launching the *Centro de Apoio Empresarial* (Business Support Centre) to provide professional training to SMEs in 2005, and Esso Angola launching new bidding processes and technical assistance for

---

[28] Model onshore PSA for the 2014/15 bid round, Article 14.7, www.sonangol.co.ao/English/AreasOfActivity/Concessionary/Documents/Licitacoes/modeloCPPonshore_en.pdf.

[29] P. Heller, "Angola's Sonangol: Dexterous Right Hand of the State" in D. G. Victor, D. R. Hults, and M. C. Thurber (eds.), *Oil and Governance: State-Owned Enterprises and the World Energy Supply* (Cambridge University Press, 2012), p. 858.

164   *Jesse Salah Ovadia*

local suppliers.[30] These programs have been important in building the capacity of local companies and resulted in noteworthy achievements, as described in Table 8.2.

On a case-by-case basis, Sonangol's Directorate of Production (D.PRO) and Directorate of Economy and Concessions (DEC) have taken advantage of their role in approving tenders to pressure companies and their subcontractors to increase local content. As an example, Sonangol very publicly rejected Total's preferred bidders for the Clov project in 2010 even though they were the lowest bid due to insufficient local content and required Total to go with a different contractor. Ovadia presents evidence that this is but one public example of the pressure D. PRO and DEC exert. Using the formal legislation that allows a 10 percent margin for local suppliers and their informal power of approval, Sonangol has, in practice, not only ensured local companies receive contracts when they are within 10 percent of the lowest bid but actually forced the international oil companies to accept both foreign and indigenous companies with bids as much as 20–30 percent higher as

TABLE 8.2 *Local content initiatives by IOCs operating in Angola*[31]

Company	Initiative	Highlights
Chevron	Angola Enterprise Program (AEP)	Funded by Spanish International Cooperation Agency for Development (AECID), this program began in 2004 and was supposed to go until 2007 but was extended until 2013. The program provides support through the Luanda Business Incubator, which graduated 6 entrepreneurs in 2009 who established companies creating 69 jobs and expecting to generate $378,000 per year.
Total	The Zimbo Fund	Partnered with Banco Totta de Angola, The Zimbo Fund created a joint guarantee fund for SMEs. The programme aimed to finance 60 projects and create 100 jobs but is now estimated to have created 300 jobs via dozens of local companies.
BP	Centro de Apoio Empresarial (CAE)	CAE maintains a database of local companies used for training and for IOCs to identify local suppliers. CAE helped Angolan firms win 289 contracts worth a total of $206 million, leading to the creation of 4,236 jobs.
Esso	Bidding Support and Assistance	Esso's program trained 78 local supplies between 2008–2009 and provided technical assistance.

[30] Ovadia, note 24.
[31] Ibid; S. Tordo and Y. Anouti, "Local Content in the Oil and Gas Sector: Case Studies," The World Bank, 2013.

suppliers when their local content on a particular tender was higher.[32] However, it is unclear whether this practice continued after the oil price shock in 2014 when the pressure to lower costs was much higher.

A more recent example of the success Sonangol has had in intervening in major projects is the high level of local content achieved in Total's most recent investment, the Kaombo project. Kaombo is located in Block 3 and involves the extraction of oil deposits across six fields in the ultradeep offshore via a large network of subsea pipelines to two floating production, storage, and offloading (FPSO) vessels named *Kaombo Norte* and *Kaombo Sul. Kaombo Norte* began production in the summer of 2018, with the second FPSO scheduled to begin operating in 2019.[33]

Learning from its experience with Clov, Total's Kaombo project is one of the biggest in terms of local content investment, surpassing US$2 billion dollars spent in-country. According to Total, this is the highest level of local content ever achieved in Angola, with around 84,000 tons of structures and equipment built in Angolan yards representing more 19 million man-hours.[34] These figures indicate the potential gains for the Angolan economy from a robust local content strategy, though again it is unclear if such gains can be replicated in the context of lower oil prices post-2014.

Given that some of Sonangol and Angola's biggest successes have resulted from the informal pursuit of local content, aided by the power Sonangol exercises over the industry, one potential impact of creating ANPG as a separate regulatory authority may be to weaken the possibilities for pursuing local content and economic development informally. However, if the government is able to give ANPG the necessary authority and capacity to formally pursue local content in a more systematic way, the move may help align local content outcomes with developmental ones.

5 CONCLUSION

Angola's local content successes are real. However, a review of the formal and informal mechanisms through which the state pursues increased local participation reveals that it is the informal mechanisms that are largely responsible for the country's gains, as well as the missed opportunities to pursue meaningful economic diversification. Governance in Angola is defined by informal exercise of power. It is therefore unsurprising that the informality with which the state pursues local content has greatly benefitted the Angolan elite at the expense of economic development.

Efforts to formalize local content policy in national legislation have stalled in Angola due to the relative lack of importance the executive places on this issue. Meanwhile local content gains are driven by the directionless activities of

---

[32] Ovadia, note 5, pp. 402–403.
[33] Total SA, "Kaombo: An Innovative Ultra-Deep-Water Offshore Project in Angola," www.total.com /en/energy-expertise/projects/oil-gas/deep-offshore/kaombo-ultra-deepwater-offshore-project.
[34] Total Angola, "Kaombo: The Energy of the Future," www.total.co.ao/en-us/kaombo-energy-future.

international oil companies and the desultory interventions of Sonangol technocrats who lack an overall strategic economic vision for Angolan development.

While less reliance on formal, and especially transparent, mechanisms may somewhat insulate the government from scrutiny of its protectionist measures in the oil and gas industry, they ultimately feed a system of governance that is unaccountable and susceptible to widespread abuse and graft. A set of laws and policies that are in many ways models for emulation across the continent, such as the innovative approach of Decree 127/03, the involvement of organizations like the Angolan Chamber of Commerce and Industry, the effectiveness with which international companies have set up small business support programs, and the role of the state oil company in using its approval power to pursue local content, are in fact limited by the lack of coordination and vision, as well as the emphasis placed on self-dealing and private gain. This is not a determined outcome of resource wealth but rather something that flows from Angola's political culture and the example set at the top – both of which have been slow to change.

9

Local Content and the Sustainable Development of Oil and Gas Resources in Nigeria

Damilola S. Olawuyi and Ayobami J. Olaniyan

1 INTRODUCTION

This chapter evaluates the efficacy of the local content requirements and policies (LCRs) in Nigeria's oil and gas industry. It identifies legal, institutional, and practical challenges that hinder the full attainment of the intended sustainable development objectives of the Nigerian LCRs. It then discusses a wide array of mutually supportive solutions that can help maximize the sustainable development potential of Nigerian LCRs.

Nigeria as an oil-producing nation takes the issue of local content seriously.[1] Efforts to put in place viable LCRs in Nigeria date as far back as 1959, when the Nigerian government began to establish policies and legal measures to give priority to Nigerians, Nigerian companies, and locally produced material, in critical sectors of the Nigerian economy, including the oil and gas sector.[2] These policy initiatives culminated in the enactment of the Nigerian Oil and Gas Industry Content Development Act (NOGICDA) of 2010,[3] which contains one of the most comprehensive legal and institutional frameworks on LCRs in the world. Based on the fundamental premise that petroleum resources, as well as its accruing benefits, belong to the Nigerian people, the fundamental objective of NOGICDA is to increase and maximize the degree of economic and social benefits from oil and gas production activities for Nigerians.[4] These intended benefits include boosting

---

[1] Nigeria's oil and gas sector accounts for about 10 per cent of gross domestic product (GDP), and revenue from her petroleum exports represents about 83 per cent of total exports revenue. See Organization of the Petroleum Exporting Countries (OPEC), "Nigeria," www.opec.org/opec_web/en/about_us/167.htm.

[2] For a discussion on the history of the development of legal and policy regimes to promote local content in the Nigerian oil and gas industry, see U. J. Orji, "Towards Sustainable Local Content Development in the Nigerian Oil and Gas Industry: An Appraisal of the Legal Framework and Challenges-Pt I" (2014) *International Energy Law Review* 30–35.

[3] Nigerian Oil and Gas Industry Content Development Act No. 2, 2010 [NOGICDA].

[4] See generally, ibid., sections 1, 2, and 3. The aim is to achieve 70 per cent Nigerian content by the year 2027. See F. Adeh, "FG Targets 70% Nigerian Content in Oil Industry by 2027" (June 9, 2020), www.thisdaylive.com/index.php/2020/06/09/fg-targets-70-nigerian-content-in-oil-industry-by-2027/.

168 *Damilola S. Olawuyi and Ayobami J. Olaniyan*

the employment of Nigerians across the entire oil and gas value chain; enhancing procurement of goods and services from companies resident in Nigeria; developing endogenous technology and infrastructure in the Nigerian oil and gas sector; improving the skills and capacity of local businesses and the domestic workforce through partnerships and knowledge transfer from foreign firms; and minimizing capital flight from the Nigerian oil and gas sector by boosting in-country economic investment, amongst others.[5] These are noble objectives that can help Nigeria reverse the resource curse conundrum that has perennially limited the ultimate socio-economic gains of the country's abundant resources to its people.[6]

However, many years after its enactment, the copious LCRs in the NOGICDA have not fully translated into increased economic and social benefits for Nigerian workers and industries, especially those in the oil-producing communities in the Niger Delta area.[7] For example, while the Nigerian LCRs specify the portion of total expenditures that must be comprised of locally sourced goods and services, lack of available capacity, technologies, and material at local level often mean that a significant proportion of goods and services in the Nigerian oil and gas sector remains foreign sourced.[8] Lack of available capacity and material is often exacerbated by lack of consistent enforcement and monitoring of applicable provisions that mandate capacity development and training for locals in oil-producing communities.[9] Similarly, perennial challenges of corruption and lack of transparency in the implementation of the NOGICDA have stifled the effective monitoring and supervision of the core tenets of the Nigerian LCRs.[10] Consequently, while the NOGICDA, in principle, aims to accelerate sustainable development in the Nigerian oil and gas sector, in practice, its LCRs have not fully translated to increased economic and social benefits for Nigerian workers and industries, especially for women and local communities in the oil-producing communities. These

---

[5] IPIECA, "Local Content: A Guidance Document for the Oil and gas Industry Second Edition," April 2016. See also K. A. Mohammed, "Nigerian Content Development: The Petroleum Technology Development Fund Initiatives" (July 2009) 2 *Petroleum Technology Development Journal* 2.

[6] See D. Olawuyi, *Extractives Industry Law in Africa* (New York: Springer, 2018), pp. 1–5; also A. Mahler, "Nigeria: A Prime Example of the Resource Curse? Revisiting the Oil-Violence Link in the Niger Delta" (2010) *German Institute of Global and Area Studies* 25.

[7] A significant proportion of Nigeria's oil and gas deposits are located in the Niger Delta area. The Niger Delta is primarily made up of the following oil-producing states: Abia, Akwa Ibom, Bayelsa, Cross River, Delta, Edo, Imo, Ondo, and Rivers. Niger Delta is home to approximately 20 million people grouped into several distinct nations and ethnic groups, amongst which is the Ogoni. See D. Olawuyi, *Principles of Nigerian Environmental Law* (Afe Babalola University Press, 2015), pp. 172–174.

[8] See J. Balouga, "Nigerian Local Content: Challenges and Prospects" (2012) *International Association for Energy Economics* 23. See also C. Nwapi, "Corruption Vulnerabilities in Local Content Policies in the Extractive Sector: An Examination of the Nigerian Oil and Gas Industry Content Development Act, 2010" (2015) 46 *Resources Policy* 93.

[9] Olawuyi, note 6, pp. 260–264.

[10] I. Ramdoo, "Unpacking Local Content Requirements in the Extractive Sector: What Implications for the Global Trade and Investment Frameworks?" E15 Initiative, International Centre for Trade and Sustainable Development (ICTSD), World Economic Forum Geneva, September 2015; also Nwapi, note 8.

Local Content and SD in Nigeria 169

concerns have resulted in increased demand for a more transparent, effective, and coherent implementation of the LCRs in Nigeria to advance sustainable development across the Nigerian oil and gas industry value chain.[11]

This Chapter identifies gaps in the Nigerian local content regime that stifle the transparent, effective, and coherent implementation of the LCRs. The Chapter is divided into five sections. After this introduction, Section 2 examines the current position on local content and sustainable development in Nigeria. Section 3 discusses the challenges or roadblocks to the successful implementation of local content in Nigeria. In Section 4, legal, institutional, and practical recommendations are put forward on how to improve the implementation of the local content legislation and its LCRs. Section 5 sets out the conclusion.

2 FRAMEWORK FOR LOCAL CONTENT AND SUSTAINABLE DEVELOPMENT IN NIGERIAN OIL AND GAS INDUSTRY

2.1 *Local Content*

The NOGICDA is the principal legal framework on local content in Nigeria. The Act provides the legal and operational basis for promoting "Nigerian Content" in the Nigerian oil and gas industry.[12] With 107 sections, the Act applies to all matters concerning Nigerian content as regards all operations and activities carried out in or linked with the Nigerian oil and gas industry.[13] The Act mandates all stakeholders (regulatory authorities, operators, contractors, subcontractors, alliance partners, and other entities involved in any project, operation, activity, or transaction) in the oil and gas industry in Nigeria to consider Nigerian content in their project development and management philosophy.[14] The Act also contains guidelines for the (i) development of Nigerian Content in Nigeria's oil and gas industry; (ii) Nigerian Content Plan;[15] (iii) supervision, coordination, monitoring, and implementation of Nigerian content by the Nigerian Content Monitoring Board; and for related matters.[16] These provisions of the Act make it an all-encompassing piece of legislation which binds everyone in the oil and gas industry as far as Nigerian Content is

---

[11] Olawuyi, note 6 at 260–264; Nwapi, note 8; also J. Ovadia, "Local Content and Natural Resource Governance: The Cases of Angola and Nigeria" (2014) 1 *The Extractives Industries and Society* 137–146.

[12] Section 106 of the Act defines "Nigerian Content" as the "quantum of composite value added to or created in the Nigerian economy by a systematic development of capacity and capabilities through the deliberate utilization of Nigerian human, material resources and services in the Nigerian oil and gas industry." The key point on Nigerian Content is the "systematic development of capacity and capabilities through the deliberate utilization of Nigerian human, material resources and services in the Nigerian oil and gas industry." This point is what distinguishes Nigerian content from other types of local contents.

[13] See NOGICDA, note 3, section 1.

[14] See ibid., section 2.

[15] See ibid., section 7

[16] Long Title, Nigerian Oil and Gas Industry Content Development Act No. 2, 2010.

concerned. All oil and gas arrangements relating to any activity in the Nigerian oil and gas industry must be in conformity with the provisions of this Act.[17]

Another notable feature of the Act, among others, is section 69, which creates the Nigerian Content Development and Monitoring Board (NCDMB), the specific functions of which are highlighted in section 70.[18] The Board has the main responsibility to implement the provisions of the Act[19] and also to manage, in its entirety, the development of Nigerian content in the Nigerian oil and gas industry.[20] Section 68 deals with noncompliance with the provisions of the Act. It provides punishment for operators, contractors, or subcontractors who carry out any project contrary to the provisions of the Act. Upon conviction, such a person is liable to a fine of 5 per cent of the project sum for each project in which the offence is committed or cancellation of the entire project.

2.2 Sustainable Development

The need for sustainable development of Nigeria's oil and gas resources – cutting across environmental, social and economic development – is extensively elaborated in several legislation and guidelines.[21] With respect to environmental protection, section 20 of the Constitution of the Federal Republic of Nigeria (CFRN), 1999 specifically provides: "The State shall protect and improve the environment and safeguard the water, air and land, forest and wildlife of Nigeria."[22] Although, this section is not justiciable under the constitution by virtue of Section 6(c) of the CFRN, its aim is to ensure environmental protection and sustainable development for Nigerian people.[23] Furthermore, section 8 of the Petroleum Act of 1969 empowers the Minister (Petroleum Resources) to exercise general supervision over all oil and gas operations in Nigeria, and to provide generally for "matters relating to

[17] See NOGICDA, note 3, section 6.
[18] The Act also gives the NCDMB various responsibilities which are scattered all over the Act.
[19] See ibid., section 70(a).
[20] See ibid., section 70(c).
[21] For general discussions on sustainable development in Nigeria's oil and gas sector, see D. Olawuyi, note 7 pp. 74–77; D. S. Olawuyi, "Legal and Sustainable Development Impacts of Major Oil Spills" (2013) 9 *Columbia University Journal of Sustainable Development* 1–15; and Olawuyi, note 6, pp. 118–121 and 303–308.
[22] See the 1999 Constitution of the Federal Republic of Nigeria, Laws of the Federation of Nigeria 2004, C23, s 20 [CFRN]. This provision is part of chapter II of the Constitution, which contains the "Fundamental Objectives and Directive Principles of State Policy." These are policies that are expected to be pursued for the realization of national ideals and aspirations, and include provisions on the protection of the environment and access to justice.
[23] CFRN, section 6(6)(c), provides that the powers of the judiciary shall not extend to "any issue or question as to whether any act of omission by any authority or person or as to whether any law or any judicial decision is in conformity with the Fundamental Objectives and Directive." See D. Olawuyi, "Increasing Relevance of Right-Based Approaches to Resource Governance in Africa: Shifting from Regional Aspiration to Local Realization" (2015) 11 *McGill International Journal of Sustainable Development Law and Policy* 113–158.

Local Content and SD in Nigeria 171

licenses and leases granted under the Act."[24] Such matters could include "safe working, the prevention of pollution of water courses and the atmosphere, and the making of reports and returns (including the reporting of accidents), and inquiries into accidents."[25] The Petroleum Minister is also empowered to revoke any license or lease where the holder fails to comply with the provisions of the regulations.[26] Pursuant to these wide discretionary powers, the Minister issued the *Environmental Guidelines and Standards for the Petroleum Industry in Nigeria (EGASPIN)*, which outlines environmental and safety standards that must be complied with by oil operators in Nigeria, to prevent, minimize, and control pollution from the various aspects of petroleum operations.[27] All oil and gas operators are required to comply with the provisions of EGASPIN in all aspects of their operations in order to minimize environmental harm to oil and gas producing communities.[28] Furthermore, the National Oil Spill Detection and Response Agency (Establishment) (NOSDRA) Act No.15 2006 outlines legal requirements and steps on the management of oil spills in Nigeria. The NOSDRA Act establishes NOSDRA as the principal agency to monitor, regulate, and respond to oil spills in the oil sector to prevent environmental harm to local communities.[29] Similarly, the Environmental Impact Assessment Act (EIA), which applies to the oil and gas industry, outlines the framework for mandatory assessments of environmental and social impacts of oil and gas projects to local communities in Nigeria. It provides for mandatory consultation with participation of local communities in the EIA process in order to minimize long term damage to the ecosystem.[30]

With respect to social development, the Nigerian legal framework aims to maximize the benefit of oil and gas production to all Nigerians, especially those in the oil and gas producing communities. The Petroleum Act 1969 provides that within ten years of the grant of an oil mining lease, the holder of the lease shall ensure that at least 75 percent of employees in "managerial, professional and supervisory grades" shall be Nigerian citizens and that "all skilled, semi-skilled and unskilled workers" are Nigerians.[31] Similarly, section 24 of the First Schedule of the Act provides that "[t]he Minister may revoke any oil prospecting licence or oil mining lease if the licensee or lessee becomes controlled directly or indirectly" by a person whose country does not offer national treatment to Nigerians. Additionally, The

---

[24] Petroleum Act of 1969, Laws of the Federation of Nigeria 2004, c P10, s. 8, Section 9(1)(b)(iii).
[25] Ibid., s. 9.
[26] Ibid., s. 8.
[27] The Department of Petroleum Resources, "Environmental Guidelines and Standards for the Petroleum Industry in Nigeria 1991, Revised Edition, 2018, https://dpr.gov.ng/egaspin/ [EGASPIN].
[28] For a review of the EGASPIN, see D. Olawuyi and Z. Tubodenyefa, "*Review of the Environmental Guidelines and Standards for the Petroleum Industry in Nigeria,*" Institute for Oil, Gas, Energy, Environment and Sustainable Development, Afe Babalola University, 2018.
[29] National Oil Spill Detection and Response Agency (Establishment) Act CAP N157, Laws of the Federation of Nigeria (LFN) 2006.
[30] Environmental Impact Assessment Act CAP E 12 Laws of the Federation of Nigeria (LFN) 2006.
[31] Petroleum Act, 1969, Schedule 1, section 38.

Petroleum (Drilling and Production) Regulations, 1969, makes local community participation and consultation mandatory before the commencement of any oil prospecting or mining activity.[32] Section 1(2)(h) of the Regulation provides an employment quota of Nigerians in the oil and gas industry, while Section 26 mandates licensees to submit "a detailed programme for the recruitment and training of Nigerians" in every phase of petroleum operations.[33] These provisions, which were in place before the NOGICDA, continue to apply in the Nigerian oil and gas industry.

Furthermore, The Niger-Delta Development Commission (NDDC) (Establishment, ETC.) Act, 2000 establishes the NDDC as an agency responsible for implementing sustainable development programs in the Niger Delta.[34] Sections 7(1)(b) and (j) of NDDC Act mandate the NDDC to "implement programmes for the sustainable development of the Niger-Delta in the area of education, employment and other key sectors."[35] Secondly, it mandates the NDDC to "execute other projects required for the sustainable development of the Niger-Delta area and its people."[36] These provisions provide a legal basis for the NDDC to work with firms, entities, and other stakeholders operating in the Niger Delta communities to implement sustainable development plans and programs.

With respect to economic development, although the NOGICDA does not clearly reference the principle of sustainable development, many of its core provisions are focused solely on ensuring that Nigerians and Nigerian entities are directly empowered to actively participate in the management of the oil and gas industry.[37] It aims to create jobs, employment, and economic advancement opportunities for all Nigerians, including those within and outside the oil and gas industry.

Furthermore, the 2017 National Gas Policy[38] and the 2017 National Petroleum Policy[39] aim to accelerate positive economic, social, and environmental development in Nigeria's oil and gas industry. For example, the main aim of the National Petroleum Policy is for Nigeria to become a nation "where hydrocarbons are used as a fuel for national economic growth and not simply as a source of income."[40] With particular reference to local content, the government commits to develop an inclusive Niger Delta, where local communities are involved in infrastructure, social, and petroleum developments in the area.[41] Pursuant to the policy, the Nigerian government also aims to focus on human capital development as a means of increasing

---

[32] The Petroleum (Drilling and Production) Regulations to the Petroleum Act 1969.
[33] Ibid.
[34] Olawuyi, note 7, 200–201.
[35] The Niger-Delta Development Commission (NDDC) (Establishment, ETC.) Act, 2000, section 7(1)(b).
[36] Ibid., section 7(1)(j).
[37] See ibid., sections 3, 12, 15, 28, 30, 51, and 52.
[38] This was approved on 28 June 2017.
[39] This was approved on 19 July 2017.
[40] KPMG, "The National Petroleum Policy (NPP)," August 2017.
[41] Ibid.

Local Content and SD in Nigeria 173

local content, including overhauling the procurement process, awarding marginal fields to indigenous people and developing human capital as a way of maximizing local and in-country value.[42] Similarly, the Policy aims to minimize environmental degradation in the oil and gas industry.[43]

The Petroleum Industry Governance Bill (PIGB) is another instrument that, if passed to law, could advance local content and sustainable development in Nigeria in the near future. In 2017, the Nigerian National Assembly passed a portion of the comprehensive PIGB.[44] The original comprehensive bill had to be split into three Bills in order for one part to be passed as the PIGB.[45] A third portion of the bill, which is yet to be passed, provides for the Host Community Fund and the management of local community participation in governance.[46] The Petroleum Host Community Fund[47] mandates MNCs in the upstream sector to remit 10 percent of their monthly net profits to the Fund, to be applied to the "development of the economic and social infrastructure" of the host communities to extractive resource projects.[48] In addition to addressing the significant infrastructure deficits in oil and gas producing communities in Nigeria,[49] this provision aims to generate jobs, social services, and environmental co-benefits to Nigerians in oil and gas producing communities.

The foregoing legislation and instruments show that Nigeria has a comprehensive framework in place that aims to accelerate local content and sustainable development in the oil and gas industry. However, despite the lofty ideals of LCRs and sustainable development in the just-discussed laws, the core precepts of Nigeria's LCRs have not fully translated to increased economic and social benefits for Nigerian workers and industries, especially those in the oil-producing communities. There are steep barriers and roadblocks that continue to hinder the successful implementation of both concepts. Some of these barriers are analyzed in the next Section.

---

[42] Ibid.

[43] Ibid.

[44] See Federal Republic of Nigeria, "A Bill for an Act to Establish the Legal and Regulatory Framework, Institutions and Regulatory Authorities for the Nigerian Petroleum Industry, to establish Guidelines for the Operation of the Upstream and Downstream Sectors, and for Purposes Connected with the Same," Petroleum Industry Bill, HB 159, 2008 [PIB]; The Senate, Federal Republic of Nigeria, "Report of The Senate Joint Committee on the Petroleum Industry Governance Bill 2017, SB 237." See further, J. Payne and C. Eboh, "Nigeria Passes Major Oil Reform Bill after 17 Year Struggle" (January 18, 2018), www.reuters.com/article/us-nigeria-oil-law/nigeria-passes-major-oil-reform-bill-after-17-year-struggle-idUSKBN1F72I2.

[45] Ibid.

[46] See, Federal Republic of Nigeria, "Petroleum Host and Impacted Communities Development Bill 2018." See further, Federal Republic of Nigeria, "Harmonized Petroleum Industry Governance Bill 2018."

[47] PIB, note 44, section 116.

[48] Ibid. The Nigerian Constitution provides for the payment of 13 percent of the revenue from the Federation Account be paid to oil producing States.

[49] Olawuyi, note 6, pp. 55–80.

174   *Damilola S. Olawuyi and Ayobami J. Olaniyan*

3 LCRS AND SUSTAINABLE DEVELOPMENT IN THE NIGERIAN OIL AND GAS INDUSTRY: GAPS AND CHALLENGES

Despite the clear sustainable development objectives of the NOGICDA, coherence, transparency, and accountability in interpretation and implementation will need to be improved. LCRs face pre-existing challenges, such as corruption, low capacities, and weak enforcement of LCRs, which weaken the sustainable development outcomes of LCRs. The key challenges to LCRs and sustainable development in Nigeria are discussed in this Section.

3.1 *Corruption and Lack of Transparency*

Transparency in the oil and gas context entails openness across all aspects of regulatory enforcement and supervision.[50] Transparency and integrity are governed by key principles such as access to information, accountability, evidence-based decision-making, and avoiding conflict of interests.[51] In order to retain public confidence and trust, an effective regulatory system must be open and transparent, meaning LCR guidelines must be clear, while efforts to enforce them should be made available for the public to review.[52] Furthermore, regulatory excellence requires frequent, timely, and detailed reporting on how LCRs are applied and enforced in project approval, construction and operations, and closure or decommissioning.[53] It is not enough for the law to mandate LCRs, the NCDMB must censoriously exercise its oversight functions in a clear and transparent manner.

For example, lack of transparency and corruption are significant stumbling blocks to the implementation of LCRs in the Nigerian oil and gas industry.[54] Estimates indicate that Nigeria has had at least $400 billion of its oil revenue stolen or misspent

---

[50] As L. D. Brandeis wrote in his very famous 1913 article, "What Publicity Can Do": "Sunlight is said to be the best of disinfectants ... open government requires that the citizenry be granted access to government records when it is necessary to meaningful public debate on the conduct of government institutions" (L. Brandeis, "What Publicity Can Do" in *Other People's Money*, chapter 5, p. 92 (1932), first published in *Harper's Weekly*, December 20, 1913).

[51] OECD. See the Rio Declaration noting that at the national level, each individual shall have appropriate access to information on hazardous materials and activities in their communities, and the opportunity to participate in decision-making processes. See also, C. Sunstein, "Informational Regulation and Informational Standing: Akins and Beyond" (1999) 147 *University of Pennsylvania Law Review* 613 at 625, stating that, "A well-functioning system of deliberative democracy requires a certain degree of information, so that citizens can engage in their monitoring and deliberative tasks ... A good way to enable citizens to oversee government action and also to assess the need for less, more, or different regulation, is to inform them of both private and public activity."

[52] See D. Olawuyi, "Local Content and Procurement Requirements in Oil and Gas Contracts: Regional Trends in the Middle East and North Africa" (2019) 37 *Journal of Energy and Natural Resources Law* 93–117.

[53] IMF Fiscal Affairs Department, "Fiscal Transparency, Accountability, and Risk," Prepared by Fiscal Affairs Department in collaboration with the Statistics Department, Approved by Carlo Cottarelli, August 7, 2012.

[54] Ovadia, note 11, pp. 137–146.

Local Content and SD in Nigeria 175

since independence in 1960.[55] There have been several allegations of bribery and misuse or exploitation of public power and position for personal or familial benefits by key regulatory agencies given the task to enforce any penalty or provision of LCRs and sustainable development across the Nigerian oil and gas industry.[56] Corruption, in the form of systematic bribes and kickbacks to regulators, patronage, and fraudulent award of contracts to cronies of regulators all prevent accountability and weaken the enforcement of LCRs in the Nigerian oil and gas sector.[57] The pervasiveness of corruption in the Nigerian oil and gas industry also manifests through lack of openness and the practice of accepting bribes on the part of regulatory officials saddled with the responsibility of implementing public procurements, and/or enforcing LCRs and sustainable development.[58] This situation has fostered an environment of lax or weak compliance with LCRs by key stakeholders.

Furthermore, Nigeria's LCRs contain gaps and vulnerabilities that foster corruption and impunity. For example, a huge opportunity for corruption under the Act is contained in section 92 of the Act,[59] which provides:

(1) The Board may accept gifts of money, land or other property on such terms and conditions, if any, as may be specified by the person or organization making the gift.

(2) The Board shall not accept any gift if the conditions attached thereto are inconsistent with the functions of the Board under this Act.

This section makes it legal for the local content Board, which is established in Section 4 of NOGICDA to guide, monitor, coordinate, and implement LCRs, to accept gratis payments and gifts from individuals and entities in the oil and gas industry. While the legislative intent for this provision could have been to widen the sources of funds available to the Board to perform its oversight functions, this provision has a significant potential to compromise the functional independence and transparency of the Board, and could entrench conflicts of interest in the Board's

---

[55] See BBC News, "Nigeria: Oil-Gas Sector Mismanagement Costs Billions," October 21, 2012, www .bbc.com/news/world-africa-20081268; K. Annan, "Momentum Rises to Lift Africa's Resource Curse," September 4, 2012, www.nytimes.com/2012/09/14/opinion/kofi-annan-momentum-rises-to-lift-africas-resource-curse.html.

[56] S. Igbinedion, "Workability of the Norms of Transparency and Accountability against Corruption in Nigeria" (2014) 3 *Afe Babalola University Journal of Sustainable Development Law and Policy* 150–155.

[57] Human Rights Watch, *The Price of Oil: Corporate Responsibility and Human Rights Violations in Nigeria's Oil Producing Communities* (Washington, DC: Human Rights Watch, 1999), p. 47 (discussing the impact of governmental corruption in the forms of systematic kickbacks for the award of contracts, special bank accounts in the control of the presidency, and fraudulent allocation of oil or refined products to political favorites, on sustainable resource governance in Nigeria). M. O. Erhun, "The Role of the Nigerian Oil and Gas Content Act in the Promotion of Sustainable Economic Development" (2015) 5 *Development Country Studies* 117.

[58] Nwapi, note 8, pp. 92–96. See also, E. Essien, G. Lodorfos, and I. Kostopoulos, "Antecedents of Supplier Selection Decisions in the Public Sector in Nigeria" (2019) 19 *Journal of Public Procurement* 15–45.

[59] Ibid., p. 93.

176   *Damilola S. Olawuyi and Ayobami J. Olaniyan*

ability to effectively sanction members of the public (individuals, organizations, and companies alike) who are in violations of the Act.[60] This kind of negative perception may hinder the activities of the NCDMB and may bias them in the many responsibilities given to them under the Act. Effective and efficient supervision of LCRs requires the independence of the regulator from industry influences; and structural and organizational autonomy in terms of finance, institutional setup, and the decision-making process of the regulator.[61] Furthermore, conflict of interest and lack of transparency brings about and feeds the public's suspicion of corruption and lack of integrity even when this is not the case. This could place a perpetual burden on the regulator to defend its actions and policies, thereby slowing down the efficacy of regulation.[62]

It is important to undertake a comprehensive reform of NOGICDA to address corruption vulnerabilities and gaps. Without addressing corruption and lack of transparency in the Nigerian oil and gas sector, LCRs in Nigeria may continue to remain ineffective.

3.2 Weak Enforcement of Relevant Laws

One of the key threats to LCRs and sustainable development in Nigeria is the weak enforcement of existing LCRs and policies.[63] While Nigeria has robust provisions on LCRs, regulatory agencies and bodies meant to enforce LCRs face several practical and structural inadequacies that reduce their supervisory capabilities and functions.[64] Inadequacies such as insufficient funds, lack of operational machinery, and dearth of technical personnel often make it difficult for government agencies to carry out their various responsibilities.[65] Thus, laws that the agencies have the responsibility to enforce are usually not enforced properly. LCRs and sustainable development programs in Nigeria are not immune from the problem of weak enforcement. Government agencies saddled with the responsibility of enforcing laws are bogged down with their own numerous challenges, such as inadequate funding, lack of required technology and manpower, and a general lack of adequate resources, which are frequent problems faced by enforcement

---

[60] For a robust discussion on the vulnerabilities for corruption under the NOGICDA, see generally Nwapi, note 8, pp. 92–96.

[61] F. Gilardi and M. Maggetti, "The Independence of Regulatory Authorities" in D. Levi-Faur (ed.), *Handbook on the Politics of Regulation* (Cheltenham: Edward Elgar, 2010), pp. 201–214.

[62] See OECD, *Governance of Regulators' Practices: Accountability, Transparency and Coordination* (Paris: OECD Publishing, 2016), pp. 24–63; A. Florini, "Introduction: The Battle over Transparency" in A. Florini (ed.), *The Right to Know: Transparency for an Open World* (Columbia University Press, 2007), pp. 1–2.

[63] Ovadia, note 11, 146, Nwapi, note8) 92–96, Olawuyi, note 6) 338–343.

[64] Erhun, note 57.

[65] Ibid. See also, Olawuyi et al., note 28.

Local Content and SD in Nigeria 177

agencies.[66] The LCRs and sustainable development plans (SDPs) also suffer from this challenge.

For instance, under NOGICDA,[67] companies (operators, contractors, and other categories of service provider) in the Nigerian oil and gas industry are expected to submit a plan, report, or compliance information to the NCDMB within a certain time frame. However, several companies (especially operators) do not comply with many LCRs.[68] Unfortunately, due to lack of funding and dearth of highly trained personnel, the ability of NCDMB to enforce compliance and apply penalties to defaulting operators in a timely manner has been perennially hampered.[69] Lack of a critical mass of staffs required to effectively monitor and enforce LCRs has stifled the regulatory capacity of the NCDMB. For example, the problem of weak institutional capacity and lack of training and expertise has been identified in several studies as key challenges that limit the ability of NCDMB to implement and monitor LCRs in Nigeria.[70] There is a need to address this gap through the recruitment of skilled and trained staff, as well as providing local content education and training for extant staffs.

3.3 Inadequate Supplier Development and Skills Acquisition Programs for Indigenous Suppliers and Workforce

As discussed in Chapter 5 of this book, supplier development programs are essential for successful LCR outcomes.[71] Bespoke skills development and local supplier development programs can help local professionals and suppliers to overcome capacity barriers that prevent them from securing highly skilled employment, winning procurement bids, or meeting the knowledge and technical requirements to operate optimally in the oil and gas industry.[72] Despite the strong emphasis in the

[66] Olawuyi et al., note 28. See also A. Olaniyan, "Imposing Liability for Oil Spill Clean-Ups in Nigeria: An Examination of the Role of the Polluter-Pays Principle" (2015) 40 *Journal of Law, Policy and Globalization* 83.

[67] See for example, NOGICDA, note 3, sections 38, 46, 49, 51, and 52.

[68] For detailed information on the level of compliance to implement LCRs on Nigerian content by companies in the Nigerian oil and gas industry in Q1 & Q2 2018, see NCDMB, "Q1 & Q2 Nigerian Content Compliance Matrix."

[69] B. Udo, "Why Local Content in Nigeria's Oil, Gas Industry Is Low – Executive Secretary, NCDMB," April 20, 2017, www.premiumtimesng.com/news/headlines/229141-local-content-nigerias-oil-gas-industry-low-executive-secretary-ncdmb.html.

[70] I. Oguinne, "Nigerian Content in the Nigerian Petroleum Industry: Legal and Policy Issues" (2011) 29 *Journal of Energy and Natural Resources Law* 405–430; also, J. Okafor and F. Aniche, "A Critical Appraisal of Enforcement of Nigerian Oil and Gas Industry Content Development (NOGICD) Act, 2010" (2014) 31 *Journal of Law, Policy and Globalization* 82–94; C. Chikezie, "Making the Local Content Law Work," NOG, May–June, 2010, pp. 11, 17.

[71] Intergovernmental Forum on Mining, Minerals, Metals and Sustainable Development (IGF), "IGF Guidance for Governments: Local content policies," 2018, pp. 28–30, defining supplier development programs as "measures and programs to help develop the capacity of local suppliers, primarily through access to markets, mentorship, training and skills development and access to finance."

[72] Ibid.

178 *Damilola S. Olawuyi and Ayobami J. Olaniyan*

Nigerian LCRs on giving preference to indigenous companies and local manpower in the Nigerian oil and gas industry, the reality is that several indigenous small and medium scale enterprises (SMEs) lack the personnel, expertise, skills, technology, and financial resources needed to be sufficiently competitive and not require preferential treatment, especially to meet the technical standards of upstream exploration and production activities.[73] Thus, there remains heavy reliance on IOCs to carry out the core and technical services in the oil and gas industry.[74]

It is not enough to prescribe LCRs that aim to empower local professionals and suppliers in the oil and gas sector. There is a need for tailored supplier development programs and training aimed at bridging knowledge and capacity gaps of such professionals and suppliers, especially through mentorship, training, and skills development.[75] The NOGICDA already contains robust provisions that mandate IOCs to train and develop Nigerian capabilities in the oil and gas sector.[76] However, only very few companies and people have been able to access training opportunities required for them to hold high-skilled jobs in the Nigerian oil and gas industry.[77] Furthermore, when such training opportunities are provided, they are not often conducted in the local dialects and languages that are accessible to the local communities.[78] The result is that several Nigerians willing to seek highly skilled employment or secure contracts to provide goods and services in the oil and gas sector simply do not have the required expertise and skills to qualify for such procurement opportunities or jobs.[79]

To enhance the competitiveness of local suppliers and indigenous workforce in the Nigerian oil and gas industry, it is important for the NCDMB to provide more opportunities for capacity development for local professionals and suppliers. For example, it is pertinent for the NCDMB to develop robust skills acquisition and training programs in conjunction with stakeholders, such as petroleum universities and technical institutes, such as the Institute for Oil, Gas, Energy, Environment and Sustainable Development (OGEES Institute), the Oil and Gas Trainers Association of Nigeria (OGTAN), and other independent training service providers in the oil and gas sector which can help bridge the current capacity gaps in the Nigerian oil and gas industry.[80]

---

[73] Ovadia, note 36.
[74] Balouga, note 8, p. 24.
[75] IGF, note 71.
[76] See NOGICDA, note 3, sections 28 and 30.
[77] Udo, note 69.
[78] Ibid. J. Aigboduwa and M. Oisamoje, "Promoting Small and Medium Enterprises in the Nigerian Oil and Gas Industries" (2013) 9 *European Scientific Journal* 244.
[79] Ibid.
[80] See Oil and Gas Trainers Association of Nigeria (OGTAN), https://ogtan.org.ng. Also Institute for Oil, Gas, Energy, Environment and Sustainable Development, www.ogeesinstitute.edu.ng.

Local Content and SD in Nigeria

3.4 Inadequate Financing for Indigenous Companies

Lack of financial capability remains a key impediment for indigenous companies working in the Nigerian oil and gas industry. The oil and gas industry is a capital-intensive industry that often requires companies to perform contractual obligations without advance financial mobilization. For example, due to the highly cost-intensive nature of oil and gas services, many domestic firms are unable to meet obligations under supply or service contracts without significant financial mobilization.[81] Consequently, only companies with strong financial and technical backing from foreign parent companies are truly able to survive and compete in the Nigerian oil and gas industry.[82] This scenario creates a situation of perennial dependence on foreign services and goods and has not produced the sustainable development aims of NOGICDA, in terms of providing economic opportunities for indigenous Nigerian oil and gas companies.

Furthermore, SMEs in the Nigerian oil and gas sector face several challenges that impact their abilities to finance oil and gas projects and meet contractual timelines.[83] These challenges include inadequate patronage; excessively long periods between completing contracts and receiving final payments; inadequate access to credit facilities and equipment financing which increases financial burden especially when purchasing expensive high-tech oil-field equipment; high cost of borrowing which erodes profitability; capital flight and inadequate access to foreign currency; and lack of financial documentation, particularly audited accounts which makes borrowing difficult.[84] These problems limit the financial capabilities of SMEs and make it difficult for them to mobilize the finances required to perform contractual obligations. These problems are further exacerbated when government entities and foreign companies fail to pay SMEs a backlog of due payments under existing contractual arrangements. These problems account for the high bankruptcy rate of SMEs in the Nigerian oil and gas industry.[85]

SMEs in the Nigerian oil and gas industry will need to be backed if they are to compete with, and have a level playing field as, foreign companies. The NCDMB has a strong role to play in creating a level playing field for Nigerian indigenous companies in the oil and gas sectors, particularly the SMEs. In realization of this, the NCDMB has launched the Nigerian Content Intervention (NCI) Fund, a pool

---

[81] M. Eboh, "Local Content, Local Troubles: How Big Firms Kill Small Businesses," December 24, 2018, www.vanguardngr.com/2018/12/local-content-local-troubles-how-big-firms-kill-small-businesses/.

[82] Ibid. See also Udo, note 69.

[83] H. U. Nwosu, I. N. Nwachukwu, S. O. T. Ogaji, and S. D. Probert, "Local Involvement in Harnessing Crude Oil and Natural Gas in Nigeria (2006) 83 *Applied Energy* 1274–1284.

[84] Ibid. See also B. Araco, "World Bank Says Less than 1 percent Nigerian Businesses have Access to Credit," Business Day, September 1, 2010, p. 5; O. Bello, "Local Content: Firms Risk Losing over \$5bn to Lack of Patronage," Business Day, September 6, 2010, pp. 1, 4, and 6.

[85] Eboh, note 81.

180   *Damilola S. Olawuyi and Ayobami J. Olaniyan*

of funds designed to provide loans to indigenous manufacturers, service providers, and firms seeking to acquire assets, especially rigs and marine vessels.[86] Beneficiaries are to get a maximum of US$10 million, repayable after five years at 8 percent interest rate.[87] This is an important initiative which, if well implemented, can significantly alleviate financial burdens of SMEs especially with respect to contract financing and the purchase of expensive equipment. However, one key concern that has to be addressed is the need to provide fair, equitable, and transparent opportunities for more SMEs to access the funds.[88]

In addition to providing opportunities for financing, the NCDMB can play a significant role in addressing lopsided contractual provisions that require SMEs to perform obligations without significant financial mobilization. Not only do such provisions fail to reflect the practical realities of SMEs, when compared to foreign companies, they also effectively set local SMEs up for failure and bankruptcy. In order to reflect the local circumstances and realities of Nigerian SMEs there is a need for the NCDMB to act against lopsided contractual terms and provisions that place indigenous companies in inequitable positions. For example, the NCDMB can provide model and template contracts for the provision of goods and services in the Nigerian oil and gas industry. Such model contracts can address issues of upfront mobilization, payment timelines and thresholds, and penalties for nonpayment after contract completion (such as high interest and default provisions) amongst others. By requiring foreign companies and government entities to comply with model contracts for the procurement of goods and services in the Nigerian oil and gas sector, the NCDMB can provide a level playing field for SMEs to compete and thrive in the oil and gas industry.

If Nigerian indigenous companies are not provided legal protection and support, they may continue to remain junior players in the industry. This challenge would erode the intention of NOGICDA, which is to encourage participation by Nigerian indigenous companies in the oil and gas industry.[89]

3.5 Gender Injustice and Inequalities in the Nigerian Oil and Gas Sector

Despite the expansive provisions of the Nigerian LCRs in terms of providing employment and participation opportunities for all Nigerian citizens, there remains a considerable gender gap in the distribution of benefits and risks, as well as access to

---

[86] NCDMB, "BOI Launch $200m NCI Fund," https://ncdmb.gov.ng/2017/08/ncdmb-boi-launch-200m-nci-fund/.

[87] Ibid.

[88] The Punch, "Nigerian Content Development Fund hasn't achieved its goals, seven years after – Wabote," April 16, 2017, https://punchng.com/nigerian-content-development-fund-hasnt-achieved-its-goals-seven-years-after-wabote/, stating that even though over $700M has been disbursed under the funds, it has gone to only three service companies.

[89] See for example, NOGICDA, note 3, s. 3, 10, 12, and 15.

Local Content and SD in Nigeria   181

socio-economic opportunities, for women in key sectors of the Nigerian oil and gas industry.[90] Several studies have compiled the growing evidence of gender injustice and inequality in oil and gas industries in Africa, including Nigeria.[91] The manifestations of gender inequality in Nigeria include uneven education, training, and empowerment opportunities for girls and women;[92] unequal access of women to, and control of, important resources such as land, property, employment, and credit facilities;[93] prevalence of social and cultural norms that assign secondary and subordinate roles to women in businesses, community, and national decision-making processes;[94] inadequate opportunities for women to hold government, and other senior leadership, positions;[95] and the increased adoption of governmental policies and programs that suppress women's experiences, perceptions, and voices.[96] These problems have over the years impacted the abilities of Nigerian women to effectively take part in and influence decision-making processes on oil and gas development activities and projects.[97] These concerns are more pronounced in oil

[90] See BBC News, "Nigeria's Growing Number of Female Oil Bosses," September 11, 2014, www .bbc.com/news/business–29127436, stating that the Nigerian "oil and gas industry is still overwhelmingly male, with surveys showing that the executive boardrooms of petroleum companies are mostly a boys' club." See also "In Search of More Women in a Male-dominated Oil and Gas Industry" (July 9, 2019), www.thisdaylive.com/index.php/2019/07/07/in-search-of-more-women-in-a-male-dominated-oil-and-gas-industry/.

[91] African Development Bank, *Women's Economic Empowerment in Oil and Gas Industries in Africa*, www.afdb.org/fileadmin/uploads/afdb/Documents/Publications/anrc/ AfDB_WomenEconomicsEmpowerment_V15.pdf, stating that in African extractive industries, "while benefits accrue mostly to men in the form of employment and compensation, the costs (e.g. family or social disruption, environmental degradation) fall most heavily on women"; also UNDP, "Africa Human Development Report 2016: Accelerating Gender Equality and Women's Empowerment Africa", 2016, pp. 1–15, stating that: African women achieve only 87 percent of the human development outcomes of men; and that endemic gender gaps costs sub-Saharan Africa $US95 billion a year. See also J. Arbache, A. Kolev, and E. Filipiak (eds.), *Gender Disparities in Africa's Labour Market* (Washington, DC: World Bank, 2010), pp. 1–10.

[92] A. Ademuson, "Women Domination and Oppression in Nigerian Society: Implications for Sustainable Development" (2016) 19 *African Journal for the Psychological Studies of Social Issues* 24–36.

[93] M. Benschop, *Rights and Reality: Are Women's Equal Rights to Land, Housing and Property Implemented in East Africa?* (Nairobi: UN-Habitat, 2002); United Nations, *Women's Control over Economic Resources and Access to Financial Resources, including Microfinance* (New York: United Nations, 2009), pp. 1–5, noting that equal access to economic and financial resources is critical for gender equality and empowerment.

[94] See UNEP, *Women at the Frontline of Climate Change: Gender Risks and Hopes: A Rapid Response Assessment* (United Nations Environment Programme, 2011), p. 6.

[95] S. Seguino, "Toward Gender Justice: Confronting Stratification and Power" (2013) 2 *Géneros* 1–36.

[96] See Ademuson, note 92; also M. O. Okome, "Domestic, Regional and International Protection of Nigeria Women against Discrimination: Constraints and Possibilities" (2002) 6 *African Studies Quarterly* 33–54.

[97] I. Ajibade and D. Olawuyi, "Climate Change Impacts on Housing and Property Rights in Nigeria and Panama: Toward a Rights-Based Approach to Adaptation and Mitigation" in D. Stucker and E. Lopez-Gunn (eds.), *Adaptation to Climate Change through Water Resources Management: Capacity, Equity and Sustainability* (New York: Routledge, 2014), pp. 264–284.

182   *Damilola S. Olawuyi and Ayobami J. Olaniyan*

and gas producing communities in the Niger Delta, where high levels of illiteracy among women, coupled with predominant marginalization and forced displacements of native women from ancestral lands, have created "double jeopardy" effects of intersecting alienation both because they are women and because they live in indigenous communities.[98]

Gender inequality in Nigeria's oil and gas sector is exacerbated by the lack of vulnerability assessment and information on the roles of, and opportunities available to, women in the Nigerian oil and gas industry value chain. The NCDMB, as well as other regulators, have yet to pay sufficient attention to studying, analyzing, and unpacking patterns of opportunity and wealth (non)creation for women in key sectors of the industry. The number of local content opportunities, such as jobs, financing, procurement contracts, and training, provided for girls and women in the Nigerian oil and gas industry are hardly measured, assessed, or documented in a clear and transparent manner.[99] Furthermore, the critical linkages between gender justice and overall sustainable development has yet to be given serious consideration in program planning, public procurement practices, decision-making, financing, training, capacity development, and program implementation in the male-dominated Nigerian oil and gas industry, cutting across government, industry, and nongovernmental agencies associated with the industry. Lack of reliable information gathering and assessment makes it difficult, if not impossible, for the NCDMB to develop tailored programs, projects, and opportunities for Nigerian girls and women, even though they are some of the most affected by oil and gas related pollution, displacements, and conflicts.[100]

Several core human rights instruments recognize equality and nondiscrimination as core pillars of international law. Articles 1, 2, and 7 of the Universal Declaration of Human Rights (UDHR) recognize that all humans are equal before the law and are entitled without any discrimination to equal protection of the law.[101] Article 26 of the ICCPR guarantees to all persons equal and effective protection against discrimination on any ground, such as gender.[102] Articles 2(3) and 3 of the ICESCR also contain similar provisions on nondiscrimination.[103] Finally, Article 7 of the Convention on the Elimination of All Forms of Discrimination against Women (CEDAW) provides for the elimination of discrimination against women in political

---

[98] Ibid.; see also L. Okolosie, "Beyond 'Talking' and 'Owning' Intersectionality" (2014) 108 *Feminist Review* 90; J. Bond, "International Intersectionality: A Theoretical and Pragmatic Exploration of Women's International Human Rights Violations" (2003) 52 *Emory Law Journal* 71 at 76.

[99] BBC News, note 90.

[100] Ajibade et al., note 97.

[101] UN General Assembly, *Universal Declaration on Human and Peoples Rights*, 10 December 1948, U. N. Doc A/810, p. 71.

[102] UN General Assembly, *International Covenant on Civil and Political*, 16 December 1966, 999 UNTS 171 [ICCPR].

[103] UN General Assembly, *International Covenant on Economic, Social and Cultural Rights*, 16 December 1966, 993 UNTS 3.

and public life, and Article 5 encourages States to take measures to eliminate prejudices and stereotyping against women.[104]

The critical intersections of environment, sustainable development, human rights, and LCRs show that the full implementation of international treaty norms in the oil and gas industry can only be effective when underpinned by gender justice and equality.[105] The human rights–based approach (HRBA) to development underscores the need for equal treatment of men and women in development efforts and projects.[106] To protect and fulfill the nondiscrimination norm of international law in the oil and gas industry, national authorities, especially the NCDMB, will need to incorporate vulnerability assessment and proofing as part of the wider human rights assessment of all development laws, policies, programs, and project.[107]

4 ADVANCING LCRS FOR SUSTAINABLE DEVELOPMENT IN NIGERIA: THE WAY FORWARD

It is imperative to develop integrated solutions to address the complex issues inhibiting the effective implementation of LCRs and SDPs in the Nigerian oil and gas industry. Holistic reforms should be put forward to solve the identified multifaceted challenges. If effectively addressed, LCRs in Nigeria can deliver practical and measurable sustainable development benefits across the Nigerian oil and gas industry. This section discusses essential legal reforms that could enhance LCRs and SDPs in Nigeria.

4.1 Enforcement of Anti-Corruption and Whistle-Blowing Initiatives in the Nigerian Oil and Gas Industry

As earlier discussed, corruption and lack of transparency are entrenched problems in the Nigerian oil and gas industry and have become the norm as to how activities are carried out. This situation must be reversed and dealt with decisively in order to actualize the broad and comprehensive provisions of LCRs in Nigeria. Although the Nigerian Extractive Industries Transparency Initiative (NEITI) has the mandate "to institutionalise accountability mechanisms and processes aimed at instilling a culture of transparency in Nigeria's

---

[104] See, UN General Assembly, *Optional Protocol to the Convention on the Elimination of Discrimination Against Women (CEDAW)*, 6 October 1999, 2131 UNTS 83.

[105] See G. Terry, "No Climate Justice without Gender Justice: An Overview of the Issues" (2009) 17 *Gender and Development* 5–18; also, D. McCauley and R. Heffron, "Just Transition: Integrating Climate, Energy and Environmental Justice" (2018) 119 *Energy Policy* 1–7.

[106] D. Olawuyi, *The Human Rights Based Approach to Carbon Finance* (Cambridge University Press, 2016), pp. 1–25, see also UN Human Rights Working Group, "The Human Rights Based Approach to Development Cooperation towards a Common Understanding among UN Agencies," 2003.

[107] See P. Tschakert, B. Van Oort, A. Lera St. Clair, and A. LaMadrid, "Inequality and Transformation Analyses: A Complementary Lens for Addressing Vulnerability to Climate Change" (2013) 5 *Climate and Development* 340–350.

184 *Damilola S. Olawuyi and Ayobami J. Olaniyan*

extractive sector for the benefit of all"[108] backed up by the NEITI Act, 2007,[109] more direct and tailored interventions could still be put in place to address corruption and transparency in the oil and gas industry. A comprehensive and bespoke regulation on oil-sector transparency is essential for the oil and gas industry. Such a regulation should criminalize corruption, bribery, and lack of transparency. For example, the Minister for Petroleum could, in exercise of the discretionary and oversight powers in the section 8 of the Petroleum Act, develop robust guidelines on oil sector transparency with respect to the provision of goods and services in the sector. This new regulation or guideline should impose stiff penalties, including loss of licenses on defaulters of all provisions relating to transparency, LCRs, and accountability across the entire oil and gas industry value chain in Nigeria. Not only will this complement the NEITI, it will also send a clear signal on government's willingness to address economic leakages and illicit practices in the industry.

The use of whistle-blowing as an alternative way of dealing with corruption and lack of transparency in the oil and gas industry is a step in the right direction which must be pursued vigorously. The Whistle-Blowing Policy (WBP) in use in Nigeria, which was introduced by the executive arm of the federal government of Nigeria in the fourth quarter of 2016,[110] has yielded positive results over time.[111] Although the total amount of money recovered so far through whistle-blowers' information is not certain, more than US$160 million is reported to have been recovered.[112] Despite this, there is no particular legislation that guarantees the protection of whistle-blowers in Nigeria.[113] However, many Nigerians have provided useful information that has led to the recovery of funds, arrest, and prosecution of individuals.[114] It is then imperative that a law protecting whistle-blowers should be enacted in Nigeria so as to encourage accountability and deter corrupt tendencies especially in the Nigerian oil and gas industry.

4.2 *Establishment of an Energy Infrastructure Bank in Nigeria*

The creation of an Energy Infrastructure Bank for the oil and gas and other related industries is recommended. This initiative, it is believed, would assist the

---

[108] NEITI, "Mission/Vision," https://neiti.gov.ng/index.php/aboutus/mission-vision.
[109] According to the explanatory memorandum to the Act, the Act is to "provide for the establishment of the Nigeria Extractive Industries Transparency Initiative (NEITI) charged with the responsibility among other things for the development of a framework for transparency and accountability in the reporting and disclosure by all extractive industry companies of revenue due to or paid to the Federal Government."
[110] Ao2 Law, "Whistle Blowing in the Nigerian Oil Industry: Matters Arising," 2017.
[111] See H. A. Salihu, "Whistleblowing Policy and Anti-Corruption Struggle in Nigeria: An Overview" (2019) 12 *African Journal of Criminology and Justice Studies* 63.
[112] Ibid.
[113] Ibid.
[114] Ao2 Law, note 110.

Local Content and SD in Nigeria 185

development of critical energy infrastructures for the Nigerian oil and gas industry. The initial funding mechanism of this bank must be well thought out to prevent a situation whereby it would be solely owned by the government. Private reputable financial investors must have input in the establishment of this bank. The focus of this bank should also be to help indigenous Nigerian oil and gas companies with loans for major energy projects so that they can compete with IOCs for major projects in the industry. A robust mechanism for running this bank must be put in place to prevent waste and embezzlement of funds meant for energy projects. The model of the current Infrastructure Bank[115] can be studied to develop a formidable Energy Infrastructure Bank of Nigeria.

4.3 *Improving Enforcement Mechanisms for Relevant Laws Dealing with LCRs and SDPs*

As earlier discussed, there are comprehensive provisions on LCRs in the Nigerian local content law, however, the implementation of the LCRs are very weak. Enforcement of LCRs and SDPs must be improved in order for meaningful growth to be recorded in the Nigerian oil and gas industry. To enhance enforcement, it is essential to provide proper funding and support (technical) to regulatory agencies saddled with the onerous task of enforcing the LCRs and SDPs. This would ensure that they meet their targets.[116] The relevant regulatory agencies should have their own adequate resources and personnel, and should not depend on the Nigerian government or oil companies for any form of assistance as provided for by the NOGICDA. A practicable guideline developed in conjunction with the oil and gas industry on mechanisms for enforcement and reporting of correct and accurate indices for the achievement of set targets on sustainable development and local content must be developed. Enforcement of LCRs and SDPs must also be transparent and seen to be transparent by the industry or else underreporting and cutting corners on compliance would continue to be the norm.

4.4 *Establishment of Specialized Training Schools for Skills Acquisition for Nigerians in the Oil and Gas Industry to enhance Local Content*

In addition to developing training collaborations with petroleum universities, institutes, and industry trainers, a bespoke training school should be created to train any Nigerian interested in working in the oil and gas industry. The development of this specialized training school and its management must be developed in conjunction with oil and gas industry experts who can give requisite technical training to students who would attend this school. This training school would bridge the skills gap and

---

[115] See Infrastructure Bank Plc, "About Infrastructure Bank," www.infrastructurebankplc.com/bank .php.
[116] Olawuyi et al., note 28.

186   *Damilola S. Olawuyi and Ayobami J. Olaniyan*

would also encourage the tenets of Nigerian content and local content in general to be implemented.

4.5 *Addressing Gender Gaps in Oil and Gas Employment*

It is imperative for the NCDMB, as well as other regulators and stakeholders in the Nigerian oil and gas industry, to give greater priority and attention to gender vulnerability assessment in the development of LCRs, programs, projects, and plans. Gender vulnerability assessment is an active process of measuring and monitoring the implications of a project or policy on a specific category of people or gender, most especially marginalized and vulnerable groups such as indigenous women.[117] By establishing an effective process for assessing gender bias and risks in LCRs, national authorities, such as the NCDMB, as well industry participants, can better understand and assess legal and customary constraints operating against the effective participation of women in project approval and decision-making processes.

Furthermore, in order to maximize the benefits of having an inclusive and gender-neutral workforce, oil and gas companies, while bearing in mind the NOGICDA, should increase the number of women in their respective organizations by putting in place the following key measures: strengthen the inflow of women at entry level positions; maintain the enthusiasm of women who are midcareer by offering them the same career advancement opportunities available to men; increase the representation of women at senior level positions; and ensure that there is strong commitment to gender balance from the top of the organization (especially from the Chief Executive Officer).[118]

5 CONCLUSION

Despite the emergence of comprehensive legislation and guidelines that aim to maximize local content benefits for all Nigerians, the quest for sustainable development in the utilization of Nigeria's abundant oil and gas resources remains incomplete. While some progress has been recorded in terms of LCR policy development, a confluence of implementation challenges continues to inhibit the full realization of both the LCRs and the SDPs across the Nigerian oil and gas industry value chain.

To ensure that LCRs move from theory to successful practical implementation, logistical concerns that stifle the abilities of NCDMB and industry participants to effectively deliver local content benefits must be carefully reviewed and addressed. Barriers to the effective implementation of LCRs can be holistically addressed by

---

[117] M. Crawley and L. O'Meara, *The Gender Proofing Handbook* (Lithuania: European Institute for Gender Equality), pp. 1–5; also F. Mackay and K. Bilton, *Equality Proofing Procedures in Drafting Legislation: International Comparisons* (Scottish Executive Central Research Unit, 2001), pp. 5–8.

[118] K. Rick, I. Marten, and U.V. Lonski, "Untapped Reserves: Promoting Gender Balance in Oil and Gas," Boston Consulting Group, July 12, 2017.

invigorating extant LCR programs, policies, and legislation with accountability and transparency safeguards; providing greater access to financing for Nigerian SMEs in the oil and gas industry; addressing training and capacity development gaps that hinder industry entry by Nigerians; as well as improving gender vulnerability assessment and gender equality in Nigeria's currently male dominated oil and gas industry.

The benefits of having implementable and practicable LCRs together with realistic SDPs executed efficiently in the Nigerian oil and gas industry are immense for an endowed nation like Nigeria. It is a like a two-way hypothetical road that ensures that Nigeria profits at both ends of the road. It will ensure that Nigeria's resources are adequately utilized for the benefits of generations to come.

10

Local Content Requirements and Treaty Implementation in Kenya's Petroleum Sector

James O. Kirwa and Melba K. Wasunna

1 INTRODUCTION

Kenya's oil and gas sector is undergoing profound changes. The country, having recently discovered roughly 560 million barrels of recoverable oil in its Northern region, is now preparing to move into the development phase of the reserves.[1] In the same vein, supportive infrastructure, comprising an 820 km crude-oil pipeline from Lokichar to Lamu, is being put in place.[2] These developments have been viewed with both excitement and concern. On the one hand, Kenya has a huge public debt and the oil sector is viewed as having the potential to significantly enhance economic development, including in the oil-producing areas which have historically remained underdeveloped.[3] The country is heavily dependent on fuel imports, importing almost 100 per cent of its fuel needs,[4] and oil discoveries could make it energy independent.[5] On the other hand, these developments have faced opposition from local communities who demand jobs, tenders, security and a share of oil revenues.[6]

Determined to address these challenges, Kenya has enacted the Petroleum Act 2019 with general local content requirements (LCRs).[7] Progress has also been made in the development of a cross-cutting Local Content Policy and the Petroleum (Local Content) Regulations.[8] While these frameworks are critical in boosting in-country value addition, promoting sustainable development through LCRs will

---

[1] Tullow Oil Plc, 'East Africa: Kenya', www.tullowoil.com/operations/east-africa/kenya.

[2] Ibid.

[3] J. Schilling, R. Locham T. Weinzierl, J. Vivekananda, and J. Scheffran, 'The Nexus of Oil, Conflict, and Climate Change Vulnerability of Pastoral Communities' (2015) 6 *Earth System Dynamics* 703 at 710.

[4] Global Legal Insights, 'Energy 2018, Kenya', www.globallegalinsights.com/practice-areas/energy-laws-and-regulations/kenya#chaptercontent2.

[5] Ibid.

[6] H. Etyang, 'No Oil Will Leave Turkana without Security and Jobs, Protesters Say' *The Star* (27 June 2018), www.the-star.co.ke/news/2018/06/27/no-oil-will-leave-turkana-without-security-and-jobs-protesters-say_c1778927, accessed 31 October 2018.

[7] Republic of Kenya, The Petroleum Act, No. 2 of 2019, 12 March 2019 [Petroleum Act].

[8] Petroleum (Local Content) Regulations 2019, Regulation 2 (unpublished) [Petroleum Regulations].

188

require a coherent and systemic implementation of the frameworks in line with Kenya's existing obligations under the World Trade Organisation (WTO) rules.[9]

This Chapter examines the provisions of these frameworks, including their alignment with international trade treaties, especially restrictions envisaged under the WTO rules. Despite limitations under the WTO rules against restrictive trade practices, LCRs can, if collaboratively implemented, provide opportunities for Kenya to promote local participation in the oil and gas value chain. Nevertheless, there is a need to ensure greater alignment of Kenya's LCRs with WTO rules, particularly regarding trade in goods. It is also essential for Kenya to adopt a multi-stakeholder approach in the design of LCRs that are flexible, sustainable and feasible to avoid environmental trade-offs and conflict with the WTO rules.

The Chapter is divided into five sections. After this introduction, Section 2 provides the context of LCRs, outlining the key drivers of LCRs in Kenya. Section 3 discusses LCRs under the Kenyan legislative and policy framework, while Section 4 explores coherence questions in Kenya's LCRs, including the possibility of mis-alignment with the WTO rules. Section 5 provides possible policy options that Kenya should consider to promote coherence in the design and implementation of LCRs. Section 6 is the conclusion.

2 KEY DRIVERS OF LCRS IN KENYA: SETTING THE CONTEXT

Local content is viewed as a performance measure adopted to address policy or market failures unique to developing countries like Kenya.[10] These failures are based on underdeveloped human, product, and capital market capacities upon which local industries cannot favourably compete in an open space without government protection. Developing countries provide this protection through 'horizontal' meas-ures (such as training and skills development, technology transfer, research and development) to foster local capacity and value addition; or 'selective' measures that aim to properly control foreign direct investment (FDI) by deliberately sheltering 'infant' sectors from foreign competition to the time they can depend on themselves.[11] The United States is historically known to have applied the 'infant sector protection' approach in trying to industrialise its economy amidst the British ascendency in the global trade.[12]

---

[9] See, e.g. I. Ramdoo, 'Unpacking Local Content Requirements in the Extractive Sector: What Implications for the Global Trade and Investment Frameworks?' Geneva, ICTSD and World Economic Forum, September 2015.

[10] R. Ado, 'Local Content Policy and the WTO Rules of Trade-Related Investment Measures (TRIMs): The Pros and Cons' (2013) 2 *International Journal of Business and Management Systems* 139; D. Olawuyi, 'Local Content and Procurement Requirements in Oil and Gas Contracts: Regional Trends in the Middle East and North Africa' (2019) 37 *Journal of Energy and Natural Resources Law* 93–117.

[11] Ibid. See also, D. Olawuyi, *Extractives Industry Law in Africa* (New York: Springer, 2018), pp. 233–40.

[12] Ibid., p. 233.

190   *James O. Kirwa and Melba K. Wasunna*

As discussed in earlier chapters of this book, the concept of local content is difficult to define, mainly because the term 'local' is vague. The term 'local' could mean a village, community or special interest group, sub-national (county), or national. This term has attracted much debate in Kenya, giving rise to two approaches to 'local' content: a localist approach that prioritises or favours local persons or firms within the oil-producing region; and a nationalistic approach that focuses on equitable participation at all stages of the oil and gas value chain. The latter approach is now reflected in the new Petroleum Act 2019, Section 2 of which defines 'local content' as 'the added value brought to the *Kenyan economy* from petroleum related activities through systematic development of national capacity and capabilities and investment in developing and procuring locally available work force, services and supplies, for the sharing of accruing benefits'.[13] Reference to 'Kenyan economy' implies that the Legislature intends to open up the petroleum sector to all Kenyan citizens, by allowing and providing for usage of locally sourced goods and services and workforce – which is well in its intent of avoiding the 'resource curse'. The draft Local Content Policy 2019 adopts a similar approach, by defining 'local' in terms of citizenship (for natural persons), ownership and control by nationals (for artificial persons), and the content of local product manufactured in Kenya (for goods).[14]

However, given the economic marginalisation of the areas where oil has been found, a combination of both localistic and nationalistic approaches in the design and implementation of LCRs can help reduce economic inequalities by stimulating sustainable participation of all stakeholders, including those living in remote and marginal areas.[15] This should be informed by the principles of value creation and retention, economic diversification and the development of sustainable local capacity and competitiveness.

The upstream oil and gas industry is new in Kenya, and so there has been a call for LCRs to cure existing capacity gaps and enhance local participation.[16] Some of these gaps include the burgeoning skills gap that impedes the inclusion of local workforce,[17] low quality of locally manufactured or available goods and services comparable to their high costs,[18] use of outdated technology in manufacturing, and

---

[13] See also, Local Content Bill 2018, Clause 2; Petroleum Regulations, note 8, Regulation 2 (unpublished).

[14] Republic of Kenya, 'Draft Local Content Policy: Maximising the Benefit of Investments and Operations through Local Content', Ministry of Industry, Trade and Co-Operatives, February 27, 2019, pp. 9–10 (unpublished).

[15] M. K. Wasunna and J. O Kirwa, 'Developing a Sustainable In-Country Value Addition Strategy: Real-Time Policy Options for Kenya's Petroleum Sector', Kenya Extractives Policy Dialogue II, Nairobi, 28–29 May 2018, p. 3.

[16] World Bank Group, Trade and Competitiveness, 'Kenya Local Content Exchange: Vision to Implementation', Kenya Local Content Exchanges, Nairobi, 4 July 2017, p. 7.

[17] Tullow Oil plc, '2017 Annual Report and Accounts', p. 28.

[18] A. Were, 'Supporting Economic Transformation: Manufacturing in Kenya: Features, Challenges and Opportunities – A scoping exercise, Supporting Economic Transformation Programme: Roundtable Discussion on Kenyan Manufacturing', Nairobi, 29 August 2016, p. 21.

poor infrastructure particularly in oil-producing areas which have historically been underdeveloped.[19]

LCRs also constitute Kenya's deliberate move to reduce overdependence on imports by creating a level playing field for domestic workforces and industries to sustainably participate in the oil and gas operations. They are also important in the realisation of sustainable development goals (SDGs), particularly: SDG 8, that seeks to promote sustained, inclusive and sustainable economic growth, and full and productive employment and decent work for all; SDG 9, on resilient infrastructure, inclusive and sustainable industrialisation, and innovation; and SDG 10, on reducing inequalities.[20]

3 LOCAL CONTENT POLICY AND LEGISLATIVE FRAMEWORKS IN KENYA

For decades, the petroleum sector in Kenya operated under the Petroleum (Exploration and Production) Act of 1986,[21] which was not informed by current industry developments. Recognising this gap, Kenya enacted the Petroleum Act 2019[22] in line with the Constitution 2010[23] and international good practices. This section explores LCRs as entrenched in this Act and other legal frameworks.

3.1 Constitution of Kenya 2010

The Constitution 2010 does not explicitly provide for local content in Kenya. However, there are general provisions that envisage the participation of the people in development processes. For instance, the principle of sovereignty[24] and the inaugural line, 'We, the people of Kenya' under the Preamble of the Constitution, aptly capture the vision and interests of the people. The Constitution defines public land to include all minerals and mineral oils,[25] which shall vest in and be held by the national government in trust for the people of Kenya.[26] This clearly sets out the question of ownership of land, and consequently the ownership of natural resources. Arguably, therefore, the people of Kenya, as the principle owners, have the constitutional right to participate in the exploitation of these resources. Article 66(2) of the Constitution mandates Parliament to 'enact legislation ensuring that investments in property benefit local communities and their economies'.[27] Article 69(1) also

---

[19] J. Obiri, 'Extractive Industries for Sustainable Development in Kenya', United Nations Development Programme, Nairobi, September 2014, p. 5.

[20] UN General Assembly, *Transforming Our World: the 2030 Agenda for Sustainable Development*, 21 October 2015, UN Doc. A/RES/70/1, Goals, 8, 9, and 10.

[21] Republic of Kenya, The Petroleum (Exploration and Production) Act, c 308, 16 November 1986.

[22] Petroleum Act, note 7.

[23] The Constitution of Kenya, 27 August 2010.

[24] Ibid., Article 1.

[25] Ibid., Article 62(1)(f).

[26] Ibid., Article 62(3).

[27] Ibid., Article 66(2).

192 James O. Kirwa and Melba K. Wasunna

requires the State to 'ensure sustainable exploitation, utilization, management and conservation of the environment and natural resources, and ensure the equitable sharing of the accruing benefits', and to 'utilize the environment and natural resources for the benefit of the people of Kenya'.[28] LCRs are essentially meant to give effect to these constitutional requirements.

3.2. Petroleum Act 2019

The Act is the main legislation that regulates upstream, midstream and downstream petroleum operations in Kenya. It requires petroleum operators to comply with local content requirements in all operations; give priority to services provided and goods manufactured in Kenya; and employ or engage qualified and skilled 'Kenyans' at all levels of the petroleum value chain.[29] The locally manufactured goods must meet the standards of the petroleum industry as prescribed by the Kenya Bureau of Standards (KBS) or any other internationally acceptable standards approved by the Energy and Petroleum Regulatory Authority (EPRA) established under the Act.[30] However, the KBS specifications envisaged under this provision are not yet in place.

The Act also requires contractors to prepare and submit long-term and annual local content plans to EPRA,[31] which has the mandate to oversee, coordinate and manage the development of local content in Kenya.[32] The local content plans provide an opportunity for the government and the contractor to agree on the expectations on local content implementation across the petroleum project phases, and the costs that are eligible for recovery (as part of cost oil).

The Act establishes a Training Fund comprising moneys paid annually by contractors for the purpose of training Kenyan nationals in upstream petroleum operations.[33] Section 52(5) of the Act stipulates that the Fund shall be used only for the purpose for which it was established, a provision that will potentially curb misappropriation of the Fund. However, the fact that the Fund only applies to upstream operations may limit the sustainability and transferability of the developed skills to other sectors and segments of the petroleum value chain. Any institution that wishes to build knowledge and technical capacity in upstream petroleum operations must be accredited pursuant to the guidelines contemplated in section 127(ll) of the new Act.[34]

Clause 20(1) of the Model Production Sharing Contract under the Act (hereinafter referred to as the 'Model PSC 2019') requires the contractors and their sub-contractors to

---

[28] Ibid., Article 69(1).
[29] Petroleum Act, note 7, sections 50(1)(b) and (c).
[30] Ibid., section 50(1).
[31] Ibid., section 50(2).
[32] Ibid., sections 51(1), (2).
[33] Ibid., section 52(2); Model PSC 2019, Clause 20(3); Petroleum (Exploration and Production) (Training Fund) Regulations 2006, Regulation 5(1).
[34] Petroleum Act, note 7, section 52(1).

LCRs and Treaty Implementation in Kenya 193

conduct training courses and programmes that will progressively increase employment of Kenyans in the upstream petroleum operations.[35] The contractors should also develop a technology transfer programme for the transfer of technology and skills to indigenous Kenyan employees and government officials on all areas of upstream petroleum operations.[36] The contractor is required to develop indigenous Kenyans to take more value-added, analytical and decision-making roles in areas of a technical or professional nature (including design engineering, project management, seismic data processing, legal, economics, auditing and accounting); and business strategic skills, such as leadership, business development, executive management and strategy development, among others.[37]

Local enterprises should be treated equally with respect to access to tender invitations and the tender evaluation criteria.[38] The contractors should submit a tentative schedule of the contemplated service and supply contracts to the Cabinet Secretary and EPRA on or before the beginning of each calendar year showing the anticipated tender dates and appropriate value and the goods and services to be provided in the forthcoming year.[39] After execution of each supply or consultancy contract, the contractor must furnish to the Cabinet Secretary and EPRA a copy of each contract and a brief description of the efforts made to find a Kenyan supplier or service provider.[40] While these provisions are critical in enhancing accountability with respect to compliance to local content requirements, the fact that they only apply to service and supply contracts with value exceeding a prescribed minimum,[41] provides leeway for contractors not to comply for contracts below that minimum. The minimum amount for each service and supply contract may be changed from time to time by the regulations made under the Act.[42]

A number of regulations are yet to be developed to operationalise the Act.[43] These include regulations with respect to local content development, capacity building and development in the upstream petroleum sector; guidelines for accreditation of institutions offering or intending to offer training in upstream petroleum operations; and regulations to govern the formation of business relationships between international oil companies and Kenyan companies for the purpose of technology, experience, knowledge and expertise acquisition. Until these regulations are made, the Petroleum (Exploration and Production) Regulations 1984, made under the repealed Petroleum (Exploration and Production) Act 1986,[44] shall remain in force.[45]

[35] Model PSC 2019, note 33, Clause 20(1).
[36] Ibid., Clause 23(1)-(3).
[37] Ibid., Clause 23(4).
[38] Ibid., Clause 22(6).
[39] Ibid., Clause 22(5)(a).
[40] Ibid., Clause 22(5)(c).
[41] Ibid., Clause 22(5)(a), (b).
[42] Ibid., Clause 22(5)(d).
[43] See, e.g. Petroleum Act, note 7, section 127.
[44] Ibid., section 128(1).
[45] Ibid., section 128(2)(e).

3.2.1 Draft Petroleum (Local Content) Regulations 2019

The Government of Kenya has made significant progress in the development of the Petroleum (Local Content) Regulations pursuant to sections 50(4) and 127(2)(bb) of the Petroleum Act 2019.[46] The Regulations, currently in draft form, underscore the LCRs entrenched under the Act, by requiring petroleum operators to establish and implement a bidding process for the acquisition of goods, works and services that gives preference to indigenous Kenyan companies.[47] In keeping with this, the operator should not award contracts based solely on the principle of the lowest bidder.[48]

The Regulations adopt a quantitative approach through specific percentages on local ownership and minimum local content targets that should be achieved over time. For instance, to be qualified to enter into a petroleum agreement or get a petroleum licence, a petroleum entity must ensure a 5 per cent equity participation of an indigenous Kenyan company other than the National Oil Corporation of Kenya.[49] However, the Cabinet Secretary in charge of petroleum may vary this requirement 'where an indigenous Kenyan company is unable to satisfy the requirement of the 5 per cent equity participation'.[50]

Non-indigenous Kenyan companies seeking to provide goods, works or services to upstream petroleum operators are required to incorporate joint venture (JV) companies or enter into favourable business arrangements with indigenous Kenyan companies and afford them a participation of at least 10 per cent of equity or contract value.[51] This means that the company cannot access the local market if it fails to comply with this requirement. This can potentially escalate the cost of doing business, particularly in setting up the business, managing risks and possibly sharing of benefits with partners whose experience may not add value to the JV. Further, while the ultimate goal is to promote technology and knowledge transfer through JVs, foreign companies may be reluctant to allow at least 10 per cent equity participation, particularly if the subject matter of the JV is of a proprietary value. The requirement is, however, not disciplined under Article XVI(2) of the General Agreement on Trade in Services (GATS).[52]

---

[46] Ibid., sections 50(4) and 127(2)(bb).
[47] Petroleum Regulations, note 8, Regulation 12 (unpublished).
[48] Ibid., Regulation 13(1).
[49] Ibid., Regulation 6(3). An 'indigenous Kenyan company' is defined under Regulation 2 as a company incorporated under the laws of Kenya that has at least 51 per cent of its equity owned by a Kenyan citizen; and at least 80 per cent of its executive and senior management positions and 100 per cent of non-managerial and other positions, held by Kenyan citizens.
[50] Ibid., Regulation 6(4).
[51] Ibid., Regulations 6(5), 13(5).
[52] GATS: General Agreement on Trade in Services, Apr. 15, 1994, Marrakesh Agreement Establishing the World Trade Organization, Annex 1B, 1869 UNTS. 183, 33 ILM 1167 (1994), Article XVI(2) [GATS], which empowers the WTO to develop 'disciplines' so as to ensure that domestic laws and regulations of WTO Members do not constitute unnecessary barriers to trade in services.

LCRs and Treaty Implementation in Kenya

TABLE 10.1 *Minimum local content levels to be attained*

Item		Start	5 Years	10 Years
1	Goods and Services	10%	As per Part 2	As per Part 2
2	Recruitment and Training			
	(a) Management staff	30%	50–60%	70–80%
	(b) Technical core staff	10%	10%	30%
	(c) Other staff	80%	90%	90%

The First Schedule of the Regulations specifies the minimum local content targets that should be achieved gradually (see, for example, Table 10.1). Products and services with higher levels of availability in Kenya, such as catering, have been assigned higher targets from the start of the project.[53] Although some of the targets may be high for the local market to meet on a competitive basis, the Cabinet Secretary is required to review them every five years (or 'more frequently if he so decides').[54] This will be critical, especially when the country has a far better line of sight of the sector to set 'realistic' local content targets.

3.3 *Natural Resources (Classes of Transactions Subject to Ratification) Act 2016*

This Act[55] was enacted to give effect to Article 71 of the Constitution of Kenya, 2010,[56] which provides for ratification by Parliament of agreements relating to natural resources. Under section 9 of the Act, some of the factors to be considered in deciding whether or not to ratify an agreement include adequate stakeholder consultation; the extent to which the agreement has struck a fair balance between the interests of the beneficiary and the benefits to the country arising from the agreement; and the benefits which the local community is likely to enjoy from the transaction. These factors speak directly to the issue of local content. The Act expressly recognises the need to ensure that frontier communities enjoy the benefits accruing from the oil and gas transactions, including employment and business opportunities, and infrastructure development. Further, the proviso regarding adequate stakeholder consultation seeks to address information asymmetry currently prevailing in the oil and gas sector in Kenya.[57]

---

[53] See ibid., First Schedule.
[54] Ibid., Regulation 11(4).
[55] Natural Resources (Classes of Transactions Subject to Ratification) Act, No. 41 of 2016, 13 September 2016.
[56] The Constitution of Kenya, note 23, Article 71.
[57] Natural Resources Act, note 55, section 9.

3.4 Public Procurement and Asset Disposal (PPAD) Act 2015

Section 155(2) of this Act[58] provides that preferential procurement shall apply only to manufactured articles, materials or supplies wholly mined and produced in Kenya, subject to availability and realisation of the applicable international or local standards. Consequently, where the products are not available or do not satisfy the applicable standards, the procuring entity is free to consider foreign products. Since only a limited range of goods manufactured or produced in Kenya can meet international standards, and since Kenya has not set its standards in relation to oil and gas, the risk of cost escalation arising from this requirement seems limited.

The Act provides for preference to materials or supplies partially mined, produced or assembled in Kenya; or firms with at least 51 per cent Kenyans shareholders.[59] Procuring entities seeking to obtain items not wholly or partially manufactured in Kenya should prepare a report detailing evidence of inability to procure local goods; and require successful bidders to cause technological transfer or create employment opportunities for Kenyan citizens.[60] The Act requires procuring entities to have in their tender documents a mandatory requirement, as preliminary evaluation criteria, for all foreign tenderers participating in international tenders to source at least 40 per cent of their supplies from citizen contractors.[61] It also provides for exclusive preference to Kenyan citizens where the tender value is below 500 million shillings; and the funding is 100 per cent from the national government, county government or a Kenyan body.[62] There is also a prescribed margin of preference, in the evaluation of tenders, to bidders offering locally manufactured, assembled, mined, extracted or grown goods.[63]

While these affirmative provisions serve as safeguards for local industry participation and sustainable development, especially in the nascent petroleum sector, the Act does not state why local participation is limited only to tenders below 500 million shillings. LCRs are essentially meant to enhance the competitiveness of local industries and natural persons to effectively participate in the petroleum sector. This cannot be achieved within a day, but in a graduated manner until the local industry is able to meet the required standards. Thus, limiting local participation to low-value tenders is clearly unsustainable. It means that major tenders (above 500 million shillings) are only reserved for foreign companies, and that no indigenous Kenyan company can ever qualify to execute such tenders.

---

[58]   The Public Procurement and Asset Disposal Act, No. 33 of 2015, 18 December 2015 [PPAD Act].
[59]   Ibid., section 155(3).
[60]   Ibid., section 155(5).
[61]   Ibid., section 157(9).
[62]   Ibid., section 157(8)(a).
[63]   Ibid., section 157(8)(b).

3.5 Technical and Vocational Education and Training Act 2013

Technical, industrial, vocational, and entrepreneurship training (TIVET) is pivotal in the development of local content in Kenya.[64] Statistics indicate that over 60 per cent of employment opportunities in Kenya's emerging oil and gas sector are expected to require vocational and technical training.[65] However, the available skills do not match sector demands.[66] The Technical and Vocational Education and Training (TVET) Act 2013[67] is therefore crucial in curing the skills gap in the sector and achieving 'globally competitive quality education, training and research for sustainable development' by the year 2030.[68] The Act requires training systems to integrate on-the-job attachment and internships at all levels in order to provide relevant training for the development of appropriate practical and innovative skills.[69] It establishes the TVET Authority to regulate and coordinate trainings under the Act, among other functions.[70] Section 38 requires TIVET institutions to adopt appropriate national and international standards in training; and establish and promote appropriate collaborative arrangements with national and international agencies on standards and quality assurance.[71] Equally, the Draft Petroleum (Local Content) Regulations 2019 envision a collaborative approach between EPRA and relevant institutions, such as the TVET Authority, in setting minimum standards, facilities, personnel, and technology for training in the petroleum industry in Kenya.[72]

A key milestone, following the discovery of oil, is the establishment of Morendat Institute of Oil and Gas (MIOG) in October 2013 to offer competence-based training in oil and gas pipelines management, operations, and maintenance to support the Northern Corridor Integration Projects (NCIP).[73] As one of the TVET institutions, MIOG should comply with the TVET Act and the standards or guidelines envisaged under section 127(2)(ll) of the Petroleum Act 2019.[74]

---

[64] S. Chinyere Ayonmike, 'Technical and Vocational Education and Training (TVET): Model for Addressing Skills Shortage in Nigerian Oil and Gas Industry' (2015) 3 *American Journal of Educational Research* 63; Republic of Kenya, 'Task Force on the Re-Alignment of the Education Sector to the Constitution of Kenya 2010: Towards a Globally Competitive Quality Education for Sustainable Development', Ministry of Education, February 2012, p. 52.

[65] Lundin Foundation, 'Education and Skills Training', www.lundinfoundation.org/education-and-skills-training/.

[66] Were, note 18, p. 21; E4D/SOGA, 'Progress Update: Employment and Skills for Eastern Africa is an Innovative Public-Private Partnership', 2017, p. 18.

[67] Technical and Vocational Education and Training Act, No. 29 of 2013, 14 January 2013 [TVET].

[68] Republic of Kenya, 'Kenya Vision 2030: The Popular Version', Government of the Republic of Kenya, 2007, p. 99.

[69] TVET, note 67, section 39.

[70] Ibid., section 6(1).

[71] Ibid., section 38.

[72] Petroleum Regulations, note 8, Clause 44(2)(b).

[73] 'Morendat Institute of Oil and Gas', www.kpc.co.ke/morendatinstitute/.

[74] Petroleum Act, note 7, section 127(2)(ll).

198   James O. Kirwa and Melba K. Wasunna

Evidently, LCRs are gaining increasing elaboration under Kenya's oil and gas legal framework. However, there is a need to ensure greater coherence in the design and implementation of Kenya's LCRs in order to achieve sustainable development and prevent overlap with international treaty obligations. The next section discusses these issues.

4 COHERENCE QUESTIONS IN KENYA'S LCRS

Kenya's LCRs are designed to stimulate economic, social and environmental development in oil and gas producing communities in Kenya. However, a number of key issues arise which may affect the coherent attainment of the sustainable development objectives elaborated in Kenya's legal framework on local content. This section highlights three such questions.

4.1 Duplication and Multiplicity of Supervision Arrangements

There are multiple bodies proposed to coordinate and monitor the implementation of LCRs in Kenya. The draft Local Content Policy 2019 proposes the establishment of a Local Content Committee that will be supported by a Local Content Unit under the Ministry of Industry, Trade, and Co-operatives.[75] EPRA is also mandated to oversee and coordinate the implementation of LCRs under the Petroleum Act 2019 and the Energy Act 2019. It is required to establish the Local Content Development and Monitoring Unit to monitor, coordinate, and implement LCRs in the petroleum sector.[76] There is also a Local Content Development Committee proposed under the Local Content Bill 2018, which seeks to provide a framework to facilitate local ownership, control, and financing of activities related to exploitation of oil, gas and petroleum resources, and increase local value capture along the petroleum value chain.[77] It is not clear how the institutions will collaborate in the implementation of LCRs. The fragmentation of responsibilities for supervising LCRs has not provided a clear and coherent picture of the roles of the different entities, particularly how to avoid overlap and duplication of

---

[75] Draft Local Content Policy, note 14, p. 55.
[76] Petroleum Regulations, note 8, Regulation 7.
[77] Therefore, the Bill only covers the petroleum sector, including upstream petroleum activities. The question that emerges is whether or not the Bill is complementary to the draft Petroleum (Local Content) Regulations (note 8). Further confusion arises from the definition of 'local content' as 'the added value brought to the Kenyan economy from extractive industry through systematic development of national capacity and capabilities and investment in developing and procuring locally available work force, services and supplies, for the sharing of accruing benefits'. The definition of 'extractive industry' under Clause 2 of the Bill (as oil, gas, and mining sectors), implies that the Bill also applies to mining operations, which are already covered under the Mining Act 2016 and attendant Regulations, namely Mining (Community Development Agreement) Regulations 2017, Mining (Employment and Training) Regulations 2017, and the Mining (Use of Local Goods and Services) Regulations 2017.

LCRs and Treaty Implementation in Kenya 199

responsibilities.[78] It is therefore important to harmonise and clarify the functions of the respective institutions.

4.2 Social Exclusions and Environmental Trade-Offs

Typically, resource extraction contracts are signed between the government and international oil companies (IOCs) with the host government focusing on the macro-economic gains (and not necessarily on the needs and welfare of host communities).[79] On the ground, oil exploration activities are associated with negative outcomes by communities, such as loss of ancestral and grazing land, socio-economic exclusion (for instance, inaccessibility of jobs by locals), insecurity, and environmental degradation, among others.[80] These highlight the trade-offs which are often inherent at the development–environment–people interfaces. More and more, there is a recognised need for IOCs to obtain a social licence to operate from the host community thereby making local communities key in the resource extraction processes.

Most IOCs in Kenya have developed corporate social responsibility (CSR) programmes to attend to some of the needs of local communities within their areas of operation.[81] While some social needs are indeed addressed, for example through building schools and hospitals, a benefit–expectation gap from communities still pervades as most of these CSR programmes fail to create broad-based growth and economic opportunities in local communities within a local content framework. These programmes are not often anchored in law. IOCs therefore enjoy the discretion of deciding the CSR programmes that should be implemented without adequate consultation with local communities. Often local communities are too weak to enter into any meaningful dialogue with IOCs and the government, or even participate in the development of local content plans and negotiation of contracts.[82]

Since the discovery of oil in Kenya, concerns of socio-economic exclusion have emerged, evidenced by a series of community protests experienced in the oil-producing areas. For instance, following violent protests in October 2013 that resulted in the suspension of oil operations,[83] a Memorandum of Understanding (MoU) was signed by Tullow Oil, in which it undertook to consult with the local

---

[78] Olawuyi, note 113.
[79] R. H. Pedersen, 'The Politics of Oil, Gas Contract Negotiations in Sub-Saharan Africa' (2014) 25 *Danish Institute for International Studies* 27 at 29.
[80] K. Mkutu and G. Wandera, 'Conflict, Security and the Extractive Industries in Turkana, Kenya: Emerging Issues 2012–2015', USIU-Africa, KSG, 2016, p. 22; Obiri, note 19, p. 13.
[81] See, e.g. Tullow Oil Plc, 'Partnering to Drive Change', Ustawi: Tullow Oil Kenya Publication, Issue 2, January – June 2019.
[82] See Pedersen, note 79, p. 42.
[83] J. Lind, 'Research Briefing: Governing Black Gold: Lessons from Oil Finds in Turkana, Kenya', Institute of Development Studies, Saferworld, October 2017.

communities in revamping its local content plans.[84] Another protest erupted in August 2014 in which subcontractors raised questions around discrepancies in wages and benefits, and unfair termination of contracts.[85] Equally, an MoU was signed in which the oil company committed to increasing the minimum wage. In June 2017, local communities invaded several sites around Ngamia oilfields, demanding more jobs and other benefits.[86] More recently, following the launch of the EOPS by the President, local communities staged protests, raising claims for more jobs, security and a share of the oil revenues.[87] Sadly, the scramble for jobs and business opportunities has been complicated by influential politicians and chiefs, who determine who is employed and from which clan or ethnic group.[88] Thus, access to jobs and tenders related to oil operations in the region tends to be easier for those who are 'well connected'.

4.3 LCRs and Treaty Implementation under the International Trade System

Despite the clear drivers and aims of Kenya's LCRs, the implementation of LCRs in Kenya raises fundamental questions with respect to how such requirements may conflict with international treaty norms, especially under the international trade system. This section discusses whether Kenya's emerging LCRs may conflict with non-restriction obligations under the WTO system.

LCRs have the potential to stimulate sustainable development in Kenya. At issue, however, is whether they amount to restrictive practices inimical to international trade instruments set by the WTO – of which Kenya is a member.[89] These instruments include the Agreement on Trade-Related Investment Measures (TRIMs), the General Agreement on Tariff and Trade (GATT), the Agreement on Subsidies and Countervailing Measures (ASCM), and the GATS.[90] The instruments endorse the 'national treatment' principle, which require member states to treat one another as they would their own nationals.

---

[84] 'Draft Memorandum of Understanding: Lifting Suspension of Operations (Block 10BB & 13T) and Establishing a Safe, Secure and Sustainable Operating Environment in Turkana', November 4, 2013, www.documentcloud.org/documents/900069-oil-mou.html.

[85] S. Stash and J. Arnold, 'SRI Roadshow', Tullow Oil Plc, April 2015.

[86] Lind, note 83, p. 6.

[87] Etyang, note 6.

[88] Mkutu and Wandera, note 80, p. 23; M. K. Wasunna, J. Okanga, and G. K. Kerecha, 'Advancing Capacity and Access to Justice in Kenya's Extractives Sector', Extractives Baraza, Strathmore University, 2018.

[89] Kenya became a member of GATT and the WTO on 5 February 1964 and 1 January 1995, www .wto.org/english/thewto_e/countries_e/kenya_e.htm. WTO rules are applicable in Kenya vide Article 2(5) and (6) of the Constitution 2010.

[90] I. Ramdoo, 'Local Content Policies in Minerals-Exporting Countries: Part 1', 2 June 2017, TAD/TC/ WP(2016)3/PART1/FINAL, p. 13.

For instance, GATT prohibits the use of quantitative restrictions on exports and imports;[91] and requires contracting states not to treat imported goods less favourably than like goods in the domestic market 'in respect of all laws, regulations and requirements affecting their internal sale, offering for sale, purchase, transportation, distribution or use'.[92] LCRs are clearly inconsistent with these provisions in so far as they condition the use of domestic over imported goods. Government procurement is excluded from the national treatment rule,[93] with the exception of procurement that falls within the ambit of the Government Procurement Agreement (GPA).

Unlike GATT, obligations under GATS are negotiable through a country's schedule of commitments. Its scope is limited to market access and national treatment that affect trade in services. Kenya is entitled to take measures to regulate trade in services in line with its policy objectives, but such measures must be 'administered in a reasonable, objective, and impartial manner'.[94] Moreover, unless expressly specified in its scheduled commitments under the GATS, Kenya should accord foreign services and service providers treatment no less favourable than it accords to its own like services and service providers.[95] Article XVI, on market access, restricts measures that protect domestic service providers;[96] limit the employment of expatriates;[97] and impose ownership requirements in the form of JVs, maximum foreign ownership and equity participation.[98] Like GATT, GATS does not regulate government procurement.

The TRIMs Agreement contains an illustrative list of prohibited TRIMs, including, 'TRIMs that are inconsistent with paragraph 4 of Article III of GATT which are mandatory or enforceable under domestic law . . . and which require the purchase or use by an enterprise of products of domestic origin or from any domestic source, whether specified in terms of particular products, in terms of volume or value of products, or in terms of a proportion of volume or value of its local production'.[99] This provision clearly prohibits quantitative LCRs relating to the supply of goods. The ASCM prohibits export subsidies granted to support local content, or contingent upon the use of domestic over imported products.[100]

---

[91] GATT 1994: General Agreement on Tariffs and Trade 1994, 15 April 1994, Marrakesh Agreement Establishing the World Trade Organization, Annex 1A, 1867 UNTS 187, 33 ILM 1153 (1994), Article XI(1) [GATT].

[92] Ibid., Article III(4).

[93] Ibid., Article III(8). Government procurement falls within the ambit of the Agreement on Government Procurement (GPA).

[94] GATS, note 52, Article VI(1).

[95] Ibid., Article XVII.

[96] Ibid., Article XVI(2)(a)–(c).

[97] Ibid., Article XVI(2)(d).

[98] Ibid., Article XVI(2)(e)–(f).

[99] TRIMS Agreement: Agreement on Trade-Related Investment Measures, 15 April 1994, Marrakesh Agreement Establishing the World Trade Organization, Annex 1A, 1868 UNTS 186, Article 2.

[100] Agreement on Subsidies and Countervailing Measures, 15 April 1994, Marrakesh Agreement Establishing the World Trade Organization, Annex 1A, 1869 UNTS 14., Article 3.1.

Kenya may be at risk of international treaty violations if it applies unfair LCRs inconsistent with the WTO rules, especially restrictions on foreign goods under the GATT and TRIMs Agreement. However, as noted by Lee, 'fair trade' in the sense of a 'level playing field' does not necessarily mean applying the same set of trade rules and conditions to every nation, but also means recognising that some countries are so disadvantaged that they need 'reasonable accommodation' under the WTO regime.[101] The 2030 Agenda for Sustainable Development recognises, thus:

> We will respect each country's policy space and leadership to implement policies for poverty eradication and sustainable development, while remaining consistent with relevant international rules and commitments. At the same time, national development efforts need to be supported by an enabling international economic environment, including coherent and mutually supporting world trade, monetary and financial systems, and strengthened and enhanced global economic governance.[102]

In addition, LCRs in Kenya may survive within some limited exceptions envisaged in the WTO rules. With regard to the ASCM, for example, domestic subsidies are actionable only if they (a) *adversely affect* the domestic commerce of another WTO member state;[103] or (b) are *specifically* granted to a company, industry or a group of industries.[104] The first exception only applies to least-developed countries and not developing countries like Kenya. Few domestic subsidies meet this threshold, based in part, on the difficulty, for the complaining party, of showing evidence of 'adverse effects' as well as on the fact that the definition of subsidy under the rules is thin. The second exception implies that horizontal measures in the form of subsidies are non-actionable under the ASCM. Subsidies that support research and development (R&D) and innovation are also non-actionable within the meaning of Article 8(2) of the ASCM.

Kenya may also rely on Article 4 of TRIMs, which allows developing countries to retain protectionist measures, provided that they are consistent with the specific derogations permitted under Article XVIII of GATT with respect to economic development needs and subject to notification to the General Council.[105]

LCRs relating to procurement and trade in services in the petroleum sector do not fall within the ambit of GATS. Kenya has made shallow commitments under GATS – particularly on services relating to telecommunication, financial

---

[101] Y. S. Lee, *Reclaiming Development in the World Trade System (2nd ed.)* (Cambridge University Press, 2016), pp. 462–463.

[102] UNGA, note 20, para. 63.

[103] C. Cimino, G. C. Hufbauer, and J. J. Schott, 'A Proposed Code to Discipline Local Content Requirements', Peterson Institute for International Economics Policy Brief No PB14–6, February 2014, p. 1.

[104] I. Ramdoo, 'Local Content, Trade and Investment: Is there Policy Space Left for Linkages Development in Resource-Rich Countries?' Discussion Paper No 205, December 2016, p. 20.

[105] I. Ramdoo, 'Do International Trade Rules Prevent Local Content Policies?' (December 2016/January 2017) 5 GREAT *Insights Magazine*.

(insurance and banking), tourism, transport and meteorological data. Most of these commitments are unbound, leaving Kenya with a lot of policy space to apply LCRs in the oil and gas sector consistent with its national goals. Thus, LCRs on JVs, equity participation, employment of Kenyan citizens and preference to domestic services and service providers, as prescribed in the Petroleum Act 2019 and the draft Petroleum (Local Content) Regulations 2019, are non-actionable. Kenya is not a signatory of GPA, hence procurement-related LCRs in the oil and gas sector are permissible.

5 PROMOTING COHERENCE IN THE DESIGN AND IMPLEMENTATION OF KENYA'S LCRS

In light of the foregoing, Kenya should consider the following recommendations in designing coherent and realistic LCRs.

5.1 Duplication and Multiplicity of Supervision Arrangements

There is a need to harmonise and clarify the functions of existing and proposed local-content institutions. The implementation, monitoring and evaluation of LCRs in the petroleum sector should be left to EPRA through its Local Content Development and Monitoring Unit. EPRA should coordinate with the Local Content Committee proposed under the draft Local Content Policy 2019,[106] which should be an umbrella institution to oversee the implementation of LCRs across sectors in Kenya. The State Department of Petroleum should coordinate with a range of stakeholders, such as EPRA, Micro and Small Enterprise Authority (MSEA), Ministry of Industry, Trade and Cooperatives, Ministry of Education, and other line agencies, to develop a sound education system, boost sector linkages, reduce business barriers and establish supplier development programmes to enhance local capabilities. Since the Petroleum Act 2019 and the draft regulations[107] already provide for a local content institutional framework, enacting the Local Content Bill 2018[108] into law will undoubtedly cause institutional overlap. This Bill should therefore not be passed.

5.2 Social Exclusion and Environmental Trade-Offs

One way that is emerging to address these gaps is promoting the robust engagement of local SMEs in natural resource extraction to ensure the benefits flow directly into communities. This therefore necessitates a policy shift from local (national) content to also touch specifically on local community content. Central in the conversation

---

[106] Draft Local Content Policy, note 14.
[107] Petroleum Act, note 7; Petroleum Regulations, note 8.
[108] Local Content Bill, note 13.

with stakeholders is a recommendation to ensure Kenya's local content regulations and policies reserve a percentage of the localisation requirements of oil and gas companies for local community stakeholders so as to stimulate growth in SMEs and business activities. The role of LCRs in these circumstances is to manage and mitigate risks that emanate from increasing community expectations regarding employment and supplier opportunities.

Moreover, the Government should create a conducive business environment by reducing regulatory constraints, especially licencing procedures; infrastructure deficits; financial constraints; cost of doing business; and information constraints. The Petroleum (Local Content) Regulations 2019 requires EPRA to maintain a database that contains details of qualified domestic suppliers, service providers and other entities.[109] This should be integrated with existing databases, such as the Kenya E-Trade Portal established by the Ministry of Industry, Trade and Cooperatives in 2017 to enable easy access to business opportunities across sectors.[110] The Government should also collaborate with IOCs to tailor the size of tenders for local SMEs.

LCRs can also help reduce market failures and foster sustainable development if they are coherent with the broader national development goals, mainly Vision 2030[111] and the Big Four Agenda.[112]

5.3 Alignment with International Trade System

Given the thin policy space under the WTO rules, Kenya should explore flexible and pragmatic options to promote sustainable local participation consistent with its treaty obligations. First, the design and implementation of LCRs should be collaborative with adequate institutional backing and clear monitoring mechanism. Second, whereas the local content targets have been designed based on the availability of products and services in Kenya, the government should work closely with IOCs in reviewing local content targets to ensure they are consistent, realistic and aligned with the WTO rules. A national survey on the capabilities of local workforce and firms, their level of participation and local supplier landscape, is imperative to gain a better understanding of the context and design feasible targets.

---

[109] Petroleum Regulations, note 8, Regulation 40(1).
[110] B. Jefwa, 'Ministry of Industry, Trade and Cooperatives launch Kenya e-trade portal' 19 October 2017, www.cio.co.ke/news/ministry-industry-trade-cooperatives-launch-kenya-e-trade-portal/.
[111] Republic of Kenya, note 67.
[112] The Big 4 Agenda, for instance, highlights technology and innovation, infrastructure, and TVET as key elements in the success of the manufacturing sector. 'The Big 4: Empowering the Nation', https://big4.president.go.ke/.

6 CONCLUSION

As Kenya develops her oil and gas sector, there is need for a timely local content strategy to ensure maximum in-country value addition while avoiding misalignment with Kenya's WTO obligations. The enactment of the Petroleum Act 2019,[113] the development of an umbrella Local Content Policy,[114] and the Petroleum (Local Content) Regulations 2019[115] provide an opportunity for Kenya to maximise gains from petroleum operations and ensure inclusive growth. These frameworks contain expansive LCRs, a key tool for promoting sustainable local participation. Despite this, there are a few gaps that should be addressed, particularly the local content targets and monitoring institutions. The central question, however, is how to implement the LCRs while remaining consistent with international trade law. Applying a mandatory approach in the design of LCRs is inimical to the GATT and TRIMs Agreement, but only if this affects trade in goods. There is also a policy space for Kenya under the GATS, which only disciplines LCRs affecting trade in services. This binds Kenya only to the extent expressly specified in its Schedule of Commitments. Government procurement is only disciplined under the GPA, to which Kenya is not a party. While taking advantage of this policy space, though thin, Kenya should adopt a multi-stakeholder approach in the design of flexible, sustainable and feasible LCRs to avoid any conflict with the WTO rules. Implementation of LCRs should be progressive and aligned with the national development priorities as well as the principle of equality encapsulated under the Constitution of Kenya 2010.[116]

---

[113] Petroleum Act, note 7.
[114] Draft Local Content Policy, note 14.
[115] Petroleum Regulations, note 8.
[116] The Constitution of Kenya, note 23, Article 27.

11

Sustainability and Local Content Requirements in Australian Oil and Gas Development: Has the Ship of Opportunity Sailed?

Tina Soliman Hunter

1 INTRODUCTION AND BACKGROUND

The development of a country's oil and gas resources has the capacity to bring not only immense wealth from the extraction of the resource itself, but also from the development of associated industries and skills. Shining examples of such local content development and economic diversification can be seen in the development of Norwegian petroleum resources since the early 1970s. Attempts to emulate the successful Norwegian approach have been made around the world, particularly in developing countries such as sub-Saharan Africa and Latin America. Less literature exists however, on the attempts and success of the implementation of local content provisions in developed countries such as Australia.

Australia commenced the exploration of its offshore petroleum resources in the 1960s, at the same time as Norway and the UK, with petroleum found in Bass Strait in 1967. Norway and the UK sought to determine their own future in relation to the development of their petroleum resources and associated industries through the development of a 'North Sea' system of regulation. The system refers to the regulatory model developed by Norway in particular, and later adopted to a lesser extent by the UK, for the exploitation of North Sea petroleum resources. The system had its origins in the regulation of hydro resources since the early twentieth century. Such a system was developed by Norway and attractive to the UK since it allowed the state to exert control over offshore petroleum activities. The hallmark of the system was the discretionary allocation of licences and state involvement in activities, from both a regulatory and participatory perspective. In this system, access to petroleum is generally granted under a discretionary system, enabling the state to direct and shape the development of petroleum offshore.[1]

---

[1] For a further discussion of the North Sea system, see T. Hunter, 'Legal Regulatory Framework for the Sustainable Extraction of Australian Offshore Petroleum Resources: A Critical Functional Analysis', Dissertation for the degree philosophiae doctor (PhD) at the University of Bergen, April 2010, pp. 83, 87–8; B. F. Nelsen, *The State Offshore: Petroleum Politics, and State Intervention on the British and Norwegian Continental Shelves* (Westport, CT: Praeger, 1991), p. 8.

206

Australia's historical origins and precedent pertaining to industry and enterprise were similar to the UK (particularly given its colonial origins), with the approach consistent with liberal-pluralism, characterised by a 'government uninvolved in capital accumulation and allocation, arm's length relations with business, the development of policies subject to societal pressures and the reliance on market solutions to economic problems'.[2] This background encouraged Australia to implement and follow the 'North American' non-interventionist regulatory system when developing its offshore petroleum policy. Originating in the USA, it is typified by a minimalist approach to state intervention (as defined by Nelsen) in the development of petroleum resources, with a preference for free market forces to influence and direct the development of petroleum resources. Under this system, petroleum licences are awarded utilising a bid system, thereby ensuring that capitalist forces influence petroleum exploitation. In this system, a 'set and forget' approach to petroleum development occurs, with the state establishing and enforcing the laws and regulations for petroleum operations, in order to protect the workers and the environment, whilst enabling private companies to maintain autonomy over petroleum operations.[3] As a result of adopting the North American system, a regulatory framework characterised by minimal intervention and regulation was implemented. Unlike the North Sea system, where state intervention stretched to all aspects of petroleum development, including field regulation, rates of depletion, and other aspects of the petroleum industry, the adoption of the North American system meant that at the time of discovery of oil in Bass Strait the Australian government sought to maintain a 'hands off' approach to regulation, focussing policy on further exploration and controlling the price of domestic oil.[4]

The issue of local content provisions was not a focus of Australia's early petroleum policy. The first time the issue of local was considered in Australia was during the 1980s and 1990s when the giant North West Shelf (NWS) petroleum reserves were discovered and development began. Two seminal reports which considered the issue of local content provisions were tabled in the Australian Parliament during the development of the NWS. The first, titled 'North West Shelf: A Sea of Lost Opportunities?' (1989) considered the need for local content provisions, recommending that such provisions be introduced by the Australian Government.[5] The second report, a decade later, considered whether Australia had missed out on benefits associated with local content provisions, and what could be done to

---

[2] T. Hunter, 'Sustainable Socio-economic Extraction of Australian Offshore Petroleum Resources through Legal Regulation: Is It Possible?' (2011) 29 *Journal of Energy and Natural Resources Law* 209–246 at 220–21.

[3] See Hunter, note 1, p. 35; Nelsen, note 1, p. 8.

[4] P. Keating, 'The Labour Approach to Petroleum Exploration Development and Pricing' (1980) 20 *APPEA Journal* 16.

[5] D. P. Beddall, 'The Northwest Shelf: A Sea of Lost Opportunities', Report from the House of Representatives Standing Committee on Industry, Science and Technology (1989).

208   *Tina Soliman Hunter*

attempt to implement local content provisions.[6] A further two decades later sees local content provisions still the subject of some discussion as new areas for exploration and production are considered in the Great Australian Bight (GAB) by the Norwegian state oil company, Equinor (formerly Statoil).[7]

As such, it is timely to consider the perceptions and role of local content requirements in Australia. This chapter examines such provisions and requirements over the last forty years: examining and analysing the history, the government perceptions of local content requirements (LCRs) in the development of Australia's petroleum resources, and their link to Australia's broader petroleum policy. After iterating an overview of the Australian petroleum industry, this chapter will first consider the concept of local content requirements within the Australian context, and the broader concept of economic diversification. It will then place the concept of LCR within the broader concept of sustainable development. The remainder, and lion's share, of the chapter is devoted to an analysis of local content provisions in Australia. Firstly, it examines and critiques the historic 'industry-based approach' to local content requirements, focussing on the Australian parliament reports from the 1989 and 1998. Finally, it examines the contemporary approach to LCRs in light of the likely development of a new petroleum province in the GAB, and the role they are likely to play in future petroleum development.

2 THE AUSTRALIAN PETROLEUM SECTOR

Australia's petroleum (oil and gas) sector is predominantly offshore, having commenced in the mid-1960s. There have been some small-scale oil discoveries onshore and large gas fields were discovered and developed in the 1970s and 1980s to supply gas to the populous east coast of Australia. In the 2000s, commercial-scale coal seam gas (CSG) was developed in the Darling Downs Region in Queensland, with the vast majority of gas produced destined for the overseas liquefied natural gas (LNG) export market in Asia.

Given that Australia's offshore petroleum resources have been explored and developed since the 1960s, its resources are a mix of mature fields[8] and frontier regions.[9]

---

[6] House of Representatives Standing Committee on Industry, Science and Resources, 'Sea of Indifference: Australian Industry Participation in the North West Shelf Project' (1998).

[7] Tina Soliman Hunter, 'Offshore petroleum drilling and risk: A study of proposed deep-sea exploration drilling in Commonwealth Regulated Waters of the Great Australian Bight' (2019).

[8] A mature field is defined as a field that has been extensively explored and high levels of production occur in these areas. Characteristics of mature areas include familiar geology, fewer technological challenges, and well-developed infrastructure. See Norwegian Petroleum Directorate, 'Facts 2009: The Norwegian Petroleum Sector' (2009) www.npd.no/en/facts/publications/, p. 30; F. Arnesen, U. Hammer, P. H. Høisveen, K. Kaasen, and N. Dagfinn, 'Energy Law in Europe' in M. M. Roggenkamp, C. Redgwell, I. Del Guayo, and A. Rønne (eds.), *Energy Law in Europe: National, EU and International Regulation* (2nd ed.) (Oxford University Press, 2008), p. 882.

[9] Frontier regions are characterised by little geological knowledge or data, significant technical challenges, and a lack of infrastructure; see Arnesen et al., note 8, p. 882. These areas have high levels of

Australia has some mature fields, particularly the Gippsland and Otway Basins in South-Eastern Australia, which were originally developed in the 1970s. Next to be explored and developed was the NWS, which comprises a mix of developing fields and fields that sit awaiting development under retention leases. There remain large tracts of frontier areas, particularly the Mentelle Basin, Lord Howe Rise, the Bight Basin (especially the Ceduna Sub-Basin), and south of Tasmania, requiring extensive exploration to realise possible petroleum reserves. The Australian Productivity Commission noted in 2009 that Australia's petroleum resources are in decline, leading to a likely decrease in the economic contribution of petroleum to the Australian economy,[10] and requiring the import of a greater percentage of its petroleum for primary energy use. Australia is vulnerable to sources of supply for petroleum, particularly at a time where 48 per cent of all global petroleum supplies are contained in the politically unstable Middle East region, and a further 10 per cent are controlled by Russia and former Soviet states.[11] Thus, a major objective for Australia today is to increase petroleum production to enable high levels of petroleum imports to meet domestic energy needs.

To meet this objective, Australia can undertake two strategies. The first is to maximise the recovery of petroleum, since the greater the recovery of resources, the greater the economic contribution of the petroleum sector to Australia.[12] Although Australia has the legal capacity to maximise production under the current legal framework,[13] governments since the 1980s have refrained from interfering in field development, instead leaving petroleum recovery to operators developing the fields.[14] This policy decision was made in order to ensure that international oil companies were encouraged to continue to explore and exploit Australia's petroleum resources. Such a policy position differs in the North Sea system, particularly Norway, which directs the exploitation, and establishes the requirement to optimise sustainable production in the legal framework.[15]

The second strategy to increase the contribution of petroleum to the Australian economy is to explore, and ultimately produce, in frontier areas. This strategy has been embraced by the Australian government, with four licences originally granted to BP (with Equinor ultimately farming-in) in the GAB. Currently, the Australian

---

uncertainty, although there are still possibilities of making substantial discoveries. See NPD, note 8, p. 30.

[10] Australian Productivity Commission, Review of Regulatory Burden on the Upstream Petroleum (Oil and Gas) Sector – Productivity Commission Research Report, April 2009.

[11] BP, 'BP Statistical Review of World Energy', June 2019, p. 13.

[12] Hunter, note 1.

[13] Part 4, Offshore Petroleum and Greenhouse Gas Storage (Resource Management and Administration) Regulations 2011 (Cth).

[14] For a detailed examination of field development and petroleum maximisation in Australia, see T. Hunter, 'The Role of Regulatory Frameworks and State regulation in Optimising the Extraction of Petroleum Resources: A Study of Australia and Norway' (2014) 1 Extractive Industries and Society 48–58.

[15] Petroleum Activities Act 1996 (Norway), ss. 1–4.

Tina Soliman Hunter

government is assessing the Environmental Plan for the drilling of an exploration well in 2,400 m in the hitherto undeveloped GAB. The reason for the push for development in the GAB is twofold. Firstly, it is likely that sweet light-grade crude, critical for Australia's needs,[16] will be found.[17] The likely influence of the exploration of the GAB on sustainability is discussed in Section 6. The second is the desire for the Australian government to attract foreign investment into the petroleum sector.

All mineral and petroleum resources in Australia are owned by the State. This is reiterated in State onshore petroleum legislation (for example in section 9 of the *Petroleum Act 1923* (Qld)), although this recognition is not expressly stated in the *Offshore Petroleum and Greenhouse Gas Storage Act 2006* (Cth) (OPAGGSA).[18] Sovereign rights in respect of exploring and exploiting the natural resources of the Australian Continental Shelf are vested in, and exercisable by, the Crown in right of the Commonwealth under the *Sea and Submerged Lands Act 1973* (Cth) (SSLA).[19] To efficiently and effectively exploit its petroleum, the State as owner of the resources assigns property rights to third parties (usually the private sector) for exploration, development, and production activities through the award of petroleum licences.[20] The petroleum licence (exploration and production) is the legal arrangement between the State and the third party.

In Australia, petroleum resource exploitation has occurred against a backdrop of changes in the focus of petroleum policy. There have been a number of changes in the policy framework governing the petroleum industry since the 1960s. These changes have been influenced by the complex interaction of changes in government, oil strikes over the last forty years, and a shifting Australian approach with successive changes in federal governments since the mid-1970s to government control over the 'commanding heights' of the economy. At the time petroleum was discovered in the 1960s, the government focused on two main areas of policy: exploration for further deposits and the establishment of petroleum price parity as a policy for the development of Australia's petroleum resources,[21] both policies remaining in place without adjustment until 1975.[22] Prime Minister Whitlam

---

[16] Equinor analysis of the geology of the Stromlo-1 well concludes that the crude is likely to be sweet light, similar to that of the Statfjord C well in the North Sea. See Equinor, 'Environment Plan for the Stromlo-1 Exploration Drilling Program, Revision 1', April 2019.

[17] See paper by Alex Warwryk and Tina Soliman, 'Risk and Regulation of Oil Drilling in the Great Australian Bight' (2019) 34 *Australian Environment Review* 110–116.

[18] However, s285(2) of the Offshore Petroleum and Greenhouse Gas Storage Act 2006 (Cth) grants title to petroleum recovered to the License holder.

[19] Sea and Submerged Lands Act 1973 (Cth).

[20] L. Hogan, 'Australia's Petroleum Resource Rent Tax: An Economic Assessment of Fiscal Settings', ABARE eReport 03.1, Prepared for the Department of Industry, Tourism and Resources, Canberra, January 2003, p. 27.

[21] Keating, note 4, p. 16.

[22] Ibid.

announced a major policy change relating to exploration in 1975; however, this was not implemented since the government was dismissed by the Governor-General in 1975 by a double dissolution of the parliament.[23] Upon a change of government in December 1975, the Fraser government returned to oil pricing parity, raising the price of local oil to full import parity.[24] This policy focus remained until a change of government in 1983.

A major shift in Australia's petroleum policy occurred at a time of increasing internationalisation and a shift toward a free market.[25] During the 1980s, the conservative federal opposition[26] indicated that its policies for the development of offshore petroleum resource would have as its primary aim a long-term sustainable indigenous energy economy.[27] This included the establishment of a national oil corporation (NOC) that would operate side by side with private oil companies but with strategic as well as commercial objectives.[28] This corporation would also provide information to the government to assist in the development of national oil and gas policy.[29] In 1983, the newly elected government undertook an assessment of Australia's offshore petroleum resource policies, recognising the importance of maintaining a program of exploration and development of the petroleum industry.[30] In 1985, the government recognised and articulated the enormity of implementing a new petroleum policy, and the need for the government to make incremental changes to the petroleum regulatory system. The petroleum industry had indicated it did not want the system to be altered, or it may prevent investment in oil and gas exploration.[31]

In response, the government announced a new offshore petroleum policy framework in 1990, with the sustainable development objective of maximising the benefit to all Australians through an efficient and competitive exploration industry that could assess Australia's petroleum resources, and develop the petroleum resources for the benefit of the Australian nation.[32] These policy goals were addressed by an offshore petroleum strategy that implemented a comprehensive program for the release of offshore acreage areas for exploration, the provision of geological data from Australian government agencies, and the provision of attractive offshore petroleum title and taxation arrangements.[33] The major elements of this new policy

---

[23] The double dissolution of the parliament is authorised under s57 of the Australian Constitution, where there is an irrevocable disagreement between the two Houses of Parliament.

[24] Keating, note 4, p. 16.

[25] G. Evans, 'The Petroleum Industry: Building Our Achievements' (1985) 25 *APPEA Journal* 22 at 23.

[26] The Federal Opposition is the political party that has not been elected to govern Australia (the federal government), rather it sits 'in opposition' to the elected government.

[27] Keating, note 4, p. 19.

[28] Ibid.

[29] Ibid.

[30] Evans, note 25, p. 23.

[31] Ibid.

[32] Department of Primary Industries and Energy, 'Offshore Strategy: Promoting Petroleum Exploration Offshore Australia', Australian Government, Public Service, 1990, p. 1.

[33] Ibid.

included the release of offshore areas for exploration by companies, the collection of exploration data, and the dissemination of data to companies exploring for petroleum.[34] However, no LCR or economic diversification policies or provisions were considered, even though a major parliamentary inquiry into such issues had been concluded the year before.[35]

The election of a conservative government in 1996 saw a review of the offshore petroleum regulatory framework. Working closely with the petroleum sector, the government set about building on some elements of the 1990 petroleum policy, as well as incorporating the policy position of the petroleum industry. This review (the Parer review) developed a policy that sought to create certainty for investors and other stakeholders.[36] It was premised on the creation of a highly competitive (in an economic sense) operating environment, allowing industry to respond confidently to international challenges and to seize international trade and investment opportunities.[37] It sought to offer high levels of certainty to investors about their rights and responsibilities and to the processes of public decision-making which it was hoped would encourage investment.[38] The policy also sought to support industry's efforts to achieve sustained wealth generation through growth, innovation, and enhancement of value.[39] It was outlined in the Minerals and Petroleum Resources Policy Statement released in 1998, which delineated a framework for the development of Australian mining and petroleum industries, and cemented Australia's commitment to provide investors with a framework of government policies that ensured certainty for investors, minimised investment impediments, and promoted investment in the Australian petroleum industry.[40]

An energy-sector-wide policy review in 2004 incorporated a consideration of Australia's petroleum policy.[41] It reiterated the 1998 policy position for Australia's offshore petroleum sector. The development of the nation's petroleum resources remains guided by the principles laid down in the 1998 policy paper,[42] which sought to ensure autonomy for oil companies in petroleum activities, with petroleum exploration, and production driven by the petroleum sector.

---

[34] Ibid.
[35] See section 5 of the Parliamentary Report North West Shelf: A Sea of Lost Opportunities? (1989) for a consideration of Local Content provisions
[36] W. Parer, 'Delivering National Prosperity' (1998) 38 APPEA Journal 7, p. 11.
[37] Ibid.
[38] W. Parer, 'Launch of the Commonwealth Government's Minerals and Petroleum Resources Policy Statement', Parliament House, Canberra, February 2, 1998. www.daff.gov.au/__data/assets/pdf_file/0003/23763/ministers_parer_speeches.pdf (last visited 2 December 2008).
[39] Ibid.
[40] Department of Industry, Sciences and Resources, 'Australian Offshore Petroleum Strategy: A Strategy to Promote Petroleum Exploration and Development in Australian Offshore Areas' (1999) pp. 2–3.
[41] Energy Task Force, 'Securing Australia's Energy Future' (2004) pp. 51–3.
[42] Ibid.

Sustainability and LCRs in Australian Oil and Gas 213

3 LOCAL CONTENT REQUIREMENTS AND ITS RELATIONSHIP TO ECONOMIC DIVERSIFICATION

The production of petroleum creates a huge demand for industrial and technical efforts to cope with the demands of the developing industry.[43] In the absence of domestic petroleum support industries, the supply of goods, services, technical expertise, and machinery requires importing (and often re-exporting once production ceases), with no benefit to the State.[44]

A way of attaining economic benefit from petroleum exploitation is to utilise the development of petroleum resources to build, and ultimately, transform, other sectors of the economy. This concept, known as cross-sectoral linkage,[45] often sees state-directed development of industrial and technological goods and services required for the development of petroleum resources and ensures that enhanced value and benefit occurs alongside petroleum resource development. Such value creation not only benefits society during the exploitation of petroleum resources, but may, through economic diversification, extend beyond the life of petroleum exploitation, creating new and innovative industries on the back of petroleum that extend after resource exploitation has ceased. The concept of cross-sectoral linkages in the exploitation of petroleum resources is not new. It was an integral part of the petroleum regulatory framework in Norway, during the 1970–1990s,[46] establishing cross-sectoral linkages that prevail today.

The establishment of cross-sectoral linkages for value creation in petroleum economies often relies on the establishment, implementation, and enforcement of LCRs (also known as local content provisions) within the petroleum regulatory framework. Such LCRs may be established as part of the licensing framework, such as the case of Norway from the Second Licensing Round in 1972, where preference for Norwegian goods and services were mandated as part of the conditions for the licence, allowing local suppliers to be up to 10 per cent more expensive than non-Norwegian suppliers.[47] The Intergovernmental Forum on Mining, Minerals Metals and Sustainable Development (IGFMMMSD) acknowledges that there is no uniform definition of LCR,[48] recognising that 'local' can be

---

[43] M. Devaraj, 'Government Policies Concerning the Discovery and Development of New Offshore Oil Provinces, with Focus on India and the North Sea' (1983) 8 *Ocean Management* 251 at 270.

[44] Ibid., pp. 270–1.

[45] T. Hunter, 'Law and Policy Frameworks for Local Content in the Development of Petroleum Resources: Norwegian and Australian Perspectives on Cross-Sectoral Linkages and Economic Diversification' (2014) 27 *Mineral Economics*, pp. 115–26 at 116–17.

[46] Ministry of Petroleum and Energy, 'Report No. 38 t the Storting (2001–2001) – Oil and Gas Activities: Unofficial translation from Norwegian', 2002, p. 11. See also T. Thune, O. A. Engen, and O. Wicken (eds.), *Petroleum Industry Transformations: Lessons from Norway and Beyond* (UK: Routledge, 2018).

[47] See a discussion of Local content Provisions and licensing in Hunter, note 1, chapter 4.

[48] Intergovernmental Forum on Mining, Minerals Metals and Sustainable Development, 'Designing Local Content Policies in Mineral Rich Countries', International Institute for Sustainable Development, October 2018, 2–3.

214 *Tina Soliman Hunter*

construed narrowly (focussing only on a geographic area), or broadly, where local is associated with a nation or citizenship.[49] The IGFMMMSD defines LCR, in relation to the mining and minerals industry, as 'specific legal provisions [to] address concerns of particular indigenous or disadvantaged communities, where "local" is meant to respond to the specific concerns of the affected community'.[50]

Such LCRs do exist in Australia and are primarily related to the development of mineral resources onshore in the various states and territories. The negotiation of these specific provisions is not mandated by legislation in any jurisdiction, with the exception of the requirements laid down in the *Native Title Act 1993* (Cth) as part of Indigenous Land Use Agreements (ILUAs).[51] Most LCR are confined to individual mining projects, negotiated by individual companies with the relevant government. In the development of Queensland's CSG in the 2000s, LCRs were not mandated, nor is there any intention to mandate such requirements in law. However, recognising the high level of spending that the resource industry makes in the Queensland economy,[52] in 2013 the Queensland resources industry developed the Queensland Resources and Energy Sector Code of Practice for Local Content (the Code). Administered by the Queensland Resources Council, the voluntary Code encourages the use of local industry.[53] It is supported by the Queensland Local Content Leader's Network's 2014 Joint Statement of Commitment: Maximising Industry Local Content in Regional Queensland.

The Joint Statement defines local content as 'the full, fair and reasonable economic contribution made to the local communities by industry investment in local goods and services, employment and training, social and community development initiatives, and local industry capability development programs'.[54] Such LCRs apply to all resource industries, but are strongly aimed at mining and mineral development. No specific LCR codes of practice exist for other states, however it is important to note that many non-mandated LCR are endorsed as part of mining agreement provisions.[55] Specific LCR or codes for the onshore Australian petroleum sector have not been established to date, probably given the small size of the industry in

---

[49] Ibid., p. 2.

[50] Ibid., p. 3. See also D. Olawuyi, *Extractives Industry Law in Africa* (Springer 2018) 233–8.

[51] For ILUA requirements under the *Native Title Act 1993* (Cth) see Division 3, Subdivisions B-E. See also the requirements to prepare and implement an Australian Industry Participation ("AIP") plan for major projects, under the *Australian Jobs Act, No. 69 of 2013*, ss. 3–8.

[52] $19.3 billion across all resources sectors (petroleum and mining).

[53] Queensland Resources Council, *Local Content* (2019), www.qrc.org.au/policies/local-content/.

[54] Queensland Local Content Leader's Network, 'Joint Statement of Commitment: Maximising Industry Local Content in Regional Queensland', July 2016, p. 2.

[55] For example, Rio Tinto's Argyle Mine's local content policy for aboriginal content is driven by its Mine Participation Agreement with the Traditional Owners and supported by a Management Plan specifically dealing with Business Development and Contracting. For examples of Agreements, see A. M. Esteves, B. Coyne, and A. Moreno, 'Local Content in the Oil, Gas and Mining Sectors: Enhancing the Benefits at Subnational Level', Policy Framework Prepared for the Revenue Watch Institute, October 2012.

relation to the minerals sector. However, the offshore petroleum sector is much larger, and legislated by a single government, the Commonwealth government. Therefore, this chapter will focus on LCR in the offshore petroleum sector.

A fundamental component for the successful use of LCR is a concomitant economic diversification policy, established to ensure that auxiliary services and industries are developed concurrently with the petroleum resources in order to attempt to avoid the resource curse.[56] Economic diversification shifts an economy away from a single income source toward multiple sources from a growing range of sectors and markets.[57] It enables a State to develop and utilise industrial activities required for the extraction of non-renewable petroleum resources for other industrial activities.[58] If a state is able to direct economic diversification to develop competent industries that can be utilised after the petroleum resources have been exhausted, then that state can sustainably develop its petroleum resources by harnessing the supply needs of the petroleum to create a domestic industrial base. This enables skills, knowledge, and competence that was gained for the development of petroleum resources to be utilised for other industrial activities, thereby building a broad industrial base the State can utilise for other industrial activities after the petroleum resources have been exhausted. As noted in Section 2 above, a policy of LCR, enforced as a requirement of the award of a petroleum license, directed all Norwegian petroleum activity at the outset, thereby encouraging economic diversification and cross-sectoral linkages. LCR, and the subsequent economic diversification and cross-sectoral linkages, were considered in Australia when the NWS was discovered, and development was planned.

4 SUSTAINABILITY IN THE CONTEXT OF PETROLEUM RESOURCE DEVELOPMENT AND ITS RELATIONSHIP TO LOCAL CONTENT REQUIREMENTS

Generally, the development of petroleum resources in an economy has the potential to cause a 'resource curse', since high levels of petroleum exploration and production create a huge influx of labour, knowledge, skills, and money into a State.[59] The requirement for the use of local industries to supply goods and services is often

---

[56] R. M. Auty, *Sustaining Development in Mineral Resource Economies: The Resources Curse Thesis* (UK: Rutledge, 1993).

[57] Economic diversification is generally taken as the process in which a growing range of economic outputs are produced. It can also refer to the diversification of markets for exports or the diversification of income sources. See United Nations Framework Convention on Climate Change (UNFCCC), 'Economic Diversification', http://unfccc.int/adaptation/sbsta_agenda_item_adaptation/items/3994 .php.

[58] An excellent example of this is the creation and development of the Norwegian diving industry. O. Wicken, 'The Layers of National Innovation Systems: The Historical Evolution of a National Innovation System in Norway', Centre for Technology, Innovation Culture (TIK) Working Paper on Innovation Studies No. 20070601, p. 57.

[59] Hunter, note 1, pp. 296–7.

216   *Tina Soliman Hunter*

implemented in order to provide benefits for the local economy. The principle is predicated on the notion that when petroleum is extracted, there is the potential for a value for the State, not only from the petroleum resource exploited, but also through the exploitation of the petroleum.[60] If domestic industries can be developed that provide goods and services for the exploitation of petroleum, then that country can recapture the production cost spending. Norway sought to use its petroleum licencing framework, particularly the award of licences and the associated Joint Operating Agreement, as a way to implement LCR and economic diversification in the 1970s, 1980s, and early 1990s.

The production of petroleum generates high levels of short-term revenue through petroleum taxation. Aside from the possible politically destabilising effects of this revenue,[61] there is a temptation by many States to utilise the revenue for the short term, in order to create a 'better' society by improving those amenities in society that are favoured by the population, including roads, healthcare, and schools. However, all of these societal resources require maintenance after they have been created. Once the petroleum revenue has ceased, the affected State needs to find a source of income in which to maintain these now essential services. But if all of the resources have been depleted, there is no continued wealth stream. By mandating LCR, which lead to economic diversification, wealth streams outside petroleum extraction can be established and maintained, thereby generating a continued source of wealth. Therefore, LCR and economic diversification are vital tools in sustainable development of petroleum resources, since they assist a State in converting resource endowments and revenue into industrial activities, knowledge, and goods that can be utilised by other industries long after the resources have gone.

5 LOCAL CONTENT PROVISIONS IN AUSTRALIA

Since the commencement of petroleum production in 1969, there has been little focus on LCR or economic diversification policies in Australia. For the last twenty years, policy has placed an emphasis on attracting international oil companies to undertake petroleum exploration and production.[62] For over thirty years, offshore petroleum licences have been allocated under the bid method, with the work program bidding (WPB) method of allocation dominating. In this form of allocation, the licence is awarded to the applicant with the highest bid (in terms of work, and its equivalent monetary value), as set out under ss. 104–7 of the OPGGSA.[63]

---

[60] Ibid.

[61] For an excellent account of the effects of petroleum revenue on political stability and instability, refer to M. Humphries, J. D. Sachs, and J. E. Stiglitz (eds.), *Escaping the Resource Curse* (Columbia University Press, 2007).

[62] Department of Industry, Science and Resources, note 40, p. 4.

[63] For a discussion of other methods of allocation of petroleum licences, and their link to the North American and North Sea systems of petroleum regulation, see T. Hunter, 'Access to Petroleum under the Licensing and Concession System' in T. Hunter (ed.), *Regulation of the Upstream Petroleum*

Under this system of allocation, there are no LCR requirements for licence holders, nor a stipulation to support cross-sectoral linkages or other forms of Australian industry economic diversification as a condition of the award of the licence. Rather, the WPB method of allocation of offshore petroleum licences seeks to encourage exploration of the Australian Continental Shelf and allow economic forces to operate in the selection of the applicant.

Although the WPB has been utilised for decades, extensive commercial finds of petroleum (especially gas) on the NWS identified a need to consider the issue of LCP, and the role of the state in encouraging economic diversification. LCPs and their role in economic diversification were first identified in the late 1980s, and articulated in the 1989 House of Representatives Standing Committee (HRSC) report, 'The North West Shelf: Sea of Lost Opportunities?' (SOLO report).[64] The SOLO report recognises the following:

> The Committee agrees with the sentiments expressed by a majority of witnesses that major natural resource projects, such as the North West Shelf Project which are exploiting a non-renewable natural resource should contribute to the economy in more ways than simply through direct revenue, royalties and taxes. They must also contribute to developing the nation's infrastructure, to creating a wider skills base, and providing real opportunities for the expansion and development of Australian industry. Since projects of this type are also contingent on government providing approval in the form of production or export licences, Government has both an opportunity and a responsibility to the Australian people to ensure that indirect benefits, as well as the direct revenue, royalty and taxation benefits are maximised.[65]

Parts of the SOLO report were scathing toward existing government departments, exhibiting bewilderment 'at the apparent lack of any real concern or consideration given by the Department of Primary Industries and Energy to the broader significance of Australian industry participation in resource development projects'.[66] The HRSC concluded that where Australian industries are competitive, in terms of cost, quality, and government policy, then the Australian government has a responsibility to ensure that Australian industry has a fair and equitable opportunity to participate in these projects.[67] Further, it identified the need that 'government has a thorough understanding of the oil and gas industry, or Australia's own industrial capacity, and of the impacts of these projects on the economy as a whole'.[68]

It is important to note that the SOLO report was not seeking mandatory LCR, similar to Norway. Rather, it supported the view that Australian goods and services

---

Sector: A Comparative Study of Licensing and Concession Systems (Cheltenham: Edward Elgar, 2015), pp. 36–58.

[64] D. P. Beddall, 'The Northwest Shelf: A Sea of Lost Opportunities', Report from the House of Representatives Standing Committee on Industry, Science and Technology, 1989.

[65] Ibid., p. 15.

[66] Ibid., p. 22.

[67] Ibid., p. xv.

[68] Ibid., p. xv.

should be encouraged where competitive,[69] and that the government undertake a coordinator role assessing, monitoring, and validating local content within these projects.[70] Further, the HRSC identified the grant of a production licence[71] as critical in developing cross-sectoral linkages and encouraging economic diversification, recommending that applicants for a production licence should be required, as part of the licence agreement, to ensure that project timescales do not discriminate against the participation of Australian industry.[72] In essence, the lack of consideration given to the 'potential economic benefits for Australian industry and the economic benefits to Australia of identifying and actively promoting opportunities for Australian industry participation' was of major concern to the HRSC.[73] On the back of such concerns, the HRSC recommended that the appropriate ministers 'urgently put in place arrangements which will compel consultation between their Departments to ensure that full account is taken of Government industry policy and the participation of Australian industry in offshore oil and gas developments'.[74]

The government of the time agreed with the aims of the SOLO report, however it disagreed with the emphasis on government intervention, stating that it was 'firmly committed to the view that the primary responsibility for ensuring industry participation in resource development projects rests with the business sector. Our general approach to industry policy is to encourage an internationally competitive and outward looking industrial sector'.[75]

Furthermore, the Government reiterated that its policy on Australian participation in major projects recognises the need to consider industry participation in an economy-wide context, bearing in mind that 'there should be a full and fair opportunity for Australian industry to participate in the development of resources';[76] and that 'any intervention should not discriminate between projects, and above all, should not adversely affect the commercial viability of individual projects'.[77] In essence, the Australian government rejected the notion of LCR and government intervention in assisting industry in value creation during the NWS project.

Nevertheless, some initiatives were established in light of the SOLO report. Of note was the establishment of the major projects facilitation unit (MPFU) in 1992 to counter 'industry perception that government approvals processes were prone to

---

[69] Ibid., p. 61.
[70] Ibid., p. 42.
[71] Granted after the licensee declares a petroleum pool as required under s129 of the OPPGSA and has decided that the development of the pool is commercially viable, and therefore requires a production licence to develop the resource.
[72] Beddall, note 64, p. 59.
[73] Ibid., p. 26.
[74] Ibid., p. 26.
[75] Government response to House of Representatives Standing Committee on Science, Industry and Technology, 'The North West Shelf: A Sea of Lost Opportunities' (1989), p. 2.
[76] Ibid., p. 2.
[77] Ibid., p. 2.

Sustainability and LCRs in Australian Oil and Gas

delays, duplication, conflict and uncertainty'.[78] The role of the MPFU was to facilitate new developments over $50 million requiring government approval, although it was duplicated with the establishment of a similar unit at the Department of Primary Industries and Energy.[79] Such duplication was noted in the SOI report, which recommended a reduction in such duplication through the streamlining of services.[80]

A second parliamentary report, 'A Sea of Indifference: Australian Industry Participation in the North West Shelf Project' (SOI report), was completed in 1998,[81] reaffirming the view from SOLO report that there was a need to champion Australian industry and demonstrated some commitment to some of the views outlined in the SOLO report.[82] Importantly, the SOI report recommended the development of a 'world class waterfront engineering facility'[83] to provide common-use facilities, and the partnering of government and the private sector to meet the industry, technological, and skilling needs of marine and resource industries. This resulted in the establishment of the Australian Marine Complex (AMC) in 2003, a 200-hectare marine industrial hub comprising shipbuilding, technology, support, and fabrication industries for the marine, defence, petroleum, and resource industries.[84] The AMC complex has contributed significantly to the development of local industries supporting petroleum and gas resource development.[85] The SOI report also recommended to the Minister for Primary Industries and Energy that the Department should require those seeking exploration permits or licences, if their project proceeds to production, to commit to maximising opportunities for local industry involvement and providing details on how this should be achieved.[86]

Essentially, the SOI report recommended that Australia should require licensees to enhance the development of local content as part of the licence application process. The Australian government argued in its response to the SOI report (affirmed its response in its petroleum policy review of 1999) that it would leave the development of local content and local industries to market forces. In rejecting the recommendation to develop and implement LCRs in the petroleum sector, the

---

[78] House of Representatives Standing Committee on Industry, Science and Resources, 'Sea of Indifference: Australian Industry Participation in the North West Shelf Project' (1998), p. 25 [SOI].

[79] Ibid., p. 25.

[80] Ibid., pp. 25–6.

[81] Ibid.

[82] Ibid., pp. 25–6.

[83] Ibid.

[84] AMC is a marine industrial hub located south of Perth. It serves as a maritime training institute, common-use business facility for marine and industrial projects, centre of technological excellence, shipbuilding centre, as well as providing support industries. See Australian Marine Complex, 'Overview of the AMC', www.australianmarinecomplex.com.au/overview-amc. (2015)

[85] Ibid.

[86] Beddall, note 64, p. xvii.

government again argued that it was committed to encouraging an internationally competitive industry.[87]

The result of the Australian government's failure to take a guiding hand in diversifying Australia's industrial base as part of its development of petroleum resources, has been that domestic industry diversification in Australia has not progressed in comparison to those countries using the North Sea system, particularly Norway. This is demonstrated by comparing the relative exports between Australia and Norway. Australia's primary exports include raw materials including iron ore, bauxite, and coal, as well as agricultural products,[88] with primary imports including machinery and transport equipment, computers, telecommunication products, and crude oil/petroleum products.[89] This differs to the diversified portfolio of exports for Norway, including petroleum and gas, machinery and equipment, metals, chemicals, ships, and fish products,[90] and imported commodities primarily comprising chemicals, metals, and foodstuffs.[91]

When oil and gas was discovered in Bass Strait in the 1960s, Australia's economy was exceptionally similar to Norway, relying on natural resources (especially wheat and wool). In the 1950s and 1960s, Australian manufacturing was assisted by protectionist policies and statutory boards, discouraging foreign investors who noted Australia's lack of competitiveness in the international manufacturing sector.[92] This prompted a decline in investment in the manufacturing sector. This did not hamper the Australian economy, since the development of mining initiatives to exploit Australia's natural resources underpinned economic expansion in the post-war period to 1974.[93]

Australia's manufacturing decline in the 1950s and 1960s, and the role of protectionist policies was addressed in the Crawford Report.[94] Australia retained high levels of tariff protection until 1973, when the first tariff cuts occurred.[95] The Crawford report identified tariff barriers as having a substantial detrimental effect on the Australian economy. Furthermore, it concluded that assistance through tariffs and quotas should be reduced in order to stimulate change in the industry sector and encourage specialisation, whilst at the same time generating increased

---

[87] For this commitment, see the Australian petroleum policy in Department of Industry, Science and Resources, note 40, as well as a discussion on the commitment to industry in Beddall, note 64.

[88] CIA, 'The World FactBook: Australia', www.cia.gov/library/publications/the-world-factbook/geos/as .html (2017).

[89] Ibid.

[90] Ibid.

[91] Ibid.

[92] S. Bell, *Australian Manufacturing and the State: The Politics of Industrial Policy in the Post-War Era* (Cambridge University Press, 1993), pp. 24–5.

[93] Ibid.

[94] J. Crawford, Study Group on Structural Adjustment (Australia), ' Report March 1979', 1979 (The Crawford Report).

[95] A. Leigh, 'Trade Liberalisation and the Australian Labor Party' (2002) 48 *Australian Journal of Politics and History* 487 at 488.

Sustainability and LCRs in Australian Oil and Gas

social welfare for the nation as a whole.[96] The Crawford report also recommended that general tariff reductions should be accompanied by industry-specific policies for highly protected industries providing specific incentives to redirect productive activities.[97] Further significant tariff cuts occurred in 1988 and 1991, with an effective reduction of manufacturing industry assistance from 1970–2001 from 35 per cent to 5 per cent.[98]

These high levels of tariffs which created industry protection had a substantial impact on the Australian economy, with Australian merchandise exports comprising only 9.5 per cent of Australia's GDP in 1973.[99] The economic position in Australia, like much of the world, changed dramatically, triggered by the increase in world oil prices in the early 1970s. The Australian manufacturing sector experienced substantial decline in employment levels between 1973 and 1980, with over 80,000 jobs lost in this period, and the industry's share of employment falling from 25 per cent in 1970 to 18 per cent in 1985. As well, its proportion of total GDP fell from a high of 29 per cent in 1960 to 18 per cent in 1985.[100] This decline continued, with manufacturing's contribution to GDP falling from 17 per cent in 1980 to 13 per cent in 1997.[101] This contrasted markedly with the manufacturing sector's virtually unchanged share of the United States GDP (19 per cent), and the slight increase in trade with Japan – from 25 per cent to 27 per cent – over the same period. In total, the contribution of manufacturing to the GDP of all industrialised countries fell by only 2 per cent, from 24 per cent in 1980 to 22 per cent in 1997.

Today, the Australian manufacturing industry is generally moribund, although there are a number of areas that have retained some strength, or been enhanced, particularly the maritime manufacturing and fabrication industry. Australia has the capacity to build and maintain defence ships,[102] as evidenced by the Department of Defence developing Australia's ship building capability in Australia.[103] The continued development of defence shipbuilding and repair capacity in NSW,

[96] O. Kingma and P. Volker, 'Structural Adjustment in the Manufacturing Sector: A Review of the Crawford Report' (1980) 5 *Australian Journal of Management* 1 at 3.

[97] Ibid., p. 4.

[98] Leigh, note 94, p. 487.

[99] K. O'Rourke and J. Williamson, *Globalization and History* (MIT Press, 1999), p. 30.

[100] Australian Bureau of Statistics, 'Yearbook Australia 2001: Manufacturing From Settlement to the Start of the New Century', January 25, 2001, www.abs.gov.au/Ausstats/abs@.nsf/Previousproducts/1301.0Feature%20Article382001?opendocument&tabname=Summary&prodno=1301.0&issue=2001&num=&view=.

[101] Ibid.

[102] P. Morris, J. Sharp, and Australian Shipowners Association, 'Independent Review of Australian Shipping, A Blueprint for Australian Shipping', January 1, 2003, p. 8.

[103] This has included the replenishment of HMAS Success, construction of two Oliver Hazary Perry Class FFG's, ten ANZAC Frigates, six Collins Class submarines, six Huon Class mine hunters, fourteen Armidale Class patrol boats, and the refit of two frigates (HMAS Manoora and HMAS Kanimbla). See Deloitte, 'Australia's Capacity to Build the LHD Ships', 2007, p. 12.

Queensland, and Victoria has created the necessary skills, resources, and infrastructure that are required for shipbuilding in Australia.[104] Australia continues to develop physical and human capital for economic diversification into maritime industries through defence shipbuilding.

The requirements of the offshore petroleum industry can be utilised to assist in the further development of Australia's shipbuilding industries. The industry itself notes that there are challenges in expanding its LNG capacity due to shortages of LNG shipping vessels.[105] This demand will need to be predominantly met by the construction of new ships in a global ship construction market that is struggling to keep up with demand.[106] Given the skills, infrastructure, and assessed capacity to construct large ships with high local content,[107] Australia has the capacity to share in the construction of LNG Ships. Ultimately, economic diversification into areas of shortage could place Australia in a position to capitalise on its limited industrial strength. This may ultimately lead to the capacity to build large ships in Australian shipyards, as the demand for LNG and floating production (FLNG), storage, and offtake (FPSO) vessels in the petroleum sector increases. Like Norway, Australia has the capacity to diversify in regional areas, providing employment and regional diversification in areas where traditional manufacturing industries have declined.[108]

6 LOCAL CONTENT PROVISIONS TODAY: HAS THE SHIP SAILED?

Whilst it is difficult to determine why Australia has failed to economically diversify, it is clear that Australia is now at a crossroads. It has the capacity and capability to utilise the experience of the AMC in Western Australia, as well as the example of Norwegian industrial diversification, to develop a petroleum-sector-driven industrial base in Australia. By investing in the human capital and physical infrastructure, Australia is sustainably developing its petroleum resources. With concentrated effort through defence department procurement and materials policies, the Australian shipbuilding industry has been salvaged. By utilising the exploitation of non-renewable resources to build industrial capabilities, Australia has the capacity to encourage sustainable development of petroleum resources for present and future Australian generations.

By implementing the recommendations relating to a need for economic diversification from the SOI report, it is possible Australia may be able to address the economic challenges associated with the development of its offshore petroleum.

---

[104] Deloitte, note 103, p. 9.
[105] APPEA, 'Australia's Upstream Oil and Gas Industry: A Platform for Prosperity', 2006, p. 12.
[106] Ibid.
[107] The Assessment of Deloitte for the construction of five large warships is that Australia has the capacity to provide 40 per cent of the total project as local content, providing an additional 800 million dollars, and divided between design (10 per cent), metal fabrication (50 per cent), and systems (40 per cent) industries.
[108] Morris et al., note 102.

Sustainability and LCRs in Australian Oil and Gas 223

Both the SOLO and the SOI report outright rejected the implementation of LCR. However, both reports, but particularly the SOLO report (undertaken during a labour government period in office) identified ways that government involvement could encourage economically sustainability. Some of these recommendations include maximising opportunities for local industry involvement and providing details of how this will be achieved; providing data which will allow analysis of value added in Australia; maximising the transfer of skills and technology to Australians; and undertaking research, development, and design in Australia to the maximum extent possible.[109]

The award of petroleum licences, as a method of encouraging economic diversification is difficult under the WPB system, since the premise of the WPB system is that the bidder that offers the highest bid is the most efficient company. The implementation of policies other than encouraging investment is difficult under the WPB system, since it is based on purely economic imperatives to encourage overseas companies. This policy position has resulted in over 150 petroleum exploration companies, many of which are non-Australian, exploring and producing petroleum from the Australian offshore region.[110] If Australia were to encourage investment in Australian industries as part of the award criteria of petroleum licencing, as recommended in the SOI report, value creation, greater diversification and investment in local industry is likely to result.[111]

Although the recommendations for government intervention in both the SOLO and the SOI report were rejected, two significant events since 2007 indicate a shifting petroleum policy emphasis in Australia. The first was the commissioning of an issues paper by the Australian Productivity Commission regarding regulatory burden in the upstream oil and gas sector,[112] with a review of regulatory policy forming a peripheral part of that review.[113]

Second, the Department of Resources, Energy and Tourism publicly declared in 2008 that 'the Australian government is committed to creating a policy framework to expand Australia's resource base, increase the international competitiveness of [the] resources sector and improve the regulatory regime, consistent with the principles of environmental responsibility and sustainable development'.[114]

---

[109] SOI, note 77, p. xvii.

[110] T. Powell, 'Discovering Australia's Future Petroleum Resources: The Strategic Geoscience Information Role of Government' (2008) 48 *The APPEA Journal* at 9–13.

[111] It is important to note that some diversification has occurred as a result of the establishment of the Australian Marine Complex in Western Australia. See T. Hunter, note 45, p. 126.

[112] Australian Productivity Commission, note 10.

[113] Ibid.

[114] The Australian Government's policy framework for offshore petroleum aims to 'expand Australia's resource base, increase the international competitiveness of our resources sector and improve the regulatory regime, consistent with the principles of leading health and safety performance, environmental responsibility and sustainable development'. See cached file:
file:///C:/Users/madel/Downloads/sub07/Department%20of%20Industry%20Innovation%20and%20Science.pdf

In 2008, the Australian government sought to build on the previous government's petroleum framework implemented in 1998, indicating its intention to encourage international competitiveness as a foundation for an improved regulatory regime, but based upon expanding Australian resources in a manner consistent with the principles of sustainable development.[115] Whilst the current policy framework, as laid down in the 1998 petroleum policy, addresses exploration and commercial aspects of Australian offshore petroleum exploration and production, it does not enunciate a commitment to encouraging sustainable development. Hence, although the Australian government has a current national petroleum policy objective to ensure stewardship of petroleum resources to increase the resource base in a manner consistent with sustainable development, the existing 1998 policy does not reflect this national petroleum objective, rather focussing on commercial interests.

From an industry perspective, in 2007, APPEA indicated its strategic objectives include developing an efficient industry; ensuring the benefits of Australia's oil and gas resources enjoyed by the Australian people are maximised; delivering petroleum energy security; and assuring the long term sustainability of the Australian oil and gas industry.[116] Furthermore, it called for an increased role for the Australian Government in the exploration for petroleum provinces: 'Whilst there is no substitute for a frontier discovery to stimulate exploration there is an important role for the Australian governments in facilitating exploration of these frontier areas by undertaking pre-competitive geoscience work required to demonstrate their petroleum potential.'[117] The government went on to say that 'it must be further developed by [governments of] all jurisdictions if the opportunity to discover new oil provinces, and thereby sustain Australia's oil industry, is to be maximised'.[118]

Arguably, current petroleum policy does not maximise the value of oil and gas resources for the Australian people. This is partly attributable to changes in the global petroleum market and Australia's petroleum reserves. Australia is generally viewed as a minor petroleum province and, in the early part of the twenty-first century, failed to be attractive in prospective terms. In the ten-year period to 2002, 154 companies commenced or recommenced exploration operations in Australia, whilst 168 companies left Australia's petroleum provinces in the same period.[119] It would appear that current petroleum policies that mandate commercial investment and strong industry control are not successful. Thus, Australia needs to rethink its petroleum policies. In addition, regulatory challenges and burdens have eroded the attractiveness of Australian petroleum provinces as a place for commercial investment.[120]

---

[115] Ibid.
[116] APPEA, note 105, p. iii.
[117] Powell, note 110.
[118] Ibid.
[119] Ibid.
[120] Australian Productivity Commission, note 10, p. 4.

However, the prospect of the GAB, and in particular the Ceduna Sub-Basin (CSB), is likely to alter the attractiveness of the region. Initial estimates, based on seismic survey and shallow geological information, place the possible resource in the GAB at between 1.6 and 6 billion BOE. Equinor, the giant Norwegian government-owned state oil company, is seeking to drill an exploration well in 2,400 m of water, and expects to find a large deposit of sweet, light crude.[121] Such a discovery is likely to bring a new wave of economic windfall for Australia, which can provide sustainable socio-economic benefit if value creation is implemented. Although public opposition to the commencement of exploration drilling in the GAB is strong, APPEA, Australia's peak petroleum industry body, commissioned a study by ACIL Allen, which concluded that the economic benefits of a full development of GAB petroleum fields are likely to be significant, with benefits to Australia in the period 2020–60, and includes 2,116 jobs during the construction phase, an 18 per cent increase in the south Australian economy, and up to $7.7 billion/annum in state and commonwealth tax revenue (petroleum and corporate tax).[122]

Sustainability in the Australian petroleum industry is at a crossroads. The present commercially focussed policy of industry attraction and investment has not achieved its objectives of developing a strong, aggressive offshore petroleum sector. The targets that were set twenty years ago, in relation to achievements for the Australian industry, have gone largely unfulfilled. Production continues to decrease, exploration continues to decline, and Australia is less attractive as a petroleum exploration province.[123] Furthermore, by its own admission, the petroleum industry is requesting more government intervention, especially in the areas of pre-competitive data to encourage exploration and frontier areas,[124] demonstrated by the Australian government undertaking a geoscientific study of the CSB and identifying world-class marine oil-prone potential source rocks.[125]

Previous Australian experience in natural resource management,[126] as well as that in Norway, demonstrates that government-led diversification of existing local industries provides countries with the opportunity to decrease its dependence on non-

---

[121] Equinor, *Draft Environment Plan for the Stromlo-1 Exploration Drilling Program* (1 February 2019)
[122] J. Nicolaou, J. Hammond, and G. Jakeman, 'Petroleum Development in the Great Australian Bight: A Preliminary View of the Economic Impact of Development', ACIL Allen Consulting, Report to APPEA, August 2018.
[123] Powell, note 110.
[124] Ibid.
[125] Geosciences Australia, 'Submission to the Senate Committee on Oil or Gas Production in the Great Australian Bight', Submission No. 70, 2017, p. 12.
[126] The Australian government has previously ensured the economic sustainability of Australia's resources through the Snowy Mountains Scheme in the 1950s and 1960s. This government-established scheme is an integrated water and hydro-electric power scheme, which dams numerous east-flowing rivers, turning them westwards to provide valuable irrigation water for the inland agricultural regions of Australia and securing Australia's post-war economic development. See Snowy Hydro, 'The Snowy Mountains Scheme', www.snowyhydro.com.au/our-energy/hydro/the-scheme/.

renewable natural resources; a dependence that can lead to economic inefficiencies and economic distortion. By encouraging sustainable development of petroleum resources through economic diversification and industry building, Australia can build its industrial capacity in the offshore petroleum industry. However, as the experience at the AMC in Western Australia has demonstrated, the guiding hand of government is required to encourage industrial diversification.

The Australian petroleum licencing system has the capacity to direct economic diversification of Australian industries. In its present form (the use of the bidding system), the licencing system cannot encourage economic diversification. A shift to the use of a discretionary system of allocation, with clearly established award criteria, would give the Australian State the capacity to encourage value creation for the Australian economy, as first suggested in SOLO report.[127] Although the use of LCR was specifically rejected, the SOLO report, and the subsequent SOI report, recognised the need for the guiding hand of government to increase local content and promote economic diversification, thereby encouraging sustainable development of petroleum resources. Given the likely potential of the GAB as a frontier petroleum region, perhaps it is timely that the Commonwealth review its method of allocation of petroleum licences. The allocation of petroleum licences should still retain a large emphasis on work program, particularly in the first three years. However, the allocation of licences should also encompass criteria that not only meet Australia's petroleum objectives of increasing international investment but also encouraging sustainability through the development of local industries, leading to value creation, and economic diversification.

7 CONCLUSION

At present, Australia is a natural resource dependent nation. It is dependent upon agricultural resources and mining resources to fuel economic growth. Some of these, such as agricultural resources, are renewable, ensuring that Australia will enjoy a steady income stream from these resources. However, much of Australia's resource wealth is non-renewable. Therefore, it is imperative to ensure that when non-renewable resources, such as oil and gas, are developed, this occurs in a manner that ensures that future generations, and not just present generations, will benefit from the exploitation of these resources. As demonstrated by the Norwegian experience, it is only through the recognition and promotion of intergenerational equity that sustainable development occurs.

An important contribution to intergenerational equity is the establishment of long-lasting industries (both goods and services) on the back of petroleum development, through value creation and economic diversification. Often a tool to attain these goals are LCR. Many jurisdictions have, or had, a clear target, policy or

---

[127] Beddall, note 64.

legislation on LCR to assist in the establishment and development of local industries in the petroleum industry. Australia has yet to fully embrace such a notion throughout the development of its petroleum resources. Two reports have identified the need for the guiding hand of the state in order to develop local industries and create economic value for Australia. Both reports were rejected, with the established petroleum policy (which prevails today), insisting that the primary focus remains on attracting international investment, reiterating a strong government 'hands off' approach.

However, Australia may be entering a new era of petroleum development. The frontier GAB, and its CSB, holds remarkable potential, predicted to be somewhere in the range of 1.6–6 billion BOE. Such potential also brings a new wave of possibility for the development of Australia's petroleum industry. Certainly, LCRs may not be fully embraced in Australia. However, state-guided policies designed to create value and encourage economic diversification may well have a place, and the next great basin may be developed with sustainability as a focus. Only time will tell.

12

Local Content for Sustainable Development in Middle East and North Africa: Current Legal Approaches and Future Directions

Damilola S. Olawuyi

1 INTRODUCTION

The MENA region, especially the Gulf countries—Kuwait, Iran, Iraq, Bahrain, Oman, Qatar, Saudi Arabia, and the United Arab Emirates (UAE) – is home to some of the world's largest exporters of oil and natural gas. MENA holds the world's largest proven gas reserves (approximately 45 per cent of the global total),[1] and approximately 48 per cent of the world's proven oil reserves.[2] In 2016, Gulf countries accounted for about a third of the world's total crude oil production, with Saudi Arabia alone producing about 12 million barrels per day.[3] Qatar holds the world's third largest natural gas reserves and is the largest supplier of liquefied natural gas in the world.[4] Iran has the second-largest gas reserves, and the fourth-largest oil reserves, in the world. Kuwait, meanwhile, holds 10 per cent of the world's proven oil reserves.[5] With abundant oil and gas resources, the MENA region has historically provided opportunities for international oil and gas companies (IOCs) to spearhead oil exploration and production activities, and to acquire interests in fields with unexplored economic potential.[6]

---

[1] This is only followed by South and Central America (19.4 per cent) and North America (14 per cent). Saudi Arabia alone holds around 16 per cent of global oil reserves, while other Gulf States also hold significant crude reserves: UAE 5.8 per cent, Qatar 1.5 percent, and Oman 0.3 per cent. See BP, 'BP Statistical Review of World Energy' (67th Edition), June 2018, p. 12.

[2] Ibid.

[3] Ibid. See also Organization of Petroleum Exporting Countries (OPEC), 'OPEC Annual Statistical Bulletin', 2017, p. 30.

[4] Due to its significant natural gas resources, Qatar is currently ranked as the richest country in the world, with the highest per capita GDP, and the largest global per capita sovereign wealth fund. See International Monetary Fund, 'World Economic Outlook Database', April 2017, www.imf.org/exter nal/datamapper/NGDPDPC@WEO/OEMDC/ADVEC/WEOWORLD.

[5] See BP, 'BP Statistical Review of World Energy, note 1, p. 16.

[6] For example, the oil and gas industry has been an important cornerstone of Qatar's economy. About 70 per cent of total government revenue, more than 60 per cent of gross domestic product, roughly 90 per cent of export earnings, and more than 90 per cent of the foreign exchange revenues in Qatar are derived from the oil and gas sector. Kuwait's oil and gas resources account for 53 per cent of GDP, 93 per cent of government revenues, and 94 per cent of export earnings. Saudi Arabia and the UAE have

Local Content in Middle East and North Africa

In search of economic diversification and sustainable development in the oil and gas sector, MENA countries are increasingly introducing LCRs in legal frameworks, extractive contracts, industry guidelines, and bidding practices.[7] For example, in 2019, Qatar's national oil company, Qatar Petroleum, announced its Localization Program for Services and Industries in the Energy Sector (TAWTEEN), which sets the target of localising Qatar's oil and gas supply chain to provide growth opportunities for indigenous small and medium enterprises.[8] The innovative programme aims to add 15 billion Qatari Riyals of 'in-country economic investment value' to the local economy. The programme aims to reward suppliers and contractors who comply with the TAWTEEN programme by meeting 'in-country value' threshold and targets.[9] Similarly, in 2015, Saudi Arabia's national oil company, Saudi Aramco, launched its In Kingdom Total Value Add (IKTVA) programme, aimed at driving, measuring, and monitoring the 'added value' brought to the Kingdom by a - contractor.[10] Participation in, and compliance with, the IKTVA programme is required for doing business with Saudi Aramco.[11] The IKTVA programme uses a complex formula to assess local content in terms of dollar amount of localised goods and services use; amount of salaries paid to Saudis; amount spent on, or allocated for, training and development of Saudis; and the amount spent on local suppliers.[12] Similarly, Oman, Kuwait and United Arab Emirates all have comprehensive legislative frameworks that require extractive companies to give priority to nationals, domestic companies, and locally produced materials, equipment, consumables, and

---

similar situations. See International Monetary Fund, 'Economic Diversification in Oil-Exporting Arab Countries', Annual Meeting of Arab Ministers of Finance, April 2016, pp. 7–8.

[7] See, for example, Organisation for Economic Co-operation and Development (OECD), Trade and Agriculture Directorate Trade Committee, Working Party of the Trade Committee, 'Local Content Policies in Minerals-Exporting Countries', June 2, 2017, TAD/TC/WP(2017)3/PART1/FINAL, pp. 6–7; also T. Acheampong, M. Ashong and V. Svanikier, 'An Assessment of Local-Content Policies in Oil and Gas Producing Countries' (2016) 9 *Journal of World Energy Law and Business* 282–302; S. Tordo, M. Warner, O. Manzano and Y. Anouti, 'Local Content Policies in the Oil and Gas Sector', The World Bank, 2013; Columbia Centre on Sustainable Investment, 'Local Content Laws and Contractual Provisions', http://ccsi.columbia.edu/work/projects/local-content-laws-contractual-provisions/; also P. Heum, 'Local Content Development: Experiences from Oil and Gas Activities in Norway', SNF Working Paper No. 02/08, Institute for Research in Economics and Business Administration, February 2008; also C. Nwapi, 'A Survey of the Literature on Local Content Policies in the Oil and Gas Industry in East Africa' (2016) 9 *School of Public Policy Technical Paper, University of Calgary*.

[8] TAWTEEN, 'Qatar Petroleum to Launch the Localization Program for Services and Industries in the Energy Sector', January 8, 2019, www.tawteen.com.qa/News-Media/Press-Releases/News-Qatar-Petroleum-to-launch-the-Localization-Pr.

[9] See TAWTEEN, 'Purpose and Definition of the In-Country Value', www.tawteen.com.qa/In-Country-Value/Purpose-and-definition-of-the-In-Country-Value. See also Qatar Petroleum, 'Qatar's Strategic Qatarization Plan', 2018, https://qp.com.qa/en/Careers/Qatarization/Pages/Qatarization.aspx.

[10] See Saudi Aramco, 'In Kingdom Total Value Add (IKTVA) Program: Program Brochure: Creating Value in the Kingdom, 2016.

[11] Ibid.

[12] Ibid.

230   *Damilola S. Olawuyi*

other goods.[13] Governments across MENA region favour LCRs as policy tools for maximising the degree of local benefits from the extractive sector through local employment, skills development, and national industry participation.[14] LCR clauses in extractive contracts could also provide investors some form of autonomy, transparency, and efficiency in sourcing goods and services for their operations.[15] The introduction of robust LCRs is a positive attempt by MENA countries to utilise oil and gas production as a key to add value to, and unlock the robust development of, other important sectors of their domestic economies.

However, while LCRs could provide a strategic tool for MENA governments to generate economic benefits for the local economy, LCRs need to be holistically balanced with other national policies on foreign direct investment (FDIs) and sustainable development, to avoid misalignments, especially in countries that are yet to establish clear legal and policy frameworks on LCRs.[16] For example, while LCRs may specify the portion of total expenditures that must be comprised of locally sourced goods and services, lack of available technology, capacity, and material at local level may delay projects and may ultimately result in loss of FDIs to less restrictive jurisdictions.[17] Such an outcome could stifle a country's path to sustainable development.[18] The undertone of conflict between the aims of LCRs and the practical sustainable development outcomes must be carefully analysed in order to avoid policy misalignments and trade-offs. Addressing the gaps between policy aims of LCRs and their practical outcomes in terms of sustainable development could help MENA countries plot a more holistic path for the reform, design, and implementation of LCRs.

This chapter examines practical challenges in the design and implementation of LCRs in the MENA region, and how such challenges may stifle the overall contributions of LCRs to sustainable development. It also discusses innovative legal

[13]   See D. Olawuyi, 'Local Content and Procurement Requirements in Oil and Gas Contracts: Regional Trends in the Middle East and North Africa' (2019) 37 *Journal of Energy and Natural Resources Law* 93–117. See also Abu Dhabi National Oil Company (ADNOC), 'In-Country Value (ICV) program', www.adnoc.ae/en/incountry-value/.

[14]   Ibid.

[15]   D. Olawuyi, *Extractives Industry in Africa* (New York: Springer, 2018) 233–243.

[16]   See Trade Arabia, 'Big boost to Saudi industries as Aramco to double local market sourcing', December 1, 2015, http://tradearabia.com/news/IND_295936.html; Tordo et al., note 7; R. Darling, 'Beyond Taxation: How Countries Can Benefit from the Extractive Industries through Local Content', Revenue Watch Institute, 2011, pp. 1–10; also Shared Value Initiative, 'Extracting with Purpose Creating Shared Value in the Oil and Gas and Mining Sectors' Companies and Communities', October 15, 2014, pp. 27–32.

[17]   D. Olawuyi, 'Legal Strategies and Tools for Mitigating Legal Risks Associated with Oil and Gas Investments in Africa' (2015) 39 *OPEC Energy Review* 247–265. D. Olawuyi and T. Mercier, 'Local Content and Procurement Requirements in Frontier African Oil and Gas Jurisdictions: One Size Does Not Fit All', December 9, 2015, www.insideafricalaw.com/blog/local-content-and-procurement-requirements-in-frontier-african-oil-and-gas-jurisdictions-one-size-does-not-fit-all.

[18]   I. Ramdoo, 'Unpacking Local Content Requirements in the Extractive Sector: What Implications for the Global Trade and Investment Frameworks?' E15Initiative, International Centre for Trade and Sustainable Development (ICTSD), World Economic Forum, September 2015.

Local Content in Middle East and North Africa 231

strategies to address the critical intersections and trade-offs between LCRs and sustainable development.

After this introduction, Section 2 examines the rise of LCRs in the MENA region and their implications for sustainable development in the region. Section 3 discusses the tensions points between LCRs and sustainable development in the region. Section 4 examines how national authorities can evolve holistic and adaptive LCRs that balance LCR goals with short- and long-term sustainable development objectives. Section 5 sets out the conclusion.

2 DRIVERS, SCOPE, AND CONTOURS OF LCRS IN THE MENA REGION

There are five key drivers of the increased adoption of LCRs in the MENA region.[19] First is the desire by MENA countries to increase the level of domestic capabilities and competencies over time. Despite the historically high level of oil and gas production activities in the MENA region, exploration and production operations have been largely spearheaded by international oil and gas companies.[20] The introduction of LCRs is based on the primary premise that domestic workforce and industries should over time develop the capacities to supply the goods, services, and human resources needed to drive the oil and gas value chain. For example, LCRs across the region emphasise the need for investors to adopt practices that foster the development of a better-trained, qualified domestic workforce over the term of the contract.[21] Virtually all of the surveyed regimes mandate preference for local goods, services, consumables, works, or enterprises. In all of the MENA jurisdictions examined, the IOC has an obligation to give due and proper consideration to preferring locally sourced services and goods when their price, quality, time of delivery, and other terms are comparable to internationally available ones. They also mandate the IOC to prepare plans and programmes for training and educating nationals during the term of the contract. The aim is to reduce excessive dependence on foreign technology, capacity, and manpower in MENA oil and gas sectors over time.

---

[19] These are extensively discussed in Olawuyi, note 13.

[20] T. Muller and M. Schitzer, 'Technology Transfer and Spillovers in International Joint Ventures', Munich Discussion Paper No. 2003–22, September 2003; also M. Levett and A. Chandler, 'Maximising Development of Local Content across Industry Sectors in Emerging Markets', Center for Strategic and International Studies, May 2012.

[21] See, for example, Iran: Maximum Utilization of Production and Services Potency in Providing Country's Needs and Promotion of Exports (2012), ss. 1–2; see also Jordan: Model Production Sharing Agreement (2007), Article 23; also Oman: Model Exploration and Production Sharing Agreement (2004), Article 19.1; Iraq (Federal) 2009 Technical Service Contract for Oil Field; Iraq Production Sharing Contract (2007) Kurdistan Region; INA Contract of 1998 for the Exploration, Development and Production of Petroleum Between the Government of the Syrian Arab Republic and Syrian Petroleum Company and INA-Industrija Nafte dd.- NAFTAPLIN, Article 17 [INA Contract]; Algeria: Law n°05–07 (2005).

232   *Damilola S. Olawuyi*

A second driver is the desire to create a level playing field for citizens, residents, and home-based industries to participate in resource production activities. Without creating a level playing field for new or emerging local industries and workforce to participate in oil exploration activities, and compete with international suppliers of goods and services, the cycle of excessive dependence on foreign goods and services may never be broken.[22] MENA countries have therefore promoted LCRs as a deliberate programme and policy aimed at ensuring that local industries are given a chance to compete with foreign suppliers. For example, the Saudi Arabia IKTVA programme emphasises the goal of creating a level playing field for local participation by adopting uniform evaluation processes in sourcing services and materials, and by promoting uniform access to project information for local suppliers.[23] Similarly, the ultimate goal of Oman's In Country Value Strategy (ICV), launched in December 2013, is to increase the country's total spend retained in order to benefit business development, contribute to human capability development, and stimulate productivity in Oman's economy.[24] Like the Saudi IKTVA Programme, the Oman ICV Programme introduces a joint supplier registration system as a single window system for registering suppliers in a 'pool'.[25] The aim is to provide equal opportunities for local industries to participate in oil and gas activities.

A third driver of LCRs across the MENA region is the desire to maximise economic benefits to citizens through job and employment opportunities. Virtually all of the surveyed regimes mandate investors to prioritise the employment of suitably qualified nationals.[26] By mandating the employment of nationals, the aim is to create opportunities for domestic employment, thereby contributing to growth in income, capacity development of nationals, and overall increased economic growth of an oil-producing country. Local employment is consistently among the topmost concerns of nationals, and often a central issue driving disputes, grievance, and conflict.[27] More local jobs could result in more support for projects. Employing more citizens and community members can also help improve company-community relations, enabling foreign investors to obtain the social license to operate.[28] Given the negative impacts of resource development on surrounding

---

[22] See Tordo et al., note 7, pp. 115–17.
[23] See Saudi Aramco, note 10.
[24] Sultanate of Oman, 'The Oil and Gas Industry: In-Country Value Development Strategy: 2013–2020', pp. 1–5.
[25] Ibid.
[26] See, for example, Republic of Yemen: Model Production Sharing Agreement (2006), Article 26; State of Qatar: Model Development and Production Sharing Agreement (2002), Article 23; Jordan: Model Production Sharing Agreement (2007), Article 23; also Oman: Model Exploration and Production Sharing Agreement (2004), Article 19.1; INA Contract, note 21, Article 17. See also TAWTEEN, note 9.
[27] Ovadia (2015) 37–38; Tordo et al., note 7, pp. 7–15.
[28] S. Tordo, B. Tracy, and N. Arfaa, 'National Oil Companies and Value Creation', World Bank Working Paper No. 218, 2011, pp. 1–10; World Bank, 'Human Capital for the Oil, Gas and Minerals

Local Content in Middle East and North Africa 233

communities, local content can help compensate the afflicted communities through job creation and value addition in the communities.[29]

A fourth driver is the desire by MENA countries to improve national technological capacity. All of the surveyed petroleum contracts mandate IOCs to give preference to locally manufactured equipment, machinery, and consumables when their price, quality, time of delivery, and other terms are comparable to internationally available ones. They also include requirements to bring some level of technology into the country, or perform research and development (R&D), so local companies can boost their competitiveness through access to state-of-the-art technology, or benefit from technology transfer.[30] Mandating IOCs to utilise locally made technology in petroleum operations directly reduces the importation of technology for petroleum operations. This could in turn compel IOCs, as well as service companies, to invest in technologies and facilities for local manufacturing and service provision.[31] For example, some IOCs operating in MENA countries have opened technology venture arms of their operations in order to speed up the development and deployment of innovative technologies that could complement oil and gas exploration activities.[32] By opening up technology ventures, IOCs can facilitate the domestic production and availability of technologies required for oil and gas exploration.

Fifth, LCRs are also used to redistribute the benefits of resource investment activities, particularly to manage social and political risks that may result from rising domestic expectations for better and more equitable distribution of wealth and authority.[33] Despite the diverse programmes designed to increase the direct financial flows of oil wealth to nationals through subsidy programmes, individuals may not perceive what they consider commensurate benefits. This can lead to pressure from the population to increase the more tangible benefits.[34] Although these

Industries', Science, Technology, and Skills for Africa's Development, March 2014, pp. 1–4; A. M. Esteves and M. A. Barclay (2011) 'Enhancing the Benefits of Local Content: Integrating Social and Economic Impact Assessment into Procurement Strategies' 29 *Impact Assessment and Project Appraisal* 205.

[29] R. Ado, 'Local Content Policy and the WTO Rules on Trade-Related Investment Measures (TRIMS): The Pros and Cons' (2013) 2 *International Journal of Business and Management Studies* 142.

[30] For example, IOCs such as Conoco Philips, General Electric, Shell, and ExxonMobil have opened up technology innovation centres and programmes at the Qatar Science and Technology Park to discover sustainable technologies for their oil and gas operations in Qatar (Qatar Science and Technology Park, https://qstp.org.qa/).

[31] Muller et al., note 20; also D. Coe, E. Helpman, and A. W. Hoffmaister, 'International R&D Spillovers and Institutions', IMF Working Paper, WP/08/104, April 2008; also A. Glass and K. Saggi, 'The Role of Foreign Direct Investment in International Technology Transfer' in A. Dutt and J. Ross, *International Handbook of Development Economics* (Cheltenham: Edward Elgar, 2008).

[32] See note 30.

[33] See M. Cook and H. Mahdavy, 'The Pattern and Problems of Economic Development in Rentier States: The Case of Iran' in M. Cook, *Studies in the Economic History of the Middle East: From the Rise of Islam to the Present Day* (Oxford University Press, 1970), pp. 435–436; A. Krueger, 'The Political Economy of the Rent-Seeking Society' (1974) 64 *American Economic Review* 291–303.

[34] C. Hanlin, 'The Drive to Increase Local Procurement in the Mining Sector in Africa: Myth or Reality?' Making the Most of Commodities Programme (MMCP) Discussion Paper No. 4,

234   *Damilola S. Olawuyi*

problems could be addressed by specific policies designed to consider the exact grievance, governments utilise LCRs as a tool for bringing jobs and income to a specific group or area where there is considerable dissatisfaction with the presence of the oil and gas operations.[35] By introducing detailed LCRs, countries can ensure that access to the control of oil wealth is evenly distributed among the local communities across the country. For example, Qatar's petroleum agreement stipulates that the Deputy Manager of the petroleum operation shall be an individual appointed by the national oil company.[36] Such a provision allows the host country to at all times monitor and ensure that a greater spectrum of the society have direct access to petroleum operations.

Despite the clear and uniform overall policy objectives of LCRs, their application and implementation continue to face practical challenges that may hinder their overall contributions to sustainable development in resource rich countries of the region. The next section discusses key practical challenges and contentions that arise in the design and implementation of LCRs in the MENA region.

3 LCRS AND SUSTAINABLE DEVELOPMENT IN THE MENA REGION: CONTENTIONS AND CHALLENGES

The overall aims and drivers of LCRs are clear – increasing host government revenue, creating a level playing field for local industries, maximizing economic benefits to citizens through job and employment opportunities, and improving national technological capacity, amongst others.[37] However, while LCRs could provide a tool for MENA governments to generate economic benefits for the local economy, LCRs may be incompatible with national policies on FDIs and sustainable development, particularly if not well designed to balance domestic development priorities and goals with LCRs and obligations. This section explores four key emerging areas of conflict in MENA countries between LCRs and overall domestic sustainable development.

First, while LCRs may specify the portion of total expenditures that must be comprised of locally sourced goods and services, the required technology, equipment, tools, and technical know-how required for petroleum operations are simply not fully available in many MENA countries.[38] The insistence on restrictive LCRs in such countries could result in negative effects. For example, lack of available technology, capacity, and material at the local level may delay projects and may

---

March 2011; J. S. Ovadia, 'The Role of Local Content Policies in Natural Resource-Based Development', Österreichische Entwicklungspolitik. Rohstoffe und Entwicklung, 2015.

[35] Ovadia, note 34.
[36] Qatar: Model Development and Production Sharing Agreement (2002), Article 23.
[37] See Olawuyi, note 13, pp. 93–117.
[38] Ibid.

Local Content in Middle East and North Africa 235

ultimately result in loss of FDIs to less restrictive jurisdictions.[39] Such an outcome may ultimately stifle a country's path to sustainable development.[40]

Second, LCRs may conflict with international treaty obligations of several MENA countries under international trade and investment regimes, especially the World Trade Organization (WTO) framework. Several bilateral and multilateral international investment treaties expressly prohibit the use of certain performance requirements – especially those related to local content, export controls, foreign-exchange restrictions, purchase of raw materials, domestic equity/ownership, technology transfer, R&D, employment, and domestic equity/ownership – that can cause trade restriction or price-distorting effects.[41] For example, the WTO Trade Related Investment Measures (TRIMs) Agreement expressly prohibits measures related to local content, trade balancing, export controls, and certain foreign-exchange restrictions, and certain bilateral treaties limit the use of other performance requirements.[42] Article 2.1 of the TRIMs Agreement requires WTO Members to refrain applying any TRIMs (trade related investment measures) that are inconsistent with the national treatment obligation under Articles III or XI of the GATT Treaty (1994).[43] Paragraph 1 of the Illustrative List in the Annex of the TRIMs Agreement itemises incompatible TRIMs to include measures which are 'mandatory or enforceable under domestic law or under administrative rulings.'[44] This specifically includes domestic measures that require an investor to purchase or use products of domestic origin, or from any domestic source, whether specified in terms of particular products, in terms of volume or value of products, or in terms of a proportion of volume or value of its local production, or limit the purchase or use of imported products to an amount related to the volume or value of local products that it exports.[45] These TRIMs provisions expressly prohibit WTO members from applying LCRs that mandate investors to make use of domestic goods, raw materials, and products that have a local origin.

Under the TRIMs Agreement, developed country members are required to eliminate the domestic application of all TRIMs within two years after the entry into force of the WTO Agreement of 1994.[46] Similarly, 'developing country'

---

[39] Olawuyi, note 17, pp. 247–65. Olawuyi et al., note 17.
[40] Ramdoo, note 18.
[41] See United Nations Conference on Trade and Development (UNCTAD), 'Foreign direct investment and performance requirements: new evidence from selected countries', 2003, p. 2, which defines PRs as 'stipulations, imposed on investors, requiring them to meet certain specified goals with respect to their operations in the host country'. In other words, they are measures requiring investors to behave in a particular way or to achieve certain outcomes in the host country. Agreement on Trade-Related Investment Measures, April 15, 1994, Marrakesh Agreement Establishing the World Trade Organization, Annex 1A, 1868 UNTS 186 [TRIMs], Preamble.
[42] TRIMs, note 41.
[43] General Agreement on Tariffs and Trade 1994, April 15, 1994, Marrakesh Agreement Establishing the World Trade Organization, Annex 1A, 1867 UNTS 187, 33 ILM 1153 (1994) [GATT].
[44] TRIMs, note 41.
[45] Ibid., Annex, Illustrative List, para. 1.
[46] Ibid., Article 5.2.

236   *Damilola S. Olawuyi*

members are required to eliminate the application of TRIMs within five years after the entry into force of the WTO Agreement, while 'least-developed country' members are required to eliminate the application of TRIMs within seven years after the WTO Agreement has entered into force.[47] WTO members are however able to request for an extension of the transition period where prevailing domestic economic circumstances did not allow for a smooth elimination of existing TRIMs within the timeframes stipulated under the Agreement.[48] The overall application of these provisions shows that many existing LCRs in MENA countries are well outside the transition period and could be in direct conflict with obligations under the TRIMs.[49] The WTO Dispute Settlement Body (DSB) has concluded in a number of cases that LCRs violate obligations under the TRIMs Agreements. For example, in the matter of *Indonesia – Certain Measures Affecting the Automobile Industry*,[50] a WTO Panel addressed issues relating to the application of LCRs in Indonesia's automobile industry within the framework of the TRIMs Agreement. The key question was whether Indonesia's 1993 car programme, which provided luxury tax exemptions and import duty exemptions to Indonesian car companies, as well as import duty reductions and exemptions on imports of automotives based on the local content percent, was in violation of Article 2 of the TRIMs Agreement and Articles I and III of the GATT.[51] The Panel concluded that Indonesia's 1993 car programme violated Article 2.1 of the TRIMs Agreement because the measure constituted LCRs which fall within inconsistent TRIMs under paragraph 1 of the list of TRIMs in the Annex to the TRIMs Agreement.[52] This case, and many others, emphasise that LCR measures that require the use of domestic products over similar imported products or provide mandatory performance targets in order to obtain a governmental advantage are all 'trade-related investment measures' that are in breach of Articles II.4 and XI.1 of the GATT.[53]

---

[47]   Ibid.

[48]   Ibid., Article 5.3.

[49]   Ibid., Article 3 provides for the application of 'all exceptions under GATT 1994' which includes the general exceptions, the security exception, and exemptions relating to restrictions for the purpose of safeguarding domestic industries from 'serious injury' as a result of importation. See GATT, note 43, Article XIX, XX (a) and (b), and XXI.

[50]   See Panel Reports, *Indonesia – Certain Measures Affecting the Automobile Industry*, WT/DS54/R, WT/DS55/R, WT/DS59/R, WT/DS64/R, adopted 15 July 1999.

[51]   See WTO Legal Affairs Division, 'WTO Dispute Settlement One Page Case Summaries 1995–2011', 2012, p. 25.

[52]   See *Indonesia—Automobiles*, note 50, paras. 14.71–14.72.

[53]   Ibid. See also *India – Certain Measures Relating to Solar Cells and Solar Modules* stating that local content measures under India's Jawaharlal Nehru National Solar Mission (JNNSM) programme constituted trade-related investment measures which is in violation of TRIMS obligations as identified in paragraph 1(a) of the Illustrative List in the Annex to the TRIMS Agreement and therefore inconsistent with Article III:4 of the GATT and Article 2.1 of the TRIMs Agreement (Paenl Reports, *India – Certain Measures Relating to Solar Cells and Solar Modules*, WT/DS456/R/Add.1, adopted 24 February 2016). See also *Canada – Certain Measures Affecting the Renewable Energy Generation Sector* where the WTO Panel stated that the Province of Ontario's Feed-in-Tariff Programme' (FIT

Furthermore, a number of Bilateral Investment Treaties (BITs) prohibit or discourage the use of LCRs mostly by reference to the TRIMs Agreement. For example, the 2012 China–Canada treaty reaffirms and incorporates the parties' obligations under the TRIMs which will include prohibitions on the use of LCRs.[54] Similarly, Article 1106 of NAFTA between Canada, Mexico, and the United States provides that no Party may impose or enforce requirements that mandate an investor to 'achieve a given level or percentage of domestic content.'[55] Article 1106.6.1 of NAFTA, however, contains exceptions that allow the use of LCRs, especially when such use is not applied in an arbitrary or unjustifiable manner.

The key question is whether LCRs utilised across the MENA region could survive close scrutiny as 'non-arbitrary or justifiable' if brought before international treaty bodies, especially under the WTO dispute resolution framework. While there is currently limited case law in this area, lessons from previous WTO decisions show that overly restrictive LCRs – that is, those that require the use of domestic products over similar imported products or provide mandatory performance targets in order to obtain a governmental advantage – may be found non-permissible and non-compliant with international investment law.[56] Furthermore, mandatory LCRs imposed after an investment is made may breach the host state's commitments and obligations under a BIT and under international investment law and could result in complex litigation and/or investor–state arbitration.[57]

Thirdly, restrictive LCRs can be detrimental to the flow of FDIs to MENA countries.[58] Many MENA countries have intensified efforts to attract FDIs in all sectors of national economies, as key ways to improve economic diversification, create jobs, and eliminate poverty in line with United Nations Sustainable Development Goals (SDG) 8 on decent work and economic growth, and SDG 1 on poverty eradication.[59] However, LCRs may limit the attractiveness of a country as

---

Programme), which required renewable energy generation facilities to use domestically produced equipment for energy generation in order to receive guaranteed prices under the FIT Programme, constituted local content requirements and violates the national treatment obligation under Article III: 4 of GATT and Article 2.1 of TRIMS (Panel Reports, *Canada – Certain Measures Affecting the Renewable Energy Generation Sector / Canada – Measures Relating to the Feed-In Tariff Program*, WT/DS412/R / WT/DS426/R, adopted 19 December 2012).

[54] See also Belgium–Guinea treaty, Article 10; India–Kuwait BIT (2001), Article 4.4; Japan–India Comprehensive Economic Partnership Agreement (CEPA 2011), Article 89; El Salvador–Peru (1996); Bolivia–Mexico (1995); Dominican Republic–Ecuador (1998); Chile–Mexico FTA (1999); Chile–South Korea FTA (2003); United Kingdom–Kenya (1999); and Burundi–Comoros (2001) all of which limit or prohibit use of LCRs.

[55] North American Free Trade Agreement, 32 ILM 289 and 605 (1993).

[56] See Mandy Meng Fang, Chapter 3, this book.

[57] R. Dolzer and C. Schreuer, *Principles of International Investment Law*, 2nd Edition (Oxford University Press, 2012).

[58] J. Jensen and D. Tarr, 'Impact of Local Content Restrictions and Barriers against Foreign Direct Investment in Services: The Case of Kazakhstan's Accession to the World Trade Organization' (2008) 46 *Eastern European Economics* 5–26.

[59] UN General Assembly, *Transforming our World: The 2030 Agenda for Sustainable Development*, 21 October 2015, UN Doc. A/RES/70/1.

a suitable and competitive location for FDIs. Given that LCRs are still relatively new in MENA countries, the direct implications of LCRs on competitiveness and flow of FDIs will have to be comprehensively measured and assessed over time. However, according to a study by the Organisation for Economic Co-operation and Development (OECD), total imports and exports have declined in every region of the world as a result of LCR policies and have shrunk world imports and exports by USD 12 billion and USD 11 billion, respectively.[60] Furthermore, according to the study, almost in all cases where LCRs are introduced, final goods exports have been reduced from 0.05 per cent to as much as 5.0 per cent.[61] For example, complying with product mandating requirements could mean project delays or higher costs on the part of the IOC, especially when suitable and reasonably priced alternatives are not immediately available locally.[62] This can have a distorting effect on the profitability and viability of a project from the investor's standpoint or affect the timeline for investment activities. The imposition of domestic level LCRs in the absence of required supporting capacity, institutional resources, or adequate technological capabilities could ultimately reduce the attractiveness of a country as a desirable location for FDIs.[63] Similarly, LCRs can significantly reduce and limit the pool of eligible investors or entrants to a country. Investors that are unable to meet a country's LCRs may seek alternate and less restrictive markets for their investments. Such an outcome could impact the ability of MENA countries to meet their sustainable development aims.

Fourthly, the rise of data localisation requirements, as seen in some LCRs in the MENA region, could raise the cost and feasibility of investing in oil and gas sectors in the region.[64] Domestic level data storage requirements that aim to restrict how information obtained locally are transferred, stored, or moved, have been increasingly introduced in the MENA region, mainly to address privacy and national security concerns by requiring investors to establish local servers in every jurisdiction in which it operates.[65] However, the increasing tendency of some countries to access and utilise investor data in a manner that undermines competitiveness have lately attracted a great deal of attention.[66] While national authorities undertake that locally

---

[60] S. Stone, J. Messent and D. Flaig, 'Emerging Policy Issues: Localisation Barriers to Trade', OECD Trade Policy Papers, No. 180, 2015, pp. 10–11.

[61] Ibid.

[62] P. Peek and P. Gantès, 'Skills shortages and local content in the Sub-Saharan African oil and gas industry: How to close the gap', Centre de recherches enterprises et societies (CRES), 2008.

[63] See United Nations Conference on Trade and Development (UNCTAD), 'Elimination of TRIMS: The Experience of Selected Developing Countries', 2007, pp. 9–10.

[64] See National Board of Trade (NBT), 'No Transfer, No Trade: The Importance of Cross-Border Data Transfers for Companies Based in Sweden', 2014.

[65] Ibid.

[66] J. Kuntze and T. Moerenhout, 'Local Content Requirements and the Renewable Energy Industry – A Good Match?' International Centre for Trade and Sustainable Development, 2013; C. Kwon and B. G. Chun, 'Local Content Requirement under Vertical Technology Diffusion' (2009) 13 Review of Development Economics 111–24.

Local Content in Middle East and North Africa   239

stored data are protected and many can only be accessed for national security reasons, recent studies have compiled instances of how data localisation can be utilised by national authorities for investment decision analysis and to promote the competitiveness of their domestic industry.[67] Furthermore, overly restrictive data localisation requirements can impose huge operating and compliance costs for investors, especially in those MENA countries where data storage infrastructure is still at early stages of development.[68] For example, recent studies show that compliance costs can increase an investor's information technology expenditure by as much as 40 per cent.[69] As the OECD notes, data localisation requirements can affect an investor's ability to adopt the most efficient technologies, increase an investor's operational cost, and may ultimately lead to missed business opportunities.[70] Overly restrictive data localisation requirements that are not backed by significant investment in reliable and affordable data storage infrastructure for IOCs, can significantly reduce the competitiveness of MENA countries as ideal locations for IOCs and can produce long-term negative implications for job creation, revenue, and overall sustainable development in the region.

Fifthly, without clarity on the role of the state in procurement processes, the practical implementation of LCRs may result in delays and an overall increase in operational costs. While LCRs may specify the portion of total expenditures that must be comprised of locally sourced goods and services, procurement procedures are frequently not well established and could raise concerns on excessive host state interference.[71] In some MENA countries, LCRs include an obligation to inform national authorities, through yearly statements, audits, or mandatory performance standards, of compliance with LCRs and procurement requirements (Oman, Iran, Saudi Arabia, UAE); in others, procurement plans must be submitted prior to the commencement of petroleum operations (Lebanon, Iraq (Federal)).[72] In some cases, the national oil company or a management committee may be directly involved in an advisory capacity (Qatar) and, in other cases, government must be informed and may participate in procurement activities above certain financial thresholds (Libya, Egypt).[73] Clarifying and understanding the variations in the designated role of the national oil company or government in the procurement

---

[67] Stone et al., note 60, pp. 10–11.

[68] Stone et al., note 60, pp. 60–2.

[69] NBT, note 64; Ponemon Institute, 'The True Cost of Compliance', January 2011.

[70] NBT, note 64, pp. 70–1.

[71] The duty of states to protect investors and their investments against unlawful interference and acts of state agencies was affirmed in *Amco v Indonesia*, Award, 20 November 1984.

[72] See, for example, Iran: Maximum Utilization of Production and Services Potency in Providing Country's Needs and Promotion of Exports (2012), ss. 1–2; Jordan: Model Production Sharing Agreement of February (2007), Article 23; Oman: Model Exploration and Production Sharing Agreement (2004), Article 19.1; Iraq (Federal) 2009 Technical Service Contract for Oil Field; Production Sharing Contract (2007) Kurdistan Region; INA Contract (1998), note 21, Article 17; Algeria: Law No 05–07 (2005); The Nigerian Oil and Gas Industry Content Development Act (2010).

[73] Ibid.

240   *Damilola S. Olawuyi*

processes is critical to avoiding disputes. As governments increasingly seek to exercise some form of influence in contractors' procurement processes to ensure total value in terms of local content, it is important for IOCs to clarify, from the outset, the level of government involvement in the contractor's procurement process. Government participation in procurement processes, as a way of monitoring LCRs and transparency, could result in significant delay and cost increase for petroleum operations, especially in some countries where government approval processes could be slow and bureaucratic.[74] This again raises the need to clarify the level of government participation and to provide streamlined processes to reduce delays, reduce costs, and enhance efficiency, in order to advance the sustainable development aims of LCRs.

The foregoing tensions and trade-offs highlight, on the broader level, the need to continually measure and balance the policy aims of LCRs with practical outcomes in terms of contributions to economic, social, and societal development. Furthermore, as MENA countries increasingly develop LCRs, they will need to do more to ensure that such LCRs are clear, specific, and aligned with international investment law in order to minimise contentions and misalignments with FDI goals. Without a strong regulatory and institutional foundation that provides clarity and certainty for investors, it will be difficult to compete with jurisdictions that provide clearer and more realistic terms and requirements for IOCs. The next section discusses innovative legal strategies to reform and address these misalignments and inconsistencies.

4 ADVANCING SUSTAINABLE DEVELOPMENT OUTCOMES IN LCR IMPLEMENTATION

Without clear safeguards, LCR regimes can reduce the overall competitiveness and attractiveness of a country's oil and gas sector. It is therefore essential for MENA countries to avoid misuse and misalignments that undermine the goals and sustainable development outcomes of LCRs.

First, as can be seen in jurisdictions such as Nigeria and Norway, where LCRs have been implemented with varying levels of success, LCRs should be backed by a clear, specific, and transparent legislative framework, including a robust performance-monitoring mechanism.[75] One key gap across the MENA region is the absence of clear, comprehensive, and specific legislation on LCRs. Across the region, LCRs are mainly expressed in policy documents and industry guidelines, as well as in petroleum contracts on a case-by-case basis. Given that such guidelines are usually oil and gas sector specific, they generally do not speak to wider questions of measuring and assessing overall impact of LCRs with sustainable development

---

[74] Olawuyi, note 13.
[75] See Acheampong et al., note 7; also Nwapi, note 7; OECD, note 7; Olawuyi, note 13.

outcomes in other key sectors of the economy. For example, some of the LCR guidelines released in the region are tailored to the oil and gas industry, and do not clearly address the interactions of such LCRs with other key sectors such as trade, investment, aviation and infrastructure development. Absence of holistic legislative framework on LCRs has not provided a chance for a robust development of clear safeguards to address wider policy issues relating to balancing LCR aims with sustainable development outcomes across multiple convergent sectors of the domestic economy. While setting national requirements and targets for local content reflects a political commitment towards ensuring domestic value creation and long-term economic growth, LCRs should be accompanied by comprehensive and holistic legal frameworks that anticipate and address wider policy implications of LCRs on broad areas of sustainable development especially economic, social, and environmental.

Second, rather than approaching LCRs from a compliance or mandatory project requirement mindset, which demands more local content or introduces more punitive enforcement measures, national authorities should adopt a more collaborative approach built on clear, transparent, and attainable LCRs, with adequate institutional support for IOCs to achieve those goals. LCRs that are primarily targeted at restricting the abilities of investors to participate in investment activities or to freely procure goods for approved projects – rather than focusing primarily on value-added and capacity development – are misguided and could ultimately hinder FDIs.[76] The starting point, therefore, is for national authorities to realign the goals of LCRs to focus mainly on creating high domestic value addition by providing full and fair opportunities for investors, irrespective of the source of the raw materials and goods, nationality of the employees, or anti-competitive or storage location of investment data. It is essential for countries to establish clear, transparent, and comprehensive local content laws that clarify the scope, content, and goals of a country's LCRs. Such laws could, among other things, provide clear and expansive definitions of key concepts such as local, local content, local company, project sum, and in-country value.[77] There is also a need to clearly identify the skills, competencies, technologies, and economic activities that a country wants to improve or build upon as part of local content implementation. Such clear definitions will reduce ambiguities with respect to the scope and content of LCRs. Local content laws can also be very helpful in addressing overlaps and limitations in other domestic laws that could hinder the successful implementation of LCRs. For example, procurement laws that have elaborate provisions on state participation in bid processes may result in unnecessary delays in an investor's procurement processes and may impact the competitiveness and ease of doing business in a country. A less restrictive approach will focus on providing as much flexibility to the investor to achieve domestic value maximization, while also ensuring oversight through periodic

---

[76] UNCTAD, note 41; United Nations Conference on Trade and Development (UNCTAD), 'Local Content Requirements and the Green Economy', 2014, pp. 10–12.

[77] Nwapi, note 7.

242   *Damilola S. Olawuyi*

procurement reports by the investor. By realigning LCRs to focus on the ultimate goals of domestic value addition, countries can better align and reconcile LCRs with key tenets of international investment law on fair and equitable treatment of investors.[78]

Third, without addressing domestic barriers to the attainment of LCRs, such as lack of domestic capacity, shortage of raw materials, technology and infrastructure gaps, amongst others, investors may face significant difficulties in complying with LCR targets and expectations which may result in defaults and contentions. It is therefore essential for national authorities to work collaboratively with investors to evolve realistic local content targets that take cognisance of domestic capabilities and also develop supportive regulatory and institutional frameworks for the delivery of the agreed targets. A collaborative approach to LCR is built on creating a supportive regulatory and business-friendly economic environment for investors to deliver greater value in the host country. Under this approach, governments have a prominent role to play in reducing regulatory and administrative barriers to domestic investments; providing fiscal incentives for investors to establish or support small and medium enterprises in the host country; updating intellectual property laws to provide greater protection for domestically produced technology; simplifying approval processes and fees for licences and permits; and providing and ensuring greater inter-ministerial coordination among key ministries and agencies that have roles to play in the employment, training, and education components of LCRs. A well-designed set of horizontal and collaborative policies and legislation targeted at creating a supportive regulatory and business-friendly economic environment for investors to deliver greater value in the host country can advance both immediate and longer-term local content objectives with fewer potential investment distortions. Apart from the fact that governments and the public will ultimately benefit more when LCRs are achieved by an investor, improperly designed LCRs could carry significant financial, legal, and reputational risks for national authorities, especially when LCRs become subjects of extensive litigation or investor–state arbitration. Furthermore, in highly competitive sectors, such as oil and gas, a country's ability to attract investors and technologies (including financial institutions and lenders) needed to develop oil resources will depend on the processes, procedures, practices, and approaches put in place to reduce contractual risks, such as those that could result from misaligned LCRs.

Fourth, many of the conflicts relating to LCRs and international treaty compliance are traceable to failure of investors and host states to fully clarify key terms of the LCRs, as well as reporting obligations, at the negotiation phase. Key questions include what constitutes local content and value addition, the role of national authorities in procurement processes, how will in-country value be measured and monitored, timelines for reporting local content compliance, and the flexibility

---

[78] Dolzer and Schreuer, note 57.

provided to the investor to develop its compliance plans and procedures. Without clear and documented agreements on these issues, LCRs may result in misalignment and contentions which may ultimately affect investor–state relations. To avoid ambiguities and misalignments, the scope of objectives must be specific, measurable, and achievable. Investment agreements should clarify the expectations of the host government, while providing the investor with the flexibility to develop its local content plans and procurement procedures. This could include providing adequate flexibility for the investor to source goods and services abroad when suitable and reasonably priced alternatives are not immediately available locally. For example, this flexible model is found in the Qatari production-sharing contract (PSC), which provides that the contractor shall, *when possible*, give first consideration or preference to locally manufactured or locally available goods.[79] This provides some flexibility for an IOC to consider other categories of goods and services if the IOC so decides for operational reasons, or in cases when suitable domestic goods or service providers are not available. The negotiation stage is also a great opportunity for an IOC and the government to agree up front on data storage requirements, especially how the cost of local data storage will be shared. As earlier noted, for example, complying with data localisation requirements could mean project delays or higher costs on the part of the investor, especially when local IT infrastructure or data storage platform is not well developed or immediately available. This can change the profit margin of a project or affect the timeline for operation activities. These trade-offs must be very well considered during contract negotiation stages to avoid long-term misalignments and contentions and to achieve a mutually beneficial and realistic contractual framework. For example, if the government insists on data localisation, fiscal terms, such as cost recovery, among others, could be amended to protect the margins of the investor, while achieving the localisation requirement stipulated by the government.

Fifth, successful LCR implementation cannot be achieved by regulation and legislation alone. Providing adequate institutional support, supplier development programs, and performance enhancement initiatives for investors to achieve LCRs and goals is also a crucial element. It is therefore essential for MENA countries to establish a focal institution, committee, or administrative unit that will coordinate the design, approval, and implementation of local content plans across the life cycle of a project. While such a focal institution can be established as a supervisory committee of a petroleum contract, a more long-term approach is to establish a national local content agency or unit that will oversee LCRs in multiple sectors of the economy. A good example is Qatar's TAWTEEN Service Centre, a unit within Qatar Petroleum, which serves as the focal point for local content information and implementation in the entire energy sector in Qatar. Apart from serving as

---

[79] State of Qatar: Model Development and Production Sharing Agreement (2002), Article 23. Qatar's TAWTEEN program also provides comprehensive information on how in-country value will be measured, monitored, and reported all through a project's life cycle. See TAWTEEN, note 9.

244   *Damilola S. Olawuyi*

a one-stop shop that will streamline the approval processes for local content implementation, such an institution would also provide methodologies and tools for operators to report and monitor their compliance with LCRs so as to minimise disputes. By empowering and establishing a focal institution on projects, investors across multiple sectors can obtain relevant information and develop a standardised approach to tracking, monitoring, and complying with LCRs. A coordinated approach can also reduce duplication and overlap, conflicting regulations, increased administrative costs, and delays.

5 CONCLUSION

The rise of LCRs in the oil and gas frameworks across the MENA region provides renewed opportunities for economic diversification and empowerment for local SMEs. However, while LCRs generally aim to boost domestic value creation and long-term economic growth in host countries, without clear safeguards, LCRs can also reduce the overall competitiveness and attractiveness of a country's oil and gas sector. For example, questions of how to ensure there is domestic availability of state-of-the-art technology, equipment, raw material, and technical know-how to advance local content mandates and targets are broader policy questions that can hinder a country's competitiveness. However, these broader policy questions are hardly addressed in many industry-specific guidelines and agreements on LCRs in the MENA region. As seen in countries such as Norway and Nigeria, clear and comprehensive legislation on LCRs can provide a framework for identifying and addressing possible misalignments and mismatch between the policy aims of LCRs and the practical sustainable development outcomes. Measuring and monitoring LCR objectives and gains in the broader context of progress in other areas such as trade, FDIs, entrepreneurship, innovation, and social development will help MENA countries to develop a more holistic assessment.

Furthermore, rather than approaching LCRs from a compliance or mandatory project requirement standpoint, it is essential to adopt a more collaborative approach built on clear, measurable, and attainable LCRs, with adequate institutional support and supplier development programs for contractors to achieve those goals. A well-designed set of horizontal and collaborative policies targeted at creating a supportive regulatory and business-friendly economic environment for investors to deliver greater value in the host country can advance both immediate and longer-term local content objectives with fewer potential investment distortions.

13

Local Content and Sustainable Development in Norway

Catherine Banet

1 INTRODUCTION

The chapter reviews the use of local content requirements (LCRs) in the Norwegian oil and gas legislation. Looking at the evolution of the regulation of LCRs over time, it reviews, successively, the legal design of the overall model for LCRs in Norway, as elaborated before the country's accession to the European Economic Area (EEA); and the legal framework for local content under liberalised and integrated energy markets after Norway joined the EEA. The ultimate purpose of the chapter is to answer the question raised by the book as to best practice in terms of a sustainability framework for LCRs with a transferable value.

When Norway discovered petroleum on the continental shelf near the shoreline of the country, its government had no petroleum legislation in place, and no local content requirements governing the sector. As a consequence, and because it was seen as a necessary step, the authorities had to both elaborate a dedicated local content policy (LCP) and adopt the associated legal requirements that would secure its implementation. And because Norway was not yet bound by any relevant European or international agreements (besides the GATT), it remained free to design its LCP regime. While pursuing those tasks, the Norwegian authorities have managed to maintain a clear line as to what was the ultimate objective of their regulatory model, that is, the maximisation of national value creation and efficient resource management.[1] Local content legal framework was in place until Norway joined the EEA and the WTO. There are currently no local content requirements per se in Norwegian legislation applicable to the petroleum industry. The fact that local content measures have been (and should be) temporary has been another key lesson from the Norwegian petroleum policy. The competences acquired by the Norwegian industry and authorities during the phase of implementation of LCRs have enabled the emergence of an internationally competitive Norwegian petroleum sector, which today competes without a national LC policy.

---

[1] See F. Al-Kasim, *Managing Petroleum Resources. The 'Norwegian Model' in a Broad Perspective* (Alden Press, 2006), chapter 8: Value Creation: A Common Objective.

245

Catherine Banet

If the Norwegian model is often described as a successful example of petroleum policy, this is largely due to a particular national context. First, when Norway discovered petroleum on its continental shelf, the country was already self-sufficient in energy supply due to rich hydropower resources. This allowed the successive governments to elaborate the national petroleum policy step by step, at a moderate pace but in a dynamic manner. The exploitation of the petroleum resources followed the same pattern. Second, Norway was already well developed before the discovery of oil and gas, and had a transparent and stable governance framework. It had high technical skills relevant for offshore petroleum operations, such as shipping expertise, advanced methods of numerical analysis, building and providing oil tankers.[2] Norway benefited from an efficient system of administrative governance with stable institutions,[3] supported by a legislative framework reflecting key principles of administrative law (rule of law, legality principle, case handling procedures, public consultation requirements, etc.). It also benefited from some more general cultural values inherent to a social democracy, such as cohesion, solidarity, accountability/responsibility of decision-makers and transparency. The population benefited from a high level of education and had a good basis for research and development (R&D) competence and learning capacity. The context may not be transferable per se to another jurisdiction,[4] but it nevertheless helps to identify some fundamental conditions that benefited the Norwegian implementation of local content measures and may inspire other national regimes.

Beyond those specific national circumstances, the core research question of the present chapter is to identify the key components of the regulatory approach adopted by Norway in terms of LCRs which successfully prepared it to compete internationally on liberalised energy markets. In doing so, it aims to identify which legal mechanisms adopted in Norway can be used in other jurisdictions to ensure a sustainable local content policy.

This chapter answers those questions following a chronological approach, structured around four main sections. After this introduction, Section 2 discusses the primary phase of the development of the Norwegian petroleum sector (1970s to mid-1990s), during which the national legislation included explicit LCRs. In the subsequent phase, the use of LCRs has been constrained by the obligations deriving from the entry into force of the European Economic Area (EEA) Agreement in 1994 (including the Licensing Directive 94/22/EC and internal market rules), and the application of the relevant WTO Agreements after Norway joined the WTO in 1995 (notably the TRIMs agreement and GATS). Norway has also entered into a series of

---

[2] Ibid., p. 58.

[3] P. Heum, 'Local Content Development – Experiences from oil and gas activities in Norway', SNF Working Paper No. 02/08, 2008, pp. 4–7.

[4] J. W. Moses and B. Letnes, *Managing Resource Abundance and Wealth: The Norwegian Experience* (Oxford University Press, 2017), p. 14. The authors describe in chapters 2 (Norwegian context) and 3 (The Norwegian Petroleum Administration) of their book the foundations of the Norwegian model and what they deem as 'non-transferable features'.

Local Content and SD in Norway   247

Bilateral Investment Treaties (BITs) which can restrain the country's ability to include LCRs. In Section 3, the chapter will review the changes introduced by Norway's accession to the EEA, to the WTO and the implementation of certain BITs for Norwegian practices. Section 4, the final section of the chapter, draws conclusions in terms of a sustainability framework for LCRs and the lessons that can be drawn from the Norwegian experience and that can serve as effective transplants – both prerequisites and barriers – in other jurisdictions. Innovative legal approaches to promote such strategies are cited when applicable.

2 PRIMARY PHASE (1970S TO MID-1990S): EXPLICIT LCRS FOR SUSTAINABLE RESULTS

The local content policy of the Norwegian authorities has been developed progressively, consolidated around some core principles (Section 2.1) which were accompanied by specific legal requirements (Section 2.2). The Section ends with some comments on this approach (Section 2.3).

2.1 *Some Common Principles in Explicit Local Content Policy in Norway*

Because Norway had no previous knowledge of the petroleum operations, attracting a diverse group of competent international companies was a key goal for government authorities that needed to secure both foreign capital and expertise.[5] The competence brought by international oil companies (IOCs) was instrumental in exploring and developing the fields and choosing the right technical solutions for enhanced recovery. The variety of IOCs present aimed to ensure competition among them and to foster efficiency, focusing on high oil and gas recovery. This competitive environment also contributed to keeping the costs low. Still today, attracting a diverse group of companies with high competences and innovative solutions is a key objective of Norwegian authorities, in particular in the context of maturing provinces.[6]

While IOCs have played a fundamental role, the Norwegian government, almost since the beginning, has planned to '*Norwegianise*' the national petroleum industry and make it capable of competing nationally and internationally.[7] Building national industry knowledge was a priority,[8] and it aimed to result in sustainable job creation,

---

[5] As stated in the Official Norwegian Report NOU 1979:43 (*Petroleumslov med forskrifter*, of 27 April 1979), at the start 'The Norwegian industry has been completely dependent on foreign capital and expertise'.

[6] Attracting a diverse group of companies with innovative solutions is a key objective of the licensing rounds system in predefined areas, so-called APA-rounds for Awards in Predefined Areas. The APA-round system relates to mature areas, while the numbered licensing rounds relate to frontier parts of the Norwegian continental shelf.

[7] St. meld. Nr. 76 (1970–1971) *Undersøkelse etter og utvinning av undersjøiske naturforekomster på den norske kontinentalsokkel m.m.*, p. 20.

[8] T. Gormley, Norway, in F. Pereira and T. Gormley (eds.), *Local Content for the International Petroleum Industry* (PennWell, 2018), pp. 393–395.

248   Catherine Banet

contributing to industrial and economic growth and social policies in the long term. Local content measures and preferential treatment were central to achieving those goals, as they required a necessary transfer of competences from the IOCs to local workforce and companies. This principle of Norwegianisation led to the establishment of national champions. Already in 1972, the government envisaged the creation of three Norwegian oil companies operating independently of one another on the Norwegian continental shelf (NCS).[9]

Government leadership was another principle applied from the start. It entailed a national steering of the direction and pace of petroleum operations, as well as wide discretion given to the government. Because governments may not always follow the same logic as private companies, assurance of government leadership was seen as a fundamental factor in enabling good resource management and in maximising local benefits. As a consequence, petroleum activities have since the beginning been subject to strict state control. This has applied to field development decisions, but also to the ability to look at the wider effects of the economic signals sent by the petroleum industry to the rest of the industry. For example, already in 1979, the government was concerned about the effects that a preferential arrangement within the upstream petroleum industry on the NCS would have for the incidental cost development in the country, as it would put pressure on prices for goods and services (local cost pressure).[10] Another manifestation of this approach has been a tradition of state participation in and state ownership of some key companies. In addition, to show sustainable leadership, Norway had to develop 'able institutions', notably through capacity building programmes.[11] National authorities should be able to promote the host country's interests but should also act in a balanced manner to maintain the interest and confidence of experienced international companies.[12]

Finally, good resources management has been and remains a mantra in Norwegian petroleum policy. It is multifaceted and is reflected in many provisions of the currently applicable 1996 Petroleum Activities Act.[13] Historically, one of the first official formulations of the good petroleum resources management policy in

---

[9] Those three oil companies were: Statoil, which was fully state-owned at its creation in 1972, and later on partly privatised; Hydro, which was part government and part privately owned; and Saga, which was fully privately owned.

[10] As mentioned in NOU 1979:43, note 5, p. 38: 'A preferential arrangement will affect the prices that the industry sets for its goods and services. In turn, this can lead to an increase in the salary levels in these businesses and in the industry in general. Businesses that do not enjoy preferential treatment but that are exposed to the full effects of international competition could struggle to cope with this higher salary level. It is hard to fully foresee the consequences for Norwegian economy of such a development'.

[11] T. Gormley, note 8, p. 388.

[12] This has been demonstrated recently by the Gassled tariff dispute in Norway concerning the competence of the Ministry of Petroleum and Energy (MPE) to amend the tariffs for the transportation of gas in the Norwegian upstream gas pipelines network (Gassled). After the MPE changed the pipeline tariffs, some shareholders in Gassled challenged the legality of the decision, which affected their revenues. The case was referred to the Supreme Court which ruled in favour of the State (HR-2018–1258-A, case no. 2017/1891, 28 June 2018).

[13] See, in particular, 1996 Petroleum Activities Act, section 1–2 (Resource management).

Norway is found in the so-called 'Ten Oil Commandments'. Those commandments have been submitted by the Standing Committee on Industry in a Storting White Paper dated 14 June 1971, and represented, in the words of the Government,[14] a clarification of what was needed to make sure that the oil activities would 'benefit the entire nation'. Commandments no. 1, 3, 6, 7 and 8 are of particular relevance for local content policy. No. 1 requires the 'national supervision and control of all activity on the Norwegian continental shelf'. No. 3 requires that 'new business activity must be developed, based on petroleum'. No. 6 requires that 'petroleum from the Norwegian continental shelf must, as a main rule, be landed in Norway'. No. 7 requires that the State develops 'an integrated Norwegian oil community with both national and international objectives'. And no. 8 requires that 'a state-owned oil company [must] be established to safeguard the State's commercial interests, and to pursue expedient cooperation with domestic and foreign oil stakeholders'.

2.2 Local Content Requirements and Associated Legal Measures

2.2.1 Evolution of the Legislative and Regulatory Framework

The Norwegian petroleum legislation has evolved progressively, structured around a few key acts supplemented by implementing rules and licensing and commercial agreements.

A prerequisite for any offshore operation in Norway was the adoption of the 1963 Royal Decree that established sovereignty over the Norwegian continental shelf.[15] Further delimitations of jurisdiction were set through bilateral treaties with Denmark and the United Kingdom.

The same year, 1963, an initial, brief (six paragraphs) framework petroleum law was adopted.[16] The law established the State's exclusive right to subsea natural resources and laid the foundation of the licensing system for the exploration and exploitation of offshore petroleum resources. Increasing interest from foreign IOCs for the resources contained in the NCS forced authorities to adopt a more complete legal framework. A committee on the continental shelf (*Kontinentalsokkelutvalget*) was established with the objective of establishing new rules for the exploration and exploitation of the submarine natural resources. In 1965, a Royal Decree implementing the 1963 framework petroleum law was adopted (hereinafter 1965 Royal Decree).[17] The first licence was awarded in September 1965, and the first big

---

[14] Storting White Paper 28 (2010 – 2011), 'An industry for the future – Norway's petroleum activities', chapter 1, Box 1.1.

[15] Royal Decree of 31 May 1963 No. 1 Relating to the Sovereignty of Norway over the Seabed and Subsoil outside the Norwegian Coast (*kgl. resolusjon av 31. mai 1963*).

[16] Act of 21 June 1963 no. 12 relating to Exploration for and Exploitation of Submarine Natural Resources (*Lov av 21. juni 1963 nr. 12 om utforskning og utnyttelse av undersjøiske naturforekomster*).

[17] Royal Decree of 9 April 1965 (*kgl.res. av 9. april 1965 om utforskning og utnyttelse av undersjøiske petroleumsforekomster*). It can be noted that the legal form of a Royal Decree was chosen for two main

250 *Catherine Banet*

discovery was made at the Ekofisk field in 1969. To consolidate the regime, a new Royal Decree was adopted in 1972 (hereinafter 1972 Royal Decree).[18] Building on the foundations of the 1972 Royal Decree, a more consistent legal framework was established by the 1985 Petroleum Act.[19] Several regulations were adopted based on this Act. Following a further evolution of the legal framework and, not least, the entry into force of the EEA Agreement, the Petroleum Activities Act No. 72 was adopted on 29 November 1996 (hereinafter 1996 Petroleum Activities Act), and remains today the main piece of legislation.[20] The Act is supplemented by a series of implementing regulations.

This legislative framework is supplemented by highly standardised agreements between licensees. The content of these agreements is based on requirements defined in the legislation. The conclusion of those agreements, such as the Joint Operating Agreement (JOA), is also mandatory for the licensees. Finally, the agreements are negotiated by the industry representatives and are subject to the approval of the Ministry of Petroleum and Energy.

As a consequence of this regulatory tradition, the LCRs have been defined in the legislation itself (both acts and implementing regulations), in the licensing requirements and in the JOA, and are reflected in contractual arrangements between parties.

2.2.2 Review of LCRs and Legal Measures

Designing a successful local content policy requires a careful balance between incentives and constraints, or in more popular terms, between carrots and sticks. In the case of Norway, the incentive for IOCs was clearly to make profits. However, looking at the legislation, most of the LC provisions put constraints on IOCs. There were not many requirements and the following sections review them successively.

(1) DUTY TO SET UP OPERATING SUBSIDIARY IN NORWAY. To be granted a production licence, the legislation required the companies to set up fully operating subsidiaries in Norway, where their principal seat of business must be located.[21] Norwegian authorities also encouraged the recruitment of Norwegian employees.[22]

reasons: first, a decree is quicker to adopt than a law which requires parliamentary discussions; second, because it was uncertain that there were any petroleum resources on the NCS, a temporary legal framework would have been easier to adapt to any new circumstances. See T. Meland, 'De første konsesjonsreglene fastsatt', Kulturminne Frigge, www.kulturminne-frigg.no.

[18] Royal Decree of 8 December 1972 relating to Exploration for and Exploitation of Petroleum in the Seabed and Subtrata of the Norwegian Continental Shelf, as amended (*Kongelig Resolusjon av 8. desember 1972 om undersøkelse etter og utnyttelse av undersjøiske petroleumsforekomster*).

[19] Act No. 11 of 22 March 1985, Petroleum Act (*Lov om petroleumsvirksomhet*, 1985).

[20] Act No.72 relating to petroleum activities of 29 November 1996.

[21] 1965 Royal Decree, section 10 (production licence); 1972 Royal Decree, section 11; 1985 Petroleum Act (original version), section 8 (production licence) and section 48.

[22] P. Heum, note 3, p. 9.

Local Content and SD in Norway 251

Although this requirement has been removed, today's legislation still contains requirements as to the domiciliation of companies. For survey licences, it is sufficient that the physical person to which the licence is granted is domiciled in an EEA state.[23] However, production licences may only be granted to a corporate body established in conformity with Norwegian legislation and registered in the Norwegian Register of Business Enterprises (insofar as other requirements are not applicable pursuant to international agreements). Production licences may also be granted to a physical person domiciled in an EEA state.[24] The Ministry may set special requirements regarding the licensee's organisation in Norway, with the purpose of ensuring that the licensee's organisation in Norway has a structure and size that enables the licensee, at all times, to make informed decisions about its petroleum activities.[25]

(II) PREFERENCE TO NATIONAL COMPANIES IN LICENSING ROUNDS, INCLUDING OPERATORSHIP. Licensing rounds became an increasingly powerful tool in LC policy by prioritising Norwegian companies, including state-owned, and developing Norwegian competencies by preparing them to compete internationally. This was done through the following legal requirements:

- *mandatory state participation* – As of 1967, the government equity participation in production licencing was required or, at least, could be imposed by the ministry as a condition for granting the licence[26];
- *establishment of National Oil Companies (NOCs)* – The most common means to secure local content is through the establishment of a NOC. It enables the state to secure national participation in the petroleum industry, pursue national policy objectives and develop national competences in addition to direct revenues. Norway did not derogate to the rule, and the Norwegian State Oil Company (*Den Norske Stats Oljeselskap A/S* – Statoil), renamed Equinor in 2018, was founded as a private limited company owned by the Government of Norway on 14 July 1972;
- *preferences given to Norwegian companies, including state-owned, when awarding licences* – NOCs are more likely than IOCs to employ local workers and use local suppliers, with long-term benefits for the national economy.[27] Therefore, Norwegian companies – in this case mainly Statoil, but also Norsk Hydro and Saga Petroleum[28] – were given preference in

---

[23] 1996 Petroleum Activities Act, section 2-1.
[24] Ibid., section 3-3.
[25] Ibid., section 10-2.
[26] 1972 Royal Decree, section 31.
[27] J. W. Moses and B. Letnes, note 4, p. 148.
[28] Statoil was a fully state-owned company when it was established in 1972, and was partly privatised and made a public limited company in 2001. Norsk Hydro is partly state-owned and had a separate oil and

licensing award decisions, getting an increasing number of blocks in general and blocks with the most promising profiles in particular. This preferential treatment in favour of Norwegian NOCs was reflected in a series of provisions, primarily included in the state participation agreements with the IOCs.[29] First, the rules for state participation were progressively strengthened. Already during the second licensing round in 1969, the government announced that it would include a clause of state participation with carried interests until commercial discoveries were made. As of the 1973 licensing round, the state participation agreements with the IOCs were amended to reflect a new obligation to automatically award the newly established Statoil 50 per cent holding in every block.[30] Second, a system of 'sliding scale' (*glideskala*) of increasing state control within the licensing group was introduced.[31] Having a state-owned company like Statoil in the licence group, often with the majority of shares and consequently voting rights, was an extremely effective tool to influence decisions and defend national policy objectives, whether in terms of economic return or maximum recovery of field resources. The award of production licences to Norwegian oil and gas companies has eased Norwegian suppliers' access those markets.[32] It also ensured quick growth to Statoil. A third tool introduced in favour of NOCs was the obligation for the foreign IOCs in the licence to cover the exploration costs for the state-owned companies (*bæring*).

- *operatorship given to Norwegian companies* – Based on the discretionary powers given to the Ministry in setting up the licensing group per block and nominating the operator, Norwegian authorities forced IOCs to enter into joint venture (JV) agreements with Norwegian companies. They also progressively gave operatorship to the Norwegian licensees within the JV. This forced collaboration was an effective tool in learning out the business and building the competence of the Norwegian companies, which became qualified and competitive operators.[33]

---

gas division (*Hydro Oil & Gas*, merged in 2007 with Statoil). Saga Petroleum was private-owned, and was acquired by Norsk Hydro in 1999.

[29] On the state participation agreements, see K. Kaasen, 'Statsdeltagelsesavtalen i norsk petroleumsvirksomhet : kontraktsrettslig form, konsesjonsrettslig innhold – eller omvendt?', Tidsskrift for rettsvitenskap (1984) p. 372.

[30] D. H. Claes, 'Statoil: between Nationalisation, Globalisation and Europeanisation', ARENA Working Papers WP 02/34, 2002.

[31] J. W. Moses and B. Letnes, note 4, p. 157.

[32] This is clearly recognized in the Official Norwegian Report NOU 1979:43, note 5, p. 38. The influence that Statoil had on the choice of suppliers – in favour of Norwegian ones – in the Statfjord field is often mentioned as example.

[33] J. W. Moses and B. Letnes, note 4, p. 156.

It should be noted that the Norwegian authorities today still exercise an important influence when putting together the licensing group per block and nominating the operator.

(III) PREFERENCE ON THE USE OF NORWEGIAN GOODS AND SERVICES ON A COMPETITIVE BASIS. A common feature of LC policies is the requirement for IOCs to use local suppliers, provided the local suppliers retained are qualified and price-competitive. A similar obligation was defined in Norwegian legislation.

At the beginning, the obligation to use Norwegian goods and services was formulated in very general terms, mirroring the fact that Norwegian authorities did not yet have an elaborated LC strategy. A reference was included in the first licensing round in 1965 that the extent to which the winning licensee will be 'contributing to the Norwegian economy' will be seen as a plus in the award procedure.[34] The explicit reference to this ad hoc criteria is to be found in a press conference declaration by the then Minister of Industry announcing the results of the first licensing round. He admitted that, while they 'had emphasised the applicant's financial strength and practical experience with oil exploration', they 'also considered the degree to which the applicant has considered marketing in Norway, building refineries in Norway, using Norwegian ships or other ways in which the applicant has or will contribute to strengthening Norway's economy in general'.[35] What happened during that period was that the IOCs entered into a 'gentlemen's agreement' with the authorities where they committed to carry out their activities from a base in Norway, to use Norwegian industry and to employ a Norwegian workforce.[36] The announcement of the second licensing round made the criteria of use of Norwegian suppliers even more explicit in the licensing award decision,[37] but one had to wait until 1972 for the introduction of an explicit LCR provision in the legislation.

The motivation for increasing the level of local content in the Norwegian petroleum policy and reinforcing LCRs in the legislation was first the need to secure long-term effects on the national economy and the wish to build a national petroleum industry able to compete internationally in the long run. It also answered criticisms from mainly two large Norwegian companies (Aker and Kværner) about how little they were called on to help in the Ekofisk project. The strengthening of the LCRs was also a reaction to the crisis the shipping industry went through in the aftermath of the 1973 OPEC oil boycott, which resulted in cancellation of orders for tankers and ships, including in Norway.[38]

---

[34] St. meld. Nr. 76 (1970–1971), note 7, p. 21.

[35] S. Kvendseth, *Funn! Historien om Ekofisks første 20 år*, Tananger: Phillips, 1988, p. 16.

[36] The practice of the 'gentlemen's agreement' is mentioned in a Government White Paper preceding the adoption of explicit legal basis for that LCR in the legislation. See St. meld. Nr. 76 (1970–1971), note 7, p. 23.

[37] The requirement was included in point 8 of the Production licences awarded in 1969. Ibid., p. 23.

[38] The effects of the international context were reported in the Official Norwegian Report NOU 1979:43, note 5, pp. 20, 38. Moses and Letnes also report that 'The Norwegian government felt an obligation to

254 Catherine Banet

As a result, the principle of the mandatory use by licensees of Norwegian goods and services when those were competitive enough was formally introduced as section 54 of the 1972 Royal Decree. The provision was re-conducted more succinctly in section 54 of the 1985 Petroleum Act, until the Act was amended, and the provision was removed in order to harmonise the Norwegian legislation with the newly signed EEA Agreement. As mentioned in the introduction, the currently applicable legislation, the 1996 Petroleum Activities Act, does not contain LC provisions.

The main components of the LC regime defined by section 54 of the 1972 Royal Decree were as follows:

- The licensees were required to ('shall') use Norwegian goods and services as long as they were competitive in terms of quality, service, delivery time and price.
- The Norwegian contractors 'shall' receive invitations to participate in a call for tenders as long as they produced goods and rendered services as required. They must be given 'real opportunities' (*reelle muligheter*) to compete and supply.[39] Pursuant to the preparatory works, this went together with an obligation imposed on tenderers to assess the Norwegian market in detail before the call for tenders can be launched.[40] It also implied that the terms and conditions of the call for tenders, the type of tender, the contracts, the size of the tenders, the standards chosen, etc. would not make it unnecessary difficult for Norwegian suppliers to participate.[41] In the original text of the 1985 Petroleum Act, applicants for the production licence were also required to submit a plan describing how they foresee collaboration with Norwegian industrial suppliers[42] (collaboration plan) in order to give the Norwegian industry 'real opportunities' to compete and supply goods and services.[43] The obligation to communicate the collaboration plan is a codification in law of a practice introduced in the fourth licensing round, based on purchased goods and services.[44] A similar obligation to disclose information on the use of local goods and services was defined in section 23 in relation to the Plan for Development and Operation (PDO) of petroleum deposit. The PDO, subject to approval by the Ministry, 'shall' include a description of the existing or planned

---

keep Norwegians employed and wanted to encourage the Norwegian shipbuilding industry to adapt in order to service the growing petroleum industry'. J. W. Moses and B. Letnes, note 4, p. 155.

[39] As mentioned in the Preparatory Works, the provision aimed to tackle the problems met by the Norwegian suppliers. The market was dominated by IOCs with established relationships with foreign suppliers and little or no knowledge about the qualifications of the Norwegian companies. Preparatory works, Ot.prp.nr.82 (1991–1992), changes to section 54 1985 Petroleum Act.

[40] Preparatory works Ot.prp.nr.72 (1982–1983) *Lov om petroleumsvirksomhet*, commentary to section 54.

[41] Ibid.

[42] In other words, not for non-petroleum related supplies, such as catering, which historically was indeed the first type of goods that the Norwegian companies supplied to the IOCs on the Norwegian Continental Shelf.

[43] 1985 Petroleum Act in its original version, section 8.

[44] In the bidding invitation of the fourth licensing rounds, the applicants who already possessed a survey or production licence were required to inform the authorities of the nature of the suppliers from Norwegian industrial suppliers. See also Official Norwegian Report NOU 1979:43, note 5, p. 38.

Local Content and SD in Norway 255

cooperation with Norwegian suppliers that will ensure the latter opportunities to supply goods and services in the construction, operation and maintenance phases of the project.[45] All those practical obligations – assessment of the available suppliers on the Norwegian market, cooperation plan, cooperation on product development, description of current and future cooperation – aimed to comply with the requirement of giving 'real opportunities' to Norwegian suppliers.[46]

- When assessing contract offers, the licensees were required to ('shall') 'take into account' the extent to which the bidders would use Norwegian goods and services.
- The licensees were made responsible for the observation of those provisions by their contractors and sub-contractors.

In this strategy on the use of local goods and services, the government has always argued that the goal was to develop local supply of competitive goods and services required by the petroleum industry, and not to demand a discriminatory use of local suppliers. What was introduced in section 54 of the 1972 Royal Decree was a requirement to give preference to Norwegian goods and services to ensure fair treatment of Norwegian suppliers.[47] At the same time, several Norwegian authorities expressed the view that the provisions should not be practiced in such a way as to exclude competitive foreign bidders and suppliers.[48] Therefore, the competitive nature of the Norwegian suppliers have been a key criterion to ensure that they gain access to the market. A slight change in the wording of the requirement was introduced in the 1985 Petroleum Law. While the 1972 Royal Decree requires licensees to use Norwegian goods and services in their activity 'as far as they are competitive with regard to quality, service, schedule of delivery and price' (section 54), the 1985 Petroleum Law requires that 'competitive Norwegian suppliers shall be given real opportunities to achieve deliveries of goods and services' (section 54).[49] This change was justified by the wish to have a more flexible wording – and application – of the requirement. Based on the 1972 wording, the competitiveness of the Norwegian suppliers was assessed on each criteria separately and cumulatively, and it happened that Norwegian suppliers were competitive enough on quality and schedule of delivery, but not on price, and were not selected on this ground.[50] The 1985 wording ensured a more general but also a more discretionary assessment of the competitiveness of the Norwegian suppliers, based on further criteria if relevant. The purpose was not to derogate from the principle of competitiveness, but to be able to take into account other relevant considerations if necessary.

[45] 1985 Petroleum Act in its original version, section 23, first paragraph.
[46] Official Norwegian Report NOU 1979:43, note 5, p. 97.
[47] Ibid., p. 38.
[48] Preparatory works Ot.prp.nr.72 (1982–1983), note 40, p. 145.
[49] Own translation.
[50] Official Norwegian Report NOU 1979:43, note 5, p. 97.

256 *Catherine Banet*

In order to supervise compliance with the previously mentioned purchase requirements, a Goods and Services Office was established within the Ministry of Industry in 1972. The main task of the Office was to control and monitor the IOCs' contracting and procurement procedures. It closely monitored the IOCs' procurement practices. To do so, the Office reviewed the tender schedule and the list of companies to be invited that the IOCs operating in Norway were required to submit. By reviewing this, the Office made sure that qualified Norwegian companies were included on the bidder's list. The Office was also entitled to set and review targets for local participation measures in personnel and monetary terms.[51] Finally, the Office also made sure that the local supply industry was stimulated through joint venture.

(IV) TECHNOLOGY TRANSFER AND RESEARCH COOPERATION. Petroleum resources on the NCS are located in deep waters, which entails that most operations face the tough conditions of the North Sea. This means that at the beginning, it required the development of new methods, skills and technologies adapted to those demanding conditions.[52] This gave Norwegian authorities a unique opportunity to design local content requirements within R&D that required innovative solutions. The need to ensure a high level of protection of workers' safety and the environment was also used as argument in favour of new innovative technological solutions. A concrete example of how technical requirements defined in legislation, on safety grounds, have favoured Norwegian companies related to the obligation to build separate platforms for drilling operations and for workers' living quarters.[53]

The preference policy for Norwegian goods and services was associated with requirements regarding research cooperation and technology transfer.

First, concerning research cooperation, it was again during the fourth licensing round of 1978 that a requirement was inserted mandating that at least 50 per cent of R&D efforts related to field development on the NCS should occur in Norway. Thereafter, the licensing terms only contained general requirements in regard to technology transfer, and details were set out in separate R&D agreements entered into with Norwegian research institutions, so-called 50 per cent agreements or 'offer agreements'. Those agreements required companies to cooperate with Norwegian research institutions within defined areas, for defined amounts, as a condition to get a licence. The agreements varied in form, from general cooperative agreements with Norwegian R&D institutions to the allocation of funds for specific R&D projects to

---

[51] J. W. Moses and B. Letnes, note 4, p. 155.

[52] Ibid., p. 151. The authors notably describe the example of the Ocean Traveler, a semi-submersible platform drilling rig which was designed to perform operations in similar situations as those found in the Gulf of Mexico but encountered major operating challenges when operations started. As stated by the authors: 'it became immediately evident that something more substantial was needed for North Sea conditions' (p. 264).

[53] J. W. Moses and B. Letnes, note 4, p. 161. See as well H. Ryggvik, *The Norwegian Oil Experience: A Toolbox for Managing Resources?*, Report number 2, Oslo: Senter for Teknologi, Innovasjon og Kultur, TIK, 2010, p 59.

be carried out by selected Norwegian institutions.[54] In addition, Norway used non-binding 'goodwill agreements' where companies declared their intent to conduct their petroleum-related R&D in Norway as much as possible.

This strategy greatly benefited the Norwegian research communities. The introduction of those technology agreements triggered an impressive development in petroleum-related technology in Norway.

The Goods and Services Office was also in charge of encouraging R&D and technology transfer.

(V) OBLIGATION TO BRING PETROLEUM ASHORE IN NORWAY. Already in the very first pieces of petroleum legislation, an obligation to bring petroleum to shore was defined. Pursuant to the Royal Decree of 9 April 1965, the King could decide that petroleum products, partly or wholly, had to be landed in Norway, should national interests require it.[55] A similar requirement, with a slightly different wording (it refers to 'produced petroleum'), is to be found in the 1972 Royal Decree[56] and the 1985 Petroleum Act in its original version.[57] The purpose was to ensure that the processing and refinement of oil and gas would be carried out in Norway. This provision was quite challenging to implement, because of the initial lack of adequate pipeline infrastructure to transport oil or gas throughout the deep Norwegian trench. Therefore, the first field development projects – Ekofisk and Frigg – were given exemptions to this provision.[58] In addition, while oil was and is still for a part processed in Norway, natural gas has traditionally been transported directly to consumer markets abroad through the pipeline network called Gassled. This is also because there is almost no consumption of natural gas on land in Norway.

(VI) TRAINING OF LOCAL PERSONNEL AND GOVERNMENT OFFICIALS. Provisions in the petroleum legislation, production licences and additional agreements requested licensees to share industrial knowledge through training of local personnel and government officials. Licensees were requested to train officials from the Ministry of Petroleum and Energy, the Norwegian Directorate or other public entities. They were also asked to train teachers in school to teach petroleum-related topics. There is also a very common requirement in LC policies.

2.3 Implementation and Compliance Strategy

The LC policy conducted by the Norwegian authorities can be deemed as successful, even in the absence of strict enforcement mechanisms.

---

[54]   J. W. Moses and B. Letnes, note 4, p. 160.
[55]   1965 Royal Decree, section 33.
[56]   1972 Royal Decree, section 34.
[57]   1985 Petroleum Act, section 26.
[58]   Official Norwegian Report NOU 1979:43, note 5, p. 33.

258   *Catherine Banet*

As noted by Moses and Letnes with reference to the St.meld.nr.53 (1979–80), in only one decade, the net share of Norwegian deliveries to the petroleum industry in Norway had increased remarkably: 'by 28 percent in 1975, by 42 percent in 1976, by 50 percent in 1977, and by 62 percent in 1978'.[59]

This result is quite remarkable considering that there was no specific supervision and no enforcement mechanisms for compliance with LCRs. The manner prescribed to monitor implementation of the previously mentioned LCRs was primarily through reporting obligation and supervision by the Goods and Services Office. Oil and Gas companies were required to submit annual reports to the Ministry of Petroleum and Energy about their activities, including the amount of Norwegian local content that was utilised. On the basis of these reports, Norwegian authorities could measure the level of local content in the Norwegian petroleum sector. What was defined as 'local' in the Norwegian context was often situated at the national interest level. Some specific requirements have had and still have direct local benefits, but the primary objective is to serve national interests.

Another characteristic of the Norwegian LC strategy is that its design has been elaborated step by step by the national authorities. When IOCs showed signs of suspicion or even resistance, the Norwegian government could adjust LC policy.[60]

The LC policy was implemented in a transparent and predictable manner, which has remained a key characteristic of the Norwegian petroleum policy. All terms and conditions for both licensing and commercial framework were communicated to stakeholders in advance, even if they had been evolving to reflect increased LCRs during this first period.

3 LCR CONSTRAINTS UNDER LIBERALISED AND INTEGRATED ENERGY MARKETS

The objective of the Norwegian authorities from the start has been to build an infant industry and prepare it to compete internationally, while maximising revenues from the continental shelf following good resource-management principles. This objective was attained by the end of the first period of explicit LCRs policy in the mid-1980s. This moment was marked by a drop in oil price (around 1986), which, given the high cost of production on the NCS, motivated a series of reforms, with the objective of remaining an attractive petroleum province.[61] Among those reforms was the revision of the local content regime, which would have been unsustainable in a tougher international competitive environment.

---

[59]   J. W. Moses and B. Letnes, note 4, p. 156; St.meld.nr.53 (1979–80), p. 27.
[60]   See, for example, the reactions among IOCs when the Norwegian government awarded the Gullfaks block 34/10 only to Norwegian companies (85 percent Statoil, 9 per cent Norsk Hydro and 6 per cent Saga Petroleum). B. V. Lerøen, 'Ettertraktet modell' (*Norsk Sokkel*, Norwegian Petroleum Directorate, 2012) p. 15.
[61]   J. W. Moses and B. Letnes, note 4, p. 162.

Local Content and SD in Norway 259

In the subsequent phase, the use of LCRs has been constrained by the obligations deriving from the entry into force of the EEA Agreement in 1994 and the application of the relevant WTO Agreements after Norway joined the WTO. Norway has also entered into a series of Bilateral Investment Treaties (BITs) which restrain the country's ability to include LCRs. This section reviews the changes introduced by Norway's accession to the EEA, to the WTO and the implementation of certain BITs for Norwegian practices.

3.1 EEA Constraints and Opportunities

The entry into force of the EEA Agreement has entailed a series of amendments to Norwegian legislation on local content and associated measures.[62]

Preferential treatment in favour of national oil and gas companies, in all forms, had to be ended as a consequence of the application of EU/EEA internal market rules and competition law. The provisions of sections 8, 23 and 54 of the 1985 Petroleum Act had to be amended. The obligation for foreign IOCs to pay state-owned companies exploration costs had to be repealed. The requirement that Statoil should get at least a 50 per cent holding in each block was removed. The technology agreement requirements were dropped. The obligation to bring petroleum ashore in Norway had to be removed, although the 1996 Petroleum Activities Act preserved Norwegian authorities' discretion to decide 'where and in which way landing of petroleum shall take place'.[63] The Goods and Services Office was closed.

Indeed, any discrimination on grounds of nationality would infringe Article 4 of the EEA Agreement. Other relevant provisions of the Agreement in terms of equal treatment and free movement relate to the prohibition against any quantitative restrictions on imports/exports and all measures having equivalent effect (Art. 11, 12 and 13), rules on State monopoly (Art. 16), freedom of establishment for EU/EEA nationals and companies or firms (Art. 31–34), free movement of services and capital (Art. 36 and 40), participation in the capital of companies of firms (Art. 124), anti-trust and competition rules (Art. 53–60) and state aid rules (Art. 61).

The purchase of goods and services by publicly owned companies on a competitive basis has been rendered mandatory following the application of EU rules on public procurement. The application of public procurement rules to the petroleum sector was discussed in detail during the EEA Agreement negotiations, since the sector was the most important one covered by the public procurement rules in Norway.[64] The relevant legislative act is currently Directive 2014/25/EU on

---

[62] For an early assessment of the range of changes required to the Norwegian petroleum regime as a consequence of the entry into force of the EEA Agreement, see F. Arnesen, 'EØS-avtalens konsekvenser for praktiseringen av det norske petroleumskonsesjonssystemet', Lov og Rett (1992) pp. 456–77.

[63] 1996 Petroleum Activities Act, section 4-11.

[64] Preparatory works, Ot.prp.nr.82 (1991-1992) *Om endringer i energilovgivningen som følge av en EØS-avtale*, p. 3.

260   *Catherine Banet*

procurement by entities operating in the water, energy, transport and postal services sectors, as inserted into Annex XVI to the EEA Agreement.

Harmonised secondary legislation put also some new constraints on the use of LCRs. Although adopted after the signature of the EEA Agreement, the Hydrocarbons Licensing Directive 94/22/EC of 30 May 1994 on the Conditions for Granting and Using Authorizations for the Prospection, Exploration and Production of Hydrocarbons restricts the capacity to use laws or regulations to implement local content. Pursuant to the Directive, the award of licences shall be done based on objective criteria published in advance, according to the principles of equal treatment, and shall not discriminate based on nationality.

Despite these new constraints, and because the Norwegian petroleum industry was able to become competitive during the first phase of explicit LCRs, the accession to the internal market through the EEA Agreement was seen as a positive development. It gave new market opportunities for Norwegian goods and services to the petroleum industry in other EEA countries.[65] Through internal market and competition law rules, the EEA Agreement offers companies a level playing field. Accession to the EEA ensures 'real opportunities' to compete that the LCRs of the original sections 8, 23 and 54 of the 1985 Petroleum Act aimed to secure. Therefore, the requirements of the EEA Agreement were mostly seen as a prolongation of this principle.[66]

3.2 *WTO Constraints and Opportunities*

Norway has been a WTO member since 1 January 1995 and a member of GATT since 10 July 1948. A direct consequence of Norway's membership to the WTO is reliance on the 'national treatment' principle, providing that foreign companies must be given the same treatment as domestic ones, and so in accordance with the different WTO agreements (i.e. TRIMS, ASCM and GATS). Under the different WTO agreements, LCRs would be either prohibited, disciplined or allowed under precise conditions. The application of those agreements to local content measures is reviewed in Chapter 3 of this book. It is therefore sufficient to point out, for the purpose of this chapter, that most LCRs as originally practiced by Norway would be inconsistent with the WTO discipline.

Similarly to the EEA, the WTO represented new constraints for the Norwegian petroleum industry, but, first and foremost, new opportunities. When Norway joined the WTO, the Norwegian companies were able to compete internationally and were therefore interested in getting access to markets abroad where they could compete on a level playing field with other

---

[65]   White paper on repeal of the local content requirements from the Petroleum Act (Instillst O. (1992–1993)); Preparatory works, Ot.prp.nr.82 (1991–1992), note 64, pp. 1–2.

[66]   Preparatory works, Ot.prp.nr.82 (1991–1992), note 64, on changes to sections 8 and 54 of the 1985 Petroleum Act, p. 15.

Local Content and SD in Norway 261

companies.[67] The multilateral regime provided by the WTO for trade in goods and services ensures minimum standards in terms of equal treatment and market access, which will facilitate entry into the foreign market for Norwegian petroleum companies.

3.3 *BITs Constraints and Opportunities*

In addition to trade agreements, reliance on LCRs may be constrained by investment-related agreements concluded between two or more contracting parties.[68] Those agreements may go further than WTO provisions on investment protection, prohibiting, for example, requirements for technology transfer and joint ventures. Like for the EEA and the WTO, an agreement like a bilateral investment agreement or treaty (BIT) will be instrumental in ensuring market access in foreign countries for the now-competitive Norwegian petroleum industry while it may prevent Norwegian authorities from putting LCRs in place at home. BITs may contain at least four types of provisions limiting the scope of LCRs policy: non-discrimination provisions, fair and equitable treatment provisions, measures to restrict performance requirements, and specific measures relating to nationality of board members and senior management.[69]

As of 2019, Norway has entered into eighteen BITs, but only fourteen are in force.[70] All those BITs were signed between 1966 and 1996. Norway has not concluded any new BITs since the mid-1990s. A rapid review of the agreements signed so far shows that the approach chosen with respect to LCRs is quite standard, reflecting some general common principles from other BITs such as the duty of non-discrimination (national treatment and most-favoured-nation treatment). As part of the mandate of a new coalition in 2015, the government planned to increase the use of BITs, where appropriate. Therefore, a new Norwegian model agreement for the promotion and protection of investments has been elaborated and subject to consultation.[71] The new model investment agreement,[72] which is still under

---

[67] White Paper, Meld. St. 28 (2010–2011), An industry for the future – Norway's petroleum activities, section 8.5.

[68] It should be noted that it has become more common over time to include provisions on investment protection in free trade agreements, including for agreements concluded between industrialised countries. In the case of Norway, one objective lately has been the definition of shared EFTA positions to be included in a separate chapter in future EFTA free trade agreements.

[69] I. Ramdoo, 'Local content, trade and investment: Is there policy space left for linkages development in resource-rich countries?' European Centre for Development Policy Management (ECDPM), Discussion Paper No. 205, December 2016, p. 26.

[70] For an overview, see the International Investment Agreements Navigator, UNCTAD, Investment Policy Hub, https://investmentpolicy.unctad.org/international-investment-agreements/.

[71] Model investment agreement – public consultation, Royal Norwegian Ministry of Trade, Industry and Fisheries, 15 May 2015, www.regjeringen.no/contentassets/e47326b61f424d4c9c3d470896492623/consultation-letter.pdf.

[72] The draft version of the new model investment agreement, www.regjeringen.no/contentassets/e47326b61f424d4c9c3d470896492623/draft-model-agreement-english.pdf.

262   *Catherine Banet*

discussion, reiterates some general provisions found in BITs, as we have discussed.[73] Of particular relevance for LC policy are the reinforced provisions on investor access to markets, where, for example, investors must be granted national treatment in connection with establishment. Importantly, the draft model investment agreement foresees detailed provisions on performance requirements (Article 8) which cover most aspects of LC policy.

4 SUSTAINABILITY FRAMEWORK FOR LCRS BASED ON THE NORWEGIAN EXPERIENCE: CONCLUDING THOUGHTS

Without doubt, Norway offers an example of successful LC policy. There is a consensus that this achievement is due to a combination of external framework conditions and carefully designed and implemented legal requirements.[74] The Norwegian LC policy also developed in a particular context as described in Section 1. Beyond those specificities, there is a series of lessons that can be drawn from the Norwegian experience that can serve as effective transplant in other jurisdictions.

A first lesson is that the elaboration of a LC policy in the petroleum sector must take into account the general energy-generation mix and sources of energy supplies of the country, as well as structural regulatory elements like governance and legal systems. An efficient system of administrative governance with stable institutions and a transparent and predictable regulatory framework will be decisive for the implementation of LC policy for the benefit of both foreign operations/investors and local industries/population. This is due to the fact that the petroleum sector is only one sector in the economy of a country, and LCRs in that sector must align with the economic development of other sectors to have long-term benefits. In the case of Norway, the ultimate goal has remained efficient petroleum resource management and maximisation of national value creation.

The LCRs should be temporary and, as far as possible, performance based, as they aim to prepare the national industry to be competitive internationally and to adapt to international norms and standards. When designing their LC policy and associated legal requirements, states should conceive them as transitory measures towards a more competitive and open international market. Norway benefited from good timing in that respect. The country had sufficient time to develop national champions and indigenous energy service companies through the use of some key LCRs before joining the EEA and the WTO. Therefore, it can be argued that, in order to benefit fully from the opportunities of liberalised and integrated markets, the national industry should have sufficient time in advance to become competitive, notably through the use of LCRs.

---

[73] Such as national treatment (Article 3), most-favoured-nation treatment (Article 4), general treatment and protection (Article 4), draft model investment agreement (2015).
[74] T. Gormley, note 8, p. 385.

The adoption of LCRs in Norway has been very progressive, step by step, and adjusted over time. This adaptive and flexible approach to LCRs made it possible to assess their benefits on the national industry while keeping a balance between sticks and carrots with IOCs. This dynamic approach was dependent on a spirit of good cooperation and openness between the industry and public authorities. It was also dependent on the close monitoring by public authorities, with elements of national control at different levels of the value chain.

In terms of legal approach, the Norwegian regulation of LCRs can be characterised as a light-touch regulation in law. There was no law on local content, but some few key provisions inserted into the petroleum legislation. Those were supplemented by a well-integrated set of licensing and contractual requirements between parties. This made the LC policy more flexible and easy to adapt to sector developments until LCRs were removed.

14

Local Content and Sustainable Development in Argentina

Marcelo Neuman

1 INTRODUCTION

This chapter examines legal and institutional frameworks that can be used to sustain local content development in Argentina by improving local content laws already established and coordinating implementation activities among the stakeholders. Argentina has twenty-four provinces, of which only ten produce oil and gas, and most oil and gas is exploited in Patagonia.[1] The ten provinces are represented in the "Organización Federal de Estados Productores de Hidrocarburos" (OFEPHI).[2] The OFEPHI strengthens the presence of the oil and gas producing provinces in the debate on oil and gas public policy. The OFEPHI's political authority is represented by the governors of the ten provinces, and its steering committee includes the provincial ministers responsible for hydrocarbon activity.

During the 1990s, the ownership of natural hydrocarbon resources was progressively passed from the national government to the provinces until they finally became whole owners of their natural subsoil resources. A series of legal instruments, and even a constitutional reform, were used to transfer the domain and administration of oil and gas resources from the national government to the respective provinces. In 2007, Law No 26197[3] granted provinces full rights to the original domain and full administration over oil and gas deposits in their territories. Consequently, all exploration permits, exploitation concessions, and any other types of contract granted or approved by the national government were transferred to the provinces. The national government retained responsibility for designing energy policy.

This transfer of oil and gas rights to the provinces greatly limited the power of the national government to design and implement local content policies at the national

---

[1] The ten provinces are: Tierra del Fuego, Mendoza, Chubut, Neuquén, Río Negro, La Pampa, Santa Cruz, Salta, Formosa, and Jujuy.

[2] Organización Federal de Estados Productores de Hidrocarburos, www.ofephi.com.ar.

[3] Honorable Congreso de la Nacion Argentina, Hidrocarburos, Ley No. 17.319 Art. 1 – Substitucion, Publicada en el Boletín Oficial del 05-ene-2007 Número: 31067 Página: 1, http://servicios .infoleg.gob.ar/infolegInternet/verNorma.do?id=123780.

264

level. Oil and gas concessions, as utilized in many countries, could not be used by the national government to increase the participation of local industry or the local workforce at the national level.[4] Therefore, this powerful tool for developing local content regulations in the bidding process was left to the provinces, hindering the possibilities of an equilibrated local content development in the country.

In addition, the provinces were not totally prepared to deal with the new responsibility of negotiating with the international and national oil and gas corporations. The transfer of the rights from the national government to the provinces was progressively done over a period of fifteen years, allowing the oil producing provinces to gradually build their public management capabilities to deal with the oil sector. However, during those years, the management capabilities of the provinces did not progress as needed, thereby preventing the public provincial officials from negotiating permissions, concessions, royalties, and other themes with the oil and gas companies on an equal basis. Simultaneously, the national government assisted the provinces in the elaboration of a consistent normative body for oil and gas and in the formation of a techno-bureaucratic staff able to carry out the activities required for guiding the industry. Although, over the years, the provinces have been able to develop a fairly good bureaucratic body to deal with these natural resources, they lack the bargaining power of national government to negotiate with the large international oil and gas corporations. This imbalance of power is reflected in the capacity of the provinces to enforce their local content regulations.

The chapter is organized in five sections. This introductory section has briefly described the particular institutional arrangement of the country's oil and gas sector under which local content initiatives can be developed. Section 2 introduces local content laws in Argentina's oil and gas producing provinces and examines the initiatives at the national level. Section 3 discusses barriers, limitations, and partial results of the local content regulations in the three most important oil and gas producing provinces of Argentina: Chubut, Santa Cruz, and Neuquén.[5] In addition, local content limitations at the national level are also considered. Section 4 highlights how those barriers can be addressed. Section 5 presents the conclusion.

---

[4] For example, in Brazil, local content is a mandatory component of the bidding processes for oil and gas licenses. See J. Guerra, M. Morales, and S. Jarrin, "Regional Evidence Papers: Local Content Frameworks in Latin American Oil and Gas sector: Lessons from Ecuador and Colombia," Research Papers Series, Evidence and Lessons from Latin America, April 2016.

[5] These provinces lead the oil and gas industry in Argentina; together they represent around 70 per cent of oil and gas production. Neuquén has become the most important oil and gas province where most of the 30,000 km^2 reservoir of "Vaca Muerta" with shale gas and shale oil are located. These resources have been ranked in third and fourth positions for gas and oil, respectively, in the world ranking of non-conventional resources. See US Energy Information Administration, "Technically Recoverable Shale Gas and Shale Oil Resources: An Assessment of 137 Shale Formations in 41 Countries Outside the United States," Independent Statistics and Analysis, US Department of Energy, June 2013.

266   *Marcelo Neuman*

2 LOCAL CONTENT IN ARGENTINA

Local content in Argentina is not only related to specific laws, decrees, and dispositions. The complex institutional arrangement between the national government and the oil and gas producing provinces sets a challenge for developing sustainable local content initiatives.

If considered broadly, local content policies can be viewed in two ways: as local content regulations and as local content development. The former typically deals with setting margins for domestic companies and percentages of nationals in the workforce, the latter with fostering the development of a competitive, sustainable, and capable local supplier base and a highly skilled workforce through local supplier development programs and local supplier investments.[6] Argentina uses both forms: local content regulations in the oil and gas producing provinces and supplier development programs at the national level.

2.1 *Local Content at the National Level*

Local content development through supplier development programs was the formula chosen by the national government to implement local content at the national level. In 2010, the national government developed a nationwide research program to assess the capabilities of local oil and gas suppliers with the objective of recommending local content policies.[7] The program recommended a series of local content initiatives at the national level, but the government was not convinced to introduce national regulations in the way other Latin American countries have done. Additionally, the recently renationalized YPF[8] did not agree to comply with local content regulations, especially if they sought to provide a domestic margin of price preference to local suppliers.[9]

The vehicle chosen to promote local content development, therefore, was the creation of a national supplier development program (SDP), first in YPF[10] and later extended to other oil and gas companies. Within one year of its implementation, the

---

[6] See, S. Tordo, M. Warner, O. Manzano, and Y. Anouti, "Local Content Policies in the Oil and Gas Sector," A World Bank Study, 2013, pp. 56, 66. See also D. Olawuyi, "Local content and procurement requirements in oil and gas contracts: Regional trends in the Middle East and North Africa" (2019) 37 *Journal of Energy and Natural Resources Law* 93–117; D. Olawuyi, *Extractives Industry Law in Africa* (New York: Springer, 2018), pp. 233–264.

[7] The author was responsible for designing and implementing the research program through the National University of General Sarmiento.

[8] YPF is Argentina's largest oil company where the state owns 51 per cent of the shares. YPF used to be the acronym for Yacimientos Petroliferos Fiscales, but since its privatization in the year 2000, the name is solely YPF.

[9] The company argued that the local supplier base was already quite competitive and that any local content regulations would add extra cost, particularly in a context where the country needed important investments to fulfil its energy requirements. There were important counterarguments to this position, but the YPF's vision prevailed.

[10] The author was asked by the Minister of Industry, with the approval of YPF, to design and implement the Supplier Development Program.

SDP was able to develop a solid network of cooperation with the support and guidance of YPF and the government.[11] Due to its success, the program was extended to other oil and gas companies over the following years, 2014 and 2015, while it continued to grow within YPF.

In December 2015, a new government with a more liberal approach came to power. YPF's CEO was changed, and after a few months of impasse, the Ministry of Production launched a new SDP, which was a continuation of the previous program[12] although extended to other industry sectors.[13] The new program, "Desarrollo de Proveedores"[14] (PRODEPRO), which was first supported by a Ministerial resolution, has been backed by law,[15] providing the supplier development program with a more robust legal instrument. The law expressly excludes YPF,[16] although its Article 24 establishes that YPF should present a supplier development program to the Ministry of Production with the objective to propose strategies that will collaborate in the increase of competitiveness of local suppliers. The program should include: the annual procurement plan, the activities to be developed and their execution, the actions for fostering local content, and enhance the competitiveness of the local supply industry to meet the demand of the national oil sector. For this objective, in February 2018, the Ministry of Production and YPF signed a Memorandum of Understanding (MoU) to start with the presentation of a Supplier Development Program by YPF. After the MoU, YPF presented its 2018 procurement plan, which was later uploaded on its webpage.

The initial steps of the program are administrated through a software platform where current and new suppliers should first register and can then offer their goods, services, or projects which are later evaluated by the Ministry of Production and by YPF. If the offers are considered, then they will have meetings with the procurement department and the technical departments of YPF. The program's benefits can include technical assistance 100 per cent subsidized; a 6 per cent bonus of the interest rate[17] for fixed capital or working capital associated with

[11] M. Neuman, "Developing Policy for Local Content in Argentina," Presentation at the 10th Global Local Content Summit, International Quality and Production Center (IQPC), London, UK, 2014.

[12] The same consultant team and methodology that has been used for the previous SDP was utilized for this new SDP.

[13] The sectors incorporated were: renewable energy, nuclear energy, the railway industry, mining, water and sanitation, the naval industry, information and communication, medical equipment, and electronics (excluding consumer electronics).

[14] In English: Supplier Development Program.

[15] See law No 27437 (*Ley de compre argentino y desarrollo de proveedores*) [Argentine purchase and supplier development Law], http://servicios.infoleg.gob.ar/infolegInternet/verNorma.do?id=310020.

[16] The exclusion of this company was done to maintain full validity of law 26741 that ordered the expropriation of 51 per cent of YPF's shares, and exempted YPF from the application of the administrative regulations regarding the management and control of the state-owned companies. The law established only that YPF should create a supplier development program.

[17] The loans are provided by the public bank Banco de Inversion y Comercio Exterior [Investment and Foreign Trade Bank].

268   *Marcelo Neuman*

a project that increases production and employment; and subsidies[18] for projects that have a relevant impact on the program. These benefits are part of the supplier development program law for all sectors considered strategic. However, in oil and gas, and specifically in YPF, there is the additional benefit of becoming a supplier to the company or expanding supplies for companies that are already suppliers.

Within the institutional arrangement of Argentina's oil and gas sector, in which provinces are entitled to grant permissions and concessions of the blocks, there is little room to develop local content regulations at a national level. The national government could use the companies' bids, contracts, and similar channels of intervention for placing local content rules, but any move in this direction will surely be resisted by the producing provinces and also by YPF.

In summary, Argentina has not yet introduced the type of national-level local content policy seen in other countries in Latin America[19] or the MENA[20] region. However, there is a series of local content regulations in the oil and gas producing provinces.

2.2 *Local Content at the Subnational Level*

The oil and gas producing provinces have advanced in more traditional local content requirements with different degrees of developments. Neuquén is the province that encompasses the majority of the geological formation of "Vaca Muerta" where most of the oil and gas investments (around 80 per cent) are being directed. It is also the province where local content requirements have advanced the furthest. Local content regulations are divided into two laws: one concerning local companies and the other the local workforce.

The first provincial local content law was passed by the provincial congress on December 2010 and enacted in January 2011.[21] The law included oil, gas, and mining industries, as well as main contractors of both sectors. The so-called Buy Neuquén law gives preferences to the goods and services of "Neuquén companies." The law specifies a series of requirements that must be met to be considered a Neuquén company; requisites that are evaluated by the application authority prior to the issuing of a document certifying qualification as a Neuquén company. Suppliers must submit this document together with their quotes and offers when participating in bids or direct contracts with oil and gas, mining, or major contractor companies in order to access the law's benefits.

---

[18] The maximum subsidy can be up to 65 per cent of the total cost of the project and with a limit of USD $150,000.

[19] Ibid., p. 2.

[20] For a complete overview of the MENA region see D. S. Olawuyi, "Local content and procurement requirements in oil and gas contracts: Regional trends in the Middle East and North Africa," OIES Paper: MEP 18, The Oxford Institute for energy Studies, University of Oxford, November 2017.

[21] See provincial law No 2755 and provincial decree No 2379/12, www.rionegro.com.ar/la-ley-del-compre -neuquino-KQRN_7661803/.

The benefits supported by the law can be classified as direct and indirect. Direct benefits comprise a 7 per cent price margin for local suppliers compared with foreign and local companies that do not qualify as a "Neuquén company." Additionally, the hiring company has the obligation to allocate at least 60 per cent of the total contract value of each of the items, or types of activities included therein, to Neuquén companies, as long as there are Neuquén companies available for each item or activity. Indirect benefits involve barriers imposed to becoming a "Neuquén company." The most significant requirements were a minimum of five years residency in the province; a real address and registered office listed on the Neuquén Public Registry of Commerce with a minimum period of five years from the enactment of the law; and that 70 per cent of the company's share capital must correspond to partners who, at the time of application, have held a real address in the province of Neuquén for a period of at least five years. The Neuquén company certificate is issued for one year and must be renewed each year.

These original barriers proved to be too restrictive for promoting investments in the supplier base and a new local content law was passed in 2016[22] to ease requirements for becoming a "Neuquén company," reducing the five years and 70 per cent prerequisites to three years and 51 per cent respectively. As for local employment, Neuquén province's hydrocarbon law[23] stipulates a preference for Argentine staff, and especially those with residency in Neuquén, at all levels in companies with exploration permissions and exploitation concessions. The proportion of national staff must be at least 75 per cent and training must be provided on the specific skills required for all activities undertaken.

In the province of Chubut, the provincial hydrocarbon law[24] passed in 2012 contains some aspects related to local content regulations in oil and gas. Chapter IV of the law, Business Social Responsibility, refers to local content in some of its articles although it considers it within compliance to wider environmental issues. It establishes that business owners of hydrocarbon projects must present an environmental impact study, including a social and economic assessment, of the areas involved in the project, as well as a set of indicators to measure and monitor socioeconomic impact and a socioeconomic action plan. It also states that oil companies should hire no less than 70 per cent of workers with residency in Chubut and stipulates a domestic margin of price preference of 10 per cent for Chubut-based suppliers when quality and delivery times are comparable between offers. In addition, the law establishes that for the studies of socioeconomic assessment, the hiring of universities, institutes, consultants, and other public or private organizations located in the province of Chubut should be prioritized. As observed,

---

[22] See provincial law No 3032, http://200.70.33.130/images2/Biblioteca/3032.pdf.
[23] See provincial law No 2453 Article 94, http://normasambientales.com/ver-norma-ley-2453-ley-de-hidrocarburos-1738.html.
[24] See provincial law XVII-102, www.chubut.gov.ar/portal/medios/uploads/boletin/Enero%2007,%202013.pdf.

270   *Marcelo Neuman*

the chapter of the law focusing on local content considers a variety of mechanisms for fostering local content; however, it lacks precision and leaves much specificity to the particular negotiations between the government and the oil and gas companies.

In the far-south Patagonian province of Santa Cruz, a local content law[25] has been in existence since year 2010. The law establishes that all hydrocarbons and mining exploration and exploitation, as well as the fishing industry, operating in the province, should give preference to the local workforce, hiring at least 70 per cent of workers with no less than two years of residency in the province. It also stipulates that companies carrying out the exploration and exploitation of hydrocarbons, mining exploitation, and industrial fishing activities should prioritize working with local companies. Companies are considered local when they have been established in the province for at least three years.

However, the law was never regulated, and it stays in a sort of a limbo. There have been complaints from supplier associations that companies do not comply with the law, especially directed towards the mining industry.[26] In year 2012, the provincial congress changed certain articles of the law, increasing sanctions for companies that do not comply,[27] but the problem seems to be the enforcement of the law by the government rather than the law itself. Seven years later, in July 2019, the government further reformed some articles of the law which had ambiguous text for an efficient supervision of hiring the local workforce. It also changed the years of residency to be considered a local worker from two to three and it further increased sanctions for non-compliance.[28] The province of Santa Cruz is an example that demonstrates that even where local content regulations have been in place for many years, they do not necessarily serve their purpose if they are not sufficiently enforced or written properly owing to a lack of capability or government will.[29] Hopefully, the new changes in the law will finally make local content work properly in Santa Cruz.

Although not as important in oil and gas production as the provinces described, there are other provinces that have applied local content regulations. One of them is the province of Mendoza in the West that, in its hydrocarbons law,[30] stipulates that specific conditions should be imposed on bids to incentivize and facilitate the participation of Mendoza-based companies in the exploration and exploitation

[25] See provincial law No 3141, http://minpro.gob.ar/legislacion/mineria/leyes/ley-3141.pdf.
[26] See Editorial RN "Se cumplieron tres años de la ley 70/30 pero la falta de controles la hace inviable" (Three years of the law 70/30 has been fulfilled but the lack of supervision makes it unfeasible), July, 2014, www.editorialrn.com.ar/index.php?option=com_content&view=article&id=163:se-cumplieron -tres-anos-de-la-ley-70--30-pero-la-falta-de-controles-la-hace-inviable&catid=14&Itemid=599.
[27] See provincial law No 3297, http://gobierno.santacruz.gov.ar/boletin/12/diciembre12/ 11diciembre2012EE.pdf.
[28] See Tiempo Sur "Promulgación de la ley 70/30 con varios cambios entre ellos los años de residencia" (Promulgation of Law 70/30 with several changes including residence years), www.tiemposur.com.ar /nota/177715-la-ley-7030-con-varios-cambios-entre-ellos-los-anos-de-residencia.
[29] Interview with Alberto Salazar, Assistant professor and researcher, Universidad Nacional de la Patagonia Austral (National University of Southern Patagonia), April 2019.
[30] See provincial law No 7526, www.saij.gob.ar/LPM0007526.

Local Content and SD in Argentina   271

stages of hydrocarbon production. It also established that a minimum of 75 per cent of workers employed should have been born in Mendoza.

Similarly, the province of La Pampa, in its provincial hydrocarbon law,[31] establishes that a minimum of 80 per cent of the local workforce and suppliers should come from La Pampa. However, it also states that if labour or supplies cannot be sourced in La Pampa, or if the costs are too high, the application authority will be able to relieve the hiring company from contracting local companies.

3 IMPLEMENTING LOCAL CONTENT REGULATIONS: BARRIERS AND LIMITATIONS

This section focuses on the barriers and limitations to sustainable local content development in the three most important oil and gas provinces: Neuquén, Chubut, and Santa Cruz. These provinces lead the hydrocarbon sector in Argentina and they have been applying local content laws for long enough to make a reasonable evaluation. In addition, an assessment on the barriers and limitations of implementing local content policies at the national level is also discussed.

3.1 *The Lack of Information on Local Industry Capabilities*

The lack of a sound assessment of the local industry capabilities severely limits the design and implementation of local content initiatives. The knowledge of local businesses' abilities to supply the oil and gas industry is a key input for elaborating local content regulations. These types of studies should not only focus on the current capabilities of the local industry but also on their potential to engage in an evidence-based learning process.[32]

None of these types of studies have been done by the subnational governments prior to developing local content regulations. The local content laws were discussed with the stakeholders (the oil and gas companies, the suppliers, and the workers) but a sound evaluation of their capabilities was lacking. Although, the absence of a study of the supplier base might not have prevented all the difficulties found in the implementation of the local regulations in the provinces, it surely would have contributed to discussion of the laws in a more positive and realistic way. These types of studies provide a solid background for elaborating local content regulations by clarifying the debate on what types of policies are the most convenient. Even today, where local content regulations have been active for years, there is a need to develop studies to evaluate the capabilities of the local industry in the provinces jointly with the impact that these regulations have had so far.

---

[31]   See provincial law No 2675, https://leyes-ar.com/ley_de_hidrocarburos_la_pampa.htm.
[32]   M. Neuman, R. Tissot, and D. Mabrey, "Are Ugandan's firms ready to take advantage of the country's new opportunities in the oil industry?" (2019) (6) *Extractive Industry Society* 293–312.

272 *Marcelo Neuman*

The province of Neuquén experienced relevant obstacles when designing and implementing local content regulations. The local content law was promoted under a context where the oil and gas companies were developing cost reduction programs and it took two years for the law to become effective. However, the law proved to be too restrictive and a few years later, in 2016, the local content law was changed for a new law loosening some requirements.[33] In the period the local content law was changed, the situation for the oil and gas industry was even worse than when the first law was enacted; the international price of the West Texas Intermediate (WTI) barrel was around $35USD. In such a tough environment, the local supplier companies were aiming at maintaining their operational activity rather than seeking additional profit.[34]

In the last four to five years, Neuquén experienced an increase in investment for developing and producing its huge reserves of shale oil and shale gas.[35] These investments have promoted the activities of the supply chain, where local companies from Neuquén, and from other parts of the country, are increasing their supplies to the oil and gas industry. The dynamic positive business environment in Neuquén is demonstrating that the new local content law is again becoming too restrictive[36] to foster sustainable local content development. New supplier companies from other parts of Argentina and from abroad with new technologies and products and are increasingly seeking to supply the oil industry in the province, but the requirements for being considered a "Neuquén company" hinder innovation in the oil sector.

Shale oil and shale gas is new for the Argentinean industry and, although the country has a relevant platform of industrial capacity built on onshore oil and gas, non-conventional resources require more intense innovation activities. There is a need to know where the local supplier industry stands, what their needs and challenges are, and what the best strategies are to promote its development. The most efficient way to get this knowledge is by a thorough study of the oil industry with focus on the supplier base.

Similarly, the province of Chubut gradually implemented local content regulations during the year 2013 after the hydrocarbon provincial law had been approved the year before. However, differently from the context of Neuquén, the law was debated when the price of the WTI barrel was at a very good price, around $85USD.

[33] Ibid., pp. 5–6.

[34] Interview with Julián Cervera, CEO of the Centro de Pequeña y Mediana Empresa de la Agencia de Desarrollo Económico de Neuquén (Small and Medium Enterprise Center of the Economic Development Agency of Neuquén), April 2019.

[35] In the period 2013–18, Neuquén received $24.6 billion in investments. The investments in year 2018 showed an increase of 30 per cent compared with year 2017. See C. Navzo, "Neuquén recibió inversions por US $24,600 millones de dólares" (Neuquén received investments for 24,600 million dollars), December 1, 2018, www.lmneuquen.com/neuquen-recibio-inversiones-us-24600-millones-n614989.

[36] In particular, the minimum period of three years required to be registered Neuquén Public Registry of Commerce, and the 51 per cent of the company's share capital belonging to partners who, at the time of application, have held a real address in the province of Neuquén for a period of at least three years.

Local Content and SD in Argentina 273

Given the context of high oil prices, the objective of the hydrocarbon law was to capture part of the additional rent of the industry by increasing the royalties by 4 per cent, from 12 per cent to 16 per cent, and direct this additional public income to public works.[37] After intense negotiations and heated debate between the government, the oil and gas companies, and other stakeholders, the law was approved. The increase of royalties lead to a rise in public income from oil and gas by 30 per cent; many infrastructure works were developed in different parts of Chubut fostering economic growth. However, regarding the development of sustainable local content, the law did not prove to be an important instrument,[38] although the law establishes a series of mechanisms for fostering local content development. Not even the most precise instruments of local content law, such as the 10 per cent premium for local suppliers and that 70 per cent of the workforce must reside in Chubut, have been totally applied. On one side, there is a lack of provincial government capabilities and willingness to implement and monitor the 10 per cent premium on price for local suppliers,[39] and on the other, more than 95 per cent of the workers in the Chubut oil fields reside in Chubut.[40]

Likewise, the law stipulating local content requirements in the province of Santa Cruz was not supported by an evaluation of the local industry of the province. In this case, the local content regulation focuses on the local workforce, rather than on the companies, in an attempt to address the internal migration of workers from other provinces.[41] The local content regulation stipulated that at least 70 per cent of the workers should reside in the province for a minimum of three years. However, the oil and gas companies bypassed this requisite by using their legal addresses for the workers who did not comply with the residency period. Recently, in April 2019, the law enforced the compliance of 70 per cent obligation of hiring Santa Cruz workers by not allowing workers from other parts of the country to use that of the companies and by increasing the fines to the companies that do not comply with this obligation.[42] But

---

[37] The extra 4 per cent of the royalties would be shared in halves between the provincial government and the municipalities.

[38] Interview with Ezequiel Cufré, president of the Cámara de Empresas Regionales de Servicios Petroleros de la Cuenca del Golfo San Jorge [Regional Chamber of Petroleum Services Companies of the Saint George Gulf Basin], former Minister of Hydrocarbons of the Province of Chubut and author of the law XVI-102, April 2019.

[39] Ibid.

[40] Ibid. The 70 per cent article was lobbied by the oil unions of Chubut in response to a law passed by the oil unions of Santa Cruz that have lobbied for a similar law in their province. In the north of Santa Cruz, just 100 kilometres away from the oil city of Comodoro Rivadavia located in the province of Chubut, there is intense oil exploitation activity. It is usual for the local suppliers based in Comodoro Rivadavia to travel with their crews to work in the oil fields of Santa Cruz.

[41] Workers from other provinces of Argentina, mostly from the Northern provinces, frequently migrate to Santa Cruz to work in the extractive industry where salaries are much higher and employment rates much better than in the Northern provinces.

[42] See ADNSUR, "Santa Cruz endurece la ley "70/30." Trabajadores petroleros, mineros y pesqueros no podrán trabajar sin acreditar 3 años de residencia" (Santa Cruz toughens the "70/30" law. Oil, mining and fishing workers will not be able to work if they do not accredit three years of residency), April 12,

the obstacle to compliance with this regulation is basically the lack of sufficient skilled labour for the oil industry in an unpopulated city as Santa Cruz,[43] especially when the oil and gas activity is operating at a satisfactory level.

As in the other two provinces, the twists and turns in the implementation of sustainable local content regulations in Santa Cruz would have been significantly eased if an assessment study had been conducted by a local supplier. This is still valid today where local regulations in this province, and the other two, seem to continue in a tortuous manner without a clear view of causes of their barriers to sustain local content development.

The local content laws in the provinces are constrained to price premiums for goods and services and to ensure percentages of local labour. In addition, local content regulations have been copied between the provinces. There is a lack of more comprehensive local content development mechanisms, such as fiscal benefits, financial support, promotion of supplier development programs in specific activities, training programs, productive agreements, and other development mechanisms. The most appropriate way to elaborate these types of local content policies is with key information about the local industry's capabilities and their needs for development.

In contrast with the provinces, the national government did develop a study to evaluate the local supplier base capabilities and the capacity of the oil and gas companies to foster local supplier development.[44] The main objective was to recommend a series of local content policies at the national level and, although the proposed legislations on local content were not accepted by the government,[45] other recommended initiatives as supplier development programs were adopted. Thus, a nationwide supplier development program for the local suppliers was designed and implemented in YPF during years 2012 and 2015.[46] Due to its success the program was extended to other oil and gas companies and was the origin of the "Programa de Desarrollo de Proveedores" (PRODEPRO), currently implemented by the national government.

2019, www.adnsur.com.ar/sociedad/trabajadores-petroleros–mineros-y-pesqueros-no-podran-trabajar-sin-acreditar-3-anos-de-residencia-_a5cbo9bfbo6e32366e62463c3.

[43] Santa Cruz has an extension of 243,943 square kilometres and a population of just above 270,000 inhabitants according to the 2010 national census. The estimation of the population for year 2018 is around 348,000, https://ahoracalafate.com.ar/nota/9105/cuantos-habitantes-somos.

[44] The Ministry of Industry, the Ministry of Economy and Finance, and the Secretary of Energy requested a study by the National University of General Sarmiento, and it was financed by the Inter-American Development Bank. The study was developed by the author, who designed and directed the research.

[45] During the study, Argentina's largest oil and gas company, YPF, was partially renationalized. The new partially state-owned company was opposed to any regulation that would increase its costs. This was the view that the company had for local content regulations.

[46] The author was the general coordinator of YPF's supplier development program reporting directly to the Minister of Industry and YPF's vice-president of share services. The general coordinator worked in close collaboration with YPF's general manager of the program.

Local Content and SD in Argentina 275

In contrast with what was happening in the provinces, the main barrier of the supplier development program at that time, which is even present today, was the lack of a sound local content regulation. Today PRODEPRO is backed up by a law,[47] but there is not any consideration by the oil company for local suppliers.

3.2 *Rigid and Unfocused Local Content Regulations*

The changing oil and gas environment in Neuquén requires flexible local content regulation that can foster cooperation between local suppliers, on both the provincial and national levels, as well as with international suppliers. Investment from the international oil and gas supplier industry is a central factor for the development of the shale gas and shale oil resources, therefore finding mechanisms of cooperation between the national and international supplier industry is a key aspect for sustainable local content development not present in the local content regulation.

The local content law presents some barriers for promoting new investments in the supplier base, which is even recognized by the current provincial authorities. The provincial authorities consider the local content law a mechanism that requires continuous adjustment to cope with the new realities of the changing oil industry environment, rather than a regulation that should be applied rigidly.[48] Currently, 600 local companies linked to the oil and gas sector have been identified by the Small and Medium Enterprise Centre of the Economic Development Agency of Neuquén,[49] a fair number for a poorly populated province of 550,344 inhabitants according to the last census.[50] However, this is a small number when compared with other regions of Argentina and also too low a number to cope by itself with demands of the continuously growing oil and gas activity in the province.

Local content regulations in Chubut are an example of the lack of focus on local content issues. The local content regulations are included in the hydrocarbon provincial law that regulates very important aspects of the oil activity, such as investments, royalties, environmental issues, and the like. Within this context, local content initiatives are discussed amidst negotiations of fundamental factors, such as extension of concessions, permissions, royalties, and investments. With such important aspects in the negotiations between the government and the oil companies, there is little room for local content initiatives, which are relegated and not prioritized. Furthermore, local content regulations include clauses that the

---

[47] Ibid., p. 4.
[48] Ibid., p. 10.
[49] In Spanish: Centro de Pequeña y Mediana Empresa de la Agencia de Desarrollo (Centro PyME-ADENEU), established by law in 1998 to promote development in the province. The Centro PyME-ADENEU is in charge of applying the local content law.
[50] National census of year 2010. The Government of Argentina develops census every ten years. The estimation of the population for year 2018 is around 650,000. Migration is increasing because of oil and gas exploitation, www.infobae.com/sociedad/2019/01/27/elecciones-en-neuquen-las-deudas-pendientes-para-la-quinta-provincia-mas-rica-del-pais/.

provincial government is unwilling to enforce, such as the 10 per cent margin of price preference for local suppliers.

The local content law of the province of Santa Cruz was elaborated for the mining, oil and gas, and fishing industries without considering their differences. The lack of focus on the oil and gas industry by the regulations limited the development of the local industry in the province. Furthermore, the articles of the law stipulating oil companies prioritise contracting local suppliers was never applied since it was not clarified how this should be implemented. In addition, the mining industry resisted the implementation of the law, especially the articles stipulating the obligation that at least 70 per cent of workers be residents of the province, while the oil industry bypassed this obligation by registering the workers in their legal addresses in the province. This behaviour by oil companies continued for years until the law was enforced in April 2019, specifically banning this practice and increasing the penalties to the companies that do not comply with this obligation.[51] Developing a local content regulation to fit the three different industries hindered the implementation of sound local initiatives in all sectors since the regulation did not cope with specific obstacles that each sector had for improving its supplier base and labour.

Regarding local content at the national level, this was basically oriented to supplier development programs. There are three main barriers in this type of local content initiative. First, the law only considers the oil and gas company YPF, leaving out more than 50 per cent of the oil and gas production. Second, the regulating decree of the law stipulates that YPF, jointly with the supplier development program, should present the annual procurement plan and the actions to promote local content in the supplier base. Without any references to numerical targets for fostering the supplier base and without any appropriate reference to the breakdown of the procurement plan, this leaves the regulation in the hands of YPF to enhance the supplier base, or not. A third limitation is that there are no penalties if YPF does not comply, leaving the regulation to the will of the company.

3.3 Non-Coordination at the Subnational and National Level

The lack of coordination between the provinces and the national government, especially in local content policies, hinders opportunities for sustainable local content development.

The national government's local content policies are basically reduced to a supplier development program by Argentina's largest oil and gas company without any mention of the provinces where YPF has upstream and downstream operations.[52] This fact could turn the supplier development programs to specific

---

[51] Ibid., p. 11.
[52] YPF has upstream operations in the provinces of Neuquén, Chubut, Santa Cruz, Mendoza, La Pampa, and Río Negro, and downstream operations in the provinces of Neuquén, Mendoza, and Buenos Aires.

Local Content and SD in Argentina

sectors or regions that do not have sustainable local content development. While it is reasonable that YPF should develop its supplier development programs based on its own needs, it is also important for the government to intervene more proactively. Close cooperation between the national government and the oil companies has proved to be synergistic in the past for both stakeholders and therefore for the local supplier base.

Lack of coordination between the oil producing provinces is another factor that prevents elaboration of comprehensive local content regulations and deters more effective development of the supplier base. When regulating local content, the oil producing provinces tend to keep local content development to themselves or base their local content regulations on what other provinces have done. The frequent quarrels between the suppliers and oil unions of Chubut and Santa Cruz are an example of how some local content regulations were elaborated in these provinces.

While the attitude of keeping oil and gas resources for the original owners is understandable and the provinces have the right to benefit the most from them, they will not be able to take advantage of full benefits without close cooperation with the national government. Sound and sustainable local content development will be achieved in each province if local content regulations are conceived of in a more holistic manner, where regulating preferences for the provincial suppliers or labour could also be present. There is a need to find mechanisms of close cooperation between the different jurisdictions in order to progress with more sound and holistic local content regulations.

4 DEVELOPING STRATEGIES FOR SUSTAINABLE LOCAL CONTENT IN ARGENTINA

While the oil producing provinces might have some specific barriers limiting sustainable local content, most barriers are common to all of them. Moreover, specific barriers are likely to be overcome if shared barriers are addressed. In this section, we highlight some recommendations on how those common barriers can be addressed. The recommendations outlined are interconnected and should be seen as an integrated approach to sustainable local content in Argentina.

4.1 Evaluate Industry Capabilities

The evaluation of different industries' capacity to supply the oil and gas sector should be performed in a consistent manner. While each province should have their own assessment, it is advisable to coordinate this task between the provinces and with the national government. A coordinated study will not only provide a better background, it will also help in the dialogue needed between the different stakeholders.

278   *Marcelo Neuman*

The type of evaluation should also be discussed between the stakeholders. Topics such as the methodology of the study, the main objectives, the basic steps or phases, and the reporting and coordinated mechanisms should be part of the discussion. An important factor to include is the performance of the local content regulations in each province and at the national level.

A study of this kind, highly articulated, will shed some light on the opportunities for improving the supplier industry and the barriers that hinder its development. Moreover, it will constitute a key input to develop more consistent and sustainable local content regulations at the national and provincial level.

4.2 *Develop More Comprehensive Oil and Gas Local Content Policies*

Frequently, local content regulations for oil and gas are shared with the mining and other industries, in an attempt to deal with all types of local content policies at once. This sort of strategy is largely ineffective since it does not consider the specific needs of the oil supplier industry, and, in an effort to standardize the incentives, it lacks specificity on the features that can be fostered in the oil and gas industry. Local content regulation in oil and gas should, among other policies, provide tax incentives for knowledge-intensive activities in an attempt to add value to the supplier chain. Similarly, specific incentives for contributing to the development of shale oil and shale gas resources should also be considered, such as developing linkages with national and international research centres, promoting joint ventures with international companies and technology-transfer mechanisms. The mining and oil and gas industries bear important differences in Argentina. While the mining industry works more like an enclave industry, the oil and gas industry encompasses the whole value chain, from upstream to downstream operations, supported by a relevant number of goods and services suppliers.

4.3 *Coordinate Local Content Initiatives*

The lack of coordination between the oil producing provinces and between them and the national government hinders important opportunities to sustain local content development. There is a need to provide a stable mechanism for coordinating local content activities between the public sectors. Coordination of the local content initiatives will help to alleviate the typical problems that arise between the oil producing provinces, and with the national government, which later are reflected in the local content regulations.

Argentina already has a mechanism for discussing oil and gas policies between the oil producing provinces and the national government. This is the OFEPHI (Federal Organization of State Hydrocarbon Producers).[53] However, the mission of the

---

[53]   OFEPHI, note 2.

OFEPHI is limited to the debate on oil and gas between the oil producing provinces and the national government. It would be important for the OFEPHI to enlarge its mission and consider additional relevant topics of the industry, such as local content regulations among others. Even the evaluation study proposed in Section 4.1 could be channelled through the OFEPHI. Therefore, the OFEPHI should be expanded from a mere institution conceived to defend the oil producing provinces' interests to a more robust institution which can cope with different aspects related to oil and gas.

5 CONCLUSION

Widespread and sustainable local development in Argentina can best be addressed by close cooperation between the national government and the oil producing provinces. The lack of coordination for elaborating a legal and institutional framework for local content hinders many opportunities that a middle-developed country with a sizeable industrial base like Argentina can exploit. An institutionalized cooperation network for industrial development based on the natural resources of oil and gas with the participation of the public and private sector and technical support of the scientific and technological community[54] can even help to counterbalance the periodic and intense shifts between interventionist and liberal governments that usually erode cumulative experience in specific areas.

Furthermore, there are constraints for developing local content policies within the framework of international treaties that regulate trade between nations.[55] There is a series of international treaties that affect local content regulations by limiting some of the options for domestic LCR implementation.[56] Argentina participates in most of these treaties and is a member of the World Trade Organization which supervises compliance of international regulations. Medium- and long-term local content development planning should also consider the barriers imposed by international regulations, on the way to developing strategies to ease these potential constraints for industrialization based on natural resources.

---

[54] The scientific and technological community encompasses research and development institutes, and universities.

[55] Ibid., p. 2.

[56] Basically within the World Trade Organization (WTO) where the most relevant agreements with implications for local content policies include the General Agreement on Tariffs and Trade (GATT), the agreement on Trade-Related Investment Measures (TRIMs), the General Agreement on Trade in Services (GATS), and the agreement on Government Procurement (GPA). S. Tordo et al., note 6.

15

The Latin American Experience in Designing Local Content Policies in the Oil and Gas Sectors: Strengths, Limitations, and Future Perspectives

Amir Lebdioui and Marcela Morales

1 INTRODUCTION

This chapter evaluates the evolution and design of local content policies in Latin America. It examines the extent to which local content requirements (LCRs) have contributed to overall sustainable development in oil and gas producing countries in the region, the gaps that remain, and policy approaches for enhancing LCR implementation in the region.

The recent resurgence of interest in local content policies in the oil and gas sectors are part of a broader policy and academic debate around harnessing non-renewable resources for sustainable development. Policy-makers in many oil and gas producing countries have considered local content policies to be an attractive option to enhance the externalities of the petroleum sector beyond the fiscal rent generated by raw material exports. However, key questions must be asked: what are the short term and long term objectives of LCRs? How can the success or otherwise of LCRs be measured? How do LCRs fit in broader sustainable development strategy? Can LCRs promote the diversification process to reduce commodity dependence, and if so, how?

For a long time, and in many countries, local content policies have been used in the petroleum sectors only to maximise local employment generation and economic benefits of oil and gas extraction, with little consideration for how local content policies can benefit the domestic industries on the long run, or help achieve the diversification of the domestic economy. However, given the more recent body of knowledge, as well as the mixed results stemming from the implementation of local content policies in recent decades, it is important to shift the discussion on the objective of LCRs towards the agenda of sustainable industrialisation and long-term diversification, as notably discussed by Ovadia.[1] In such a perspective, several key

---

[1] J. S. Ovadia, 'Is Natural Resource-Based Development Still Realistic for Africa?' February 10, 2016, www.e-ir.info/2016/02/10/is-natural-resource-based-development-still-realistic-for-africa/; J. S. Ovadia, *The Petro-Developmental State in Africa: Making Oil Work in Angola, Nigeria and the Gulf of Guinea*

Latin American Experience Designing LCPs 281

factors can be underlined for the successful design and implementation of local content policies.

The Latin American experience is particularly informative in the study of the different factors that impact local content outcomes. Indeed, Latin America has a long history of oil and a gas production, and most countries in the region have adopted a diverse range of local content measures to maximise the economic benefits of the petroleum sector, in a rather heterogeneous manner, and achieving diverse outcomes.[2] Brazil and Mexico have adopted local content policies in the most comprehensive way, with important reforms and adaptations over time, but local content policies in the rest of the region have been somewhat inconsistent and broad, especially in comparison with other regions of the world.[3]

This chapter reviews the experience of several oil and gas producing countries in Latin America by analysing the local content policies and their sustainable development outcomes in terms of local employment, national industry participation, and skills development. The chapter identifies the strengths and limitations of the different local content frameworks implemented in Latin America. It then explores the factors that influence the outcomes of local content policies as a tool for sustainable development and diversification. Four key factors are highlighted for discussion: the role of specificity of local content frameworks; the role of national oil companies; the role of capability-building programmes and opportunities for learning by doing for long-run competitiveness; as well as the role of regional cooperation to avoid the fallacy of composition and maximise economies of scale.

To be successful and sustainable in the long run, local content requirements and policies need to be accompanied by capacity-building programmes to provide the skills required for local content activities, as well as provide opportunities for learning by doing. In contrast, broad protectionist approaches focused on short-term goals, such

---

(London: Hurst, 2016) 1-25; J. S. Ovadia, 'Local content policies and petro-development in Sub-Saharan Africa: a comparative analysis' (2016) 49 *Resources Policy* 20–30.

[2] M. Morales, J. J. Herrera, and S. Jarrin, 'Local Content Frameworks in Africa and Latin America: Experiences from Ecuador And Colombia,' Research Paper Series, Evidence and lessons from Latin America, Regional Evidence Papers, April 2016; M. Morales, J. J. Herrera, D. Mushemeza, and J. Okiira, 'What Matters When It Comes to Adopting Local Content in the Oil and Gas Sector? A Comparative Analysis of Success Factors in Africa and Latin America,' Research Paper Series, Evidence and lessons from Latin America, Comparative Evidence Paper, 2017.

[3] S. Tordo and Y. Anouti, 'Local Content in the Oil and Gas Sector: Case Studies,' A World Bank Study, 2013; G. A. Musik Asali, R. Espinasa, and M. Walter, 'Energy Reform and Local Content In Mexico: Effects in the Mining Sector,' Inter-Development Bank, Energy Division, Infrastructure and Environmental Sector, Technical Note No. IDB-TN-771, April 2015; C. Kennedy, 'Mexican Local Content Rules Could Complicate Oil Investment' April 1, 2014, https://oilprice.com/Latest-Energy-News/World-News/Mexican-Local-Content-Rules-Could-Complicate-Oil-Investment .html; R. O'Connor and L. Viscidi, 'La Reforma Energética en México: Cerrando la Brecha de Habilidades (The Energy Reform in Mexico: Bridging the Skills Gap),' Inter-American Dialogue, June 2015; M. Place, 'Brasil Revisará Contenido Local para Atraer Inversionistas Petroleros,' May 5, 2015, www.bnamericas.com/es/news/petroleoygas/brasil-revisara-contenido-local-para-atraer-inver sionistas-petroleros1.

282 Amir Lebdioui and Marcela Morales

as local employment, are unlikely to increase the capabilities and competitiveness of local suppliers in the long run. Also, the role of a strategic regional approach to local content policies has often been neglected. Increased regional cooperation to foster industrial complementarities can help address the challenge of gradual competitiveness and scaling up for local suppliers in Latin America. This chapter provides policymakers in Latin America, and elsewhere, with insights and perspectives on how local content strategies can be improved to promote sustainable development and diversification further.

This chapter is divided into four sections. After this introduction, Section 2 examines local content frameworks in six Latin American countries, while Section 3 focuses on the factors that impact the outcomes of these frameworks. Finally, Section 4 presents conclusions and recommendations.

2 LOCAL CONTENT FRAMEWORKS AND OUTCOMES IN LATIN AMERICA

This section evaluates local content frameworks of major oil and gas producing countries in Latin America and their outcomes.[4] This section provides a synthesis of the review conducted on local content frameworks in six Latin American countries.[5]

As stated in the introduction of this chapter, Latin American countries feature divergent and heterogeneous approaches to local content laws and policies. On the one hand, Brazil and Mexico offer the most comprehensive strategies to local content policies and have defined and revisited these measures to adapt them to the changes and challenges of the oil and gas industry.[6] On the other hand, Argentina, Bolivia, Colombia, Ecuador, and Venezuela have established provisions within their respective national laws to promote local employment (and to a much lesser extent national industry participation and skills development) within the oil and gas sector but have not developed comprehensive, institutionalised, and explicit local content strategies.

2.1 Legal Mechanisms

The adoption of local content in Latin America has been diverse and has shown different approaches to this strategy. Various aspects of local content, such as the promotion of national industries or the generation of local employment along the oil and gas value chain, are included in most legislation across the region. Most

---

[4] The seven countries selected in the Morales et al. (2016) study, note 2, are Argentina, Bolivia, Brazil, Colombia, Ecuador, Mexico, and Venezuela.

[5] Morales et al. (2016), note 2; ELLA, 'Outline of Learning Alliance on Oil And Gas – Local Content: Boosting the Benefits from the Oil and Gas Sector through Local Content,' Learning Alliance Highlights, Oil and Gas Local Content, 2016.

[6] Kennedy, note 3; Musik Asali et al., note 3; O'Connor et al., note 3.

countries in the region have not developed specific local content laws. Local content provisions are embedded in sectorial laws, mostly in the legal instruments that regulate the hydrocarbons sector in each country.

In Brazil, the central government is in charge of all the decisions related to the oil and gas sector. The national strategies have prioritised the participation of the national industry in the value chain. The National Petroleum Agency was created under the Hydrocarbons Law with the mandate to implement, regulate, supervise, and monitor local content across the country.[7] This entity has a separate legal framework that details how local content should be implemented and measured. The main focus of this framework is on the promotion of the participation of the national oil and gas industry.[8] Brazil promotes local content in all exploration and exploitation contracts. The provisions in the contracts are very detailed and include local content quotas applied to all bidding processes. Beyond local content requirements, the national local content policy also establishes the mandate of the national oil company, *Petróleo Brasileiro S.A* (Petrobras) as a key institution in the enhancement of the competitiveness of local suppliers.[9] Brazil has one of the most comprehensive local content strategies in Latin America, which often serves as an example to other countries.

Mexico, after Brazil, is among the countries in the region with the most detailed local content legal frameworks in the region. The national development strategy is built around the country's ability to foster local content and strengthen the local industry and the local providers across the value chain. Mexico's Hydrocarbons Law supports local content through specific provisions that seek to strengthen local providers at the national level. These provisions include criteria to measure local content during bidding and contracting processes, and also define fines and sanctions in case of non-compliance.[10]

Mexico's oil and gas industry has a strong history of protectionism and nationalisation since the 1930s. The national industrialisation strategy had achieved positive outcomes, such as the development of a competitive industrial base outside the oil sector, but Mexico's monopoly and protectionism over the oil and gas industry have resulted in some challenges such as reduced investment levels in exploration, among other issues.[11] However, a different national content policy for the hydrocarbons sector was initiated in 2008 as a result of a legislative reform, called 'Ley de Petróleos Mexicanos.' This law required the national oil company, *Petróleos Mexicanos* (Pemex) to increase its local content level by 25 per cent by establishing mandatory local content provisions in its contracts, as well as enhance its suppliers

---

[7] Morales et al. (2016), note 2.
[8] Ibid.
[9] Ibid.
[10] Ibid.
[11] H. Nordas, E. Vatne, and P. Heum, 'The Upstream Petroleum Industry and Local Industrial Development: A Comparative Study', Institute for Research in Economics and Business Administration, May 2003; Morales et al. (2017), note 2.

284 Amir Lebdioui and Marcela Morales

and contractors' capacity to fulfil the upstream needs of Mexico's oil and gas industry.[12] Pemex was consequently required to publish a supplier development strategy which resulted in the issuance of the Strategy for Developing Suppliers, Contractors and National Content in 2009.[13] In Mexico, Pemex's actions towards supporting domestic suppliers are thus guided by the Hydrocarbons Law and the Strategy for the Development of Local Contractors and National Content.

In Ecuador, local content provisions are strongly concentrated in the labour market. The Hydrocarbons Law establishes provisions regarding quotas to promote local employment and requires oil and gas companies to implement programmes and internships for local students and workers to develop their capabilities.[14] Related provisions that support this mandate are also present in the general laws such as the Ecuadorian Labor Law. The Hydrocarbons Law also regulates the participation of national industries in the oil and gas sector. The law indicates that local providers and companies should be given preference over international companies.[15] Overall, the legal framework is very detailed about local content; however, it does not include monitoring or evaluation mechanisms to oversee the implementation and effectiveness of local content measures.

Local content provisions in Colombia are scattered across various laws. Most local content provisions are related to the promotion of local employment and are present in the country's legal framework for employment.[16] What is interesting in the case of Colombia, is that there are not any legal provisions to encourage a preference for national companies over foreign companies. Overall, legal provisions encourage competition to promote innovation and growth. The country strongly emphasises the development of training programmes to develop skills among employees. The National Innovation Fund has been created for this purpose.

In Bolivia, local content provisions are mainly concentrated in the Hydrocarbons Law. The main focus of the local content strategy is to ensure that contracts held between the National Oil Company and private companies include a local content strategy.[17] However, other measures or requirements are not mentioned in the law.

In Argentina, local content is not openly mentioned in sector legal frameworks. The Constitution and the Hydrocarbons Law indicate that oil resources and their related decisions are under the responsibility of the provinces. Each province has the liberty to establish specific conditions and requirements in their dealings with

---

[12] M. Grunstein and C. Diaz-Wionczek, 'Local Content in The Petroleum Industry – Mexico' (Baker Institute, February 2017), pp. 2–8. Before 2008, no local content requirements were considered mandatory in Mexico.

[13] In this strategic plan, the local content baseline estimated was 35.1 per cent, and the target was to increase it to 43.9 per cent in 2019. See Grunstein and Diaz-Wionczek (2007), note 12.

[14] Morales et al. (2016), note 2.

[15] Ibid.

[16] Ibid.

[17] Ibid.

Latin American Experience Designing LCPs

national and international companies and suppliers. However, local laws do not mention local content regulations.[18]

The next section discusses the approaches and objectives of different local content frameworks across Latin America.

2.2 *The Focus of Local Content Frameworks*

In its broadest meaning, local content policies now generally refer to the actions a country can take to increase local participation in the extractive sector through promotion of the local supply of labour, goods, and services. A survey of LCRs in Latin America reveals two distinct approaches: prioritisation of local employment; and focus on national industry participation. Interestingly, most Latin American countries, with the exceptions of Brazil and Mexico (and Colombia to a lesser extent), have local content laws that focus much more on local employment than skills development and national industry participation in the supply chain.[19]

The prioritisation of local employment is a popular strategy and can be explained by the fact that local employment quotas are easy tools to adopt in the short term with limited investment required (in comparison to other strategies such as quotas for national industry participation or skills development programmes), while benefits can be seen relatively quickly, especially for communities living close to extraction areas.[20] The resistance from foreign extractive companies to local employment quotas is also lower, as local labour is usually cheaper than foreign extraction and can contribute to cost reduction in the long run. Nevertheless, local employment tend to be limited to low-skilled activities, unless there are incentives for firms to train and/or hire local managers and highly skilled professionals or local content provisions target different types and levels of professional activities for which local staff is preferred (this notion is further elaborated in Section 3.1 on the specificity of local content laws).

On the other hand, Brazil and Mexico show a stronger focus on national industry participation (followed by skills development), which is explained by the establishment of local content minimums for bidding processes and capacity-building programmes for suppliers.[21] In terms of skills development (and capacity building more broadly), Colombia, Brazil, and Mexico (to a lesser extent) are the countries

---

[18] Ibid.

[19] Morales et al. (2016), note 2; ELLA, note 5. For instance, Ecuador, Venezuela, and Bolivia have established the most provisions regarding local employment within their frameworks but none of those countries has developed specific provisions regarding national industry participation and skills development (Morales et al., 2015). In Venezuela, local content provisions found in the Hydrocarbon Law and General Labour Law mainly focus on local employment and set minimum quotas for Venezuelan workers, as well as fines if those quotas are not met (ibid.). Bolivia features a similar approach, although the government recently begun to promote national industry participation as well.

[20] Morales et al. (2016), note 2.

[21] Ibid.

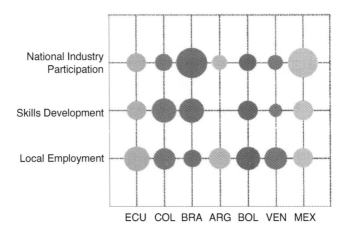

FIGURE 15.1 Local content strategies in Latin America[22]

that have made the most provisions to enhance technology transfer and skills development (the importance and impact of capacity building and learning by doing in Brazil and Mexico is further examined in Section 3.2).

The countries that have focused their local content policies more on local employment while neglecting national industry participation and skills development, namely Bolivia, Ecuador, and Venezuela, also registered the lowest scores in terms of local content outcomes, as shown by Figure 15.2. Indeed, Ecuador, Bolivia, and Venezuela have achieved high rates of local employment and skills development in the hydrocarbons industry, but without witnessing the development of a local suppliers base that can contribute to industrial development and diversification. In contrast, as observed by Morales et al.[23] and as illustrated by the cases of Brazil, Mexico, and Colombia, countries that place a stronger emphasis on skills development and national industry participation tend to achieve better local content outcomes.

The neglect of national industry participation can thus be quite problematic given that national industry participation is the dimension of local content that holds the most significant potential for maximising industrial spillovers. Also, while countries at early stages of local content implementation tend to focus more on local employment generation rather than knowledge transference and national industry participation, the emphasis on national industry participation seems to be correlated with advanced stages of local content implementation.[24] Hence, it appears that with more experience in local content implementation, countries tend to move their

---

[22] Ibid.
[23] Ibid. See also D. Olawuyi, *Extractives Industry Law in Africa* (New York: Springer, 2018), pp. 233–264.
[24] Morales et al. (2016), note 2; ELLA, note 5.

local content laws towards national industry participation and skills development, beyond local employment alone.

In the case of Brazil, similarly to Colombia, local content has been introduced as an important criterion in the bidding processes for oil and gas contracts. Such innovative measures enabled the successful incorporation of local content considerations in bidding processes in competitive terms, as contractors were left to compete in terms of displaying higher local integration with national suppliers. Nevertheless, in Brazil, from 1997 with the issuance of the Brazilian National Petroleum Law until recently when the government decided to waive local content rules for offshore exploration to attract foreign investment, a minimum threshold for local content was introduced in competitive biddings for concession contracts. It can be argued that such inclusion of local content consideration in competitive bidding has been extremely successful with average local content commitments resulting from bidding rounds increasing from 27 per cent in 1999 to 84 per cent in 2008 in Brazil.[25][26]

In Mexico, the other successful case in Latin America in terms of local content outcomes, local content policy has evolved through time. Since its creation, Pemex had a mandate to source capital goods locally, and local content provisions in bidding processes are established in the Mexican Hydrocarbons Law. While contractors must prove compliance with at least 40 per cent of local content in their operations, procurement proposals that include higher participation of Mexican personnel, goods, and services, receive favourable treatment during the selection process, similarly to Colombia and Brazil's approach.[27] However, the local content policy in Mexico has been plagued by corruption, technological shortcomings, and lack of competitiveness. Since 2008, the Government of Mexico has adopted legislative reforms to align local content policies with strategic and competitiveness considerations, including the promotion of capacity development programmes and intra-industry dialogue alongside mere local content requirements.

3 FACTORS THAT SHAPE LOCAL CONTENT OUTCOMES IN LATIN AMERICA

Despite the enactment of comprehensive policies and laws on LCRs in the Latin America region, LCRs have not resulted in expected levels of economic, social, and environmental development in these countries. The application of LCRs in oil and gas

---

[25] Mechanisms to ensure compliance are also an important part of the Brazilian local content model with fines to contractors that fail to meet their local content obligations.

[26] Tordo et al., note 3; F. Neuhaus, 'New Local Content Rules for the Brazilian Offshore Oil Exploration Sector and the Challenges for the Next Decades in the Ultra-Deepwater Pre-Salt Layers,' iManagementBrazil, 2014; Morales et al., note 2.

[27] O'Connor et al., note 3.

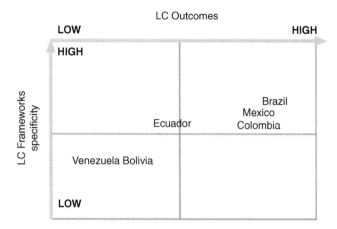

FIGURE 15.2 Relation specificity – outcomes[30]

producing countries in Latin America has achieved mixed results, notably because of high barriers to local participation, especially in countries with little existing capacity.[28] These barriers to localisation are notable because the oil and gas industries are characterised by high capital investment, specialised and technologically complex inputs, as well as consolidated global supply chains to reduce costs and guarantee quality standards. Hence, the fact that an activity is related to a country's natural resource endowment does not necessarily mean that this country has 'easier' or privileged access to such action. This section provides an overview of critical factors that influence the sustainability and successful impact of LCRs on economic development.

3.1 The Specificity of Local Content Laws

Morales et al. compared the local content outcomes in the region and have shown that the degree of specificity of the local content framework is positively correlated with higher local content outcomes.[29]

Countries such as Argentina, Bolivia, and Venezuela have achieved low levels of both local content outcomes and local content frameworks specificity, mainly due to a lack of local content provisions in their legal frameworks and the poor quality of available information. In contrast, Brazil, Colombia, and Mexico have achieved a high level of specificity of local content provisions in national law, policy, and contracts, as well as high levels of local content outcomes.

---

[28] Tordo et al., note 3.
[29] For more information on the methodology to assess local content outcomes and specificity, see Morales et al. (2016), note 2.
[30] Ibid.

For instance, in contrast to the countries that achieve low specificity scores, the Brazilian Hydrocarbons Law also included the creation of a National Petroleum Agency (ANP) to implement, regulate, and supervise local content policies and practices, as well as provide a detailed framework on how local content should be measured in the country.[31] The Brazilian local content framework also outlines different provisions regarding local content and minimum percentages to be observed by the concessionaires, as well as includes a local content certification system, which established a methodology and transparent rules to calculate the percentage of local content in goods and services in Brazil.[32] While the 'local' dimension of local content can be understood in several ways, the Brazilian constitution of 1988 also used to distinguish companies incorporated in Brazil but controlled by non-Brazilians from companies incorporated in Brazil and controlled by Brazilians.[33]

In contrast to Brazil, in Argentina, which featured the lowest specificity score among the countries studied, the National Constitution and the Hydrocarbons Law confer the ownership of oil and gas to the local provinces. As a result, while national laws contain provisions regarding the percentage of local employees that must be hired in oil and gas operations, local content policies remain very basic and broad at the national level. At the provincial level, only four of the ten oil-producing provinces have a Hydrocarbons Law, and only some of those include necessary provisions for local content.[34]

Hence, it appears that countries that have more specific local content frameworks have achieved better local content outcomes than countries with broad and general local content provisions that enabled contractors to exploit loopholes. However, it is interesting to note that even though Ecuador and Colombia scored similarly in terms of the specificity of their local content frameworks, they feature divergent local content outcomes, with Colombia's outcome being much higher than that of Ecuador. This difference between Ecuador and Colombia sheds light on the fact that local content performances can be influenced by other factors, which Morales et al. identified as the role of the divergence in business-friendly environments.[35] However, the similar level of specificity of local content provisions does not necessarily mean that the two countries' frameworks also featured

---

[31] V. Galante, 'Local Content in Brazil,' May 8, 2013, www.mayerbrown.com/local-content-in-brazil-05-08-2013/.

[32] Ibid.

[33] However, with the Constitutional Amendment no.6/1995, such distinction was revoked, and companies incorporated in Brazil were considered 'Brazilian companies' for all legal purposes, no matter the origin of the capital or the nationality of the shareholders (ibid.).

[34] Morales et al. (2016), note 2; Morales et al. (2017), note 2.

[35] In contrast to Colombia, Ecuador features a more protectionist system, not only with limited incentives to develop the capacities of local suppliers but also featuring a challenging business environment (which was identified by private oil companies as the main reason impeding local content, despite the existence of preferential measures in favour of national suppliers, heavy taxation, and import barriers); Morales et al. (2016), note 2, pp. 29–30.

similar strategies and approaches towards local content, which leads us to the next sections of this chapter that highlight additional factors that matter when implementing local content policies.

3.2 The Role of NOCs

The role of National Oil Companies[36] in boosting national industry participation can also be emphasised, as notably evidenced through country experiences reviewed throughout the Learning Alliance[37] on local content policies in the oil and gas sectors.[38] In Latin America, the countries that tend to display high local content outcomes in the oil and gas sectors, such as Brazil, Mexico, and Colombia, for instance, Petrobras (Brazil), Pemex (Mexico), and Ecopetrol (Colombia) have played proactive roles in the implementation of industrialisation plans and supplier development programmes to develop the skills and capacity of local suppliers. This trend is also reflected outside the region. In Malaysia for instance, Petronas, the national oil corporation, has played a key role in investing in upstream capabilities as well as developing the capacity of local suppliers through a vendor development programme, a 'touring clinic' for suppliers, and investment in technical training institutes.[39]

While the experiences of Petrobras in Brazil and Pemex in Mexico show that NOCs can have generated positive local content outcomes when NOCs follow clear institutional guidelines on local content that are embedded within the companies' corporate strategies, the experiences of PDVSA in Venezuela, YPFB in Bolivia, or Petroamazonas in Ecuador, show that strong NOCs do not necessarily play an active and positive role in the implementation of local content policies. Indeed, the importance of the NOC does not necessarily translate into positive local content outcomes. What Section 3.1 shows is that what matters is not the 'strength' of the NOC, but whether or not the NOC gets involved in capacity-building programmes to achieve local content objectives.

3.3 Capacity Building, Learning by Doing, and Long-Term Competitiveness

This section discusses innovative strategies and approaches for improving sustainable development outcomes of LCRs in Latin American countries. While several

[36] NOCs in Bolivia, Ecuador, Mexico, and Venezuela are owned by the state whereas in Argentina, Colombia, and Brazil, NOCs function under a private-public mixed ownership. In all seven countries, NOCs are the main oil and gas producers.

[37] The 'ELLA Learning Alliance on Local Content Policies in the Oil and Gas Sectors' ran from May 2016 to November 2016, bringing together participants from a number of African and Latin American countries, as part of the Evidence and Lessons from Latin America program, a south–south cooperation initiative facilitating comparative research and knowledge exchange between Latin America and Africa.

[38] ELLA, note 5.

[39] A. Lebdioui, 'Local content in extractive industries: Evidence and lessons from Chile's copper sector and Malaysia's petroleum sector' (2019) 7(2) The Extractive Industries and Society, 341–352.

petroleum producers in Latin America have relied on local content requirements to increase value addition and domestic job creation, those requirements have often led to adverse outcomes, as outlined in the first section of this chapter. Quotas have often been either too high, scaring away investors, or too broad, enabling investors to exploit ambiguities.[40] More importantly, the government has often used local content quotas (through regulations) without investing in the process of capabilities accumulation in parallel, leading to a trade-off between local content and competitiveness. The salient challenge is thus to find the balance between local content requirements and competitive, efficient, and quality supply-chain development.[41] The following recommendations can help Latin American countries to achieve this balance.

3.3.1 Integration of Local Suppliers into the Value Chain

One of the key factors that determine the success of LCRs is indeed the extent to which local content frameworks envision long-term competitiveness and the integration of local suppliers to international supply chains, which is crucial to reduce commodity dependence and promote industrial development. While it is generally accepted that global supply chains in the oil and gas sectors are highly consolidated, several cases across developing countries prove that such high entry barriers to established international supply chains can be overcome.[42] Also, looking at several historical experiences of petroleum producing countries, such as Norway and Malaysia, it is striking that several internationally competitive activities within the extractive sectors had initially begun as a domestic need to develop capabilities to extract domestic oil resources (such as offshore extraction equipment in Norway).

In contrast with the experience of Latin American countries that achieved lower local content outcomes, in the countries that deliver the highest local content outcomes in Latin America, Mexico, and Brazil, the NOCs (Pemex and Petrobras) developed and participated in capacity-development programmes designed to support local content objectives.[43]

---

[40] Columbia Center on Sustainable Investment, 'Local content in Malaysia,' 2016.

[41] Grunstein et al., note 13.

[42] For instance, West African oil producers such as Cameroon and Nigeria, generated ecosystems of internationally competitive firms providing support functions to operations, logistics, and maintenance in the sector (J. Bond and J. Fajgenbaum, 'Harnessing Natural Resources for Diversification' (2014) 6 *Global Journal of Emerging Market Economies*). In Malaysia, several SMEs that were appointed as suppliers to Petronas have now become globally competitive suppliers (such as Proeight, SCOMI, and Sapura Kencana, amongst others) and now operate in more than twenty countries worldwide. See Lebdioui (2019), note 39.

[43] In Ecuador for instance, despite the strong role of the NOC (PetroAmazonas), and the adoption of local content laws, PetroAmazonas has not been involved in meaningful capacity-building programmes for local suppliers.

The following section examines the implementation of capacity-building programmes in Mexico and Brazil more closely.[44] More particularly, we have divided the experience of each country according to four primary mechanisms of capacity building: frameworks and legislation for the promotion of capacity building; funding and credit financing for suppliers; supplier development programmes; and intra-industry dialogue.

3.3.2 Supporting Capacity Building and Competitiveness

To be successful and sustainable on the long run, local content requirements and policies need to be accompanied by capacity-building programmes to provide the skills required for local content activities as well as provide opportunities for learning by doing.

Beyond mere local content requirements alone, sustainable local content policies thus require capacity building programmes (through supplier development programme, intra-industry dialogue to share information and quality requirements) to build competitiveness in the long run. The gradual accumulation of expertise, technology, knowledge, and engineering skills through learning by doing, enables local firms to gradually meet the demand for inputs and services required in petroleum operations but also to produce more sophisticated inputs over time and consequently add more value to the petroleum sector.

As a result of such holistic approaches to local content in the petroleum sector, even though countries gradually phase out local content requirement because of their commitments with the WTO, they would have built a competitive supplier base that will no longer need infant industry protection. To achieve positive local content outcomes, local content policies need to be part of a broader strategy and long-term vision for value addition in the petroleum sector.

In such a context, it is perhaps useful to contrast the Latin American experience with the Malaysian case, for instance, where Petronas notably incites international oil companies based in Malaysia to train and use local suppliers but also integrates local suppliers in its international operations (notably in Vietnam and Sudan), further helping them in their internationalisation efforts and developing economies of scale. Those internationalisation efforts in upstream activities of both Petronas and its local suppliers can notably also be explained by the relatively limited national hydrocarbons reserves and the need to compete for international markets to reach economies of scale and maintain productivity.

---

[44] Although the focus is on Mexico and Brazil, it can be noted that Ecopetrol in Colombia, which ranks as the third country in Latin America in terms of local content outcomes, has also developed a series of programmes to strengthen the capacities of local suppliers and enhance skills among the local workforce, notably through various training programmes and the set up of a National Innovation Fund. Morales et al. (2016), note 2.

In contrast, in Mexico, the methodology underlying Pemex's supplier development strategy (which both forecasted Pemex's future demand and assessed the production level and competitiveness capacity of local providers), had only looked at domestic demand while neglecting the importance of regional and global demand and supply. The Mexican strategy does not seem to include an aggressive export strategy, despite the Pemex supplier development strategy mentioning export considerations as one of its objectives. In fact, instead of listing actions to promote the long-term international competitiveness and exports of domestic suppliers, the Pemex strategy has mostly addressed the ability of suppliers to export in the context of identifying them to close the domestic gap between national supply and Pemex demand.[45] As also noted by Grunstein and Díaz-Wionczek,[46] the real purpose of local content policy – industrial development – would be achieved if the Mexican strategy prepares local suppliers to expand beyond Mexican boundaries. For the time being, it is too early to determine whether the current local content policy in Mexico will lead to regional global competitiveness, and consequently follow the path of the country's thriving export-oriented automotive industry, which also benefited from a targeted supply-chain development policy, strengthening the export orientation of the industry.[47]

Brazil has been relatively more successful than Mexico in promoting the export orientation of its local suppliers, as evidenced by the case of the globally competitive shipyard industry in Brazil. Petrobras' internal local content policy also aims to support capacity development of local suppliers by overcoming technology gaps, and it identifies the business areas that are considered a priority for the oil and gas sector and where local content goals need to be achieved.[48]. In addition, the local content legislation also encourages operators to invest 1 per cent of gross revenue in research and development activities, which holds the potential to boost their competitiveness and export orientation.[49]

It appears that local content frameworks in the petroleum sectors across Latin America have not achieved such levels of export orientation yet and domestic suppliers in Latin America still lack competitiveness in the provision of specialised goods and services to the extractive sector. However, the experiences of Brazil and Mexico reveal on-going efforts to promote the competitiveness of local suppliers.

---

[45] Pemex, 'Estrategia de Petróleos Mexicanos para el Desarrollo de Proveedores, Contratistas y Contenido Nacional' (Pemex´ Strategy for the Development of Local Contractors and National Content), 2009 [Pemex 2009].
[46] Grunstein et al., note 13.
[47] Ibid.
[48] Morales et al. (2017), note 2.
[49] Tordo et al., note 3.

3.3.3 Funding Mechanisms and Credit Financing for Suppliers

The role of funding mechanisms and credit financing is key for supplier development, given that access to credit is one of the major financial obstacles for local small or medium sized businesses (SMEs) to integrate into the oil and gas supply chain. Mexico and Brazil developed funding mechanisms to encourage financing for domestic suppliers.

In Mexico, the legislation also required the creation of the FISO Pemex Trust Fund, through the National Development Bank, Nacional Financiera (NAFIN), to strengthen the development of local suppliers and the integration of national companies into the oil and gas supply chains. The FISO Pemex fund provides technical assistance, subsidies, and financial support, notably through credits, for domestic firms wishing to become Pemex suppliers. Between 2009 and 2014, NAFIN offered 300 million Mexican pesos (about USD 23 million) in credits to companies that had a contract with Pemex, while the technical assistance group only channelled around about US$3 million in subsidies through supplier and contractor development programmes.[50]

In Brazil, the PROGEDIR programme was established to support credit financing from the National Bank for Economic and Social Development (BNDES) for SMEs wishing to become Petrobras suppliers. Also, in a similar objective, the credit right investment funds initiative (*Fundos de Investimento em Direitos Creditórios* – FIDCs) was aimed to enable Petrobras suppliers to secure capital and funding at rates lower than those available on the market.[51]

3.3.4 Supplier Development Programmes

While local content requirements offer a protected environment that could be used for learning by doing, both Mexico and Brazil have seen the implementation of supplier development programmes in parallel with local content requirements to help local suppliers achieve long-run competitiveness. Supplier development programmes are particularly helpful in enhancing the industrial capabilities of local suppliers. Indeed, such programmes allow vendors to benefit from more stable intra-industry relationships, exposure to best practices and quality standards, as well as to develop marketing capabilities.[52]

---

[50] Grunstein et al., note 13. There seems to be a discrepancy regarding the amount of funding offered through the FISO Pemex, because according to Pemex (Pemex 2009, note 55), a contribution of 5 billion pesos was considered for 2009 as well as an additional 2.5 billion pesos for 2010, which is 17 times higher than the amount reported for the period 2009–14 by Grunstein (Grunstein et al., note 13).

[51] Morales et al. (2017), note 2.

[52] In Malaysia, the NOC also holds touring 'clinics' that offer a platform for local suppliers to interact with Petronas staff and learn about company's procurement system, receive help in registering and accessing future opportunities, both domestically and abroad (Tordo et al., note 3).

Pemex's supplier development programme contributed to identifying potential suppliers, as well as to organising skills development programmes for registered Pemex suppliers. Such initiatives had a considerable impact on local content outcomes in Mexico. Indeed, local integration has shown a stable increase from 40.5 per cent in 2009–10 to 41.5 per cent in 2010–12 and seems to be going in the right direction to achieve the local content objective of 43.9 per cent in 2019 set by the law.[53] Some 87 per cent of Pemex's providers during 2015 were Mexican, although we do not know how much value that 87 per cent captures for Pemex's overall spending (of about USD 11 billion) on suppliers that year.[54]

In Brazil, Petrobras has an extensive track record of collaborations with local suppliers to promote local content. Some of those initiatives, which support the process of capacity building for local suppliers, are outlined in this section. For instance, Petrobras implemented a national programme, in collaboration with the Ministry of Mines and Energy, for the mobilisation of the national oil and gas industry (PROMINP). PROMINP aims to maximise the productivity and competitiveness of the local supply of goods and services in the oil and gas sectors in Brazil and abroad. Indeed, it is worth noting that PROMINP also aims to promote the export of goods and services by domestic suppliers.[55]

Petrobras has also collaborated with the Brazilian Agency for Micro and Small enterprises, SEBRAE, to promote the integration of micro and small enterprises as suppliers into the domestic oil and energy value chain.[56]

3.3.5 Intra-Industry Dialogue

In Brazil, the PROMINP programme has provided the many players involved in the oil and gas industry with a standing discussion forum for the development of initiatives that can improve the domestic supply of good and services competitively and sustainably. Indeed, PROMINP's discussion forums involve the government, oil operators, associations, financial institutions, and suppliers, as well as educational institutions.[57]

In Mexico, as a result of the 2008 legislative reforms, an intra-industry dialogue between Pemex and its suppliers was fostered by demand-and-supply analysis groups to better understand Pemex's expenditures and future domestic supply opportunities

---

[53] Grunstein et al., note 13.

[54] Morales et al., note 2.

[55] P. S. Rodrigues Alonso. 'The PROMINP 10th Anniversary: Results, Challenges and Perspectives for the Maritime Industry in Brazil'. May 6 2014. www.investidorpetrobras.com.br/enu/4397/OTCLocalContentinBrazil6MAY14.pdf.

[56] Rodrigues Alonso, note 55; Tordo et al., note 3.

[57] P. Andrews, J. Playfoot, & S. Augustus, *Education and Training for the Oil and Gas Industry: The Evolution of Four Energy Nations: Mexico, Nigeria, Brazil, and Iraq* (Amsterdam: Elsevier, 2015); World Bank, *A Practical Guide to Increasing Mining Local Procurement in West Africa* (Washington DC: The World Bank Group. 2015).

through polls. A total of 4,025 firms participated in the supply analysis and polls to provide insights regarding their obstacles in becoming suppliers to Pemex or in scaling up to meet the domestic demand. On the demand side, Pemex forecasted its demand for the next five years and published it in a widely accessible document. This task not only enabled support of long-term planning efforts of companies to better serve Pemex's demand but also helped Pemex define a supply-chain development strategy and invest critical resources in targeted activities for which providers would have to be developed.[58]

The demand forecast task was also key to ensure more stable and long-term contracts for suppliers, which is crucial for the efficiency of local suppliers. Before 2008, local suppliers in Mexico were not guaranteed permanent contracts by Pemex because Pemex, considered a public sector entity, had to procure all its goods and services through public bids according to the acquisitions law. However, Pemex's new procurement rules and organisational structures were amended to fix this gap.[59]

Pemex also recently set up several initiatives to smoothen the intra-industry dialogue with its current and prospective suppliers. In 2010, Pemex notably created the Unit for Development of Suppliers, Contractors, and National Content, which is responsible for the implementation of the local content policy and overview of the progress of suppliers. Pemex also established a Supplier Relationship Programme (RPC), which aims to 'perform actions beyond the established limits by the contractual relationship Pemex-Company,' and enables smoother dialogue in the interest of quality, delivery time, logistics, and quality improvements, which benefit both parties (Pemex). As a result, gains by local suppliers have exceeded the established conditions of their contract and enable them to distinguish themselves in competitiveness terms.[60]

3.4 Regional Coordination and Approach to Local Content Policies

Despite their long history as oil and gas producing countries, local content has been adopted across Latin American countries not only in a heterogeneous manner but also with very little regional cooperation. It is essential to reshape local content policy and practices towards the promotion of a regionally integrated industrial ecosystem in the oil and gas sectors in Latin America. A development policy that includes the creation of regional clusters for local content in the oil and gas sectors would help achieve the strategy of localisation that progressively develops the scale and capacity of local suppliers to achieve competitiveness.[61] Such a regional strategy is justified by several factors.

[58] Grunstein et al., note 13.
[59] Ibid.
[60] As part of this Supplier Relations Programme, Pemex has also developed initiatives that contribute to lower the entry barriers for local suppliers, such as Pemex Pass, an online platform to register and evaluate suppliers (Morales et al. [2017], note 2; Pemex, 2018).
[61] A. Lebdioui, 'Uncovering the High Value of Neglected Minerals: Development Minerals as Inputs for Industrial Development in North Africa' (2020) 7(2) *The Extractive Industries and Society*, 470–479.

Firstly, local suppliers need to increase their ability to enjoy economies of scale and drive cost down. Integrating local suppliers in regional/supranational supply chains can thus also enhance their productivity. Secondly, regionalising local content policies to promote industrial complementarity can help prevent duplication of efforts in the same activities and fallacy of composition between neighbouring countries operating in the same regional markets.

Thirdly, for the time being, Latin American suppliers cannot compete with European, North American, and Asian firms when it comes to bidding for contracts, so there is a need for regional infant industry protection to protect market shares with opportunities of learning by doing to increase productivity.

Lastly, the creation of an efficient regional supply chain that foreign operators and contractors can plug into and rely on would reduce switching costs for international oil companies operating in Latin America. This would increase the reliability of the Latin American supply chain in the petroleum sector and increase the bargaining power of Latin American counterparts to attract FDI within the region.

As similarly argued in the case of Africa,[62] regional agencies such as the Latin-American Energy Organisation (OLADE) could play an instrumental role in undertaking the appropriate and necessary actions to regionalise issues of local content design and implementation. For instance, OLADE or networks such as *la Red Latinoamericana de Industrias Extractivas* could play an active advocacy role in raising awareness of the neglected opportunities for regionalisation of Local content policies.

A coherent regional local content agency across Latin America could be created with an overall objective of shaping the vision of regional clusters for oil field services and equipment (OFSE). The key responsibilities of such an agency would include recommendations of a road map for the regional OFSE industry to increase its competitiveness, as well as recommendations to create an attractive environment for investments in OFSE, suggestions for streamlining administrative processes for intra-regional trade, and investments in supply-chain development to facilitate the creation of regional clusters.

A successful strategy to deal with the problem of national industry participation and regional supply chain development must be much more far-reaching than current efforts and should include a platform where Latin American petroleum exporters can tackle issues of regional integration through an interconnected local content policy, to guide and promote economically sustainable market opportunities. Local content policies in Latin America need to be shaped by the vision of new regionalism, promoting fairness, and mutually beneficial regional partnerships.

---

[62] A. Lebdioui, 'Promoting Local Content Policies for Industrial Development: Challenges, Opportunities and the Need for a Regional Vision in Africa,' 2017.

4 CONCLUSION

As demonstrated by the Latin American experience, to achieve positive local content outcomes, local content laws need to be part of a broader strategy and long-term vision to be a valuable addition to the petroleum sector and industrial diversification. On the one hand, short-term vision in terms of LCRs across Latin America tend to prioritise the generation of local employment through local labour quotas. On the other hand, countries that achieved positive long-term local content outcomes have accompanied locally employed provisions with skills development programmes and promotion of the national suppliers of goods and services. Local content objectives thus need to be carefully adapted to the local context through a holistic approach, taking into account the combination of requirements, incentives, skills transfer, state-led investments, and opportunities for learning by doing.

Indeed, supplying national demand of goods and services in the oil and gas sectors through LCRs may offer a protected environment to build capabilities and increase learning by doing. Historical experiences show that some of the current approaches are mostly failing to deliver developmental and economic outcomes because of the lack of strategic capacity-building programmes to support local content policies. The challenge that lies ahead for the sustainable economic impact of LCRs is to maximise the economic spillovers of the hydrocarbons sector with a strategy of localisation that progressively develops the scale and capacity of local suppliers on a path to become internationally competitive. NOCs consequently have an essential role to play in successful design and implementation of local content policies in Latin America through supplier development programmes, as well as maintaining a flow of information with local firms to enable potential suppliers to learn and adapt to quality and market standards, among other things. Increased regional cooperation to foster industrial complementarities can help address the challenge of gradual competitiveness and scaling up for local suppliers in Latin America.

These findings have important implications for development policy in Latin America's petroleum-rich countries that are trying to harness their natural resources for economic growth. Several realistic actions could be taken to address the issues raised in this chapter, and would considerably contribute to increasing the impact of local content policies on sustainable development, further helping Latin American oil producing countries to meet the industrialisation challenge.

However, local content in the oil and gas sectors is not a one-size-fits-all development strategy. Local content policies have often been assessed on their cost relative to their benefits, but we must not forget about the potential opportunity costs of local content policies, especially in countries with limited resources and budget constraints. Indeed, whether local content policies are the best avenue for diversification and reduction of commodity dependence depends on several country-specific factors. In some contexts, downstream value addition should not be neglected as a suitable avenue for industrial diversification. Indeed, we should keep in mind that local content in the oil and gas sectors is not an objective in itself, but a means to achieve sustainable development, especially in the context of exhaustible resources. Policymakers must thus first decide how local content policies fit into their country's overall industrial strategy. If local content is an objective to be pursued seriously, policy-makers must be aware of the potential challenges and factors to take into account to maximise the positive externalities and industrial spillovers from upstream diversification in the oil and gas sectors.

16

Local Content and Sustainable Development in Brazil

Eduardo G. Pereira, Rafael Baptista Baleroni, Fernanda Delgado, Jose Vicente Duncan de Miranda, Aaron Koenck, and Pedro Henrique Neves

1 INTRODUCTION

The Brazilian Federal Law 12,351 ("Pre-Salt Law") defines local content as the proportion between the value of the goods produced and services rendered in Brazil for the performance of the upstream contracts and the total value of the goods used and services provided for this purpose.[1] Despite other regulatory sources discussed in the following, this is the only Brazilian law that clearly defines local content in the oil industry.

Brazil is a fairly interesting case to analyze from a local content perspective in the oil and gas sector as it has been evolving for several decades. Since the opening of the Brazilian upstream sector to the private sector,[2] local content has been a part of

---

[1] Brazil: Law No. 12,351 [Pre-Salt Law], regulates the exploration and production of oil, natural gas, and other fluid hydrocarbons, under the production share regime, in the Pre-salt polygon and other strategic areas, it establishes the Social Fund and amends provisions of Law 9478, of August 6, 1997.

[2] Such opening began in 1995, with Constitutional Amendment No. 9, which ceased the national oil company Petrobras" role as the monopolist in exploration and production activities. Law No 9,478, dated August 6, 1997 (referred to as "Brazilian Oil Law") regulated the sector. In general, terms, Brazil then adopted a tax and royalties system, where oil companies (including Petrobras) in open bidding rounds for exploration and production concessions in which (i) oil and gas companies completely assume the exploratory risk, and (ii) have the right to the entire production in case of success, paying taxes, and royalties over its revenues. Major legal changes came in 2010 when the country adopted more interventionist policies, driven by the large pre-salt findings. Two laws implemented the main changes: (i) Law 12,276, dated June 30, 2010 ("ToR Law"), which introduced the "Transfer of Rights", a direct grant of rights to Petrobras, under which it can explore and produce up to 5 billion barrels of equivalent (BOE) in certain areas, which was valued at approximately US$ 42.5 billion and was made together with a capital increase from the government and a public raising of equity by Petrobras; and (ii) Law 12,351, dated December 22, 2010 ("Pre-Salt Law"), which introduced a production sharing regime for areas in the pre-salt region, in which (initially) Petrobras was determined as the sole operator in all areas, with a minimum interest of 30 per cent in them. More recently, from 2016 onwards, the Brazilian federal administrations have introduced more liberal measures in the sector. Petrobras ceases to be the sole operator and to have a minimum 30 per cent interest; instead, it now has preferential rights to become a member of consortiums in case it loses in competitive bids of areas in which it was previously nominated. There are bills of law and talks of removing all Petrobras' special rights; even to extinguish the production-sharing regime and another one to create a local content law.

300

Local Content and SD in Brazil 301

governmental policies to a certain extent. The Brazilian regulatory framework concerned with this matter was developed over the past decades. Local content requirements are included in all granting instruments – except in Round Zero. However, as demonstrated in this chapter, the terms and conditions of the governmental policies have varied throughout the different rounds.

This chapter aims to address the evolution of LCRs and procedures in Brazil. It evaluates the key contributions of LC rules to sustainable development in Brazil's oil and gas industry. This chapter is divided into five sections. After this introduction, Section 2 provides a brief history of LC rules in Brazil. Section 3 evaluates key gaps that limit the effectiveness and overall sustainability of the Brazilian LC rules. Section 4 provides recommendations on pathways for reforms. Section 5 sets out the conclusion.

2 A BRIEF HISTORY OF LOCAL CONTENT RULES IN BRAZIL

The following subsections briefly describe the history of LC rules in Brazil. The key focus of this section will be the relevant granting instruments signed between the Brazilian governmental authority and the relevant oil and gas companies.[3]

2.1 *Petrobras' Monopoly (pre-1995)*

Both the exploration and production of hydrocarbons in Brazil have been strongly regulated since the mid-twentieth century. The Brazilian Federal Constitution of 1946,[4] and later Law No. 2,004, dated October 3, 1953,[5] established the state monopoly over research, drilling, refining, and transportation of petroleum and its by-products, and created *Petróleo Brasileiro S.A.* (Petrobras) to enact the monopoly. Petrobras' monopoly was preserved in subsequent Federal Constitutions and was not revoked until 1995.[6]

Although not particularly relevant, early initiatives to promote local suppliers date back to 1986, with the creation by Petrobras of the PROCAP initiative.[7] Until the early 1980s, equipment used in the Brazilian oil and gas sector was mostly imported. Only when Petrobras moved to new offshore frontiers between water depths of 600 m and 1,000 m did it start to foster the local development of technology to meet the new challenges. PROCAP 1000 (re. 1,000 m depth) followed in 1986–92, PROCAP 2,000 in 1993–9.[8] These, however, were initiatives driven by Petrobras, not governmental policies.

[3] Based on the relevant granting instruments and tender protocols at ANP's website: www.rodadas.anp.gov.br/en, last accessed January 18, 2020.
[4] *Constitution of Brazil*, 1946.
[5] Brazil: Law No. 2,004, *establishing "Petróleo Brasileiro Sociedade Anonima" (Petrobras)*, 3 October 1953.
[6] Federal Constitucional Emente n° 9/1995.
[7] *Programa de Inovação Tecnológica e Desenvolvimento Avançado em Águas Profundas e Ultraprofundas* (PROCAP) or Program for Technological Innovation and Advanced Development in Deep and Ultradeep waters.
[8] E. de Almeida and D. C. Martinez Prieto, "Impactos do Conteúdo Local Sobre a Dinâmica dos Investimentos em E&P de Petróleo no Brasil" (2014) *Rio Oil and Gas* at 3–4. PROCAP 3,000 followed in 2000–11 and PROCAP *Visão Futuro* began in 2012.

2.2 End of Petrobras' Monopoly: Round Zero and Local Preference (1998)

In 1995, Brazil began opening the upstream sector. The Federal Constitution was changed in 1995 to allow the Federal Government to concede exploration and production rights to companies other than Petrobras. The 1997 Brazilian Oil Law created the independent national petroleum agency (ANP), established the concession system, and forced Petrobras to operate in a competitive environment.[9]

This law respected Petrobras' rights over areas in which it was already developing production activities or blocks in which it had made commercial discoveries or investments and exploration.[10] Such rights were recognized by means of concession agreements granted in what became known as "Round Zero." In 1998, Petrobras entered into 397 concession contracts, for 115 exploration blocks, 51 development areas, and 231 production fields.

Although Round Zero contracts contained no local content percentage requirements, they provided a local preference clause.[11] According to it, Petrobras should ensure preference in contracting national goods and services whenever they were available at a similar price, term, and quality when compared to those in the foreign market.[12] This provision was kept in subsequent concessions.

2.3 Rounds 1 to 4: No Mandatory Minimum Local Content (1999–2002)

The requirement of a minimum local content percentage began in Round 1 and, with minor changes, was kept constant until Round 4 (in 2002). This coincided with the end of the presidency of Mr. Fernando Henrique Cardoso.

Upstream concessions are granted through competitive bids. Rounds 1 to 4 established that proposals should include two factors: (1) signature bonus (i.e. down payment to the government), weighting 85 per cent of the final score; and (2) a percental commitment of acquiring locally goods and services (i.e. local content) weighing a total of 15 per cent. The practice of allocating some weight to local content commitments as a judgment criterion was used from Round 1 until Round 13, albeit with variations on its relative weight. Rounds 14 and 16 no longer considered local content as part of the bid parameter. Table 16.1 summarizes such local content bid parameter development:

From Round 1 to Round 4 (1999–2002), bidders faced no mandatory local content minimum requirements (floor) in their bids but were subject to maximum percentages (ceiling). Percentages were capped at 50 per cent for the exploratory phase and

---

[9] Brazil: Law No. 9,478, Deals with the national energy policy, activities related to the oil and gas monopoly, creates the National Council for the Energy Policy (Conselho Nacional de Política Energética) and the National Petroleum Agency (Agência Nacional do Petróleo) and makes other provisions [Brazil], 6 August 1997.
[10] Ibid., Arts. 32 and 33.
[11] Section 18.1 of the Concession Contract in effect at that time.
[12] Ibid.

Local Content and SD in Brazil

TABLE 16.1 *Local content bid parameter development*

Round	R1 to R4	R5 and R6	R7 to R13	R14 to R 16
Weight	15%	40%	20%	0
Exploration	3%	15%	5%	0
Development	12%	25%	15%	0

Source: Table prepared by authors based on bidding protocols issued by ANP of each bidding round.

TABLE 16.2 *Non-compliance penalties in Rounds 3 and 4*

Local content		Penalty	
Range (%)		Achieved (up to, %)	Penalty (progressive and cumulative)
0	30	30	200% of the difference until 30%
30	40	40	160% of the difference until 40%
40	50	50	120% of the difference until 50%
50	60	60	80% of the difference until 60%
60	100	100	50% of the difference until 70%

Source: Table prepared by authors based on bidding protocols issued by ANP of each relevant bidding round.

70 per cent for the development phase. There were vague requirements of concessionaires keeping an inventory of the purchases and then sending them to the ANP. How the assessment of compliance would occur was then unclear, other than by the presentation of reports regulated under ANP Regulation 36 of 2001. Nonetheless, failure to comply was subject to penalties. Rounds 1 and 2 set a penalty of 200 per cent of the non-fulfilled amounts, while Rounds 3 and 4 adopted a sliding scale summarized in Table 16.2.

2.4 *Rounds 5 and 6: Minimum Percentages (2003–4)*

In Rounds 5 and 6 (2003 and 2004), minimum local content percentages were introduced, with minimum percentages depending on the exploratory environment,[13] as summarized in Table 16.3:

However, there were, no ceilings for local content commitment. Commitments beyond the floor resulted in additional points when judging the proposals. In these rounds, the weight of local content as a judgment criterion was 40 per cent

---

[13] "Local Content Policy, Upstream Guide" (*Deloitte*) www2.deloitte.com/br/en/pages/energy-and-resources/upstream-guide/articles/local-content.html#, last accessed January 18, 2020.

304 Pereira, Baleroni, Delgado, Miranda, Koenck, Neves

TABLE 16.3 *Minimum local content percentages in Rounds 5 and 6*

Environment*	Exploration Phase	Development Phase
A	30%	30%
B	50%	60%
C	70%	70%

Source: Table prepared by authors based on bidding protocols issued by ANP of each relevant bidding round.

(15 per cent for the exploration phase and 25 per cent for the development phase). There were five sub-items of local content for which a percentage had to be committed and compared with other offers.

Penalties were also changed: (1) a 50 per cent penalty over the difference until the minimum required percentage, and (2) a 20 per cent penalty over the difference until the offered percentage that is above the minimum.

The multi-item judgment criteria, the large weight of, and the change in, the penalty mechanism created confusion as well as a possibility of exaggerated commitments in scenarios where paying the penalty was more cost-efficient than buying locally or it was strategically important to acquire the area.

In addition to changes in the bid auction, ANP adopted Regulation 180 on June 9, 2003, to replace Regulation 36 and further detailed the mechanism to evidence compliance with local content. Also in 2003, the Brazilian government launched PROMINP (Oil and Natural Gas Industry Mobilization Program) through Decree No. 4,925, in order to maximize participation of the national goods and services industry, on a competitive and sustainable basis, in the implementation of investment projects in the oil and natural gas sector in Brazil and abroad.

The main consequence was the adoption of the Local Content Booklet (*Cartilha de Conteúdo Local*) in July 2004. This booklet defines a methodology for calculating the local content of goods, systems, subsystems, and services related to the sector. Additionally, this booklet seeks to identify the manufacturing origin of the components that make up equipment, weighs the value of imported inputs against the value of the good, and consolidates both values in the local content Index.

2.5 *Rounds 7 to 10 (2005–8): Minimum and Maximum Percentages, Certification System*

In 2005, during Round 7, ANP established both minimum and maximum local content percentages, according to the location of the block. The percentages

Local Content and SD in Brazil

TABLE 16.4 *Minimum local content percentages in Round 7*

	Exploration Phase		Development Phase	
Location of the Block	Min %	Max %	Min %	Max %
Deep Waters (Depth over 400 m)	37	55	55	65
Shallow Waters (Between 100 m and 400 m)	37	55	55	65
Shallow Waters (Less than 100 m)	51	60	63	70
Onshore	70	80	77	85

Source: Table prepared by authors based on bidding protocols issued by ANP of each relevant bidding round.

considered the location of the blocks according to four criteria: onshore, shallow waters up to 100 meters, shallow waters between 100 and 400 meters, and deep waters, as summarized in Table 16.4:

For each block location, there was a spreadsheet defining the minimum percentage of each item and sub-item in the exploration and development phases. The overall percentage is calculated from the percentages of items and sub-items by their respective weights. The weight of each item or sub-item was to be proposed by the bidding company based on the total cost of the venture. This additional level of detail considerably increased the complexity of proposals and the risk of non-compliance with specific items.

Penalties changed again. If the non-performed local content percentage (NR%) was under 65 per cent, the penalty (M) would be 60 per cent of the value of the non-performed local content. If the non-performed local content percentage was equal or greater than 65 per cent, the penalty would escalate from 60 per cent until 100 per cent when the non-performed local content was equal to 100 per cent.[14] Local content accounted for 20 per cent of the final bid score, with 5 per cent in the exploration phase and 15 per cent in the development phase.

In addition to specifying partial local content commitments (for items and sub-items) and creating limited ranges for offers and reducing the weight of the local content item in the bidding judgment, Round 7 also changed the method for measurement and verification of local content, introducing the Certification System in 2005. The Local Content Booklet was included as part of Round 7's

---

[14] Mathematically: If $0 < NR(\%) < 65\% \Rightarrow M(\%) = 60(\%)$
If $NR(\%) \; 65\% \Rightarrow M(\%) = 1,143 \, NR(\%) - 14,285$

306   *Pereira, Baleroni, Delgado, Miranda, Koenck, Neves*

concession contracts (as Annex III thereto). This created the burden of additional transaction costs to manage concession contracts.

It was only in 2007 (in Round 9), however, that a detailed local content manual was issued, defining the methodology for performing a certification. ANP Resolution 36 (2007) established the updated Local Content Booklet as the criterion to assess local content, removing the need of it being attached to concession contracts. Rules for accreditation and auditing of certifying entities were also passed, as per ANP Resolutions 37 (2007) and 38 (2007) (later revoked by ANP Resolution 25 (2016)).

Under the certification system, each concessionaire is responsible for local content information and must require its suppliers to certify their products and to maintain all necessary information for local content measurement, which is thereafter evidenced by the submission of certificates issued by companies accredited by ANP.

2.6 *Round 11 to 13: Impacts from Pre-Salt Discoveries, PEDEFOR*

Due to the pre-salt findings, there was a five-year interval between Round 10 (2008) and Round 11 (2013). Both Mr. Lula da Silva and Mrs. Dilma Rousseff's administrations had in mind that a new regime had to be put in place to reflect the then-perceived, almost inexistent exploratory risk in pre-salt areas, as well as the then-existing high oil prices. In 2010, both the Transfer of Rights (ToR) and the Pre-Salt law were adopted.[15] While the ToR agreement was entered into in 2010, the first production sharing agreement in the pre-salt area was only entered into in 2013. By then, only Petrobras was authorized to be the operator in the pre-salt.

Meanwhile, criticism of the local content system increased, given the high complexity and costs involved. The judgment criteria to grant concessions in Rounds 11 to 13 (2013–15) did not change in comparison with Round 10 (hence, rounds 7 to 13 had the same criteria, except that Round 13 removed some of the sub-items in the spreadsheet).

However, the pre-salt areas, both under the TofR and the production sharing regimes, innovated in the sense of removing local content as a judgment criterion. A predefined percentage was established to be met.

In 2016, still under Mrs. Rousseff's administration, the federal government launched the PEDEFOR initiative (Program for Stimulus to Competitiveness in the Supply Chain, Development and Enhancement of Suppliers in the Oil and Natural Gas Sector), under Decree No. 8,637, dated January 15, 2016.[16] PEDEFOR

---

[15] Brazil: Law No. 12,276, authorizes the Union to directly assign to Petrobras, with due compensation, the activities of research and production of oil, natural gas and other fluid hydrocarbons in areas that contain up to 5 billion barrels of oil equivalent, 30 June 2010 [Transfer of Rights or ToR Law]; Pre-Salt Law, note 1.

[16] Brazil Decree No. 8,637 of January 15, 2016.

Local Content and SD in Brazil

seeks to improve the local content policy in the oil and gas sector through the recognition and valorization of initiatives and investments that contribute to increasing the competitiveness of suppliers in Brazil; stimulate national engineering; promote technological innovation in strategic segments; expand the supply chain of goods, services, and systems producing in Brazil; increase the local content level of suppliers already installed; and stimulate the creation of technology-based companies.

The program acts mainly through (1) incentives to suppliers in the country, through the valuation of a higher percentage of local content than effectively existing for goods and services of strategic character; and (2) bonuses, with the granting of local content units to consortiums or companies that, in the exercise of their activities, promote certain investments in the country. In other words, the program tried to foster investments in the country and targeted to favor certain selected sectors. In addition, PEDEFOR provides for committees with representatives appointed by various government entities (ministries, ANP, development bank). During its activities, the committees may invite industry representatives to collect information from civil society. This has been used to improve dialogue between the government and industry associations.[17]

2.7 Round 14 (2017) Onwards: Liberalization

The year 2016 was politically turbulent in Brazil. Due to the unfavorable market response faced by the local content policy and the negative impact it had on investments in the oil and gas sector, the new federal administration (under Mr. Temer) decided to implement major changes to local content requirements and certification methods.

In 2017 and 2018, a new local content model was established to be applied in the Bid Rounds, as per the National Council for Energy Policies (CNPE) Resolutions No. 07 (2017), 22 (2017), 01 (2018) and ANP Resolution No. 726 (2018).

Given the irrelevance in outcomes[18] and pervasive incentives from Round 14 onwards, local content ceased to be a scoring factor in bids but remained as

[17] More details on the Program: www.mdic.gov.br/index.php/competitividade-industrial/pedefor, last accessed January 14, 2020.

[18] Irrelevance was observed despite the variation in the weight of local content commitments towards the bidders' final scores. The table here summarizes the number of areas granted per group of rounds and the number of those that would have had a different outcome if local content was not a criterion:

Round	R1 to R4	R5 and R6	R7 to R10	R11 to R13
Granted	88	255	422	251
Different Outcome	1	4	1	1

Source: L. Andrade, "Impacto do Conteúdo Local como Critério de Oferta nas Rodadas de Licitações para Concessão de Blocos Exploratórios" (2016) Rio Oil and Gas.

TABLE 16.5 *Local content requirements from Round 14 onward*

Segment	Onshore	Offshore
Exploration	50%	18%
Construction of Wells	N/A	25%
Production Development	50%	N/A
Subsea Equipment	N/A	40%
Platforms	N/A	25%

Source: Table prepared by authors based on bidding protocol issued by ANP.

a minimum requirement in the E&P Contract. Additionally, given the high complexity, compliance, and monitoring costs, local content requirements were simplified and cover only five macrosegments as summarized in Table 16.5:

A similar approach of preset local content commitments was also adopted in production-sharing agreements for pre-salt areas.[19] Additionally, each concession contract provided for a mechanism to seek waivers from the local content commitment. Its evidentiary burden was considerable. There was a large backlog of waiver requests and an overarching solution was sought. ANP adopted a general waiver policy.

Resolution 726 (2018) regulated the possibility of a waiver of local content commitments, based on specific criteria (e.g. no national supplier, excessive pricing, new technology, among others).[20] Concessionaires were also allowed to amend concessions (until Round 13), production sharing, and ToR agreements to reflect the new local content requirements. Criteria and procedures are detailed in the Resolution and increased the level of certainty as to waiver requirements.

Looking forward, in October 2019, ANP started a public hearing[21] to simplify current mechanisms to verify the local content in imported products. This process will likely result in efficiency gains, control, and auditing of the local content reports. This is an additional impact of the new local content policies introduced by the CNPE since 2017.

---

[19] More details on the production sharing agreements: http://rodadas.anp.gov.br/pt/partilha-de-producao, last accessed January 14, 2020.

[20] More details on the companies that sought it: www.anp.gov.br/exploracao-e-producao-de-oleo-e-gas/conteudo-local/aditamento-da-clausula-de-conteudo-local, last accessed January 14, 2020.

[21] Public Hearing No. 21/2019, scheduled to occur on November 27, 2019.

Local Content and SD in Brazil

3 LESSONS LEARNED

3.1 *Local Content as an Instrument of Economic Development*

One of the main goals of any government should be the creation of an environment that promotes sustainable development of the economy on behalf of its citizens and companies. Attracting investments effectively demands a complex and aligned policy to allow internal development and returns. All stakeholders involved should jointly work to fix the errors that have hindered growth and reinforce those that spurred development. This objective can be achieved through dynamic rules weighed against stability and certainty needed by investors.[22] For society as a whole, the creation of skilled job opportunities, income, and long-term business opportunities should be leveraged.

The conditions established for the execution of the LCRs can be an instrument for enhancing the local industry. The proportion of investment by the operating companies in national goods and services can directly promote the economy where the oil and gas activities are explored/produced, and it may cascade to other regions of the country. Local content requirements may be an effective way of preventing the "Dutch disease."[23]

There is also an expectation of technological development, improvement of human resources capacity, generation of new jobs, and fiscal income-expanding benefits to various segments of the economy and society. Because of these expectations, the Brazilian local content policy has been subject to signs of progress and has become an important topic of debate when involving the participation of international companies in the exploration of oil and gas activities.

Because of its developed local content policies, Brazil has seen some success cases. Its local content policies boosted involvement by the national industry from 57 per cent in 2003 to 75 per cent by the first half of 2010.[24] This includes the revitalization of its naval industry[25] in the early 2000s, along with expansion in capacity in certain capital goods, fabrication, machinery, equipment, metallurgy, subsea equipment, and control systems, to name a few examples.[26] The number of suppliers to Petrobras increased from 1,800 firms at the end of the 1990s to 3,400 by

---

[22] F. G. Pereira, C. Matthews, and H. Trischmann, "Local Content Policies in the Petroleum Industry: Lessons Learned" (2019) 4 *Oil and Gas, Natural Resources, and Energy Journal* 631 at 642.

[23] Dutch disease, broadly speaking, refers to the phenomenon of increase in export revenues (denominated in a foreign strong currency), which appreciates the local foreign exchange rate and results in loss of competitiveness of local firms. This may also be combined with means of production being pulled to the extraction of the relevant resource. See W. M. Cordem and J. P. Neary, "Booming Sector and De-industrialization in a Small Open Economy" (1982) 92 *The Economic Journal* 825–848.

[24] Program for Mobilization of the National Oil and Gas Industry (PROMINP).

[25] The number of industry workers increased from around 3,000 employees to 70,000 employees from 2003 to 2013. N. N. Filho, "Brazil's Oil & Gas Local Content Policy: Lessons Learned," Institute of The Americas, September 2017, p. 3.

[26] Ibid.

2009.[27] As mentioned before, the employment of local citizens is also a key indicator of the success of local content policies.[28] Lastly and maybe most importantly, Brazil saw the generation of 875,000 jobs during this same period.

The determination of LCRs to incentivize contracts with national companies can be well designed by competent authorities but if market factors, mainly the proven strengths and deficiencies, are not considered, LCR implementation may be a threat to achieve the objectives and disincentivize further investments.

Although improvements over time are necessary (and desired), any process for changing rules requires a deep discussion with all impacted parties and a sustainable plan to be monitored through the years. Stability and dialogue are important for long-term planning. Frequent rule changes without previous debate increase the perception of risk. In this sense, initiatives of dialogue between companies and government – such as PEDEFOR – help mitigate such risks and permit a "reality check" of local content parameters. For instance, such dialogue resulted in major changes to local content requirements, even retrospectively (via a waiver policy).[29] Means of dialogue with a variety of stakeholders is certainly a positive lesson.

Furthermore, Brazil adopts a cost-based approach of supplied goods and services rendered in the country, regardless of the nationality of controlling shareholders, the nationality of the workforce during the production of assets, or other criteria.[30] This could be considered another positive lesson learned so the rules and policies are focused on the actual benefits developed in the country regardless of the ownership of the relevant companies, which could lead to bogus companies, nepotism, and/or corruption in certain cases.

Finally, the certificate system is most likely one of the best initiatives developed by the Brazilian government. Such a system helped to reduce the administrative burden to audit a massive amount of local content compliance, as well, it assisted the industry with a more efficient system and more certainty in the process.

3.2 Brazil: Developed Local Content Policy with Improvements Needed

Although Brazil made some progress with local content practices, it still faces challenges. The Brazilian reality of excessive protection defined and hindered the absorption of technology, while also reducing incentives for investment in

[27] S. Borschiver and G. R. Freitas, "Políticas de Conteúdo Local na Indústria de Óleo e Gás" (2016) *Rio Oil and Gas Conference Proceedings.*

[28] Filho, note 25.

[29] M. Nogueira, "Relaxing of Brazil local content rules will boost oil output capacity: report" (*Reuters*, 20 June 2018)

[30] Trench Rossi Watanabe, "Doing Business in Brazil 2018," 2018, www.bakermckenzie.com/-/media/files/expertise/ma-resources/Doing/Business/In/Brazil.pdf, last accessed January 18, 2020.

Local Content and SD in Brazil

research and development and innovation.[31] The country has not been gradually exposed to international competition to advance the provision of incentives for innovation.[32]

One could presume that the policy execution lacked a central strategic plan to gradually implement the reforms in accordance with the country's supply chain reality. The excessive levels of LCRs percentage requirements did not take into account the Brazilian-installed capacity, which generated, in many cases, targets that were impossible to achieve and totally disconnected from the market reality. Yet, some requirements granted a level of protectionism that resulted in expensive prices and longer delivery times.

Also, it is important to mention the length and inflexibility of the local content table. The table featured over 90 items, each one carrying commitments, and very well detailed.[33] The need to determine local content requirements for activities that should occur six, eight, or even ten years in the future made model efficiency difficult. The model surpasses relevant market variants, such as macroeconomic conditions, oil prices, or even breakthrough technologies coming down the line. Further, Brazil's high requirement for local suppliers' competitiveness is also due to the reduction of the so-called *Custo Brasil*[34] and the improvements in infrastructure and workforce.[35] However, the policy was designed to focus, mainly, on the establishment of local purchase obligations, which does not lend itself to the increase of competitiveness in the local industry, especially when there is only one buyer. So, these local content policies led to reduced efficiency and higher costs to comply with such rules as not all of them were readily available or at least led to a fairly lengthy and uncertain process to obtain waivers of certain obligations.

The high costs involved in the acquisition of the equipment and services using the latest technology, in addition to uncertainties of the agreed terms when facing the market (i.e. availability, purchase, delivery, price, quality, term, sale, and replacement), raise layers of risk in the execution of the local content policy. The contractual and regulatory terms are challenges faced by operating

---

[31] F. B. Reynolds and B. R.Schneider, 'Introduction' in F. B. Reynolds et al. (eds.), *Innovation in Brazil: Advancing Development in the 21st Century* (Routledge, 2019) 1–10.

[32] Ibid.

[33] Filho, note 86,

[34] *Custo Brasil* refers to the increase in operational costs associated with doing business in Brazil, making Brazilian goods and services more expensive when compared to other countries. There are several factors that contribute to the extra costs, including high levels of public deficits; inefficiency of public services; maintenance of high interest rates; exaggerated net interest spread of financial institutions (among the highest in the world); excessive bureaucracy for imports and exports, creating difficulties for foreign trade; low education levels and lack of qualified labor; excessive layers of bureaucracy (e.g. starting a company in Brazil takes at least 120 days); high levels of corruption within the public sector; high tax burden; expensive labor costs; high social security costs; complex and inefficient fiscal legislation; economic instability; high electricity costs; legal uncertainty; among others.

[35] Pereira et al., note 22.

companies. The chronogram during the project execution needs to be adjusted, anticipating or postponing the foreseen activities. The companies face delays due to several elements, including lack of availability of products, services, technology, qualified labor, regional differences, logistics, and beyond. The exploration, development, and production of oil and gas demand continuous duty of control and care of the activities performed. A complex and stringent local content regulation increases the likelihood of financial penalties due to the breach of strict contractual or regulatory terms or even misinterpretation of the extensive regulatory framework. Those uncertainties may generate higher and unforeseeable costs in the acquisition of national goods and services. The geological and exploration risks faced by the operating companies may potentialize the need to import unique technology and equipment that may threaten the overall local content percentage commitments.

Local content must be one of the tools in a sector's industrial policy, but not the country's industrial policy itself. As such, it must be combined with other measures capable of elevating the competitiveness of local suppliers, such as incentives to oil companies to participate in R&D projects with universities and local research centers, as well as opening up the market to foreign companies, both key to the development of local industry capacity. These were success cases in both Norway and the UK. In Brazil, 76 per cent of suppliers remained focused on the local market, evidencing low international competitivity, and the transfer of technology was not effective as most of the local oil and gas industrial complex is made of subsidiaries of international companies.[36]

As a response to the excess of items to be realized and the fact of them being extremely detailed, Brazilian local content policy is highly punitive: the elevated minimum percentages make the penalties grow exponentially, a phenomenon that demonstrates the disproportion between the companies' demands and the local industry's ability to meet those demands (Figures 16.1 and 16.2). Beyond the fact that the fines do not contribute to the increase of the sector's efficiency, they also charge the regulatory agency even more with waiver requests. The fact that local content requirements are defined in advance, generally seven to ten years prior to the bidding round, is also ineffective because market variants, such as oil price and macroeconomic conditions, are not taken into account. In addition, considering the lifecycle of an upstream project, each phase, as well as their expected returns, can take many years. The exploration phase can take three to ten years, while development usually takes two to four years, and production fifteen to twenty-five years or even longer (see Figure 16.3).

---

[36] Borschiver et al., note 27.

Local Content and SD in Brazil 313

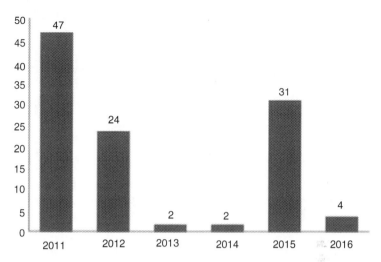

FIGURE 16.1 Number of fines applied to non-fulfillment of local content requirements in the oil and gas sector
Source: Brazilian Petroleum, Gas and Biofuels Institute (IBP) and University of Rio de Janeiro (UFRJ) (2016).

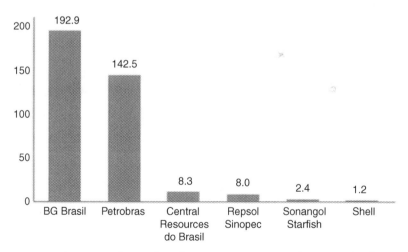

FIGURE 16.2 Fines issued to oil and gas companies in relation to local content requirements (in R$ million)
Source: Adapted from Valor Econômico (2017).

Additionally, the adopted local content policy in Brazil does not follow metrics or indicators that could quantify its results. The absence of a formal assessment is connected to the institutional fragmentation of the policy's governance, as well as to the great diversity of public institutions involved in the different stages of the local

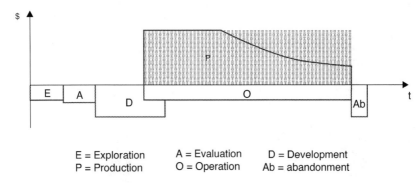

FIGURE 16.3 Upstream project typical cash flow
Source: Pereira (2000).[37]

content policy cycle. This makes it hard for institutional leadership to emerge and coordinate the process.[38]

The obligation of a minimum local content share in concession contracts of exploration blocks demands the creation of a unique metric system that assures uniformity, transparency, and credibility to the many acting agents in the Brazilian oil and gas sector.[39]

Unfortunately, it is not clear to society if this was effectively realized, since oil and gas companies, with the exception of Petrobras, are not obligated to make purchases in a transparent manner. Petrobras, on the other hand, follows public purchases norms that obligate them to have more transparency in the process, despite the mechanism alone not being able to guarantee the transparency and clarity desired.[40] Nevertheless, Petrobras illustrates another key concern with LCRs as shown during investigations known as "car washes."[41] If local content and procurement rules are not well designed nor properly audited nor fully transparent it could lead to corruption cases.[42]

[37] Figure 16.3 shows the duration of each of the steps in an upstream project, with production and operation being the longest ones. Thus, a local content policy determined in the event of a bidding round, or before (which is the case in Brazil), becomes out of date through the lifecycle of the project.
[38] E. de Almeida et al., *Custos e Benefícios da Atual Política de Conteúdo Local* (IBP – UFRJ, 2016) pp 23–34, www.ibp.org.br/personalizado/uploads/2017/01/2016/TD/Custos-e-Benef%C3%ADcios-da-Pol%C3%ADtica-Conteúdo/Local.pdf.
[39] C. E. R. Xavier Junior, "TD 1775 – Políticas de Conteúdo Local no Setor Petrolífero: O Caso Brasileiro e a Experiência Internacional," Instituto de Pesquisa Económica Aplicada (IPEA), October 2012.
[40] Ibid.
[41] "Operation Car Wash" is the massive corruption probe into former President Luiz Inácio Lula da Silva. High-level Petrobras employees were identified as actors in serious corruption practices and subsequently arrested. J. Watts, "Operation Car Wash: Is This the Biggest Corruption Scandal in History?" *Guardian* (June 1, 2017).
[42] S. Pearson, "Petrobas Scandal Knocks Broader Brazilian Oil Industry," March 25, 2015, www.ft.com/content/9080ccd2-cdaa-11e4-8760-00144feab7de. For risk of local content and corruption, see, for instance: M. Martini, "Local content policies and corruption in the oil and gas industry," *Transparency International*, September 12, 2014, and S. Rose-Ackerman, *Corruption and Government: Causes, Consequences, and Reform* (Cambridge, UK: Cambridge University Press, 2016), chapter 4.

Another criticism related to the local content policy is that it does not differentiate small from large projects when it comes to requirements and the approval process. Hence, smaller projects with minor volumes are subject to the same rules as larger projects, such as deep-water.[43] Because of that, there are constant problems with bureaucracy and compliance, affecting the profitability of small oil and gas companies.

In addition, it may be very complex and risky to add local content as a bid parameter as it may create the "wrong" incentives for companies to bid unrealistic numbers and later claim for waivers due to the unfeasibility of such an offer/commitment. Alternatively, the host government might ignore waivers but have to impose large fines, which may discourage investments.

Ultimately, the local content policy is criticized for not having a core strategy with well-defined metrics and for not agreeing with the country's reality. Also there is a lack of selectivity, which prohibits purchase strategies of operators focused on the most competitive segments of the chain, considered key segments. According to a study prepared by Bain & Company for the Brazilian Petroleum, Gas and Biofuels Institute (IBP) in 2015,[44] the segments with the highest potential for employment and technology should be the focus of the local content policy. They are (i) projects, fabrication, and installation of modules and topsides, (ii) subsea equipment, and (iii) subsea installation services (see Figures 16.4 and 16.5).

Those segments were found through a multi-criteria analysis, where two matrices were elaborated, one focusing on employment and the other on technology. The vertical axis is the same on both and represents local demand significance in terms of global demand. The horizontal axis considered distinct ponderations in five macroeconomic criteria (billing, CAPEX, employment, EBITDA, and R&D investments). The main goal was to compare results and observe convergence in attempts to prioritize different approaches.[45]

In both cases, all three sectors were located more to the right and up than the others, concluding that they enhance all five criteria and are more attractive to Brazil's long-term development. Moreover, the bigger the circle, the bigger its capacity of generating benefits to the country, consequently to the business scale.[46]

---

[43] Pereira et al., note 22.
[44] IBP and Bain & Company. "Propostas de Políticas Públicas para o desenvolvimento socioeconômico a partir dos investimentos em exploração e produção offshore." Final Report, 2015, www.ibp.org.br/personalizado/uploads/2017/01/ESTUDO-DF-POLITICAS-PUBLI CAS.pdf, last accessed January 18, 2020.
[45] Ibid.
[46] Ibid.

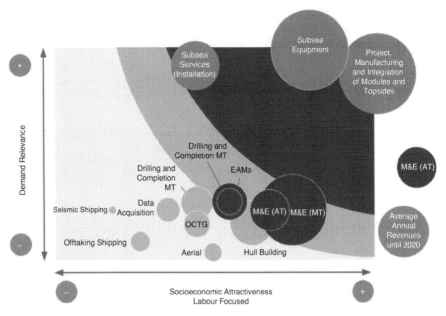

FIGURE 16.4 Priority matrix focused on employment
Source: Brazilian Petroleum, Gas and Biofuels Institute (IBP) and Bain & Company (2015) (note 44).

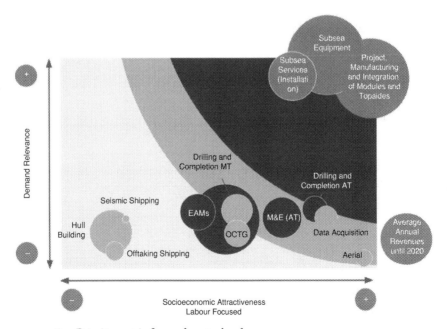

FIGURE 16.5 Priority matrix focused on technology
Source: Brazilian Petroleum, Gas and Biofuels Institute (IBP) and Bain & Company (2015) (note 44).

Local Content and SD in Brazil 317

Local content should be the focus for technology advancement in coordination with all related and connected industries (including but not limited to shipyards, heavy industries, construction, etc.) in order to maximize employment and benefits to the economy in a wider sense.

4 ADVANCING SUSTAINABLE DEVELOPMENT IN LCR IMPLEMENTATION: RECOMMENDATIONS

It is important to make clear policies and goals in order to achieve any sustainable development. Local content is not an afterthought. In fact, it can be an important tool to help prevent the surge of Dutch disease.[47] To do that, these policies must focus on strengthening technology-intensive sectors and be guided by certain factors such as accountability, performance measurement metrics, efficiency, access to information, progress monitoring, financing, R&D incentives, and taxes.

Unfortunately, this is not the case in Brazil on most fronts. Brazilian local content policies has lacked strategic long-term planning and at best has had different governmental policies, which changed from one government to the next. Lack of political stability and continuity affected long-term planning: this fact became obvious as the terms and conditions for local content parameters kept changing in different bid rounds without consistency. LCR formulation in Brazil took a trial-and-error approach which came with a heavy cost, delays, and uncertainties.

Furthermore, most local content policies fail to encourage better compliance by offering fiscal and/or financial incentives to increase compliance with local content instead of higher fines for lack of compliance only. Furthermore, LCRs should have a foreseeable plan to cease their requirements. Otherwise local companies and industries might not be competitive in an international market, as has happened in the North Sea.[48]

In summary, the current formulation of local content policy has not yet translated into competitiveness for the local industry and has not allowed them to compete in the international market, similar to the UK[49] and Norway,[50] for example. Brazilian LCRs should provide a long-term vision and better focus on technological cooperation with local universities and research centers as has happened in the North Sea.[51] Instead, it has burdened the Brazilian economy, in most cases by reducing the attractiveness of investments and efficiency in the upstream sector, which did not entirely translate into employment and income for the country as the policies and rules might have expected,

---

[47]   See note 23.
[48]   F. G. Pereira and T. Gormley, "Conclusion" in Eduardo G. Pereira and Tonje Gormley (eds.), *Local Content for International Petroleum Industry* (Pennwell, 2018) 435–448.
[49]   Ibid.
[50]   Ibid.
[51]   Ibid.

318 *Pereira, Baleroni, Delgado, Miranda, Koenck, Neves*

except for a few initiatives and certain industries as discussed previously. The gaps in the development of those tools (i.e. the policy management model) include: the establishment of governance mechanisms and institutional coordination; development of a planning model for strategies where the objectives to be achieved; and generation of jobs, increased productivity, and dynamic competitive capacity generation.

In addition, the performance of an entire oil and gas project, including decommissioning of facilities, lasts more than thirty years. The local content policy should target the attraction of new local and foreign investments for the long term. It should not impact the commitments towards the government, and should always benefit the people, the environment, and the institutions. As a result of the established strategic objectives, the following shall be defined: the resources needed for development of strategies; the industrial policy instruments to be used whether they are light or heavy policies; externalities measurement indicators adhering to the defined strategic objectives; the role of science, technology, and innovation in the development of the policy; structured measurement of the way the relationship between the costs associated with the resources are applied; the benefits from the implemented policies; and a timeframe to end such LCRs.

Unfortunately, these institutional goals and long-term policies are severely affected by a lack of political stability and different approaches by different political parties in power. This was clearly the case in Brazil for the past decade. Nevertheless, Brazil is not alone with such a lack of political stability, as it seems to be the norm in a number of oil and gas jurisdictions as we have seen in the UK,[52] the USA,[53] Mexico,[54] Argentina,[55] Venezuela,[56] among others in the past years.

5 CONCLUSION

Local content can be a powerful and effective tool to boost the wider local economy. However, it can also reduce the development of the petroleum industry, impact the local level of competitiveness, and increase corruption, among other issues. These are some reasons why local content should be well designed and take into account the reality of each country with a progressive system in order to avoid most pitfalls behind local content policies and regulations.

[52] K. Prescott, 'Brexit Uncertainty Is Harming My Business', www.bbc.com/news/business-50116368, last accessed January 14, 2020.

[53] 'Trump's Policies Are Bringing Instability to a Fragile World Economy', www.washingtonpost.com /opinions/trumps-policies-are-bringing-instability-to-a-fragile-world-economy/2019/08/01/ d926ea94-b486-11e9-8f6c-7828e68cb15f/story.html, last accessed January 14, 2020.

[54] N. P. Flannery, 'Political Risk Analysis: What to Expect after Mexico's 2018 Presidential Election', www.forbes.com/sites/nathanielparishflannery/2018/06/26/political-risk-analysis-what-to-expect-from-mexicos-2018-presidential-election/#6488fa695a76, last accessed January 14, 2020.

[55] A. Cummins, 'Argentina's Political Uncertainly Is Stoking Financial Fear', www.ft.com/content/ f31bfofc-ce3f-11e9-bo18-ca4456540ea6, last accessed January 14, 2020.

[56] 'Venezuela Crisis: How the Political Situation Escalated' www.bbc.com/news/world-latin-america -36319877, last accessed January 14, 2020.

The Brazilian experience is not an exception. It demonstrates positive and negative lessons learned from a local content perspective. Positive lessons may include the efficient certified system to increase compliance and reduce governmental administration procedures[57] and the increase in the development of certain sectors, such as the naval sector and related industries. Negative lessons may include unrealistic parameters and pervasive incentives to bid unrealistic local content terms.[58] Another negative example might be the lack of distinction from small to large projects.

In any case, it will be interesting to follow the LCRs in Brazil, how they will evolve and until when they would survive. Arguably, one of the reasons why local content succeeded in the UK and Norway was the end of its regime and obligations. Although some initial protection to the local industry may make sense (such as via local content requirements), the true goal should be fostering an industry able to compete globally – or at least, some competitive industrial niches.

---

[57] F. Pereira and T. Gormley, note 48.
[58] Ibid.

17

Industrial Policy and Local Content Rules in US Energy Policy

Zachary Sturman and Timothy Meyer

1 INTRODUCTION

The United States (US) has a long history of using local content requirements (LCRs) – laws, regulations, or governmental measures that condition a benefit, often financial support, on the use of a certain percentage of inputs from the local jurisdiction – to promote the development of favored domestic industries. The energy sector, as well as related infrastructure industries, have been no exception. Historically, the US has used LCRs and similar measures to promote the development of fossil fuel industries. More recent interest by policymakers in the US have spurred the use of local content rules tied to pipeline construction, as well as extensive use of LCRs to spur investment in renewable energy. Moreover, LCRs are used at every level of government in the US, from the federal to state and local governments.

This chapter describes the use of LCRs and similar measures in the US, first generally and then in the energy sector specifically. Section 2 argues that the initial turn toward LCRs in the US came at the state and local level as a result of constraints placed on tariffs. Tariffs provide a relatively transparent means of protecting domestic industries from foreign competition, while at the same time raising government revenues. The US, however, is a federal country. Very early in its history, the US banned the use of tariffs by its constituent states. US states responded by substituting regulatory protection for tariff-based protection, including some of the earliest local content rules in the US.

Section 3 describes the migration of local content rules from the state and local level to the federal level, beginning most importantly with the Buy American Act of 1933. Just as occurred at the state and local level within the US, the emergence of LCRs at the federal level coincides with reductions in tariffs, in this case as a result of the emergence of the modern international trade system. Rapid growth in federal spending as a means of spurring economic activity during the Great Depression also contributed to federal interest in LCRs.

Section 4 describes the use of LCRs in the energy sector. Not surprisingly, given the history of LCRs at the state and local level, energy-related LCRs appear very

320

Industrial Policy and Local Content Rules in US   321

common subnationally. At the same time, they also exist at the federal level, and a renewed interest in industrial policy has led to a number of proposals from policymakers across the political spectrum to expand their use in the energy sector.

Section 5 considers the role that LCRs might play in promoting sustainable energy practices. There are at least two reasons to think LCRs might not promote sustainable energy practices. The first is the conventional view that LCRs distort product markets and lead to economic inefficiency. The second is that LCRs are used to promote investment in both fossil fuels and renewable energy, meaning that LCRs do not uniquely promote the development of lower carbon energy options. We suggest, however, that LCRs may nevertheless promote renewable energy more than fossil fuels for several reasons. For instance, by magnifying local benefits, LCRs may encourage policymakers to subsidize the development of new industries, like renewable energy, that create public goods and are therefore likely to be underfunded relative to what would be optimal from a social welfare perspective. Section 6 concludes.

2 PROTECTIONISM IN EARLY AMERICAN HISTORY

In the nineteenth century, Great Britain sought to arrest colonial inroads into the British manufacturing sector and envisioned American colonies as mere suppliers of raw materials. To that end, England levied restrictions and duties on colonists in order to shelter English dominance of global manufacturing.[1] Subsequent to American independence, leaders of the new Republic pushed to develop an internationally competitive manufacturing sector. George Washington and Alexander Hamilton viewed protection for domestic industries, in the form of tariffs, not only as a tool to jumpstart American manufacturing, but also as a necessary antidote to reliance on foreign nations. True American independence, they thought, required economic independence.[2]

The first century and a half of American history reveals high tariff policies, averaging over 25 percent for imports after the War of 1812. During this time period, tariffs played a two-fold role. First, before the creation of the income tax, tariffs served as the primary revenue generator for the new nation.[3] Second, tariffs provided protection for young US industries.[4] In the earlier part of the nineteenth century, Henry Clay's American system used tariffs to protect infant industries in the

---

[1] R. Dewey, *Financial History of the US*, 4th ed. (New York: Longmans, Green, and Co., 1912), pp. 9–10 (noting that the British crown did not levy duties on colonies to "enrich the treasury" but rather to protect manufacturing).

[2] P. Bairoch, *Economics and World History: Myths and Paradoxes* (University of Chicago Press, 1993).

[3] J. Dobson, "Two Centuries of Tariffs: The Background and Emergence of the US International Trade Commission," US International Trade Commission, December 1976, pp. 1–2. This revenue-generating function of tariffs persisted until ratification of the 16th Amendment in 1913, which legalized the government's direct taxation of individual income.

[4] See F. W. Taussig, *The Tariff History of the US: A Series of Essays*, 6th ed. (Cornell University Library, 1913), pp. 1, 23 (describing "protection to young industries").

northeastern part of the US, while devoting much of the revenue tariffs generated to building the infrastructure of westward expansion.[5] By the late nineteenth century, protection for industry and labor in the face of the economic upheaval created by industrialization became a dominant rationale for the tariff.[6]

Critically, this period predated the modern international trade regime, with its focus on reducing tariffs via rounds of reciprocal tariff negotiations. As a consequence, protection at the federal level did not need to take the form of regulations (although of course it could). Tariffs provided a generally more attractive means of protection – one that benefitted domestic industry and labor while simultaneously funding the government.

The story within the US was different. The US was initially composed of thirteen former British colonies that thought of themselves as sovereign states after the American Revolution. The initial charter governing their relationship, the 1781 Articles of Confederation, permitted each state to set its own foreign tariffs and also apply tariffs to goods moving between the states within the US.[7] In 1789, however, the US Constitution replaced the Articles of Confederation. The Constitution granted the US government, not the state governments, control of taxation and foreign commerce, and it explicitly forbade the states from imposing interstate or foreign tariffs on goods.[8] The US Constitution thus created an early version of what we might now call a customs union – a zone with no internal tariffs and a common external tariff.

Abolishing the states' ability to impose internal tariffs did not, of course, remove political pressures for protection at the subnational level. It simply removed the primary tool of protection. Unable to use tariffs anymore, states turned to regulatory protection, including measures that look very much like modern LCRs. The use of these measures only accelerated as the US economy became increasingly integrated.[9] As a consequence, in the nineteenth and early twentieth centuries, US cities and states created a range of policies that sought to give preference to local products or services as a condition of accessing local markets. US courts evaluated the constitutionality of these measures under a doctrine known as the Dormant Commerce Clause, which holds that the US Constitution "denies the States the power unjustifiably to discriminate against or burden the interstate flow of articles of commerce."[10]

---

[5] For an overview, see M. G. Baxter, *Henry Clay and the American System* (University of Kentucky Press, 1995). See D. Irwin, *Clashing over Commerce: A History of US Trade Policy* (University of Chicago Press, 2017), p. 157 (explaining how the Senate used internal improvements to incentivize tariff votes).

[6] See J. L. Huston, "A Political Response to Industrialism: The Republican Embrace of Protectionist Labor Doctrines" (1983) 70 *Journal of American History* 35–57.

[7] C. R. Drahozal, "On Tariffs v. Subsidies in Interstate Trade: A Legal and Economic Analysis" (1996) 74 *Washington University Law Quarterly* 1127 at 1180–1181.

[8] US Constitution § 9, cl. 6, § 10, cl. 2.

[9] Localities in early America were more self-sufficient (prior to the development of a complex manufacturing sector in the US) and less interconnected, which meant that the role of intra-colonial or intra-state protectionist efforts would be limited. Dobson, note 3, pp. 14–15.

[10] *Oregon Waste Systems, Inc. v. Department of Environmental Quality*, 511 US 93, 98 (1994).

For instance, in the mid-nineteenth century, Pennsylvania required vessels coming into the port of Philadelphia to employ a local pilot – a measure designed in part to boost local employment. Although conditioning access to the local port on the use of local labor, the Supreme Court upheld the measure as a justifiable way to take into account local concerns.[11] By contrast, in 1890 the Supreme Court struck down a Minnesota law requiring any meat sold within the state to be inspected by local Minnesota authorities no longer than 24 hours prior to slaughter. The effect of the law was to require meat producers to use Minnesota slaughterhouses as a condition of accessing the Minnesota market.[12] Similarly, in *Dean Milk Company*, the Supreme Court struck down a municipality's ordinance in Wisconsin that required milk sellers to pasteurize and bottle commercial milk within five miles of the city center.[13] More recently, in 1984 the Supreme Court struck down a law requiring timber harvested in Alaska to be processed in Alaska before it could be exported.[14] A raft of similar state measures require the use of in-state service providers as a means of forcing out-of-state industries to do business with in-state service providers as a condition of accessing the local market.[15]

Although not necessarily thought of LCRs historically, and not all unconstitutional, these measures all create forms of local content requirements. They discourage interstate trade in various products by requiring an out-of-state actor to employ local service providers within the state in which the goods are ultimately sold. More generally, these measures attest to how legal rules limiting protection interact with a persistent political demand for protection of local interests. Legal rules that limit one form of protection, such as tariffs, spur innovation in other forms of protection, such as regulatory protection and local content rules.

3 MODERN LCRS IN THE US

While LCRs and similar forms of regulatory protection flourished at the state level during the nineteenth century, they did not migrate to the federal level until the early decades of the twentieth century. In this section, we discuss the rise of LCRs at the federal level. Three changes made regulatory protection, and LCRs in particular, more attractive during this period.

---

[11] *Cooley v. Board of Wardens*, 53 US 299 (1851).

[12] *Minnesota v. Barber*, 136 US 313 (1890).

[13] *Dean Milk Co. v. Madison*, 340 US 349 (1951), para. 356.

[14] *South-Central Timber Development, Inc. v. Wunnicke*, 467 US 82 (1984), para. 100 (holding unconstitutional Alaska's requirement that timber produced in-state be processed in-state before it could be exported).

[15] E.g., *Pike v. Bruce Church, Inc.*, 397 US 137 (invalidating Arizona's requirement that cantaloupes sold in-state also be packed in-state). Other measures simply impose regulatory burdens on out-of-state products not imposed on in-state products. *Voit v. Wright*, 141 US 62(1891), paras, 64–65 (holding unconstitutional a Virginia statute requiring only out-of-state flour to be inspected prior to sale within the state). Although similar, these measures are not LCRs because they do not condition a benefit (usually market access) on using local goods or services.

324   *Zachary Sturman and Timothy Meyer*

First, the income tax supplanted the tariff as the primary source of the federal government's revenue. In the nineteenth century, many doubted the constitutionality of an income tax. In 1913, the 16th Amendment to the US Constitution established the income tax's constitutionality. With a superior source of revenue, the tariff lost one of its major policy justifications.

Second, the US began to negotiate international trade agreements that called for tariff reductions. As a policy matter, these agreements were justified by a belief that tariff increases – especially the Smoot–Hawley Tariff of 1930 – had contributed to the Great Depression. Legally, the Reciprocal Trade Agreements Act of 1934 provided the basis for the US to reduce its tariffs in accordance with tariff-reduction agreements with other nations. The decrease in tariffs accelerated after World War II with the creation of the General Agreement in Tariffs and Trade (GATT). Over the latter half of the twentieth century, GATT parties negotiated trade liberalization in a series of negotiating "rounds." The US reduced its average industrial tariffs by 26 percent in the first GATT negotiating round alone.[16] More modest cuts followed in the 1950s, with significantly deeper cuts (as a percentage) from the 1960s onward during the so-called Kennedy, Tokyo, and Uruguay Rounds of GATT negotiations.[17] Just as the elimination of tariffs within the US was associated with increased forms of regulatory protection, so too did the decline in tariffs increase interest in regulatory protection at the federal level.[18]

Third, the 1930s also saw the birth of the modern administrative state and, along with it, a significant increase in the federal government's expenditures. US voters elected Franklin Roosevelt president in 1932. Upon taking office, Roosevelt reversed his predecessor's austerity policies and moved to rapidly increase domestic spending as a way to jumpstart the nation's economy. Perhaps not surprisingly, if the government makes expenditures with taxpayer dollars, citizens often expect those dollars to flow primarily, if not exclusively, to US citizens and businesses. LCRs, of course, achieve this purpose by requiring the recipients of federal funds to spend those funds on the consumption of domestic goods and services.

To that end, the Buy American Act of 1933 constitutes the oldest and most well-known federal LCR.[19] Like most modern LCRs, the Buy American Act deals primarily with government procurement. It establishes price preferences for American products and American construction materials when the federal government acts as a buyer. If the cost of a bidder's American-sourced components is at least half the total cost of all the components in that bidder's offer, then this

---

[16]   World Trade Organization, "World Trade Report 2007: Six Decades of Multilateral Cooperation: What Have We Learnt?" 2007, p. 207.
[17]   Ibid.
[18]   See, e.g., E.J . Ray, "Changing Patterns of Protectionism: The Fall in Tariffs and the Rise in Non-Tariff Barriers Symposium: The Political Economy of International Trade Law and Policy" (1987–1988) 8 *Northwestern Journal of International Law and Business* 285.
[19]   *Buy American Act of 1933*, Act of March 3, 1933, 47 Stat 1520 (codified, as amended, at 41 USC. §§8301–8305) [Buy American Act].

domestic-sourcing bidder will receive favorable treatment from federal agencies.[20] Specifically, bidders who meet these domestic content conditions are not subject to the addition of an above-bid percentage that agencies tack onto noncompliant bids in order to account for foreign sourcing of products.[21] This ranges from 6 to 50 percent, but agencies are free to adopt higher percentages by regulation.[22] Although Congress permits agencies some discretion in complying with the Act, agencies are required to track purchases via submissions to the Federal Data Procurement Data System and must indicate if procured goods are domestically sourced "in accordance with the Buy American Act."[23] From the bidders' side of the equation, vendors must provide a Buy American certificate if they wish to win bids for supply contracts with the federal government.[24]

Importantly, several exceptions to the Buy American Act free agencies from the requirement to apply this markup. For example, goods in small purchasing orders[25] or goods to be used outside the US are not within the purview of the Buy American Act.[26] But the most important exception to the Buy American Act comes from the Trade Agreements Act of 1979.[27] The Trade Agreements Act permits the President to waive the Buy American Act or other domestic procurement requirements for countries that are party to, or otherwise comply with, the WTO's Government Procurement Agreement (GPA) or a US free trade agreement, such as the North American Free Trade Agreement.[28] The GPA requires parties to treat foreign and domestic bids for procurement contracts equally.[29] Therefore, for the majority of federal procurement contracts, products from the more than 60 countries with whom the US has trade agreements are treated the same as American products.[30]

---

[20] Ibid.; K. Manuel, "Buy American Act – Preferences for 'Domestic' Supplies: In Brief," Congressional Research Service, April 26, 2016, pp. 1, 3 (also discussing that bidders can receive favorable treatment if products are commercially available off-the-shelf, or "COTS," items).

[21] Buy American Act, note 19.

[22] Ibid.

[23] "GSA Federal Procurement Data System-Next Generation (FPDS-NG) Data Element Dictionary," Version 1.5, October 25, 2019, chapter 9H.

[24] 48 CFR § 52.225–2(a).

[25] Manuel, note 20 (explaining that "micro-purchases" under $3,500 are not subject to the Buy American Act).

[26] Ibid., pp. 1, 6 (outlining several exceptions to the Buy American Act, including cases wherein domestic products are unavailable, domestic product prices are "unreasonable," purchasing domestic products would be "inconsistent with the public interest," the bid is for a commercial item in the information technology sector, and when the procured goods are for the express purpose of commissary resale).

[27] 19 USC § 2511; 48 CFR § 25.403.

[28] K. M. Manuel, A. M. Dolan, B. J. Murrill, R. M. Perry, and S. P. Mulligan, "Domestic Content Restrictions: The Buy American Act and Complementary Provisions of Federal Law," *Congressional Research Service, September* 12, 2016, pp. 1, 7. As of the time of writing, the North American Free Trade Agreement may be, but has not yet been, replaced by the US–Mexico–Canada Agreement.

[29] Ibid., pp. 1, 7–9.

[30] Public Citizen, "How Overreaching 'Trade' Pact Rules Can Undermine Buy American and Other Domestic Preference Procurement Policies," 2018.

326 *Zachary Sturman and Timothy Meyer*

Although waivers of Buy American requirements based on these trade agreements limit American producers' advantages in securing procurement contracts with the US government, they also, of course, allow American producers to more equitably compete for procurement contracts with foreign governments.[31]

Beyond the Buy American Act, a range of federal statutes creates LCRs in a number of areas.[32] We highlight four here – defense, federally financed projects, international development, and sustainable energy.

3.1 NATIONAL DEFENSE

The Berry Amendment requires nearly all Department of Defense purchases to be US-sourced.[33] It requires that "specialty metals" – which comprise the armed forces' aircraft, missiles, tanks, weapons systems, and ammunition – come exclusively from American producers.[34] The Amendment surfaced in World War II as a yearly appropriations measure and ultimately gained permanence in 1993.[35] Significantly, the Trade Agreements Act has no bearing on these military-related domestic content requirements. In fact, many trade agreements include express language assuring that the trade agreements have no effect on domestic content requirements for military purchases.[36] National security concerns propel this sacrosanct insulation of defense purchases from foreign competition in procurement.[37]

3.2 *Federally Financed Programs*

While LCRs at the federal level began with government procurement, increasingly the US government attaches local content rules to federally financed programs – programs in which the government gives money to other entities, such as state and local governments, to pay for a project.[38] Under international law, the US is legally responsible for the actions of its subnational governments. As a matter of US

---

[31] Ibid.

[32] Manuel et al., note 28, pp. 1, 24–28, provides a detailed list of LCRs in federal law.

[33] There are some exceptions provided in the Berry Amendment. For instance, if domestic products are not available or if there are wartime, urgent needs for materials that can be more easily fulfilled with foreign products, then some substitution for foreign supplies can take place. See ibid., pp. 1, 15.

[34] 10 USC §2533(b).

[35] *Department of Defense Appropriations Act*, 1994, PL 103–139, § 8005, 107 Stat 1488 (Nov. 11, 1993). Manuel et al., note 28, pp. 1, 12.

[36] Manuel et al., note 28, pp. 1, 14. See also Revised WTO Government Procurement Agreement, US Appendix I, Annex I (outlining that the GPA WTO does not apply to mostly all Department of Defense purchases).

[37] US Government Accountability Office, "Defense Acquisition: Rationale for Imposing Domestic Source Restrictions," GAO/NSIAD-98-191, July 17, 1998, p. 1. See also Manuel et al., note 28, pp.1, 12–13.

[38] G .C. Hufbauer, J. J. Schott, C. Cimino, M. Viero, and E. Wade, "Local Content Requirements: Report on a Global Problem," Petersen Institute for International Economics, June 28, 2013, pp. 1, 120–122.

domestic law, however, international agreements do not automatically bind subnational governments, such as US state governments. This discrepancy, common in federal countries, creates a situation in which a subnational government can create international liability for the nation that the central government cannot easily avoid.[39] In response to this problem, some international agreements, including the GPA, exempt local measures unless they are specifically included.[40] As a result, US states are either actually exempt from the GPA's rules or, at a minimum, cannot easily be compelled to comply as a matter of domestic law.

For example, when local or state governments accept federal dollars for transit projects, any iron or steel purchased must come from American manufacturers.[41] When the Federal Aviation Administration, Federal Highway Administration, Federal Transit Administration, Federal Railroad Administration, or Amtrak oversee subnational government projects, LCRs usually attach to this federal oversight.[42] Some of these statutes even explicitly permit states to impose more stringent LCRs than those imposed by federal law.[43] By way of example in the energy sector (to which we will return in greater detail), in 1936, Congress sought to catalyze the development of electricity and telephone infrastructure in rural areas through the Rural Electrification Act. Any state participation in this federal program had to be accompanied by the use of American materials and supplies.[44]

3.3 International Development

LCRs also surface in the context of federal agencies' selection of grants for international development projects. The US Agency for International Development (USAID) administers a number of grant projects that outline preferential treatment for American-sourced bidders. The USAID "renewable energy technology transfer program" considers the extent to which a bidder's equipment has been produced in the US, and awardees' materials costs must be at least 50 percent from American producers.[45] Interestingly, Congress made clear that its purpose in passing this program was to promote "the export of US renewable energy technologies and

---

[39] T. Meyer, "Local Liability in International Economic Law" (2017) 95 North Carolina Law Review 261. In most, if not all, cases, federal legislation could preempt subnational action that was inconsistent with an international agreement. As a practical matter, however, getting Congress to pass such legislation, or the executive branch to bring a lawsuit to preempt a subnational measure, is very difficult. Ibid.; see also Medellin v. Texas, 552 US 491 (2008).

[40] Revised WTO GPA, note 36, Annex 2. In fact, a surprisingly large number of US state executive branch programs are subject to the GPA's rules.

[41] 23 USC §313(a) (for projects administered by the Federal Highway Administration); 49 USC § 50101 (a) (for Federal Aviation Administration projects); 49 USC § 5323(j) (for Federal Transit Administration projects); 49 USC § 24405(a)(1) (for Federal Railroad Administration projects).

[42] Manuel et al., note 28, pp. 1, 17–20; Hufbauer et al., note 38, pp. 1, 120–21; Public Citizen, note 30.

[43] 23 USC §313(d).

[44] Manuel et al., note 28, pp. 1, 24–25; Rural Electrification Act of 1936, Pub L No. 115–334.

[45] 42 USC § 13316.

328   *Zachary Sturman and Timothy Meyer*

technological expertise; retain and create manufacturing and related service jobs in the US;" and only secondarily to "assist foreign countries in meeting their energy needs through the use of renewable energy in an environmentally acceptable manner."[46] USAID's "innovative clean coal technology transfer program" stipulates the same LCRs.[47] In a similar vein, for projects unrolling outside the US, LCRs often apply. The federal statute creating the International Clean Energy Foundation, a government corporation, requires the Foundation to give preference in its grant-making procedures to US companies and to technologies substantially manufactured in the US.[48] In 2003, Congress passed legislation requiring that any US participation in international research in nuclear fusion must guarantee that the percent of high-technology components in the program is greater than or equal to the US' financial contribution to the project.[49]

3.4 *Sustainable Energy*

Finally, the federal government uses LCRs to promote sustainable energy domestically through its own procurement practices. For instance, Congress passed legislation requiring the federal government prioritize energy-efficient lighting in procurement contracts, and the legislation specified that these energy-efficient lighting purchases should align with the Buy American Act.[50] Another federal statute mandates federal agencies opt "to the maximum extent possible" to purchase vehicles that run on alternative fuel sources. This statute provides that the federal government should give preference to vehicles that use *domestically* sourced alternative fuels.[51] Yet another statute requires that the Department of Defense give favorable treatment in procurement contracts for photovoltaic devices that rely on American-manufactured components.[52]

4 THE PREVALENCE OF LCRS IN THE US ENERGY SECTOR

As the prior sections have demonstrated, LCRs are deeply embedded in the US constraints on tariff-based protection and have channeled pressure for protection into regulatory protection, including LCRs, while political pressure to spend tax dollars locally have caused LCRs to proliferate throughout government-spending

[46] Ibid.
[47] 42 USC § 13362.
[48] 42 USC § 17353.
[49] 42 USC § 16312.
[50] Use of Energy Efficient Lighting Fixtures and Bulbs, Pub L No 40–3313, www.law.cornell.edu/uscode/text/40/3313.
[51] Alternative Fuel Use by Light Duty Federal Vehicles, Pub L No 42–6374, www.law.cornell.edu/uscode/text/42/6374.
[52] 10 USC § 2534; Miscellaneous Technology and Base Programs, Pub L No 10–2531, www.govinfo.gov/app/content/pkg/USCODE-2014-title10/html/USCODE-2014-title10-subtitleA-partIV-chap148-subchapV.htm.

programs of various kinds. In this section, we describe the use of LCRs in the energy sector more specifically. We begin with a description of energy-specific LCRS at the state level. While LCRs and LCR-like programs have historically been common in the oil and gas industry, they have become especially significant in the renewable-energy context, where they have been the subject of a WTO dispute. Energy-related LCRs can also be found at the federal level, although as we will explain in Section 4.3, it is the renewed interest in such LCRs at the federal level that is particularly important.

4.1 State-Level Oil and Gas LCRs

States have for many years used LCRs and similar programs to encourage companies to invest in and extract natural resources located within their borders. These programs often straddle the boundary between regulations designed to attract business and outright LCRs. States often give benefits in the form of tax breaks or subsidies to companies that agree to locate within the state. For instance, Wisconsin legislators hurled government benefits at multinational manufacturing giant, Foxconn, to induce the company to move its manufacturing plant to the state.[53] Amazon's well-publicized campaign to launch its second headquarters has garnered similar state and local government efforts to lure the technology giant in hopes of producing jobs and economic growth.[54] These programs differ from traditional LCRs, however, in that – while they typically grant companies benefits, like tax exemptions, that are justified on the expectation that they will ultimately lead to greater local economic growth – they do not legally condition benefits on the use of local products, labor, or services.

Similarly, when states implement oil and gas policies, they are often trying to attract energy companies to do business in the state on the hope, but without the legal requirement, that the business will create new jobs. But these programs are more like ordinary LCRs in one important respect: they legally condition benefits on the extraction (i.e., use) of local oil and gas. Without such consumption, the benefits flowing from complying with the LCR do not apply.

For example, Alaska awards 30 to 40 percent tax breaks for any oil and gas expenditures for companies engaging in exploratory projects.[55] In Oklahoma, lawmakers seek to attract new oil and gas exploration by taxing new wells at just 2 percent

---

[53] S. Cohn, "Wisconsin Governor Says Foxconn Is Again Likely to Miss Job Targets," July 9, 2019, www .cnbc.com/2019/07/08/wisconsin-governor-says-foxconn-is-again-likely-to-miss-job-targets.html. Despite Foxconn's purported intent to hire more than 13,000 Wisconsin workers, it has fallen well short of its goals and hired just 156 workers from Wisconsin in 2018.

[54] M.J., "How America's Cities Are Competing for Amazon's Headquarters: with a Mixture of Tax Incentives, Task Forces, and Cacti," December 5, 2017, www.economist.com/the-economist-explains /2017/12/05/how-americas-cities-are-competing-for-amazons-headquarters.

[55] Alaska Department of Revenue: Tax Division, "Alaska Tax Credits," http://tax.alaska.gov/programs/ programs/credits/index.aspx.

330 *Zachary Sturman and Timothy Meyer*

for the first thirty-six months of operation.[56] Then, the wells face the normal 7 percent tax rate thereafter. Texas, the US' largest producer of oil and gas,[57] administers an array of tax programs aimed at incentivizing oil and gas production. Tax exemptions vary depending on whether the well is new, "previously flared," high cost, or a marginal well.[58] North Dakota provides special exemptions for oil projects outside the so-called Bakken and Three Forks regions, such that the normal 5 percent tax is lowered to 2 percent.[59] Other projects can qualify for complete tax exemptions (0 percent).

State-level oil and gas LCRs do not appear to be losing relevance. In fact, some credit these types of tax exemptions as pivotal launchpads for firms' development of the technology necessary to engage in hydraulic "fracking," wherein companies extract deeply encased shale gas.[60] This technological breakthrough has contributed to a boom in the amount of domestic fossil fuels that companies are able to access in the US.[61]

4.2 *State-Level Renewable Energy LCRs*

The pattern is even more stark in renewable energy. States routinely condition government benefits on renewable energy companies' use of products, labor, or services within the state.[62] The terms vary by state, with some states requiring the use of local equipment (like solar panels or wind turbines), while others require local feedstock or biofuels.[63] For example, the Louisiana Code exempts gasohol – a biofuel that contains at least ten percent alcohol and is thus more sustainable than traditional fuels – from the state sales tax, but only if the alcohol in the gasohol has been "produced, fermented, and distilled" in Louisiana.[64] Another Minnesota

---

[56] D. Blatt, "Cost of Oil and Gas Tax Breaks Continues to Approach $400 Million," May 2, 2019, https://okpolicy.org/cost-oil-gas-tax-breaks-continues-approach-400-million/.

[57] US Energy Information Administration, "Monthly Crude Oil and Natural Gas Production," October 31, 2019, www.eia.gov/petroleum/production/.

[58] Railroad Commission of Texas, "Present Texas Severance Tax Incentives," www.rrc.state.tx.us/oil-gas/publications-and-notices/texas-severance-tax-incentives-past-and-present/presenttax/.

[59] North Dakota: Office of State Tax Commissioner, "What is the Current Severance Tax Rate for Oil and Gas Produced in North Dakota?" www.nd.gov/tax/faqs/articles/160-/.

[60] Associated Press, "Tax Breaks, US Research Play Big Part in Success of Fracking," January 12, 2019, www.cleveland.com/nation/2012/09/tax_breaks_us_research_play_bi.html.

[61] PPI Energy and Chemicals Team, "The Effects of Shale Gas Production on Natural Gas Prices," US Bureau of Labor Statistics: Beyond the Numbers, May 2013.

[62] T. Meyer, "How Local Discrimination Can Promote Public Goods" (2015) 95 *Boston University Law Review* 1939 at 1959–1963.

[63] Indiana Code Title 5. State and Local Administration § 5–22-5–8.5(f) (requiring a preference for clean energy vehicles from Indiana); Kan. Stat. Ann. § 74–50, 136 (compelling domestic preferences for solar and wind projects), La. Stat. Ann. § 3:3712 (mandating a preference for Louisiana feedstock); La Stat. Ann. § 47:305.23(A) (offering a tax exemption for a biofuel known as "gasohol" if more than ten percent of inputs come from Louisiana).

[64] La Stat. Ann. § 47:305.23(A).

statute provides that any state project that entails the installation of solar panels purchased or installed must be made in Minnesota.[65]

These state-level renewable energy LCRs appear in at least twenty-three states, a number that does not account for similar city-based renewable energy LCRs.[66] Another striking feature of the state-level renewable energy LCRs is that they appear in both politically conservative and politically liberal states. Finding renewable energy LCRs surface in politically liberal states like California, Oregon, Massachusetts, and Connecticut is perhaps unsurprising, given that in the US, political liberals have tended both to support renewable energy policies and, at least until recently, also support greater levels of protectionism.[67] But more conservative states not traditionally pictured as climate change innovators,[68] like Indiana, Kansas, Louisiana, Mississippi, South Carolina, Texas, and Utah, have likewise conditioned government benefits on local content provisions in renewable energy programs.[69] The political milieu surrounding enactment of these renewable energy LCRs in more conservative states likely reflects local job creation and economic considerations alongside any concerns for the health of the planet.[70] It may also reflect path dependence. The use of LCRs and other forms of regulatory protection in the oil and gas sector (as well as other sectors) may influence the future use of LCRs in renewable energy.

The prevalence of renewable energy LCRs has turned out to be a problem for the US. These LCRs are not limited to (although they do include) government procurement programs. As a consequence, they are clearly subject to the general nondiscrimination rules of the GATT.[71] In a 2013 case, the WTO's Appellate Body upheld a ruling that an LCR in the Canadian province of Ontario's feed-in tariff program violated the national treatment obligation found in the WTO's Agreement on Trade-related Investment Measures (TRIMs Agreement) and GATT article III.[72] Based on

---

[65] Minn. Stat. § 174.187(2).

[66] Meyer, note 62, pp. 1959–1963.

[67] Ibid., pp. 2015–2027.

[68] J. Marlon, P. Howe, M. Mildenberger, A. Leiserowitz, and X. Wang, "Yale Climate Opinion Maps 2018," August 7, 2018, https://climatecommunication.yale.edu/visualizations-data/ycom-us-2018/?est=happening&type=value&geo=state; C. Funk and B. Kennedy, "How Americans See Climate Change in 5 Charts," April 19, 2019, www.pewresearch.org/fact-tank/2019/04/19/how-americans-see-climate-change-in-5-charts/.

[69] Meyer, note 62, pp. 2015–2027.

[70] Ibid., p. 1969.

[71] They would also be subject to the subsidies' disciplines in the Agreement on Subsidies and Countervailing Measures, although in practice subsidies claims have been less important in challenging renewable energy LCRs than have ordinary nondiscrimination rules. See T. Meyer, "Explaining Energy Disputes at the World Trade Organization" (2017) 17 *International Environmental Agreements: Politics, Law and Economics* 391.

[72] Appellate Body Reports, Canada – Certain Measures Affecting the Renewable Energy Generation Section, Canada – Measures Relating to the Feed-in Tariff Program, WTO Doc. WT/DS412/AB/R, WT/DS426/AB/R (adopted May 24, 2013).

Zachary Sturman and Timothy Meyer

that decision, the US brought a successful WTO challenge to an LCR in India's Jawaharlal Nehru National Solar Mission program.[73]

India responded by bringing a WTO challenge against a subset of state and local renewable energy LCRs in the US. A dispute panel upheld India's claims that these programs violated GATT article III's national treatment obligation because they provide less favorable treatment to foreign products, as compared to domestic products.[74] The US' appeal of that decision is pending as of the time of writing. Similar decisions, such as the one against Canada, have been followed by the withdrawal of financial support for renewable energy programs.[75] And while it appears the decision against the US is unlikely to receive legal effect until the WTO Appellate Body is reconstituted,[76] India may retaliate against the US anyway.

4.3 Federal LCRs for Energy

The federal government in the US has a number of LCRs for energy. As discussed in Section 3.2, for instance, the Rural Electrification Act – a statute designed to spur investment in electricity infrastructure – contains an LCR. Likewise, government programs designed to procure sustainable energy products often have Buy American requirements, as do international development programs that aim to boost sustainable energy practices in foreign countries.[77] In the last several years, though, an increased interest in industrial policy has led to a rise in the use of LCRs in the energy context.

President Trump heavily campaigned on protectionist sentiments, with a special emphasis on taking measures to revive domestic steel, iron, and coal production.[78] Although he has had difficulty getting legislation through Congress, President Trump has used executive orders to promote the use of LCRs in the context of energy and energy infrastructure.

---

[73] Appellate Body Report, India – Certain Measures Relating to Solar Cells and Solar Modules, WTO Doc. WT/DS456/AB/R (adopted Oct. 14, 2016).

[74] Panel Report, US – Certain Measures Relating to the Renewable Energy Sector, WTO Doc. WT/DS510/R (circulated June 27, 2019).

[75] T. Meyer, "Free Trade, Fair Trade, and Selective Enforcement" (2018) 118 *Columbia Law Review* 491 (documenting the withdrawal of support for renewable energy programs after adverse trade decisions).

[76] As a practical matter, the US' appeal likely prevents the adoption of any adverse decision. The US, as is well known, has blocked the appointment of new members of the WTO's Appellate Body. As of December 2019, the number of Appellate Body members has fallen below the quorum necessary to resolve the appeal. As a result, the implications of the decision are uncertain.

[77] The federal tax code also contains significant tax breaks for oil and gas companies. 26 USC § 263(c) (depending on the time horizon of a project, companies can deduct 30, 70, or 100 percent of taxes they would otherwise owe for the cost to drill wells), 26 USC § 451 (provides a tax credit for "marginal wells," which are wells that do not produce large amounts of oil and gas), and 26 USC § 199 (providing a 6 percent income tax deduction for US oil and gas production).

[78] C. Deppen, "Trump Promised to Bring Back Pennsylvania's Coal, Steel, and Energy Jobs. But Can He?" November 17, 2016, www.pennlive.com/news/2016/11/trump_promised_to_make_pennsyl.html.

Industrial Policy and Local Content Rules in US

For instance, in January 2019, President Trump signed Executive Order 13858, "Strengthening Buy-American Preferences for Infrastructure Projects," instructing the federal government to prioritize the use of American iron and steel in procurement and construction projects.[79] President Trump explicitly linked this last executive order to energy infrastructure projects, in particular the construction of pipelines.[80] Despite this connection, however, the Trump administration has not produced specific guidelines that it promised on the use of domestic content in pipelines.[81] Nor is the executive order likely to have significant real-world impacts. Although it calls for domestic preferences in federal government expenditures, it contains language that cabin its effectiveness to actions "consistent with the law." In other words, the executive order has little effect on any existing laws that disallow preferential treatment of domestic sources.[82]

President Trump's most recent relevant executive order appears potentially more significant for at least any government-funded energy infrastructure projects. Executive Order 13881, "Maximizing Use of American-Made Goods, Products, and Materials," re-defines what counts as American-sourced pursuant to the Buy American Act.[83] Prior to this executive order, in implementing the Buy American Act, agencies gave preferential treatment to products whose US subcomponents'

---

[79] Federal Register, "Executive Order 13858: Strengthening Buy-American Preferences for Infrastructure Projects," January 31, 2019, www.federalregister.gov/documents/2019/02/05/2019–01426/strengthening-buy-american-preferences-for-infrastructure-projects. Although not really LCRs, President Trump also signed a number of "America First" executive orders aimed at promoting the oil and gas industries. Federal Register, "Executive Order 13796: Implementing an America-First Offshore Energy Strategy," April 28, 2017, www.federalregister.gov/documents/2017/05/03/2017–09087/implementing-an-america-first-offshore-energy-strategy. See also Federal Register, "Executive Order 13868: Promoting Energy Infrastructure and Economic Growth," April 10, 2019, www.federalregister.gov/documents/2019/04/15/2019–07656/promoting-energy-infrastructure-and-economic-growth (discussing preferences for catalyzing American energy production). More generally, President Trump also signed Executive Order 13788, which calls for administrative agencies and the federal government more broadly to use goods and products produced in the US and to hire American workers (Federal Register, "Executive Order 13788: Buy American and Hire American," April 18, 2017, www.federalregister.gov/documents/2017/04/21/2017–08311/buy-american-and-hire-american.

[80] President Trump famously called for the Keystone Pipeline to use American steel, but this rhetoric has not been transformed into any codified requirement that steel be sourced from American producers. T. Benning, "Trump's Idea for 'Buy American' Mandate on U.S. Pipeline Projects has 'Vanished': The Inaction Could Reflect Concerns That the Pipelines Mandate Would Be Unfeasible and Potentially in Violation of International Trade Law," February 7, 2018, www.dallasnews.com/business/energy/2018/02/07/trump-s-idea-for-buy-american-mandate-on-u-s-pipeline-projects-has-vanished/.

[81] Ibid.

[82] See T. Kertscher, "Trump Overstates Effect of Memo Of American Steel in Pipelines," April 21, 2017, www.ajc.com/news/national-govt–politics/trump-overstates-effect-memo-american-steel-pipelines/ft4xwNR042p6mqmHhQWNEL/ (discussing the inoperability of Trump's executive order pertaining to steel, and highlighting its inapplicability to the Keystone Pipeline).

[83] Federal Register, "Executive Order 13881: Maximizing Use of American-Made Goods, Products, and Materials," July 15, 2019, www.federalregister.gov/documents/2019/07/18/2019–15449/maximizing-use-of-american-made-goods-products-and-materials.

costs amounted to more than 50 percent of total costs. President Trump changed this so that preferential treatment only applies if the costs of US products included in the final product are more than 55 percent of total costs, instead of the traditional 50 percent. In the case of iron and steel products, he went even further, making preferential treatment contingent on sourcing 95 percent of the components of the final product in the US. To be sure, this executive order affects only the small portion of government procurement contracts and expenditures that are subject to the Buy American Act without being subject to waiver under the Trade Agreements Act. Still, for that subset of procurement purchases, this executive order makes the preference for US products considerably stricter.

If President Trump (a Republican) has at least attempted to use LCRs to boost or otherwise influence oil and gas production in the US, similarly Democratic policymakers have called for the use LCRs to boost renewable energy. Most notably, Senator Chuck Schumer, the Democratic leader in the US Senate, has called for subsidies for the purchase of American-made electric vehicles.[84] His plan aims to simultaneously reduce fossil fuel consumption in the transportation sector and spur the growth of the US auto manufacturing sector. Similarly, Senator Elizabeth Warren, one of the leading candidates for President in the 2020 Democratic primaries, called for the use of LCRs to spur a more rapid transition to clean energy while also establishing US leadership in green technology.[85]

Taken together, these policies and proposals signal a renewed interest in energy-related LCRs at the federal level. However, they differ significantly in the forms of energy they support. President Trump's efforts seek to promote the fossil fuel industries, while Democratic policymakers have sought to use LCRs to promote renewable energy technologies. In the next section, we consider the implications of these differing approaches.

5 DO US LCRS PROMOTE SUSTAINABLE ENERGY?

In this section, we consider whether the use of LCRs in the US is likely to promote sustainable energy. As we explain below, the conventional economic answer to this question is no. LCRs distort markets, causing efficiency losses, and therefore are likely to inhibit the development of markets for new products, such as renewable energy products. This economic view, though, ignores the role of law and politics in promoting sustainable energy. Once one considers the role of law and politics, the case for LCRs, especially in the promotion of public goods in federal countries like the US, becomes significantly stronger.

---

[84] C. Schumer, "A Bold Plan for Clean Cars," October 24, 2019, www.nytimes.com/2019/10/24/opinion/chuck-schumer-electric-car.html.

[85] E. Warren, "Leading in Green Manufacturing," June 4, 2019, https://elizabethwarren.com/plans/green-manufacturing.

5.1 Economic Effectiveness of LCRs

Putting aside both legal restrictions and politics for the moment, from a purely economic point of view, LCRs appear to be suboptimal tools for US industrial policy goals generally and the energy sector in particular. LCRs create economic inefficiency because they use regulation to direct funds to particular products or services favored by the government, and away from similar products that might otherwise meet the consumer needs. The private market, be they consumers or private firms considering investments, do not make their choices based on commercial factors like cost and quality. Rather, they choose based on price considerations driven by regulation, rather than qualities of the product. An oil company, for instance, may invest in one state but not another because the tax exemption is larger, even though the costs associated with actually drilling for oil are higher in that state. Likewise, a consumer may purchase costlier or less efficient domestically produced solar panels because doing so qualifies them for a government credit. These choices are inefficient if a non-local alternative – extracting oil in another state or purchasing cheaper or higher quality foreign solar panels – would be cheaper or of higher quality. The total cost of the product, in other words, is higher because of the LCR. Moreover, directing funds to less-efficient products or investments can dampen innovation by reducing the incentives that relatively inefficient firms have to adapt.

Apart from its effect on individual product markets, LCRs may also be relatively less desirable in terms of achieving broader policy aims. Much energy regulation, for instance, aims to reduce carbon emissions. Through LCRs, the government selects favorite technologies, when lower-cost alternatives could better achieve the same broader policy aims. For example, Connecticut deploys LCRs for solar panel installation programs.[86] However, solar panels might not be the most cost-effective way for every firm to reduce carbon emissions. Instead, one particular wind turbine manufacturer who is more effective than any solar manufacturer in reducing carbon emissions will be hampered by these solar LCRs; these state governments favor a less efficient solar firm over a more efficient wind firm. Moreover, by selecting favorites, the government discourages innovation because new firms will be less likely to find creative solutions in reducing carbon if solar is already determined to be the preferred solution.[87] In this sense, LCRs channel investment into what could be undesirable, inefficient sectors.

By comparison with LCRs, general subsidies and taxes can promote broad policy aims while allowing the market to select the cheapest and most effective solution. LCRs are, at least usually, a form of subsidy.[88] Both general subsidies and LCRs

---

[86] Conn. Gen. Stat. § 16-245ff.

[87] V. de Rugy, "Subsidies Are the Problem, Not the Solution, for Innovation in Energy," March 24, 2015, www.mercatus.org/publications/government-spending/subsidies-are-problem-not-solution-innovation-energy.

[88] A LCR does not necessarily have to provide a subsidy in the strict definition contained in the WTO's Agreement on Subsidies and Countervailing Measures, but it virtually always provides support in the colloquial sense in which the word subsidy is used.

involve the government choosing particular policy goals to promote and therefore, implicitly or explicitly, choosing winners and losers. But LCRs exacerbate subsidy-related economic concerns because they are less direct than general subsidies. Instead of straightforwardly favoring targeted industries, LCRs circuitously do so through requirements that artificially limit the choices available to private actors. For example, Louisiana's LCR targeting the biofuel known as "gasohol" for renewable energy goals conditions benefits on the use of Louisiana gasohol.[89] Not only does this favor a particular industry, it favors a particular industry within a particular state. If the goal were to combat climate change, then the world's atmosphere does not care whether emissions stem from Louisiana-sourced or Mississippi-sourced gasohol. In fact, if Mississippi-sourced gasohol is less costly than Louisiana-sourced gasohol, then this LCR funnels resources into consuming inefficient Louisianan inputs.

Taxes, for their part, disfavor one undesirable outcome and allow firms to compete in finding the remaining lowest-cost solutions.[90] Taxes are also less administratively burdensome than LCRs. LCRs require the government to pick particular industries to favor and to determine exact percentages of domestic inputs that trigger government benefits. In addition, the government must regularly dole out benefits and determine which firms qualify for benefits implicated by LCRs. The government also foots the bill for these benefits.[91] For all these reasons, LCRs require that the government incur monitoring and administrative expenses. Conversely, taxes are revenue positive because, instead of paying "good" actors, the government charges "bad" actors.

5.2 Political and Legal Effectiveness

In contrast to their economic ineffectiveness, LCRs can be politically and even legally effective instruments of industrial policy in the sustainable energy space, although they remain no better than second best as compared to other policy instruments. The conventional economic story posits that LCRs, as a convoluted breed of subsidy, are inefficient in bringing about policy aims.[92] LCRs favor particular industries, creating administrative burdens and discouraging innovative solutions that could otherwise compete with the government's chosen industries. In this sense, LCRs induce wasteful activity because taxes provide a more cost-efficient way to attack the same policy objectives. This would mean that LCRs are welfare-reducing. But this does not capture the entire welfare analysis. First, the most economically

---

[89] La Stat. Ann. § 47:305.23(A).

[90] J. Bundrick, "Tax Breaks and Subsidies: Challenging the Arkansas Status Quo" (Arkansas Center for Research in Economics, 2016), pp. 1, 19–20.

[91] E. Hutchinson, *Principles of Microeconomics* (University of Victoria Creative Commons, 2019), Topic 4 part 2: Applications of Supply and Demand: Taxes and Subsidies.

[92] de Rugy, note 87.

Industrial Policy and Local Content Rules in US

efficient mode is not always politically viable. Second, the most economically effective tools may be more likely to face legal challenges. In fact, given the recent heightened interest in US industrial policy and legal boundaries, LCRs might be some of the most effective tools available. Finally, in an absolute sense, a suboptimal tool like an LCR can still be welfare-enhancing if its benefits are sufficiently high, which is likely to be true when LCRs promote public goods.

5.2.1 Comparative Political Benefits of LCRs

The widespread use of LCRs points to their political attractiveness, a feature which has several explanations. First, tax increases are unpopular, especially in the US, in which a small-government ethos and associated objections to tax increases have been organizing political principles for decades.[93] Although LCRs may create economic deadweight losses that are greater than that created by taxes, LCRs are not viewed as being as heavy-handed as taxes. As a result, LCRs are often easier to enact. Whatever their long-term economic effects, LCRs take the form of a benefit to a particular industry, while a tax negatively impacts a particular industry. Where the benefits are targeted, and the costs diffuse – as in the case of LCRs – building a coalition to oppose the measure becomes more challenging and thus political opposition is muted.[94] LCRs compound this effect because they often take the form of a double benefit. Consumers, which can include industries, receive a subsidy from the government for the purchase of a product produced domestically. In effect, LCRs attached to fiscal subsidies spend tax-dollars twice – first to the consumer who is the direct recipient of the government subsidy, and second to the downstream domestic producer whose product must be purchased to qualify for the subsidy.[95] Especially in a political environment, like that in the US, in which political spending often arouses opposition, spending the same tax dollars to support multiple political constituencies is likely to appeal to legislators. For this reason, LCRs that contain fiscal subsidies may be more attractive than other forms of subsidies that are less economically distorting.

Taxes, on the other hand, are more salient[96] to opposing parties than are LCRs. A tax on fossil fuels surely finds political resistance from fossil fuel stakeholders, but a LCR that favors domestic biofuels lacks the same transparency in its negative impact on fossil fuel producers. From a behavioral economic standpoint, LCRs are framed in terms of "gains" to domestic beneficiaries, while taxes are perceived as

---

[93] A. S. Blinder, "Is Government Too Political?" (1997) 76 Foreign Affairs 116 ("Americans abhor paying taxes and are constitutionally incapable of favoring 'big government' in the abstract").

[94] See generally M. Olson, Jr., *The Logic of Collective Action: Public Goods and the Theory of Groups* (Harvard University Press, 1971).

[95] Meyer, note 62.

[96] See J. Brooks, B. Galle, and B. Maher, "Cross-Subsidies: Government's Hidden Pocketbook" (2018) 106 *The Georgetown Law Journal* 1229 at 1249 (discussing how subsidies can be effective because they are "less salient to individuals" than taxes).

338 Zachary Sturman and Timothy Meyer

"losses" to affected industries. Collective loss aversion[97] predicts that constituents will detest taxes more than LCRs that have the same economic effects.

LCRs offer two additional political benefits. First, a LCR can act as a commitment device[98] that ties policymakers, long term, to the promotion of a particular industry, like solar, for example. In this way, the LCR may have longer-term political benefits in spaces like climate change, where political action is otherwise inadequate or nonexistent. Second, LCRs can precipitate a snowball effect. Heavy-hitting legislation, like a nationwide carbon tax, might seem politically futile.[99] However, the likelihood of enacting this sort of weighty legislation may increase in the presence of climate-focused LCRs – in politically conservative and politically liberal states – more than without them. Current solar and wind LCRs in a politically conservative state like Kansas,[100] for example, appear to move the needle closer toward, rather than away from, broad-sweeping climate-change legislation.

5.2.2 Comparative Legal Benefits of LCRs

LCRs may also be less likely to face legal challenges than other forms of support for renewable energy. This claim needs to be qualified. LCRs are often straight-forwardly illegal under both international trade law and, in the US, the Dormant Commerce Clause. The WTO's Agreement on Subsidies and Countervailing Measures, for instance, prohibits subsidies that are contingent on the use of domestic products over imported products,[101] and a broader range of LCRs are unlawful under GATT article III's national treatment rules. Despite this fact, LCRs are often less obviously illegal than at least certain kinds of taxes and also less likely to be challenged. Within the US, this comparative legal advantage is clearest at the state and local level. As discussed above, states are categorically not allowed to impose tariffs. As a result, LCRs are – as a relative matter – more likely to be legal than are state-level tariffs. At the state and local level, LCRs are also less likely to be challenged in federal court. As discussed,[102] state and local LCRs are rampant in the energy sector but appear not to have drawn constitutional challenges in US federal courts. The nature of the US federal system thus increases the attractiveness of LCRs, relative to other policy instruments.

---

[97] See generally A. Tversky and D. Kahneman, "Loss Aversion in Riskless Choice: A Reference-Dependent Model" (1991) 106 *Quarterly Journal of Economics* 1039.

[98] For an explanation on how commitment devices operate, see generally T. Rogers, K. Milkman, and K. Volpp, "Commitment Devices: Using Initiatives to Change Behavior" (2018) 311 *Journal of the American Medical Association* 2065–2066.

[99] See generally S. Anderson, I. E. Marinscu, and B. Shor, "Can Pigou at the Polls Stop Us Melting the Polls?" National Bureau of Economic Research, July 31, 2019 (working paper) (offering economic explanations for the inability of policymakers to enact a carbon tax).

[100] Kan. Stat. Ann. § 74-50, 136.

[101] Agreement on Subsidies and Countervailing Measures, April 15, 1994, Marrakesh Agreement Establishing the World Trade Organization, Annex 1A, 1869 UNTS 14, Art. 3.1.

[102] See also Meyer, note 62.

Industrial Policy and Local Content Rules in US 339

Internationally, tariffs are not categorically unlawful, although they are subject to the tariff bindings imposed under the WTO and may be entirely unlawful under free trade agreements.[103] Precisely because they are transparent, the legality of tariffs is usually relatively easy to judge. By contrast, subsidies, and LCRs in particular, can function as layers of legal ambiguity. For instance, proving the existence of a subsidy under the SCM Agreement is necessary before the prohibition on LCRs can be invoked. Yet proving the existence of a subsidy is notoriously difficult and has prevented WTO panels from finding the existence of a prohibited subsidy in certain cases.[104]

5.2.3 Welfare Effects of LCRs

The combination of the legal and political benefits makes LCRs particularly attractive within the US as a means of supporting industries. Legally, subsidies are less likely to draw scrutiny than are protective tariffs. Politically, LCRs have advantages over both general subsidies and taxes in terms of framing effects and political coalition building. But the question remains whether LCRs are beneficial from a welfare point of view.

The crucial question in decomposing the welfare consequences of LCRs is constructing what the counterfactual world looks like. In general, of course, renewable energy offers welfare advantages over fossil fuels due to the environmental externalities that fossil fuel consumption creates. Consider, therefore, a world in which LCRs are less common for both fossil fuels and renewable energy. One possibility is that LCRs might reflect nothing more than political signaling, which would mean they might be closer to welfare neutral. Under this account, politicians impose LCRs not so much to promote particular industries but rather to merely signal support for those industries. This theory posits that LCRs are overall ineffective (and thus inconsequential from a welfare perspective) when compared to other policy tools, but politicians use LCRs to easily signal policy preferences to voters without having to deliver substantive results.

The US uses LCRs of various kinds to support both fossil fuels and renewable energy. Globally, however, the size of government support for fossil fuels dwarfs the support for renewable energy. Getting rid of LCRs across the board might thus create a welfare gain by reducing relative support for fossil fuels. On the other hand, however, LCRs may be particularly useful in generating support for new industries

---

[103] See, e.g., GATT 1994: General Agreement on Tariffs and Trade 1994, April 15, 1994, Marrakesh Agreement Establishing the World Trade Organization, Annex 1A, 1867 UNTS 187, 33 ILM 1153 (1994), Art. II.

[104] See Appellate Body Reports, Canada – Certain Measures Affecting the Renewable Energy Generation Section, Canada – Measures Relating to the Feed-in Tariff Program, WTO Doc. WT/DS412/AB/R, WT/DS426/AB/R (adopted May 24, 2013). This ambiguity may be specific to the subsidies' rules, however. These cases have more often been successful under GATT, ibid., Art. III's national treatment rules.

that rely on innovation to become financially competitive with incumbent industries. That suggests that an across-the-board crackdown on local content rules may harm renewables, and thus sustainability, relative to fossil fuels. For example, when the US government hurled tens of millions of dollars into finding a cure for polio in the mid-twentieth century, this likely had the short-run effect of stalling economic development in other areas and it relied on choosing a particular industry for government favoritism. Moreover, like renewable energy LCRs, US grants for polio research had positive externalities and the funding supported domestic researchers. When Jonas Salk discovered a vaccine for polio in 1955, it was hailed as one of the greatest medical triumphs in the history of public health, not as an inefficient government resource allocation.

This example raises a larger point. LCRs may be economically distorting within the product markets in which they operate, but they may be welfare-increasing when they are used to support the development of products that create positive externalities. Products, like renewable energy, that create positive externalities will likely be undersupplied relative to the optimal amount precisely because no single actor is able to capture the benefits from investing in innovation. The political benefits of LCRs allow legislators to capture this benefit, thereby incentivizing them to invest in products that are globally welfare-increasing.

This benefit may be especially important in federal systems like the US, where a significant amount of government support can come from subnational governments. Smaller jurisdictions are even less likely to subsidize products that create public goods, since their small size means that they will capture even less of the public benefits than would the nation as a whole. By creating additional local benefits, LCRs create incentives for smaller jurisdictions to fund investment in public goods projects. This investment, in turn, may be especially important in the energy sector, where renewables must compete with a heavily subsidized and established fossil fuel sector.

5.2.4 Making Local Content Work for Sustainability

If LCRs can promote sustainability in the energy sector, the question then becomes how trade rules can be adapted to further that end. Because LCRs can and do support both sustainable and non-sustainable energy, and because they are (at least in their clearest form) presumptively unlawful under trade rules, the easiest way to carve out a role for LCRs in promoting sustainable energy is to make lawful the use of LCRs when they are used for sustainable purposes. By making LCRs lawful when used for sustainable purposes, but not otherwise, the economic discrimination inherent in LCRs can be channeled into areas in which the economic costs are balanced by offsetting public benefits that the market might otherwise undervalue.

This task can be accomplished in several different ways. The most straightforward would be to exempt LCRs tied to renewable energy (or more broadly to environmental protection) from nondiscrimination rules in the context of the ongoing negotiations on the Environmental Goods Agreement (EGA). At present, the EGA negotiations focus on eliminating tariffs on environmentally related products.[105] While reducing tariffs on sustainable products would indeed promote their development and availability globally, a narrow exemption for LCRs tied to funding investment in such products could further stimulate development of markets for sustainable products. Indeed, the exemption could, in principle, be limited to dispute resolution, leaving renewable LCRs presumptively unlawful but leaving what to do about them to diplomatic negotiations. Such sector-specific carve-outs have precedent, most recently in the Comprehensive and Progressive Trans Pacific Partnership's exemption from investor–state dispute settlement for tobacco control measures.[106]

A second method would be to level the playing field on enforcement of trade rules between sustainable technologies and nonsustainable technologies. Research has shown that trading rules, especially the nondiscrimination rules that drive challenges to LCRs, are disproportionately enforced against policies that support renewable energy, as compared to fossil fuels.[107] As a result, trade enforcement policies act as an additional de facto subsidy for fossil fuels.[108] Simply leveling the playing field in enforcement policy would thus provide a boost for renewable energy. Eliminating discrimination in enforcement policy could be done at the national or international level through monitoring the effects of enforcement policies on sustainable products and their nonsustainable market competitors and bringing cases designed to address the resulting imbalance.

Yet a third approach would be to modify how GATT article XX is applied to measures that fit within the scope of the article XX exceptions.[109] Discrimination allows a government to shift some of the costs of a measure to those outside the jurisdiction, creating negative economic externalities. A doctrinal modification to article XX would ask (a) whether the shifting of costs was necessary (or related to) passing and implementing a measure pursuing an objective permitted by article XX, and (b) whether the multilateral benefits created by the measure pursued exceed its costs. At the first stage, a WTO panel would evaluate whether the enacting legislature needed to rely on discrimination to ensure pursuit of the permitted objective. This inquiry could examine the prevalence of discriminatory provisions in the jurisdiction's code more generally, as well as the scope and justification for including the discriminatory provision in this piece of legislation. For instance, a jurisdiction that discriminated broadly in its legal code would have a difficult

---

[105] World Trade Organization, Environmental Goods Agreement (EGA), www.wto.org/english/tratop_e/envir_e/ega_e.htm (last visited Jan. 24, 2020).
[106] Comprehensive and Progressive Trans Pacific Partnership art. 29.5.
[107] Meyer, note 75.
[108] Ibid.
[109] Meyer, note 62.

342   *Zachary Sturman and Timothy Meyer*

time showing that discrimination was necessary to pass a particular provision, while a jurisdiction that used discrimination only in limited circumstances could presumptively claim that it only invoked discrimination here in order to secure support necessary to pass the challenged measure. Second, a panel would then evaluate whether the negative economic externalities created by the measure are outweighed by positive environmental externalities.

Programs that on balance provide global public goods that fall within the scope of GATT article XX should survive review under both the exceptions and chapeau of GATT article XX. Such a narrow exception would encourage governments to tailor LCRs and similar programs to produce positive externalities. Moreover, this doctrinal change would not allow discrimination more broadly. The doctrinal shift would only benefit programs that are both politically necessary and create multilateral benefits.

Within the US, a similar trend has already taken hold. Federal courts applying the dormant commerce clause have been reluctant to find renewable energy programs that have out-of-state effects that arguably are discriminatory unconstitutional.[110] More generally, in the dormant commerce clause context courts have become more skeptical of judicial balancing inquiries that second-guess the benefits of economic policies pursued by elected governments. Finally, given the prevalence of renewable energy LCRs and similar programs within the US, the dearth of challenges in federal court suggests that the wisdom of LCRs in this space has primarily been left to the political branches.

6 CONCLUSION

As demonstrated in this chapter, LCRs have been used in the US to support both fossil fuels and renewable energy. Ultimately, if LCRs make it easier to support products, like fossil fuels, that create negative externalities, then they may not promote the development of sustainable energy markets. But evidence suggests that fossil fuel subsidies, including fossil fuel LCRs, are even less likely to attract challenges than are renewable energy subsidies.[111] As a consequence, rules limiting the use of LCRs are more likely to reduce support for renewable energy than fossil fuels. While LCRs can in theory render unlawful support regimes for both kinds of fuel, in practice legal challenges are more likely for one than the other. Conversely, relaxing rules on local content could create political incentives for governments to invest in renewable energy at a time in which a rapid energy transition is increasingly critical for averting the catastrophic environmental, economic, and human consequences of climate change.

[110]   *Energy and Environmental Legal Institute v. Epel*, 793 F.3d 1169 (10th Cir. 2015).

[111]   Meyer, note 71; D. De Bievre, I. Espa, and A. Poletti, "No Iceberg in Sight: On the Absence of WTO Disputes Challenging Fossil Fuel Subsidies" (2017) 17 *International Environmental Agreements: Politics, Law and Economics* 411.

18

Oil and Gas Sector Local Content Decision Processes: Canadian Indigenous Participation

Alastair R. Lucas, and David K. Laidlaw

1 INTRODUCTION

Local content requirements (Lcrs) are used by countries to capture a share of benefits from petroleum development for that country. In many countries these are implemented in inflexible instruments, such as laws, or decrees.[1] Canada had experimented with national LCR in the 1980s but does not currently have them.[2] However, it has what has been called the *Fourth World* of Indigenous people living in Canada, who are subject to material poverty and constrained circumstances due to colonial practices.[3] In 2016, 4.9 per cent of Canada's population were Indigenous[4] and they trail other Canadians in every socioeconomic category, such that Canada's First Peoples as a separate country, would rank 78th (out of 193) on the United Nations Human Development Index.[5]

This chapter considers Indigenous Nations as analogous to developing countries wishing to capture a share of the benefits from petroleum development in

[1] F. G. Pereira, C. Mathews, and H. Trischmann, "Local Content Policies in the Petroleum Industry: Lessons Learned" (2019) 4 *Oil and Gas, Natural Resources and Energy Journal* 631; D. Olawuyi, "Local Content and Procurement Requirements in Oil and Gas Contracts: Regional Trends in the Middle East and North Africa" (2019) 37 *Journal of Energy and Natural Resources Law* 93.

[2] Canada's National Energy Program (1980–5) was a mixture of federal legislation and policies directed towards capturing the benefits of petroleum developments for all Canadians, which ultimately failed due to resistance from oil producing provinces, a drop in world oil prices, and changing political climate.

[3] G. Manuel and M. Posluns, *The Fourth World: An Indian Reality* (Don Mills, ON: Collier-Macmillan, 1974); O. O. Odulaja and R. Halseth, "The United Nations Sustainable Development Goals and Indigenous Peoples in Canada," National Collaborating Centre for Aboriginal Health, 2018; P. D. Palmater, "Stretched Beyond Human Limits: Death by Poverty in First Nations" (2011) 65/66 *Canadian Review of Social Policy* 112.

[4] "Aboriginal Peoples in Canada: Key Results from the 2016 Census," Statistics Canada, October, 2017. There are 1,673,785 Indigenous people in Canada with 51.8 per cent living in urban areas; 744,855 First Nations are entitled to live on Reserves but only 44.2 per cent can be accommodated; Indigenous Nations are small, 70 per cent have fewer than 500 inhabitants, and 96 per cent have fewer than 2,000 inhabitants. "Aboriginal Demographics from the 2011 National Household Survey," Statistics Canada, May 2013.

[5] Palmater, note 3, p. 8. First Peoples are First Nations and Inuit. Canada currently ranks 12th.

344   *Alastair R. Lucas and David K. Laidlaw*

a sustainable fashion.[6] This analogy is not perfect. Indigenous Nations are embedded within Canadian society and are reliant on Canada to create LCR to provide local benefits (LB) to Indigenous Nations, defined as added value brought to an Indigenous Nation, by procurement of local goods, services, and workforce development, including strategic community investments.[7] Indigenous Nations make rules for the distribution of LB within themselves.[8]

This chapter is divided into six sections. After this introduction, Section 2 examines the historical relationship between Canada and Indigenous Peoples while Section 3 reviews constitutional aboriginal rights. Section 4 outlines Canada's petroleum sector and Section 5 describes and assesses Canada's LCR. The final section includes recommendations on how to implement LCRs in light of the Canadian example.

2 CANADA AND INDIGENOUS PEOPLES

Canada is a recovering colonial country. Canadians have appropriated for their use 99.97 per cent of the lands and resources of the original occupants, the Indigenous peoples, living in Canada.[9] As detailed in *Report of the Royal Commission on Aboriginal People* (1996)[10] after centuries of dispossession, marginalization, and failed assimilation efforts, including the *Indian Act* (1876+),[11] Residential Schools (1883–1980s),[12] Enfranchisement Policies (1876–1969),[13] and culminating in the rejected 1969 assimilationist White Paper, *Statement of the Government of Canada on Indian Policy*,[14] Canada has moved to reconsider its relationship with Indigenous

---

6   B. J. Richardson, "The Ties that Bind: Indigenous Peoples and Environmental Governance" (2008) Comparative Research in Law and Political Economy, Research Paper No. 26/2008; D. A, Lertzman and H. Vredenburg, "Indigenous Peoples, Resource Extraction and Sustainable Development: An Ethical Approach" (2005) 56 *Journal of Business Ethics* 239; N. Houde "The Six Faces of Traditional Ecological Knowledge: Challenges and Opportunities for Canadian Co-management Arrangements" (2007) 12 *Ecology and Society* 34.

7   M. Hackenbruch and J. D. Pluess, "Commercial Value from Sustainable Local Benefits in the Extractive Industries: Local Content," BSR, March 2011, p. 2.

8   T. Rodon, I. Lemus-Lauzon, and S. Schott, "Impact and Benefit Agreement (IBA) Revenue Allocation Strategies for Indigenous Community Development" (2018) 47 *The Northern Review* 9.

9   The use of "Canadians" is deliberate. Canadian society has, since 1867 inherited the territories, resources, and obligations of Britain arising from historical encounters, as well as incurring new obligations to Indigenous Peoples.

10 *Report of the Royal Commission on Aboriginal People* (Ottawa: Supply and Services Canada, 1996) [RCAP].

11 *Indian Act*, RSC 1985, c I-5. It required the registration of Indigenous citizens and their children into "Indian Bands" and distributed benefits and imposed disabilities for individuals on the basis of their status as an Indian.

12 Indian Residential Schools forcibly removed children from their families, to distant Boarding Schools where they were taught Canadian languages, abused (including sexual abuse), and given sub-standard education in an attempt to assimilate them. "Truth and Reconciliation Commission" 2015, trc.ca.

13 Indians had no right to vote in Canadian elections until the 1960s. Enfranchisement was the practice of encouraging or compelling members of Indian Bands to give up their Indian status in return for the right to vote.

14 *Statement of the Government of Canada on Indian Policy*, 1969 (Ottawa: Queen's Printer, 1969).

peoples. A significant step was government willingness to consider land claims following the Supreme Court's decision in *Calder v Attorney-General of British Columbia*.[15]

Canadians have always made agreements with Indigenous Nations, who had a long history of such agreements, beginning with the eighteenth-century *Peace, Trade and Alliance Treaties* in Eastern Canada that were critical in France's defeat by Britain and its Indigenous Allies in the French and Indian Wars of 1754–63. The *Treaty of Paris, 1763* saw France surrender its colonies to Canadians, with the *Royal Proclamation, 1763* including measures addressing Indigenous Nations' territorial concerns about colonists by drawing a boundary called "the frontier" along the borders of colonies beyond which Colonial governors could not give private land grants. Lands beyond the frontier were Indigenous lands. *Any unpurchased land* within the colonies were "Indian Hunting Grounds," the purchase of which was a government monopoly after a public meeting of Indians for that purpose.[16] The *Royal Proclamation, 1763* is the basis for 500+ Historical Treaties with Indigenous Nations under which Canada would acquire most, but not all of its territory.[17] Written land-surrender Treaties were made in northern Ontario and three western provinces, whereby Indigenous Nations surrendered rights to territory in return for promises. They could continue traditional ways of life on surrendered lands (subject to tracts being taken up by governments for settlement and other purposes). Lands based on population would be reserved for exclusive Indigenous use (Reserves), with annual annuities, supplies, and other benefits.[18] Land-surrender Treaties were not made in the Maritime colonies; Québec; British Columbia; or Canada's Artic, where the *Royal Proclamation, 1763* provisions on unpurchased lands were regularly disregarded or avoided by extra-legal means, as Canada merely asserted sovereignty.

The relationship between Canadian governments and Indigenous peoples is governed by the *honour of the Crown* requiring fidelity in agreements, including the interpretation of Treaties and constitutional promises.[19] Treaties are nation-to-nation agreements, as they bind peoples in perpetuity, and are sacred agreements between Canada and Indigenous Nations that require common intention to create legal relationships, mutually binding promises, and negotiations concluded with

---

[15] *Calder v Attorney-General of British Columbia*, [1973] SCR 313 [*Calder*], leading Canada to establish Land Claims processes to negotiate Modern Treaties.

[16] In RCAP, note 10, vol. 1, Appendix D, p. 680 [*Royal Proclamation, 1763*]; T. Fenge and J. Aldridge (ed.), *Keeping Promises: The Royal Proclamation of 1763, Aboriginal Rights, and Treaties in Canada* (Montreal: McGill-Queens University Press, 2015).

[17] J. Borrows, *Crown and Aboriginal Occupations of Land: A History and Comparison* (Toronto: Ipperwash Inquiry, 2005).

[18] A. Morris, *The Treaties of Canada with the Indians of Manitoba and the North-West Territories, Including the Negotiations on Which They Were Based, and Other Information Relating Thereto* (Toronto: Belfords, Clarke and Co., 1880).

[19] *Haida Nation v British Columbia (Minister of Forests)*, 2004 SCC 73 [*Haida*]; *Manitoba Métis Federation Inc v Canada (Attorney General)*, 2013 SCC 14 [*Manitoba Métis*]; *Province of Ontario v. Dominion of Canada* (1908), 42 SCR 1; affd [1910] AC 637.

346 Alastair R. Lucas and David K. Laidlaw

solemnity.[20] Treaties are not confined to land issues and attract special rules of interpretation incorporating Aboriginal perspectives.[21] Canadians have historically failed to uphold Treaty promises, leading to ongoing disputes.[22]

Canada is a constitutional monarchy and a federation. Its constitution is a blend of vestigial but important Crown prerogatives, unwritten conventions, and written instruments, notably *The Constitution Act, 1867* that divides jurisdiction between the federal and provincial parliaments.[23] Overarching federal powers are listed in section 91 including section 91(24) power over "Indians, and Lands reserved for the Indians,"[24] with provinces, subject to pre-existing interests, owning the lands, and legislating within the Province under provincial powers listed in section 92 including 92(13) "Property and Civil Rights in the Province."[25]

On April 17, 1982, Canada patriated its constitution from the United Kingdom in *The Constitution Act, 1982* to become the supreme law of Canada.[26] It included a *Charter of Rights and Freedoms* in Part I with equality, civil, and political rights held by all Canadians against government actions, and Aboriginal rights in Part II. Section 35(1) provides that "The existing aboriginal and treaty rights of the aboriginal peoples of Canada are hereby recognized and affirmed," with protection from the *Charter* and any rights previously acquired in section 25.[27] Aboriginal rights were included as the legal mechanism to reconcile Canada's assertion of sovereignty over aboriginal peoples and de facto control of land and resources formerly owned by them, in an ongoing process of reconciliation with new Treaties being the preferred outcome.[28]

3 ABORIGINAL CONSTITUTIONAL RIGHTS

3.1 *Aboriginal and Treaty Rights*

Currently, constitutionally protected aboriginal rights are activities central to the lifestyle of Indigenous Nations, being practised in a current form that relates to the

---

[20] *R v Sioui*, [1990] 1 SCR 1025. Solemnity is commonly evidenced by the exchange of symbolic gifts.
[21] *R v Marshall*, [1999] 3 SCR 456 [*Marshall*] at para. 78, in dissent but not on this point.
[22] To resolve these, Canada established a Special Claims Tribunal, sct-trp.ca/hom/index_e.htm.
[23] *Constitution Act, 1867* (UK), 30 & 31 Vict c 3.
[24] Other relevant federal powers include Navigation and Shipping (10) and Sea Coast and Inland Fisheries (12). Inuit are subject to federal jurisdiction, *Reference whether "Indians" includes "Eskimo"* [1939] SCR 104, as are the Métis, descendants of the inter-marriage of Indigenous and Canadian persons, in *Daniels v Canada (Indian Affairs and Northern Development)*, [2016] 1 SCR 99 but neither were included in the *Indian Act*.
[25] Other relevant provincial powers include Local works and Undertakings within the Province (10).
[26] *The Constitution Act, 1982*, being Schedule B to the *Canada Act 1982* (UK), 1982, c. 11. Prior to 1982, amending Canada's constitution required legislation from the United Kingdom's Parliament.
[27] Ibid., s 35(2) defines "aboriginal peoples" as including "Indian, Inuit and Métis peoples," because "aboriginal law" refers to Canada's mechanism to govern its relationship to Indigenous People, this will be used in addition to the Indigenous nomenclature. The *Charter* did not include economic or environmental rights.
[28] *R v Van der Peet*, [1996] 2 SCR 507 [*Van der Peet*] at para. 19; *Haida*, note 19; *Manitoba Métis*, note 19.

original practice prior to Canadian contact that have not been extinguished by explicit federal legislation prior to April 17, 1982.[29] Treaties can embody aboriginal rights and provide additional rights. However, they are not a complete code as aboriginal rights can be practised in the same territory unless barred by the applicable Treaty or private land grants.[30] Aboriginal and Treaty rights include ancillary rights,[31] and cannot be restricted unless there is a valid legislative object, such as public safety or conservation. The restriction must be proportional and accord with the historical relationship between Canada and aboriginal peoples, including the *honour of the crown*.[32] Where the government has assumed control over a central aboriginal interest such as land, the Crown has a *fiduciary duty* to uphold that aboriginal interest.[33] Treaties can surrender aboriginal title in surrender language, if any, in accordance with the Treaty terms with Reserves remaining aboriginal title lands.[34] Aboriginal and Treaty rights, take priority over other uses as they pre-date them.[35]

3.2 *Aboriginal Title*

Aboriginal title is a unique fusion of common law where extended possession gives rise to title and aboriginal legal systems of control over territory where permissions are required to share or transit that land. This fusion has several aspects: aboriginal title lands can only be sold to the Crown and are based on the prior exclusive occupation by Indigenous Nations before Canadian sovereignty. Aboriginal title is held communally as a collective right of Indigenous Nation members, with the Indigenous Nation having exclusive rights over and control of their aboriginal title lands (including subsurface resources) with the restriction that uses be consistent with their group nature and be preserved for enjoyment of future generations.[36] Like aboriginal rights, aboriginal title may be infringed, with valid objects expanded to general development subject to finding a specific justification, provided the duty to consult is satisfied and infringement is consistent with the

---

[29] *Van Der Peet*, note 28, paras. 46–60; *R v Sappier; R v Gray*, 2006 SCC 54. In *R v Powley*, 2003 SCC 43, Métis rights arise in the post-contact *pre-control* period before Canadians gained political and legal control in an area.

[30] *R v Adams*, [1996] 3 SCR 101.

[31] Ancillary rights are rights necessarily and reasonably incidental to the exercise of the protected right, *R v Sundown*, [1999] 1 SCR 393.

[32] *R v Sparrow*, [1990] 1 SCR 1075 [*Sparrow*]. The valid legislative object was chosen as "public interest" was too vague a test and did not reflect the honour of the crown.

[33] *Sparrow*, note 32; *Wewaykum Indian Band v Canada*, 2002 SCC 79; *Manitoba Métis*, note 19.

[34] *R v Badger*, [1996] 1 SCR 771; *Guerin v The Queen*, [1984] 2 SCR 335.

[35] *Sparrow*, note 32; *Marshall*, note 21. Commercial exercise of aboriginal rights to fish are dependent on evidence of trade at contact, and the priority is limited to the modern equivalent of a moderate livelihood.

[36] *Delgamuukw v British Columbia*, [1997] 3 SCR 1010; *Tsilhqot'in Nation v British Columbia*, 2014 SCC 44 [*Tsilhqot'in Nation*]. Métis aboriginal title is doubtful with the trial decision finding that the Red River Métis People held land individually not communally, *Manitoba Métis*, note 19.

348 Alastair R. Lucas and David K. Laidlaw

Crown's fiduciary duty.[37] Aboriginal title arises in areas without land-surrender Treaties and may extend offshore.[38]

3.3 The Crown's Constitutional Duty to Consult and Accommodate

Aboriginal peoples do not have the right to free, prior, and informed consent to developments on their traditional lands under the *United Nations Declaration on the Rights of Indigenous Peoples* (2007).[39] Instead they have the constitutional right to Crown consultation and accommodation prior to governments making decisions about those developments (duty to consult/duty to accommodate).[40] The duty to consult flows from the honour of the Crown and arises when the Crown has knowledge, real or constructive, of the potential existence of the aboriginal right or title and contemplates *new conduct* that might adversely affect them.[41] It requires meaningful, good-faith dialogue from and with each aboriginal group affected consistent with that group's strength of claim or, when the claim is established by Treaty, the territorial extent of the current exercise of that right, and the potential impact of the decision on those aboriginal interests.[42] There is a spectrum of consultation, from weak claims and weak impacts with lower consultation requirements to strong claims and high impacts which require a greater depth of consultation, that may change in the process as new information is provided.[43] The consultation process may reveal a need to change government conduct, giving rise to a duty to negotiate reasonable accommodation that may range from decision modifications to

[37] *Tsilhqot'in Nation*, note 36, paras. 75–77.
[38] The *Oceans Act*, SC 1996, c 3, was the first legislation to claim ownership by Canada of the seabed and is subject to aboriginal rights in section 2.1.
[39] UN General Assembly, *United Nations Declaration on the Rights of Indigenous People*, 2 October 2007, UN Doc. A/RES/61/295, is a non-binding declaration. Canada initially voted against this Declaration but adopted it on November 10, 2010, with qualifications. Canada has yet to incorporate this into domestic law despite political promises to do so.
[40] *Haida*, note 19, in areas without completed Treaties and extended to Treaty areas in *Mikisew Cree First Nation v. Canada (Minister of Canadian Heritage)*, [2005] 3 SCR 388 [*Mikisew*].
[41] *Haida*, note 19; *Taku River Tlingit First Nation v British Columbia (Project Assessment Director)*, [2004] 3 SCR 550 [*Taku River*]; *Rio Tinto Alcan Inc v Carrier Sekani Tribal Council*, [2010] 2 SCR 650 [*Rio Tinto*]. Project approvals may require additional permissions and the duty to consult will be engaged for each new stage of decision-making.
[42] *Haida*, note 19, found consultation inadequate while the companion case, *Taku River* found adequate consultation in the environmental approval process. In *Mikisew*, note 40, Treaty 8 allowed the government to take up lands and the honour of the Crown required the government to consult with affected aboriginal groups.
[43] *Haida*, note 19; *Mikisew*, note 40. Lower consultation depths require giving notice of the proposed decision, disclosing information, and discussing any issues in response with the intent to minimize impacts, with deep consultation including but not limited to, opportunities to make submissions for consideration, formal participation in the decision-making process, and written reasons to show that aboriginal concerns were considered and the impact they had on the decision.

cancellation.[44] Agreement is not required and aboriginal peoples are not given a veto on the use of their traditional lands.[45]

Procedural aspects may be delegated by governments to industry proponents as they can modify proposed projects to mitigate impacts, but governments remain responsible to fulfill the duty.[46] Courts can review decisions when it is alleged that government has failed to fulfill this duty, with the standard of review for government's assessment of aboriginal claims or impacts being correctness. If the assessment is correct the decision will be set aside only if the government's consultation process was unreasonable.[47]

3.4 Modern Treaties and Self-Government Agreements

Canada has signed twenty-six Modern Treaties with Indigenous Nations covering 40 per cent of Canada's land mass and twenty-one Self-Government Agreements negotiated under Canada's *Aboriginal Self-government Policy* recognizing Indigenous Nations' inherent right to self-government in internal matters within the framework of Canada's Constitution.[48] The first modern Treaty in 1976, *The James Bay and Northern Québec Agreement*, set the template for other Modern Treaties, establishing three general categories of land: core lands for exclusive use by Indigenous peoples, shared jurisdiction lands, and public lands with specified aboriginal rights.[49] Within core lands, Indigenous Governments exercise

---

[44] *Haida*, note 19; *Beckman v Little Salmon/Carmacks First Nation*, [2010] 3 SCR 103 [*Beckman*].

[45] *Haida*, note 19; *Taku River*, note 41; *Tsilhqot'in Nation*, note 36. Modern Treaties define the duty to consult and include processes for fulfilling it, supplemented by principles of Treaty interpretation including honour of the Crown. The Yukon Umbrella Final Agreement (1993) includes a definition of consultation, in chapter 1.

[46] *Haida*, note 19; D. Laidlaw and M. Passelac-Ross, *Alberta First Nations Consultation & Accommodation Handbook* (Calgary: Canadian Institute of Resources Law, 2014); D. K. Laidlaw, *Alberta First Nations Consultation and Accommodation Handbook – Updated to 2016* (Calgary: Canadian Institute of Resources Law, 2016).

[47] *Haida*, note 19; *Taku River*, note 41; *Rio Tinto*, note 41, speculated that properly structured administrative tribunals could satisfy the duty to consult and *Clyde River (Hamlet) v Petroleum Geo-Services Inc*, 2017 SCC 40 and *Chippewas of the Thames First Nation v Enbridge Pipelines Inc.* 2017 SCC 41 gave the federal energy regulator the power to satisfy the duty to consult in some applications. See also *Tsleil-Waututh Nation v. Canada AG)*, 2018 FCA 153. These standard-of-review principles are consistent with the rebuttable reasonableness standard-of-review framework outlined by the Supreme Court of Canada in *Minister of Citizenship and Immigration v. Vavilov*, 2019 SCC 65, and *Bell Canada v. Canada (AG)*, 2019 SCC 66.

[48] Crown–Indigenous Relations and Northern Affairs Canada, "General Briefing Note on Canada's Self-government and Comprehensive Land Claims Policies and the Status of Negotiations," 2015; Minister of Indian Affairs and Northern Development, "Federal Policy Guide, Aboriginal Self-Government: The Government of Canada's Approach to the Implementation of the Inherent Right and the Negotiation of Aboriginal Self-Government," 1995.

[49] *The James Bay and Northern Québec Agreement* (Québec: Éditeur official du Québec, 1991). This is discussed in D. Laidlaw and M. M. Passelac-Ross, *Sharing Land Stewardship in Alberta: The Role of Aboriginal Peoples* (Calgary: Canadian Institute of Resources Law, 2012) [*Land Stewardship*].

350 Alastair R. Lucas and David K. Laidlaw

governance over the use of lands. Within shared jurisdiction lands a number of Indigenous majority Boards give recommendations to governments on land and water use.[50]

3.5 Joint Stewardship Arrangements

Negotiating Modern Treaties within the Provinces requires federal and provincial government cooperation, which can be done but requires additional time.[51] *Joint Stewardship Arrangements* with Provincial governments may provide an interim solution by restoring bilateral trust and progressing to Modern Treaties, although they may only be possible in regions subject to intense resource development pressure.[52] Approximately 200 *Shared Decision Making Agreements*, have been entered into in British Columbia with other provinces having similar initiatives.[53]

4 CANADA'S OIL AND GAS SECTOR

4.1 Natural Resources in Canada's Economy

Canada has a number of policies directed at improving socio-economic conditions in Indigenous Nations. However, progress has been slow, in part because of the inadequacy of funding and lack of economic opportunities.[54] Natural resource development is seen as a source of economic opportunities, particularly in the mining and petroleum sectors.[55]

Historically, Canada has been reliant on natural resources that continue to play a significant role in Canada's modern service economy. In 2018, energy production, the majority from the petroleum sector, totalled 10.6 per cent of Canada's GDP, provided 900,000 jobs (4.8 per cent), $111 billion in exports (15 per cent), and provided on average $17.8 billion in government revenue (11 per cent).[56] The oilsands of northern Alberta hold the world's third-largest reserves and production

---

[50] For example, the Yukon Umbrella Agreement includes a definition of sustainable development at page 7 which applies to Land Use Planning (chapter 11) and Development Assessment (chapter 12) and the Surface Rights, Heritage, Water Management, Fish and Wildlife, and Forest Resources Board(s).

[51] Nisga'a Final Agreement (1998) required 25 years of negotiation after *Calder*. Government delay was one of the motivating factors in *Haida*, note 19.

[52] *Land Stewardship*, note 49.

[53] "Step by Step: Final Report for the Shared Decision Making in BC Project," Centre for Dialogue, Simon Fraser University, March 2015.

[54] Indigenous Governments receive half of the per capita funding for services in comparison to non-Aboriginal Canadians who also have the added benefit of provincial funding. Palmater, note 3.

[55] Indian Affairs and Northern Development, "Federal Framework for Aboriginal Economic Development," 2009.

[56] Natural Resources Canada, "Energy Fact Book 2018–2019," 2018; Global Affairs Canada, "Canada's State of Trade 2019," 2019. These are not uniformly distributed with Alberta, Saskatchewan, and, to a lesser extent, British Columbia being reliant on petroleum development.

LCRs and Indigenous Participation in Canada   351

has outstripped declining conventional production since 2010; oilsands production in 2017 was 2.8 million barrels of synthetic diluted bitumen equivalent per day.

This development of the petroleum sector has been facilitated by Canadian legislation, where governments hold *mineral rights* and lease them to Proponents, with regulation focussed on conservation of petroleum reserves (and government revenue); while private owners, if any, hold *surface title* subject to pre-emption and compensation for the surface affected by development.[57]

4.2 *Environmental Protection and Assessment*

The rise of environmental concerns in the 1970s led every jurisdiction to pass legislation for environmental protection and environmental impact assessment under their respective powers.[58] Environmental protection legislation generally involves prohibitions on emissions into the environment or elements of the environment, unless a licence was applied for and granted by government departments with inspection, investigative, and prosecution powers.[59]

Environmental Impact Assessment (EIA) is a systematic analysis of the potential impacts of a proposed project on the natural and human environment to obtain project approval in the public's best interest.[60] This started in 1973 with the federal policy *Environmental Assessment and Review Process*, legislated in 1992 as the *Canadian Environmental Assessment Act*,[61] and amended in 2012 to restrict EIA to designated projects and reducing environmental consideration with EIA Tribunals providing approval recommendations to government who make the approval

---

[57]   F. .L. Hughes, A. J. Kwasniak, and A. R. Lucas, *Public Lands and Resources Law in Canada* (Toronto: Irwin Law, 2016). In Alberta, public land legislation has excluded mines and minerals from any transfer to private interests since Alberta acquired them from Canada in 1930, *Public Lands Act*, RSA 2000, c P-40, s 35(1). Surface rights compensation started in 1947, *Surface Rights Act*, RSA 2000, c S-24. Surface Rights Board granting entry orders to proponents with compensation for owners of surface title. The first energy regulator in 1938 was the *Petroleum and Natural Gas Conservation Board* with a focus on proper petroleum development through licencing well location, its successor the Alberta Energy Regulator [AER] has been delegated authority over upstream production and environmental regulation of energy projects under the *Responsible Energy Development Act*, SA 2012, c R-17.3 [REDA].

[58]   Environment jurisdiction is shared, *Friends of the Oldman River Society v Canada (Minister of Transport)*, [1992] 1 SCR 3, 1992. S. Wood, G. Tanner, and B. J. Richardson, "What Ever Happened to Canadian Environmental Law?" (2010) 37 *Ecology Law Quarterly* 981.

[59]   *Canadian Environmental Protection Act*, 1999, SC 1999, c 33. Specific components of the environment may be addressed in other legislation for example the *Fisheries Act*, RSC 1985, c F-14, section 35 (1) says "No person shall carry on any work, undertaking or activity that results in the harmful alteration, disruption or destruction of fish habitat."

[60]   Public interest was initially considered protection of the environment, transitioning to sustainable development during the 1980s: J. F. Glenn, "Decision-Making Regimes Governing Environmental Assessment in Canada," Report for the Canadian Environmental Assessment Research Council, 1992.

[61]   *Canadian Environmental Assessment Act*, SC 1992, c 37, applied to all projects with a federal aspect unless excluded by regulation; it addressed aboriginal rights by defining environmental effect as any changes in the "current use of lands and resources for traditional purposes by aboriginal persons" in s 2(1).

352 Alastair R. Lucas and David K. Laidlaw

decision within set timelines.[62] These changes were partially reversed in 2019 as amendments restored evaluation of environmental components, added a pre-assessment process to gauge public controversy, and revised the public interest definition to include consideration of aboriginal rights but retained government EIA approvals.[63]

Proponents for a petroleum project generate a project description detailing potential project impacts and mitigation measures for screening by the Impact Assessment Agency of Canada (IAAC) to determine if an EIA is required and, if so, the project will be referred to the Canadian Energy Regulator (CER) for approval.[64] Other jurisdictions have similar but differing environmental protection and assessment regimes that require a complex web of intra-governmental substitutional and cooperation processes to avoid duplication.[65]

5 CANADIAN LOCAL CONTENT RULES

Developing the petroleum sector, in light of the prior occupation of Canada by Indigenous peoples holding aboriginal rights and title, has presented new challenges. Current Canadian LCRs providing LB are through mandated or commercially prudent Proponent Impact Benefit Agreements with Indigenous Nations and, to a limited extent, Canadian regulatory approval conditions.

5.1 Impact Benefit Agreements in the North

Discovery of petroleum reserves in Alaska and Canada's Mackenzie Delta in the 1970s, led to proposals to develop a pipeline along the Mackenzie River valley to Alberta connecting existing pipelines for export to the United States. These proposals coincided with uncertainty over Indigenous land claims and led to Justice Thomas Berger's *Mackenzie Valley Pipeline Inquiry* (1977) that heard from a number of groups, including Indigenous peoples whose traditional territory

---

[62] *Jobs, Growth and Long-term Prosperity Act*, SC 2012, c 19, amended 109 pieces of legislation including the *Fisheries Act* and *Navigable Waters Protection Act* resulting in *Canadian Environmental Assessment Act*, 2012, SC 2012, c 19, that maintained the existing treatment of aboriginal rights. Projects subject to EIA were listed in *Regulations Designating Physical Activities*, SOR/2012–147.

[63] *An Act to enact the Impact Assessment Act and the Canadian Energy Regulator Act, to amend the Navigation Protection Act and to make consequential amendments to other Acts*, SC 2019, c 28. Effective August 28, 2019.

[64] *Impact Assessment Act*, SC 2019, c 28, s 1 [IAA], s 43. Projects subject to EIA are in *Physical Activities Regulations*, SOR/2019–285; notably, it only includes projects with more than 75 km of right of way that are not adjacent to previous disturbances. CER continued in *Canadian Energy Regulator Act*, SC 2019, c 28, s 10, cer-rec.gc.ca; D. Laidlaw, "Bill C-69, the Impact Assessment Act, and Indigenous Process Considerations," March 15, 2018, Ablawg.ca.

[65] Substitution agreements can be challenged: *Coastal First Nations v British Columbia (Environment)*, 2016 BCSC 34 [*Coastal*].

LCRs and Indigenous Participation in Canada   353

the pipeline would traverse. He recommended a ten-year pipeline postponement.[66]

Other natural resource projects continued to be developed, with the uncertainty around Indigenous land claims being resolved by confidential Proponent access agreements with local Indigenous Nations, intended "firstly to address the impacts of development on aboriginal communities and secondly to obtain both short and long term benefits of that development" (Impact and Benefit Agreements (IBAs)).[67] IBA use coincided with the negotiation of Modern Treaties and Indigenous Nations, which included a requirement to negotiate IBAs *in addition* to settlement of land issues in all of the Inuit Treaties, other Modern Treaties and consequent Territorial legislation.[68] Some Modern Treaties do not explicitly require them but their use has become standard, driven in part by selection of core territory with developable resources in the Modern Treaty negotiations.[69]

In 1999, Kennett recommended negotiating IBAs with consideration of matters in the Nunavut Agreement's Schedule 26–1.[70] IBAs have become more complex, with similar recommendations from other authors giving a sense of this complexity.[71] There is a limited set of academic cross-disciplinary and business literature on IBAs supportive of their implementation but expressing concerns about confidentiality and lack of government oversight.[72] There have been calls for reforming IBAs[73] but these have not been implemented for many reasons, including:

---

[66] T. R. Berger, "Northern Frontier, Northern Homeland: The Report of the Mackenzie Valley Pipeline Inquiry: Volume One, Minister of Supply and Services Canada, 1977, p. 196. There are two volumes.

[67] S. Kennett, "A Guide to Impact and Benefits Agreements," Canadian Institute of Resources Law, 1999, pp. 1 and 7.

[68] C. Knotsch and J. Warda, "Impact Benefit Agreements: A Tool for Healthy Inuit Communities?" National Aboriginal Health Organization, 2009; The Tłı̨chǫ (Tåîchô) Agreement (2005), s 23.4.1; *Oil and Gas Act*, RSY 2002, c 162, s 68; Indian and Northern Affairs Canada, "Agreement between The Inuit of The Nunavut Settlement Area and Her Majesty The Queen in Right of Canada," May 25, 2018, Article 8 [Nunavut Agreement].

[69] For example, Nunavut Agreement, note 68, Article 17 describes the purpose of Inuit Owned Lands [core lands] as 17.1.2 (b) areas of value principally for reasons related to the development of non-renewable resources. During selection negotiations Canada shared its geological information.

[70] Nunavut Agreement, note 68, Article 26 required the negotiation of an IBA for a Major Project.

[71] Knotsch and Warda, note 68; G. Gibson and C. O'Faircheallaigh, "IBA Community Toolkit: Negotiation and Implementation of Impact and Benefit Agreements," The Gordan Foundation, 2015; M. Lewis and S. Brocklehurst, "Aboriginal Mining Guide : How to negotiate lasting benefits for your community," Canadian Centre for Community Renewal, Tr'ondëk Hwëch'in and the Canadian Northern Economic Development Agency, 2009; M. W. Browne and K. Robertson, "Benefit Sharing Agreements in British Columbia: A Guide for First Nations, Businesses, and Governments," prepared by Woodward and Company for the Ecosystem-Based Management Working Group.

[72] A Draft Bibliography is at B. Bradshaw and A. Wright, "Review of IBA Literature and Analysis of Gaps in Knowledge," ReSDA Draft Gap Analysis Report #9, 2013.

[73] S. A. Kennett, "Issues and Options for a Policy on Impact and Benefits Agreements," Canadian Institute of Resources Law, Prepared for the Mineral Resources Directorate, Department of Indian Affairs and Northern Development, May 27, 1999; G. Shanks and S. Lopes, "Sharing in the Benefits of

354 Alastair R. Lucas and David K. Laidlaw

- Indigenous Nations prefer to negotiate confidential IBA with Proponents: they are aware of circumstances in their community, of their distinct needs and the urgency of them, and direct negotiation provides the flexibility to address them. Proponents, concerned about access certainty and timely project development, can obtain them in an IBA.
- For Canada, some speculate this allows governments to withdraw from their responsibility to govern as, "IBAs allow governments to reconcile both the pressure to ensure more ecologically and socially 'sustainable' practices in the mining sector while maintaining economic development and competitiveness."[74]
- Confidentiality concerns for Indigenous Nations are significant: IBAs are privately negotiated attempts to provide for their needs, in the absence of government funding and they will be sensitive to disclosure, as inclusion of IBA benefits in Canada's Own Source Revenue Policies would deduct a portion of those benefits from normal funding.[75]

IBAs are now prevalent in the mining sector, with official estimates in 2016 of 480 IBAs negotiated since 1974 covering 300 projects, with 374 signed in the last ten years providing significant LB.[76]

Petroleum development in the North with IBAs include the Norman Wells oilfield and Norman Wells Pipeline Project (1985).[77] The revived McKenzie Gas Project (2004) with extensive IBAs was approved but cancelled because of a drop in natural gas prices.[78] The majority of current petroleum development is in southern Canada in the development of oilsands in Alberta and supporting export pipelines.

Resource Developments: A Study of First Nations-Industry Impact Benefits Agreements," Public Policy Forum, 2006.

[74] G. Peterson St-Laurent and P. Le Billon, "Staking Claims and Shaking Hands: Impact and Benefit Agreements as a Technology of Government in the Mining Sector" (2015) 2 *The Extractive Industries and Society* 590; T. Levitan and E. Cameron, "Privatizing Consent? Impact and Benefit Agreements and the Neoliberalization of Mineral Development in the Canadian North" in A. Keeling and J. Sandlos (eds.), *Mining and Communities in Northern Canada: History, Politics, and Memory* (Calgary: University of Calgary Press, 2015), p. 259.

[75] Own-source revenue for self-governing groups [OSR]. These are currently suspended until 2020 to negotiate implementation. Proponents share the same concerns, as OSR policies would be an indirect development tax raising the cost of access.

[76] Intergovernmental Working Group on the Mineral Industry, "Mining Sector Performance Report 2006 to 2015," Conference Presentation for Energy and Mines Ministers Conference, Winnipeg Manitoba, August, 2016; Resources and Sustainable Development in the Arctic (ReSDA) has summaries of resource development project in all three territories, http://yukonresearch .yukoncollege.yk.ca/resda/knowledge-sharing/resda-atlas/. See also Natural Resources Canada Indigenous Participation in Mining, www.nrcan.gc.ca/our-natural-resources/indigenous-natural-resources/indigenous-participation-mining-activities/7815.

[77] IBA negotiations are ongoing. Pipeline Profiles: Enbridge Norman Wells, www.cer-rec.gc.ca/nrg/ ntgrtd/pplnprtl/pplnprfls/crdl/nbrdnrmwlls-eng.html.

[78] "Mackenzie Gas Pipeline," 2004, https://apps.cer-rec.gc.ca/REGDOCS/Item/View/338661. The Aboriginal Pipeline Group would own 33 per cent of the project, and IBA with the Inuvialuit Settlement Region, the Gwich'in and Sahtu Settlement Areas but not the Dehcho region;

Lcrs and Indigenous Participation in Canada

5.2 Regulatory Approval Conditions as LCR

5.2.1 Canadian Energy Regulator

Canada's petroleum sector is regulated by the Canadian Energy Regulator (CER) established under the *Canadian Energy Regulator Act*, as an independent quasi-judicial regulator over energy infrastructure with powers, on application to recommend approval for inter-provincial pipelines or intra-provincial designated projects, including environmental assessment.[79]

Regulated projects will be directed to the CER for approval. The CER Filing Manual requires Proponents to engage with affected aboriginal groups prior to application, with those efforts and results described in the CER Application and updated periodically.[80] Applications will contain Proponent information for each affected aboriginal group on the anticipated impacts of the project on their aboriginal interests, and proposed mitigation efforts. Aboriginal groups will review massive detailed Project Descriptions,[81] to confirm or provide additional information and make suggested project changes to the Proponent. The Proponent will review those changes and may change the Project's design, location, or plans (practical accommodations) and respond, potentially triggering another round of discussion.[82] Practical accommodations are not benefits; they are lessened impacts.

The Proponent usually offers confidential Contribution Agreements to fund engagement, and may, at any stage, enter into IBAs with aboriginal groups in return for supporting the Project although the CER does not require these. Approval recommendations are contingent on satisfactory Proponent engagement with aboriginal groups, which may include plans for future engagement.

The CER will, after receiving a completed Application, conduct oral or written evidentiary hearings and once the CER is satisfied the evidence is adequate, it will prepare Draft Conditions and call for written arguments addressing them. The CER will consider the evidence, comments, and arguments and prepare a Report with its

---

C. A. Dokis, *Where the Rivers Meet: Pipelines, Participatory Resource Management, and Aboriginal-State Relations in the Northwest Territories* (Vancouver: University of British Columbia Press, 2016).

[79] IAA, note 64. Applications for approval commenced with the predecessor National Energy Board [NEB] established in 1959 under the *National Energy Board Act*, RSC 1985, c N-7, will continue under that regime, and references to CER practices are equivalent to the NEB, unless otherwise noted. Provincial energy regulators are similar.

[80] CER Board Filing Manual at 3.4.2 and 3.4.3, uses "Proponent consultation," which has been confusing for all parties given "Crown consultation"; we distinguish this as Proponent engagement.

[81] Proponents are required to provide increasing detail in project description, with the IAA, note 64, s 22(1) listing twenty factors to be assessed including, among other things, project impacts on climate change, gendered impacts, and cumulative impacts. P. N. Duinker and L. A. Greig, "The Impotence of Cumulative Effects Assessment in Canada: Ailments and Ideas for Redeployment" (2006) 37 *Environmental Management* 153.

[82] K. Lambrecht, *Aboriginal Consultation, Environmental Assessment, and Regulatory Review in Canada* (Regina: University of Regina Press, 2013) makes useful definition at 108 to 109.

findings, recommendations, and conditions of approval. Canada will normally make approval decisions within 90 days.

5.2.2 Crown Consultation in EIA

Canada has developed Consultation Policies incorporating the duty to consult into EIA, delegating procedural aspects of the duty to project Proponents, with subsequent direct consultation as may be required.[83] EIA requires information about project impacts on the natural and human environment and incorporation is justified on that basis.[84] Canada encourages aboriginal groups to participate in the CER process, and will record aboriginal issues, and after the CER Report is delivered, Canada will directly consult each aboriginal group separately within self imposed timelines to make approval decisions.[85]

Project approval is dependent on the Crown's fulfilment of the duty to consult which is outside of the Proponent's control. While Proponents are delegated procedural aspects, they cannot provide government-only compensation measures for impacts on aboriginal rights. Elements within Proponent control, such as significant financial compensation, may obtain regulatory consent but this distorts the reconciliatory purpose of aboriginal rights and perpetuates dissatisfaction.[86] Proponents face manageable regulatory approval risk in obtaining CER approval and uncontrollable Crown consultation risk should Courts quash Canada's approval. Both risks include lost revenue from delayed approval.

Aboriginal groups' difficulties include:

- limited input into a compulsory process as they cannot frustrate Crown consultation;[87]
- challenging EIA Tribunal decisions and Canada's approval is difficult where, crown consultation will be informed by the EIA Tribunal's recommendations; additional crown consultation will extend until Crown approval; and

---

[83] Government of Canada, "Aboriginal Consultation and Accommodation – Updated Guidelines for Federal Officials to Fulfill the Duty to Consult," March 2011 [Federal Consultation Policy]. Provincial treatment of the duty to consult, Laidlaw, note 46.

[84] Lambrecht, note 82; N. Craik, "Process and Reconciliation: Integrating the Duty to Consult with Environmental Assessment" (2016) 53 *Osgoode Hall Law Journal* 632-680; *Taku River*, note 41.

[85] *Gitxaala Nation v Canada*, 2016 FCA 187 [*Gitxaala*]. This process was a complete code with the Canadian government as decision-maker.

[86] Proponents may perceive this as overpayment while Indigenous governments, under constant fiscal constraints, will be forced to choose between compensation and continued exercise of their rights. Laidlaw, note 46.

[87] Federal Consultation Policy, note 83, p. 13. Lower courts said governments have absolute discretion in structuring Crown consultation: *Cold Lake First Nations v Alberta (Tourism, Parks & Recreation)*, 2013 ABCA 443 [Cold Lake]; *Gitxaala*, note 85. The Supreme Court has not ruled on this. Government consultation funding is limited to a fraction of requested funding.

LCRs and Indigenous Participation in Canada

additional crown consultation may be required in subsequent licensing processes;[88] and

- EIA Tribunals assess the impacts on current uses only. They cannot decide aboriginal title and rights, though their determinations on the underlying claim carry weight in future decisions, such that, from a practical point of view, EIA Tribunal decisions will de facto determine aboriginal rights and title on a reasonableness standard rather than correctness.[89]

5.2.3 Regulator Approval Conditions as LCR

Recent CER Reports have included a standard aboriginal package of conditions with reporting requirements.[90] Proponent Commitments to an aboriginal group are included in a general approval condition requiring Proponents to comply with all their commitments.

5.2.3.1 CONTINUAL ENGAGEMENT WITH AFFECTED INDIGENOUS NATIONS. The CER has imposed conditions requiring Proponents to prepare and fund Aboriginal Engagement Plans during project operation and decommissioning with input from aboriginal groups. For example, Enbridge's Line 3 Pipeline Project traversed settled lands with 95 per cent in private hands with minimal impacts on aboriginal rights, but CER, after hearing evidence from aboriginal groups, imposed conditions to file a Report for approval on an *Operational Consultation Plan for Aboriginal Groups*, developed in consultation with Aboriginal groups respecting the cultural interests of Aboriginal groups regardless of the nature of the land use in the Project area.[91]

5.2.3.2 EMPLOYMENT OF ABORIGINAL ENVIRONMENTAL MONITORS. The CER now imposes conditions requiring Reports for approval, on plans for employing Aboriginal Monitors during construction, operations, and decommissioning. For example, Enbridge Line 3 was required to file a Report for approval on an *Aboriginal Monitoring Plan*, describing participation by aboriginal groups including: a list of all

---

[88] *Métis Nation of Alberta Region 1 v Joint Review Panel*, 2012 ABCA 352; *Tsleil-Waututh Nation v Canada (National Energy Board)*, 2016 FCA 219.

[89] *Council of the Innu of Ekuanitshit v Canada (Attorney General)*, 2014 FCA 189; leave denied 2015 SCC 10578, after this it would take a well funded and determined Innu of Ekuanitshit to advance title claims.

[90] Reports for CER approval will not allow the specified aspect of the Project to proceed until CER approval, while Reports for information do not; both may impose service requirements to interested parties.

[91] Enbridge Line 3 replaced an aging pipeline from 1968 from Alberta to the US border in Manitoba, with a new line in the same corridor and decommissioning the old pipeline. Enbridge Line 3 NEB Report, April 25, 2016, https://apps.neb-one.gc.ca/REGDOCS/Item/View/2949686. Volume 2, Condition No. 29, p. 224 and Condition No. 37, p. 228. A Report on plan effectiveness for information filed after five years.

groups consulted; groups agreeing to participate in monitoring (with explanation for those not agreeing); project components to be monitored with monitoring methodologies including a summary of engagement with aboriginal groups in the preparation of them; and information on how monitoring information will be used by Enbridge and distributed to aboriginal groups.[92]

5.2.3.3 ABORIGINAL TRAINING, EMPLOYMENT, AND PREFERENTIAL PROCUREMENT. In order to address the socio-economic situation of Indigenous peoples, Proponents will, in their engagement with aboriginal groups, provide standardized plans for training, aboriginal employment, and preferential procurement for aboriginal firms.[93] Many Project employment opportunities will be short term, providing limited indirect benefits, such that aboriginal groups may request voluntary Proponent funding for community facilities to provide longer-term social benefits.

The CER imposes conditions requiring a Report for approval, on training, aboriginal employment, and preferential procurement prior to construction. For example, in Trans Mountain, it imposed conditions requiring Reports on *Aboriginal, Local, and Regional Skills and Business Capacity Inventory* for information, with Reports for approval on *Training and Education Monitoring Plan*, and *Socio-Economic Effects Monitoring Plan*.[94]

5.2.4 Summary of LB from CER Approval Conditions

While the various Reports described have yet to be filed, other Reports have been filed to give an idea as to potential LB. Of the post-construction Reports, *Towerbirch Project Aboriginal Monitoring Plan* (January 12, 2017) reported the hiring of five members of affected aboriginal groups,[95] and *Towerbirch Employment, Contracting and Procurement Report* (April 11, 2018) indicated 11 per cent of person hours involved aboriginal employees, with aboriginal subcontractor procurement totaling $14,892,588. However, the breakdowns did not specify aboriginal groups.[96] General

---

[92] Ibid., Vol. 2 Condition No. 12, pp. 219–220.

[93] For example, in "Trans Mountain Application," December 16, 2013 [Trans Mountain Application] https://apps.cer-rec.gc.ca/REGDOCS/Item/View/2385938. These plans are Appendices F and G in "Document B1-45 – V3B_APPE_TO_APPH – A3S0V1."

[94] "National Energy Board Report: Trans Mountain Expansion Project," May 20, 2016 [Trans Mountain Report].

[95] The Towerbirch Project was a 90 km pipeline project adjacent to existing disturbances. Towerbirch Aboriginal Monitoring Plan, January 12, 2017, https://apps.cer-rec.gc.ca/REGDOCS/Item/View/3160060, NEB Filing Doc: A81268. It appears that affected aboriginal groups did not have an IBA with the Proponent.

[96] Towerbirch Employment, Contracting and Procurement Report, April 11, 2018, https://apps.cer-rec.gc.ca/REGDOCS/Item/View/3539379. Breakdowns limited to Local/Regional and Provincial categories.

LCRs and Indigenous Participation in Canada

conditions may be improving for some Indigenous Nations but CER Approval conditions provide relatively limited LB to specific Nations.

5.3 Impact Benefit Agreements in the South

5.3.1 Alberta Oil Sands

The largest market for Canada's petroleum sector has been the United States, but with increased US domestic production Canadian imports are trading at significant discounts from world prices. The higher world prices are required to expand oilsands production and require additional export pipeline capacity to coastal ports. There have been two proposals, Northern Gateway (2002–13)[97] and Energy East (2014–17)[98] which have not received approval, and Trans Mountain Expansion Project (2014–) which is approved but under appeal.[99]

Alberta has made it a policy priority to increase oilsands production, projecting a rise to 4 million bpd by 2024, and in order to do so,[100]

- AER was established in 2012 as an up-stream energy regulator with environmental responsibility for energy projects and no jurisdiction over Crown consultation;[101]
- Alberta amended Consultation Policies in 2013, centralizing the Crown's aboriginal consultation in the Aboriginal Consultation Office to rule on the duty to consult and give directions to the AER;[102] and
- to address cumulative impacts from rapid development, Alberta implemented Regional Development Plans as cabinet-level planning documents listing land use priorities and requiring compliance from all arms of the government, including the AER with the plan in the oilsands region, stating oilsands development is a priority use.[103]

---

[97] Joint Review Panel Report Enbridge Northern Gateway Project, December 19, 2013, https://iaac-aeic.gc.ca/050/evaluations/document/97260 [JRP Report Northern Gateway]. Involving 1,000 km of new twin pipelines to Kitimat, British Columbia.

[98] Energy East Project (2014–2016), https://apps.cer-rec.gc.ca/REGDOCS/Item/View/2540913. Involving reversing 3,000 km of existing pipeline with new construction of 1,000 km to Saint John, New Brunswick.

[99] Trans Mountain Application, note 93. Involving 1,000 km of new construction adjacent to existing pipeline to Vancouver, British Columbia.

[100] Government of Alberta, "The Provincial Energy Strategy," 2008; Government of Alberta, "Responsible Actions: A Plan for Alberta Oil Sands," 2009; L. E. Adkin (ed.), First World Petro-Politics: The Political Ecology and Governance of Alberta (University of Toronto Press: Toronto, 2016), J. P. Findlay, The Future of the Canadian Oil Sands: Growth Potential of a Unique Resource amidst Regulation, Egress, Cost, and Price Uncertainty (Oxford: Oxford Institute for Energy Studies, 2016).

[101] REDA, note 57, s 21.

[102] Laidlaw, note 46.

[103] Alberta Land Stewardship Act, SA 2009, c A-26.8; Lower Athabasca Regional Plan (2012) described in Alberta Energy Regulator, "ABAER 017: Teck Resources Limited, Application for Oil Sands Evaluation Well Licences Undefined Field," October 21, 2013, p. 63.

Alastair R. Lucas and David K. Laidlaw

Alberta approves oilsands projects in the normal course. For example, in the Jackpine Oilsands Mine Expansion (2007), the Proponent proposed to expand the existing mine to include additional mining, and Alberta's environmental regulator approved it in 2010.[104] This was a Project with federal aspects, requiring a Joint Review by the AER and CER.[105] The Joint Panel Report (July 2013) found significant unmitigable adverse effects on the environment and aboriginal rights, but recommended approval in the public interest, which was duly granted.[106] Canada's approval was contested, but the Court said Canada had fulfilled the duty to consult and the issues complained of were within provincial jurisdiction.[107] There is only one case in Alberta where governments' conduct was successfully challenged.[108]

5.3.2 Impact Benefit Agreements in the Oilsands

Negotiating IBAs is both possible and prudent, and there is evidence of negotiating IBAs in the oilsands, as several First Nations withdrew their objections immediately prior to the Jackpine Hearings saying the Proponent had entered into agreements addressing their concerns.[109] In this way, they maximized their information on the Project and their capacity to delay approval absent an IBA.[110] Similarly in the Joslyn North Mine Project, First Nations withdrew their opposition after entering into IBAs.[111] Although the LB from these IBAs may be limited, if a Project is likely to be approved, which is the case in Alberta, then the perception that a "bad deal is better than no deal" governs.[112]

---

[104] The 2008 Jackpine Application to Alberta's regulators, LB were limited to "[i]ndirect benefits from the projects will be created by using local suppliers, including First Nations and Métis companies, provided that they are competitive and meet the project and operations requirements." Shell Canada Limited, "Application for the Approval of the Jackpine Mine Expansion Project Volume 1: Project Description," December 2007, P-iii.

[105] Alberta refused to participate in the Joint Review Panel Hearings citing its previous EA approval.

[106] Alberta Energy Regulator, "Report of the Joint Review Panel Established by the Federal Minister of the Environment and the Energy Resources Conservation Board Decision 2013 ABAER 011: Shell Canada Energy, Jackpine Mine Expansion Project, Application to Amend Approval 9756, Fort McMurray Area," July 9, 2013 [Jackpine Review]. The only effective mitigation measures would be conservation offsets for maintenance of aboriginal livelihoods, but this was not possible given Alberta's refusal to participate.

[107] *Adam v Canada (Environment)*, 2014 FC 1185.

[108] *Cold Lake*, note 87. Additional consultation was ordered on a Métis Harvesting Agreement (1980).

[109] Jackpine Review, note 106.

[110] B. Gilmour and B. Mellett, "The Role of Impact and Benefits Agreements in the Resolution of Project Issues with First Nations" (2013) 51 *Alberta Law Review* 385.

[111] Energy Resources Conservation Board and Canadian Environmental Assessment Agency, "Report of the Joint Review Panel Established by the Federal Minister of the Environment and the Energy Resources Conservation Board: Decision 2011–005: Total E&P Joslyn Ltd., Application for the Joslyn North Mine Project," January 27, 2011.

[112] S. McCarthy, "First Nation Chief Who Opposed Oil Sands Signs Deal with Teck Sharing Benefits of Bitumen Extraction," September 23, 2018, www.theglobeandmail.com/business/article-first-nation-chief-signs-deal-with-teck-to-participate-in-frontier-oil/.

LCRs and Indigenous Participation in Canada 361

5.3.3 Impact Benefit Agreements in Export Pipelines

Similar considerations drive the negotiation of IBAs in export pipelines but they are uniquely vulnerable. Trans Mountain has 43 IBAs (out of 131 aboriginal groups) with groups sharing in excess of $400 million.[113] Northern Gateway had entered into a number of IBAs, claiming agreement with 80 per cent of affected aboriginal groups.[114] However, IBAs were not made with coastal aboriginal groups who adamantly opposed both pipelines fearing a repeat of the 1989 Exxon Valdez disaster.[115]

Unlike oilsands projects, pipelines are linear disturbances, generating additional complexity with hundreds of EIA participants leading to regulatory delays, with numerous aboriginal groups (some with aboriginal title claims) requiring fulfillment of the Crown's duty to consult.[116] Private Proponents of export pipeline projects will assess the financial viability of the project during EIA with estimates of direct costs to obtain approval ranging from 4 to 11 per cent of total project costs; costs in excess of these limits jeopardize pipeline viability.[117]

In Northern Gateway, after lengthy hearings, the Joint Review Panel Report (December 19, 2013) cited adverse effects to specific species and the Great Bear Rainforest, but recommended approval subject to 209 conditions.[118] Canada conducted direct consultation and gave approval on June 17, 2014. Aboriginal groups challenged this in Court and two years later in *Gitxaala Nation v Canada* the approval was quashed.[119] Northern Gateway having spent $500 million to obtain approval on a $7.9-billion project (16 per cent), not only faced additional proceedings, but unanticipated *political risk* in the form of a proposed Tanker Ban off the

---

[113] Trans Mountain Pipeline Expansion, www.transmountain.com/news/2018/43-aboriginal-groups-have-signed-agreements-in-support-of-the-trans-mountain-expansion-project; T. Hopper, "What Do First Nations Really Think about Trans Mountain?" April 20, 2018, https://nationalpost.com/news/canada/what-do-first-nations-really-think-about-trans-mountain.

[114] The exact number of which is uncertain; unusually IBAs included Equity Agreements with a capped 10 per cent share of the $5.5 billion project shared equally with aboriginal groups. S. Narine, "Wording of Enbridge Equity Agreement Draws Criticism" (2012) 19 *Alberta Sweetgrass*.

[115] The Alaska Oil Spill Commission Final Report, *SPILL: The Wreck of the Exxon Valdez* (Anchorage: Alaska Oil Spill Commission, 1990); National Transportation Safety Board, "Marine Accident Report, Grounding of the U.S. Tankship Exxon Valdez on Bligh Reef, Prince William Sound Near Valdez, Alaska, March 24, 1989," Washington: National Transportation Safety Board, 1991.

[116] Northern Gateway had 206 Intervenors (108 aboriginal groups), Trans Mountain had 482 Intervenors (131 aboriginal groups), and Energy East had 350 Intervenors (123 aboriginal groups).

[117] G. Holburn and M. Loudermilk, "Risks and Costs of Regulatory Permit Applications in Canada's Pipeline Sector," Submission to the National Energy Board Modernization Expert Panel, Ivey School of Business, 2017. Regulatory delay risks are double-ended as shipping contracts will carry an in-service deadline after which shippers may cancel them.

[118] JRP Report Northern Gateway, note 97, Volume 2, p. 4, "There were 206 intervenors, 12 government participants, and 1,179 oral statements before the Panel. Over 9,000 letters of comment were received. The Panel held 180 days of hearings, of which 72 days were set aside for listening to oral statements and oral evidence."

[119] *Gitxaala*, note 85.

362 · Alastair R. Lucas and David K. Laidlaw

northeast coast of British Columbia.[120] Canada reconsidered its decision and denied approval on November 25, 2016.[121] Similarly in Energy East, Trans-Canada Pipelines (now TC Energy) having spent $700 million to reach the Application stage on a $12 billion project (5.8 per cent), facing a lengthy approval process, uncertain *Crown consultation risk*, and potential Tanker Ban, ultimately withdrew the project on October 5, 2017.[122]

In Trans Mountain, the CER Report (May 20, 2016), noting that 85 per cent of the pipeline route parallels the existing pipeline thus reducing impacts, recommended approval with 157 conditions.[123] Canada conducted direct Crown consultations,[124] and gave approval on November 29, 2016.[125] Aboriginal groups challenged this in Court. Kinder Morgan, having spent $1.1 billion dollars in receiving an approval, on a $7.7 billion project (14 per cent), faced with additional judicial risks and British Columbia's continued opposition, stopped work.[126] Canada acquired Trans Mountain in early 2018 for $4.5 billion, pledging to complete Trans Mountain and sell the enterprise, generating concerns that major pipelines require government support.[127]

Twenty-one months after approval, the Court in *Tsleil-Waututh Nation v Canada (Attorney General)*[128] quashed the Canada's approval of Trans Mountain, saying the Report findings within its mandate were reasonable, but they incorrectly interpreted the EIA mandate by excluding Project-related shipping, rendering government reliance on it invalid.[129]

---

[120] The Tanker Ban was a proposal from the Liberal party (in a draft Ocean Protection Plan applicable to both coasts) they were elected in October 19, 2015, and passed the *Oil Tanker Moratorium Act*, SC 2019, c 26.

[121] Order-In-PC-Council 2016–1047 (November 25, 2016), Citing the original impacts in the Report.

[122] CER Major Applications and Projects, cer-rec.gc.ca/pplctnflng/mjrpp/nrgyst/index-eng.html.

[123] Trans Mountain Report, note 94. EIA was confined to written evidence and argument with the exception of reception of Aboriginal Oral Tradition by thirty-five Aboriginal Groups over twenty-two days of hearings. It included Condition No. 145, that could require annual public disclosure of aboriginal Mutual Benefit Agreements (IBAs).

[124] "Joint Federal/Provincial Consultation and Accommodation Report for the Trans Mountain Project," November 2016; A joint Consultation Report was required as the result of Northern Gateway challenges in *Coastal*, note 65.

[125] Order-In-PC-Council 2016–1069 (November 29, 2016).

[126] Kinder Morgan Press Release (April 8, 2018).

[127] Canada Department of Finance News Release, "Agreement Reached to Create and Protect Jobs, Build Trans Mountain Expansion Project," May 29, 2018. NEB, "Optimizing Oil Pipeline and Rail Capacity out of Western Canada: Advice to the Minister of Natural Resources" (Ottawa: NEB, March 2019). There have been a number of unsolicited proposals from aboriginal groups to purchase the Project, C. Varcoe "New Indigenous coalition aims to buy a piece of Trans Mountain pipeline," June 5, 2019, https://calgaryherald.com/business/energy/varcoe-new-indigenous-coalition-aims-to-buy-a-piece-of-trans-mountain-pipeline.

[128] *Tsleil-Waututh Nation v Canada (Attorney General)*, 2018 FCA 153. Released August 28, 2018.

[129] Ibid. The Court also said the CER Report did not "include all of the subjects where consultation was required [as] it did not assess the nature and scope of asserted or established Indigenous rights including title, including governance rights," that were not properly addressed in Crown consultation at 570 to 573. This was also the finding in *Gitxaala* (note 85), P. B. Wood and D. A. Rossiter,

Canada did not appeal, directed the CER to conduct a Hearing on missed aspects, and immediately commenced direct Crown consultations.[130] The CER Report of February 22, 2019, determined Project-related shipping would incur significant adverse impacts but recommended approval subject to seven revised and sixteen new conditions.[131] Canada concluded direct consultations[132] and gave approval on June 18, 2019.[133] The Court issued leave to appeal this approval on September 4, 2019.[134] Canada is proceeding with the Trans Mountain Project despite this – targeting completion in mid-2022.

6 CONCLUSION AND RECOMMENDATIONS

In Canada, CER approval conditions can provide limited LB, but Indigenous Nations prefer to negotiate confidential IBA with Proponents to provide LB. Recent studies show a 12.7 per cent improvement on Community Wellbeing scores for Indigenous Nations with an IBA.[135]

IBAs are common in northern Canada, but negotiating IBAs where provinces are involved is less common – with Proponents' motivations to negotiate an IBA focussing on regulatory approval delays, including Crown consultation risks. This is driven in part by governments' policy to delay Crown consultation until after an EA Report is received, leaving Proponents in their mandated engagement with aboriginal groups limited to offering financial measures to compensate for impacts on aboriginal rights and title. One option is involving governments in negotiations at an earlier stage to provide government-only remedies for impacts, in concert with Proponents providing a share of benefits from that development, ideally in confidential IBAs. This appears possible in Saskatchewan's Consultation Policy (2010) where the Saskatchewan government may have Proponents meet with aboriginal groups in Crown consultation meetings.[136]

"The Politics of Refusal: Aboriginal Sovereignty and the Northern Gateway Pipeline" (2016), 61(2) *Canadian Geographer* 165.

[130] Order-In-PC-Council #2018–1179 (September 20, 2018), Government Announces Part II of Path Forward on the Trans Mountain Expansion Project, Natural Resources Canada Press Release (October 3, 2018).

[131] NEB Reconsideration Report (February 22, 2019) and Errata Letter (March 15, 2019) both https://apps .neb-one.gc.ca/REGDOCS/Item/View/3754555. It did not change Condition No 145.

[132] Trans Mountain Expansion Project Crown Consultation and Accommodation Report (June 2019).

[133] Order-In-PC-Council #2019–0820 (June 18, 2019).

[134] *Raincoast Conservation Foundation v Canada (Attorney General)*, 2019 FCA 259 limited to CER Reconsideration Report.

[135] D. Meerveld, "Assessing Value: A Comprehensive Study of Impact Benefit Agreements on Indigenous Communities of Canada," Major Research Paper, Graduate School of Public and International Affairs, University of Ottawa, 2016.

[136] Government of Saskatchewan First Nation and Métis Consultation Policy Framework (2010) at 8.

364   *Alastair R. Lucas and David K. Laidlaw*

Recent Court decisions may mandate this, as *Tsilhqot'in Nation* confirmed that the honour of the Crown applies to both the federal and provincial governments. Thus, in the Jackpine Mine Expansion, where Alberta took up lands under a land surrender treaty for mining purposes, combined with the Joint Review Panel findings that the only appropriate mitigation measures are conservation offsets, ought to have required Alberta, in fulfilling the honour of the Alberta Crown, to provide offsets under the logic of *Mikisew*.[137] A change in governments' approach to Crown consultation would address long-standing concerns of industry and Indigenous Nations.

For countries contemplating LCR, Canada's experience suggests the need for flexible IBA agreements prior to granting access to petroleum developers. Following the example of Alberta's new *Co-Management Agreement for Métis Settlements*, one process for consideration may include competition between qualified Proponents by way of proposing a program of local content benefits to that country [Proponent Proposal].[138] This would shift the burden onto Proponents to assess local needs and propose programs to provide them, under two equally important concepts:

- compensatory purposes: for impacts of petroleum development that invariably fall on local communities,[139] with potential Proponent mechanisms to directly compensate local communities, provide a separate compensation fund to which citizens could apply for displacement or economic impacts or any other proposals to fulfill this purpose; and
- beneficial purposes: for obtaining both short- and long-term sustainable benefits, with potential Proponent mechanisms including technology and revenue sharing directed at governments, health providers, and social and community services; local hiring, training, and professional development; local procurement with support for commercial capacity or any other proposals to fulfill this purpose.

Proponents Proposals could be formulated in accordance with government-recommended considerations derived from the IBA literature.[140] The selection of Proponent Proposals and negotiations of final IBAs could be managed by government or independent agencies. We suggest however that approval of a final IBA should proceed through some form of public approval process to assure Proponents

---

[137]   *Mikisew*, note 40.

[138]   The *Co-Management Agreement for Métis Settlements* was changed in 2013 to allow a number of qualified bidders to compete with proposals to provide LCB; W. Renke, "Alberta's Métis Settlements and the Co-Management Agreement" (2014) 23 *Constitutional Forum* 5.

[139]   B. Docherty, S. Knox, L. Pappone, and A. R. Siders, "Bearing the Burden: The Effects of Mining on First Nations in British Columbia," International Human Rights Clinic, Harvard Law School, October 2010.

[140]   See notes 66–74, 76, 78, and 139. That guidance should not restrict Proponent programs or methods for addressing those considerations.

of public support and lead to Proponent Proposals providing sustainable benefits for a wide part of the public.

These are tentative suggestions, but Canada's experience, in reconciling petroleum development and Indigenous Nations' efforts to obtain sustainable short- and long-term benefits of petroleum development, may provide insights and prompt additional research.

PART III

Lessons Learned and Future Directions

19

Local Content, Community Content, and Sustainable Development in the Oil and Gas Industry: Perspectives from Legislation, Policy, and Community Development Agreements

Ibironke T. Odumosu-Ayanu [*]

1 INTRODUCTION AND CONTEXT

This chapter examines the critical distinctions between the measures that are regarded as part of local content, that is, local content requirements (LCRs), community content initiatives, and community development agreements (CDAs). It analyzes these distinctions from the lens of the sustainable development goals (SDGs) outlined as part of the 2030 agenda for sustainable development.[1] While not necessarily endorsing any initiative that has been regarded as part of local content, this chapter demonstrates that it is necessary to clearly delineate the scope of each initiative in order to appropriately assess their contributions, if any, to the SDGs. For their part, community content measures appear to have a greater potential to reflect the SDGs, although as currently crafted, mostly as an addendum to LCRs and as mechanisms that do not provide much choice to the local communities that host and are impacted by oil and gas development ("local communities"/ "host and impacted communities"), they ultimately lack the capacity to fully reflect what many local communities view as "development."[2] The SDGs incorporate three aspects of sustainable development, that is the economic, social, and environmental aspects. A report prepared in partnership between IPIECA, "the global oil and gas association for environmental and social issues," the United Nations Development Program (UNDP), and the International Finance Corporation (IFC) outlines the oil and gas industry's "potential to contribute to all 17 SDGs."[3] Local content is one of the major initiatives that the report addresses noting *inter alia* that "[l]ocal content

---

[*] Parts of this chapter appeared as a post titled "Sustainable Development and Community Content in the Oil and Gas Industry" (November 27, 2019) on AfronomicsLaw and the Dalhousie Law Journal Blog.

[1] UN General Assembly, *Transforming Our World: The 2030 Agenda for Sustainable Development*, 21 October 2015, UN Doc. A/Res/70/1.

[2] See the discussion in Section 2 of this chapter.

[3] IPIECA, IFC, UNDP, "Mapping the oil and Gas Industry to the Sustainable Development Goals: An Atlas," 2017, p. vii.

policies, which promote the sourcing of goods and services from local businesses, can help foster economic growth and development, especially when pursued in the context of improving the enabling investment and business environment."[4] The scope of local content and the relevance of that scope for assessing the contributions of local content to achievement of the SDGs forms the focus of this chapter.

In 2012, an article titled "Foreign Direct Investment Catalysts in West Africa: Interactions with Local Content Laws and Industry-Community Agreements" was published.[5] It assessed LCRs and agreements between local communities and industry, generally known as CDAs, and determined the extent to which LCRs and CDAs may be reconciled with the investment promotion initiatives of Nigeria and Ghana. LCRs[6] and CDAs[7] are generally adopted as measures to ensure that nationals of a country and local communities are direct beneficiaries of resource development.[8] While the 2012 article assessed LCRs as government-led initiatives and CDAs as mostly private initiatives, it acknowledged that separating government-led and private initiatives is not always apposite.[9] In fact, it adopted the view that both initiatives involve some government presence and both are market-based initiatives.[10] As this chapter will demonstrate, LCRs (policy and/or legislative requirements that usually have a national focus), CDAs (agreements between specific host/impacted communities and industry), and community content (policy and/or legislative requirements that usually have a community focus) are increasingly being subsumed under the general scope of local content. Recognizing that "the lines between the public

[4] Ibid., p. 42.
[5] I. T. Odumosu-Ayanu, "Foreign Direct Investment Catalysts in West Africa: Interactions with Local Content Laws and Industry-Community Agreements" (2012) 35 *North Carolina Central Law Review* 401.
[6] A complete analysis of LCRs is beyond the scope of this chapter. On arguments in favor of and against LCRs, see C. Nwapi, "Defining the "Local" in Local Content Requirements in the Oil and Gas and Mining Sectors in Developing Countries" (2015) 8 *Law and Development Review* 187. For arguments against LCRs, especially from the perspective of World Trade Organization requirements, see Nwapi, pp. 193–196; Odumosu-Ayanu, note 5, pp. 426–427; C. Cimino, G. C. Hufbauer, and J. J. Schott, "A Proposed Code to Discipline Local Content Requirements," Policy Brief: Peterson Institute for International Economics, February 2014. See also H. Deringer, F. Erixon, P. Lamprecht, and E. van der Marel, "The Economic Impact of Local Content Requirements: A Case Study of Heavy Vehicles," European Centre for International Political Economy Occasional Paper 1, January 25, 2018, for a critique of LCRs and situating these arrangements within the context of non-tariff barriers.
[7] On CDAs, see generally, C. O'Faircheallaigh, "Community Development Agreements in the Mining Industry: An Emerging Global Phenomenon" (2013) 44 *Community Development* 222; E. Oshionebo, "Community Development Agreements as Tools for Local Participation in Natural Resource Projects in Africa" in I. Feichtner, M. Krajewski, and R. Roesch (eds.), *Human Rights in the Extractive Industries: Transparency, Participation, Resistance* (New York: Springer, 2019), p. 77.
[8] On the purpose of local content, see J. S. Ovadia, "Local Content and Natural Resource Governance: The Cases of Angola and Nigeria" (2014) 1 *The Extractive Industries and Society* 137.
[9] While CDAs are mostly negotiated between local communities and industry, they are sometimes mandated by government. On the public–private distinction and CDAs, see I. T. Odumosu-Ayanu, "The (Legal) Nature of Indigenous Peoples' Agreements with Extractive Companies" in I. T. Odumosu-Ayanu and D. Newman (eds.), *Indigenous–Industry Agreements, Natural Resources and the Law* (New York: Routledge, 2020 – Forthcoming).
[10] Odumosu-Ayanu, note 5, p. 424.

Local Content, Community Content, and SD 371

and private are increasingly blurred," this chapter argues that the scope of local content remains unclear and contested, especially in its interaction with host and impacted communities and, ultimately, with sustainable development.[11]

In Nigeria's oil and gas industry, from which this chapter draws examples, local content is generally understood as the legislative requirements enunciated in the *Nigerian Oil and Gas Industry Content Development Act* (NOGICDA/Act).[12] The Nigerian Content Development and Monitoring Board (NCDMB), created under the Act, recently published a separate set of community content guidelines to address LCRs in host and impacted communities.[13] The NCDMB's "Community Content Guideline" attempts to connect the Guideline with the Act and the Guideline also seeks to incorporate Nigeria's oil and gas industry's version of CDAs, that is, the Global Memorandum of Understanding (GMOU). In light of these interconnected layers that are evident in Nigeria's local content initiative – that is, legislated LCRs, community content guidelines, and GMOUs that are referenced in the NCDMB's Community Content Guideline – Nigeria serves as an apt illustration of the arguments that this chapter advances.

In their assessment of local content, other commentators have also alluded to the relationship between LCRs, CDAs, and, in some cases, a specific category of community content.[14] Warner's analysis of local content incorporates what he calls "community investment programmes."[15] These community investment programmes are driven by oil and gas companies and not by government-mandated local content policies that seek to promote "local participation" or "local capability development."[16] Warner argues that the companies' "underlying motivation" in investing in "community projects in proximity to facilities is about building for the business an informal 'social license to operate.'"[17] He situates GMOUs in his conceptualization of community investment programmes. In identifying three challenges of community investment programmes, that is, sustainability, relevance, and political visibility, he asks whether "the closer integration of community investment programmes with the local content capability development programmes of the

---

[11] Ibid., at 424.
[12] *Nigerian Oil and Gas Industry Content Development Act*, 2010 Act No. 2 ["NOGICDA"].
[13] Nigerian Content Development and Monitoring Board, "Community Content Guideline," 2017, https://ncdmb.gov.ng/images/Downloads/CCGHCCChecklist.pdf.
[14] Odumosu-Ayanu, note 5; D. S. Olawuyi, "Enhancing the Benefits of Local Content in Extractive Industry Agreements: Legal Approaches and Trends in Frontier Extractive Jurisdictions" in I. T. Odumosu-Ayanu and D. Newman (eds.) *Indigenous-Industry Agreements, Natural Resources and the Law* (New York: Routledge, 2020 – Forthcoming); Nwapi, note 6; M. Warner, "Incentivising Community Content: The Interface of Community Investment Programmes with Local Content Practices in the Oil and Gas Development Sector" Overseas Development Institute, June 2007. See also, A. M. Esteves, B. Coyne, and A. Moreno, "Local Content Initiatives: Enhancing the Subnational Benefits of the Oil, Gas and Mining Sectors," Natural Resource Governance Institute, July 2013.
[15] Warner, note 14.
[16] Ibid., p. 1–2.
[17] Ibid., p. 4.

372   *Ibironke T. Odumosu-Ayanu*

parent oil company" will "improve the prospects for long-term economic sustainability in affected communities" and argues that the integration of community investment programmes with local content initiatives offer responses to these challenges. Warner's principal contribution is, perhaps, what he calls "community content," that is, "the interface of community investment programs with local content."[18] His approach to community content appears geared toward oil companies as he notes that "[u]ltimately, community content is about realising a competitive advantage for the oil company in the eyes of both the local population and the country's guardians of economic policy."[19] Community content is a "merit good," that is, it targets host and impacted communities and therefore somewhat "exclusionary" while conventional local content programmes are not as exclusionary and are more of a "public good," although when situated in the global context, local content can also be regarded as a merit good.[20]

Nwapi has also turned attention to local content policies and host and impacted communities. His primary argument is that the mainstream approach to local content, which seeks "to promote increased local participation in FDI by directing the utilization of indigenous companies in the procurement of goods and services, employment of locals and the use of local raw materials by foreign investors," "impedes the potential of local content requirements to engender real economic development."[21] Nwapi insightfully argues that LCRs can do more than serve national interests. They can also "meet the demands of subnational stakeholders, such as local governments and communities, which will in turn enable companies to obtain the social license to operate."[22] However, for this to occur, LCRs need to "adopt a bottom-up approach that gives proper recognition to the citizens of the localities where the extractive activities take place."[23] This "localist approach" can "promote inclusiveness with regard to the resource-rich communities who often feel excluded from the benefits of the resources located within their territory and as a mechanism to reallocate resource wealth within the country."[24]

In one of the essays in a collection on *Indigenous-Industry Agreements, Natural Resources and the Law*, Olawuyi presents an account of LCRs that incorporates

---

[18] Ibid., p. 5.

[19] Ibid., p. 5. Warner notes at page 8 that: "community content is a means to satisfy two sets of interests. Public authorities are looking for ways to position the talents and resources of their dominant upstream energy industries as a catalyst for wider sustainable economic development. And, the established multinational oil and gas development companies need to maintain a visible competitive advantage against the globally competing national oil companies, and against each other. Elevating their contribution to local content capture and local capability development, and integrating these new practices with the need to sustain a 'social license to operate' through community investment programmes, offers just such competitive differentiation."

[20] Ibid., p. 5.

[21] Nwapi, note 6, pp. 187–188.

[22] Ibid., p. 188.

[23] Ibid.

[24] Ibid., p. 205.

CDAs within local content.[25] He argues that LCRs are included in extractive industry agreements and other instruments in order to maximize the benefits of extractive industry development to nationals and host and impacted communities. He presents LCRs as serving similar functions to CDAs that facilitate employment and skills development for host and impacted communities.

The views that Odumosu-Ayanu, Warner, Nwapi, and Olawuyi express in the essays highlighted, are not uniform and not without nuanced differences. For example, while Olawuyi reads LCRs and CDAs as part of local content, Odumosu-Ayanu recognizes their potential impacts and benefits but mostly reads them separately. The central organizing frame in the authors' pieces, which this present chapter captures, is the potential close connection between LCRs and community-related initiatives, either in the form of CDAs or similar initiatives that seek to privilege host and impacted communities. As Esteves, Coyne, and Moreno note, "[c]ommunity development obligations are relevant to local content because they tend to support enterprise development, skills development programs and other social and physical infrastructure that contribute to a healthy local economy."[26]

Clearly, there is a close connection between LCRs and community-related initiatives such as CDAs with Esteves, Coyne, and Moreno also referring to "local indigenous content."[27] However, this connection has yet to be fully and deliberately explored by the relevant policy makers. What currently entails is a muddying of mechanisms that have developed as state-led LCRs that mostly apply nationally; mostly industry-led CDAs although in parts of the world such as Australia and Canada, Indigenous peoples are also primary drivers of CDAs; and some recent efforts at developing community content guidelines.[28] This chapter argues that instead of assuming that legislated/policy-mandated LCRs and negotiated or standard form CDAs serve the same functions in practice or transposing the functions of one on the other, it is necessary to systematically and intentionally reflect on their contributions to locally beneficial natural resource development. For instance, while CDAs are by their nature intended to focus on local communities, using Nigeria as an example, the country's local content legislation is designed to apply nationally and has been a subject of a critique to the effect that "the Nigerian elite" are "the primary beneficiaries of Nigerian content."[29] This chapter highlights the need to develop mechanisms that appropriately account for the benefits and limitations of these mechanisms,

---

[25] Olawuyi, note 14.
[26] Esteves et al., note 14, p. 14.
[27] Ibid., p. 16.
[28] On agreements between Indigenous peoples and industry in Australia, Canada, Ghana, and Nigeria, see Odumosu-Ayanu, note 9.
[29] J. S. Ovadia, "The Making of Oil-Backed Indigenous Capitalism in Nigeria" (2013) 18 *New Political Economy* 258 at 259.

both at a national level and for local communities. In addition, LCRs are designed and implemented by the state[30] and it is not clear that self-governing Indigenous nations in many parts of the world would consider mandated CDAs with predetermined parameters set by the state as an opportunity to express free, prior, and informed consent.[31] At the same time, in other places, CDAs may not materialize in the absence of state intervention, assuming that CDAs are more beneficial to host communities than detrimental, as CDAs exist within legal, political, and socioeconomic contexts that cannot be separated from the agreements.[32] Essentially, while there appears to be developing understanding of the relationship between local content and local communities, there remains a need to clearly articulate visions for the different forms of engagement with host and impacted communities in the oil and gas industry, either as separate nationally focused LCRs, specific community content policies, or CDAs; or to clearly develop these as part of a single bundle of engagement with well-defined parameters.

The balance of this chapter makes a case for the need to be more deliberate about conceptualizing and contextualizing the relationship between and purpose(s) of LCRs and other initiatives that appear to serve similar purposes in communities. In light of the fact that the SDGs are crafted in the nature of "goals," it is necessary to critically assess whether local content in the broad sense or each initiative that is being regarded as part of local content are meeting the SDGs. This is particularly relevant given that these measures, especially CDAs, are not value-neutral and could be detrimental to, or even rejected by, host and impacted communities. In Section 2, this chapter analyzes the economic development rationale for the three main types of interconnected initiatives that the chapter discusses, that is, LCRs, CDAs, and community content guidelines. Section 3 discusses community content, situating it within Nigeria's local content laws and the SDGs. Section 4 turns attention to GMOUs (a form of CDAs in Nigeria's oil and gas industry), noting the limitations of adopting them as a proxy for local content and their significant limitations as instruments that reflect any measure of communities' self-determination. Section 5 analyzes the initiatives in light of the SDGs while Section 6 concludes.

---

[30] CDAs are mandated in Nigeria's mining industry. See section 116 of the *Nigerian Minerals and Mining Act*, Act No. 20, 2007.

[31] On free, prior, and informed consent, see UN General Assembly, United Nations Declaration on the Rights of Indigenous Peoples, 2 October 2007, UN Doc. A/RES/61/295; C. M. Doyle, *Indigenous Peoples, Title to Territory, Rights and Resources: The Transformative Role of Free Prior and Informed Consent* (New York: Routledge, 2015).

[32] On detriments of CDAs, see O'Faircheallaigh, note 7, pp. 231–235.

Local Content, Community Content, and SD 375

2 RATIONALE FOR LCRS, COMMUNITY CONTENT, AND CDAS

Private investment – domestic and foreign – has been a major area of policy focus of many countries, including Nigeria.[33] States adopt several measures to ensure that investment is beneficial to the local economy. From indigenization policies to liberalization to measures such as local content policies adopted as a middle ground, investment policies occupy a major area of policymaking. Local content policies and requirements vary across jurisdictions and so do the definitions of local content.[34] Usually, local content is mostly viewed from the perspective of LCRs. Countries adopt LCRs in order to "maximize the gains" of FDI "through the promotion of local participation in FDI and the use of local raw materials."[35] LCRs usually require local procurement of goods, local service provision, employment of citizens of host states as well as active participation of local companies.

Some commentators regard local content as measures that extend beyond government-mandated requirements. In their definition of local content, Tordo et al. mostly outline the government-mandated view of LCRs but also note that "[l]ocal content *may even refer* to the provision, by the oil company, of infrastructure (schools, medical facilities) that is not an input into its own production but intended for the benefit of the local population (either of the nation generally or the neighborhood of the installations)."[36] They argue that many oil and gas companies adopted the view that local content is part of corporate social responsibility (CSR).[37] Local content is now, however, mostly viewed through the lens of a "compliance regime."[38] Between the voluntary CSR view and the (government) compliance regime lies the agreement model (CDAs), where companies pledge to provide benefits, including infrastructure development, to host and impacted communities. In addition, governments may choose to provide incentives to firms in order to foster local content. Such incentives may coexist with mandatory LCRs as is the case in the NOGICDA.[39] In this broad view of local content, there are the compliance/mandatory LCRs, mandatory community content measures, government incentives to facilitate local content, and CDA provisions. In this frame, local content measures are located in legislation, such as the NOGICDA, which is directed specifically toward LCRs and incentives; in other

---

[33] United Nations Conference on Trade and Development, "Investment Policy Review: Nigeria," United Nations, UNCTAD/DIAE/PCB/2008/1, 2009.

[34] For a case study of LCRs in multiple jurisdictions, see S. Tordo and Y. Anouti, *Local Content in the Oil and Gas Sector: Case Studies* (Washington, DC: The World Bank, 2013) (discussing LCRs in the oil and gas sectors in Angola, Brazil, Indonesia, Kazakhstan, Malaysia, and Trinidad and Tobago).

[35] C. Nwapi, "A Survey of the Literature on Local Content Policies in the Oil and Gas Industry in East Africa" (2016) 9 *The School of Public Policy Technical Paper* at 2.

[36] Silvana Tordo, Michael Warner, Osmel E. Manzano and Yahya Anouti, Local Content Policies in the Oil and Gas Sector (Washington, D.C.: The World Bank, 2013) 3 [emphasis added].

[37] Ibid., p. 63. Although some would situate CDAs within the broader context of CSR, CDAs are largely treated separately for the purpose of this chapter.

[38] Ibid.

[39] NOGICDA, note 12, s. 48.

pieces of legislation such as Nigeria's *Petroleum Act*, oil and gas contracts between governments and industry actors[40]; and, as some have argued, in CDAs.[41]

The dominant view of local content remains the compliance model-type LCRs mandated by government in legislation, policy instruments, and investor–state contracts. Many Third World countries that adopt the compliance model of LCRs do so to foster economic development. However, local content has been critiqued as having "a dual nature: it is both a mechanism for promoting large-scale economic development and at the same time a mechanism for the elite to capture oil rent by legitimising policies that play favourites and privilege particular capitalists."[42] Economic development is, itself, a complex and contested concept.[43] It has been argued that the "theory behind local content is that by encouraging Nigerian participation in the oil and oil services sectors, more of the money invested annually in extracting the country's resource wealth ... can be captured domestically and used to spur growth in other sectors of the economy."[44]

Ovadia situates local content within the development conversation. For him local content could be viewed in terms of "indigenization" or "domiciliation," with indigenization representing Nigeria's policies in the 1970s and 1980s and domiciliation accounting for the current view regarding local content. Ovadia notes:

> The developmental effects of local content can be thought of as falling into two broad categories: policies designed to increase national ownership premised on the assumption that profits will trickle down to the general populace (premised on a notion of "trickle down effect") and policies designed to increase economic activity and job creation through "knock-on effects" from the oil industry. ... [T]he former, though still very much a part of the current local content drive, were the explicit focus of "indigenization" or "Nigerianization" policies in decades past, while the latter newly emphasized "domiciliation" within Nigerian content.[45]

---

[40] LCRs are usually framed as legislative or policy requirements. However, in some cases, these requirements are included in agreements between the state and extractive companies. In fact, Joint Operating Agreements, which are common in Nigeria's oil and gas industry between upstream oil and gas companies and Nigeria's national oil and gas company (the Nigerian National Petroleum Corporation ("NNPC")) are regarded in some quarters as local content strategies. Warner, note 14, p. 1. For the contents of Joint Operating Agreements regarding local content, see J. S. Ovadia, "Indigenization versus Domiciliation: A Historical Approach to National Content in Nigeria's Oil and Gas Industry" in T. Falola and J. Achberger (eds.), *The Political Economy of Development and Underdevelopment in Africa* (New York: Routledge, 2013), p. 54.

[41] See I. Ramdoo, *Designing Local Content Policies in Mineral-Rich Countries* (Winnipeg: The International Institute for Sustainable Development, 2018), pp. 7–8.

[42] Ovadia, note 8, p. 138.

[43] See I. T. Odumosu-Ayanu "Local Communities, Environment and Development: The Case of Oil and Gas Investment in Africa" in Kate Miles (ed.), *Research Handbook on Environment and Investment Law* (Edward Elgar, 2019) 480 at 486.

[44] Ovadia, note 40, p. 49.

[45] Ibid., p. 49.

Local Content, Community Content, and SD 377

While indigenization, which was the first wave of government-mandated local content, focused on "national ownership" and the current wave directs its attention toward increased "economic activity and job creation" for all Nigerians, the approach for fostering the participation of host and impacted communities in the local content conversation and practice remains unclear. The Nigerian government adopted measures to address challenges in the Niger Delta, including the establishment of the challenge-prone and now defunct Oil Mineral Producing Area Development Commission, and the Niger Delta Development Commission.[46] Oil companies have also adopted efforts to form nonbinding GMOUs with communities to provide services. In spite of these government and industry initiatives, significant challenges remain in the Niger Delta. More recently, the government, through the NCDMB, issued community content guidelines in a bid to address host and impacted communities' place in the local content regime. Given its relatively recent publication, it is too early to assess the effectiveness of this measure and its contribution to economic development in the Niger Delta.

The meaning, implications, and impacts of economic development are contested.[47] For many policy makers, economic development is linear, suggesting that society 'progresses' from one stage to another in a predetermined fashion.[48] Critical scholars, such as Esteva, argue that development suggests "a favourable change, a step from the simple to the complex, from the inferior to the superior, from worse to better. The word indicates that one is doing well because one is advancing in the sense of a necessary, ineluctable, universal law and toward a desirable goal."[49] Many African states are not as critical but adopt policies that seek to reduce poverty and meet economic needs both in the immediate and long term.[50] LCRs mostly fit within this vision of economic development, that is, adopting measures to facilitate economic growth at a national level. Local community-specific benefits have mostly been at the periphery of government-mandated LCRs.

In light of the national focus of many of the policies regarding the oil and gas industry, including LCRs, host and impacted communities have a complex relationship with the development message that drives these policies and the measures through which they are implemented. Oil and gas projects alter the lives of host and impacted communities and often have significant impacts on their livelihoods.[51] National-focused policies not specifically tailored to these challenges mostly do not

---

[46] See J. Shola Omotola, "From the OMPADEC to the NDDC: An Assessment of State Responses to Environmental Insecurity in the Niger Delta, Nigeria" (2007) 54 *Africa Today* 73.

[47] See Odumosu-Ayanu, note 43, p. 486.

[48] See generally, W. W. Rostow, "The Stages of Economic Growth" (1959) 12 *The Economic History Review, New Series* 1; W. W. Rostow, *The Stages of Economic Growth: A Non-Communist Manifesto* (Cambridge University Press, 1960).

[49] G. Esteva, "Development" in W. Sachs (ed.), *The Development Dictionary: A Guide to Knowledge as Power* (Witwatersrand University Press; Zed Books, 1993), p. 10.

[50] Odumosu-Ayanu, note 43, p. 487.

[51] Ibid., pp. 487–488.

respond to communities' concerns and experiences. Even the visions of community development that most governments and oil and gas companies espouse are significantly limited. Governments and oil and gas companies mostly view community development as philanthropic and voluntary CSR[52] or through the lens of GMOU-type agreements.[53] Meanwhile, scholars argue that community development "goes beyond the narrowly economic to encompass social and cultural well-being."[54] More importantly, local communities espouse views regarding well-being that do not necessarily fit within definitional boxes. These community perspectives on development "rely on individuals' views and needs and on community expectations and aspirations."[55] Sometimes, those views may favor oil and gas production and at other times, local communities may prefer that oil and gas production should not proceed. Drawing an example from Kenya, the Endorois community expressed their view in terms of "choice and self-determination" as well as "effective and meaningful participation in projects" arguing that development is "an increase in peoples' well-being, as measured by capacities and choices available."[56]

LCRs do not reflect this choice and self-determination view. In their mandatory form as government policy or legislative requirements, they mostly fit the general/national conception of economic development. Community content guidelines that are adopted as a type of addendum to LCR legislation also do not reflect much choice and self-determination as they presuppose that oil and gas production will proceed. While CDAs have the potential to reflect a community development perspective, GMOUs, which are a form of CDAs, are very limited instruments. As such, while incorporating community content into the local content frame may provide direct benefits to communities, the parameters, scope, and other important factors regarding local content are determined by the state and/or industry without much, if any, insight from the communities. If LCRs and most of the other measures that some argue are part of local content address development issues, they are mostly limited to economic growth-related issues that sometimes have a social impact. They do not fully address the interrelated economic, social, and environmental dimensions of sustainable development.

---

[52] N. Yakovleva, "Models for Community Development: A Case Study of the Mining Industry" in T. Marsden (ed.), *Sustainable Communities: New Spaces for Planning, Participation and Engagement* (Oxford: Elsevier, 2008), p. 47.

[53] Ramdoo, note 41.

[54] J. Loxley, *Aboriginal, Northern, and Community Development: Papers and Retrospectives* (Winnipeg: Arbeiter Ring Publishing, 2010), p. 20.

[55] Odumosu-Ayanu, note 43, p. 488.

[56] *Centre for Minority Rights Development (Kenya) and Minority Rights Group International on behalf of Endorois Welfare Council v. Kenya*, African Commission on Human and Peoples Rights, 273/2003 (25 November 2009), para. 129.

Local Content, Community Content, and SD

3 LOCAL CONTENT REQUIREMENTS, COMMUNITY CONTENT, AND SUSTAINABLE DEVELOPMENT

Nigeria exemplifies the relationship between LCRs and community content. The country was under colonial administration until its political independence in 1960. Political independence did not, however, automatically translate to economic independence. The decolonization period of the 1960s and 1970s was a time when many Third World countries sought to assert economic independence domestically and in the international arena. This was a time when dependency theory garnered prominence,[57] nationalization of sectors that were germane to national identity were relatively common occurrences, and international relations saw the emergence of efforts to develop a new international economic order.[58] Nigeria, at this time, turned efforts toward ensuring that its oil and gas industry generated significant benefits for the country. Since this time, the country has adopted a myriad of mechanisms to reflect this view. The journey from indigenization[59] to liberalization[60] of the oil and gas industry has culminated in what appears to be a middle ground in the form of the NOGICDA.[61] In addition to establishing the NCDMB, the Act requires that all entities involved in Nigeria consider "Nigerian content" as an "important element" of their "management philosophy."[62] Essentially, Nigerian content is the philosophy that currently drives the execution of projects and other activities in Nigeria's oil and gas industry. The Act defines Nigerian content as "the quantum of composite value added to or created in the Nigerian economy by a systematic development of capacity and capabilities through the deliberate utilization of Nigerian human, material resources and services in the Nigerian oil and gas industry."[63] It focuses on "Nigerian" content with almost no specific references to the host communities.[64]

---

[57] See for example, W. Rodney, *How Europe Underdeveloped Africa* (London: Bogle-L'Ouverture Publications, 1972).

[58] See UN General Assembly, *3201 (S-VI). Declaration on the Establishment of a New International Economic Order*, 1 May 1994, UN Doc, A/RES/3201(S-VI); UN General Assembly, *Charter of Economic Rights and Duties of States*, 6 November 1974, UN Doc. A/RES/3281.

[59] See generally, C. Ogbuagu, "The Nigerian Indigenization Policy: Nationalism or Pragmatism?" (1983) 82 *African Affairs* 241; S. Megwa, "Foreign Direct Investment Climate in Nigeria: The Changing Laws and Development Policies" (1983) 21 *Columbia Journal of Transnational Law* 487; T. J. Biersteker, *Multinationals, the State and Control of the Nigerian Economy* (Princeton, NJ: Princeton University Press, 1987).

[60] *Nigerian Investment Promotion Commission Act* (Decree No. 16 of 1995), Cap. 117 Laws of the Federation of Nigeria, 2004. See generally, K. U. K. Ekwueme, "Nigeria's Principal Investment Laws in the Context of International Law and Practice" (2005) 49 *Journal of African Law* 177.

[61] NOGICDA, note 12.

[62] Ibid., s. 2.

[63] Ibid., s. 106.

[64] See ibid., s. 27. As discussed in this section, a subsequent NCDMB guideline has turned attention toward host and impacted communities.

380 Ibironke T. Odumosu-Ayanu

The NOGICDA promotes development of Nigerian content as "a major criterion" for awarding licenses and permits as well as bidding for exploration, production, and other operations.[65] From the Act's commencement, "all subsequent oil and gas arrangements, agreements, contracts or memoranda of understanding relating to any operation or transaction in the Nigerian oil and gas industry" are obliged to conform to the Act's requirements. Nigerian content has, essentially, become an overarching component of Nigeria's oil and gas industry. NOGICDA is a vast piece of legislation that addresses an array of issues including principles to be adopted in evaluating bids,[66] technology transfer,[67] training,[68] and a 5 percent maximum for expatriates in management positions.[69] In addition, by Section 3(1), "Nigerian independent contractors shall be given first consideration in the award of oil blocks, oil field licences, oil lifting licences and in all projects for which contract is to be awarded in the Nigerian oil and gas industry." "[E]xclusive consideration" is given to Nigerian indigenous services companies in certain instances.[70] The Act privileges goods made in Nigeria as well as services provided in Nigeria in furtherance of Nigerian content.[71] Nigerian Content Plans that operators send to the NCDMB shall include details of the plan to give "first consideration" to services and goods from Nigeria.[72] First consideration shall also be given to Nigerians for employment and training.[73] All insurable risks related to the "oil and gas business, operations or contracts" in Nigeria's oil and gas industry must be insured "with an insurance company, through an insurance broker registered in Nigeria."[74] A similar requirement applies to the services of legal practitioners.[75]

Nigerian content, which is the hallmark of LCRs in Nigeria's oil and gas industry, is perhaps also its greatest most unacknowledged challenge. That focus, perhaps inadvertently, results in LCRs that do not reflect the interests of host and impacted communities. The NCDMB's Community Content Guideline seeks to rectify this challenge. Like local content, the meaning of community content is contested. If arrangements such as GMOUs are regarded as part of local content, GMOU-type arrangements would also form part of community content. However, in this section, community content measures are government-led initiatives akin to the type of LCRs in the NOGICDA. The distinction lies in community content policies being directed specifically toward host and impacted communities. In this sense, community content is a "sub-component" of LCRs.[76] Essentially, in effecting LCRs

[65] Ibid., s. 3(3).
[66] Ibid., s. 16.
[67] Ibid., s. 44.
[68] Ibid., s. 30.
[69] Ibid., s. 32.
[70] Ibid., s. 3(2).
[71] Ibid., s. 10.
[72] Ibid., s. 12.
[73] Ibid., s. 28.
[74] Ibid., s. 49. See also s. 50 of the NOGICDA.
[75] Ibid., s. 51. See s. 52 for requirements regarding retaining financial services in Nigeria.
[76] Nwapi, note 35, p. 12.

under community content, host and impacted communities receive preference regarding employment, training, procurement and other relevant areas of LCRs. Community content has been viewed as a measure for industry's acquisition of a social license to operate, mitigating conflict in oil-producing areas as well as furthering economic growth in the communities.[77]

Although Nigeria's oil and gas local content initiative has focused on Nigerian content without significant attention to host and impacted communities, a few provisions of the NOGICDA direct attention to host communities. For example, section 27 of the NOGICDA states that the NCDMB may require an "operator to maintain an office in a Community where the operator has significant operations." In an ambiguous provision in section 28(2), the Act states that the NCDMB "shall ensure that the operator or project promoter maintains a reasonable number of personnel from areas it has significant operation."

One of the local content initiatives that is directly related to host communities is the Nigerian Content Intervention Fund, which is a NCDMB fund that the Bank of Industry manages.[78] The Nigerian Content Intervention Fund is derived from the Nigerian Content Development Fund that was created under section 104 of the NOGICDA. By section 104(3), the Nigerian Content Development Fund is "employed for projects, programmes, and activities directed at increasing Nigerian content in the oil and gas industry." As a result, the Intervention Fund must also be directed toward facilitating Nigerian content. Given that the Intervention Fund has been directed toward the promotion of community content, it appears that community content is now being interpreted as an important part of Nigerian content. One of the "strategic objectives" of the Intervention Fund is to "facilitate the growth of community based companies in the upstream oil and gas sector."[79] While this objective does not necessarily lead to an incontrovertible conclusion that the Fund applies to community content, other provisions support that indication. One of the key indicators is that the Nigerian Content Intervention Fund is accessible, inter alia, to "community contractors of any of the oil producing communities."[80] A community contractor is defined as "a company operating in the upstream/ midstream sector of the oil and gas industry, that has a valid contract with an IOC [international oil company] for a job in any of the oil and gas communities and whose chief promoter is also an indigene of an oil and gas producing community."[81] One of the specific funding arrangements available as part of the Intervention Fund is the community contractor finance scheme. The community contractor finance scheme has, perhaps, the most favourable loan terms as the loan limit is the highest

---

[77] Ibid., p. 11.
[78] The Nigerian Content Intervention Fund/Bank of Industry, "The Nigerian Content Intervention Fund," https://ncifportal.boi.ng/ncif/public/.
[79] Ibid.
[80] The Nigerian Content Intervention Fund/Bank of Industry, "The Nigerian Content Intervention (NCI) Fund Frequently Asked Questions," https://ncifportal.boi.ng/ncif/public/faq.
[81] Ibid.

of the five types of funding arrangements available under the Intervention Loan as well as the lowest interest rate.

More specifically, the NCDMB has adopted a Community Content Guideline. Like GMOUs, it has been reported that the NCDMB's Community Content Guideline was adopted, in part, as a mechanism for fostering security and peace in the Niger Delta.[82] The Guideline "was borne out of the necessity to boost peace and security in the Niger Delta and address the lingering squabbles between host communities, operators and service companies over participation in oil and gas activities."[83] While the Guideline does not reference stability in the Niger Delta in setting out the key aspirations of the NOGICDA, it lists integration of oil producing communities into the oil and gas value chain as a major impetus. It asserts that the NOGICDA places "premium consideration" on community participation. Observers would, however, be divided on this assertion because, as noted earlier, communities are sparsely referenced in the NOGICDA. If community content has been an area of interest in Nigeria's LCR regime, such interest is mostly communicated through the NCDMB's Community Content Guideline, which, unlike the NOGICDA, is not a statutory document but a Guideline without the same legislative and implementation force as the NOGICDA. Nevertheless, the Guideline incorporates some implementation mechanisms, such as the NCDMB's ability to refuse to issue a Certificate of Authorization if a plan to open a project office is not submitted.[84] General implementation requirements also apply, with penalties for noncompliance including under the NOGICDA.[85] In addition, provisions of the Guideline must be incorporated into all operators, project promoters, and contractors' Nigerian Content Plan required under the NOGICDA.[86]

The Community Content Guideline defines both host and impacted communities. A host community is "the community where oil and gas operations/projects take place" while an impacted community is a "right of way community due to pipeline passage, road access or any other 'conduit' . . . that is significant to the success of the operations in the host community."[87] In the case of offshore oil fields, host communities are those "communities along the coastal areas bordering the offshore field."[88] Definition of host and impacted communities is significant as it creates exclusion and inclusion criteria for the application of the Guideline. It determines those communities to which the Guideline applies. It is significant that impacted communities are defined as right of way communities and do not include

---

[82] A. Sanyaolu, "NCDMB to Develop Policy on Community Content," November 7, 2016, www .sunnewsonline.com/ncdmb-to-develop-policy-on-community-content/.

[83] C. Olayinka, "Unfolds Rules on Community Engagement," February 23, 2017, https://guardian.ng /appointments/ncdmb-unfolds-rules-on-community-engagement/.

[84] NCDMB, note 13, 4.1.1.

[85] Ibid., 7.0.

[86] Ibid., 5.0(1).

[87] Ibid., 1.0.

[88] Ibid.

communities that are affected by the negative impacts of upstream activities, for example, through oil spills or gas flaring, but are not right of way communities.

The objectives of the Community Content Guideline include youth engagement, infrastructure development, attracting business, and funding support for community entrepreneurs.[89] The Guideline relies on four pillars – project offices in the communities, employment and development of human capital, procurement of goods and services, and funding.[90] The project office pillar relies on sections 25 to 27 of the NOGICDA. Based on section 27, which indicates that the NCDMB may require a project office in the community, the Community Content Guideline includes criteria for the establishment of these offices.[91] The Guideline provides specific requirements regarding the employment pillar. All unskilled jobs, 50 percent of semi-skilled jobs and 10 percent of skilled positions are to be exclusively reserved for indigenes of host communities.[92] In addition, at least 20 percent of the personnel employed during the operations phase of a project must be indigenes of the host communities.[93] The human capital development requirements are akin to some of the types of initiatives that industry undertakes through GMOUs. These requirements include development training programmes that are based on "periodic needs assessments" and which are directed toward the unique needs of the industry and of the host communities.[94] The human capital development provisions also include guidelines regarding scholarships that are sponsored by industry as well as empowerment programmes sponsored by industry and the NCDMB. In addition, 30 percent of the positions available for project-based trainings are reserved for members of host communities or, if the host community lacks the requisite number of people with the relevant qualification, members of neighboring communities.[95] Regarding procurement, at least 30 percent of goods and services must be procured from the host communities.[96] The NCDMB, through the Guidelines, also indicates an intention to provide funding in partnership with financial institutions to businesses in the host community for opportunities in the oil and gas industry.

The Community Content Guideline does not only include some similarities with GMOUs, especially with regard to human capital development, the Guideline specifically references these instruments. It states that the NCDMB "shall adopt provisions of existing and valid GMOUs/MOUs (e.g. governance structure,

---

[89] Ibid., 3.0

[90] Ibid., 4.0.

[91] See ibid., 4.1.

[92] Ibid., 4.2.1. See s. 4.2.1(iii) for rules regarding instances where communities do not have the requisite capacity for skilled roles.

[93] Ibid., 4.2.1(iv).

[94] Ibid., 4.2.2(iii).

[95] Ibid., 4.2.2(vi).

[96] Ibid., 4.3(i).

384   *Ibironke T. Odumosu-Ayanu*

obligations of parties, etc.), where such provisions do not conflict with the provisions of the CCG [Community Content Guideline], NOGICD Act 2010 or other policy directions of the NCDMB."[97] Incorporation of GMOUs supports the position that the lines relating to the different aspects of economic engagement with communities in the oil and gas industry are being blurred but without systematic consideration of the rationale for such connections or their implications. The Community Content Guideline addresses some issues that are similar to the issues that GMOUs contemplate but with the Guideline, government determines all the parameters. Unlike agreements, it does not leave room for community choice. The communities may have the benefit of capacity development, but they do not participate in fundamental decision-making. In a way, that position reflects a classic LCR perspective where communities are not consulted. With regard to the measures that this chapter discusses, the NCDMB's Community Content Guideline is a local content initiative along the lines of the type of requirements enunciated in the NOGICDA. The impact of the Community Content Guideline is, however, yet to be determined given its relatively recent publication. However, an assessment of community content measures in light of the SDGs is possible. Given their direct attention to host and impacted communities, some of which are the poorest groups of peoples partly as a result of the sometimes-negative impact of oil and gas production on the lives and livelihoods of these people, community content has the potential to more effectively contribute to the achievement of SDGs such as SDG 1 on the elimination of poverty. Nevertheless, as Section 5 will demonstrate, both LCRs and community content are limited sustainable development measures.

4 THE GMOU MODEL AND ITS LIMITATIONS AS A PROXY FOR LOCAL CONTENT

Beyond community content measures, agreements between oil companies and local communities are sometimes regarded as part of local content and some have argued that they have the potential to contribute to achievement of the SDGs. These agreements somewhat mirror community content measures although they are grounded in agreement rather than policy. Oil companies in Nigeria, such as Chevron Nigeria Limited (Chevron) and Shell Petroleum Development Company (SPDC), which formerly adopted Memoranda of Understanding (MOUs) as a means of engaging with host and impacted communities in the Niger Delta,[98] have reformed their mechanism of engagement to the GMOU

---

[97] Ibid., 5.0(3).
[98] See M. Hoben, D. Kovick, D. Plumb, and J. Wright, "Corporate and Community Engagement in the Niger Delta; Lessons Learned from Chevron Nigeria Limited's GMOU Process," Consensus Building Institute, November 2012, for a discussion of Chevron's approach to "community engagement" prior to the GMOU. The pre-GMOU model involved agreements with individual communities.

Local Content, Community Content, and SD

starting with Chevron in 2005.[99] As mentioned previously, GMOUs are a type of CDA. CDAs are known by different terms, one of which is Nigeria's oil and gas industry's GMOUs. CDAs vary in content and scope across the world and some are more beneficial for local communities than others.[100] Given that this chapter draws its examples from Nigeria, it relies on Nigeria's oil and gas industry's form of CDAs, that is, GMOUs.

GMOUs may not be appropriately termed legally enforceable common law contracts[101] but they are "signed" agreements.[102] As Chevron's Legal Counsel notes, a Chevron "GMOU is not a legal contract."[103] Rather, "it is an agreement with the intention to create a moral responsibility" on the company to do what it says it will do.[104] GMOUs are crafted as CSR commitments that mostly focus on service provision.[105] Authors have often considered GMOUs in this light, in one case analyzing the "ethical and philanthropic responsibilities" of oil companies.[106] GMOUs have also been referred to as community development or community engagement mechanisms.[107]

It was recently reported that SPDC had spent about 17 billion Naira in Rivers State of Nigeria and a total of 44.35 billion Naira in Abia, Bayelsa, Delta, and Rivers States pursuant to GMOUs.[108] As the report indicated, the projects and programmes addressed issues related to "health, education, water and power supply improvement, sanitation and infrastructure development."[109] While these are laudable

---

[99] For a critique of GMOUs, see O. Adunbi, *Oil Wealth and Insurgency in Nigeria* (Indiana: Indiana University Press, 2015), pp. 143–158; I. T. Odumosu-Ayanu, "Governments, Investors and Local Communities: Analysis of a Multi-Actor Investment Contract Framework" (2014) 15 *Melbourne Journal of International Law* 473. See also O. Egbon, U. Idemudia, and K. Amaeshi, "Shell Nigeria's Global Memorandum of Understanding and Corporate-Community Accountability Relations" (2018) 31 *Accounting, Auditing and Accountability Journal* 51 for a critique of Shell's GMOUs. See generally, "GMOU Participatory Stakeholder Evaluation: A Joint Evaluation of the Global Memoranda of Understanding between Chevron, Community Organizations and State Governments in the Niger Delta," October 2008.

[100] Odumosu-Ayanu, note 9.

[101] Ibid.

[102] SPDC, "Global Memorandum of Understanding," www.shell.com.ng/sustainability/communities/gmou.html.

[103] Chevron, "Roots of Change: Chevron's Model Community Empowerment Program in the Niger Delta," 2017, p. 3.

[104] Ibid., p. 3.

[105] On CSR in Nigeria's oil and gas industry, see generally, O. Ojo, "Nigeria: CSR as a Vehicle for Economic Development" in S. O. Idowu and W. L. Filho (eds.), *Global Practices of Corporate Social Responsibility* (New York: Springer, 2009) 393.

[106] O. Okoro and U. Ejekwumadu, "The Challenge of Balancing Ethical and Philanthropic Responsibilities by Companies in Extractive Communities" (2018) 11 *OIDA International Journal of Sustainable Development* 17.

[107] Hoben et al., note 98, p. 8. On GMOUs and "sustainable community development" see K. K. Aaron, "New Corporate Social Responsibility Models for Oil Companies in Nigeria's Delta Region: What Challenges for Sustainability?" (2012) 12 *Progress in Development Studies* 259.

[108] E. Chinwo, "Nigeria: Shell Spends N17 Billion on GMOU Clusters in Rivers," May 28, 2019, https://allafrica.com/stories/201905280627.html.

[109] Ibid.

386   *Ibironke T. Odumosu-Ayanu*

initiatives that the report claims the communities had the "opportunity to decide and implement," they, except perhaps education, do not necessarily fit within the empowerment-type initiatives that LCRs focus on. Some GMOUs also help facilitate training toward entrepreneurship.[110] GMOUs typically do not address environmental issues.[111]

GMOUs have been regarded as a "public-private approach to community engagement" which involves participatory development processes that help resolve conflict and address community needs" in the Niger Delta.[112] They fit within the CDA tradition although they are one of the most limited of the CDA arrangements. They closely mirror philanthropic CSR. Chevron's GMOUs, which are sometimes touted as contributing to the SDGs,[113] are "signed between clusters of communities, Chevron and state governments."[114] In conjunction with state and local governments in the Niger Delta as well as nongovernmental organizations, Chevron formed Regional Development Committees (RDCs) for the GMOUs. Each RDC includes elected members of the communities "who represent local interests and oversee GMOU implementation in a specific region."[115] Chevron provides the funds while the communities select projects. Chevron's participation also extends to the committees and the boards that review the projects and determine their approval.[116] The funds that Chevron provides to the RDCs are "partially tied to Chevron's operational performance," thereby ensuring that communities that do not disrupt Chevron's operations "earn a funding bonus."[117] The GMOUs are essentially used as a mechanism for addressing violence in the Niger Delta and as a means for the company to acquire a social license to *continue* to operate. And, some have argued, "[t]hrough structures such as RDCs, communities become accomplices in their own marginalization."[118]

SPDC adopts a similar organizational structure for its GMOUs by working through Community Trusts (CTs) and Community Development Boards (CDBs) that include members of the communities. CDBs include representatives from the CTs, that is, "chairpersons, secretaries and members of the CT."[119] CDBs also

---

[110]   O. Dania, "GMOU: 438 Itsekiri Youths Begin Entrepreneurship after Training," September 12, 2018, www.vanguardngr.com/2018/09/gmou-438-itsekiri-youths-begin-entrepreneurship-after-training/.

[111]   Aaron, note 107, p. 267.

[112]   C. Neff (President, Chevron Africa and Latin America Exploration and Production Company), cited in Chevron, "Roots of Change: Chevron's Model Community Empowerment Program in the Niger Delta," 2017, p. 2.

[113]   "Chevron's GMOU to Enhance Nigeria's Sustainable Development Goals – Negrese," April 24, 2018, www.vanguardngr.com/2018/04/chevrons-gmou-enhance-nigerias-sustainable-development-goals-negerese/; Chevron, note 103, p. 5.

[114]   Chevron, note 103, p. 2.

[115]   Ibid.

[116]   Ibid.

[117]   Ibid., p. 3.

[118]   Adunbi, note 99, p. 158.

[119]   Egbon et al., note 99, p. 61.

include a representative each from the SPDC, the local government, the state government, Niger Delta Development Commission, and the National Petroleum Investment Management Services.[120] Regardless of these mechanisms, it has been argued that Shell GMOUs remain "squarely under the control of Shell."[121]

As unenforceable arrangements that rely on the largesse of the oil companies, GMOUs cannot be regarded as mechanisms that foster "choice and self-determination." In addition, they largely do not capture many of the elements of LCRs, including local procurement and service provision that could contribute to empowering entrepreneurs within communities. Rather, they provide benefits mostly in the form of infrastructure development, as well as education and training. GMOUs are a means for acquiring the social license to operate and quell violence in the Niger Delta rather than for achieving the goals of local expertise and contribution that local content policies seek to achieve.

5 LOCAL CONTENT AND THE SUSTAINABLE DEVELOPMENT GOALS

The oil and gas industry has situated itself within the SDGs. IPIECA's joint report with the UNDP and IFC outlines the industry's potential to contribute to each of the seventeen SDGs. In particular, the report severally references the potential contributions of local content measures in the achievement of the SDGs. However, it acknowledges that:

> [O]il and gas production can foster economic and social development by providing access to affordable energy, opportunities for decent employment, business and skills development, increased fiscal revenues, and improved infrastructure. However, oil and gas development has historically contributed to some of the challenges that the SDGs seek to address – climate change and environmental degradation, population displacement, economic and social inequality, armed conflict, gender-based violence, tax evasion and corruption, increased risk of certain health problems, and the violation of human rights.[122]

Like LCRs, the SDGs focus on governments, the private sector, citizens, and several other stakeholders.[123] Clearly all the SDGs are interlinked, yet some lend themselves better to analysis from the lens of local content initiatives. SDG 1 – "end poverty in all its forms everywhere" – according to the joint report, requires investment in local development. Without labelling it local content, the description of investment in local development in this context is the quintessential description of what governments typically include in LCRs. It would involve integrating local businesses into oil and gas companies' supply chains, investing in skills development, adopting

---

[120] Ibid.
[121] Ibid., p. 67.
[122] IPIECA, note 3, p. vii.
[123] Ibid., p. 1.

"inclusive recruitment and hiring practices," as well as training and educational programmes.[124] The report's engagement with SDG 1, however, exceeds this conventional view of local content. It extends to CDAs, with the report noting that CDAs "can be an opportunity to support the self-determined economic development of local communities near oil and gas projects."[125] They "can help provide the enhanced development cooperation needed to implement anti-poverty programmes."[126] Here, CDAs are separated from LCRs especially when one considers the later reference to "gender-sensitive local content" that is listed as part of the measures for reducing gender inequality, thereby facilitating an end to poverty.[127]

SDG 4 – "ensure inclusive and equitable quality education and promote lifelong learning opportunities for all" – also lends itself to a local content analysis. The report encourages oil and gas companies to invest in education and training as part of efforts to garner a social license to operate and meet local content requirements.[128] It specifically calls on oil and gas companies to "[e]stablish a company strategy for local content to promote sustainable development."[129] Here local content also appears to mean LCRs as the report goes on to add that "companies benefit from a strategy that balances their priorities and *local content requirements*."[130] According to the report, SDG 5 in its quest to "achieve general equality and empower all women and girls," would require, inter alia, implementation of "gender-sensitive local content policies."[131] These "gender-sensitive local content policies" could be cast in the frame of LCRs as they "include gender-equality targets for employment and preference in local procurement to companies that meet similar targets" or they could form part of a company's CSR efforts.[132] In particular, implementing an increase in "employment opportunities for women and female representation in management" is likely to be included as a CSR measure.[133]

SDG 8 – "promote sustained, inclusive and sustainable economic growth, full and productive employment, and decent work for all" – addresses employment, which is a staple of LCRs. The report acknowledges that "many developing countries have local content policies requiring certain levels of local employment."[134] While a good part of the discussion of SDG 8 in the report relies on industry contributing to the achievement of the goal through local content, its reference to the "local" bears mentioning. It states: "Policies should also establish what 'local' means, because the developmental impact of procurement from companies located

[124] Ibid., p. 10.
[125] Ibid.
[126] Ibid.
[127] Ibid.
[128] Ibid., p. 22.
[129] Ibid., p. 23.
[130] Ibid. Emphasis added.
[131] Ibid., p. 27.
[132] Ibid., p. 28.
[133] Ibid., p. 28.
[134] Ibid., p. 42.

near the project will likely be quite different from procurement from a company merely located within the host state."[135] This call for clarification of the local is particularly relevant for a distinction between LCRs crafted for a national audience and specific community content requirements. Again, it demonstrates the need for clarity regarding the measures that are being addressed within the broader label of local content.

It is also relevant that LCRs are hardly mentioned with regard to SDGs that specifically address environmental issues. While sustainable development addresses the economic, social, and environmental dimensions of developmental activities, LCRs are mostly directed toward economic and, sometimes, social issues. However, some appropriately drafted CDAs address environmental issues.[136] To then conflate LCRs and CDAs, or even community content initiatives and CDAs, is to make it difficult to determine whether LCRs or other measures are contributing to the achievement of the SDGs and which SDG they are advancing. Similar to the environmental issue is active efforts to seek community participation and consent to projects, which is one of the targets of SDG 16. Target 16.7 requires "responsive, inclusive participatory and representative decision-making at all levels."[137] LCRs are not mechanisms that foster community participation in decision-making and consent. They are government-mandated initiatives. Even community content guidelines are not consent based. On this issue, community content functions much like national-focused LCRs. However, appropriately negotiated and well-drafted CDAs typically involve community participation in decision-making although most of them also lack the element of consent to projects. In fact, local content broadly or narrowly defined is not consent based. If local content, as LCRs or as the broad initiative that encompasses the measures that this chapter has discussed, is to facilitate sustainable development in the manner that the SDGs contemplate, they must move beyond the government- and industry-centric view of decision-making.

Still, beyond the SDGs, measuring the success or otherwise of local content broadly conceived or viewed more conventionally as LCRs, must proceed from a local community-centered perspective. While community content is directed toward host and impacted communities, as mentioned earlier, community content itself is not consent based. As discussed in Section 2 of this chapter, Kenya's Endorois people have articulated a view of development that policy makers that design local content policies, and industry actors that respond to these policies and draft their own local content plans, will do well to incorporate in their designs.

In light of the chapter's discussion and its call for caution in defining local content, especially following this present discussion of the SDGs, a number of points are apparent. First, it is necessary to mainstream community content. In the

---

[135] Ibid., p. 43.
[136] See generally, Odumosu-Ayanu and Newman, note 9.
[137] UNGA, note 1.

case of Nigeria, this will involve directly incorporating it as part of the NOGICDA instead of addressing it as secondary guideline adopted several years after the Act entered into force. This call for legislation, however, only extends to the community content guideline. Legislating CDAs, or GMOUs in the case of Nigeria's oil and gas industry, is a more complicated issue. Although communities that lack strong organizational capacities will not do well with the superior bargaining power of companies without some assistance from government, especially in a country such as Nigeria that does not recognize the Indigenous status of any community of Nigerians, mandatory CDAs may not be apposite in all cases because they may become legalistic and serve as contractual re-enactments of community content. Rather, if concluded, these agreements should serve as separate mechanisms for negotiating aspects of the relationship between communities and companies as the parties deem necessary.

Second, in the spirit of sustainable development that addresses economic, social, and environmental issues as interrelated, community content guidelines that omit specific environmental requirements in the relationship between industry and local communities are incomplete. The suggestion is not that environmental provisions in community content guidelines should replace environmental legislation. Rather, it is to provide a comprehensive outlook of the interrelationship between economic, social, and environmental issues. Third, compared to national-focused LCRs, this chapter has somewhat favored measures that are directly community-focused such as community content measures. Yet, it bears emphasizing that even community content is limited when it is measured against the SDGs. But beyond the SDGs, both LCRs and community content lack the essential element of fostering communities' economic self-determination that respects community choice and consent toward increased wellbeing for the communities. Hence, in developing these measures, choice and self-determination must be emphasized.

Finally, the definitional issues should be addressed in order to appropriately design policies that meet the needs and aspirations of the relevant actors. Each initiative that has been included as part of local content has its goals and place in advancing realization of benefits from oil and gas production in host countries. In one sense, they all have the potential to advance "local content." Yet, they serve different purposes and are designed by different actors. LCRs are a government tool to mostly facilitate national economic development. They are mostly directed to a national audience to serve national purposes of localizing the oil and gas industry. Community content closely mirrors LCRs, but it is directed at local communities. They are also a mechanism designed by the government to foster what it believes to be the economic development goals of host and impacted communities. To the extent that they are government driven, LCRs and community content measures are similar, but their beneficiaries are sometimes different. These two measures are the purview of government and they should continue to be developed as such.

In many parts of the world, CDAs are not government-regulated and the debate as to the extent of regulation, if any, that should be directed toward these instruments continues. Nigeria's oil and gas industry's GMOUs are private instruments and as this chapter has argued, they are significantly limited instruments. While they may yield results similar to LCRs and community content, these are instruments that governments cannot and should probably not rely upon as mechanisms for meeting their local content goals. Hence, when analyzed in light of sustainable development and the SDGs, the need to clearly delineate the scope and purpose of each of these measures cannot be overemphasized. Clearly, both government-led and private initiatives are essential for achieving the SDGs but not all can necessarily form part of government's planning process toward meeting the SDGs. Regarding all as local content may inadvertently suggest that these mechanisms equally have the same capacities and influence.

6 CONCLUSION

Definitions matter and so does the scope of local content. Local content has been interpreted to include a number of measures, including government-mandated LCRs, government-defined community content, and CDAs. Some of these measures are mandatory; others are voluntary. Some are government-defined; others, such as Nigeria's GMOUs, are industry driven. As this chapter has demonstrated, each of these measures offers different benefits to the interested actors and provides unique challenges for host and impacted communities. For policy makers to uncritically regard them all as part of local content, without exploring the policy and practical implications of such definitional exercise, is to proceed without caution regarding the impacts on the national economy, the economic well-being of the host and impacted communities, and sustainable development. It is also to proceed without much attention to the impact on industry's decision-making and the implication of such decision-making ultimately on the oil producing country in question.

20

Local Content Requirements and Social Inclusion in Global Energy Markets: Towards Business and Human Rights Content

Oyeniyi Abe and Ada Ordor

1 INTRODUCTION

This chapter examines the intricate connections between local content requirements (LCRs) and business and human rights concerns, particularly, how LCR implementation can produce social exclusions and complex human rights violations in global energy markets. Drawing examples from the Global South generally, and Nigeria in particular, it discusses the drivers of social exclusions in LCRs implementation as well as legal and institutional pathways for integrating business and human rights norms into the design and implementation of LCRs.

The scholarship behind business and human rights concerns has been shaped to a great extent by the United Nations Guiding Principles on Business and Human Rights (GPs).[1] The GPs have underscored the emergence of a rapidly developing set of international law norms on the human rights responsibilities of states and multinational corporations (MNCs). Understanding these human rights responsibilities, impacts and socially responsible behaviour, in particular for companies, is an essential component of corporate risk management.[2]

Oil and gas production globally continues to be linked with complex human rights violations.[3] Because of the sheer size of their wealth, power and influence, the question that bogs policy makers and political actors revolves around the impact of MNCs on the well-being and legal protection of citizens, as well as how extractive projects create the social exclusion and marginalisation of vulnerable members of the society.[4] For example, Nigeria's responsibility to ensure effective legal protection vis-à-vis MNCs in the extractive sector has been weakened by the recalcitrant

---

[1] UN Human Rights Council *Guiding Principles on Business and Human Rights: Implementing the United Nations 'Protect, Respect and Remedy' Framework: Report of the Special Representative of the Secretary-General on the issue of Human Rights and Transnational Corporations and Other Business Enterprises*, 21 March 2011, UN Doc. A/HRC/17/31 [GPs].

[2] D. Olawuyi, 'Climate Justice and Corporate Responsibility: Taking Human Rights Seriously in Climate Actions and Projects' (2015) 34 *Journal of Energy and Natural Resources Law* 27–44.

[3] D. Olawuyi, *Extractives Industry Law in Africa* (New York: Springer, 2018), pp. 331–7.

[4] Ibid.

Local Content Requirements and Social Inclusion 393

attitude of non-state actors to remediate the impact of their activities.[5] This has exacerbated local remonstrations in the face of weak enforcement mechanisms, ineffective judicial regimes and lack of political will to stymie corporate excesses.

The nexus between conflict and resource production is often pronounced when host communities, corporate actors and the state disagree on the management, revenue distribution, protection and control of the natural resources.[6] Further, there is a dearth of human rights consideration or human rights language in energy contracts, domestic corporate laws and institutional regulations. The key questions, therefore, are: What does business and human rights content or language mean for the energy markets? How can human rights norms be integrated into the design and implementation of LCRs?

These concerns have unified the world by creating a shared approach towards the GPs. A fundamental part of these GPs is enshrined in the concept of corporate responsibility to respect human rights.[7] Demonstrating a corporate respect for human rights is vital to building a culture of trust and integrity amongst local communities, investors, shareholders and the state. Indeed, both corporate impact and a healthy relationship with host communities reduce litigation, financial and reputational risks.[8] The GPs are essentially a 'product of social and power relations and a tool for challenging and reshaping those relations'.[9] With particular reference to the extractive sector, this chapter investigates how business and human rights principles are producing social inclusions and human rights concerns through the lens of LCRs. Such investigations extend to the fact that extractive projects that often lead to virulent and extreme remonstrations have forged resilient communities who are more buoyed by the capability to promptly recover from complications arising from these extractive resource projects.

---

[5] Ibid.

[6] A. Akonnora and F. Ohemeng, 'Towards a More Accountable Resource Governance in Developing Countries: The Case of Ghana's Oil and Gas Sector' (2019) *The Extractive Industries and Society* 1 (noting that the revenue management requires effective institutional framework to ensure transparency and accountability). See also R. Lima-de-Oliveira, 'Corruption and Local Content Development: Assessing the Impact of the Petrobras' Scandal on Recent Policy Changes in Brazil' (2019) *The Extractive Industries and Society* 9 (arguing that local content policies in Brazil's oil and gas sectors facilitates industrial development and job creation). In 2016, for instance, Mozambique produced over 200 billion cubic feet of natural gas, while its economic growth rose at an annual average of 7.3 per cent over the last decade. Despite this, it recently defaulted on repaying its debt, and therefore unable to leverage this wealth (See 'Mozambique Default on Eurobond Was Unnecessary', January 23, 2017, www.cnbcafrica.com/news/financial/2017/01/23/mozambique-default-on-eurobond-was-unnecessary/. Likewise, Equatorial Guinea has become a classic example of the 'resource curse' mystery in Africa (see 'Equatorial Guinea: Squandered Riches', February 3, 2014, www.ft.com/content/a06d499a-8a99-11e3-ba54-00144feab7de.

[7] See D. Olawuyi, 'Increasing Relevance of Right-Based Approaches to Resource Governance in Africa: Shifting from Regional Aspiration to Local Realization' (2015) 11 *McGill International Journal of Sustainable Development Law and Policy* 113–58.

[8] Olawuyi, note, 2.

[9] World Bank, 'World Development Report: Governance and the Law', 2017, p. 83.

Unquestionably, states have struggled to ensure that institutions, policies and investments reinforce structural transformation.[10] Resource extraction in Nigeria has been associated with economic stagnation, weak democracy and unsatisfactory development outcomes. While oil significantly accounts for the government's revenue, the impact of resource extraction has, however, created environmental problems, weak institutions and uncertain economic outlook.[11] Furthermore, there have been concerns and debates as to whether such proceeds benefit the host communities in particular and the populace generally.[12]

Nigeria has committed to addressing some of these teething problems, through the integration of human rights protection into resource extraction policies and programs, particularly LCRs.[13] This leads to the debate on how effective Nigeria's local content laws and policy are in addressing business and human rights concerns, particularly, whether and to what extent Nigeria's LCRs have been able to address social exclusions (or inclusions) and other perennial human rights concerns.[14]

To address these questions, this chapter investigates the extent to which Nigeria has been able to integrate business and human rights norms into the design and implementation of LCRs. It further examines the competing approaches towards implementation of LCRs in Nigeria. This chapter is divided into five sections. After this introduction, Section 2 discusses the drivers of social exclusions in the design

[10]   UN Economic Commission for Africa, 'Governing Development in Africa – The Role of The State in Economic Transformation', Economic Report on Africa, 2011, www.uneca.org/publications/eco nomic-report-africa-2011.

[11]   See E. Chinedu and C. Chukwuemeka, 'Oil Spillage and Heavy Metals Toxicity Risk in the Niger Delta, Nigeria' (2018) 8 *Journal of Health and Pollution* 180905 (noting that Nigeria loses over 40 million litres of crude oil to oil spillage annually). See also D. Olawuyi, *Principles of Nigerian Environmental Law* (Afe Babalola University Press, 2015), pp. 172–89.

[12]   C. Hufstader, 'Where Does Oil Money Go? I Went to Nigeria to Find Out', July 20, 2015, https:// firstperson.oxfamamerica.org/2015/07/where-does-oil-money-go-i-went-to-nigeria-to-find-out/.

[13]   See O. Abe, 'The Feasibility of Implementing the United Nations Guiding Principles on Business and Human Rights in the Extractive Industry in Nigeria' (2016) *Afe Babalola University Journal of Sustainable Development Law and Policy* 137–57. Some initiatives have called for more openness and transparency in extractive resource management. For instance, the Extractive Industries Transparency Initiative (EITI) is a multi-stakeholder approach which promotes openness, transparency and accountability in the management of natural resources in the decision-making process. Member states are obliged to disclose information on tax payments, licences and contracts. Nigeria not only signed the initiative, it enacted the EITI Act, 2007 to pave way for the implementation of the initiative. See further the Publish What You Pay (PWYP) coalition which aims at promoting transparency; the Open Government Partnership (OGP) which aims to 'secure concrete commitments from governments to promote transparency, empower citizens, fight corruption, and harness new technologies to strengthen governance'. The Natural Resource Charter is a set of principles designed for civil society and government and details the best approach for harnessing the opportunities created by extractive resource governance. Other initiatives include the UN Global Compact, www.unglobalcompact.org; OECD Guidelines for Multinational Enterprises (2011), www.oecd.org /daf/inv/mne/48004323.pdf.

[14]   The Nigeria Oil and Gas Industry Content Development Act (2010) aims at increasing indigenous participation in the oil and gas industry by prescribing minimum standards for the use of local services and materials besides promoting the transfer of technology and skill to Nigerian labour in the industry.

Local Content Requirements and Social Inclusion

and implementation of LCRs in Nigeria. Section 3 advances the argument that integration of human rights principles is fundamental to the effective implementation of LCRs. Section 4 discusses the pathways for leveraging extractive resources for sustainable development through local content requirements. Section 5 concludes this chapter.

2 SOCIAL EXCLUSION AND LCRS: THE NIGERIAN EXAMPLE

This section demonstrates that if not designed with business and human rights safeguards, LCRs can result in complex human rights violations. Drawing examples from Nigeria, this section examines how LCRs have occasioned the social exclusion of local communities and stakeholders in extractive projects.

Conceptually, social exclusion encompasses a process whereby individuals are precluded from fully engaging and participating in the socio-economic and political life of their environment, thus disabling them from fully asserting their rights.[15] According to Lenoir, 'marginalised people from formal labour markets and welfare benefits experience a rupture of the social bond that constitutes the undergirding of the rights and responsibilities of citizenship'.[16] Social exclusion as a result of extractive projects is more obvious in the way and manner in which people fail to gain access to social, economic and political benefits at the same time, and how social institutions are at the vanguard to ensure this is achieved.[17] This causes poverty, reduced production capacity and reduced access to maternal healthcare, a leading cause of the high infant mortality rate in Nigeria. Host communities to extractive projects are also prone to gender inequality, insecurity and resource conflicts.[18] For example, in Nigeria, extractive contracts are shrouded in secrecy.[19] The result is that the state, far disconnected from the people, enters into resource contracts on behalf of these same people. These contracts do not take human rights concerns into consideration. Thus, the state, and by extension the companies, created economic values for themselves – in a way that does not produce values for society. As a result, societal needs and challenges can not be met – thereby creating a phase of social exclusion.[20]

The polemics associated with gender disparities often heighten the tensions surrounding allocation of responsibilities by the companies. In Nigeria's Niger

---

[15] F. Fisher, 'Occupying the Margins: Labour Integration and Social Exclusion in Artisanal Mining in Tanzania' (2007) 38 *Development and Change* 738.
[16] R. Lenoir, 'Les Exclus: Un Francais Sur Dix' cited in J. Beall, 'Globalization and Social Exclusion in Cities: Framing the Debate with Lessons from Africa and Asia' (2002) 14 *Environment and Urbanization* 41–51; see also A. de Haan, 'Social Exclusion: Towards a Holistic Understanding of Deprivation', Department for International Development, London, 1999 (arguing that the concept has been numerously applied when analysing facets of deprivation in developing countries).
[17] Haan, note 16.
[18] Ibid.
[19] Olawuyi, note 3.
[20] M. E. Porter and M. R. Kramer, 'Creating Shared Value' (2011) *Harvard Business Review* 89.

396   *Oyeniyi Abe and Ada Ordor*

Delta, social gender roles significantly determine the nature of the impact of the extractive industry, resulting in unequal benefits and risks for men and women. For instance, the exclusion of women from employment, procurement, community meetings and decision-making processes is a challenge to the actualisation of the Free, Prior and Informed Consent (FPIC) principle.[21] In the Degema and Asari-Toru local government areas of Rivers State, community residents largely agree that companies hardly ever hire educated women from their community because they believe oil and gas-related engineering and technical work is a male preserve.[22] The same reasoning is applied in the mining industry. Besides, the companies cannot afford to lose human resource time during the women's statutorily mandated maternity leave. Women were employed only in low-paying house-maintenance, cleaning and helper positions, and the community meeting times often conflicted with their working hours.[23]

The debate about the level of Nigeria's local content policy has been mired in controversy. In principle, LCRs are designed to achieve a level of domestication that ensures that the procurement of goods and services, local employment and the security of key installations should be done in a way that gives priority to domestic companies and locally produced materials.[24] However, as discussed in Chapter 4 of this book, the Nigerian LCR has failed to achieve much result in practice, as MNCs come up with different ways to circumvent and avoid compliance. The convoluted application of LCRs in Nigeria's local market has exacerbated tensions between host communities and extractive projects and extractive companies. This effect is observed in not only how MNCs have been able to chase lower production costs in ways that undermine local community's rights but also how the host communities to extractive projects have mobilised in collective action in response to the limited regulation of such MNCs in lieu of their job insecurity. In some instances, worker mobilisation has been met with violence (and often deadly responses).[25]International oil and gas companies (IOCs)

---

[21]   The Free, Prior, Informed Consent (FPIC) principle has its foundation in the ILO Convention 169 – Convention on Indigenous and Tribal Peoples in Independent Countries – 169/1989. Adopted in 1989 and entered force in 1991. This is a legally binding instrument that deals with indigenous and tribal people's rights. The Convention provides that indigenous peoples are entitled to free and informed consent before they are relocated from their land.

[22]   O. Abe, 'The Rights Based Approach to Extractive Resource Governance in Nigeria through the Lens of the UN Guiding Principles on Business and Human Rights: Lessons from South Africa', Unpublished PhD thesis, University of Cape Town, South Africa, June 2018, p. 174.

[23]   Ibid.

[24]   D. O. Olawuyi, 'Local Content Requirements in Oil and Gas Contracts: Regional Trends in the Middle East and North Africa' (2019) 37 *Journal of Energy and Natural Resources Law* 93–117; J. Korinek and I. Ramdoo, 'Local Content Policies in Mineral-Exporting Countries', OECD *Trade Policy Papers*, No. 209; M. Eboh, 'Local Content, Local Troubles: How Big Firms Kill Small Businesses' December 24, 2018, www.vanguardngr.com/2018/12/local-content-local-troubles-how-big-firms-kill-small-businesses/.

[25]   See UNEP 'Environmental Assessment of Ogoniland', 2011.The report revealed that the activities of MNCs have systematically contaminated most of Ogoniland, with serious consequences for human life and well-being. These consequences include large-scale evidence of contamination of land and underground water courses; high levels of harmful substances and pollutants, such as benzene, found in community drinking water; residues of harmful substances still found on sites claimed to have been

Local Content Requirements and Social Inclusion 397

continue to frustrate small-and medium-scale enterprises to the point of bankruptcy,[26] surprisingly due to late payment for work done. In some instances small firms are encouraged to bid for tenders from the IOCs without guarantee of timely payment in return.[27] Nonetheless, they still bid and are expected to carry out the work without any form of down payment or mobilisation fee, and this challenge transcends completion of the contract.[28] In addition, the procurement process is marred by corruption and there is no guarantee that the LCRs are actually observed. The implication of the foregoing is that severe human rights violations occur within the context of evasion of LCRs by MNCs, as well as lax enforcement of LCRs, which deprive locals' socio-economic benefits. This misalignment between government and investors creates an avenue for socially excluding citizens, especially in the face of this blatant disregard for human rights and human lives. The lack of clarity on integration of human rights norms in LCRs further complicates the expectations of businesses with regard to human rights compliance. For instance, is there a requirement or provision requiring companies to conduct a social and environmental impact assessment? If so, who validates such assessments as complying with extant laws?[29] Are there specific human rights standards explicitly stated in extractive contracts that include provisions for local content and procurement plans? These uncertainties can result into legal risks and the breakdown of relationships between investors and communities. Investors should be able to understand how LCRs can contribute to social inclusion and a validation of social license to operate to avoid these legal risks.

2.1 *Drivers of Social Exclusion in Resource Projects*

There are basically four key drivers of social exclusion in extractive communities.[30] First, the exclusion of marginalised people from having access to and exercising rights over oil, gas and other mineral resources.[31] Under this categorisation, artisanal miners, and other small-scale independent miners, have often been classified as illegal due to their inability to have access to flexible licensing systems, inadequate institutional support and insufficient land.[32] On the other hand, oil is a concentrated resource that requires large-scale investments. As such, it presents opportunities for government and

---

cleaned by the oil companies; and failure of the oil companies to operate according to Nigerian standards or any recognised global standard.

[26] Eboh, note 24.

[27] Ibid.

[28] Ibid.

[29] See the Reciprocal Promotion and Protection Agreement between the Government of the Kingdom of Morocco and the Government of the Federal Republic of Nigeria (signed 3 December 2016 – not yet in force) [Morocco-Nigeria BIT].

[30] C. Gore, 'Social Exclusion and Africa South of the Sahara: A Review of the Literature', International Institute for Labour Studies, ILO (IILS), January 1994.

[31] Ibid.

[32] G. Hilson and C. Potter, 'Why Is Illegal Gold Mining Activity so Ubiquitous in Rural Ghana?' (2003) 15 *African Development Review* 237–67.

398   *Oyeniyi Abe and Ada Ordor*

companies. Opportunities for oil bunkering do, however, provide financing prospects for non-state actors in Nigeria.[33] In most instances, the state favours the IOCs at the expense of small-scale independent miners who are victims of poor education and low living standards.[34] This reveals how local competition and the assertion of power influence the dynamism of social and political institutions over entitlements to extractive resources.[35]

Second, the relationship between small-scale independent miners and large-scale international miners on the one hand, and 'protectors' of natural resources on the other, is intricate.[36] Exclusion in this context refers to the way people are allowed access to the mining sites on terms that instigate inferiority and dependency to the authority.[37] This is pegged on their social identity – for example, age, gender, race, religion – and their positions in the mining industry by virtue of their identity.[38] Berry asserts that

> if access to the means of production is predicated on social identity, then the definition of property rights hinges on the demarcation of social boundaries, and exploitation operates through the subordination of some people within access-defining groups rather than complete exclusion.[39]

Given that literature emphasises age (minors) and gender (women), women miners and child labour in small-scale independent mining is a common occurrence. Often the involvement of children and women in mining is due to diverse reasons, including socio-economic factors like poverty.[40] Thus, the extraction of resource

---

[33]   O. H. Boris, 'The Upsurge of Oil Theft and Illegal Bunkering in the Niger Delta Region of Nigeria: Is There a Way Out?' (2015) 6 *Mediterranean Journal of Social Sciences* 563 (examining the methods, actors, causes and impacts of oil theft and the measures adopted by Nigerian governments to combat oil theft); M. Obenade and G. Amangabara, 'The Socio-Economic Implications of Oil Theft and Artisanal Refining in the Niger Delta Region of Nigeria' (2012) 3 *International Journal of Science and Research* 2390 (noting the significant economic cost of artisanal refining and oil bunkering); G. Ezirim, 'Oil Crimes, National Security, and the Nigerian State, 1999–2015' (2018) 19 *Japanese Journal of Political Science* 80–100 (noting that deprivation of oil benefits to Nigerian citizens manifested in illegal oil bunkering, pipeline vandalisation, cross-border smuggling of petroleum products, attacks on oil installations, kidnapping, and piracy, with attendant threats to national security).

[34]   D. F. Bryceson, 'The Scramble in Africa: Reorienting Rural Livelihoods' (2002) 30 *World Development* 725–39.

[35]   T. A. Benjaminsen and C. Lund, 'Formalisation and Informalisation of Land and Water Rights in Africa: An Introduction' (2002) 14 *European Journal of Development Research* 1–10.

[36]   MMSD, 'Breaking New Ground: Mining, Minerals and Sustainable Development', International Institute for Environment and Development, 2002.

[37]   C. Jackson, 'Social Exclusion and Gender: Does One Size Fit All?' (1999) 11 *European Journal of Development Research* 125–46.

[38]   Eboh, note 24, p.67.

[39]   S. Berry, 'Concentration without Privatization? Some consequences of Changing Patterns of Rural Land Control in Africa' in R. E. Downs and S. P. Reyna (eds.), *Land and Society in Contemporary Africa* (University Press of New England, 1988), pp. 53–75.

[40]   E. O. Ofei-Aboagye, 'Gender Dimensions and Gender Impacts of the Paradigm of Mining-Led Economic Development in Africa' in TWNA (ed.), *Mining, Development and Social Conflicts in Africa* (Third World Network Africa Ghana, 2001), pp. 69–82.

Local Content Requirements and Social Inclusion

materials create inequalities of income, injustices and social exclusion. LCRs requirements are initiated to ensure that indigenous companies and the local community benefit from such international companies by developing their capacity to supply factors of production needed to 'drive the oil and gas value chain by substituting domestically produced goods for imported goods, and to create more local employment by substituting domestic labour for imported or foreign-based labour.'[41]

Third, a key driver of social exclusion in extractive communities is the desire on the part of 'governance and people's ability to take part in decision making or access institutions related to management of mineral resources'.[42] This concerns issues like citizenship and people's involvement in governance bureaucracies that 'affect their ability to make a livelihood from mineral resources'.[43] It also relates to the way institutions define exclusionary and inclusionary practices, how they are implemented and the sanctions that affect their enforcement.[44] Commonly asked questions in this area include whether extractive communities play a role in the decision-making process concerning decisions that directly affect their entitlement to the extractive resources, and whether they can access their social and political institutions managing such sites.[45]

Fourth, extractive companies in Nigeria have failed to interact with their host communities on the basis of respect, inclusion and meaningful participation.[46] The idea of corporate social responsibility providing material goods is not necessarily what communities want or need to meet their objectives of long-term sustainability. The mere mention of Shell in Nigeria triggers resentment and tension.[47] Meaningful consultation with stakeholders is an integral part of due diligence that companies should implement.[48] Insufficient avenues for public participation and inadequate regulation led to frustration and violence on the part of communities in the Niger Delta.[49] Government inaction to enforce LCRs led local communities to

[41] Korinek and Ramdoo, note 24, pp. 8–10.
[42] Gore, note 30.
[43] Ibid.
[44] P. Gibbon, 'Privatization and Foreign Direct Investment in Mainland Tanzania, 1992–98', Danish Institute for Institutional Studies, January 1999, www.eldis.org/document/A28124
[45] N. Kabeer, 'Citizenship and the Boundaries of the Acknowledged Community: Identity, Affiliation and Exclusion' (2002) IDS Working Paper 171.
[46] Principle 18; see also Olawuyi, note 3.
[47] D. Olawuyi, 'Fostering Accountability in Large Scale Environmental Projects: Lessons from CDM and REDD+ Projects' in J. Wouters, A. Ninio, T. Doherty, and H. Cisse (eds.), Improving Delivery in Development: The Role of Voice, Social Contract, and Accountability (Washington, DC: The World Bank Legal Review, 2015), pp. 127–47.
[48] GPs, note 1, Principle 18.
[49] B. R, Konne, 'Inadequate Monitoring and Enforcement in the Nigerian Oil Industry: The Case of Shell and Ogoniland' (2014) 47 Cornell International Law Journal 181; U. Etemire and M. Muzan, 'Governance and Regulatory Strategies Beyond the State: Stakeholder Participation and the Ecological Restoration of Ogoniland' (2017) 26 Griffith Law Review 275; Amnesty International, 'Negligence in the Niger Delta: Decoding Shell and Eni's Poor Record on Oil Spills', 2018.

resist projects that had acquired a legal licence to operate.[50] Participation is the hallmark of local capacity.[51] In the context of energy projects, participation improves responsibility and the 'inclusion of local people who have been excluded by the command and control model'.[52] The locals must be adequately consulted and meaningfully engaged in a free and informed manner,[53] to the extent that this process will create a consequential contribution to any project affecting their socio-political, cultural and environmental rights.[54] What are these barriers to effective engagement? In South Africa, for instance, despite the ingenuity in the passage of the Broad-Based Black Economic Empowerment (BBBEE) law, empirical evidence suggests that implementation has been riddled with 'tender corruption', economic strain and lack of sincerity on the part of oil and gas companies.[55] Some corporate executives enlist the names of black professionals to circumvent the crux of the legislation. As a result, BBBEE as a LCR fails the threshold of equality and inclusion.[56] Similarly, although many IOCs employ locals in Nigeria, they do so to project an appearance of LCR compliance and to skirt legal requirements. These locals do not enjoy procurement or employment benefits. While the IOCs meet legal requirements, the reality is that they undermine local companies rather than aid them.

The concept of local content is designed to construct relationships between local and foreign companies that allow for transfer of technical know-how in strategic skills areas. LCRs mandates require quotas, establish goals for locals and allow these locals to increase their own participation in employment. Through training and employment generation locals are fully integrated into corporate structure and governance. For host communities who are impacted by extractive projects, a heightened share of local content outcomes is expected. In the context of integrating human rights to produce social and 'local' inclusion, rights must be labelled broadly to encompass a wide variety of outcomes, such as community engagement, health and safety, treatment and training of employees, and grievance mechanisms. The key questions are: How does a company validate the significance it ascribes to

---

[50] Etemire and Muzan, ibid.

[51] Ibid.

[52] See further V. Mauerhofer, 'Public Participation in Environmental Matters: Compendium, Challenges and Chances Globally' (2016) 52 *Land Use Policy* 481 (noting that participation in environmental matters covers decision-making, access to information and justice).

[53] H. Mostert and H. V. Niekerk, 'Disadvantage, Fairness and Power Crises in Africa: A Focused Look at Energy Justice' in Y. Omorogbe and A. Ordor (eds.), *Ending Africa's Energy Deficit and the Law: Achieving Sustainable Energy for All in Africa* (Oxford University Press, 2018), p. 63 (all individuals must be fairly represented in decision-making process and full information disclosure by government and industry are very important).

[54] See commentary to GPs, note 1, Principle 18.

[55] A. Pike, J. Puchert, and W. T. Chinyamurindi, 'Analysing the Future of Broad-Based Black Economic Empowerment through the Lens of Small and Medium Enterprises' (2018) 18 *Acta Commercii* 1.

[56] A. Wehmhoerner, *Correcting the Past–Losing the Future? Black Economic Empowerment in South Africa* (FEPS Studies, 2015).

Local Content Requirements and Social Inclusion 401

the realisation of its human rights commitment? What types of human rights issues are discussed by senior management and by the Board, and how does that produce social exclusion? How does the company engage with stakeholders with regard to human rights compliance? This chapter proceeds on the basis of these four dimensions of social exclusion. The next section addresses the importance of business and human rights content in the design and implementation of local content policies in Nigeria, and how LCRs can balance human rights and other objectives.

3 BUSINESS, HUMAN RIGHTS AND IMPLEMENTATION OF LCRS

Observing human rights principles in business can provide a framework for addressing social exclusions in the design and implementation of LCRs. The GPs on Business and Human Rights constitute a normative framework for preventing and addressing corporate-related human rights abuses, as well as providing for local content. They have prescribed minimum standards of behaviour for companies and bring to the fore the less-talked-about separation of human rights from corporate objectives. This section examines the scope and content of the GPs, as well as their potential for addressing social exclusions in the design and implementation of LCRs. The GPs re-emphasised the significance of states' existing obligations in protecting human rights, the need for businesses to comply with domestic laws and rules and the provision of adequate remedies to victims of human rights violations. Thus, the GPs seek to enhance corporate practices in order to achieve concrete results for victims of human rights violations – as well as communities that are hosts to extractive projects and are recipients of a corporate-induced environmental disaster.[57] GP 23 enjoins business enterprises to comply with all domestic laws and applicable international human rights instruments, where they operate. They must also consider the risk of triggering or contributing to gross human rights abuses as a legal compliance issue wherever they operate.[58] Though local context may affect the human rights risks of a company's relationship, it must ensure compliance with internationally recognised human rights.[59] Indeed, the GPs could serve as a yardstick for states to adapt local laws in conformity with human rights benchmarks. This section discusses four strategic areas where fundamental elements of the business and human rights content can be integrated into domestic law and corporate practice.

---

[57] See L. C. Backer, 'From Institutional Misalignments to Socially Sustainable Governance: The Guiding Principles for the Implementation of the United Nations' 'Protect, Respect and Remedy' and the Construction of Inter-Systemic Global Governance' (2012) 25 *Pacific McGeorge Global Business and Development Law Journal.*

[58] Ibid.

[59] GPs, note 1, Commentary. See GPs, note 1, Principles 1 and 11.

3.1 *Applying Business and Human Rights Principles to the Nigerian Corporate Content*

The legality of corporate existence in any jurisdiction is the enactment of corporate law and securities regulation. In Nigeria, the Companies and Allied Matters Act, 1990 (CAMA), regulates corporate activities. In 2018,[60] after three decades of existence, the CAMA was amended by the Senate. While the amended Act, amongst other things, sought to establish the means of regulating businesses, ensuring transparency and shareholder engagement as well as promoting a friendly business climate in Nigeria, it failed to incorporate human rights provisions in its over 600 sections.[61] The sustainability of corporate practice in the extractive sector can best be served if businesses maximise value for the communities where they operate. The dearth of human rights content in Nigeria's corporate law means companies have an easier path to externalise the cost of human rights violations to other bodies, especially the state, and to avoid corporate responsibility for host communities which are often labelled saboteurs.[62] The implication, therefore, is that corporate entities in Nigeria are at a heightened risk of alienating host communities or losing their social licence to operate.[63] Furthermore, s. 279 of the CAMA provides that directors should have duty of care towards their shareholders and act in utmost good faith towards the company; that is, the corporate Board should take rational decisions, which include extending good faith practices to local communities, employees and other stakeholders.

A consideration of human rights responsibilities is fundamental to ascertaining the best interest of the company. Comparatively, South Africa's corporate law has far-reaching implications for integrating business and human rights content.[64] Section 7(a), provides that the Companies Act must 'promote compliance with the Bill of Rights as provided in the Constitution'.[65] Thus, in the management of the affairs of the company, directors and officers of the company must ensure that activities of their company are geared towards promoting and encouraging human rights as contained in international legal instruments. By their nature, human rights risks demand the direct engagement of corporate board, management and leadership. Section 15(a) thus provides that a company's 'Memorandum of Incorporation must be consistent with the Companies Act'. This is where the GPs becomes

---

[60] The Companies and Allied Matters Act (Repeal and re-enactment) Bill was passed by the Senate on 15 May 2018.

[61] Abe, note 13, p. 152.

[62] O. Abe, 'Utilisation of Natural Resources in Nigeria: Human Right Considerations' (2014) 70 *India Quarterly* 6.

[63] Shift, 'Developing Indicators of Rights-Respecting Leadership and Governance: An Overview', September 2019, www.shiftproject.org/valuing-respect/the-conversation/duplicate-of-the-current-use-of-metrics-in-company-human-rights-reporting-in-southeast-asia/

[64] See also articles 20(1), 260 of the Constitution of Kenya.

[65] Chapter II of the Constitution of the Republic of South Africa, 1996 provides for the Bill of Rights which binds a 'natural or a juristic person'.

Local Content Requirements and Social Inclusion

instructive. Essentially, each provision of the Memorandum must be conscious of the fact that it must comply with the Bill of Rights contained in the Act and in the Constitution. The failure to consider human rights implications led to the silicosis case in South Africa.[66] Thus, there is the 'duty' on the part of corporate actors to go beyond the 'do no net harm' requirement in respecting human rights when operating in weak zones.

The discretionary nature of the exercise of fiduciary duties of directors impedes the ability to say, with certainty, that companies act in accordance with human rights obligations. To promote transparency and accountability, the Institute of Directors, South Africa (IoDSA) published the *King IV Report on Corporate Governance for South Africa*.[67] The *Report* obliges companies to document their social responsibility projects.[68] Thus, documents submitted by a company for incorporation must commit to human rights standards. Likewise, under India's Companies Act 2013, a class of companies that meets a designated profit threshold is required to spend 2 per cent of its average annual net profit on corporate social responsibility (CSR). Incentivised companies are expected to have focused on the following areas: human development, economic development, welfare, the environment and sustainable development.

The dearth of human rights content has facilitated the social exclusion of local communities in obtaining resource dividends, resulting in citizens' recourse to alternative means of sustenance. Recently, the Nigerian government banned mining activities in Zamfara State due to the unregulated artisanal mining activities of gold and lead in the community.[69] These activities have resulted in numerous deaths, kidnappings and other social evils.[70] Extractives industry laws in Nigeria must integrate human rights into their provisions.

3.2 Corporate Due Diligence

The GPs are clear about the ability of a company to distinguish human rights risks that are integral to its operations. GP 17 clarifies that business enterprises must be able to prevent and mitigate adverse human rights impact where it occurs. To do this effectively, business entities 'should carry out human rights' due diligence which must be geared towards reducing the risk of compliance with human rights norms.[71]

---

[66] *Bongani Nkala & 68 ors v. Harmony Gold Mining Company & 31 ors* Consolidated Case Number: 48226/12.

[67] See Institute of Directors, Southern Africa, 'King IV Report on Corporate Governance for South Africa', November 1, 2016.

[68] Ibid.

[69] S. Tukur, 'Zamfara Violence: Nigerian Government Bans Mining Activities in Troubled State', April 7, 2019, www.premiumtimesng.com/news/headlines/324348-breaking-zamfara-violence-nigerian-govt-bans-mining-activities-in-troubled-state.html.

[70] Ibid.

[71] See generally GPs 17, note 1.

404 Oyeniyi Abe and Ada Ordor

Extractive industries in Nigeria must periodically assess actual and potential human rights impacts of their activities. Not only do they have the technical and scientific capabilities to detect, prevent and, where it occurs, mitigate human rights violations, they possess the financial capability to remedy corporate harm.

Due diligence and impact assessments are important tools in complying with business and human rights principles. It is not only important to conduct due diligence: it validates a sustainable business model. This model depicts a sustainable corporate entity as one that is economically viable on the one hand, and integrates human rights into its core operations on the other hand. Both legal and social licences are imperative to corporate sustainability. Companies must build long-term, equally constructive relationships with communities and strive for continuous open dialogue. Sometimes, the impact of corporate activities in the extractive sector, for instance, occasions negative consequences of economic decisions, and creates adverse concerns for these decisions. It is important for extractive companies to observe and scrutinise any financial benefits accruable to the company. This can only be achieved through human rights impact assessments and effective due diligence. When these are done, the company is able to function in a cohesive and progressive system in which human rights integration and economic benefits are synchronised, further projecting such companies as human rights compliant.

A due diligence strategy should be established in cooperation with the stakeholders. Details of this policy should incorporate potential risks from their activities and a map showing how to recognise, analyse and prioritise the evident risks. Businesses should articulate procedures to regularly assess the compliance efforts of subcontractors or suppliers, in line with the risk mapping, while appropriate actions to mitigate risks or prevent serious impacts must be articulated effectively. Nigeria's whistleblowing policy encourages voluntary disclosure of information about fraud, bribery, financial misconduct and other forms of corruption or theft to the Federal Ministry of Finance.[72] Companies must adopt a whistle-blowing policy where employees or anyone with knowledge of the company's activities can report them to the appropriate authorities. In evaluating the due diligence requirement of the corporate entities, a system must be devised to monitor the executed actions and assess their effectiveness.

Globally, countries are adapting business and human rights norms to shape domestic due diligence requirements. For example, the French 'Duty of Vigilance' law creates a broad responsibility to prevent human rights and environmental impact for French-based companies with over 5,000 employees in France and 10,000 employees globally.[73] The due diligence requirement covers the

---

[72] Federal Government of Nigeria, Federal Ministry of Finance, 'FMF Whistle Blowing: Frequently Asked Questions', http://whistle.finance.gov.ng/_catalogs/masterpage/MOFWhistle/assets/FMF%20WHISTLEBLOWING%20FREQUENTLY%20ASKED%20QUESTIONS.pdf.

[73] JORF n°0074 du 28 mars 2017; texte n° 1. LOI n° 2017–399 du 27 mars 2017 relative au devoir de vigilance des sociétés mères et des entreprises donneuses d'ordre (1). NOR: ECFX1509096L, www.legifrance.gouv.fr/eli/loi/2017/3/27/ECFX1509096L/jo/texte.

Local Content Requirements and Social Inclusion 405

activities of parent companies and those of their subsidiaries, suppliers and subcontractors, wherever located. Companies are required to establish, publish and implement an annual 'vigilance plan' and to report on its implementation. Failure to comply with this requirement will result in judicial enforcement coupled with financial penalties. The vigilance plan must be detailed enough to include 'adequate, reasonable vigilance measures to identify risks and to prevent serious impacts' on human rights, the health and safety of individuals and the environment, resulting from the activities of the company and of the companies it controls.[74] This protection and provision also extends to the activities of the company's subcontractors 'with whom they have established commercial relationship'.[75] Consequently, Total–France can be held liable for activities of Total–Nigeria that impact on human rights and foster the social exclusion of Nigerians.[76]

Integrating human rights is indicative of how well governance structures are put in place in the control and management of a company. It further strengthens the behaviour of the board, with the resultant effect on board decisions. Companies must be able to develop realistic mechanisms for evaluating business respect for human rights, and provide practical indicators and tools for measuring human rights compliance. Periodic due diligence is one of those mechanisms. An observance of human rights norms is therefore critical to the sustenance of any business model.

3.3 Promoting 'Local' Consultation and Participation

To adequately measure human rights risks, GP 18 urges businesses to 'identify and assess any actual or potential adverse human rights impacts' of their activities. One of the avenues to measure these risks is to engage in meaningful consultation with affected groups and other relevant stakeholders. The lack of local community consultation and participation in resource contract negotiations and decision-making processes between state and investors lays the foundation of several human rights violations. For instance, in Ghana, the extractive laws do not provide any role for local communities in decision-making processes, although oversight responsibilities were placed on traditional rulers.[77] It is imperative for businesses to connect and communicate with local communities at different stages of an extractive project. The granting of a social licence to operate guarantees shared values and

---

[74] Ibid.

[75] Ibid.

[76] On 23 October 2019, an international NGO, Friends of the Earth, in a coalition of some NGOs, brought Total before the French courts for its failure to elaborate and implement its human rights and environmental vigilance plan in Uganda. This case is novel in that it is the first of its kind to make sure Total answers for its non-compliance with its legal obligations under the French duty of vigilance law. See further, J. Renaud and T. Bart, 'Oil company Total faces historic legal action in France for human rights and environmental violations in Uganda', Friends of the Earth International, October 23, 2019, www.foei.org/news/total-legal-action-france-human-rights-environment-uganda.

[77] Mandela Institute, University of the Witwatersrand, 'Public Regulation and Corporate Practices in the Extractive Industry', 2017, p. 9.

benefit sharing at the local and national level. For example, community impact and benefit agreements[78] create a form of relationship amongst stakeholders,[79] integrate local experience and offer the public opportunities to provide their views about and obtain reactions to continuing projects. Corporate–community extractive investments create a shared value system and effective partnerships for local stakeholder development.[80] In Zimbabwe, the Indigenisation and Economic Empowerment Act guarantees local communities a minimum of 50 per cent shareholding in mines through the Community Share Ownership Schemes.[81] Local community resistance and the lack of hydraulic fracturing technologies prevented the exploration of shale gas in South Africa.[82] Citizens were concerned about water and air contamination and threats to existing economies and human health. The estimated reserve in the Karoo is significant but it comes with serious environmental and infrastructural challenges. Development must be 'locally' and not investor driven.

Consultation and meaningful engagement provide a basis for clear, accurate and timely information to be provided to 'locals' in respect of potential impacts on their community. To fulfil the right to participate, local communities must be able to freely and fairly express their views – without any form of coercion, manipulation or use of force. This is the trademark of compliance with LCR. The locals know what is best for them and can decide how that transformative project can be best achieved.

The participation of local community is indispensable to understanding the local context. Citizens must lead their own development and build their own institutions. In effect, there must be rewards when companies have incorporated local community participation into their policies. At the same time, sanctions should be meted out to those who have failed to comply with established human rights benchmarks. For example, when participation fails, the community is left with no choice but to resist any projects that may be sited on their land. Consequently, encouraging local community participation reduces conflicts in the resource zones.

The application of the principle of integration of human rights into business as a moral imperative, coupled with consultation and awareness will contribute to the implementation of LCRs in Nigeria's extractive resource industry. Conversely, comprehensive consultation continues to be a Herculean task for most local communities. This is due to leadership structures that are characterised by power struggles, making it difficult for companies to engage with community leaders. Linked to this is the fact that vulnerable members of the community, especially

---

[78] W. Plessis, 'Responsible Mining: Key Principles for Industry Integrity' (2017) 20 *Potchefstroom Electronic Law Journal* 2. See further, Odumosu, Chapter 19, this volume.

[79] S. Utterwulghe, 'Public-Private Dialogue for Specific Sectors: Extractive Industries', Nuts & Bolts: Technical Guidance for Reform Implementation, Investment Climate, World Bank Group, 2012.

[80] Shared Value Initiative, 'Extracting with Purpose Creating Shared Value in the Oil and Gas and Mining Sectors' Companies and Communities', October 25, 2014.

[81] Section 5 of the Indigenisation and Economic Empowerment Act 14 of 2007 (chapter 14: 33).

[82] M. Louw and J. Minnaar, 'Hydraulic Fracking in the Karoo, South Africa', February 11, 2015, https://ejatlas.org/conflict/hydraulic-fracturing-fracking-in-the-karoo-south-africa.

Local Content Requirements and Social Inclusion

women, are deprived of involvement in the participatory process, due, in part, to cultural hegemonic structures. Engagements must be with all strata of the society, through community meetings, opinion surveys, community liaison officers and employee and community hotlines. These forms of engagement must consider the political, cultural and legal sensitivities of host communities.

It is important that consultation forms the bedrock of meaningful engagement. The mere fact that 'locals' have consented to an extractive project does not mean they should be deprived the opportunity to withdraw consent. This could arise where the development of a project has led to a reasonably unforeseen destruction of their livelihoods and potentially irredeemable human rights violations.

3.4 Grievance and Complaints Mechanisms

Where companies have determined that they have caused human rights violations, it is imperative that they provide adequate remedial processes for victims.[83] This could be through due diligence processes or effective engagement in remediation. A more potent approach, however, is to effectuate operational-level grievance mechanisms.[84] This approach creates an avenue for businesses to engage in dialogue with those socially excluded, and victims of human rights, as a means to address and resolve grievances.[85] An effective grievance mechanism, either judicial or non-judicial, must be anchored on legitimacy, availability, predictability, transparency and rights compatibility.[86] An operational-level mechanism enables socially excluded citizens to trigger an early stage recourse and resolution system. Companies must ensure there is easily accessible grievance machinery within the company or contracted to an independent expert. This ease of access expedites identification of human rights violations as an integral part of a company's conduct of human rights due diligence. The idea that the socially excluded and victims of human rights violations are able to directly raise concerns about corporate impact validates sustainable development of the energy and extractive sectors in Nigeria.[87] These complaints will also provide an opportunity for companies to self-assess their practices and tackle systemic problems where identified.

As part of their international human rights obligations, states have a duty to ensure that their judicial, administrative and legislative arms are effectively utilised in protecting against business-related human rights abuse.[88] This is where the Nigerian National Human Rights Commission has a prominent role to play. Nigeria's business and human rights policy must enhance its governance structures

[83] GPs, note 1, Principle 22.
[84] See ibid., Principle 31.
[85] Ibid., Principle 31(h).
[86] Ibid., 31.
[87] See ibid., Commentary to Principle 29.
[88] Ibid., Principle 25.

408   *Oyeniyi Abe and Ada Ordor*

and systems so as to allow communities to address grievances and complaints to such a degree that the national scale involved can respond adequately to it, especially when human and environmental costs supersede the human and economic benefit of the extractive industries processes. Extraction, investment and development need adequately to prevent, reduce and resolve any compromising impact on livelihoods, employment and sustenance, whilst improving the social contract, economic empowerment, education and active citizenry in the governance of extractive resources.

3.5 *Trade Agreements*

One area in which the lack of business and human rights content has socially excluded 'locals' is that of state–investor trade agreements. GP 9 clarifies that states must preserve satisfactory 'domestic policy space to meet their human rights obligations when pursuing business-related policy objectives with other States or business enterprises', especially through investment treaties or contracts. Investor–state agreements, in principle, are meant to encourage and protect sustainable development and investment. The sustainability of such investments can be determined if they contain human rights provisions and safeguards. International trade agreements must not prioritise investors' rights ahead of the country's best interests. In complying with the multilateral trading system encouraged by the WTO, Nigeria entered into a bilateral trade agreement (BIT) with Morocco in December 2016.[89] This BIT contains several provisions that enshrined corporate social responsibility, human rights provisions and deference to local content, making it the most progressive BIT in modern times. Not only does the BIT impose binding obligations directly on investors, it obliges investors to carry out social, human and environmental impact assessments.[90] Article 13(3) obliges each Party to respect and observe social responsibility owed to the other Party. Articles 18(2) and 18(3) of the BIT state that: 'Investors and investments shall uphold human rights in the host state' and 'act in accordance with core labour standards as required by the ILO Declaration on Fundamental Principles and Rights of Work 1998'. Article 24 obliges investors to comply with all local laws and regulations. In addition, investors and their investments are must endeavour to contribute maximally to the sustainable development goals of the host states and 'local community through high levels of socially responsible practices'.[91]

The foregoing shows the progressive tendencies of a domestic regime to facilitate human rights compliance. What is needed is strong political will to enforce extant laws and thus leverage natural resources for sustainable development. Section 4 provides the guiding principles for ensuring LCRs are efficacious and essential to achieving a substantial local value added.

---

[89] Morocco-Nigeria BIT, note 29.
[90] See ibid., articles 14, 15.
[91] Ibid., article 24(1). See also articles 17 (anti-corruption), 19 (corporate governance and practices).

Local Content Requirements and Social Inclusion 409

4 INTEGRATING BUSINESS AND HUMAN RIGHTS NORMS INTO THE DESIGN AND IMPLEMENTATION OF LCRS

Tackling the core problems and tensions inherent in LCR development and implementation, ranging from economic growth to social provisioning and environmental sustainability, requires a holistic integration of business and human rights norms into LCR development planning and processes. To guarantee an integration of business and human rights norms into project design and the implementation of LCRs, Nigeria must intensify its efforts to expand the regulatory capacity, institutional efficacy and democratic legitimacy of governance institutions that shape development. These institutions are responsible for labour standards, social provisioning and democratic participation, amongst others. What follows are recommendations for an integration of business and human rights into Nigeria's legal and institutional structure.

4.1 *Determine Business and Human Rights Content Threshold*

The determination of local content remains pivotal to ascertaining the social dimension of the design, application and implementation of LCRs in Nigeria. A cursory look at the description of a 'Nigerian company' shows that a company incorporated in Nigeria and having no less than 51 per cent equity shares held by Nigerians will be classified as 'local'.[92] The Nigerian Oil and Gas Industry Content Development Act also describes 'Nigerian content' as the 'quantum of composite value added to or created in the Nigerian economy by a systematic development of capacity and capabilities through the deliberate utilization of Nigerian human, material resources and services in the Nigerian oil and gas industry'.[93] In relation to employment, procurement and operation, the Act stipulates that preference is to be given to Nigerian nationals and independent operators respectively.[94]

In determining the threshold, the Act provides general specification for companies to give preference to local services, equipment and other factors of production if the prices of such local services, equipment and other factors of production are comparable to their international counterparts. Section 14 of the Act encourages

> all operators and project promoters to consider Nigerian content when evaluating bids where the bids are within 1% of each other at commercial stage and the bid containing the highest level of Nigerian content shall be selected provided the Nigerian content in the selected bid is at least 5% higher than its closest competitor.

Section 106 of the Act also describes the Nigerian content indicator as 'a percentage rating of a company based on specific criteria defined on the basis of values ascribed

---

[92] Nigerian Oil and Gas Industry Content Development Act, 2010 Act No. 2 (22 April 2010), Section 106 [NOGICDA].
[93] Ibid.
[94] Ibid.

410   *Oyeniyi Abe and Ada Ordor*

to each criterion'. The elastic method that Nigeria adopted to establish its threshold for local content gives an operator some room to adjust the local content requirements to reflect the market realities.[95] Such elasticity allows operators to preserve the quality of goods and services they produce.[96] In addition, such flexibility minimises the legal risks of operator non-compliance with the requirements of local content. The downside of this, however, is that without proper oversight, operators have leeway to determine the extent to which they implement the requirements. To ensure proper oversight and enforcement, human rights principles relating to accountability, access to information, citizen participation and equitable distribution of opportunities have to be clearly reflected in setting LCR thresholds and in performance-reporting requirements of extractive companies.

4.2 *Advance Social Inclusion and Oversight Responsibilities*

The level of participation in the employment and procurement process by the 'locals' must be addressed and enforced.[97] Understanding such variation prevents dispute, especially where the government seeks to exert more influence than is necessary in the procurement process.[98] Whereas the Nigerian government specifies its local content threshold, its instructions on the procurement process are not well cemented. The elastic approach adopted by the government enables operators to come up with their own procurement procedures as long as such procedures comply with the requirements of its local content development and other international standards, especially human rights considerations. It is noteworthy that such procedures are reviewable by the Nigerian Content Development and Monitoring Board (NCDMB).[99] The essence of this Board is not only to ensure compliance with local content requirements but also to guide, monitor, coordinate and implement the LCRs. Thus, governments, companies and local communities must work together to obtain truthful and representative goals of ensuring local content in the extractive industry.

Institutional coordination and monitoring lie with government. According to Olawuyi, governments have a role to play in reducing 'regulatory and administrative barriers to domestic investments … simplifying approval processes and fees for licenses and permits'.[100] Collaborative and effective oversight reduces duplicity of functions, bureaucracy, delays and administrative costs. The NCDMB must ensure continuous and periodic growth of local content in its oil and gas operations in the industry when reviewing content plans submitted during applications for licence,

---

[95] Olawuyi, note 24, p. 109.
[96] Ibid.
[97] Ibid.
[98] Ibid., p. 110.
[99] NOGICDA, note 92, Section 4.
[100] Olawuyi, note 24, p. 113.

Local Content Requirements and Social Inclusion 411

permit or interest. Also, a certificate of approval must be issued by the Board only if it is satisfied that the intended operator meets the requirements of local content. However, companies also need incentives. This will create a shared value approach to achieving maximum effects of LCRs.

Where the company fails to adhere requirements under the Act, a penalty of a fine of up to 5 per cent of the project sum for each project becomes due to the Board, upon conviction.[101] Fines paid are deposited into a Local Content Development Fund,[102] which can be used to empower local communities. Furthermore, the Fund defrays the expenditure of the Board and funds the implementation of the Nigerian content development. The Fund consists of, inter alia, revenue accruing from the proceeds of investments made by the Board or any other source. For every contract awarded to an operator, 1 per cent of the sum of such contract, subcontract or project shall be deducted at source and paid to the Fund.

4.3 Establish a Business and Human Rights Unit (BHRU)

The concept of creating a human rights agency within the extractive sector in Nigeria has come of age considering the extensive human rights violations that have characterised the industry over the years. Undoubtedly, there is the linkage between human rights and the environment, trade and socio-economic factors that face host communities in the extractive sector. A BHRU would ensure that from design to implementation, extractive resource projects do not infringe the human rights of local communities. It would serve as the linkage and rallying point between the local community and MNCs, as well as other stakeholders, NGOs and pressure groups. A BHRU will ensure that MNCs keep to their obligation to respect human rights in their spheres of operation, will be responsible for investigating human rights abuses and will be authorised to certify a project for having fulfilled human rights obligations. Personnel of the BHRU should cut across various disciplines, and include environmentalists, labour and human rights experts from academia and those who have sufficient training in extractive resource governance. Mere training in environmental law does not suffice. Staff must understand and show commitment to processes for integrating rights into corporate practices and conduct. The guarantees of social inclusion necessitate the maintenance of open, ethical standpoints, respect for diversity and inclusion of local cultures and customs.

5 CONCLUSION

The adoption of LCRs aim to provide a framework through which resource-rich countries can maximise the benefits and value from the oil and gas industry, to the

---

[101] NOGICDA, note 92, Section 68.
[102] Ibid., Section 90.

advantage of the host communities to extractive projects. However, a lack of widespread and sustained implementation of local content laws defeats the ingenuity inherent in the capability of these laws to ensure social inclusion and participation in the extractive industry. An examination of these laws still shows a dearth of human rights consideration or human rights language, as evident in Nigeria's company law.

Where local communities are socially excluded, remonstrations, bickering and distrust arise. Rather than demonise host communities as saboteurs, companies should engage closely with local communities to accomplish social change. Young volunteers from each host community can be trained and drafted to monitor company installations. Such installations or projects will be seen as a joint project between the communities and companies, thereby fostering business respect for human rights.

The legal barriers that stifle enforcement of local content – such as lack of institutional coordination, absence of business and human rights institutions, and absence of business and human rights content threshold in LCRs, will need to be addressed. While IOCs struggle to comply with these requirements, government must create a pathway for incentivising companies, and institutional support, to do much more than the law requires. Effective implementation of the policy and legislation can only be achieved where local firms are empowered in terms of capacity and in procurements that guarantees local participation in the provision of goods and services and the employment of locals.

21

Advancing Sustainable Development in Local Content Initiatives: Summary for Policy Makers

Damilola S. Olawuyi

1 SUMMARY

This book set out to examine the values, assumptions and guiding principles that underpin the growing adoption of LCRs in global energy markets, as well as how questions of social exclusion, gender injustice, corruption, lack of transparency and inadequate stakeholder engagement in LCR formulation and implementation have been, and could be better, addressed. This final chapter reviews salient themes discussed and highlights directions for future action and research.

There are few regulatory measures and instruments that have divided opinion in global energy markets in the twenty-first century more than LCRs. Existing studies in the field have satisfactorily compiled the meaning, nature and scope of LCRs as a revolutionary and innovative regulatory measure that could unlock the competitiveness of the local economy, while allowing a country to strengthen its national industry and achieve other social benefits.[1] LCRs could stimulate economic development; minimise capital flight; and unlock the competitiveness of the domestic workforce, while allowing a country to diversify and strengthen its national industry. LCRs could also promote other social benefits such as job creation, development of endogenous technology and infrastructure, and the redistribution of wealth and authority to address concerns of particular indigenous or disadvantaged communities.[2] The focus of LCRs on wealth creation, small- and medium-scale entrepreneurship, skill development, social equality, stakeholder engagement and community empowerment all reinforce the fundamental roles that LCRs can play

---

[1] See D. Olawuyi, 'Local Content and Procurement Requirements in Oil and Gas Contracts: Regional Trends in the Middle East and North Africa' (2019) 37 *Journal of Energy and Natural Resources Law* 93; T. Acheampong, M. Ashong, and V. C. Svanikier 'An Assessment of Local Content Policies in Oil and Gas Producing Countries' (2016) 9 *Journal of World Energy Law & Business* 282; Intergovernmental Forum on Mining, Minerals Metals and Sustainable Development, *Designing Local Content Policies in Mineral Rich Countries* (2018), www.iisd.org/sites/default/files/publications/local-content-policies-mineral-rich-countries.pdf, p. 2–3; also S. Tordo et al., *Local Content Policies in the Oil and Gas Sector* (World Bank 2013).

[2] Olawuyi, ibid.

414   *Damilola S. Olawuyi*

in advancing the United Nations Sustainable Development Goals (SDGs) in global energy markets. Achieving all of the SDGs, especially those relating to poverty eradication (SDG1), zero hunger (SDG2), education and lifelong learning (SDG4), equality and gender justice (SDG5), energy for all (SDG7), employment and decent work for all (SDG8), climate change (SDG 13), stakeholder participation (SDG16.7), as well as systemic coordination and partnerships (SDG17) will require local capacity development.[3]

However, despite the promise and potential of LCRs, they have also been linked, in a number of countries, with producing misalignments with extant national obligations under core international treaty provisions on trade, investment, gender justice, environment, human rights and sustainable development. While several studies have documented the increasing adoption of LCRs across the world, what remained absent was a detailed examination of the intersectional nature of LCRs and sustainable development, especially how protectionist and restrictive LCRs could produce negative outcomes in terms of foreign direct investment, technological development, renewable energy and low carbon transition, distributive justice and human rights protection. Drawing examples from energy markets in Africa, Asia, Europe, North America, Latin America, South America and Australasia, the twenty-one chapters of this book provide a far more complete, multijurisdictional and systematic exposition of how LCRs have evolved in energy jurisdictions countries across the world, as well as a comparative analysis of the key implementation challenges that arise, and legal and negotiation techniques for managing those challenges.

This central research question has been explored in a diversity of settings across the themes of oil and gas regulation, renewable energy development, World Trade Organisation (WTO) measures, economic tools, environment, equity, human rights, aboriginal treaty rights, racial equality, distributive justice and sustainable livelihoods. Starting in Part I with a discussion of the evolution, scope and tenets of LCRs in global energy markets, the book examined the relationship among LCRs, sustainable development, participatory development, distributive justice, social licence to operate and corporate social responsibility; and introduced some of the normative frameworks that have been utilised to analyse the conceptualisation, design and implementation of LCRs. The thirteen chapters in Part II consist of a series of geographical case studies that apply these frameworks to selected energy markets in the Global North and the Global South. The case studies identify concerns of social exclusion, environmental trade-offs, corruption, lack of transparency, gender injustice, use of performance requirements, and incoherent application of LCRs that have been raised in different energy markets. This part also identifies compatible and high-leverage local content strategies, the contexts in which they are being implemented, barriers to their effective implementation and

---

[3]   See Chapter 19 of this book; D. Olawuyi, 'Sustainable Development and Water-Energy-Food Nexus: Legal Challenges and Emerging Solutions' (2020) 103 (1) *Journal of Environmental Science and Policy*, https://doi.org/10.1016/j.envsci.2019.10.009.

Advancing Sustainable Development in Local Content Initiatives 415

innovative legal approaches to promote such strategies. The chapters demonstrate how inappropriately designed and implemented LCRs can produce distributive injustice, local resistance, misalignment of a country's fiscal policies and sustainable development goals, and may ultimately serve as disincentive to foreign participation in a country's extractive market. The case studies then discuss innovative legal strategies to address these misalignments and inequities.

This final chapter of the book offers reflections on the case studies and addresses how lessons from the diverse jurisdictions may inform thoughts on how to effectively design, apply and implement sustainable and rights-based LCRs. As demonstrated in the twenty-one chapters of this book, the growing tensions between LCRs and contemporary sustainable development treaties do not necessarily mean that LCRs are intrinsically incompatible, or cannot be reconciled, with the goals of international sustainable development law. Rather these conflicts demonstrate that LCRs can be misguided and misused at the domestic level in a manner that conflicts with and undermines the key goals of international sustainable development law, which, as expressed in a number of international law instruments, including the recent SDGs, is to enhance policy coherence for sustainable development by eliminating barriers to FDIs and the transfer of environmentally sustainable technologies. Furthermore, if carefully designed and implemented, LCRs can also provide a basis for energy companies and indigenous communities to negotiate mutually beneficial terms that could address social, economic and environmental concerns of energy operations in indigenous communities. It is therefore essential for countries stipulating LCRs to avoid misuse and misalignments that undermine the goals and long-term success of LCRs.

2 RECOMMENDATIONS

Without adequate sustainable development safeguards, LCRs designed to expand economic benefits from energy operations and projects risk exacerbating treaty violations, social exclusion, corruption, lack of transparency, human rights violations, delayed progress on climate and environmental action and loss of FDIs in many countries. LCRs must be carefully designed, implemented and monitored to reduce ambiguities and misalignment between the overall policy aims of LCRs and its practical outcomes. While there is no one-size-fits-all success formula for ensuring sustainable development outcomes in LCR design and implementation, this section presents a number of positive lessons, optimal strategies and steps that energy regulators, project proponents, and other energy sector stakeholders should be aware of when implementing LCRs.

First, LCRs should be backed by a clear, specific and transparent legislative framework, including a robust performance-monitoring mechanism.[4] As Nwapi

---

[4] See Chapter 15, stating that countries such as Argentina, Bolivia and Venezuela have achieved low levels of both local content outcomes, mainly due to a lack of local content provisions in their legal frameworks and the poor quality of available information. In contrast, Brazil, Colombia and Mexico

416 *Damilola S. Olawuyi*

demonstrates in Chapter 2, ambiguities in terms of what constitutes 'local', especially failure to cater for the interests of subnational localities where energy operations occur when setting national LCRs, can result in significant backlash for operators in terms of maintaining stability in a resource-bearing locality and retaining a social licence to operate.[5] It is essential for countries to establish clear, transparent and comprehensive local content laws that clarify the scope, content and goals of a country's LCRs. Such laws could, among other things, provide clear and expansive definitions of key concepts such as local, local content, local company, project sum and in-country value.[6] This requires facilitating dialogue by actors across the energy value chain and agreeing on, and enforcing, mutual commitments. There is also a need to clearly identify the skills, competencies, technologies and economic activities that a country wants to improve or build upon as part of local content implementation. Such clear definitions will reduce ambiguities with respect to the scope and content of LCRs. Local content laws can also be very helpful in addressing overlaps and limitations in other domestic laws that could hinder the successful implementation of LCRs. For example, procurement laws that have elaborate provisions on state participation in bid processes may result in unnecessary delays in an investor's procurement processes and may impact the competitiveness and ease of doing business in a country. A less restrictive approach, on the other hand, will focus on providing as much flexibility as possible to the investor to achieve domestic value maximisation, while ensuring oversight through periodic procurement reports by the investor.

Second, rather than approaching LCRs from a compliance or mandatory project requirement mindset, which demands more local content or introduces more punitive enforcement measures, national authorities should adopt a more collaborative approach built on clear, transparent and attainable LCRs, with adequate institutional support for IOCs to achieve those goals. As demonstrated by Fang, blatantly discriminatory and restrictive LCRs may not be able to pass muster in terms of the WTO disciplines. However, the fact that the TRIMs Agreement, as well as many BITs that prohibit LCRs, also include a wide range of exceptions for their use, strongly suggest that when designed and implemented within the frame of permissible limits, LCRs can be compatible and reconciled with the goals of international trade and investment law, and can help countries to substantially increase the economic, social and environmental benefits of FDI. It is therefore essential for countries stipulating LCRs to avoid misuse and misalignments that undermine the goals and success of LCRs.[7] LCRs that are primarily targeted at restricting the

---

have achieved a high level of local content outcomes due to specificity of local content provisions in national law, policy and contracts.

5 Ibid.
6 Chapter 2.
7 See also Chapter 17, discussing the need to relax and align the objectives of LCRs in order to advance progress in energy diversification and investment in renewable energy technologies that create positive externalities.

Advancing Sustainable Development in Local Content Initiatives   417

abilities of investors to participate in investment activities or to freely procure goods for approved projects – rather than focusing primarily on value-added and capacity development – are misguided and could ultimately hinder FDIs. The starting point therefore is for national authorities to realign the goals of LCRs to focus mainly on creating high domestic value addition by providing full and fair opportunities for investors, irrespective of the source of the raw materials and goods, nationality of the employees or storage location of investment data. By realigning LCRs to focus on the ultimate goals of domestic value addition, countries can better align and reconcile LCRs with key tenets of international investment law on fair and equitable treatment of investors.

Third, without addressing domestic barriers to the attainment of LCRs – such as lack of domestic capacity, shortage of raw materials, technology and infrastructure gaps, amongst others – investors face an unrealistic task of complying with national expectations which may result in failures and contentions. The result, as Karamanian demonstrates in Chapter 4, is that energy companies have developed all forms of negative strategies and artificial shell entities to evade unrealistic LCR obligations. Karamanian rightly notes that such developments, along with associated corruption, 'have profound human rights implications, whether as to fundamental principles of equality and dignity or more specific matters, such as the right to work, the right to pay for work, and the right to property'.[8] It is therefore essential for national authorities to work collaboratively with investors to evolve realistic local content targets that take cognizance of domestic capabilities, and also develop supportive regulatory and institutional frameworks for the delivery of the agreed-upon targets.[9] A collaborative approach to LCR is built on creating a supportive regulatory and business-friendly economic environment for investors to deliver greater value in the host country. Under this approach, governments at all levels, especially subnational levels where energy operations occur, have prominent roles to play in providing required institutional and governance support for local suppliers to achieve LCRs. Such supportive governance measures include reducing regulatory and administrative barriers to domestic investments; providing fiscal incentives for investors to establish or support small and medium enterprises in the host country; updating intellectual property laws to provide greater protection for domestically produced technology; simplifying approval processes and fees for licences and permits; and providing and ensuring greater inter-ministerial coordination among key ministries and agencies that have roles to play in the employment, training and education components of LCRs.

Fourth, as Ezenagu and Eze-Ajoku demonstrate in Chapter 5, while LCRs have significant potential of upgrading domestic products and services and promoting relevance and competitiveness of local suppliers, implementation of LCRs can be

---

[8] Chapter 4.
[9] See Chapter 16, discussing how Brazil's LCR has been hindered by unrealistic targets, as well as lack of clear and well-defined metrics for measuring success.

418   *Damilola S. Olawuyi*

bedevilled by negative externalities if not backed by knowledge clusters, networks, learning and monitoring, and collaborative governance. The geographical case studies in Part II of the book unpack such negative externalities to include a general disconnect between overarching goals and outcomes of LCRs;[10] failure to carefully align LCRs with national development objectives;[11] lack of measurable targets and milestones in terms of empowerment under LCRs;[12] lack of political will;[13] corruption;[14] social exclusion and inadequate attention to gender bias and lopsidedness in the design and implementation of LCRs;[15] conflicting local content legislation, regulatory and policy proposals;[16] environmental trade-offs;[17] industry-based approach to LCRs that fail to adequately protect the interests of future generations;[18] limited availability of domestic resources and capacity;[19] conflict with international investment obligations; and inadequate data protection frameworks to maintain the sanctity of data obtained by governments under mandatory LCRs, amongst others.[20] These negative externalities reinforce Ezenagu and Eze-Ajoku's thesis that some supporting infrastructure must be present prior to the enforcement of LCRs in order to achieve measurable positive results. According to them, these include clusters, networks, learning, monitoring and collaborative governance. Successful LCR implementation cannot be achieved by regulation and legislation alone. Providing adequate institutional support and supervision for investors to achieve LCRs and goals is a crucial element. A well-designed set of horizontal and collaborative policies and legislation targeted at creating a supportive regulatory and business-friendly economic environment, as well as supplier development and training programs, for investors to deliver greater value in the host country can advance both immediate and longer-term local content objectives with fewer potential investment distortions. As Lebdioui and Morales demonstrate in this book, countries that tend to display high local content outcomes, such as Brazil, Mexico and Colombia, for instance, 'have played proactive roles in the implementation of industrialisation plans and supplier development programmes to develop the skills and capacity of local suppliers'.[21] To be successful and sustainable on the long run, LCRs 'need to be accompanied by capacity-building programmes to provide the

---

[10]   See Chapter 6, discussing the key challenges and struggles in the implementation and enforcement of local empowerment initiatives in the South African petroleum industry.
[11]   See Chapter 7.
[12]   Ibid., also Chapter 6.
[13]   See Chapter 8
[14]   Ibid.
[15]   Ibid.
[16]   Chapter 10.
[17]   Ibid.
[18]   Ibid., also Chapter 11.
[19]   Chapter 12
[20]   Ibid.
[21]   See Chapter 15.

Advancing Sustainable Development in Local Content Initiatives   419

skills required for local content activities as well as provide opportunities for learning by doing'.[22]

Apart from the fact that host countries and the public will ultimately benefit more when LCRs are achieved by an investor, improperly designed LCRs could carry significant financial, legal and reputational risks for national authorities, especially when LCRs become subjects of extensive litigation or investor–state arbitration. Such risks may also manifest themselves in project disruptions due to disputes, such as community protests over a perceived lack of benefits from a project, including potential harm to employees due to such protests. Furthermore, in a highly competitive sector such as oil and gas, a country's ability to attract investors and technologies (including financial institutions and lenders) needed to develop oil resources will depend on the processes, procedures, practices and approaches put in place to reduce contractual risks, such as those that could result from rigid or misaligned LCRs.

Fifth, the Norwegian case study provides a good example of successful LCR implementation and how countries can progressively phase out LCRs. As demonstrated by Banet, Norway's success is due to a combination of external framework conditions and carefully designed and implemented legal requirements.[23] According to Banet, 'an efficient system of administrative governance with stable institutions and a transparent and predictable regulatory framework will be decisive for the implementation of LC policy for the benefits of both foreign operations/investors and local industries/population'.[24] It is therefore essential for countries to establish a focal institution, committee or administrative unit that will coordinate the design, approval and implementation of local content plans across the life cycle of a project. Such an administrative body will also ensure that the use of LCRs in one subsector aligns with the economic development of other sectors, in line with the country's national development vision and priorities.[25] While such a focal institution can be established as a supervisory committee of a petroleum contract, a more long-term approach is to establish a national local content agency or unit that will oversee LCRs in multiple sectors of the economy. Apart from serving as a one-stop shop that will streamline the approval processes for local content implementation, such an institution would also provide methodologies and tools for operators to report and monitor their compliance with LCRs so as to minimise disputes. By empowering and establishing a focal institution on projects, stakeholders across multiple sectors and government tiers can obtain relevant information and develop a standardised approach to tracking, monitoring and complying with LCRs. A coordinated approach can also reduce duplication

[22] Ibid.
[23] Chapter 13.
[24] Ibid.
[25] Ibid.

420 *Damilola S. Olawuyi*

and overlap, conflicting regulations, unnecessary administrative costs and delays.[26] Regional cooperation is also important to share experiences and best practices, foster industrial complementarities and maximise economies of scale.[27]

Sixth, LCRs in the energy sector have wide implications for the fulfilment of several human right obligations in local and aboriginal communities where energy activities take place.[28] If carefully designed and implemented, LCRs could be an effective way of preventing and addressing the natural resource curse or the "Dutch disease" that has affected social, economic and environmental progress in many oil and gas rich countries.[29] Furthermore, as the South African example demonstrates, LCRs in tailored Broad-based black economic empowerment (BEE) programs have provided veritable tools for redressing systemic human rights violations, racial inequality and uneven distribution of benefits and burdens in historical marginalized black or Aboriginal communities.[30] Similarly, as Lucas and Laidlaw argued, LCRs could provide a tool for channeling economic, social and environmental benefits to such historically marginalized groups by ensuring Indigenous content, that is 'procurement of local goods, services, and workforce development, including strategic community investment' in such communities.[31] Implementing tailored LCR programs in Aboriginal communities could provide an opportunity for governments to respect, protect and fulfil fundamental human rights obligations in extant nation-to-nation treaties between the government and Indigenous Nations. This includes human rights relating to: Participation and inclusion; Access to information; Non-discrimination and equality; Empowerment and accountability; and Legality and access to justice (the "PANEL Principles").[32] Design and implementation of LCRs therefore need to carefully integrate and reflect the PANEL Principles to address human rights concerns relating to inadequate consultation and

---

[26] See Chapter 14, discussing the need for institutional coordination at all levels of government to ensure successful LCR implementation.

[27] Chapter 15, discussing regional cooperation, knowledge sharing and capacity development as key factors for the successful design and implementation of local content policies.

[28] See Chapter 18, discussing the need to better integrate the right to consultation and accommodation concerning proposed oil and gas development in Canada that may adversely affect aboriginal communities.

[29] See Chapters 9, 15 and 16.

[30] Chapter 6.

[31] Chapter 18.

[32] See D. Olawuyi, 'Energy (and Human Rights) for All: Addressing Human Rights Risks in Energy Access Projects', in R. Salter, C. G. Gonzalez and E. Kronk Warner, *Energy Justice: US and International Perspectives* (Edward Elgar, 2018) 73–104; also see the preamble to chapter 23 of Agenda 21, approved by the UN Conference on Environment and Development on 13 June 1992: UN doc A/CONF.151/26 (vols. I–III) (1992), stating that fundamental prerequisites for the achievement of sustainable development is broad public participation in decision-making. 'This includes the need of individuals, groups, and organizations to participate in environmental impact assessment procedures and to know about and participate in decisions, particularly those that potentially affect the communities in which they live and work.'

Advancing Sustainable Development in Local Content Initiatives 421

accommodation of stakeholders, lack of transparency, gender discrimination, social exclusion, amongst others. As Odumosu-Ayanu rightly notes, in developing LCRs and community content, human rights principles relating to choice, self-determination and respect for the choice and consent of local and aboriginal communities are crucial and must be respected and protected.[33] Odumosu-Ayanu calls for a holistic integration of 'community content' into legislation and industry guidelines on LCRs. Community content, like LCRs, aim to integrate social, economic and environmental well-being of host and impacted communities in the energy sector by ensuring that their choices, preferences and will are reflected and respected at all stages of the energy industry value chain.

The rights of local and aboriginal communities can be comprehensively protected by mainstreaming human rights content, especially the PANEL Principles, into the design and implementation of LCRs, in line with the United Nations Guiding Principles on Business and Human Rights (GPs).[34] As Ordor and Abe rightly argued, tackling the core problems and tensions in LCR development, 'ranging from economic growth to social provisioning and environmental sustainability, requires a holistic integration of business and human rights norms into development planning and processes.'[35] This will include giving greater priority and attention to gender vulnerability assessment in the development of their LCRs, programs, projects and plans. As extensively discussed in Chapter 8, evidence suggests that there remains a significant gender bias in the distribution of risks, benefits and access to economic opportunities in energy markets, especially in developing countries in Africa.[36] The need to integrate gender dimensions into decision-making processes to avoid inequality and gender-based discrimination is well recognised by several core international human rights instruments.[37] To respect, protect and fulfil equality and non-discrimination norms of international human rights law, national authorities must take active steps to address gender bias in the distribution of risks and benefits in energy industries.[38] Gender proofing the design and implementation of LCRs could help national authorities and industry stakeholders to assess how the benefits and risks generated from LCRs and

---

[33] See Chapter 19.
[34] See Chapter 20.
[35] Ibid.
[36] African Development Bank, *Women's Economic Empowerment in Oil and Gas Industries in Africa*, www.afdb.org/fileadmin/uploads/afdb/Documents/Publications/anrc/AfDB_Women EconomicsEmpowerment_V15.pdf, stating that in African extractive industries, 'while benefits accrue mostly to men in the form of employment and compensation, the costs (e.g. family or social disruption, environmental degradation) fall most heavily on women'.
[37] See D. Olawuyi, *The Human Rights Based Approach to Carbon Finance* (Paperback edition, Cambridge University Press, 2018).
[38] Ibid.; see also United Nations, 'The Human Rights Based Approach to Development Cooperation towards a Common Understanding among UN Agencies' (2003), www.undg.org/archive_docs/6959-The_Human_Rights_Based_Approach_to_Development_Cooperation_Towards_a_Common_Un derstanding_among_UN.pdf, para 4(d).

422   Damilola S. Olawuyi

empowerment initiatives has resulted in greater economic development, job creation, access to procurement and supply contracts and increased capacity, and
increased representation for women in decision-making processes.[39] By establishing
an effective process for assessing risks on the basis of gender, national authorities, as
well industry participants, can better understand and assess legal and customary
constraints operating against the effective participation of women in project
approval and decision-making processes.[40] It is essential for countries to establish
and maintain an effective database for assessing the effectiveness of LCRs on the
basis of gender roles, risks, opportunities and the constraints operating against
women's participation in decision-making processes in the energy sector.
A comprehensive integration of 'human rights content' into the design and implementation of LCRs can help social and human rights concerns and trade-offs.[41]

As for the role of lawyers representing companies and investors in negotiating
energy agreements, it is important to clarify and clearly document the expectations
of the host state with respect to reporting, LCR measurement, role of state agencies
in procurement processes, key members of the local communities that are to be
involved in engagement processes, as well as how cost implications of data localisation requirements are to be allocated. Nearly all cases of conflict over incompatibil-
ity of LCRs with international law arise from lack of clarity and guidelines on
practical expectations of the host state with respect to LCRs. International investors,
and their business and legal advisers alike, can avoid such uncertainty and backlash
by fully clarifying and understanding host country expectations on LCRs, and the
risks embodied within such expectations and requirements, for the countries within
which they seek to operate and to structure their projects accordingly. There is
a strong business case, in terms of cost, reputation and effectiveness, for investors and
host countries alike, to do so.

Finally, the importance of continuous research, benchmarking and monitoring
cannot be overemphasised. Setting clear and comprehensive LCRs is only one
aspect of the task; establishing research programs and funds for continuous monitoring of LCR outcomes, in light of overall sustainable development goals and aims of
a country, is a second crucial requirement for success. For example, Nigeria has
already announced a Nigerian Content Research and Development Fund
(NCR&DF) for the purpose of promoting robust research and development
(R&D) that will bridge technology, local capacity and interoperability gaps in the
implementation of LCRs in the country.[42] Establishing similar R&D innovation

---

[39] M. Crawley and L. O'Meara, *The Gender Proofing Handbook* (Lithuania: European Institute for
      Gender Equality, 2002), pp. 1–5; also F. Mackay and K. Bilton, *Equality Proofing Procedures in
      Drafting Legislation: International Comparisons* (Scottish Executive Central Research Unit, 2001),
      pp. 5–8.
[40] Chapter 9.
[41] See Chapter 19.
[42] The US$50 Million Fund is designed to cover four broad intervention areas, namely: research (basic
      and applied); establishment of Centers of Excellence in academic and research institutes; sponsorship

Advancing Sustainable Development in Local Content Initiatives 423

funds and programs can help countries to make timely and informed decisions in terms of adjusting LCR thresholds and expectations to align with contemporary realities. For example, as economic and political conditions, international treaty obligations and energy outlook change, there could be a need to relax LCRs or progressively phase them out, as was the case in Norway. As Sturman and Meyer demonstrate,[43] relaxing or updating rules on local content could also create political incentives for governments to attract and retain investment in the energy sector in a low oil price economy, when rapid global energy transition is increasing to avert the catastrophic environmental, economic and human consequences of climate change, and also when many countries are accelerating economic recovery plans in the aftermath of the global economic downturn resulting from the COVID-19 pandemic. To maximize their sustainable development outcomes, LCRs must be flexible, adaptable and constantly monitored and updated in light of best available information and technology.

3 CONCLUSION

If coherently implemented and aligned with broader obligations under different treaty regimes, LCRs can be key enablers of sustainable development in global energy markets. This book has developed a profile of the multifarious human rights, sustainability, regulatory and institutional gaps that limit the coherent application of LCRs at national levels. While the manifestations of these challenges may be escalating in some jurisdictions, the scope and intensity are uniform across global energy markets. Lessons learned from the success or failure of LCRs in one context, may therefore inform thoughts on reforming LCRs to achieve optimal outcomes in other national contexts.

The success or otherwise of integrating human rights content into LCRs at national levels will to a large extent depend on local circumstances and contexts, most especially the human rights culture, frameworks, institutional capacity, supplier development programs and resources for R&D that are available to support broad sustainable development outcomes, especially respect for human rights, in the design, approval and implementation of energy projects. Answers to these questions would also depend to a large extent on the political will by national authorities and industry stakeholders to support a comprehensive reform process that aligns LCRs with international treaty norms on trade, investment, gender, environment, human rights and sustainable development.

---

of commercialization of research; and sponsorship of endowment of professorial chair on local content in research universities. See O. Bello, 'NCDMB Governing Council Approves $50m for Research and Development' (July 05, 2020), https://businessday.ng/news/article/ncdmb-governing-council-approves-50m-for-research-and-development/.

[43] Chapter 17.

Index

CDAs, 369, 370, 371, 373, 374, 375, 378, 385, 388, 389, 390, 391

business enterprise, 75, 80, 81

civil Society, 8, 153, 307, 394

comparative analysis, xi, 5, 12, 13, 161, 414

corporate social responsibility, xi, 11, 14, 30, 151, 199, 369, 399, 403, 408, 414

Development
diversification, 3, 10, 39, 138, 147, 148, 158, 165, 190, 206, 208, 212, 213, 215, 216, 217, 218, 220, 222, 223, 225, 226, 227, 237, 416

economic growth, 8, 10, 32, 33, 35, 43, 45, 63, 76, 83, 86, 120, 124, 128, 147, 172, 191, 226, 232, 237, 241, 244, 248, 273, 329, 370, 377, 378, 381, 388, 393, 409, 421

environmental, 1, 4, 7–12, 14–16, 30–33, 35–45, 64, 71, 74, 83, 95–96, 132–137, 145, 152, 154, 168, 170–175, 178, 181, 183, 189, 192, 198, 199, 202–204, 207, 210, 241–242, 256, 269, 272, 275, 287, 294, 298, 328, 339, 341, 351–353, 355–360, 370, 377, 386–395, 400–406, 420

industrialisation, 191

poverty, 10, 27, 63, 83, 127, 202, 237, 343, 377, 384, 387, 388, 395, 398

renewable energy, 3, 4, 5, 6, 7, 41, 42, 43, 44, 45, 46, 47, 48, 49, 50, 51, 53, 57, 59, 60, 61, 62, 64, 237, 267, 320, 321, 327, 328, 329, 330, 331, 332, 334, 336, 338, 339, 340, 341, 342, 414, 416

SDG, 1, 9, 10, 191, 237, 369, 370, 374, 384–391, 414, 415

SDP, 266, 267

SRM, 8

sustainable, xi, 4, 5, 7, 8, 9, 10, 11, 12, 13, 14, 15, 17, 42, 46, 57, 73, 74, 98, 130, 132, 142, 145, 154, 156, 157, 158, 161, 167, 168, 169, 170, 172, 173, 174, 175, 176, 177, 179, 182, 183, 185, 186, 188, 196, 197, 198, 200, 202, 204, 208, 211, 216, 222, 223,

224, 226, 229, 230, 231, 234, 235, 238, 239, 240, 241, 244, 301, 309, 317, 350, 351, 369, 371, 378, 384, 388, 389, 390, 391, 395, 403, 407, 408, 414, 415, 420, 423

Distributive justice, xi, 14, 132, 149, 150, 151, 153, 154, 414

FPIC, 396

Globalisation, 29, 32

Good governance
accountability, xi, 8, 14, 102, 133, 174, 175, 183, 184, 187, 193, 246, 317, 403, 420

corruption, xi, 14, 15, 64, 68, 71, 74, 78, 80, 81, 123, 135, 153, 154, 162, 168, 174, 175, 176, 183, 184, 310, 311, 314, 318, 387, 394, 397, 400, 404, 408, 413, 414, 415, 417, 418

transparency, xi, 14, 15, 75, 77, 78, 133, 138, 144, 148, 151, 154, 162, 168, 174, 175, 176, 183, 184, 187, 230, 240, 246, 314, 337, 393, 394, 402, 403, 407, 413, 414, 415, 421

Human Rights
aboriginal rights, 344, 346–351, 356, 357, 360, 414

business and human rights, 65, 77, 79, 82, 392–395, 401–412, 421

gender, 4, 11, 12, 14, 20, 22, 117, 121, 132, 149–151, 154–155, 180–184, 186–187, 387, 395–396, 398, 413–414, 418, 421–423

non-discrimination, 8, 37, 39, 41, 44, 49, 53, 64, 72, 73, 77, 108, 111, 115, 119, 181–183, 259, 261, 340, 341, 421

racial equality, 108, 400, 414, 420

Indigenisation policies, 6, 406

International Petroleum Industry Environmental Conservation Association, 16, 31, 168, 369, 387

Index

IOCs, 139, 146, 150, 231, 238, 243, 381

oil and gas, 6, 10, 11, 23, 33, 41, 67, 68, 71, 90, 91, 93, 94, 95, 96, 99, 108, 141, 151, 152, 158, 166, 167, 168, 169, 170, 171, 172, 173, 174, 175, 176, 177, 178, 179, 180, 181, 182, 183, 184, 185, 186, 187, 188, 189, 190, 191, 195, 196, 197, 198, 203, 204, 205, 206, 208, 211, 217, 218, 220, 223, 224, 226, 228, 229, 230, 231, 232, 233, 234, 238, 240, 241, 242, 244, 245, 246, 247, 252, 257, 259, 264, 265, 266, 267, 268, 269, 270, 271, 272, 273, 274, 275, 276, 277, 278, 279, 300, 301, 302, 307, 309, 312, 313, 314, 315, 318, 329, 330, 331, 332, 333, 334, 343, 369, 371, 374, 375, 376, 377, 378, 379, 380, 381, 382, 383, 384, 385, 387, 388, 390, 391, 393, 394, 396, 399, 400, 409, 410, 411, 413, 414, 419, 420

PSA, 159, 162, 163

International Trade

ASCM, 200, 201, 202, 260

FDI, 34, 37, 38, 189, 240, 372, 375, 416

foreign investors, 35, 65, 66, 67, 70, 71, 73, 75, 82, 110, 160, 220, 232, 372

GATS, 9, 194, 200, 201, 202, 205, 246, 260, 279

GATT, 9, 10, 47, 48, 49, 50, 52, 53, 54, 55, 56, 57, 58, 59, 60, 61, 200, 201, 202, 205, 235, 236, 237, 245, 260, 279, 324, 331, 332, 338, 339, 341, 342

protectionist, 4, 7, 10, 61, 82, 84, 85, 86, 88, 97, 99, 100, 103, 166, 202, 220, 322, 332, 414

trade agreement, 325

TRIMs, 6, 9, 47, 52, 58, 189, 200, 201, 202, 205, 235, 236, 237, 246, 279, 331, 416

Local Content

empowerment, 28, 107, 109, 111, 112, 113, 115, 117, 118, 119, 120, 123, 124, 125, 127, 128, 129, 181, 383, 386, 408, 418, 422

gaps, 14, 169, 175, 176, 178, 181, 187, 190, 203, 205, 230, 301, 318, 423

grievances, 17, 407, 408

legislation, 338, 373, 375, 390, 418

legislative frameworks, 128, 240, 241, 246, 250, 415

linkage, 33, 127, 132, 141, 147, 411

policy, 22, 26, 29, 37, 67, 69, 75, 93, 107, 108, 109, 161, 165, 214, 245, 246, 247, 249, 250, 268, 307, 309, 311, 312, 313, 314, 315, 317, 318, 396

localism, 18, 28, 29, 36

stakeholders, 9, 17, 31, 75, 91, 102, 114, 161, 169, 172, 175, 178, 186, 190, 203, 204, 212, 249, 258, 264, 271, 273, 277, 278, 309, 310, 337, 372, 387, 395, 399, 401, 402, 404, 405, 406, 411, 419, 421, 423

subsidy, 48, 202, 233, 268, 335, 336, 337, 339, 341

suppliers, 33, 37, 45, 66, 83, 84, 88, 90, 103, 124, 161, 162, 164, 165, 177, 178, 204, 213, 229, 232, 251, 252, 253, 254, 255, 266, 267, 268, 269, 271, 273, 274, 275, 276, 277, 278, 301, 306, 307, 309, 311, 312, 321, 360, 404, 405, 417

supply chain, 114, 115, 118, 229, 272, 307, 311

Regional content, 18, 149

Resource curse, 155, 156, 168, 175, 215, 393

Small and Medium Enterprises (SMEs), 70, 136, 143, 178, 229, 242, 272, 275, 397, 400, 412, 417

state-owned, 113, 125, 248, 249, 251, 259, 267, 274